The Los Angeles **Metropolis**

Howard J. Nelson

University of California, Los Angeles

KENDALL/HUNT
PUBLISHING COMPANY
Dubuque, Iowa

Cover design by Noël L. Diaz

B   402939   01

Marco Polo describes a bridge, stone by stone.

"But which is the stone that supports the bridge?" Kublai Khan asks.

"The bridge is not supported by one stone or another," Marco answers, "but by the line of the arch that they form."

Kublai Khan remains silent, reflecting. Then he adds: "Why do you speak to me of the stones? It is only the arch that matters to me."

Polo answers: "Without stones there is no arch."

Italo Calvino, *Invisible Cities*. New York: Harcourt Brace Jovanovich, 1972. p. 82.

Contents

Preface

Anyone is fortunate to have the Los Angeles Metropolis as a subject for investigation, but perhaps a geographer is the luckiest of all. Seldom is as wide a variety of natural landscapes, economic activities and human communities found within such a tiny fraction of the earth's surface. More than that: rarely does a single metropolitan area include so much that is of significance to the nation at large, and of interest to much of the world.

Within the Los Angeles Metropolis, in dramatic display, are many diverse natural features. There are rugged mountains, fertile valleys, extensive plains, miles of sandy beaches, and a bordering ocean. The climate is one of the world's rarest, and exhibits more variety within this one region than is found in many countries. As a challenge to human ingenuity, each natural feature seems to present its special problem for urban living: earthquake faults lace the area, hillsides crumble, subsidence occurs in spots, floods happen with distressing frequency, and wildfires in the chapparal present a unique urban hazard. Ironically, the gentle winds, marine air and abundant sunshine are not only a delight to the occupants, but also create an atmosphere uniquely subject to the modern era's gaseous pollutants.

Changes in human activity within the region over the last two centuries boggle the mind. Hunting and gathering Indians, occupants for centuries, were displaced by Spanish-Mexican ranchers, who were in turn superseded by American farmers and town-founders. For more than fifty years the area prospered as a unique agricultural region, foisting the breakfast orange on a bemused nation. It was the developments of the twentieth century, however, that transformed the Los Angeles region into a world class Metropolis whose population exceeds that of forty-five states. Unrecognized resources and industries based on new inventions—petroleum, motion pictures, aircraft—propelled the region to economic importance and attracted millions of migrants. These earlier arrivals have been joined recently by additional millions from foreign lands, adding a rainbow of color to a monochromatic past.

Exploring the built-up landscape of the Metropolis is as rewarding as probing its past. Its residential districts are composed of neighborhoods of easily recognized house-types whose widely varying styles reveal the popular taste of the period in which they were built. Furthermore, they are occupied today by a suprising variety of Americans: Anglos, blacks, Latinos and "new immigrants" from everywhere. Now the familiar East Los Angeles barrio has been joined by scores of others, and to Little Tokyo and Chinatown has been added Koreatown, Little Armenia and Little Saigon. The region also includes a newly booming downtown, bustling ports on an artificial harbor, and widespread specialized districts of all sorts—commercial, service, manufacturing, wholesaling and more.

Although tied together today by its famous freeways, the Metropolis boasts a traditional transportation background. Horsecars, cable-cars, and electric streetcars flourished here. So, too, did the interurban, the much lamented Pacific Electric, responsible for much of the region's sprawl. In the 1920s, however, the Metropolis did not follow the lead of other cities into subways. Residents found the newly available automobile convenient and well suited to the region, and enthusiastically supported the building of ever better roads. Some form of rapid transit, however, may lie in the future. Finally, although the Metropolis is logically considered as a single unit, it is actually fragmented into five counties and more than a hundred cities, a situation of consequence for its inhabitants.

The topics outlined above indicate the scope of the twenty-two chapters in this book. Although written as a text for a course, "The Los Angeles Metropolis," offered in the Geography Department at UCLA, it assumes no previous geographic background. It is designed for anyone with a curiosity about the nature, evolution and operation of this complex and important area. A major goal is to provide the general reader with the kind of information needed in order to make wise decisions on issues of vital concern to the Metropolis. Finally, it is hoped that this book will be of interest to individuals everywhere who have a desire to know more about one of the world's great Metropolitan centers, its successes and its failures, and the lessons it has to teach about urban development and city life in the modern world.

A book of this sort would be impossible were it not for the work of literally hundreds of people who have had the Los Angeles area as the object of their interest. Working in academic institutions or governmental agencies, writing for journals or newspapers, or as authors of books in the past or today, these individuals have produced an immensely useful literature. They all have my acknowledgment and gratitude. Special thanks are due several persons who have read large portions of the manuscript. I would particularly like to thank J. E. Spencer, longtime colleague and carpool companion, who arrived in Los Angeles almost seventy years ago, and whose affection for the region and interest in its evolution has never waned. Thanks are also due a fellow native of Gowrie, Iowa, Carl P. Strand, literate engineer, and sometime resident of California cities, both north and south. Most of all I would like to thank my wife, Betty, who has shouldered the drudgery of proofreading seemingly endless pages of manuscript in the various stages of the production of this lengthy volume.

Noël L. Diaz, Principal Cartographic Illustrator, Department of Geography, UCLA, supervised the production of the maps and advised in the selection of photographs. His skill is appreciated, as is that of his assistant, Dominique Pahlavan. Many of the photographs are from the collection of Robert E. Spence, the pioneer aerial photographer of southern California. His photographs, which record the growth of the area during the period 1920–1968, have been donated to the UCLA Department of Geography. They are a rich treasure. Scattered throughout the book are a number of quotations from Cary McWilliams, *Southern California, An Island on the Land.* Peregrine Smith, Inc., 1973. They are reprinted by permission. Acknowledgment of other quoted material and photographs appears in the text.

Howard J. Nelson
Los Angeles, California

CHAPTER 1

Los Angeles: Image and Reality

Figure 1.1. A sandy beach and nearby mountains have been a part of the image of the Los Angeles Metropolis through the years. This view, taken August 28, 1931, shows Santa Monica and a proposed breakwater. (Photo courtesy Spence Collection / Department of Geography, UCLA.)

"Nowadays one can see that the Spaniards were right after all . . . California is, indeed, 'at the right hand of the Indies', and, in Southern California, it does have a Terrestrial Paradise, an Amazon Island, abounding in gold and, certainly, 'infested with many griffins.' " Carey McWilliams (1946, pp. 377–378).

"I had already begun to wonder whether God intended for people to live in Los Angeles. Certainly He never meant for millions of them to live here." Richard Reeves (1981, p. 5).

The Los Angeles Metropolis is a loosely knit community of more than eleven million people which today extends from Ventura to Palm Springs, and from Lancaster to San Clemente. It is not an ordinary place but a region that inspires strong and contrary feelings.

The Los Angeles Metropolis is second in size in terms of population to the New York City Metropolitan area, and unlike it, it is still growing. In the last fifty years it has been the destination of more Americans who have moved from one region to another than any other metropolis. Further, in the last decade or two, it has been the most desired goal for the millions of "new immigrants" now arriving in our land. Its residents, in their scramble for homes in the Metropolis, have bid up the price of dwellings in many neighborhoods to heights that must be unprecedented in America. Throughout the twentieth century, millions of people, Americans and foreigners alike, have behaved as though the region were indeed a legendary Terrestrial Paradise, the fabled Big Rock Candy Mountain.

During this same period a chorus of disparaging voices has been heard in the land, its stridency rising in concert with the growth of the Metropolis. Choking smog, tangled freeways, dangerous earthquakes, poor taste, and fast bucks are common critical themes. So, too, is the notion that by building a city here nature has been transformed more than in building other cities. Implicit in much of the criticism, and sometimes explicitly proclaimed, is the idea that it wasn't intended for people, or at least many people, to live in Los Angeles. Los Angeles, in the view of some, is simply not supposed to be here. "It is difficult to find any good reason why the city of Los Angeles should have come into existence" (Dasmann, 1965, p. 139). The ordinary person, American and foreigner alike, doesn't seem to have been listening. Even so, it is ironic that as Los Angeles has grown to Metropolitan size it has acquired a negative image, for that is not the way it used to be.

In its first hundred years as an American city, Los Angeles, although not so well-known, was widely admired. When it was thought of at all, and it was increasingly as the years went by, it was seen as a lovely place set in a tropical land where the living was easy and perhaps even glamorous and exciting. It became the goal of millions of hopeful migrants. It is true that American cities generally have lost much of their appeal. No urban area has undergone such a complete revision of its image in the last quarter of a century as has Los Angeles—none had so much to lose. How did the most desired come to be the most despised? More importantly, how much of the present negative image of the area is justified and to what extent is Los Angeles still Lotus Land?

Los Angeles as Lotus Land

The image of Los Angeles as Lotus Land sprang from the general American view of California in the 1850s as a promised land, a "land of new beginnings," a part of the persistent American dream. The European peasant struggled to migrate to an America of hope, promise, and the chance for a better life, if not for himself then surely for his children. In similar fashion, the American in drought-plagued Kansas, in a lonely Chicago rooming house, or even in a reasonably profitable urban or rural situation could still dream of a place where he could start again, where there was more opportunity, where he could live an easier and more pleasant life. Americans are a restless people, and the pursuit of happiness wherever it might be found, has been believed to be an inalienable right for more than two hundred years.

California came vividly to the nation's attention with the discovery of gold in 1848, and for many citizens it became the locale of the American dream. At first it was northern California and its gold fields that caught their fancy and was the goal of their real or imagined treks. The gold fields were soon worked out, and California, for a time, meant the fruit groves and wheat fields of the Central Valley. Surprisingly early the nation's image of California was, however, transferred to *southern* California, particularly to the area of the Los Angeles Metropolis. Here was a different place where the winters were mild and the summers were without rain, a place where men of energy could produce an earthly paradise.

Information about the region reached the East in various ways, through letters written by early settlers, through the advertising of the railroads, and through articles in newspapers and magazines. Perhaps the most influential sources were travel books, widely read in the nineteenth century to satisfy the curiosity of the stay-at-homes about their vast country. One of the most widely read and most influential of these was Charles Nordhoff's 1872 volume, *California for Health, Pleasure and Residence.* The very title sets the theme. One chapter was entitled, "A January Day in Los Angeles," and a few paragraphs from it reveal what the nation was beginning to hear about Los Angeles.

"As I drove out from Los Angeles into the country on a January morning with a friend, we met a farmer coming into town with a market-wagon of produce. It was a cloudless, warm, sunny day, and the plain where we met him was covered with sheep suckling their lambs, for in January it is already lambingtime here. The farmer's little girl sat on the seat with him, her shawl, which her careful mother had wrapped about her shoulders, carelessly flung aside. To me, fresh from the snowy Plains and Sierras, and with the chill breath of winter still on me, this was a pleasing and novel sight; but the contents of the man's wagon were still more startling to my Northern eyes. He was carrying to market oranges, pumpkins, a lamb, corn, green peas in their pods, sugar-cane, lemons, and strawberries. What a mixture of Northern and Southern Products! What an odd and wonderful January gathering in a farmer's wagon!

"Around us the air was musical with the sweet sound of the baa-ing of young lambs. Surely there is no prettier or kindlier sight in the world than a great flock of peaceful, full-fed ewes, with their lambs, covering a plain of soft green, as far as the eye can reach. All the fence corners, where there were fences, were crowded with the castor-oil plant, which is here a perennial, twenty feet high—a weed whose brilliant crimson seed-pods shine like jewels in the sunlight. Below us, as we looked off a hilltop, lay the suburbs of Los Angeles, green with the deep green of orange-groves, and golden to the nearer view with their abundant fruit. Twenty-one different kinds of flowers were blooming in the open air in a friend's garden in the town this January day; among them the tuberose, the jessamine, and the fragrant stock or gillyflower, which has here a woody stalk, often four inches in diameter, and is of course a perennial. The heliotrope is trained over piazzas to the height of twenty feet, and though the apple and pear orchards, as well as those of the almond and English walnut, will continue bare for some time, and the vineyards, just getting pruned, look dreary, the vegetable gardens are green as with us in June, and men and boys are gathering the orange crop. . . .

"The architecture of this region will remind you that you are in a land where it is never very cold. The dwelling is a secondary matter here, and it results that many people are satisfied to live in a very small and slight house. Muslin and paper inside walls are common; a barn is like Jack Straw's house, neither wind-tight nor water-tight. In the Pico House, at Los Angeles, you must walk across an open, brick-paved court, containing a fountain and flowers, to get from your room to the dining room; at San Bernardino, most of the rooms in the hotel have no entrance from within at all; you go on to an open corridor, and enter your chamber from that; and, as the stores and shops are mostly without chimneys, at San Bernardino I saw clerks and shopkeepers on a cool day warming their coattails by a fire built in the middle of the street. I should say that what a farmer from the East would spend in bringing his family out here he would more than save in the cost of his farm buildings.

"The price of land at first strikes the stranger as high. Near Los Angeles they ask from thirty to a hundred dollars per acre for unimproved farming land. 'If I can get two crops a year from farming land which I buy already cleared, and can plough in December; if I can raise from ten to fifteen tons of alfalfa hay by successive cuttings in a year; if I can support two cows from a quarter of an acre of beets; if my peach-trees bear a peck to a tree in the second year from the pit; if my apple-trees give a full crop in five years; if my vines yield grapes the second year after I plant them; and if my kitchen garden is green and productive all the year round, and I need not provide shelter for stock or fire wood for my house, why am I foolish to pay one hundred dollars per acre?' (asked a farmer to whom I told my impressions). . . .

"The pepper-tree, an evergreen, and one of the most beautiful shade-trees, can be transplanted safely and easily when nine inches in diameter, and being closely trimmed will make a grateful shade the first season. Vines do actually bear at two years from the first cutting. Strawberries ripen abundantly in January. Mr. Rose, at the Mission San Gabriel, has a eucalyptus tree (the Australian blue gum), which in eight years from the cutting which he planted has made a sound and stately growth of seventy-five feet, with a trunk proportioned to its height. I accepted the invitation of a farmer to see a field of mangelwurzels, half an acre, which he said were 'as big round as a nail keg, and mostly two feet and a half long', and I saw them. I should add that they had been eighteen months growing. . . .

"Next, irrigation means a dry summer, which is one of the greatest possible conveniences to the farmer. From the first of May till November the skies are serene, and there is no rain. Crops are put in here in December and January. The barley is already sprouting in some fields. When grain ripens and is harvested, the farmer has no rainstorm to fear. He does not cut in haste, or at the wrong time, for fear of a storm; he need not hire an extraordinary force to get his crop into barns. In the Sacramento and San Joaquin valleys, as well as here, the grain is thrashed on the field, put into bags, and lies there in the open air until it is sold. Hay, in the same way, when it is cut in spring, is stacked in the field or barnyard, and rests, without even a shed, until November. The harvest may last a month or six weeks. . . .

". . . Last, I come to the orange. 'All these trees do well, and are profitable,' said an orange cultivator to me; 'but they don't compare with the orange; when you have a bearing orange orchard,

it is like finding money in the street.' I have satisfied myself, by examination of nearly all the bearing orchards in the southern counties, and by comparing the evidence of their owners, that at fifteen years from the seed, or twelve years from the planting of three year old trees, an orange orchard which has been faithfully cared for, and is favorably situated, will bear an average of 1000 oranges to the tree. This would give, at twenty dollars per 1000—a low average—a product of $1200 per acre. One man can care for twenty acres of such an orchard; and every other expense, including picking, boxes, shipping, and commissions in San Francisco, is covered by five dollars per 1000. The net profit per acre would, therefore, be a trifle less than nine hundred dollars." (Nordhoff, 1872, pp. 136–141, 170.)

What a fabulous region. Strawberries in January. Oranges, corn, and peas harvested in the middle of winter. Beets as big as a nail keg. A warm sunny climate. Blooming flowers of all sorts, and lush orange groves, golden with their abundant fruit. What a place—hotels with fountains and plazas instead of halls. Houses without chimneys. What a life—no need to cut firewood, no need to provide shelter for live stock. No need to worry about the vagaries of rain or destructive thunderstorms. Irrigation water is always available. Furthermore, is growing oranges really as profitable as finding money on the streets? No wonder that for many it was "Goodbye New York," "So long Indiana," "On to Los Angeles."

A New Life in a California Bungalow

The attraction, clearly, was not profitable agricultural crops alone. Implied throughout was a vision of a better life. No more winter snows, no more furnaces to stoke, no more expensive and tedious winter care of livestock. Here was a place where a new kind of life was possible, where an entirely different lifestyle had become the subject of another widely circulated book, significantly entitled, *Under the Sky in California,* by Charles F. Saunders, published in 1913. California, of course, means southern California, for Saunders is living and

4

writing in Pasadena. His most revealing chapter is, "Residence in the Land of Sunshine, Life in a Bungalow." Here are a few excerpts:

". . . Though it is not possible to draw a hard-and-fast line at which the California bungalow style stops and something else begins, there is one thing sure: that when you see a cozy one or one-and-a-half-story dwelling with low-pitched roof and very wide eaves, ample porches, lots of windows and an outside chimney of cobble or clinker-brick half hidden by clinging vines—that is a bungalow, whatever other houses may be. In Pasadena and Los Angeles there are literally miles of these delectable little dwellings, hardly any two just alike. Those two cities appear to be the special places where the bungalow habit seriously began, though the fashion has spread very largely through the State. In size, the popular taste is for five or six rooms (exclusive of the bath), but eight or nine rooms are not uncommon, though this greater number usually necessitates an upper story. Nowadays, since the luxury of outdoor sleeping has come to be appreciated, the sleeping-porch is an indispensable adjunct, and this may be part of the ground plan or set jauntily, like a yacht's cabin, on the roof.

"The building material is generally redwood on an Oregon pine framework, the foundation being cobble or concrete; and there may or may not be a cellar. . . . An artistic effect is produced by the use, in some cases, of cypress shakes for the sides. . . . Within there is usually paneling half way up the walls in the beautifully grained Oregon pine, stained, not painted; there is a built-in buffet in the dining-room, and in the living-room and den built-in bookcases and settlers, and open fireplaces.

"The properly appointed bungalow inside stands for comfort, leisureliness and cheerfulness, comporting with a climate which makes for the same qualities. Bungalow life is informal but not necessarily bohemian, and at its best is simple, without being sloppy. If it is winter, the open fire that greets you as you enter directly from outdoors into the living-room—there is no hallway—is a pleasant thing for the spirit, even if hardwood does cost fifteen dollars a cord. The ample windows fill the house with light, not glaring, but subdued by the generous overhang of the eaves; and there is the perfume of violets or roses, or both, in the air—they have not come from a florist's, but from under the window outside.

If it be summer, the house is cooler than the outdoors; and the lowered awnings outside the windows and the dropped screens on the porches, temper the indoor light to a restful half-light. Opened doorways and windows admit the breeze with its manifold fragrances from hedge and garden, while complete screening throughout the house keeps out insect life. Rugs and couch-covers in cheerful colors, Oriental or Indian; Indian *ollas* of quaint designs for flower holders; Indian baskets set here and there for receptacles or hung on walls as plaques; pictures of characteristic California scenes, such as snow-capped mountains, cool cañon depths, the crumbling Missions—all such things help to give the unconventional touch which goes with bungalow living.

"While the delight of bungalow life in California is largely attributable to the quality of climate which, winter and summer, calls you out of doors, or failing that, to open wide your casements and invite outdoors in, a generous share of credit is due also to good architects and first-class builders who have brought into the country the best ideas of their art and craft. There is not a facility to comfortable living known to the world that may not be found in the better class of California towns and at reasonable rates. Electricity for lighting, electrical devices for cooking or for otherwise lightening labor, gas-ranges and grates, and gas water-heaters, the most approved plumbing, telephone connections both local and long-distance—these are matters of course in every modern bungalow in California tourist towns. . . .

"To the family of moderate means a very appealing feature of bungalow life is the ease of keeping house which it offers, and the independence of servants. The servant problem, indeed, has been solved in Gordian-knot fashion by doing away with the servant; for, given a reasonable degree of strength and skill on the part of the womankind of the household, a servant is not needed, and in the democratic West no lady loses caste by the fact of doing her own housework. As there are in most bungalows but one floor and few rooms, the housewife's daily steps are reduced to a minimum. The kitchen is a compact little room, airy and light, and provided with various ingenious modern helps to lessen labor. Adjoining is the invariable screen-porch where are laundry-tubs, ice-box, cooling closets, et cetera, the cooling closet being a built-in cupboard with open, screened bottom and top and perforated shelves through which a vertical current of air ascends continually from under the house to roof, and, in this land of cold nights, makes the housekeeper measurably independent of ice even in summer. Gas is the usual fuel for cooking, though some bungalows have electric kitchens, and by it the work of preparing meals is reduced to as little as may be. If the housewife desires to be spared the labor of cleaning, which is necessary much less frequently in the relatively non-humid climate of California than on the Atlantic slope, she may arrange to have someone come from outside at stated times and take this off her hands. . . .

"As to heating the bungalow, the mildness of the climate reduces this to a comparatively simple matter. Even in winter, unless during an abnormal cold-snap or on rainy days, fire cannot be regarded as a necessity, except in the early morning and during the evenings. One wood-fire in the living-room fireplace is, therefore, all the average family need count on, as bathroom and sleeping-chambers are customarily supplied either with gas heaters or a certain kind of little sheet-iron stove with a furious draught, that can be made red hot with twisted newspapers in a few minutes. . . .

"As to the cost of bungalow living in California, it is pretty much what one chooses to make it. Our own small family of sometimes four, and sometimes three, found by experience that we lived in Pasadena for about one-third less than in Philadelphia and lived better; and we could have reduced the cost still further in Pasadena had we chosen to work our kitchen garden as we might have done instead of only playing with it. . . .

"In speaking of bungalow life a word is in order about the part the porches play. Like many other people, we made an outdoor living-and-dining room of our rear veranda, a quiet, retired spot on whose roof and sides were climbing roses and honeysuckles that hid us from our neighbors. From this flowery bower we looked out upon our little 60 × 90 foot garden, and beyond to the Sierra Madre, with its lovely lights and shadows and exquisite colors in the evening glow. Old-hickory chairs and settees, with a similar table or two, indifferent to the weather, make a suitable furnishing to such a nook. We added, in our case, the sewing-machine, and all through the long dry season—it lasts from May sometimes till November—it stood ready to hand, giving the porch a pleasant touch of domesticity

which a low work-table, piled high every week with the family mending, served to complete. Here the daily mail was brought and discussed, the newspaper read, letters written, the vegetables prepared for dinner, callers entertained; and here often our meals were served not only in summer, but on sunny days in winter. We began this practice impulsively as a sort of frolic—we were fond of picnicking—but it proved so delightful and satisfying that it soon became a habit. Dished up on hot plates in the kitchen and brought quickly to the veranda on a tray, the eatables suffered nothing from their outing, while appetite and digestion throve; for we did not allow the meals to degenerate into "pick-up snacks" but kept them on the plane of serious repasts. An alcohol lamp on a side-table served for the heating of water, and the warming up of small matters. The extension of electrical connections to the porch simplifies proceedings still further." (Saunders, 1913, pp. 236–243.)

Not only did the Los Angeles area permit the production of new and exotic crops, but it was also a place where the environment permitted the development of a new and more casual lifestyle. To enable the resident to live in this carefree way and to take full advantage of the new environment a new house type evolved—the California Bungalow. It was designed to bring the outside in, and was characterized by light and airy rooms, outdoor living and sleeping, and a work-saving design. All this, of course, at a cost less than that "on the Atlantic shore." The American now had a new facet for his dream of California. Today many California bungalows still stand in the parts of the urban area built up generally in the 1900–1925 period. Many feel the style was brought to its ultimate perfection by the architectural firm of Greene and Greene—a sample of their work, the Gamble House, can be seen at 4 Westmorland Place, Pasadena.

Additional Glamour—Motion Pictures

At the very time (1913) that Saunders was writing of a new California life style, a new industry was being established in the area, an industry that was to glamourize the region all over again. The motion picture was being developed, and Los Angeles was the place where it was happening. It was something the world had never seen before and had two significant effects. Now more people than ever before would be exposed to the same kind of entertainment. In addition, the entertainment industry itself, for the first time, would be concentrated in a single place. And the place, the land of make-believe, adventure, happiness, and glamour would be Los Angeles— or Hollywood, as the newspapers would have it. Soaring to importance in the nineteen twenties, the movies reinforced the earlier glamorous image of the area. Not only was Los Angeles still an exotic place, it was thought of as a land of marvelous opportunity once again. Now, at least in fantasy, any girl from Anyplace could simply seat herself at the soda fountain in Schwab's Drug Store, be discovered by a producer, and soon she would be a movie star famous around the world.

Much later, as the period was coming to a close, a movie-spawned entrepreneur, Walt Disney, was to carry the image a step further by the creation of an entire amusement park devoted to fantasy: Disneyland. By then, however, the era had ended, spoiled in large measure by its own success.

Was the Dream a Nightmare?

One should not be deceived, since even during the period when Los Angeles was thought by many to epitomize the American Dream there were others who remained skeptics. At the root of some of the unease was the odd climate: the arid appearance of the place, the lack of summer rain, the absence of the traditional four seasons—in short, the strangeness of it all. B. F. Taylor, arriving in midsummer (1878) described the dry landscape. "Tree and shrub, except where transfigured with the witchery of water, are powdery as a miller's coat, and the dry fields and highways are strewn with Graham flour that rises

without yeast. Palm leaves are as grey as elephants' ears, and portions of the landscape have a disused air . . . while the heat dances a hot-footed hornpipe upon the top of your head. . . ." (Taylor, 1878, p. 261.)

Other critics were mainly concerned with the people, their boosterism, their rootlessness, and the recency of their arrival. Lucious Beebe was no admirer of the city and would write, "Every time I find myself in Los Angeles I wonder what I've done to displease God" (Robinson, 1968, p. 4). Beebe was a society writer from the East, and in truth there was no "society" here, although Pasadena or Santa Barbara might have disputed the assertion. Detractors, too, were the novelists and playwrights who were moved in from their free-lancing days in the East or England and assigned to writing scripts. They didn't like their work and they didn't like the people involved in the movies. Their employers were not "cultured gentlemen" but rather ex-New York fur merchants or clothing salesmen. Of course they were unhappy, and some took out their frustration by satirizing both the movies themselves and southern California.

There was much to satirize: the movies themselves, with their emphasis upon "box-office," showmanship, and mass appeal; the crudity of the producers, directors, and actors; the broken dreams of many who had hoped for success in "Hollywood." The region, too, had its vulnerable spots. Where else would a cemetery prove to be the biggest tourist attraction for more than three decades? Actually, it wasn't called a cemetery, but Forest Lawn Memorial Park. It didn't look like a cemetery since it had no prominent headstones. It was a landscaped garden filled with statues and fountains. You weren't supposed to act as if it were a cemetery for happiness was encouraged everywhere. Its chapels celebrated more marriages than funerals. Similarly, in what other city would the most prominent theologian be a white-robed blonde—Aimee Semple

McPherson—who liked to ride into her 5,000 seat church on a white horse and chase an evil-looking devil around the stage? She was not the only example of peculiarity. As *Life* wrote from Los Angeles in the 1930s, "This lovely, cuckoo land . . . nowhere else do eccentrics flourish in such close abundance. Nowhere do spiritual or economic panaceas grow so lushly. Nowhere else is undisciplined gullibility so widespread" (Meyer, 1981, p. 79).

Other criticism was directed toward the things that made Los Angeles "different" from other metropolitan areas and therefore somehow not "quite right." It was a sprawling city, with interurbans and automobiles for transit instead of elevated trains and subways. People lived in single family houses instead of apartments. Thus it did not seem to be really urban, but rather, "forty suburbs in search of a city." The area generally missed the large influx of migrants characteristic of the early part of this century, and Eastern critics deplored the lack of the colorful ethnic enclaves, the lively streets, and the bustling tenements familiar in the cities back East. Instead they found, in the 1890–1930 period, a land of transplanted Midwesterners, and the writers subjected the area to the scorn usually reserved for the Midwest. In truth, some of the local residents also longed for a return to the more open, cosmopolitan atmosphere of an earlier period. Williard Huntington Wright in 1913 complained about the lack of night life, the puritanism of the city's leaders, and, finally, exploded, "Virtue has become virulent" (Wright, 1913, p. 99).

One would suspect, also, that a portion of the disenchantment with Los Angeles represents simply the fact that for many the dream of California was unattainable. Not everyone could achieve the good life. Most migrants did not make a fortune in Los Angeles real estate, nor did their land prove to be underlain with oil. Not every girl who sipped a cherry coke in Schwab's Drugstore became a movie star, or even a bit player. Not everyone who made the journey to Lotus Land found a satisfying job, or even a job at all. Furthermore, discrimination has always been a feature of life in Los Angeles; segregation has been around for a hundred years. For many, life had the same frustrations here as elsewhere, and the disappointment was great because the hope had been so high. For many it really was "a land of shattered dreams."

"Eden in Jeopardy"

It has been only in the last quarter century, however, that the criticism of the Los Angeles Metropolis has become almost universal. Several years ago a geographer at UCLA, Gerald Zeck, surveyed attitudes of college students around the country toward various American cities. When asked about Los Angeles, derogatory images dominated, with smog and freeways the most common characterization. Images of Los Angeles as big, large, crowded, and sprawling were much more numerous than allusions to its warm and sunny climate. Northern Californians, especially, tended to favor such evaluations as "cesspool," "horrible," "mistake," "plastic people," "phony everything," and "just plain ugly" (Zeck, 1972, p. 213). Negative images are not confined to students. In the new edition of the *Encyclopaedia Britannica* John A. Weaver begins his article on Los Angeles with some comments on growth and "palm trees and oil derricks." Then, "it has paid for its spectacular growth by acquiring such urban attributes as smog-filled skies, a polluted harbour, clogged freeways, explosive ghettos, overcrowded schools, and annual budgets teetering on the brink of bankruptcy" (Weaver, 1980, p. 107).

Ironies abound. The Los Angeles area, which had escaped the coal smoke pollution of Eastern cities, now had its air filled with a new form of gaseous garbage with its own name— "smog." The automobile, which had given the Angeleno unprecedented freedom of move-

Table 1.1
Population by Race and Ethnic Group
By County, Adjusted by the Area of the Metropolis, April 1980

County	Number	Percent				
		Anglo	Latino	Black	Asian	Indian
Los Angeles	7,477,657	52.4	27.6	12.6	5.8	0.6
Orange	1,931,570	78.7	14.8	1.3	4.5	0.7
San Bernardino	740,427	73.4	18.5	5.3	1.7	1.1
Ventura	508,173	72.6	21.4	2.1	3.0	0.9
Riverside	405,656	74.1	18.8	4.6	1.4	1.1
	11,063,483					

Source: U.S. Bureau of the Census, *Twentieth Census, 1980. Population and Housing, Summary Tape, File 1A.*

ment, was now present in such large numbers that its network of freeways were reputed only to "provide parking lots for the area's seven million cars and trucks." The single family house, once thought to be a graceful response to a balmy climate, was now seen as a wasteful use of high quality agricultural land, a contributor to urban sprawl, and the refuge of the despised suburbanite.

The Reality of the Eighties

The People

The Los Angeles Metropolis today is the home of more than eleven million people, the second largest metropolis in the United States (after New York) and one of the world's major concentrations of population. Urbanization is now dominant; the former agricultural areas have been engulfed by urban forms. Subdivisions, shopping centers, and industrial buildings fill the lowland from the promontories of the Palisades to the plains of San Bernardino and from the coast of Ventura to the far corners of Orange County's Irvine Ranch. The agricultural landscape was forced into retreat, orange groves and walnut orchards yielded to the subdivider, and the dairy farmer cried, rhetorically: "Where now, brown cow." Even the wild landscape has felt the mark of urbanites. They ride their cycles over it, camp in it,

and get lost in it. They burn it and litter it until the wild landscape, too, has become urbanized.

The existence of this massive population cluster in the Los Angeles area is a remarkably recent phenomena. In 1900 the population of the city of Los Angeles was only 102,000, compared to 3.5 million in New York City that same year. The entire Metropolis boasted only 325,000 persons. By 1940, after several significant growth periods, there were 3.25 million persons, ten times as many as in 1900. However, since 1940 about 6,000,000 persons have migrated to the Los Angeles area, one of the most extensive and rapid movements of people to an urban area this country has ever seen. In the decade of the seventies the Metropolis grew by more than 100,000 persons a year; perhaps half of this was in-migration. No wonder Frank Lloyd Wright is reported to have exclaimed, "If you tilt the whole country sideways, Los Angeles is the place where everything loose will fall."

The population is not only large but has also become cosmopolitan once again. No longer is the region dominated by transplants from "Middle America," but the population now contains racial and religious mixtures of the sort that characterize metropolitan areas elsewhere. For example, three million or more Latinos, mainly of Mexican origin, live in the

9

Metropolis, the largest concentration anywhere save for Mexico City. There are about one million Canadians in the Metropolis, about the same number that live in Montreal, Canada's largest city. The Metropolis is the home of the largest group of Armenians in America, about 150,000. A similar number of persons of Japanese ancestry form the largest concentration on the American mainland. There are about 100,000 each of Korean, Chinese, and Israeli in the Metropolis. There are large and growing numbers of Filipinos, Thais, Vietnamese, Iranians, Germans, Norwegians, British, and Hungarians in the area—many people from almost every land. A portion of each group are not on the citizenship track: students who have overstayed their visas, tourists who have not gone home, immigrants who arrived illegally. In addition, there are about 1.1 million blacks—only New York and Chicago have larger numbers.

Cosmopolitan quality is augmented by a variety of religious groups. Catholic archdioceses in the Metropolis count about 2.5 million adherents; only New York and Chicago have more. The Jewish Federation Council estimates that there are about 550,000 Jews living in the area, second in numbers in the world, behind New York, but ahead of Tel Aviv. Even if the region did miss the influx of European immigrants so important to the structure of Eastern cities early in this century, its array of ethnic and religious groups today is as varied as that of any American Metropolis. In the eighties, "Los Angeles has become what New York was at the turn of the century, the port of entry, or at least of first sojourn, for most of the immigrants to the United States" (Grimond, 1982, p. 11).

The Place—Is It Still Here?

What of the *Place* itself, the southern California of the American dream, is it still here? It was the natural environment, the sunny climate, the encircling mountains, and the sandy beaches washed by the vast Pacific that comprised a large part of the good life of the emigrant's dream. The earlier images: the lush green valleys, the snow-capped mountains, the surfer on a curling wave—are they with us still?

The answer is obvious to an English visitor, Reyner Banham. Writing in 1970 he did not hesitate to use the familiar natural features to organize his book, *Los Angeles and the Architecture of Four Ecologies* (Banham, 1970). The foothills, the plains, and the beaches are his dominant "ecologies" (the fourth is "autopia"—the freeways). Apparently the newly arrived observer, today as always, feels that the natural features are the key to understanding the region. With all their problems, the topography, the climate, the vegetation, and the beaches, remain as remarkable assets.

The earth abides. The topography remains basically as it was when people first arrived. The Sierra Madre looms as always behind the inland valleys, lending a feeling of stability and providing a sense of orientation to the lowland dweller. The lower ranges still give form to the valleys, and from a distance appear remarkably unchanged. Seen closer up, the highway passageways are visible, as are the many residential areas that cover their close-in sections, particularly in the Santa Monicas. Urban forms cover the lowlands, but modification of the contours of the land have been relatively minuscule.

The dynamics of the topography continue also, but now create severe problems. Landslides, slumps, and soil creep were always with us; today, if you live in the "wrong" site in the hills, the result may be your neighbor's house arriving in your yard, or yours in his. The Palisades fall into the sea as before; today this action destroys homes and covers highways, and we are concerned. Earthquakes, noticed by the first explorers, still jolt the Metropolis at irregular intervals, occasionally with considerable damage, and there is much uncertainty in the future. The broad sandy beaches, formerly stable, now have to be artificially re-plenished. The topographical variety of the region, fascinating to the earlier Midwester-ner, remains to charm the modern English-man today.

Similarly, climatic changes are likely to be measured in centuries rather than in years. January days remain sunny; the numbing cold of the Midwest winter is unknown. The sum-mers are dry; thunderstorms and tornadoes are generally absent. Cool breezes waft in from the Pacific, comforting the beach communities on summer afternoons; evenings are warm in the valleys, confirming the utility of swimming pool and barbecue. The summer humidity of the East is but a memory. Rainfall totals con-tinue low and water must be imported for ir-rigation. As always, winter rains occasionally bring floods, but now the surplus waters do not sink harmlessly into the floors of the valleys, or wash blithely over the coastal plain seeking a new and easier way to the sea. Now, if un-controlled, they have the potential for much damage and, in spite of much expensive effort, flood damage is occasionally extensive. Santa Ana winds still blow. These "northers," in the past mainly an annoyance to the residents, now occasionally fan wildfires in the brush, and if the brush covered hills are strewn with resi-dences the potential for disaster is great.

Vegetation, the most frail of nature's ele-ments, has changed repeatedly as the region has been overrun by people. Although many of the mountains retain their chaparral (charmingly labeled the "Elfin Forest" by one author), the lowlands have been completely altered. The native bunchgrass, needlegrass, wild rye, and numerous forbs provided ade-quate pasturage for early ranchers, but were dry and brown most of the year and far from scenically attractive to many. The wild oats, burr clover, and mustard that spread so widely after European settlement also turn brown and are no more attractive to the Easterner. To those long resident in the West, the gentle yel-lows and browns of the autumn landscape do

hold an attractiveness of their own. Only a few oaks broke the monotony of the arid plains. It has been the numerous introduced species of trees and shrubs, and their multiplication into hundreds of thousands or even millions of in-dividuals, that now give the landscape its lush, green, exotic appearance the year around, an aspect so pleasing to the eye of the migrant.

What is new and deleterious in the envi-ronment is smog. It is an ironic quirk of ca-pricious fate that the long hours of bright sunshine and the light winds, so appealing in an earlier era, are today the villains in the smog formation process. For the sunlight is the cat-alyst in the energizing action that transforms the products of combustion (from automobile, power plant, and home furnace alike) into eye-smarting, plant-damaging, health-hazardous smog. In spite of much local effort and ex-pense smog persists.

In fairness, without in any way minimiz-ing its damaging effect, one must correct the national impression: smog is not a daily oc-currence; when present it is not ubiquitous. Smog has its season, and the prevalence and intensity of smog have a very complex geo-graphic distribution, affecting some areas, generally downwind, more severely than oth-ers. Nonetheless, Mount Baldy is not an un-usual sight from Santa Monica Boulevard and a resident of the Hollywood Hills can still see Catalina on a clear day.

The environment of the Metropolis, with all of its virtues and broad scale stability, does not readily accommodate itself to human beings. A successful future will require more understanding of its nature and vigilance in its use, than we have demonstrated in the past.

The Economy

The economy of the Los Angeles Metrop-olis is no longer based on agriculture, no longer does the Chamber of Commerce promote tourism and geraniums, no longer is manufac-turing stunted. Nearly five million jobs are

11

available in the Metropolis in the 1980s. Furthermore, the economic structure of the Metropolis is generally similar to the economies of the other large metropolitan areas. That is, about the same proportions of our labor force are employed in the major economic activities as in the average American metropolitan area. Estimated local proportions for 1980 were about the following: manufacturing 25%, trade 23% (retail and wholesale), service 22%, government 14%, finance, insurance, and real estate 6%, and so on. In terms of total numbers employed in these broad categories the region is usually second to New York and ahead of Chicago, as would be expected from the size of their population and labor force. The one exception is manufacturing in which Chicago has a slight numerical lead over Los Angeles.

On a more detailed level some familiar characteristics of the Metropolitan economy can still be seen. A highly developed aerospace industry and its spinoffs—scientific research and development, electronics, scientific instruments, oceanography, and so on—are reputed to give the area the greatest collection of advanced-technology industries in the nation. Similarly, the area is reputed to have the greatest concentration of mathematicians, scientists, engineers, and skilled technicians in the United States. In addition, it has the leading port complex on the Pacific Coast; the Los Angeles Customs District is the seventh largest in the United States in terms of the value of international trade.

The Metropolis also ranks first in the entertainment industry—television, radio, motion pictures, records, and tapes. Tourism is still significant, with more than twelve million tourists visiting the area annually, drawn not only to the area itself but to such attractions as Disneyland, Knott's Berry Farm, Universal Studio Tours, Magic Mountain, and so on.

The agriculture that remains is often consumer-oriented. Citrus now accounts for only fifteen percent of the area's agricultural production. The Metropolis is the nation's leader in the production of nursery stock and cut flowers, however, and Riverside County produces more eggs than any other county in the country. Specialty crops are still produced in quantity: lima beans, broccoli, strawberries, spinach, cantaloupes, and watermelon. Avocados are also important on the margins.

"Life in Los Angeles Is a Tonic . . .": *Los Angeles Times,* 1906

What of the life? If the economy is much like that of other American cities, and if the population mix is also not far from the urban norm, is the life, too, losing its unique qualities? Perhaps it is, for the area is becoming more like other cities in several ways, and other cities are taking on some of the characteristics that formerly distinguished Los Angeles. The trend here is strongly away from the single-family house and has been since the 1950s. By 1980 perhaps sixty percent of the families in the city of Los Angeles lived in multiple dwellings. As a result, population densities over parts of the region are beginning to approach those in the other urban areas. For example, a broad belt running from Hollywood to the Santa Monica Freeway has a density of more than 15,000 persons per square mile, comparable to densities found in Chicago or San Francisco. Smaller areas as diverse as Boyle Heights, the Sunset Strip, Westwood, and a portion of Long Beach have similar densities. Too, since World War II, the dispersed single family suburb has become characteristic of all American metropolitan areas. Finally, even in terms of automobile ownership the region is losing its uniqueness. Minneapolis-St. Paul and Denver have more automobiles per household, and the ratios of Detroit, Cleveland, and San Francisco are similar to those of Los Angeles. Some of the area's distinctiveness, then, does appear to have vanished.

Furthermore, it is true that the almost bucolic quality of the southern California landscape, remembered with such fondness by those who knew it, is no more. Poppies no longer grow on the slopes above Altadena. Foothill Boulevard today eastward from Pasadena no longer leads one between groves of oranges, and the San Fernando Valley is not now sown to wheat. The agricultural age and the agricultural landscape is gone, presumably forever.

Even in an age of heightened appreciation of nature and rusticity, however, one should not fall into the trap of the earlier critics. A great many citizens of the Metropolis have no desire to return to the "good old days". Many would forgo the poppies for the excitement of the Dodgers (and other sports teams). Others prefer a delicatessen on the corner to an orange grove and, perhaps to most, the view of the evening lights of the San Fernando Valley from Mulholland Drive surpasses the sight of its earlier endless wheat fields. One can no longer take the Pacific Electric to Venice or to Mount Lowe. It is a truly disadvantaged or disingenuous youth, however, who cannot find his way on some occasion to a sandy beach or secluded mountain path even today. Finally, there is something to be said for the people of a region who permit its assets, once enjoyed by thousands, to be appreciated by many millions. Perhaps that is what the American Dream is all about.

1. Suggested Readings

Banham, Reyner. *Los Angeles: The Architecture of the Four Ecologies.* New York: Harper and Row, 1971.
This delightful volume is an English architect's sympathetic view of the Metropolis. Banham's "ecologies" are: Surfurbia, Foothills, The Plains of Id, and Autopia.

Cameron, Robert. *Above Los Angeles.* San Francisco: Cameron and Co., 1976.
A stunning collection of aerial photographs, in color, this atlas-size volume includes a few matching shots from the 1920s.

Donley, Michael W. et al. *Atlas of California.* Culver City: Pacific Book Center, 1979.
This atlas maps a variety of data for the state, emphasizing historical and cultural geography, economic systems and the natural environment. Some insets emphasizing the Metropolis are included.

Grenier, Judson A. ed. *A Guide to Historic Places in Los Angeles County.* Dubuque, Iowa: Kendall/Hunt, 1978.
The book opens with a short history of the area, but the main body is a guide to some four hundred historic spots and buildings.

McWilliams, Cary. *Southern California Country, An Island on the Land.* Santa Barbara: Peregrine Smith, 1973.
Although first published in 1945 this book remains as perhaps the best single work on the Metropolis. McWilliams was a keen observer, understood the area well and wrote vividly.

Nunis, Doyce B. ed. *Los Angeles and its Environs in the Twentieth Century.* Los Angeles: Ward Ritchie Press, 1973.
This is an annotated bibliography and is particularly useful in that it has both a subject and author index.

Rubin, Barbara, et al. *Forest Lawn, L. A. in Installments.* Santa Monica: Westside Publications, 1979.
This sympathetic appreciation of Forest Lawn is a fragment of a Ph.D. dissertation in Geography at UCLA.

Spencer, J. E. ed. *Day Tours in and Around Los Angeles.* Palo Alto: Pacific Books, 1979.
Fourteen daylong automobile expeditions around the Metropolis are featured in this guidebook sponsored by the Los Angeles Geographical Society.

Steiner, Rodney. *Los Angeles: The Centrifugal City.* Dubuque, Iowa: Kendall/Hunt, 1981.

Well illustrated with many maps and photographs, this thoughtful geography emphasizes the sub-regions within the Metropolis.

Wurman, Richard S. *LA/Access.* Los Angeles: Access Press, 1981.
Produced for the Los Angeles Bicentennial, this pocket-sized volume provides an excellent guide to both traditional and non-traditional destinations. Features unusually fine maps.

Maps. The best maps of the Metropolis are those of the Automobile Club of Southern California (available free to members, some for a price to others). Most useful sheets are *Los Angeles and Vicinity* and *Metropolitan Los Angeles* (both of these have wall-size editions), *Los Angeles and Long Beach Harbors,* and *Downtown Los Angeles.* Another excellent set is the U.S. Geological Survey, 1:250,000 series, which covers the Metropolis in four sheets. For maps showing social and economic patterns (from U.S. Census data) a fine set is available from the Western Economic Research Company, 13437 Ventura Blvd., Sherman Oaks, 91423. (213) 981–9762.

CHAPTER 2

Landscape of the Metropolis

Figure 2.1. The valleys are visibly bounded by nearby mountains as shown in this view of Pasadena taken from above the San Rafael Hills, December 16, 1934. (Photo courtesy Spence Collection / Department of Geography, UCLA.)

"The Los Angeles region, as a geographical unit, stands out from its surroundings in a way that can hardly be appreciated by people living in lands of less pronounced topography. Nothing can be more striking than the change from the steep, eroded slopes of the mountains to the flat, smooth, alluvial floors of the filled valleys. There are, in reality no foothills. One steps from plain to mountain . . ." Jonathan Garst (1931, p. 10).

It is the physical site that gives a region much of its personality. In Chicago, it is the location on the lake front, and the level prehistoric lake floor over which the city has spread that is reflected in its gridiron regularity. The character of the San Francisco or the Vancouver regions comes from their half land, half water sites and the juxtaposition of hills and mountains. The Los Angeles Metropolis, similarly, has a complex arrangement of terrain features. It comprises a group of inland valleys and a coastal plain separated by low but steep mountains with many passes all lying between an arc of high rugged mountains and the dual crescents of Santa Monica and San Pedro Bays. The shore, the plains, the fingers of mountains within the urban region, the inland valleys, and even the high mountains provide a variety of environments for home, work, and play that are rare features in metropolitan areas around the world.

Features of the Terrain

The high mountain wall surrounding Los Angeles is easily observed from an airplane approaching the city. Northwest to the Pacific lies a complex of mountains known as the Santa Susanas as they appear north of the western San Fernando Valley. Directly north of Los Angeles are the San Gabriels, extending eastward for some sixty miles to Cajon Pass, ranging in height from 3,000 to 10,000 feet, with the familiar Old Baldy (Mount San Antonio) 10,080 feet high, visible as a snow covered peak on many clear winter days. Eastward of Cajon Pass, which also marks the line of the famous San Andreas fault, are the San Bernardino Mountains, also about sixty miles long. Mount San Gorgonio, their dominant peak, at 11,485 feet is the highest in southern California. Finally, the San Jacinto Mountains angle southward into Mexico, with their dominant peak taking its name from the mountains and rising 10,786 feet into the sky.

The two peaks are only twenty miles apart and provide a spectacular entryway into the region through San Gorgonio Pass, some 8,000 feet below the summit.

These remarkably precipitous and rugged ranges constitute a significant barrier to the region and are penetrated by only a few narrow passes. Further, they provide an impressive backdrop; their ascent from valley to mountaintop is equal to that of the Rocky Mountain Front behind Denver or Colorado Springs. The mountains provide a visible wall, a comfortable enclosure, and separate the Los Angeles Metropolis from its hinterland—often inhospitable lands of desert climate. Moreover, as one writer puts it, "When you have mountains in the distance, or even hills, you have space" (Pirsig, p. 263). The Spaniards called these encircling ranges the "Sierra Madre," source of their water of life and literally the mother of the region. An appropriate name, it deserves revival.

The land in front of the Sierra Madres is a land of much topographic variety, as has been indicated previously. Two mountain ranges run parallel to the Sierra Madre some distance in front, one arising in the west, the other in the south. Appearing first as the Santa Barbara Channel Islands, then as the Santa Monica Mountains, one range extends with declining elevation until it almost touches the San Gabriels at the Los Angeles River, forming the Glendale Narrows. The second range starts as the spine of Baja California and continues northward as the Santa Ana Mountains, and the Puente and San Jose Hills, until it, too, almost touches the San Gabriels. Between the ends of the Puente Hills and the Santa Monica Mountains lie the Repetto Hills, forming a low arc cut by many gaps.

In the alluvial filled troughs between these ranges are three inland valleys. The San Fernando Valley is in the trough between the Santa Monica and the Santa Susana-San Gabriel Mountains, terminated at the west by the Simi Hills block. The San Gabriel Valley,

16

Figure 2.2. The major landforms of the Metropolis.

shaped like a half moon, lies in front of the San Gabriel Mountains and behind the Repetto Hills. And the San Bernardino Valley is in the trough between the Puente Hills and the San Bernardino Mountains.

What is the significance of this topographic arrangement? "It is noteworthy," Garst (1931, p. 6) explained, "that whereas the Sierra Madre is highest behind the Los Angeles region, the Santa Monica–Santa Ana Range is very low in the section that crosses the region. It is this peculiar circumstance which has been responsible in large part for the building of the region and for its favorable conditions for human occupance. The low range in front has allowed the sea breeze to penetrate to some extent into the valleys, and the storms to break against the Sierra Madre in the rear. The height of the Sierra Madre has enabled it to gather a large proportion of the moisture from the storm clouds, and the rock waste that this water has washed down has filled the valley basins. The comparatively

easy drainage through the Santa Monica–Santa Ana Range has resulted in sufficient outwash to keep the elevation of the valley floors largely between 500 and 1500 feet above sea level. The outwash has built up a great area of plain outside of the Santa Monica–Santa Ana range." The plain meets the sea in sickle-shaped beaches, and the open bays of Santa Monica on the west and San Pedro to the south.

The Los Angeles plain, lying in front of the Santa Monica–Santa Ana range, has been built in recent geological time by the eroded material carried through the mountains by three rivers, the Los Angeles, the San Gabriel, and the Santa Ana. Today the plain reaches from the spurs of the Santa Monica Mountains, which come down to the sea fifteen miles west of downtown Los Angeles, in a southeasterly direction about fifty miles, and has a maximum width of about twenty miles. The free flow of this sediment to the ocean has been partially blocked by a line of hills—Baldwin

Hills, Dominguez Hills, Signal Hill—marking the underlying folds of the Inglewood-Newport fault zone, and a great area of delta plain has developed. West and southwest of this line of hills an additional lowland has been built—an accumulation of materials between them and the Palos Verdes Hills, formerly an island.

Topography and People

The human occupance of the Metropolis is involved with the varied topography in many ways. The mountains act as barriers to movement, provide a vast nearby recreational area, furnish spectacular homesites, and are prime factors in the region's amazing variety of micro-climates. The inland valleys and the coastal plain were favored for agriculture in an earlier era, and in a later period could be developed with urban forms easily and economically. Today they are the home of the vast majority of the region's people. The miles of coast are the scene of extensive white sand beaches and provide the possibility of harbors and marinas. The ocean itself is both an economic resource and a precious amenity. Even the subsurface has utility as a source and storage basin for water, and in a number of places petroleum is present. Finally, the varied topography of the area, evidence of a dynamic past, has left a heritage of numerous problems—earthquakes, landslides, subsidence, and all the rest.

Mountains as Barriers

The small number of routes connecting the Los Angeles Metropolis with the rest of the country clearly show the barrier effect of the encircling mountain ranges. Highways leaving the region traverse mountain canyons and relatively high passes, or skirt the coast just above the high tide line.

The traveler heading east has two choices. Interstate 10 and the Southern Pacific Railroad (to Yuma and New Orleans) use San Gorgonio Pass some 2,600 feet high at Beaumont, the pass site city. Interstate 15 (and the traditional Route 66) and both the Santa Fe and Union Pacific Railway cross the mountains through Cajon Pass (or Box Pass, as it is actually a box canyon) 4,257 feet high and opening into the high desert of the Antelope Valley and the route to Las Vegas, Salt Lake, and the East.

Travel directly northward to the Central Valley and San Francisco has always been difficult. Traditionally the traveler left the San Fernando Valley by a low but steep pass of the same name (for years a dreaded obstacle) and then swung either east or west in the valley of the Santa Clara River. The Antelope Valley could be reached by going eastward up the valley (Soledad Canyon) over Soledad Pass (3,210 feet). However, to achieve the Central Valley the Tehachapis must still be crossed at about 4,000 feet. The area's first rail line (1876) arrived this way via a tunnel more than a mile long under San Fernando Pass. Today Highway 14 follows essentially the same route. An alternative was to go down the Santa Clara River Valley to Ventura, and then work northward through the Coast Ranges, a route followed later by the Coast Line of the Southern Pacific. An indication of its difficulty is that the line reached Santa Barbara in 1887, but did not connect with San Francisco until 1901. Directly north of Los Angeles toward the Central Valley lies a knot of mountains avoided by the early road builders. Finally a passable route was opened to automobiles. The road, which wound through the mountains, had so many curves it is reported that the driver had to make more than one hundred complete circles on the forty-eight mile road. Even today, the grades on Interstate 5, over Tejon Pass (4,144 feet), are the steepest permissible on Federal highways.

The route along the seaward flank of the Santa Monicas northward along the coast, was shunned as impassable by early explorers and never used by the Spaniards. The traditional routes northwestward were through the San

Fernando Valley. No public right-of-way ever developed along the steep coastal front of the Santa Monica Mountains and, as engineering skills improved, land for a highway had to be purchased. Many delays were encountered, and the first coastal highway was not completed until 1929. Highway 101 today follows one route, through a series of valleys and down the steep Conejo Grade to the Oxnard Plain. A rail line, the modern coast route, follows another, via a tunnel (1902) through the Santa Susana Pass into the Simi Valley.

The significance of the few high pass entrances to the region may seem to be limited to roadside mountain scenery and a few slow-moving trucks most days of the year. On an occasional winter day, however, the traveler will find snow blocking the highway in Cajon Pass or at Gorman, on Tejon Pass, and on more occasions chains will be required for safe passage. The modern commercial airliner soars at will over the highest portions of the ranges. However, pilots of small planes with unpressurized cabins still seek out the few breaks in the mountain wall almost as avidly as the highway builder.

Mountains as Habitats

Mountains have been a part of the area's life style for almost a century. An observatory on Mount Wilson was reached by a toll road (1889), and an inclined railway up neighboring Echo Mountain (1893), and the Mt. Lowe Railway stimulated interest in the ranges behind Pasadena as a recreational area. Acquired as a forest reserve in the 1880s, the area has seen rapidly increasing use for hiking, fishing, camping, weekend cabins, and occasional winter skiing. Romantically named roads, "Angeles Crest Highway," "Rim of the World Drive," "Pines to Palms Highway," provide access into the mountains for the weekend excursion or Sunday drives. Alternatively, one can take a tram from Palm Springs to the wilderness area of Mount San Jacinto.

The slopes of the high mountain rim are generally too precipitous for homesites. The San Gabriels particularly, much shattered and fractured, atop the San Andreas fault, have sharp crestlines and are generally uninhabited. The exception is a small settlement at Wrightwood on the north-facing slope. The San Bernardinos, younger, less worn, not as much shattered by earthquakes, have broader crests with more habitable land. Here a number of resort communities have developed around mountain lakes formed where valleys have been dammed as reservoirs for irrigation projects. Bear Valley was dammed in 1884, creating Big Bear Lake. Lake Arrowhead, 1901, and Lake Gregory, 1939, were later undertakings. Today, numerous communities have developed along their shores as mountain resort-suburbs among the pines at elevations of about 6,700, 5,100, and 4,850 feet, respectively, still accessible to downtown Los Angeles by a ninety minute drive.

It is as weekend and holiday recreational areas within the Metropolis that the high mountain ranges have their greatest utility. As only one example, twice as many people visit the San Bernardino Mountains annually as visit the most popular national park—some seven and a half million as long ago as 1964. Scenery is somewhat limited because of the general aridity of the lower slopes. However, there are spectacular drives; in winter, if the weather has been cooperative, there are numerous skiing opportunities; camping is popular in the summer, as is fishing and hunting in season. Recently, an additional facility, Lake Silverwood, created as part of the California Water Plan, has become available for boating, fishing, and picnicking.

Far and away the most important highlands for homesites are the lower ranges that penetrate like fingers into the very heart of the metropolitan area. These include the Santa Monicas, Santa Anas, the Repetto Hills, and the more distant Palos Verdes Hills. At the margins of these heights, there have developed unusually desirable residential neighborhoods, some of which extend into the canyons, and others wind up the ridges above. Along the south slopes of the Santa Monicas, for example, are Hollywood, West Hollywood, Beverly Hills, Bel Air, Brentwood, and Pacific Palisades. As one writer puts it, "Here high class home sites are available for those who enjoy spectacular views from the hillsides, or the seclusion of their 'laurel privacies' in the canyons."

Mountains and Climate

The mountain ranges, both high and low, are major factors in the area's climatic characteristics and their influence will be detailed in a chapter on climate. The high mountains themselves add a separate climatic zone to the region, characterized by much rainfall and regular winter snow, but their influence on climate permeates the Metropolis. They block off winter storms. They impede the flow of the sea breeze into the interior valleys. They are mainly responsible for the wide regional variations of rainfall, from an average of fifteen inches in downtown Los Angeles to thirty-five inches on Mount Wilson, for example. Finally, it is the arrangement of the mountains that provides the area with its distinguishing microclimates, producing variations in summer temperatures between locations only ten or fifteen miles apart that are greater than those found in the East between places 1,000 miles distant.

The Precious Lowlands

The two thousand square miles of generally flat lowlands are the most densely settled and the heart of the Metropolis. The lowlands are not as picturesque as the mountains, nor as romantic as the seashore, but it is on these prosaic areas that the action was, is now, and, in all likelihood, will be in the future.

It was the lowlands, watered by the mountain streams, that attracted the first settlers. They provided the pastures for the cattle ranches; they were the scene of the great agricultural developments of the American irrigator and orchardist. The lowlands could be easily crossed by railroads and interurban, thus bringing the mountains and seacoast within range of the urban settler. The subdivider, too, was attracted to the lowlands where roads and other improvements could be built at reasonable costs. It is on the lowlands, today, where the vast majority of the people live. It is on these areas that the manufacturing plants have been built, shopping centers erected, and office buildings sited. The presence of expansive lowlands makes possible the Metropolis as we know it.

"Los Angeles Is the Greatest City on the Shore in the World"
Reyner Banham (1971, p. 37).

The Pacific Ocean, the coastline with its miles of sandy beaches, the developed harbors, and the numerous small boat marinas have become one of the greatest assets of the Metropolis. For a city that was not founded on the coast, its coastal development and the influence of the beaches and ocean is remarkable.

First there are the beaches, some seventy miles or more of them from Zuma to Balboa, an almost continuous double arc of white sand, nearly all of it open to the public. To quote Banham (1971, p. 39) again, "One way or another, the beach is what life is all about in Los Angeles." He points out that this beach life style has its own artifact, the surf-board. The Pacific Electric made access to the beaches easy early in this century. To stimulate traffic they introduced surfing in 1907 by bringing George Freeth, a pioneer surfer from Hawaii, to Redondo Beach to give demonstrations. The surfer on a curling wave has been a symbol of the area ever since.

Then there are the marinas. Strung along the coast from the Ventura Marina to Newport Bay are seven man-made havens for thousands of small pleasure craft and headquarters for a lifestyle pleasurable to tens of thousands of people. *The* marina, though, at least in terms of local parlance and national fame, is Marina del Rey. Dredged out of the swamps behind Playa del Rey (the King's Beach) from 1957 to 1965, with tidelands oil money and the backing of Los Angeles County, it is now advertised as the largest marina in the country and has slips for nearly 6,000 boats. Its complex of apartments, condominiums, restaurants, and shops cater to a way of life geared to youth, the sun, and the sea.

More important to the economic base of the area are the artificial harbors of Los Angeles and Long Beach. Dredging of the tidal mud flats began in 1887, and the construction of a breakwater (1899) converted an open roadstead into a well protected harbor. The continuously improved complex today comprises one of the most extensive manmade deepwater harbors in the world. Today the dual harbors handle more ship traffic and more gross tonnage than any other west coast port. These twin harbors are not only an efficient contact with the resources and markets of the world, but the complex includes sites for manufacturing plants, a naval base, a marina for small boats, and attractions for the general public such as the Queen Mary and the shops and restaurants of "Ports of Call."

Beyond the shore lies the Pacific, a major resource for all people who live along its borders. The Indians found it an inexhaustible source of food and an efficient surface for local travel. It eventually brought explorers from Spain, England, and Russia. Later sea otters provided a basis for Russian (mainly) sea hunting. Salt was made from its waters. In this century it has supported a productive fishing industry. First sardines and then tuna were caught in quantities sufficient to make Los Angeles the chief fishing port in the nation in the 1920s. Today the Pacific has inestimable value as a recreational resource for the sometime sailor, an amenity for watchers of its waves and gulls, and as a neutral, non-polluting region over which masses of clean air arrive unceasingly.

The Subsurface

In most metropolitan areas the only thing of value under the ground is gravel. In Los Angeles, however, two other subsurface products have been significant, water and petroleum-natural gas.

Water was the first essential, and the arrangement of mountain and plain has created a number of basins of porous alluvium, ideal for the storage of water. They make possible, in effect, vast underground lakes. Consider the water that falls on or runs from the surrounding mountains into the San Fernando Valley. Percolating into the alluvium, some gradually flows toward its outlet at the Glendale Narrows in sufficient volume and regularity so that originally the Los Angeles River was a perennial stream. The water that remains underground can be pumped out and used as needed. In addition, water brought into the area by aqueduct can be stored in these underground basins until needed. Similar reservoirs exist under the San Gabriel and San Bernardino valleys and under much of the coastal plain. In some areas at an earlier period artesian water was available, water that flowed naturally from wells by hydrostatic pressure. The availability of water in these underground basins helped open the inland valleys to irrigation agriculture and is a continuing asset.

Further, portions of the Metropolis are underlain with petroleum bearing strata. Early evidence was the bubbling tar pits (the present Hancock Park), and the pitch was used to waterproof roofs and caulk ships. Gradually, bonafide petroleum deposits were found, first just north of downtown Los Angeles, then in a variety of locations. Fortuitously, the major oil fields were discovered in the early 1920s at just the time a great demand for gasoline for automobiles was developing. The effect of oil fields on the Metropolis has been mixed. The drilling of thousands of wells provided employment for many and generated much revenue at a time both were rare. Further, for the first time, the area now had a local source of energy. By nature an ephemeral form of land use, the presence of oil fields has had an important effect on the development of neighborhoods, blighting some spots for a time and delaying their development until the resource was exhausted. Then large blocks of land, formerly by-passed, became available and occasionally they have resulted in communities designed as a unit, such as the La Brea Apartment complex and Century City.

2. Suggested Readings

California Geology.
> A monthly publication devoted to articles and news related to the earth sciences in California. Each issue includes book reviews and lists new publications. Available from: California Division of Mines and Geology, P. O. Box 298, Sacramento, CA 95812, for $3.00 a year.

Jahns, Richard H. ed. *Geology of Southern California. Bulletin 70.* Sacramento: California Division of Mines, 1954.
> The classic description of many aspects of the physical geography of the Metropolis; includes articles, maps and guides.

Lockmann, Ronald F. *Guarding the Forests of Southern California.* Glendale: Arthur H. Clark, 1981.
> Describes the preservation of the mountain backdrop of the Metropolis as national forest through the efforts of local residents and the federal government.

Robinson, John W. *The San Gabriels.* San Marino: Golden West Books, 1977.
> A large scale book with many pictures and maps this volume tells the story of the human use of the San Gabriel Mountains.

Sharp, Robert P. *Geology Field Guide to Southern California.* Dubuque, Iowa: Kendall/Hunt, 1972.
> This book features a layman's discussion of the geology of the mountains and valleys of the Metropolis, plus a number of self-guided tours, both within and beyond the region.

CHAPTER 3

Earthquakes, Landslides, and Other Hazards of Terrain

Figure 3.1. The Palisades crumble from time to time, occasionally covering the Pacific Coast Highway, as on April 23, 1958. (Photo courtesy Spence Collection/Department of Geography, UCLA.)

"The farther we are from the last earthquake, the nearer we are to the next." Bailey Willis (Crowell, 1975, p. 4).

"Anyone who would deliberately attempt to ride out an ocean storm in an improperly designed or constructed ship would be considered foolhardy. Yet here we sit, most of California's communities, in and below many tens of thousands of old structures designed and built with little or no knowledge of earthquake engineering or foundation geology, waiting to ride out a severe earthquake next year or in five years or, with great good luck, in twenty years." Wesley G. Bruer (Clark, 1973, p. 4).

Earthquake History

When the Spanish explorer Portolá arrived at the Santa Ana River in 1769 he experienced a severe earthquake and promptly named the stream *Santa Ana de Los Temblores*. Before the party left the San Fernando Valley four days later they had felt the earth shake twelve more times. From the first European account of the region its dynamic geology has been an important part of the description. At least seventy-five earthquakes of various magnitudes have been reported in the period 1812–1971. For example, an earthquake on July 11, 1855 is reported to have damaged almost every building in Los Angeles, left large cracks in the adobe walls, and toppled chimneys and roofs. At San Gabriel Mission the bells were shaken down, and the Hugo Reid adobe house (now part of the Los Angeles County Arboretum) was wrecked.

Repetitive descriptions of damage caused by the area's many earthquakes would be tedious, if sobering, but this is how Los Angeles fared during the three strongest quakes in California's history:

A quake was felt in the city January 9, 1857. An eyewitness reports, ". . . the quake grew in power until houses were deserted, men, women and children sought refuge in the streets, and horses and cattle broke loose in wild alarm," (Newmark, 1970, p. 204). This was the result of an earthquake along the San Andreas Fault centered near Fort Tejon (estimated magnitude 8.0) where lateral displacement was thirty feet.

On the morning of March 26, 1872 sleepers were thrown out of bed in Los Angeles by a sharp earthquake. When "excited riders" (Newark, 1970, p. 440) reached the area from the Owens Valley, they reported what may have been the strongest earthquake in California history (estimated magnitude 8.3). The Sierra Fault Block rose twenty-three feet, movement along the fault was noticed for seventy miles and at Lone Pine fifty-two out of fifty-nine homes were destroyed.

The San Francisco earthquake, April 18, 1906 (estimated magnitude 8.25) was scarcely felt in Los Angeles, but there resulted identification of the San Andreas Fault over its entire length, it having moved in some amount over a distance of two hundred seventy miles. Knowledge gained from it became clues to the nature of faulting, and the kind of damage common in buildings, all provided data that would eventually be used in developing building codes and other standards.

The Long Beach Earthquake

The most significant earthquake for the Los Angeles area was the Long Beach earthquake of March 10, 1933. On the Newport-Inglewood fault, it was not very strong as earthquakes go (magnitude 6.3) but it occurred in a densely populated area with much poor construction—building codes up to that time did not consider the possibility of earthquakes. As a result it was devastating, particularly in Long Beach, Garden Grove, Compton and Torrance, with one hundred two fatalities in the area and some forty million dollars in damage, all out of proportion to the strength of the quake.

Perhaps it is best described by an eyewitness. The following is a condensed excerpt from an article by Gordon B. Oakeshott (1973, pp. 55–59) in recalling the event of fifty years ago.

"It was about 5 minutes to 6:00 on March 10, 1933 and twilight was beginning to dim the landscape on this rather dull day as seen from our home on the border of Compton and north Long Beach. We were preparing dinner and I stood at the kitchen window facing south toward what was to be the earthquake epicenter about 20 miles away. I looked up sharply when I heard a peculiar, low-pitched rumbling sound. Then, within 2 or 3 seconds, came the sounds of crashing buildings, explosions of dust into the air, and violent shaking of our one-story frame-and-stucco house. So fast did the violence follow the first tremors that we barely had time to plant ourselves desperately in the kitchen doorway.

My mother and two-year-old son were thrown to the living-room floor and our small, squat, open gas heater was up-ended. Our modest house was twisted and rocked by such intense ground motion that we marvelled that our later inspection revealed no real damage.

"Seismologists and geologists now recognize that local ground acceleration in a moderate earthquake—like the 6.3 Richter magnitude Long Beach earthquake—may be as high as in a truly great earthquake, like the magnitude 8.25 San Francisco earthquake. At Compton and Long Beach in 1933, water, electricity, gas and phones were all turned off within minutes of the main shock. Water, electricity, and phone service were restored within a few hours, but restoration of gas service took longer while emergency utility crews checked systems for leaks.

"Judging from the intensity and duration of shaking, ground cracking, and concentration of building damage, the intensity of the earthquake was higher in Compton than it was in Long Beach, although Long Beach was closer to the epicenter (two miles offshore southwest of Huntington Beach). There appear to be good geologic reasons for this: Compton lies at sea level in a water-saturated basin of sediments formed by overflow of the Los Angeles River and Compton Creek while Long Beach is mostly over the geologic high of the Newport-Inglewood structural zone which is relatively more stable. Only a few years prior to the earthquake Compton had enjoyed artesian water from shallow wells.

"How long did we feel the intense shaking? A long, long 10 seconds, or more!—during which time I wondered: to what climax of intensity could this build up? Would the house utterly collapse around us? I experienced the same uptight apprehension in the strongly felt 'aftershock' of October 2, 1933 (Richter magnitude 5.4), which originated near Signal Hill northwest of the epicenter of the March 10 earthquake.

"In my wisdom (?) as a young geologist, I told my wife that we had certainly experienced the main shock and all aftershocks would be lesser. Therefore, there was no sense in following the neighbors who were moving out onto their front lawns for the night's rest. So, we stayed inside and heard all night long the screaming sirens of the ambulances taking the injured along nearby Long Beach Boulevard into Los Angeles emergency hospitals, and experienced one bed-shaking aftershock after another. Before morning, my seven-months pregnant wife was shaking in resonance. Needless to say, we moved out on the lawn for the next several nights!

"Our house fared well—as did most of the other modern single-story, woodframe houses—but others were not so fortunate. Many of the older, larger woodframe houses—often set on 'cripples', or pedestals, instead of continuous concrete foundations, and not bolted to their foundations—were displaced horizontally a foot or two and collapsed. Many of the old business buildings, built of unreinforced brick, with poor mortar, and designed only for vertical load and not resistant to the horizontal loading of an earthquake, failed. Even a moderate earthquake imposes stresses and strains on structures which expose weaknesses in design and construction that years of static load might not uncover! I shall never forget one of the 'classic' building failures in Compton. My good friend, Dr. Firkins, a dentist who had gone on geologic field trips with me (through the diversion tunnels in the gorge of the Colorado River before the Hoover Dam was built, for example) was killed by a falling beam as he was working on a patient. His office was on the second floor, supported only by vertical 'stilts' above an open market. His patient was hurt slightly, but survived. My wife and I attended outdoor services for him a few days later, held in the backyard of the mortuary as the aftershocks continued.

"The worst of all building failures were those which affected the schools of Long Beach and Compton. I shall cite the buildings of the Compton Union High School and Junior College, both because they were typical of 'schoolhouse' failures and because in 1933 I was teaching surveying and the earth sciences at the College and so have poignant memories.

"Our three-story high school and college classroom-and-administration building was so badly damaged that it had to be razed and rebuilt. My basement classroom was filled with rubble and a central chimney structure had come down through classrooms on two floors into the basement. I managed to salvage surveying equipment in a few days, after the aftershocks died down. It was indeed a godsend that the earthquake happened at a time of day when school buildings were nearly unoccupied.

Compton College's beautiful, tile-roofed arcades between buildings collapsed completely. The great and lasting good that came from the tragic and scandalous failures of school structures in this earthquake was the passage of the Field Act by the State Legislature. The Field Act requires state approval and inspection of school buildings, plans, and construction practices. Experience in later earthquakes—notably Arvin-Tehachapi 1952, San Francisco 1957, and San Fernando 1971—has amply demonstrated the efficacy of the Field Act in increasing seismic safety of school buildings.

"At Compton, it was many months before we occupied our classrooms again. The school semester closed abruptly on March 10 and regular classes were not resumed until the beginning of the fall semester. Beginning with the fall semester we taught quite happily in open tent structures on the grass floors of the athletic field.

"The swampy estuarine lowlands just north of Newport Beach, Huntington Beach, Alamitos Bay, and Bolsa Chica were sites of ground and road cracking, separation of bridge structures from their approaches, and evidence of shallow soil-liquefaction as shown by sand boils and mud volcanoes. Fracturing and dislocation of streets and curbs in the water-saturated, lowland sediments of the Compton basin were extensive. For example, the carefully laid-out benchmarks I had set on curbs around the College for the use of my surveying students were rendered useless by the extensive breaking and dislocation of the concrete curbs. Settling cracks in the lowlands and earth slumps and slides along the steeper slopes of the structural and topographic hills of the Newport-Inglewood uplift gave testimony of strong ground shaking. In adition to the direct effects of ground shaking, the many ground failures contributed significantly to building and street damage.

"Perhaps 90 percent of Compton's business and professional center was concentrated in an area a few blocks long on the wide main street and a couple of blocks into the side streets. Prompt and decisive action, with the official threat of death to looters, and the lack of fires had left much of the merchants' goods damaged but intact. However, most of the business and professional buildings were demolished or had to be vacated as structurally unsafe.

"How could business be carried on? What about essential goods and services for the public? On the edge of the city—only a few blocks from the old business center—stood the unoccupied huge, boxlike steel-and-galvanized-iron structure of the Fry Roofing Company. A day or two after the earthquake the plan was conceived to lay out 'streets' in this vast structure and to allocate to each businessman prorated space in the same relative position and with the same street names to which we were all accustomed. Thus, we all had a big, convenient market for months after the earthquake, while downtown Compton was being rebuilt."

San Fernando Earthquake

The most recent temblor of significance in the Metropolis was the San Fernando earthquake which occurred at 6:00 A.M. February 9, 1971. It lasted ten seconds, and caused considerable damage mainly in the northern San Fernando Valley. The epicenter was about seven miles north of San Fernando and twenty-four miles from downtown Los Angeles. Shaking was intense in the northern valley, strong in central Los Angeles, and rather weak in Long Beach. In effect a portion of the San Gabriel Mountains rose several feet and moved southward several inches. This motion caused very strong ground shaking waves, with intensity decreasing with distance. The earthquake had a Richter magnitude of 6.4, stronger than the earlier Long Beach quake.

Sixty-four people died, and damage was estimated at half a billion dollars, yet it was a shock of only intermediate magnitude. It caused considerable damage because it was located at the edge of a densely populated region. Fatalities undoubtedly would have been higher had the earthquake been centered twenty miles farther south, close to the center of population and near the location of many old buildings. Had it occurred a few hours later many more occupants would have been in the buildings that did collapse, many more motorists would have been on the freeway bridges

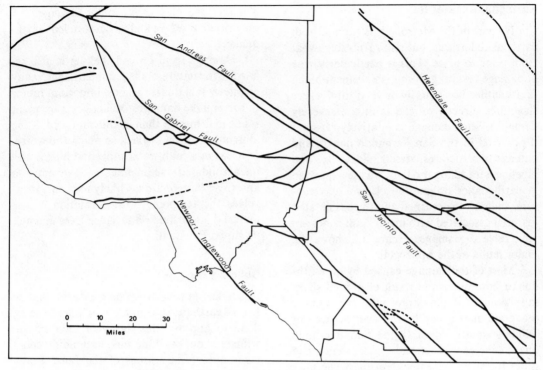

Figure 3.2. The major earthquake faults of the Metropolis.

that were destroyed, and many more pedestrians would have been on the streets risking casualties from falling debris.

The Metropolis as Earthquake Country

The earth's surface seems to consist of about a dozen giant, seventy-mile-thick rock plates floating on the earth's semimolten mantle. These plates are in constant though microscopic motion. At the junctions of the plates, friction temporarily locks them in place, causing stresses to build up. Eventually the rock fractures allowing the plates to resume their motion. It is this sudden release of energy that causes earthquakes. In California two great plates are sliding past each other along the San Andreas Fault. The narrow portion west of the fault is moving northwest, whereas to the east the North American plate is moving southeasterly. For at least ten million years the relative velocity of these plates has averaged two or two and a half inches a year or about twenty-three feet a century. The San Andreas fault and its associated faults in southern California are visible results of this motion, and the uplift of the San Gabriel Mountains and the opening of the Gulf of California are products of deformation along the boundary between the two plates.

As our Metropolis is located adjacent to the San Andreas and its system of faults, earthquakes are inevitable. Experts assert that a quake of about the magnitude of the San Fernando earthquake occurs somewhere in California once every four years, and that there is a reasonably high probability that a great earthquake will occur within the next thirty years. As earthquakes are certain to occur we should understand their forces and endeavor to design our Metropolis in such a way that loss of life and damage to property is minimized.

Earthquake Hazards

No part of the Metropolis is exempt from earthquake hazards, but risk varies somewhat from place to place. This is particularly true of damage resulting from displacement along faults, either horizontally or vertically, where structures directly on the fault are severely damaged. Such damage is relatively rare but it occurred in the San Fernando quake, and damage to structures, streets, sidewalks, and pipelines straddling the fault was severe. Even in earthquakes originating elsewhere, structures built on the crushed and unconsolidated material associated with major fault zones are vulnerable to damage. Figure 3.2 shows the major faults in the Metropolis.

Most of the damage caused by an earthquake, however, is the result of ground shaking because of the large area involved—a moderate quake may be felt over an area of 100,000 square miles. In the San Fernando quake damage was noticeable more than thirty miles from the epicenter. Normally the bulk of the damage and the vast majority of the deaths in an earthquake are the result of structural collapse, falling cornices of older buildings and so on, caused by ground shaking. The effect of ground shaking is related to the intensity of the quake, the distance from the epicenter, the period of motion, the duration of shaking, and the nature of the ground involved.

The most common measure of the intensity of earthquakes is the Richter Magnitude, named after its developer, Professor C. F. Richter. This scale uses a seismograph to measure the energy of an earthquake at its source. The magnitude of the quake is expressed in whole numbers and decimals. Comprehending the scale is difficult because the magnitude increases logarithmically. Each higher number represents a ten fold increase in the magnitude of the tremors, and a thirty to sixty fold increase in the energy released. Thus a 2 point quake is barely perceptible, a 5 magnitude may cause minor damage, a 7 magnitude is severe and an 8 is a violent earthquake.

Damage from ground shaking is also related to the nature of the ground. In fact, many engineers feel this is the most important factor in earthquake damage. Oscillatory movement is less in firm rock than in alluvium, and, if the alluvium is water soaked, so much the worse. In areas of a high water table and fine, sandy unconsolidated sediments a phenomenon known as *liquefaction* is likely to occur. It involves the temporary transformation of the material into a fluid mass which loses much of its supportive quality.

Building Design

It has gradually become evident that to live in earthquake country much needs to be done to improve the ability of buildings to withstand quakes. Our current building codes come out of the lessons of the Long Beach earthquake and further experience has brought additional modifications.

In 1933, many wood frame houses were shaken from their foundations and often collapsed, unreinforced brick walls failed, and many school buildings with brick or hollow block walls and wooden roofs and floors fell down. Most of the loss of life occurred when persons were struck by falling cornices, parapets, or other ornamentations as they tried to leave shaking buildings. Out of this experience came building codes that have proven effective. Lateral bracing, a continuous foundation with sills bolted to it, reinforcing steel rods in brick walls, and the elimination of outside ornamentation were included in the Los Angeles building codes enacted after 1933. As a result, the typical one-story, single family dwelling withstood the San Fernando earthquake quite well. Although about 20,000 homes were damaged, and eight hundred thirty were destroyed or nearly destroyed, no occupied residential structure collapsed as a result of shaking. In spite of the fact that perhaps ninety percent of the affected population were in residential structures at the time of the quake, there were only two fatalities in dwellings as compared to fifty-six associated with other structures. The casualty factor in dwellings, therefore, was somewhat less than one per million (Slosson, 1975, p. 237). Damage did occur in structures immediately adjacent to the fault displacement. At these locations split level structures with the second story over the garage were particularly vulnerable. Other damage was associated with poor fill, laid down before the grading codes were strengthened in 1963. Damage was also high in older (pre-1933) masonry structures.

Continuing Problems for the Area

As earthquakes are an ever present menace, an assessment of the current hazards and means for their alleviation seems appropriate. It is estimated, for example, that some 28,000 pre-1933 buildings in Los Angeles County still stand, buildings that do not conform to the current Uniform Building Code in relation to earthquake shaking. About 5,000 of these buildings are residential, but only about two hundred are single family dwellings. The majority are clustered around the downtown area, but others are widely scattered. Outright abandonment of these structures is difficult as they have a value of eight billion dollars, are the home of 200,000 people and provide workplaces for some 35,000. The difficulty is compounded as many of the residents are elderly and poor and many of the businesses are marginal. Immediate demolition or renovation would be practical only if combined with relocation assistance or grants for renovation.

At least the hazardous buildings might be prominently identified, and priorities established for occupancy reduction, renovation, or demolition.

Many high rise buildings have been built since 1957, constructed to modern standards that presumably will withstand expected quakes. They have not been tested by really severe shaking, however. Problems of elevator operation, evacuation, fire fighting, falling glass, and debris may be ameliorated by advance preparation. In addition, it is thought by some that standards for earthquake resistance of nonstructural components of tall buildings—partitions, lighting fixtures, furnishings, and external veneers—need further strengthening.

There are perhaps twenty dams in Los Angeles County that may be endangered by a quake, and hazards lie both in the loss of function, i.e., storage capacity, and the threat to life and property in the spillway of the dam. An increase in the earthquake resistance of these dams may be called for.

An additional problem with no obvious solution results from the fact that all of the area's "lifelines" cross fault lines. All of the major aqueducts bringing water into the region cross the San Andreas fault as do the two natural gas lines serving the region. The same is true of four petroleum pipelines and the major telephone trunk lines. Much of the electricity brought into the area also crosses the San Andreas fault; other generating plants are located near the Newport-Inglewood fault. Three major sewage disposal systems either cross or are near the latter fault.

For the long run the region's zoning ordinances should be brought into conformity with seismic risk regions. Land use planning that prohibits the settlement of high risk areas by dense populations and complex structures should be a primary goal. Areas adjacent to faults should be reserved for open ground uses, and areas of fill and unconsolidated sediments avoided by uses that attract large populations.

One adjustment to living in earthquake country would be to share the cost of quakes through insurance. Earthquake insurance is available on a special risk basis, but is not commonly bought. Rates range from $1.50 to $2.50 per $1,000 and have a five percent deductible provision. Thus, on coverage of a $100,000 home the first $5,000 of damage would be excluded from compensation.

The Future: Prediction and Prevention

In the mid 1980s work is in progress that may make possible the prediction of the place, time, and magnitude of a future earthquake. Instruments of various sorts are being installed in fault zones: seismometers, laser strain gages, resistometers, tiltmeters, and others, and data being recorded. A report by the National Academy of Science assesses progress: "Earthquake prediction is still in a research stage . . . but theory and experience are advanced enough to justify confidence that an expanding prediction capability may be imminent. By prediction we mean the specification of place, time and magnitude of earthquakes within sufficiently narrow limits to permit short-term and accelerated long-term actions to save life and property." (National Research Council, 1975, p. 24.) The reaction of the public to this new knowledge, if it becomes available, is a worrisome unknown.

Just as intriguing is research that may lead to the management of earthquakes. The goal is to control the slippage between the continental plates by pumping out water in sections that need strengthening and injecting water at other points to induce slippage. By inducing slippage of a short section of a fault between two strengthened portions it is thought the natural strains could be released gradually. The idea is that once or twice a year you would slip a five-kilometer section of a fault like the San Andreas two or three centimeters. That would probably be enough to keep the two plates moving at about the same average rate of displacement as they have moved at for some time. Some slight damage to structures near the fault could result, but most people would

likely prefer a movement of a couple of centimeters a year every year to five meters (sixteen feet) all at once every hundred years.

Landslides, a Hazard of Hillside and Bluff

Geologists have mapped about 3,800 landslides in the area of the Metropolis, a concentration probably unequaled in any other American Metropolitan Region. Landslides have been natural events throughout the region during all recent geological time. Generally, they have resulted from the association of steep hillside slopes, youthful and weak earth materials, adverse geologic structure and, occasionally, heavy rainfall. Only some ten to fifteen percent of the slides derive from human activity.

Most of the hillsides in our area are composed of sedimentary rock, much tilted, folded, and broken by faults. Sometimes layers of clay or similar materials are present. Often it is these clay layers which turn to mush when saturated with water that so weaken the slopes that landslides occur. Sometimes this is a natural occurrence, but in other instances it is the result of human alteration of the drainage pattern, or a humanly-derived change in the angle of the slope, loading the top of the slope, or undercutting the toe of the slope.

Occasional historic slides have reached massive proportions. A view of the Pacific Palisades from the coast highway reveals a scalloped appearance from ancient and active slumps and rockfalls. "On April 4, 1958, a slide involving 90,000 cubic yards of material plunged down on the Pacific Coast Highway. The movement took place so suddenly that an engineer was killed and several pieces of equipment were buried; the engineer, incidentally, was inspecting the removal of a slide which had taken place a month earlier. Rather than risk a third slide, it was decided to build the highway around the toe of the slump." (Pipkin and Ploessel, 1973, N.P.) A second famous landslide is in the Portuguese Bend area of the Palos Verdes Hills. In 1956 a large section that had been built up with single family homes began moving seaward. Eventually over three hundred acres were involved and more than one hundred fifty of the homes destroyed. The land has moved more than one hundred forty feet since the slide began, and as recently as 1973 it was moving at a rate of a foot a month.

Other, less spectacular slides take place almost every year, often after heavy rains. In 1960 landslides after one storm took two lives, forced the evacuation of one hundred hillside homes and did millions of dollars of property damage. Although damage is localized as far as homes are concerned, the cost of repairing roads, utilities, and drainage channels comes from taxpayers in general, so in a real sense the problem is a regional one.

The City of Los Angeles began enacting increasingly stiff grading codes after the severe winter seasons of 1951–52, during and after which many cases of flooding and sliding occurred. The grading Ordinance of 1952 was the first of its kind and has been widely emulated. Hillside terrain was defined, permits for cuts and fills in these areas were required, and inspections were required to see that certain engineering standards were met. In 1956 the city began requiring geologic reports prior to the issuance of grading permits and, later, geologists preparing these reports had to be certified by an Engineering Geologists Qualifications Board. The code was further strengthened in 1963, tightening up specifications for cut and fill slopes, compaction of fill materials, and provisions for surface drainage. The final inspection requires certification by a soils engineer, a geologist and a civil engineer stating that the originally approved plat has been translated into reality.

Subsidence

Earthquakes, slumps, and slides are instantaneous and dramatic phenomena, but an additional type of geologic hazard affects the Metropolis that is gradual and almost unnoticed: subsidence. One cause may be the result of the removal of ground water by artesian flow or pumping. The area around La Verne, for example, sank nearly three feet in the twenty-seven year period 1923–1950 (about 1.2 inches a year), a phenomena which was correlated with the decline in levels of artesian wells. Water is now injected into the aquifer. Such slight sinking is generally unnoticed, but it must be taken into account by engineers in designing canals, sewers, and drains which are sensitive to slight change in elevation.

More commonly in our area, however, subsidence has been associated with the removal of petroleum. The Inglewood Oil Field in the Baldwin Hills area was observed to have sunk about ten feet between 1917, when oil was discovered, and 1960. On December 14, 1963, the Baldwin Hills Reservoir was destroyed by failure of its foundations, and the released water did extensive damage, rushing down through residential neighborhoods on its way to Ballona Creek and the sea. The dam was located on the northeast flank of the oil field, and a Board of Inquiry concluded, "the earth movement which triggered the reservoir failure evidently was caused primarily by land subsidence." (California, 1964, p. 3.)

For several decades the harbor area, the location of the Wilmington oil field, experienced a costly and spectacular subsidence. Production began in 1937; by 1951 subsidence had reached sixteen feet, and by 1966, twenty-nine feet in the center of a twenty square mile bowl-shaped basin. This was not only a world record depth but embarrassing and costly, for the center, on Terminal Island, was only five or ten feet above sea level to begin with. In addition, the area was heavily industrialized, the location of a Southern California Edison Plant, and a U.S. Naval Shipyard, as well as hundreds of oil wells. A massive rescue operation was started: building levees and retaining walls, adding fill and raising of structures. As early as 1962 it was estimated that the damage was $100 million dollars.

The many legal problems resulting from subsidence (unitization of the oil field, for example) were solved in 1958. Subsidence was stopped by repressuring the field through injection of seawater in conjunction with secondary processes of oil recovery. The subsidence zone was stabilized by 1966 and, more recently, the surface has rebounded upward about one foot.

Problems of the Seashore

Even the broad sandy beaches that rim the region's oceanward edge are not without their problems. Early in this century they are believed to have been in a general state of equilibrium between sand deposited and sand lost due to wave and current action. Sand is carried into the sea by streams during the winter rains, and the strong littoral drift southeastward moves sand into the area from as far north as the Santa Clara River eighty miles away. As there is no sand accumulation in the Palos Verdes area it is thought that much sand is lost in the deep Redondo submarine canyon. With the spread of urban forms, however, the extension of flood control fixtures, and the building of breakwaters and harbors, this equilibrium has been upset. Today we have both a condition of general beach starvation and sand maldistribution: unnatural beach widening in some places, unnatural erosion in others.

The fine, soft sand of our beaches was once a part of the surrounding land, and it reaches the sea through the combined processes of denudation. Now, many structures, streets, parking lots, and so on have been built on potential sand-producing surfaces, reducing denudation and cutting off the sand supply at its source. Our flood control devices, check dams, debris dams, and large water-retarding dams, as well as the concrete channel linings all act to drastically reduce the supply of sand reaching the sea. Efforts to stabilize the coastal palisades and preserve the foreshore also reduce the material which might be ground to sand by the pounding waves. General sand starvation of the beaches has been the result, and without artificial replenishment a general narrowing of our beaches would be inevitable.

The construction of breakwaters in connection with harbors have been major contributors to the maldistribution of sand on our beaches, and a variety of measures have been attempted to correct these imbalances. For example, the jetties built up the coast at Port Hueneme connect the head of a submarine canyon with the harbor and effectively prevent harbor silting. They also form a nearly perfect barrier to sand from the Santa Clara River that would normally work its way onto the local beaches. To overcome this obstacle it has been necessary to dredge 1,800,000 cubic feet of sand each year from the accumulation zone above the jetties and to transport it across the harbor entrance where it is released onto the downcoast beaches. (Place, 1970, pp. 103–105.)

When the Santa Monica breakwater was built in 1933 to provide a yacht harbor, the reduced wave action caused the shoreline in its lee to widen. As early as 1948 the beach behind the breakwater was seven hundred fifty feet wider than before; a mile upcoast some three hundred fifty feet had been added to the beach, and as far north as Santa Monica canyon an additional two hundred feet of sand had been deposited. It is thought that eventually the beach will grow all the way out to the breakwater.

At the same time the entire shoreline from Santa Monica pier to Redondo Beach suffered from sand starvation. The recession of the beach amounted to something like seventy-five feet at Venice by 1945, and storms that formerly did no damage now found beachfront property vulnerable. A temporary solution was found when the Hyperion Sewer Plant was enlarged in 1947 amid sand dunes built when the Los Angeles River was emptying into Santa

Monica Bay. Leveling of the site resulted in the removal of 14,000,000 cubic yards of sand which were distributed hydraulically to beaches extending as far north as Ocean Park. These six miles of beaches were widened an average of six hundred feet, but, of course, they were still subject to gradual erosion, and movement of sand downbeach. An additional 2,400,000 cubic yards of sand became available for beach widening with the construction of a power plant at El Segundo in 1956. Construction of Marina del Rey (1958–62) and its jetties also affected sand movement. The jetties provided a barrier to the natural movement of sand southward, so the 3,200,000 cubic yards of sand produced in the dredging of the entrance channel were spread to the south, where it was thought it would compensate for about twenty years of erosion without natural replenishment.

For the future, several steps toward reducing beach starvation are possible. They include the sluicing of coarse sediment from behind dams during periods when the flow of water will carry the material to the sea, the physical transport of sand to the coast, the bypassing of sand around the heads of submarine canyons, and artificial filling, using sand from dunes or offshore deposits of suitable sand. In addition, a series of small properly engineered groins might be used to hold or moderately prograde the beach. Such long-term solutions must await ecological planning over wider units and on a larger scale than is yet possible.

3. Suggested Readings

Barrows, Allan G. ed. *A Review of the Geology and Earthquake History of the Newport-Inglewood Structural Zone, Southern California. Special Report, 114.* Sacramento: California Division of Mines and Geology, 1974.
Running diagonally from Newport Beach to Culver City this fault is of vital interest to many in the region. This volume describes the fault zone, discusses the earthquakes that have occurred along it, and speculates briefly on future possibilities.

California Division of Mines and Geology. *Landslides in the Los Angeles Region, California. Open File Report OFR 79-4LA.* Sacramento: California Division of Mines and Geology, 1979.
This report describes the effects of the February-March 1978 rains. It is strikingly illustrated and includes an extensive bibliography on local landslides.

Crowell, John C. ed. *San Andreas Fault in Southern California. Special Report 118.* Sacramento: California Division of Mines and Geology, 1975.
Although written for a geological conference and field trip, the twenty-eight papers in this report will provide much of value to anyone in search of information about this famous fault.

Oakeshott, Gordon B. ed. *San Fernando, California, Earthquake of 9 February, 1971. Bulletin, 196.* Sacramento: California Division of Mines and Geology, 1975.
A detailed, well-illustrated volume, that will tell you all you ever want to know about this recent earthquake.

Tank, Ronald W. *Focus on Environmental Geology.* New York: Oxford, 1976, 2nd. ed.
This volume comprises a collection of readings, a number of which focus on the Metropolis: subsidence in Long Beach, the San Fernando earthquake, speculation on earthquake prediction and control and so on.

Yanev, Peter. *Peace of Mind in Earthquake Country.* San Francisco: Chronicle Books, 1974.
A popular account that describes measures anyone can take to reduce the earthquake hazard.

4

Land of Sunshine and Many Microclimates

Figure 4.1. Smoke from a brush fire in Topanga Canyon, started by an unauthorized dynamite blast in Calabasas, is fanned by Santa Ana winds October 1, 1927. (Photo courtesy Spence Collection/ Department of Geography, UCLA.)

"Hell, we're giving away the land. We're selling the climate." "Lucky" Baldwin, 1881 (Glass-cock, 1933, p. 222.)

"The climate of Southern California is palpable: a commodity that can be labeled, priced and marketed. It is not something that you talk about, guess about, complain about. On the contrary, it is the most consistent, the least paradoxical factor of the environment. . . ." Carey McWilliams (1946, p. 6).

The Los Angeles Metropolis is blessed with the rarest of all the earth's climates, that known to climatologists as Mediterranean. It is characterized here by warm, sunny winters with occasional rains, and hot rainless summers cooled to some extent by sea breezes. A vast pool of placid air (a high pressure system) lies off the coast in summer, forcing the storm tracks northward. The summer climate is characterized by day-to-day similarity, even monotony. The most accurate forecast in this season is that the weather tomorrow will be much like that of today. In the winter, however, the high pressure cell shrinks and an occasional storm from the high latitudes sweeps across the coast breaking the monotony with refreshing rain.

General Characteristics of the Local Climate

The region faces the ocean, and the wind from it, the sea breeze, is a major characteristic of the climate. Shielded as it is from summer storms, only the sea breeze stirs the air in this season. As the daytime temperature of the land increases, the air above it is also warmed and rises, creating a low pressure area. Air from the cool ocean blows in out of the west, reaching velocities of up to twenty miles an hour along the coast although the force decreases rapidly inland. The effects of the sea breeze eventually reach into the inland valleys, resulting in a complete change of air over the region each day. During the night, surface radiation cools the air in the mountains and hills, and it flows into the valleys and meanders to the coast, producing a gentle "land breeze."

In May and June the sea breeze brings in fog caused by the condensation of moisture from the saturated ocean air as it crosses the belt of cooler water near the coast. The lower few hundred feet are evaporated by the heat of the land and the haze hangs over the country as a "high fog," making for dreary days.

In early summer, it is carried far inland and may last all day; later, it is dissipated by the afternoon sun, and by midsummer it is almost entirely absent. It is not until about July that all the region except the immediate coast has daytime temperatures that may be uncomfortably hot.

The sea breeze has a major effect on summer temperature. In August, the hottest month, the high temperature averages sixty-eight degrees in Santa Monica, and eighty-two in downtown Los Angeles, fourteen miles away, or an increase of one degree per mile. (Even this temperature is lower than that of either Chicago or New York, cities located some five hundred miles farther north.) Beyond the Santa Monica-Santa Ana mountain ranges in the interior valleys the temperatures are much higher. On the average, maximum summer temperatures in the San Bernardino Valley are ten degrees higher than at Los Angeles or twenty-five degrees higher than at Santa Monica. Surprisingly, the temperatures everywhere sink to about the same range at night, making the nights in the hot valleys pleasantly cool. (The August mean low at Santa Monica is fifty-four degrees, at San Bernardino fifty-six degrees.) Furthermore, the relative humidity of the valley air is low, greatly ameliorating the high temperatures.

After September the daytime temperatures decrease rapidly in the interior valleys but only slowly along the coast. October is often warmer than June in downtown Los Angeles. By January, the coldest month, most places have generally similar maximum temperatures, with monthly mean maxima varying from fifty-eight at Santa Monica to sixty-six at San Bernardino. The sea acts only as a modest warming agent in winter, producing slightly warmer nights close to the coast (January mean minima at Santa Monica is forty-two, at San Bernardino it is thirty-seven).

The entire Metropolis is well warmed by winter sunshine. In this season, it is the valleys that have the most comfortable weather. The

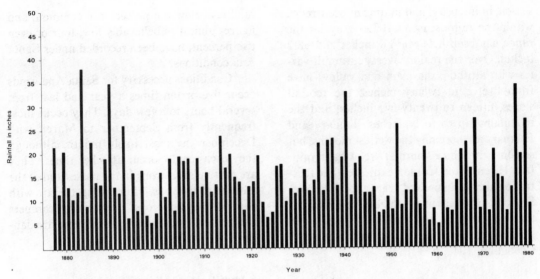

Figure 4.2. One hundred-four year rainfall record at Los Angeles. Based on data from: Metropolitan Water District, *Annual Report, 1981.* Figure 7.

daytime temperatures are high, with an extreme maxima above eighty-five and a mean maxima above sixty-six reported every month for all valley stations. Then, too, the sun shines over three-fourths of the possible hours until the first of the year and over two-thirds for the remainder of the winter.

Nighttime frost in the interior valley bottoms is not infrequent, but marginal moderate slopes with good air drainage are little subject to killing temperatures for any but the most delicate plants. There is, however, great local variation in the frost hazard owing to topography and, in low pockets where cold air accumulates, freezing usually occurs several times each winter.

Usually air temperature decreases at a constant rate with altitude: the warmest air is at the surface, and it is cooler aloft. We take advantage of this when we go to the mountains to "cool off." As warmer air is lighter (less dense) than cool air, normally rising air currents result in considerable mixing throughout the lower atmosphere. However, on days when a layer of cool, moist, marine air moves inland, and when the air above it is warm, as occurs on many days in the Metropolis, we have what

is known as an *inversion.* On these days little vertical mixing of the air occurs: the cooler, heavier air is near the ground, the light, warm air is above. The point where they meet is called the inversion base. "The inversion base acts as a barrier to vertical mixing, not because it is a lid that cannot be penetrated by thermals, or rising air currents, but because air that pushes through the inversion base is heavier than the air in the inversion and returns to equilibrium by sinking below the base" (Keith, 1980, p. 71). Any pollution that enters the atmosphere below the inversion base will stay trapped near the surface, as it does on most days during the summer photochemical smog season.

The rainy season extends from November through April although rainy days come with great irregularity. Between rains, the bright days and untroubled skies of summer return. Heavy rains are not uncommon; five inches in twenty-four hours have been recorded in Los Angeles and a single storm has left as much as thirty inches at mountain stations. In one year a total of sixty-seven inches fell on Mount Wilson. The outstanding characteristic of the rainfall is its great variability, from season to season, in intensity, and in time of occurrence within the rainy season. At Los Angeles the range has been between 4.8 inches and 38.2 inches. Over the region, average rainfall varies with altitude; the plain and valleys have from twelve to twenty inches; the foothill slopes, fifteen to twenty-five inches; and the mountains up to forty inches. January and February are normally the wettest months, but seldom is anything "normal" relating to rainfall. Helen Hunt Jackson expressed her frustration almost a hundred years ago. "The Wet Season is the season in which it can rain but may not; and the dry season is the season in which it cannot rain, but occasionally does" (Robinson, 1942, p. 32).

Santa Ana Winds

One of the more uncomfortable episodes of the Los Angeles climate are the occasional Santa Ana winds, named for one of the canyons through which they often flow. Usually warm, always very dry, these north or northeast winds are often full of dust; "Harsh and burning winds, they rip off palm leaves, snap branches, topple over eucalyptus trees, and occasionally carry off a flimsy roof," as McWilliams (1946, p. 10) describes them. They make the natives restless. It is when these winds are howling, according to Raymond Chandler (1976, p. 7) that "Meek little wives feel the edge of the carving knife and study their husbands' necks."

Santa Anas occur when there is a high pressure system over the Great Basin and low pressure to the southwest. The air, originally from the Arctic, has been warmed a bit, but has had no chance to absorb moisture. Further warming occurs as it moves southward, and compression raises the temperature still higher—the Great Basin is at least a mile high; compressional heating alone would raise its temperature about twenty-eight degrees by the time the air mass reaches sea level. The air is not only hot but extremely dry; relative humidities below ten percent are common, and figures almost unbelievably low, four or even two percent, have been recorded under Santa Ana conditions.

Conditions necessary for Santa Ana winds occur five or ten times a year and last from several hours to a few days. They occur most frequently from September to March with December the most likely month, although they occasionally occur at other times. They are particularly strong in the passes and at the mouths of canyons, often filling the air with dust, damaging crops, overturning campers and trailers, and creating an extreme fire danger.

A Multitude of Microclimates

To the Easterner the climate of the Metropolis is unique and distinctive, vastly different from what he is accustomed to. One of these uncommon traits is great variations in climate from place to place, a phenomena unknown in regions of similar size in the East or Midwest. They were first revealed to the agriculturalist who might see his orange grove turn brown with frost, while his neighbor's grove, only a bit farther upslope, came through the winter essentially undamaged. Today, urban folks also find the microclimates significant in a different way—they make possible distinctly different lifestyles within surprisingly limited distances.

Consider two families living only about twenty-five miles apart, one a resident of Santa Monica while the second lives in Woodland Hills. In Santa Monica, a July day may begin with the sky overcast with "high fog" and with the humidity above sixty percent. The sun may "burn through" late in the morning, with the temperature reaching a maximum of about seventy degrees, although the sensible temperature may seem lower due to the brisk sea breeze. High clouds and a temperature of sixty-five or so come with the evening. In the winter time, however, temperatures here are the highest in the region, averaging fifty degrees in January. Afternoon temperatures in that month average about sixty-five degrees. Bougainvilleas, Burmese honeysuckle, cup-of-gold vine climb arbor and house; cherimoya and other tropical fruits grace an occasional back yard.

The same July day in Woodland Hills may dawn bright and clear, with the temperature climbing rapidly to an afternoon maximum of ninety-five degrees. However, the humidity is low and the high temperature is not uncomfortable in the shade. The evenings remain warm, but the night temperatures of the clear air may fall to nearly sixty degrees. Swimming pools abound, and air-conditioning is common in both home and car. Winter days, too, tend to be sunny, with January maximums averaging nearly seventy, although the nights are quite cold, averaging about forty degrees. Frost occurs on about ten nights in winter. Attempts to grow tender tropical plants risk severe winter kill.

Thus, the resident of Santa Monica might feel comfortable in a sweater or jacket on the same July day that the Woodland Hills citizen finds a dip in the pool a relief from the heat. Balmy evenings make the inland location the home of the backyard barbecue and patio living. In January, however, cars parked in the open overnight in Woodland Hills might be covered with frost (which the owner will wash off with his omnipresent garden hose), whereas an automobile outdoors in Santa Monica will only pick up a layer of dew.

Microclimatic Regions of the Metropolis

The significant differences in climate within the Metropolis illustrated above were responsible for much of the region's agricultural variety in an earlier period. Today they may account for some of the extensive commuting patterns, as workers seek to live in a climate more to their liking than that of their workplace. Because of their importance and

uniqueness it is useful to identify and characterize in a general way some of the microclimatic regions within the Metropolis.

Marine

The zone completely dominated by the ocean has what may be called a *Marine* climate. It includes the beaches and extends inland varying distances—a short way where the ocean is bordered by cliffs, and as much as two to three miles in low areas. It has the mildest winters in the region and the coolest summers, with summer days often of limited sunlight because of the daily high fog. The air fresh off the sea is seldom really dry. This is tuberous begonia and fuchsia climate, one that is kind to very tender plants that need only moderate summer heat. Some stations have never recorded frost. For these mild temperatures one must forego much clear sky and tolerate moist air. The Los Angeles airport has fog on some fifty-three days, mainly in the cooler half of the year. This zone has a climate where neither large furnaces nor air conditioning are needed; a fireplace will handle the evening chill nicely and a sweater may be a much used item of clothing.

Semi-Marine Climate

The region of *Semi-Marine* climate takes in most of the Los Angeles Lowland back from the immediate coast from Brentwood to Irvine. It extends inland about to downtown Los Angeles, Anaheim, and Santa Ana. Although behind the fog belt generally, it is under the influence of the ocean most of the time. Winters are seldom cold, frost is rare, and the temperatures generally never fall below twenty-eight degrees. Spring days may be cloudy due to the presence of high fog. Summers are warmer than along the coast, but the entire area is reached by sea breezes and is seldom really hot. It has lower winter temperatures than the Marine, but is somewhat warmer and has less fog in the summer. Humidities tend to be lower than close to the coast.

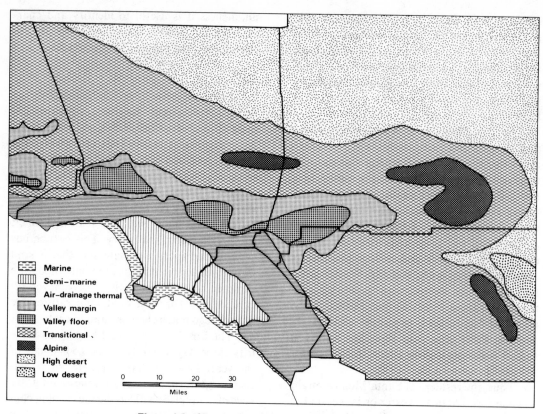

Figure 4.3. Climatic zones in the Los Angeles Metropolis.

Legend:

- Marine
- Semi-marine
- Air-drainage thermal
- Valley margin
- Valley floor
- Transitional
- Alpine
- High desert
- Low desert

0   10   20   30

Miles

Air Drainage Thermal Climatic Zone

The Santa Monica Mountains, Santa Ana Mountains, the connecting Repetto and Puente Hills, together with land with some elevation at their seaward base, have what might be called an *Air Drainage Thermal Climate*. Sunset Boulevard might be thought of as a border in the section where it appears. With more heat than the neighboring Semi-Marine Climate, yet with little danger of frost on winter nights, it is one of the most favored orchard climates. Where arable land is available, avocados, lemons, and Valencia oranges do well, and sloping land favors drainage of cold air on winter nights.

Valley Margin Climate

The margins of the interior valleys, that is, the high ground at the base of the surrounding hills, have a distinct and important climate. Located far enough from the ocean to escape the damp air and fog, the summers are hot and the winters are sunny and warm. Hot summer days are trademarks of the climate—half the days in July, August, and September reach or exceed ninety at Burbank and one hundred degrees at Redlands. Summer nights are pleasantly cool, however. In addition, the slopes are sufficient to drain off the cool air near the ground on clear winter nights, thus providing almost frost-free sites for orange groves. The extra heat of summer enables the region to grow sweet fruit and these areas were the classic navel orange orchard areas.

Valley Floor Climate

The floors of the interior valleys have a climate similar to the margins in summer—bright, sunny, and hot days, comfortable nights. But in the wintertime, their occasional frosty nights set them apart from the margins agriculturally. Cool air collects in pools on the valley floors, and it is common to have from ten to twenty nights with frost. Although to residents today this is of slight importance, it is critical to plants. Agriculturalists grew deciduous fruits, apricots, walnuts, and peaches, as well as alfalfa and truck crops, and today the home gardener must stick to hardy plants.

Alpine and Transitional Mountain Climates

The tops of the mountains have a distinctive type of climate, *Alpine,* with distinct seasons based on temperature. Sharp seasonal differences are the rule; at Big Bear Lake (6,800 feet), while summer daytime temperatures are comfortably warm, winters are distinctly cold, and have reached an all-time low of twenty-five degrees below zero. Snow is a usual winter phenomena at elevations over 4,000 feet; Mount Wilson, for example, averages forty-one inches of snow, distributed over a number of small storms. The sky is clear and usually cloud-free in all seasons; at Mount Wilson, solar photography is possible from three hundred five to three hundred twenty-five days in a year.

Between the Alpine and Valley Margin climates is a broad belt along the steep inner face of the Sierra Madre that we are simply calling *Transitional.* Generally an uninhabited area, precipitation increases with elevation and temperature decreases.

Climates beyond the Mountain Wall

Strictly speaking, this region is outside our Metropolis; however, several distinctive climate zones are encountered as one enters or leaves our area. The Antelope Valley (around Lancaster, for example) has a *High Desert* climate. Rainfall is less than ten inches a year.

To a visitor from the Metropolis, summer seems terribly hot and the winter unusually cold, and there is often a great deal of wind. The most pleasant seasons are spring and fall. However, the region is famous for the constancy of its sunshine and the clearness of its skies. The U.S. Air Base near Lancaster boasts that for ninety-nine percent of the hours of every month visibility is good enough for contact flying.

The climate of the *Low Desert* is experienced at Palm Springs. Here rainfall averages less than five inches a year and the sun shines ninety percent of the time it is above the horizon. Normal temperatures of one hundred degrees characterize summer days, but the area enjoys sunny and warm winter weather and is free from the dreary high fogs of spring.

Urban Wildfire, an Unusual Hazard

Wildfires are not new to the Los Angeles Metropolis. The best evidence of a long fire history comes from the vegetation itself which seems to have evolved under conditions of occasional burning. Some species of the chaparral have seeds that need high termperatures to sprout; temperatures reached three to six inches below the surface during a fire. Other species have a root with a knotty platform that enables the plant to regenerate after the branches have been burned. Fire almost seems to be the climax of the vegetative cycle and the plant material is capable of rapid recovery. When Cabrillo, lying off the coast in October, 1542, saw the fires that impelled him to call San Pedro *Bahia de las Fumos,* the question of whether the conflagration was set by the Indians or was of natural causes was not terribly important. In either case, fires seem to have been commonplace.

They still are. In November of 1961, the Bel Air Fire swept through the Santa Monica Mountains in the Bel Air-Brentwood community, destroying four hundred eighty-four residences and twenty-one other buildings in less than two days, and insured losses alone totaled twenty-four million dollars. In November, 1966, the Loop Fire started near the city of Los Angeles, spread over 2,028 acres of watershed destroying thirty-two homes, and killed twelve experienced firefighters caught in a narrow canyon. On September 27, 1970, the area was ablaze from Newhall to Malibu, a distance of thirty-five miles. Three men were burned to death, two hundred ninety-five homes were destroyed, and some 180,000 acres were burned; so it goes year after year.

Significantly, however, the region's fire hazard is of a different nature than its earthquake danger: serious, out-of-control wildfires are broadly predictable both as to location and time. The places likely to burn are the hills and mountains within the Metropolis that are still covered with native brush as well as the districts immediately adjacent to them. The disastrous fires occur on the relatively rare days with Santa Ana winds. The structures that are endangered are usually only those in locations where dwellings and chaparral are in close proximity. Wildfires are only a hazard to those who choose to build their dwellings in such locations. Others can avoid this danger entirely.

It should be understood that wildfires in the Metropolis do not have the same causes or receive the same treatment as mountain forest fires in many parts of California. Many of the latter are caused by lightning and often spread mainly because of the rugged terrain and lack of accessibility. Fires of this type occasionally occur in the Sierra Madre, but they are of a different genre—our concern here is not with them. Within the Metropolis the wildfire often is caused by human accident or by arson.

Destructive wildfires in the Metropolis involve four elements: chaparral, Santa Ana winds, human structures, and the spark that sets them off. In a general way, all of these elements are subject to human action save for the wind.

Vegetation

The natural vegetation of the Santa Monica and other low mountain ranges in the Metropolis is commonly known as chaparral. It is made up of brush and low trees such as chamise, ceanothus, scrub oak, red shank, sagebrush, deerweed, manzanita, sumac, sugar bush, and buckwheat. Chaparral areas contain massive amounts of fuel. With an average height of four feet, but rising from eight to fifteen feet on south slopes, it contains from six to forty tons of vegetation per acre. As the chaparral, in order to survive in the dry summer, has a high oil content and during periods of low humidity becomes desiccated, it is hardly surprising that it is reputed to be among the fastest burning brush land in the world.

Wind

Santa Ana winds are the second ingredient that "turn the hilly areas into a vegetative and meteorological time bomb." When they are blowing, small, normally easy-to-manage brush fires suddenly rage out of control and become destructive wildfires. Santa Ana winds, described earlier, not only arrive after the long, hot, rainless southern California summer, but are so desiccating that they can, in a few hours, negate the effects of recent rainfall—thus, the rainy season and the fire season overlap. Under such conditions, the chaparral quickly becomes tinder dry, as do the wooden shingles—everything is then highly combustible.

Although the Santa Ana winds create a serious fire problem, they have some ameliorating characteristics. They blow only a few days in the year, perhaps six to ten. Normally they can be predicted a day or two in advance. Further, the direction of the winds is known—they blow from the north or northeast, and their paths through the mountains have been repeatedly mapped.

Human Structures

Wildfires do relatively little damage except to watershed unless they burn in areas occupied by buildings. In the lowland areas of the Metropolis, urban forms have now completely replaced natural vegetation, and in these areas little fire hazard exists. In developing the hilly areas, however, hazardous juxtaposition of structures and vegetation was almost inevitable. The steep canyon walls have restricted most street building to the narrow winding canyon bottoms or the equally narrow and sinuous ridge lines. Houses have been built in the canyons backing up to the brush, and on the ridges. In between lie the brush covered slopes left in their natural state for both economic and esthetic reasons. In many instances, the brush comes right up to the homes; sometimes, if the house is cantilevered out over a steep slope, brush actually is growing beneath the building.

The houses in question are of all architectural styles, but many are one or two story structures with light wood frame or stucco construction. Most roofs are covered with wood shingles or shakes and have wide overhanging eaves. Large picture windows are common. Spacing between the houses varies with the size of the lot, but where lots are small it may be as little as twelve feet, with the distance even less between the eaves.

The Other Element Is Man

Whereas wildfires have always been with us, the number of wildfires in the surrounding hills seem to have increased roughly in proportion to the entry of people into their vicinity. As population has spread westward along both flanks of the Santa Monicas, for example, fires in these areas have been more frequent. Origins of the destructive wildfires in the Santa Monicas are widely varied. Of the twenty-one major fires in the Los Angeles County portion of the mountains between 1925 and 1966, four were started by smokers, three

by gasoline engine exhaust or sparks, two each resulted from fallen power lines, camp fires, and hot ashes; and a single fire was started by each of the following: brush burning, blasting, automobile, truck backfire, faulty incinerator, friction from farm implements, sparks from a welding torch, and an overheated electric pump. Seven were thought to be of incendiary origin. Although this sample is probably not extensive enough to be statistically valid, it does illustrate most of the common ways by which human action produces the spark to begin the conflagrations.

Living with Wildfire

A metropolitan area that must live with wildfire may reduce the hazard in a number of ways. One procedure would be to minimize the contact between human structures and the chaparral. Current regulations requiring brush to be cut back at least thirty feet from a dwelling is a start, but perhaps overly modest. If people must live in the brush-covered hills, perhaps cluster-type housing developments should be encouraged, with each cluster of homes surrounded by a band of fire-resistant vegetation (ivy or ice plant, for example), weeded and watered by a home owners association.

What can be done about the chaparral itself that annually becomes almost explosively combustible? Suggestions include selective thinning—reducing the amount of vegetation to specimen plants—thus, in effect, introducing fuel breaks into the pattern. One school of thought argues that our current practice of actively preventing fire allows enormous amounts of fuel to accumulate over the years and thus creates conditions for a disastrous fire when one does occur. As an alternative, it is proposed that a program of controlled burning be introduced, whereby selected portions of the hills would be burned off in the early spring. However, this alternative is presently resisted by local fire authorities as too dangerous. Another drastic alternative suggests the wholesale substitution for the chaparral of plants that will grow in our climate but will not burn. A number of rock roses and saltbrush species have those characteristics. It is a question, however, whether or not this expensive solution would be more than a temporary one. The natural vegetation has strong recuperative powers and might take over the hills again in a relatively few years.

A great deal can be done architecturally to reduce the fire damage to houses in and near brush country. The greatest fire hazard to homes is wood shingle and shake roofs. Not only do they catch fire easily but they add to the fire hazard. Burning shingles and shakes are blown off, rise in the thermal columns from burning roofs, and are carried long distances by winds, falling, still flaming, onto brush and other roofs. Often these burning brands are carried over the fire lines to start new fires in previously unendangered areas. Further, to protect houses with wood shingle roofs requires the time, effort, and water that under other conditions could be used to fight the fire itself. Wood shingle and shake roofing should be eliminated in fire hazardous areas. In addition, overhanging combustible eaves tend to trap heat and sparks, large windows facing brush covered slopes break, or sometimes home furnishings catch fire from radiant heat alone, and houses or porches cantilevered over brush-covered slopes almost invite combustion.

Finally, what can be done to prevent fires from starting in the first place? Brush could be cleared away from the vicinity of highways as a start. Since dangerous fire conditions—periods of Santa Ana winds—are predictable and last only a few days, a wildfire alert could be called, warning the public of the potential risk. Special rules could be implemented for these brief periods. For example, any construction or agricultural equipment likely to cause sparks could be forbidden to enter brush

areas. Hiking and camping could be prohibited. Power lines, where not underground (as is desirable) could be subject to constant patrol.

It has now been many years since a major fire in the Santa Monica Mountains came nearly up to the UCLA campus. The ashes were not yet cool when a representative of professional fire agencies and insurance companies began investigating the event. His story is still one of the most informed and also exciting accounts of fire in the chaparral and is well worth reading. Here is Rexford Wilson's story, "The Los Angeles Conflagration of 1961—The Devil Wind and Wood Shingles." Reprinted from the January 1962 *NFPA Quarterly,* (Vol. 55, No. 3), Copyright © 1962 National Fire Protection Association, Quincy, Massachusetts. Reprinted by permission.

"In the brush-covered Santa Monica mountain range of Los Angeles, California, real concern is felt when the U.S. Forest Service brush burning index climbs to the mid-twenties. On Monday morning, November 6, 1961, the local burning index was being raised from the incredible 84 of the day before to a predicted 98. At 8:03 A.M. the fire department, like a cat preparing to pounce, began moving engine companies into the mountain district to reinforce the protection there. The brush on the mountains was so dry it crumbled to the touch. The wood shingles and shakes on many roofs were light in weight from lack of moisture. The surface wind was increasing. Those in the fire service hoped there would be no ignition today.

"Yet, at approximately 8:10 A.M. a fire of accidental origin started at the end of the road in a deep gully called Stone Canyon on the north side of the Santa Monica mountains in the city of Los Angeles. Before the embers of this fire cooled, over 513 homes and 24 other buildings in the Bel Air and Brentwood residential districts would be destroyed or heavily damaged causing an insured building loss of an estimated 24 million dollars which includes insured losses to vehicles, art objects, and jewelry. The uninsured losses, damage to watershed, and subsequent flood damage have not yet been estimated. This fire would destroy the largest number of buildings of any single conflagration on the North American continent since September 17 1923, when a fire in brush spread sparks onto the wooden roofs of homes in Berkeley, California, where 640 buildings were destroyed.

Weather

"Southern California has a sunny, semiarid climate with a relatively even year-round temperature usually running from the mid 50's to the mid 70's in the Los Angeles area. The relative humidity usually ranges between the 40's and the 80's. Annual rainfall varies between 4 and 31 inches for a mean of 15 inches compared with 33 inches in Chicago, 42 in New York, and 45 in Houston. The last three years, however, have not been average. Of the 17.49 inches of rain which fell in 1958, only 1/2 inch fell in the last eight months of that year. From May 1, 1958, to November 6, 1961, only about 19 inches of rain had fallen. Thus, November 1961, has been preceded by a long, dry period.

The Santa Ana Winds

"One of the peculiarities of Southern California weather is a phenomenon called the Santa Ana winds. These winds are known as "The Desert Winds" but this is not an accurate description. It is popularly known that these winds are caused by a high pressure area over the great basin between the Sierra and the Rocky Mountain ranges and a low pressure trough to the southwest. Air rushing from the high pressure area to the low pressure area cuts through mountain passes at velocities recorded occasionally over 80 mph.

"What is not popularly known about the Santa Anas is that the air coming from the desert is arctic continental air. Super-chilled above the arctic, it moves at a high level over the northwest area of the country. Chilling of the air has removed most of its moisture. If this cold, heavy air finds a particular pressure trough, the air can flow down the trough into the great basin. As this arctic air fills the basin it spills over the mountain passes creating a wind velocity of its own. Under the influence of the pressure areas already mentioned, this wind velocity is increased. When this pressure gradient is high, the wind becomes a gale.

"The path this air has taken has warmed it somewhat but has given it no opportunity to gather moisture. Thus, it can pour from the desert region at 65 degrees F or hotter bearing little or no measurable humidity. As this super-dry air roars through the mountain passes and spills into the valleys and across the ridges of southern California, it draws moisture from every plant, every bush, every roof, every building, and every person it passes. As these winds rise, the relative humidity plummets to values unknown in many areas of this continent. Ground level humidities below 20 per cent are common and below 10 per cent are often found. Humidities of 4 per cent and 2 per cent are occasionally recorded.

Topography

"The Santa Monica mountains point like a finger from the west into downtown Los Angeles. The 1600- to 2000-foot-high range separates the 200- to 300-foot-high coastal plain of downtown Los Angeles and harbor area on the south from the 400- to 700-foot-high San Fernando Valley plain of city residential and business areas on the north. Of Los Angeles' 457 square miles, 112 square miles are mountain area.

"Because of the view, the rustic setting, and the expense of clearing and grading land in this mountain range, it has become a very fashionable place to live. Builders have scooped out canyon bottoms, built roads, and placed small homes along both sides of these roads. Ridge tops have been flattened off and graded to provide for a central road with homes built on each side.

Ground Cover

"The natural ground cover of the Santa Monica range is commonly known as chaparral. The chaparral is made up of indigenous brush and low trees, such as greasewood, mesquite, manzanita, sage, sumac, wild walnut, live oak, and buckwheat brush. This brush, in order to live in the semiarid summer months, has a high oil content, which provides sustenance for the plant when the moisture levels are too low for it otherwise to survive. Thus, as the humidity drops, this material becomes more and more combustible. Under low humidity conditions, it is thought to be the most combustible brush in North America.

"Its burning characteristics are unusual as it appears to burn twice. After the brush is preheated by the approaching fire, the leaves and small twigs appear to burn off, and this burning preheats the larger brush members. Then about 30 seconds to a minute later, the larger members burn.

"The brush in the fire area had been growing unburned for over 25 years and in this lush state was estimated at about 50 tons per acre. If this ground cover is burned off due to the steepness of the canyon sides, a severe flood threat exists until reseeding can be completed.

Dwelling Construction

"With the steep canyon walls, there is little choice in this area on street layout. In addition, builders have attempted to keep every square foot of land in its most saleable condition. The result is that streets are narrow and winding, partly due to the contour of the land, and partly due to the attempt to make the homesites exclusive and private.

"Construction of the homes was light wood frame with stucco, or brick veneer and wood walls. Roof coverings were predominantly wood shingle or wood shake with some rock roofs, some gravel roofs and occasional tile roofs. The rock roof is a standard built-up roof, but instead of gravel, stone is used. In some cases these stones are screened to be fist size or larger.

"Most of the homes were built within 50 feet of the brush while occasional ridge homes on curves were able to be set back 100 to 150 feet from the brush. Many homes had brush within 10 to 15 feet of the house.

"Average daily water consumption in the fire area is about 20,000,000 to 22,000,000 gallons. Most individuals have installed underground sprinkling systems for their lawns, which are controlled by two or three valves. The systems are capable of distributing water over the entire lawn at once. Some persons have golf course type sprinklers called "rain birds" permanently installed in the surrounding brush that can also be controlled from a house valve. A few persons have installed sprinklers permanently on their wooden roofs in an attempt to reduce the hazard of the roofing. Thus, a mountain area homeowner with a lawn sprinkler system and three rain birds is capable of using about 100 gallons of water a minute on his premises. One hundred such homeowners using water at once could draw 10,000 gallons per minute easily and 1,000 could draw 100,000 gallons per minute with little trouble.

"Many of the homes in this area have pools located behind the houses. These pools contain from 30,000 to 50,000 gallons of water each. In order to provide privacy, they are either located behind the home or surrounded by a fence or heavy hedge. No provisions have been made to put a connection near the driveway or street which would allow the fire department to take suction from these pools, and very few of the homeowners have any portable means of utilizing the water from these pools for the protection of their property.

"One hundred of these swimming pools would provide about 4 million gallons of water, which is more than many small towns have in their entire town water supply, and is almost 7 times as much water as the fire department has used in other recent large scale brush fires in the area.

"Mobile defensive tactics have been developed by the Los Angeles Fire Department to deal with the threat to homes in their mountain areas. These tactics call for apparatus to be moved down a street immediately behind the burning brush. Men from a unit stop at the first threatened house that is unprotected by another unit. They then try to extinguish ignited spots on the exterior of the home and, when done, move on down the street to the next involved but unattended building. This "leapfrogging" of the apparatus gives maximum coverage from minimum men and equipment.

"If time and manpower permit, the property is prepared for the oncoming fire by removal of as much exterior combustibles as possible, closing of all windows and doors, and preparation of garden hoses and ladders.

"It has been found that, where the department can prepare ahead of the fire and where the fire is from direct exposure of the brush, one man can handle up to five of the small ranch type homes if they have fire-retardant roofing, but only one or possibly two of these homes, if they have wood shingle or shake roofs. If the fire exposure is from flying brands or embers, then the man guarding the fire-retardant roof can handle more than five homes while the man guarding the wood roof must usually restrict his operations to one roof. Thus, within a shower of brands and embers, it takes about 20 companies to protect 100 wood-roofed homes but only three or four companies to protect 100 fire-retardant roofed houses.

Monday, November 6

"At dawn, winds on the dry floor of the San Fernando Valley were 17 mph with gusts to 23 mph from the north, northeast. Between 7 A.M. and 8

A.M., wind velocity increased to 29 mph with gusts to 35. Because of the extremely low humidity and high winds of the Santa Ana, the Los Angeles City Fire Department declared a "high hazard" at 8:03 A.M., initiating the preplanned move-up of companies into the mountain protection area to reinforce the initial striking companies for this section.

The Brush Fire Phase

"Just after 8:10 A.M., fire started at the end of Stone Canyon Avenue in an area illegally used for dumping beyond the end-of-the-road barrier. The fire was seen by a grading contractor 30 seconds after he and his "cat skinner" had walked over the area, and was reported by telephone from a nearby house to the Van Nuys Signal Office at 8:15 A.M. from whence the alarm "Fire at 3651 Stone Canyon Avenue" was sounded. Four engine companies, a tank wagon, a ladder company, and the mountain patrolmen for that area responded.

"First-arriving companies found a brush fire about one acre in size in progress at the bottom of Stone Canyon just north of Mulholland Drive. Four additional engines were sent at 8:18 A.M. By now all three signal offices had received the alarm, and all incoming lines were jammed and would be for the next 1/2 hour. Two extra engine companies were ordered at 8:20 A.M., three additional engine companies at 8:22 A.M. At 8:26 A.M., as the fire spread up the west side of the canyon wall toward Mulholland Drive, Chief Sawyer declared a "major emergency" and called for 15 additional engine companies, 2 borate air tankers, tractors, and 6 sector chiefs. Shortly thereafter, the fire jumped across Mulholland and was burning on the south slope of the Stone Canyon area. A helicopter was ordered, time 8:28 A.M. About 40 homes were being threatened by the fire north of Mulholland and 200 homes, two apartments, a store and school were threatened on upper Roscomare Road.

"The department went immediately into its mobile defensive tactics for saving homes as the fire spread rapidly south. The command post equipment was being sent to a graded spot on Mulholland Drive overlooking Stone Canyon to the south. Chief officers from downtown were being dispatched to take over staff positions here. As it would take about 30 minutes for the equipment and chiefs to arrive, preliminary command post operations were

set up from a chief's car at 8:33 A.M. The commercial helicopter on contract to the fire department was grounded for its 100-hour inspection. A call was made for the Los Angeles police helicopter but it was also grounded for its 100-hour inspection. The first of the two aerial tankers was air-borne at 8:42 A.M. and despite general policy regarding their use in populated areas, they began working the western flanks near the homes.

"Reports to the Water and Police Departments brought action. While police began sealing off the northern roads from Sunset Boulevard, regulator crews began moving into the area on Water Department orders. The Beverly Glen pumping plant lost its electric power, but the automatic diesel power unit took over.

"The 161 students who had arrived for class at the Roscomare Elementary School were evacuated to the Brentwood Elementary School south of Sunset Boulevard. Many school buses and parents turned back at the early signs of smoke and returned the children to their homes.

"By 9:00 A.M., 49 Los Angeles fire department units had been dispatched and the homes on the northeast side of the upper part of Roscomare Road were being successfully defended. A call was placed for one of the Los Angeles County helicopters.

"The fire spread rapidly southward jumping over upper Roscomare at 9:05 A.M., spreading south on the west side of Roscomare. At 9:10 A.M. radio station KMPC's helicopter was commandeered for fire service use. Fire department radio contact with this helicopter depended upon a small "handy-talkie." This would prove ineffective later in the fire.

"With the fire now spreading on both sides of Roscomare Road, the defensive fire crews were spread out but were still successful in saving homes. The fire was hooking southeasterly across Stone Canyon above the reservoir. From the command post and motor pool on Mulholland Drive many pumps, men, and four tractors were sent to make a stand on the west ridge of Beverly Glen.

"When the south edge of the fire reached the intersections of Roscomare Road, upper Stradella, and upper Linda Flora, the defensive forces were split, some going to protect the west side of Linda Flora and some to protect the east side of Stradella.

This division required more men, and, at 9:30 A.M., a Phase I recall was instituted. Both radio frequencies were now beginning to show signs of crowding. Pumper-to-pumper water-pressure requests, officer-to-chief reports, chief-to-chief sector reports, and command post-to-alarm headquarters requests were increasing as the number of units at the fire continued to rise and as the defense was spread farther and farther apart. At 9:30 A.M., eight additional aerial tankers were requested to take additional action for control of the eastern flank. Because of the favorable terrain, control would be attempted by air attack at the west ridge above Beverly Glen, coordinated with engine company and tractor support. At 9:36 A.M., the fire jumped Stradella into the Roscomare Canyon area. The fire now forced defense on both sides of Linda Flora, Stradella, and Roscomare Road, as well as in the Beverly Glen area. The fire had spread over a large portion of Stone Canyon and was moving quickly south and southeast. The defense was now stretched dangerously thin but continued to save homes for a few more minutes.

"From the helicopter it was obvious that this was going to be a bad brush fire as the fire was spotting 300 or more yards ahead of itself as it moved south.

"The 578 children at the Bellagio Road School were evacuated by school bus to the Brentwood Elementary School. News media were notified of this as parents tried to locate their children.

"The third air tanker for the fire was air-borne at 9:42 A.M., followed soon by 12 others. The new Stone Canyon emergency pumping unit was started on the line for the first time at 9:05 A.M. The fire was beginning to pick up speed in a southward direction.

"At 10:00 A.M., other difficulties began to appear. The smoke cloud had spread south on ground level winds and southwest on the upper level winds causing concern of people south and west of the fire, some miles from the fire area. Water consumption jumped significantly as residents began to operate their lawn and brush sprinklers and those with wooden roofs began wetting them down. Some fire fighters entering homes to pull down curtains and close windows found all faucets going and water flowing across the floor from overflowing tubs, showers, and sinks. Demand from the 1,000,000-gallon and 500,000-gallon tanks on the north end

of lower Linda Flora Drive drained the remaining water from these tanks in about 10 minutes. Lower Linda Flora Drive and the connecting ridge section of Chalon Road thus went dry about 10:00 A.M.

"The main section of the brush fire was now down to about the middle of Stone Canyon reservoir and measured surface wind gusts in the valley had increased to 40 mph, while in the fire area even stronger fire-caused winds were bending hose streams about 45 degrees to the side as braced fire fighters tried to get the water into critical spots on roofs and eaves. Companies were being moved up Stone Canyon Road and Bel Air Road to set up defenses there. By 10:35 A.M., 59 Los Angeles City units were at work. Twelve Los Angeles County units, 6 county camp crews, plus 5 county chiefs had been called.

"Men defending upper Linda Flora Drive were still able to hold the fire from the homes. They were sweeping, kicking, and wetting embers on the roofs, wetting down smoldering eaves, and in some cases even ripping burning shingles and shakes off with their bare hands. The fight here would be successful but it took a lot of men and equipment.

"The fire finally broke through the thinning defense lines to involve 8 wooden-roofed homes and one gravel-roof home on upper Stradella Road and to ignite 16 homes with wooden roofs on Roscomare Road, in the 1945 to 1743 section.

"Fire fighters reported that even if they were on a roof with a hose, an ember could be blown up under a shingle and cause ignition on the dry undersurface to involve the attic and force them from the roof.

The Wood Shingle Phase

"Sometime in the next fifteen minutes, the fire changed character and forced a general shift of technique. The fire started jumping into the populated section to the south ahead of the spreading brush fire. Borate pilots, making drops in these areas as a desperate measure of defense, reported seeing debris of embers and burning shingles in the air. They also reported house roofs burning well in advance of the brush fire. Twenty-three wood roofs on Roscomare below number 1570 were becoming involved.

"Water pressure was failing in the north end of Bel Air Road, on Stradella, Chantilly, and Somera. The new, never tested, East Ridge pumping plant was now put on the line and began pumping the first of 4,000,000 gallons it would contribute to the fight. Communications across the fire area and from the helicopter were impossible. Both frequencies were in massive use and constantly jammed with critical messages. Acknowledgments were practically impossible.

"At this point the planned defensive strategy broke down and operations became a local defend-what-you-can-and-move-on operation. About 1,000 Bel Air homes were being threatened, 78 per cent of them with wood roofs. At 10:50 A.M., eight additional Los Angeles City units and ten additional Los Angeles County units were ordered—the largest single call of the fire.

"In this same period of 10:50 A.M. to 11:30 A.M., the largest hazard to life occurred in the fire. With the difficult fights now being waged on Roscomare, upper Linda Flora, upper Stradella, in Stone Canyon on Bel Air Road, no equipment had been available to send to the previously uninvolved Chantilly Road, Somera Road or to lower Linda Flora, and the connecting section of Chalon Road.

"Suddenly, residents of Somera and Chantilly Road found themselves in a fire area when roofs began to burn. The fire had been hidden from view, though smoke had been seen for some time over the rise to the immediate north. One witness said that he was preparing to leave about 11:00 A.M. when suddenly his house's wood roof ignited and seven minutes later the building was ablaze. The first chief into Chantilly Road found "about 30 roofs involved," and the brush not yet burning. Of the 67 homes on this street, 42 would be destroyed—all with wooden roofs.

"On Somera Road, residents were also taken completely by surprise. One woman was inside cleaning, and she stepped outside to find the roof of her neighbor's house on fire. Four workmen painting a new house across the street suddenly found roofs burning up the street. Two of them found a young mother and her baby in the street. They took her by the arms and, holding her baby, ran south to the end of the road and down the steep brush-covered, not yet alight, canyon slope. The other two workmen leaped into a pool at the end of the street with the elderly owners of the home and their dog. Despite the fact that they thought at one point they would die from the heat, all survived. One old lady hid under a large-leaved plant near the street and survived. Another woman jumped into her car and

drove north "through the flames" to Chantilly Road, then south and out. Of the 55 buildings on this street, 45 would be destroyed. Of the destroyed, 40 had wooden roofs. Of the 10 saved, 7 had fire-retardant roofs.

"Lower Linda Flora and connecting Chalon Road experienced a similar occurrence approximately at the same time. A woman on Linda Flora reports that the fire came from the north over Orum Road from Roscomare Canyon. The first things to ignite were three wooden roofs. With no water she could do nothing so she left. Sixty-four homes were lost on her street, 50 of which had wooden roofs. South of Linda Flora on Bellagio Road one chief saw a small 1 1/2 foot circle burning on a shingle roof. He tried to get a request through on the radio and found it impossible. In five minutes, the house roof was gone and brands from this roof had ignited the neighbor's home 100 feet away, taking most of the roof off it before an engine arrived. No brush was burning in the area. As homes were destroyed, they collapsed, breaking water piping, creating additional demands on the water system.

"At the same time (11:30 A.M.) on the west side of Sepulveda Boulevard, the Tigertail pumping unit suffered a power failure. Because the upper wind carried smoke over these western areas, some units were patrolling there though no fire had yet crossed Sepulveda Boulevard.

"During the hour from 11:30 A.M. to 12:30 P.M., 19 additional Los Angeles City units had been ordered into the fray as more and more homes and brush were involved. All defense lines were now gone and operations on narrow side streets, on long private driveways, on dead-end and ridge roads were abandoned because of the extreme danger to personnel.

"By now the 523 students of the Kenter Canyon School on the west side of Sepulveda had been evacuated by school bus to the Brentwood Elementary School.

"By 12:50 P.M., 96 Los Angeles City Fire Department units were working on the fire with most on the east side of Sepulveda boulevard. Then suddenly in the Brentwood residential district, fires were reported up to a mile west of Sepulveda Boulevard 1 1/2 miles southwest of the Bel Air fire—not one or two fires, but 60 to 70. Roofs and brush were alight. At 12:56, 16 additional units were called and ordered into this area. All available equipment from the Bel Air section of the fire was also moved over, along with a call for Civil Defense units. All units were forced to enter the area from Sunset Boulevard. As they entered, they found homes with roofs alight. They had to stop and fight. The last units in were those to go the farthest up canyon.

"In the northern half of Brentwood homes were built in many cases right back into the brush. Witnesses from Tigertail Road report that the shower of brands from over the hills to the northeast ignited the brush in many places at about 1:00 P.M. They also reported that the evacuees then clogged the road bumper to bumper preventing any entrance by fire equipment to the area. The brush fire directly exposed and destroyed approximately 90 homes. About 60 of these homes hung out over the canyon side or had large expanses of glass. Fire fighters attempting to reach the northern half of the Brentwood area had to deal first with the fires in the southern section. Three buildings exposed by the brush burned at Mount St. Mary's College. On one, the fire penetrated the attic when brands and embers ignited birds' nests under the eaves; another apparently ignited when the fire-exposed windows broke.

November 7, 1961

"At 8:00 A.M. the following morning a Phase IV total recall was ordered as fire spread to the north and west near Sepulveda Boulevard but was halted by ground forces and coordinated aerial attack by noon when the conflagration was declared officially contained.

November 8, 1961

"By Wednesday, November 8, residents had begun to worry about the flood threat that now was so large. Homes untouched by the fire were in danger of ruin or collapse by the tide of mud sure to come if the rains came. By Sunday, November 12, the flood control people were distributing sand bags and sand to residents. Salvaged pipes were being used to build temporary surface sprinkler systems on the hillsides. Rye grass seed was being distributed by the truck load. The feverish activity continued until Monday, November 20, when it rained and rained hard. This 1.88 inch rainfall was not the last to occur during the next few weeks. Damage created by the November 20 downpour was increased by the heavy rains of December 2 and 3, 1961.

Conflagration Statistics

"The conflagration had burned at an average rate of 13 acres a minute during the first six hours, had covered an area of 6,090 acres and had a perimeter of 19.6 miles. No one was killed. Four hundred and eighty-four homes and 21 other structures had been totally destroyed. Twenty-nine homes and three other buildings had been damaged more than 30 per cent. Total structural dollar losses are estimated presently at $24,135,000. Fire losses to vehicles, art and jewelry are included in this figure. Cost of fire control was estimated at $3,000,000. Estimates on the damage to watershed and the subsequent flood damage are not available as this is written.

"In all, 154 engines and 54 other tactical vehicles were used on the conflagration. Los Angeles city units alone used 135 miles of hose.

"Fourteen air tankers flew over 93 hours to deliver 266,200 gallons of borate slurry on the three fires.

Lessons, Comments, and Recommendations
Lessons

"Three major lessons are emphasized by the experience of this conflagration. They are, in order of their importance to the destruction of buildings: the hazardous nature of wood shingles and shakes; the conflagration threat of California brush; and the problems of large-scale fire fighting.

Wood Shingles and Shakes

"The planned mobile defensive tactics worked against the spreading brush fire until wood shingle and shake roofs became involved. When this happened, the character of the fire changed. Whether homes in the southern part of the Bel Air district became involved because of embers from burning brush or from flying brands from the 24 wood-roofed homes burning upwind on Roscomare and upper Stradella is a matter of academic interest only. The fact is that many wood roofs downwind became ignited before the surrounding brush and sometimes without having any brush burned around them at all.

"When the first wood roofs burned, the surface wind was still the main factor in the direction of the fire and brand travel. But when many homes and brush in areas on the southern part of the Bel Air district became involved, the tremendous burning drew air from all directions and the thermal currents carried smoke and debris up to 6,000 feet high. From 2,000 feet up, northeast winds carried the burning debris southwesterly depositing the brands in the Brentwood residential district, igniting brush and wooden roofs there.

"Embers and roofing brands burn as they go and thus have a definite range before they burn to a size too small to ignite anything. The larger pieces take longer to burn and thus have a greater range.

"Burning embers from brush have been known to travel 1,000 to 3,000 feet, and in a few cases as much as a mile and a quarter down surface winds, to start spot fires in front of a running brush fire. Burning wood shingles and shakes, on the other hand, create larger flaming brands and, therefore, have a recorded range in previous conflagrations of one to three miles and in one instance traveled a distance of eight miles to a deck of a ship at sea. Thus, while burning brands from roofing and embers from the brush probably were carried on the same thermal currents into the upper level winds, only the larger pieces of shingles and shakes had enough fuel to burn for the two- to three-mile distance up, over and down into the Brentwood area. This explains why the embers and charred remains on lawns and in pools of Brentwood were flat thumbnail to palmsize brands, clearly showing the weathered grain of roofing.

"The second important point about the wood roofing in this fire was that tremendous amounts of water, time, men, and machinery were required: (1) to try to prevent ignition of the wooden roofing; (2) to try to control small fires once they started on the roofing; and (3) to try to prevent ignition of neighboring homes. Nothing could be done to prevent the roofing brands from being carried overhead once the fire gained its overwhelming advantage over manual fire fighting efforts.

"No amount of fire fighting—no matter how skilled—can defend a city against a wood-shingle conflagration that has started. Fire department tactics require defense lines to be drawn. This defense requires time to act. With such defense lines can come intelligent tactical use of men and equipment. Such use is not possible with the fire leaping overhead, finding ready sources of ignition in other wooden roofs scattered at distances downwind—roofs which will produce more flaming brands to continue the chain reaction. The speed of a leaping

fire like this one, under adverse weather conditions that breed conflagrations, does not give the needed time to act.

"Had all the roofing in this area been fire retardant, it is certain that the men used on roof protection would have been available for defensive protection of the homes directly exposed by the brush fire. It is also certain that the home loss in the Bel Air district would have been significantly less, and it is probable that the fire would never have crossed Sepulveda Boulevard to destroy homes in the Brentwood district.

The California Brush

"With the exception of the wood shingle and shake roof ignition already discussed, fire gets into brush-exposed homes in four basic ways. Each of these ways involves direct fire exposure from burning brush. Thus, only those homes in the area of the actual burning brush are in danger of ignition.

"ATTIC VENTS OR LOUVERS form one route. Though these vents can be covered with mesh, it is still possible for small sparks to pass through and these sparks have, in some cases, caused ignition of the attic space. With unscreened vents, the problem is even greater.

"OVERHANGING EAVES are sometimes left open to act as attic vents. These eaves form hoods to trap the heat sweeping up from the brush fire. The built-up heat can then enter and ignite the attic space. Some homeowners close the eaves with soffits of plaster and other material that will stay in position and thus be suitable in keeping fire out.

"LARGE GLASS AREAS are vulnerable to the heat caused by the fire. They crack and allow heat, smoke, sparks and sometimes fire itself into the home, causing ignition. Because of the view these large glass doors and windows are popular.

"OVERHANGING PORCHES and overhanging houses also form traps for heat which can cause ignition underneath.

"No home, however, regardless of its construction, is certain to survive a heavily exposing brush fire when no one is there to protect it.

"The amount of heat and fire exposing a house is increased by the burning of combustible fences, outdoor furniture, diving boards, and combustible debris, as well as by exterior-mounted gas meters which can melt.

"The amount of heat can be reduced by the removal of the above items and of the brush 30 feet from the home. Brush height out to 100 feet from the home can also be limited to 15 or 18 inches to reduce this exposure.

"Tactics developed for fighting fire in this particular brush area due to the short, fast burning characteristics of this brush allow a fire fighter to step inside a home until the fire runs past. He then can step outside and usually extinguish spot fires on the eaves, siding or trim if a wooden roof has not become involved and if the fire has not entered the attic.

Recommendations

Roofing
"This Los Angeles conflagration was one of many which have proved that wooden roofing has the potential of starting or contributing to a conflagration which is completely beyond the capabilities of modern fire department forces.

"At this time, the only way to control this potential is to eliminate wood single and shake roofing.

"Thus, the most important recommendation to prevent a fire of this size in the future is that the types of roofing allowable for all future construction and major repair have an Underwriters' Laboratories, Inc., Class C or better rating.

Brush
"The second most important recommendation deals with the brush fire problem.

"In Los Angeles long range planning includes the development of a less combustible ground cover which will survive on these hills and reduce the severity and speed of the burning in the area. Immediate steps to reduce the exposure include the removal of brush within 30 feet of the home and the reduction in height of it back at least 100 feet from the house. During the week after the fire, 850 tons of brush above the usual amount were removed from the surrounding hillside areas.

"The ignition of a home can be reduced by the protection of the eaves, vents and louvers, as well as by the removal of all unnecessary combustibles from the exterior and provisions for the quick removal of necessary combustibles, in the event of fire.

"Additional brush area recommendations deal with rezoning, life safety of stilt-type homes, road and drive construction, adequate numbering of dwellings, adequate street marking and many other details."

4. Suggested Readings

Bailey, Harry P. *The Climates of Southern California.* California Natural History Guide, No. 17, Berkeley: University of California Press, 1966.
Although brief, this small volume provides a professional description of the Metropolitan climate. It covers all of southern California, so paints with rather broad strokes.

California Department of Forestry. *Chaparral Management Program. Final Environmental Impact Report.* Sacramento: The Resources Agency, 1981.
This report is a discussion of the benefits and problems of proscribed burning as a tool for managing California brush lands. Alternative techniques are also evaluated.

Edinger, James G. *Watching for the Wind.* Garden City, N.Y.: Anchor Books, 1967.
A small paperback that is written for anyone who is interested in his local weather. Edinger lives in Los Angeles, however, so much of the volume applies to the Metropolis. It includes good material on the marine layer, smog, wildfires and Santa Anas.

Keith, Ralph. W. *A Climatological Air Quality Profile, California South Coast Air Basin.* El Monte: South Coast Air Quality Management District. 1980.
This document is the best available discussion of the climate of the Metropolis and its relationship to atmospheric pollution. It includes much data in tables and on maps.

Kimball, Marston. *Plant Climates of California*.

This is a series of maps prepared for the University of California Extension Service. Although these maps are difficult to locate, much of what they contain has been incorporated in the "Climate Maps" found in Sunset Magazine's *New Garden Book,* Menlo Park, Calif.: Lane, 1977.

CHAPTER 5

Pollution in the Balmy Air

Figure 5.1. Smoke from backyard incinerators and industrial plants combines with photochemical smog to define the base of the inversion, January 15, 1940. View from over Vernon toward Palos Verdes Hills. (Photo courtesy Spence Collection / Department of Geography, UCLA.)

"On . . . October 3 (1542, Cabrillo and his men left San Diego) and . . . sailed . . . along the coast, where they saw many valleys and plains and many smokes and sierras inland. . . . The Sunday following . . . they came to the mainland in a large bay (San Pedro) which they named "Baia de los Fumos" on account of the many smokes they saw there. . . ." (Wagner, 1941, pp. 46–47.)

". . . smog is an unholy alliance between a substantially constant daily dose of aerial contaminants and a highly variable amount of natural ventilation. It is the weather that calls the tune, smog or no smog. . . ." James G. Edinger (1967, p. 113).

"We have met the enemy and they are us." Pogo.

It was in the summer of 1943 that smog came to Los Angeles to stay. However, it had been around, on occasion, since at least 1940, and periodic complaints of eye and throat irritation by workers in the Civic Center had been reported in the newspapers. Then the days would become clear again and the nuisance would be forgotten. In July, 1943, it remained—a thick smoky cloud descended over the downtown and visibility was cut to three miles. The Los Angeles City Council requested an investigation into the "peculiar atmospheric conditions" and the County Board of Supervisors commissioned their Health Officer to cooperate in discovering the source of the "nuisance." A butadiene plant on Aliso Street producing synthetic rubber for the war was blamed by many. The smog worsened. In September the *Los Angeles Times* reported: "Thousands of eyes smarted. Many wept, sneezed and coughed. Throughout the downtown area and into the foothills the fumes spread their irritation. . . ." Pasadena and other nearby communities seemed to be particularly affected.

Thus began one of the most memorable and poignant episodes in the human occupancy of the Los Angeles Metropolis. The health-giving qualities of the southern California climate were legendary. The area's lovely, soft air, free from the gusty winds of the East, was a delight. Its long hours of bright sunshine were highly prized. The cool, marine air made living in low latitudes comfortable. It was distressingly painful to discover that many of these beloved climatic assets were meteorological qualities most conducive to smog formation and now liabilities in the struggle for pure air.

Even the attractive California life style was to be a part of the problem. Single family houses surrounded with spacious yards, in far flung, uncrowded neighborhoods, had set this urban area apart from the Eastern cities with their lines of row houses and huddled apartments. Further, the automobile had seemed to

be the ideal solution to movement in this generously spaced metropolis. Now this living arrangement, which required much long distance travel to multi-centered work and shopping locations, was to be a significant element in the smog problem. Finally, the millions of additional people, attracted to this area in the mobile period after World War II, and their automobiles, were to make the search for a clean atmosphere a race after a rapidly retreating goal.

There was intense irony, too, in the timing of the southern California predicament. Coal had been unavailable and unused as a fuel in the area, so Los Angeles had been spared the smoke, soot, and grime that afflicted cities in Europe and the American East. In the 1940s, new methods of controlling smoke and soot pollution were coming into use at the same time that photochemical smog was becoming a problem in Los Angeles. For the first time since coal had been discovered it became worthwhile to wash the stone buildings of London and Paris to restore their forgotten whiteness. For the first time in a hundred years, the skies of Pittsburgh and St. Louis were reasonably free from smoke. And, for the first time, a cloud of whiskey-colored, eye-irritating, vegetation-killing fumes was settling over the "land of sunshine." Of course, the full realization of what was happening was to be discovered only bit by bit over a period of many years. It may be instructive to trace the activities that gradually revealed the awful truth to the inhabitants of the "City of the Angels."

The Stung City Strikes Out at Obvious Offenders

What should be done about the newly poisoned atmosphere? As the butadiene factory seemed to be the main villain, public pressure was applied to clean it up. After some resistance the operators promised to install pollution control devices, and the *Los Angeles Times* reported "relief . . . within 60 days the entire elimination of the nuisance within four months was promised yesterday." But health officials, who had begun sampling the air in July, had noticed that eye irritation was just as severe upwind from Aliso Street as downwind and were aware that the problem had been building up for some years. When controlling the fumes from the offending factory failed to relieve the pollution, the public looked around for other culprits. Visible or smelly emissions were the first to attract attention, and the blame was put on a long list of polluters: dumps, factory chimneys, incinerators, oil refineries, and "many small contributors." Most of these were the traditional producers of smoke and dirt and were the logical beginning targets of control efforts. No one realized that the area had a different problem. Hence, the word "smog" was automatically applied to the local pollution, although smog was a word that had been coined by an Englishman, H. A. Des Voeux, in 1905 to describe the atmospheric conditions over British cities where smoke combined with fog to form killing smoke-fogs.

The citizens cried for action. Pleas from health officials, the Pasadena Chamber of Commerce, and threats by elected officials were made to the obvious polluters. Laws followed. In 1945 the City of Los Angeles passed an ordinance limiting the amount of smoke permissible from a single source. The County Board of Supervisors extended the law throughout unincorporated areas. But while twenty-two of the other forty-four cities enacted similar laws, twenty-two did not, and they, needless to say, were often the location of the worst polluters.

The *Los Angeles Times* formed a citizens' advisory smog committee. It also employed Prof. Raymond R. Tucker to assess the local problem and to recommend a course of action. Tucker, a mechanical engineer, had served as Smoke Commissioner of St. Louis during the period in which that city cleaned its air of soft coal particle pollution. The *Times* headlined

his findings on January 19, 1947. His first concern was with organization, and he recommended the creation of a unified smog control district in Los Angeles County, headed by a chief enforcement officer with sufficient power to crack down on offenders. He identified many sources of pollution: factories, backyard fires, public dumps, lumberyard incinerators, automobiles, buses, diesel trucks, heating plants, railroads, home and municipal incinerators. As the beginning of remedial action, he recommended the outlawing of open burning, whether by individuals or by public dumps. Perhaps his St. Louis experience was behind his suggestion that all factories should be required to provide a chemical analysis of smoke and fumes discharged from their chimneys. He further recommended the setting of strict standards as to the type of smoke that could be legally discharged from their chimneys. What would an expert say about the automobile in 1947? "It is quite probable that the auto does contribute, but not in proportions that it is the sole cause." Tucker could not determine the source of tear producing gases, which he called "lachrymatic," and insisted that a research program must be set up. However, "as this work may require only a few months or it may require many years . . . all known sources of pollution should be rigidly controlled while the research program is carried on." Finally, he pointed out the problems of the area's "monsoon" type of climate with its shallow layer of marine air and temperature inversions (Ainsworth, 1947, pp. 1,8). One would have to say from the vantage point of thirty years that Tucker's report was remarkably perceptive. For example, research did require many years; in fact, it is still going on, and one of its major findings was to be that the automobile was the source of much of the "lachrymatic gases."

Action followed shortly. In April, the Board of Supervisors drafted a bill along the lines proposed by Tucker, and at their instigation it was introduced in the state Legislature. After much lobbying by newspapers, local officials, and the general public, it was passed and signed by the governor. This act established air pollution control districts in each county, to be activated only when the local Board of Supervisors decided that there was a need for it. Then they could make rules and regulations to control air pollution. Further, they were authorized to establish a permit system, with permits required to construct or operate any equipment capable of producing smog. Violators could be sued "in the name of the people of California." The Los Angeles County Supervisors activated the district immediately and became its directors. An administrator was hired, as was a technical and enforcement staff, and operations began in February, 1948.

Less than five years after the problem was first recognized a reasonably effective administrative apparatus to deal with the trouble had been created. If we remember that for much of this time it was hoped that the problem could be solved by action against a particular plant or two, and that the skies were their normal blue between widely spaced attacks of smog, perhaps this was a reasonably rapid community response in a democratic society to a complex problem. Almost no one realized the difficulties that lay ahead.

Early Attempts to Identify and Control Smog

The Los Angeles County Air Pollution Control District (popularly known as the APCD) was now in action. Louis C. McCabe, Chief of the Coal Branch of the United States Bureau of Mines, was appointed as the director. Controls were ordered for the obvious sources of pollution. Acid sludge-burning at oil refineries was halted, and injunctions were issued to stop open burning at fifty-five dumps. Standards were set limiting the emission of smoke, fumes, and dust from process industries. Eye irritation was first attributed to sul-

furic acid mist released by refineries and other chemical industries. Such emissions were ordered reduced, and in 1949 the Hancock Chemical Company developed a sulfur recovery system which transformed the sulfur-laden refinery fumes into solid sulfur—the only known example of a pollution control device producing a profitable product. Thousands of smudge pots were ordered replaced by a newly developed "smokeless" orchard heater. Other early regulations included the control of fumes and dust at foundries, smelters, and steel mills, and odor control at rendering plants. When hydrocarbons were discovered to be an ingredient in smog, refinery operations were converted to a closed system and all large gasoline storage tanks were covered. Open fires were banned, and one and a half million backyard incinerators were outlawed as of October 1, 1957, the first regulation that affected the average citizen. Power plants were required to switch from fuel oil to natural gas, first during the smog season, later whenever natural gas was available. In the first decade tens of thousands of pollution control units were installed at a cost of more than a hundred million dollars to the areas' industrialists. The area now had the cleanest factories in the world. The controls were all on stationary sources of pollution, of course. However, it is now estimated that in the 1940s and 1950s, about forty percent of all pollution came from these sources, so even in retrospect, it was a logical and worthwhile place to start the smog control battle.

More than action against the obvious polluters was required. Also essential was a program of research and experimentation—not enough was known about the nature and cause of the region's air pollution. Further, even when polluters could be identified with certainty, methods or devices for their control often were unavailable. They had to be created. The research and engineering sections of the APCD were to develop through the years until the agency was recognized as the leading authority on air pollution and its control in the world.

Numerous scientists were employed as consultants. One of these, Professor Arie J. Haagen-Smit, a biochemist at the California Institute of Technology, made a startling discovery in his laboratory in 1950. He put a mixture of hydrocarbons and nitrogen dioxide (the ingredients of automobile exhaust) into a laboratory flask and exposed it to sunlight. The resulting product looked like smog, it smelled like smog, tests proved it was smog. Now, for the first time, the automobile was tagged as a major contributor to the area's pollution problem.

However, from a laboratory experiment to universal acceptance of the result was a long and weary road. First, smog control officials and then the general public had to be convinced that the automobile, needed and used by everyone, was the real culprit. Even gaining local conviction was child's play compared to getting the automobile industry to admit their guilt and clean up their engines. As early as 1953 Supervisor Hahn wrote Henry Ford II asking what his company knew about automobile pollution and if it had any plans for a research and abatement program. The answer was that exhaust gases were dispersed and so no research was necessary. All through the 1950s the APCD appealed to the auto industry and independent manufacturers to develop control devices. Nothing happened. As late as 1959, C. A. Chayne, Vice President of General Motors, was telling the California Legislature that "smog cannot be produced by a normally tuned automobile."

Other moves toward controls were met by the opposition of those affected. The metal industries, financially powerful, resisted the installation of electrical precipitators on open hearth and steel furnaces and the requiring of "bag houses" (gigantic vacuum cleaners) to control fumes. The subdividers, who were bulldozing orchards and burning the trees, ob-jected to the prohibition on open burning. The orchardists put up a fight before abandoning their old "smudge pots." Even the housewives, in the name of individual freedom, joined the makers of incinerators in resisting the elimination of that malodorous contraption. John Anson Ford, one of the Supervisors, relates how discouraged they became because they "could never prove the enactment of any one of these restrictions, or all of them put together, was eliminating smog." (Ford, 1961, p. 124).

The oil industry, too, proved to be a vociferous opponent of the activities of the APCD. Its organ, the Western Oil and Gas Association, originally hired the Stanford Research Institute to carry on investigations paralleling that of the APCD. Later, in 1954, they joined with citizens groups, industrialists, commercial enterprises, and universities to form the Southern California Air Pollution Foundation, seemingly to act as a counterweight to the APCD. At first, these organizations stressed the many factors that might contribute to smog—apparently to take the heat off the petroleum industry and automobiles. The Supervisors accused them of "making propaganda." Eventually, however, the Air Pollution Foundation confirmed the APCD findings. An automobile was driven on a dynamometer to simulate traffic conditions in a closed chamber; the exhaust was exposed to sunlight and smog was produced. The organization disbanded in 1961.

Control of Mobile Sources of Pollution Shifts to the State Level

The events of the turbulent fifties demonstrated that controlling pollution from automobiles, which involved putting pressure on the automobile industry, was beyond the ability of a single county, however large and populous. Then, too, the problem was becoming widespread; nine counties in the Bay Area created the second APCD in 1955, others were to follow. In 1960 the state of California established a Motor Vehicle Control Board, to set emission standards, approve control devices, and enforce their installation and maintenance. (Its functions were assumed by the California Air Resources Board in 1967.) No technical difficulty existed in the control of crankcase fumes, and the automobile industry was persuaded to include control devices on the 1961 models sold in California. In the same year, standards were set requiring the phased reduction of hydrocarbon emissions by eighty percent, and carbon monoxide emissions by sixty percent. The first reduction of these two pollutants was mandatory with 1966 model automobiles; evaporation losses from fuel tank and carburetor were to be controlled in 1970. Oxides of nitrogen were to be reduced in 1971 with reductions gradually increasing through 1975—to meet this last stringent standard, catalytic converters were necessary on most cars.

In 1967, the Federal government preempted all emission control in the country through the Federal Clean Air Act. However, under certain circumstances, California was to be exempt. First, California's standards must be more strict than Federal standards. Secondly, a waiver must be obtained each year from the Environmental Protection Agency.

Although all of this activity has brought many benefits, there still are at least two problems involved. One is that the emission control devices have not remained fully effective and automobiles began exceeding permitted emission standards after only a few thousand miles of use. In an attempt to assure that all vehicles (rather than just a few test samples) met the required criteria, at least when they were new, assembly line testing of all vehicles sold in California began in 1973. A second problem is the direct result of the method used by the automobile industry to meet the hydrocarbon emission standard. The American automobile manufacturers chose to modify the operation of the engine through leaner carburetion,

changes in timing, and by injecting air into the exhaust ports. The result was that the emissions of oxides of nitrogen were now increased from fifty to one hundred percent. Over the years the reduction of hyrdrocarbons and the increase of oxides of nitrogen resulting from the operation of the 1966–1970 automobiles has changed the proportions of these gases in the air over the Los Angeles Basin. Now the conditions for a reaction between them was even more favorable, and there were more ozone alerts in the area in 1970 than in any year since 1956. And there were more oxides of nitrogen blown into the air than there were before the control program began.

Meanwhile, additional action has taken place on the local level. In 1960, the APCD restricted the olefin content of gasoline sold in the county—a regulation designed to reduce eye irritation caused by automobile exhaust but thought to be ineffective by some critics. Further, it began to regulate processes involving organic solvents, even to the extent of banning the use of paint containing photochemically reactive liquids. A rule adopted in 1971 required the installation of newly developed devices to reduce nitrogen oxides by power plants and manufacturing concerns. Then, too, any fuel burned in the county must contain no more than 0.5 percent sulfur. Most recently, it has required the installation of vapor recovery equipment at filling stations to recover vapors from the gas tanks of automobiles as they are filled. In addition, gasoline tank trucks are required to have vapor recovery systems.

Beginning July 1, 1975 there was a change in the organization of the local agency. The Los Angeles APCD was combined with similar bodies in Orange, Riverside, and San Bernardino Counties. The new regional agency is called the "South Coast Air Quality Management District." Presumably the shift resulted from the fact that smog is no respecter of county boundaries.

The Local Atmosphere, the Other Half of the Problem

There are still many smog free days in the Metropolis. The distant landmarks of Mount Baldy and Catalina can be seen clearly from the top of UCLA's Bunche Hall. Automobiles, factories, power plants, and everything else are pouring out pollutants every day, yet some days are smoggy, some are clear. Why the difference? Simple enough: when the marine layer and its shallow temperature inversions (discussed in the previous chapter) are not present, there is no smog. At such times the pollutants mix freely with the vast ocean of air and they soon become so thinned out as to almost completely disappear. When there is a temperature inversion, however, the pollutants are trapped below the inversion level and accumulate. If the inversion level persists for several days at a time, as it does in its seasonal weather sequences, the smog thickens and fills the air space below the inversion. Clearly, smog is a function of two distinct systems: one which produces the pollutants, and another which receives, converts, and spreads them. This is not a new discovery, since the operators of the butadiene plant, first thought to be the smog villain, offered to gear operations of the facility to changing atmospheric conditions.

What are the atmospheric conditions in the Los Angeles area that are conducive to smog formation? They include the following: frequent temperature inversions that trap pollutants in the shallow layer of air near the ground, breezes which are too gentle to blow the pollutants away, the high mountainous arc which tends to confine the pollutants within a limited area, and the bright, omnipresent sunshine, which converts the gaseous pollutants into photochemical smog. We will consider each factor separately.

On three days out of every four, the air over the Metropolis is composed of two layers: a moist, relatively cool marine layer near the ground and a dry warm or hot layer above. Because of expansional cooling, air temperatures usually decrease with altitude. However, under these conditions, a cool layer beneath abnormally warm air aloft, we have a reversal of the normal temperature gradient, hence the term, inversion. As the cool air is heavier than the warm, little or no mixing occurs between the layers of air. When the marine layer is thin, and the base of the inversion is only a few hundred feet above the ground, all of the pollutants are trapped in a relatively small volume of air and heavy smog may be the result.

Even on some days when the marine layer is shallow, there is no smog. On these days there is considerable wind—now more air will pass a given spot and dilute the pollution. But this does not happen very often; the average wind speed in Los Angeles is from three to six miles an hour—less than that of any other metropolitan area in the country. Usually this is considered a desirable quality—gentle breezes are more pleasant than heavy gales for life and leisure. It means, however, that the atmospheric mechanics of the Basin are poorly designed to disperse contaminants horizontally. The normal wind pattern is a daytime sea breeze (from west to east) and a nighttime land breeze (from east to west). On most days in spring and early summer the sea breeze and the general eastward movement of air move the pollution produced each day through the area and out the mountain passes. This daily "flushing" of the Basin is less pronounced in late summer and winter as wind speeds are lighter and the land breeze begins earlier. On some days with stagnant air, land breezes may begin near the mountains by late afternoon, and the pollutants remain in the Basin through the night. Winter storms break the pattern, as do occasional Santa Anas.

During Santa Anas, the normal wind pattern reverses, and air arrives over Los Angeles from the northeast. This is dry and warm air (discussed in the previous chapter) that sweeps away the marine layer and brings desert air to the beach communities. When the air flow is weak, a very stable layer of air is formed near

Table 5.1
Daily Emissions: South Coast Air Basin Pollution Sources

Contaminate	Tons Per Day	Percentage—each source Motor Vehicles	Other Mobile*	Stationary Permitted**	Stationary Other
Carbon monoxide	7876	75.8	3.9	3.4	16.9
Reactive organic gases —(mainly hydrocarbons)	1512	51.6	3.9	21.2	23.3
Oxides of nitrogen	1337	57.2	7.7	23.2	11.9
Oxides of sulfur	276	15.8	8.4	71.3	4.5
Suspended particulates	621	14.0	1.1	9.4	75.5

* Other mobile: ships, aircraft, trains, off-road vehicles.
** Stationary permitted: operating under District permit or exempt.
Source: South Coast Air Quality Management District, *Air Quality Digest*, September, 1981, p. 5.

the ground under another temperature inversion, and again smog is the result. If the Santa Ana is mild, it is the beach communities that are hot, and it is to these areas that the tertiary pollutants find their way. Normally, however, Santa Anas with normal wind speeds blow quite strongly and clear the air entirely of smog, producing hot, but beautifully clear days.

The high mountainous arc surrounding the Basin plays a varying role in the region's air pollution problem. At night and during the early morning the mountains function as barriers restricting the inland movement of the marine air. However, as their slopes heat up in the daytime they act a bit like chimneys, venting the smog from the area. Edinger, visiting Mount Wilson, some 6,000 feet high, found that its crest was right in the smog, and that visibility was only a mile or so. He explains, "The daytime thermal upslope winds had pulled the smog, like a dirty rug, right up the southern slopes of the San Gabriels" (Edinger, 1967, p. 111).

Finally, and most ironically, it is the bright sunshine that occurs with pleasing regularity which provides the energy to activate the chemical reaction in the atmosphere which transforms the original innocuous gases from automobile and factory into the noxious stuff we call smog.

To keep matters in perspective, it should be remembered that the same meteorological conditions that make for poor ventilation of the local atmosphere today have always been with us, and, even without modern pollution, there were days when the air was not clear. Cabrillo in 1542 noted the accumulation of natural haze and smoke from Indian campfires that remained in the air. Sea fog or haze, droplets of moisture condensed in the air, are a common feature in mornings in many areas. In the winter, fog often occurs far inland after cool, clear winter nights. Dust kicked up by the wind, plant pollen, particles of ocean salt all contribute to a natural haze that made the air under the inversion layer murky even before man arrived in the region. Donald Carr describes the view in his youth (1920s) from Mount Wilson as seeing a "little city overhung with a rather becoming mistiness, like a light scarf on a woman's hair."

After All This, What Still Fouls Our Lovely Air?

In the 1980s, what pollutants still foul our balmy air, and from whence do they come? Data for the most recent available year are shown in Table 5.1. These five items, carbon monoxide (CO), hydrocarbons (HC), oxides of nitrogen (NO_x), sulfur dioxide (SO_2), and particulates (TSP, total suspended particulate), are the major *primary* pollutants. That is, they are the compounds produced directly by automobiles, power plants, petroleum refineries, factories, home furnaces, and so forth. In our atmosphere, however, sparked by the energy of the sunshine, some of these gases react with the oxygen and nitrogen in the air and with each other to produce several new gases that appear in no table as we have no way to measure their volume. As one of these, nitrogen dioxide (NO_2), is a product of the reaction of primary gases, it is called a *secondary* pollutant. It eventually enters into a further reaction. The most important of the *tertiary* pollutants, or the final products of the reaction, is ozone (O_3). Ozone is so significant in the Basin that it is sometimes used as a surrogate for "smog." Other tertiary pollutants produced in small quantities are peroxy acetal nitrate (PAN), and various aldehydes. In addition, sulfur dioxide (SO_2), in a separate reaction, combines with oxygen and water to form sulfuric acid in an aerosol haze.

Primary Pollutants

Hydrocarbons (HC), compounds composed of the elements carbon and hydrogen, are of several different types. Methane is an example of one type (alkanes), another type is called alkenes or olefins. This distinction is important because the two types vary greatly in reactivity and thus in their contribution to smog. Methane is relatively unreactive, but olefins react rapidly. About sixty percent of the hydrocarbons come from mobile sources (mainly motor vehicles) and about forty percent from stationary sources. Oxides of nitrogen (NO_x, mainly nitric oxide) are colorless, odorless gases, formed from the nitrogen and oxygen in the air during all burning processes. If the temperature and pressure are both high, as in motor vehicle engines, large amounts of oxides of nitrogen are produced. Motor vehicles account for about sixty percent of this pollutant in the Metropolis; power plants, aircraft,

ships, factories, and home furnaces add the remaining forty percent. Carbon monoxide (CO) is a colorless, odorless, toxic gas, formed by the incomplete combustion of any fuel containing carbon such as gasoline. Almost all of the carbon monoxide produced in the Basin comes from motor vehicles. Sulfur dioxide (SO_2) is a colorless gas with a sharp, irritating odor, formed when fuels containing sulfur are burned. It comes from power plants, chemical plants, petroleum refineries, and metal processing plants especially. Particulates, or total suspended particulate (TSP) are tiny particles of solid or liquid droplets in the atmosphere and include dust, soot, aerosols, fumes, and mists. They are produced in industrial and agricultural operations, from combustion, from auto exhausts, and from photochemical reactions in the atmosphere. Wind blown dust and the salt in the ocean spray also add particulates to the atmosphere. In the air they both scatter and absorb sunlight, producing haze and reducing visibility.

Secondary and Tertiary Pollutants

The chemical reaction that takes place in the "witches brew" of the Los Angeles atmosphere is so complex that it is not yet completely understood. Scores of things are going on at the same time. The main outlines, however, are known. Hydrocarbons, when only partially oxidized, produce "literally thousands of different compounds, most of which are undesirable." In the atmosphere, oxides of nitrogen and reactive hydrocarbons, in a multistep reaction, produce nitrogen dioxide (NO_2), itself highly reactive. It is a gas with a yellowish-brown tint, easily visible in the air, the color we associate with smog. Nitrogen dioxide absorbs ultraviolet light from the sun which starts an additional reaction with the same ingredients and produces a group of tertiary pollutants. Of these the most significant is ozone (O_3), a nearly colorless (faintly blue) gas, with a faint chlorine odor (like bleach). Ozone is continually being formed and used up during the photochemical reaction process, and cannot accumulate until all of the nitric oxide has been converted to nitrogen dioxide. Another chemical produced in the final smog reaction is peroxy acetyl nitrate, commonly called PAN. It is beastly stuff, particularly toxic to leafy vegetables and will make a grown person cry.

Off doing its own thing is sulfur dioxide. Instead of being part of the smog-forming chemical reaction, in the presence of sunlight and moist air, it simply becomes converted to tiny droplets of sulfuric acid. This acid is what eats away marble and turns plant leaves yellow. Further, it is not good for the human respiratory tract. Carbon monoxide, also, is not part of the smog-forming reaction. It is objectionable by itself.

The Distribution of Smog

Maps showing the distribution of smog in Los Angeles have not been published widely in local newspapers and magazines. Why? Have they been suppressed by land owners and communities in areas that might show heavy smog concentrations? Maybe. Actually, smog maps that mean anything are extremely difficult to produce. Each pollutant, and we have now identified nine of them (and there are more), has its own individual distribution pattern. Not only that, but the distribution is different for each hour of the day. Further, the distribution changes from spring to summer and fall and winter. What can one say about their distribution? Let us see.

Each of the primary pollutants has an area of concentration originally related to the varying sources of pollution. Their distribution is affected by the prevailing winds: generally from the coast to inland, stronger in summer than winter, with the exact direction related also to the topography. The volume of pollutants also varies both hourly and seasonally. Lower winter temperatures result in increased fuel consumption. Too, substitution of fuel oil for scarce natural gas in winter increases the amounts of nitric oxide and sulfur dioxide that are produced in that season. Pollutants produced by automobiles reach their peak during the weekday morning rush hours. The secondary and tertiary contaminants, of course, have their own distribution patterns.

In the Los Angeles area, stationary sources of pollution, power plants, oil refineries, and heavy manufacturing, are located mainly in the south and southwest coastal areas and in the eastern San Fernando Valley. These plants produce considerable quantities of sulfur dioxide and nitric oxide, the latter formed during the combustion of all fuels. Pollution from motor vehicles is heavily concentrated in the same areas plus the central district, and, in a limited way, is widespread. These mobile sources emit mainly carbon monoxide, nitric oxide, and hydrocarbons.

Carbon monoxide comes almost entirely from automobiles. It has similar distributions in both summer and winter, although summer concentrations are generally lower as there are far fewer morning surface inversions during that season. During the winter morning traffic peak, for example, high concentrations of carbon monoxide are found over all areas of heavy vehicle concentration. As the day progresses, levels do not increase, but the polluted air simply diffuses downwind. Figure 5.2a, based on twelve hour carbon monoxide concentrations, shows that the densely populated and heavily traveled areas of Los Angeles and Orange Counties have the greatest number of days in violation of standards.

Particulates may be either natural things such as sea salt dust, or material from human activities. Measurements of particulates do not distinguish between wind blown dust and man-made materials, and the greatest number of violations of state air quality standards occur in a band running from El Monte to Riverside: see Figure 5.2b.

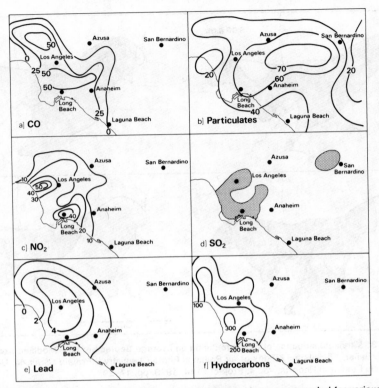

Figure 5.2. Number of days on which state or federal standards were exceeded for various pollutants in 1980. Based on data from: South Coast Air Quality Management District. *Summary of Air Quality in the South Coast Air Basin of California. 1980.*

Nitric oxide, a product of fuel combustion, has its highest atmospheric concentrations close to major source areas. It reacts with the air to become nitrogen dioxide, an intermediate product of the photochemical reaction, which is characterized by great seasonality. Nitrogen dioxide reaches its greatest concentration in winter because, with short days and less intense sunlight, the reaction often fails to proceed beyond this (nitrogen dioxide) stage. In summer, however, with intense sunlight present over many hours, the reaction usually continues, with the nitrogen dioxide forming ozone and other things. During the summer, when the prevailing winds sweep from the coast to the inland valleys, the coastal stations show relatively low nitrogen dioxide readings; the central area and east San

Gabriel Valley, higher readings; and the more distant valleys, almost none. Figure 5.2c shows that most violations of nitrogen dioxide standards on an annual basis, occur at locations near the source of the pollutants. If only summer months were used, the coastal stations would show fewer violations, and the central area and east San Gabriel Valley, more. In all seasons, the more distant valleys have almost no violations.

The end product of the reaction discussed above, ozone, has a distributional pattern that is the most complicated of all. Areas of high concentration are sometimes far from the sources of pollutants. Ozone formation begins shortly after sunrise, but does not become a significant pollutant until all of the nitrogen dioxide from the morning traffic peak is consumed. Peak ozone levels occur between noon

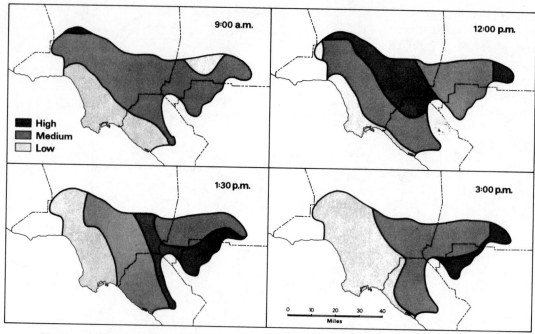

Figure 5.3. Varying distribution of oxidants during an average September day. Modified from: Joseph V. Behar, "Simulation Modes of Air Pollution Photo Chemistry," *Project Clean Air*, University of California Research Reports, vol. 4, Project 5-14, 1970, pp. 17-29.

and 2:00 P.M., with declining levels later in the afternoon, reaching a minimum at night when ozone formation stops because there is no sunlight. The changing distribution of ozone levels is shown in Figure 5.3 for four periods during the day—A. mid-morning, B. late morning, C. early afternoon, and D. mid-afternoon. The changing pattern of ozone distribution clearly reflects the effect of additional hours of sunlight as well as the gradual movement toward the eastern valleys due to the prevailing daytime winds.

Sulfur dioxide, almost entirely produced by power plants and heavy industry, has a much more restricted distribution. It tends to be confined to its source areas, mainly the southwest coast and south coast, and around Fontana, with the pattern of pollution extending downwind, following a plume-shaped dispersion pattern as illustrated by Figure 5.2d.

Warning: Breathing Smog May Be Hazardous to Your Health

In August, 1968, some sixty members of the UCLA medical faculty sent a statement to the *Los Angeles Times* asserting that "air pollution has now become a major health hazard to most of this community during much of the year." They advised "anyone who does not have compelling reasons to remain, to move out of smoggy portions (of the basin) to avoid chronic respiratory diseases like bronchitis and emphysema." They admitted that hard evidence to support this statement was not yet available, but insisted that by the time it was collected it might be too late for many people.

Although this has been the most dramatic statement yet concerning the effects of smog on health, no one would argue that breathing smog is good for the human body. The most obvious deleterious effect is eye irritation. Although individuals vary considerably in their sensitivity, this one symptom is sufficiently widespread to prove that smog is injurious to humans. Other effects are more subtle, and positive proof of injuriousness is not easily produced. It does seem clear, however, that the several components of smog aggravate a wide variety of respiratory diseases such as emphysema, bronchitis, and asthma, and, in general, contribute to coughing and chest discomfort. Some medical opinion believes it possible that smog contributes to a chronic state of illness and increases the incidence of lung cancer. Oxidants have been implicated as accelerators of the aging process. Carbon monoxide decreases the oxygen-carrying capacity of the blood, to the detriment of vital tissues. It is also possible that there is a correlation between air pollution and such things as heart disease and even the frequency of automobile accidents, although this has not, so far, been proven medically.

Smog seems to affect various groups of people differently. Some persons are genetically susceptible to such things as lung disease, asthma, arteriosclerosis, and the development of coronary heart disease. Exposure to carbon monoxide, oxidants, oxides of nitrogen, and such things as lead would be expected to aggravate the genetically conditioned abnormality of such susceptible persons.

Plants seem to be particularly sensitive to smog and effects are often noticed on them before humans seem to be affected. Some agricultural crops, romaine lettuce, spinach, Cattleya orchids, and carnations, once of major importance, can no longer be grown commercially in the basin. Others, carrots, beets, tomatoes, and beans, suffer reduced yields, and ozone causes damage to alfalfa. In 1969, smog reportedly caused a loss of about forty million dollars in the agricultural returns of the Metropolis, much of it from reduced citrus yields. Four species of trees in the San Bernardino National Forest have been severely damaged by smog, with the Ponderosa Pine particularly affected, shedding their needles and dying prematurely. With the pines, as with people, however, individuals seem to fare differently, with some trees essentially immune. Hopefully, their offspring will be immune to smog as well, and will provide the young trees needed to replace the many thousands which have died in recent years.

The harmful effects of smog on health was recognized as early as 1955, and an air monitoring network and emergency control system was begun. At first, a three stage "alert" system was developed, in which air contaminant levels were set for the major pollutants. When they were exceeded, action was taken depending on the stage of the alert attained. This was the first system of its kind in the country. In 1969 a "School and Health Warning System" was initiated, designed to protect students and others with cardiac and respiratory problems by advising them to avoid exercise when pollution reached designated levels.

In recent years, both the federal and state governments have established air quality standards and emergency episode criteria for various pollutants. When concentrations of a pollutant above a specified level is either reached or predicted, a Stage One Episode is declared. Persons with respiratory or coronary heart disease are notified through the mass communications media to take precautions against exposure. Schools are notified so they can curtail student participation in strenuous activities. Actions to reduce pollutants are voluntary. When pollutants reach or are predicted to reach Stage Two concentrations, major stationary polluters: power plants, petroleum refineries, and other large polluters are required to reduce their emissions of hydrocarbons and oxides of nitrogen by twenty percent. Inspectors are out in force and the rate of compliance is high. In addition, an effort is made to substantially reduce automobile traffic. At first, large employers (those 2,700 firms and institutions that employ more than one hundred people at a single location) were required to close off two-thirds of their parking places. The result was chaos: employees drove to work anyway and cruised around for miles looking for alternate parking places. Today, these large employers are encouraged to institute employee carpooling and vanpooling programs so there is an alternative to single person commuting. The results are mixed. A Stage Two Episode is thought to cost the region about two million dollars a day. Stage Three Episodes require a state of emergency, can be proclaimed only by the governor, and would result in a "summer holiday," like the Fourth of July or Labor Day, with most businesses and industry shut down. The estimated cost would be about a billion dollars a day.

Stage One Episodes are declared quite often. For example, during 1980, in some portion of the South Coast Air Basin, Stage One ozone Episodes occurred on one hundred one days, and Stage One carbon monoxide Episodes occurred on four days. Stage Two ozone Episodes were called on fifteen days in 1980, about average—the range is from ten to twenty. Obviously, benefits gained in a Stage Two or Stage Three Episode come mainly if they can be predicted far enough in advance that effective action can be taken. No Stage Three episodes have ever been called in the South Coast Air Basin.

Cleaner Air in the Future?

The air pollution problem is dynamic; sources shift and goals change. As automobiles become cleaner, some remaining uncontrolled stationary sources assume more significant roles, as do the dirty engines of motorcycles. In 1968, Haagen-Smith was quoted as saying: "The smog hasn't gotten any worse—it's more or less stabilized." In 1981, with the exception of nitrogen dioxide, an examination of the data seems to indicate a downward trend throughout the basin for most contaminants. Although there is variation from

one year to another, tied to variations in the weather, the grim years of the 1960s seem to have been put behind us.

Our goals are changing, too; both the state and nation through Clean Air Acts have established goals—statistical criteria for clean air that must be met by every locality. They are somewhat different, but presumably the Metropolis must meet the more stringent of the conflicting standards, and its aim is to do just that. Although these standards are legally binding, it is safe to say, however, that some of them are so unrealistically stringent that they cannot be achieved. There is evidence, for example, that natural (or residual) background emissions come close to reaching the standards in many urban and some rural environments. Once again, the folly of enacting comprehensive laws applying to the natural environment for as diverse a region as the United States is clearly demonstrated.

Let us see how the South Coast Air Basin fared in 1980. The state standard for ozone was exceeded on one hundred eighty-one days at Fontana, for carbon monoxide on forty-three days, and for nitrogen dioxide on twenty-three days. The state standard for particulates was exceeded on more than seventy percent of the days in a broad band extending from Pico Rivera to Riverside. There is no state standard for hydrocarbons, but the national standard for this pollutant was exceeded on more than three hundred days at Lennox. On the other hand, the state sulfur dioxide standard was met on every day of the year—Los Angeles is the cleanest metropolitan area in the nation by this standard. To be fair, the record is not as dismal as it may seem. Although on fifty percent of the days the air at Fontana did not meet the state standard for ozone, to take one example, this does not mean that the standard was exceeded half of the time. The standards are such that if they are exceeded during a single hour during any day, that day has not met the standards. The Environmental Protection Agency is charged, as a last resort, to prepare plans for areas that will enable them to conform to the National Clean Air Standards. Their plan of July 2, 1973, for the Los Angeles area, in desperation, called for a one hundred percent reduction in gasoline use, and a sixty percent reduction in diesel fuel sales. Granting the unrealism of some of the standards of the Clean Air Act, what can be done that will enable the region to approach desirable standards?

As current state law gradually requires cleaner and cleaner engines in new cars, proposals for cleaning up cars already on the road are a logical additional move. One set of ideas focuses on the pre-1970 automobile, which by modern standards is quite dirty. One proposal, currently dormant, is to require that smog control devices be installed in 1960–65 cars, evaporative control devices on 1966–69 cars, and NOX devices on the whole batch. A more imaginative, and perhaps more politically practical, suggestion is to offer a bonus for every pre-1970 vehicle exported for sale outside of the region. A second course of action involves periodic mandatory inspection and maintenance of all vehicles within the basin. (Such a bill was passed by the Legislature in 1972, but "blue penciled" out of the budget by Governor Reagan.) A pilot inspection program was begun in Riverside County in 1976.

Further reduction of pollutants from both stationary and mobile sources can be accomplished by state and local regulation. Current stationary-source action centers around requiring the substitution of non-reactive materials by users of organic solvents—degreaser substitutes, nonreactive paint thinners, and dry cleaning vapor recovery.

Enforcement procedures on the local level may also need revision. Whereas the South Coast Air Management District apparently has an effective program for reducing visible emissions and odor problems, it is alleged that it is less effective in keeping track of invisible sources, the gases that are the primary sources of photochemical smog. The solution is not easy; there are some 60,000 pollution sources in Los Angeles County alone and, once they have been given permission to operate, their equipment is rarely checked by surprise inspections—the good faith of the operator is relied on. Although a good many violators of smoke ordinances are brought to court, first offenders are fined from fifty to one hundred dollars, and it is charged that it is often more economical to pay the fine than to solve the problem. A shift to the use of injunctions, or civil suits for damages, has been suggested as a more effective enforcement procedure.

There are instances of retrogression; fuel for power plants is the clearest example. By about 1970, some plants had completed the switch to clean-burning natural gas. As a shortage in natural gas developed, reconversion to fuel oil is taking place. Even if low sulfur fuel oil is available, significant additional pollution is inevitable. Too, in the long run, the local utilities had hoped to phase out their plants in the basin entirely, shifting to nuclear or coal-burning equipment outside the region. However, environmentalist opposition to the building of coal burning or nuclear plants almost anywhere in the West is making that hoped for move a more distant dream.

In the category of moving sources of pollutants, aircraft, both jet and propeller-driven, as well as motorcycles, remain problems. Federal opposition to control of aircraft set back the enforcement program a bit, but limitations on smoke applied to most jet engines by the end of 1978, and became more stringent after 1980. Aircraft venting of fuel was prohibited in 1975. Hydrocarbons from planes are pretty well controlled, but carbon monoxide and nitrogen oxide remain problems. Motorcycles, especially the two stroke variety, are particularly dirty. In lieu of a method of controlling emissions, the prohibition of their use from 6:00 A.M. to 8:00 P.M. in the May to October period has been suggested by the Environmental Protection Agency.

A package of transit improvement programs, usually coupled with a means of reducing the convenience, or increasing the cost, of automobile travel is normally a part of all air-cleaning programs. Ideas include exclusive bus-carpool lanes (Diamond Lanes), on-ramp metering, favored access to freeways for buses and carpools, carpool matching programs, free parking for carpoolers, and reduced parking spaces for others at many destinations. Another series of suggestions include the assessment against the owner of an automobile, an emissions tax tied to miles driven (feasible with mandatory annual inspection), higher taxes on gasoline, limiting total consumption of gasoline to 2.7 billion gallons per year by a system of freely auctioned coupons, or gas rationing at the wholesale level. Transit could be made more attractive by subsidizing buses, providing additional bus service to poorly served areas, shortening headways on existing routes, coupled with favored access and use of freeways. More ambitiously, a spine of generally radial fixed rail rapid transit focused on the Central Business District (supplemented by express and local bus service) might be constructed.

There is little agreement, however, as to the effectiveness of many of these strategies (see, for example, Table 5.2). A major problem is that only thirty-two percent of the total vehicle miles driven in the Basin are attributable to commuting between home and work. In addition, commuting by freeway accounts for less than twenty-five percent of total vehicle miles driven. Attempts to reduce freeway commuting by carpooling, exclusive bus routes, and so on, can only make a small dent in the proportion of total miles driven. Too, people on a four-day work week would likely simply do more leisure and recreational driving on other days. Another disturbing statistic casts doubt on the usefulness of any strategy that simply reduces the length of the trip through "park and ride" plans, or carpooling, where cars are used as transportation to the

Table 5.2
Summary of Impacts for Various Control Strategies

Strategy Description	Approximate Percentage Vehicle Miles Traveled Reduction
Much improved public transit	3
Improved transit and tax on auto use	4
Auto free zone in Los Angeles central business district	0.6
Increased parking costs	Negligible
Four day work week	3.6
Exclusive bus and carpool lane	2.5
Exclusive bus and carpool lane with 3¢/mile tax	3.2
Increased commuter carpools to achieve an average automobile occupancy of 1.5 on freeways	4.4

Source: Compiled from *Transportation Control Strategy Development for the Metropolitan Los Angeles Region,* prepared by TRW, Inc. for the Environmental Protection Agency, APTD-1372, January, 1973, pp. 129-170.

assembly point. "Preliminary data indicate that emissions generated during the first few minutes of vehicle operation represent a large portion of the total emission during any individual vehicle trip." (Lelong, 1974, p. 138.) If this data stands up, it implies that as far as air pollution is concerned the reduction in the number of trips is the important thing, not simply a reduction in total vehicle miles traveled.

For the long run, twenty years or more, possible approaches that would allow the area to move nearer to the goals of the Clean Air Act, are both esoteric and more likely to be effective. What seems to be needed is an entirely new technology; for example, electric cars, the replacement of oil-fueled burners with electric devices, and with all electricity coming from outside the Basin. Another help would be the use of solar energy for space conditioning and water heating. Helpful too would be the guidance of growth, if any, in such a way that a reduction in emissions would come naturally, for example, through interspersing of commercial/industrial and residential areas so that people could live closer to their work. Perhaps advances in electrical communications might reduce the need to travel from home to office. Maybe in some way the entire region's activities could be varied in accordance with the changing ability of the atmosphere to absorb pollutants. Perhaps additional changes in our personal life style might be developed.

5. *Suggested Readings*

Lees, Lester, et al. *Smog, A Report to the People*. Pasadena: Environmental Quality Laboratory, California Institute of Technology. 1972.
A panel of scientists, in this small volume, consider the kind of control measures necessary to achieve the reduction in the number of smoggy days mandated by the Clean Air Act.

South Coast Air Quality Management District. *Air Quality Management Plan 1982 Revision*. El Monte: South Coast Air Quality Management District, 1982.
This report outlines a series of proposals by which the local District hopes to accomplish the almost impossible task of eventually meeting the goals mandated by the state and federal governments. An *Environmental Impact Report* and an *Appendix* are included as separate volumes. The same organization also publishes an annual report, *Air Quality Trends in the South Coast Air Basin,* as well as occasional specialized documents. All are available from the District's office at 9150 Flair Drive, El Monte, CA. 91731.

Water for a Thirsty Land

Figure 6.1. The city of Los Angeles stores Owens Valley water in the Hollywood Reservoir. This view is through Cahuenga Pass toward the eastern San Fernando Valley, January 12, 1960. (Photo courtesy Spence Collection / Department of Geography, UCLA.)

"A drop of water, taken up from the ocean by a sunbeam, shall fall as a snowflake upon the mountain top, rest in the frozen silence through the long winter, stir again under the summer sun and seek to find its way back to the sea down the granite steeps and fissures. It shall join its fellows in mad frolics in mountain gorges, singing the song of falling waters and dancing with the fairies in the moonlight. It shall lie upon the bosom of a crystal lake, and forget for a while its quest of the ocean level. Again it shall obey the law and resume its journey with murmurs and frettings; and then it shall pass out of the sunlight and the free air and be borne along a weary way in darkness and silence for many days. And at last the drop that fell as a snowflake upon the Sierra's crest and set out to find its home in the sea, shall be taken up from beneath the ground by a thirsty rootlet and distilled into the perfume of an orange blossom in a garden of the City of the Queen of the Angels." Allen Kelly (Los Angeles Board of Public Service Commissioners, 1916, p. 10).

"Little drops of water on little grains of sand,
Make a hell of a difference in the price of land." Anonymous parody on a Julia Carney poem.

Cities can exist only if resources are brought to them. For thousands of years roads have been built over which food and fuel could be transported to cities, and aqueducts have been constructed to bring in water. A stone aqueduct, the "Marcia—the pride of Rome," built in 145 B.C., brought water fifty-eight miles from the Anio Valley to that city. In 1608 an aqueduct was built to carry fresh water thirty-eight miles to London, and as early as 1892 Manchester received water from a source ninety-six miles distant. Since 1913 the Catskill Aqueduct has transported water one hundred thirty miles to New York City. San Francisco dammed the wild Tuolumne River, inundating the spectacular Hetch Hetchy Valley (twin to Yosemite Valley) and transported the water one hundred fifty miles to serve its needs in 1923. The southern California aqueducts, then, are by no means unique. Their fame lies in their length and in the ingenuity of their engineering rather than in their novelty. However, they were to come only after the region had been settled for more than a hundred years.

Early Sources of Water

Although it is the aqueducts that have caught the public eye, the region's local sources of water have had both early and continued importance. The Spanish settlers were experienced irrigators and recognized that the mountain streams could compensate for the lack of year-round rainfall. San Gabriel Mission was founded at a site where irrigation water was plentiful. Similarly, the pueblo of Los Angeles was located on a small mesa near the Los Angeles River, above the reach of all but the worst of floods, where water from the then perennial stream could be diverted and would run by gravity to the pueblo's fields. All through the nineteenth century this stream provided all the water the growing settlement needed.

Similarly, Americans coming into the area after 1850 secured the services of engineers who were skilled in irrigation practices, and scores of settlements were founded using water from distant mountain streams. To serve Riverside, for example, a brush weir diverted water from the Santa Ana River through a canal (fourteen feet wide, four feet deep) fifteen miles to the town. Wooden flumes on trestles carried the water over intervening arroyos. In the mountain reaches of the same river, a "remarkable dam was built across Bear Valley in 1884, where water could be stored before being conducted through canals, tunnels, flumes (over two arroyos and "the great barranca known as Mill Creek Wash") more than twenty miles to Redlands in the valley below. Some individuals, like George Chaffey, were part engineer, part innovator, and part promoter. Chaffey introduced water saving concrete pipes, developed the idea of using his irrigation system to generate electric power and invented the concept of the "mutual water company" to transfer riparian rights to more distant land. All this was in conjunction with the settlements he founded—first Etiwanda, and later Ontario—the latter chosen in 1903 as the model irrigation colony in the country.

Although mountain streams and reservoir sites are few, by good fortune the valleys between the high mountains and the sea provide natural reservoirs—extensive ground-water basins with great storage capacity lie beneath them. Water coming down the mountain streams spreads out over the alluvial fans and the gravel of the river beds and filters into the basins. Best of all, it was discovered that in many areas wells drilled into this alluvium were artesian, that is, they would flow naturally by hydrostatic pressure. In 1910 there were 1,596 artesian wells in the area. In that same year, spurred by the invention of the deep well turbine pump, there were also 3,494 pumped wells operating. Over much of the area every farmer and fruit grower had a well for his own use and these wells provided water for

Table 6.1
Member Agencies Local Water Production and MWD Deliveries
Metropolitan Water District
In Acre Feet, Fiscal Year 1980-1981

Member Agencies	Local Production	Total Deliveries MWD	MWD Deliveries, Per Cent of Total*
Anaheim	32,792	30,292	48
Beverly Hills	—	14,034	100
Burbank	551	23,152	98
Calleguas MWD	26,019	79,339	75
Central Basin MWD	157,476	78,996	30
Chino Basin MWD	171,372	34,381	10
Coastal MWD	1,186	37,324	97
Compton	5,411	3,373	38
Eastern MWD	103,990	36,868	26
Foothill MWD	6,518	9,267	59
Fullerton	9,864	22,681	70
Glendale	2,692	25,073	90
Las Virgenes MWD	—	10,282	100
Long Beach	31,301	40,072	56
Los Angeles**	571,163	45,710	6
MWD of Orange County	175,000	227,548	53
Pasadena	17,164	19,772	54
San Fernando	3,263	211	6
San Marino	4,921	4	—
Santa Ana	27,310	15,270	36
Santa Monica	4,533	13,484	73
Three Valleys MWD	48,163	48,322	50
Torrance	4,365	20,099	82
Upper San Gabriel Valley MWD	231,622	42,201	3
West Basin MWD	44,077	163,458	75
Western MWD of Riverside County	162,740	52,018	24
Total	1,843,493	1,093,231	37

* Does not include deliveries used for groundwater replenishment.

** Water from the Owens-Mono Valleys is considered by the MWD as a local source, i.e., water supplied by the member agency.

Source: Metropolitan Water District of Southern California, *Annual Report, 1981*, Table 14.

some 342,000 acres. These basins are like banks, and heavy drafts in excess of replenishment soon lowered the water table drastically. Until about 1900, however, these local supplies seemed adequate.

Even today about half the water needs of the Metropolis come from the diversion of the local streams or by the pumping from the local ground basins. Each water district has a different ratio of local and imported water in its use pattern, and the ratios change somewhat from year to year. However, Table 6.1 shows the situation in 1980–1981.

The City of Los Angeles Has Its Own Water Supply: the River

Under the laws of Spain the original pueblo of Los Angeles was "invested with a perpetual and permanent right to take and use" the waters of the Los Angeles River—in fact, the very purpose of the settlement was to utilize these waters. The river's headwaters gather moisture from the entire San Fernando Valley drainage basin and much of the runoff accumulates in the alluvium beneath the valley floor as an underground lake. The valley slopes toward its opening at the Glendale Narrows where an impervious rock layer forces much of the water to the surface. As a result, the Los Angeles River carried flowing water every month of the year to the site of the pueblo and beyond. For almost a hundred years water was diverted by a brush "toma," or weir, upstream from the plaza into a primitive system of "zanjas" (ditches) which not only irrigated the fields but served the domestic needs of the growing settlement. The main conduit was called the "Zanja Madre" and from it a number of branches ran to different parts of the town. (The line of one of these can still be seen on Olvera Street.) Later, a ditch was built on the east side, and a third diverted water considerably above the city for the irrigation of higher ground. The pueblo jealously guarded its water rights and, when the padres at San Fernando Mission dammed the river in the vicinity of the present North Hollywood, the *Ayuntamiento* began legal proceedings and the dam was ordered removed in 1810.

When the city was incorporated in 1850, the Act of Incorporation confirmed to the city the same water rights formerly held by the pueblo. A city Water Department was soon organized but, in an attempt to secure a more modern distribution system than open ditches and water carts, it was leased to a private company in 1869. The annual rental was four hundred dollars and the lease ran for thirty years. Some up-grading occurred, and by 1888 there were fifty-two miles of water lines, of which about half were pipelines, with the rest of the mileage as open ditches. Unsatisfied, the city refused to renew the lease. It took, however, a long court battle and the payment of two million dollars to recover the system.

Improvements to the water system that were started under private ownership were completed after the city regained control. In the 1890s the area experienced a period of less than normal rainfall. William Mulholland, then a water company engineer, proposed a scheme to catch the underground flow by building infiltration galleries under the river where it passed through the Glendale Narrows. As the spot was privately owned, condemnation proceedings were necessary. In 1899 the state Supreme Court confirmed the right of Los Angeles to all of the water it needed from the Los Angeles River for its municipal supply. Included was the right to prevent farms upstream in the San Fernando Valley from pumping water from wells. (An earlier decision held that Los Angeles had no right to sell water from the river outside the city limits, but it could supply newly annexed territory.)

Dry years continued, and the infiltration galleries planned earlier were built in 1902. Water from the galleries (located above the present Los Feliz Boulevard) was used for domestic purposes, and surface water from the river was diverted near the present Headworks Spreading Grounds for irrigation use. In addition, wells were drilled, both above the Narrows and in the south part of the city. As a conservation measure, one of the first acts of the new Los Angeles Water Department was to order the universal installation of water meters. In 1902 there were only three hundred nineteen meters in service, mainly on large users. By 1905 the program was essentially complete for all domestic and irrigation users, with 35,955 meters in operation. Water consumption, after the installation of meters, dropped drastically from two hundred forty-five gallons per capita to one hundred thirty-five gallons in 1907. Even so, the Los Angeles River was now fully utilized, the city was still short of water, and the residents of the San Fernando Valley were suffering real hardship. Additional water from outside the area seemed essential.

Since the city resumed distributing water, it has been involved in dozens of lawsuits concerning its pueblo water rights. One case involving Burbank, Glendale, and Los Angeles lasted twenty years and was finally decided in 1975. The transcript was nearly 50,000 pages long, the appeal brief consisted of eleven printed volumes with a combined thickness of ten inches, the most voluminous record in the one hundred eighteen year history of the Los Angeles Superior Court. But in the end, the decision was the same: the pueblo rights of Los Angeles to the water in the Los Angeles River were confirmed. Today the galleries still collect water from under the Narrows, and some one hundred sixteen deep wells (they are large wells, of from twelve to fourteen inches in diameter) pump water from the underground aquifers, mainly in the San Fernando Valley. Even so, these local sources provide only about twelve percent of the water needed by the densely populated city.

Water from the Outside: The Owens Valley and the City of Los Angeles

As the dry years continued, it was evident that if Los Angeles was to sustain future growth it needed more water. Other nearby streams in the Metropolis were already completely utilized, and acquiring rights to them would simply reduce supplies for nearby agricultural communities. The Mojave River was considered, but securing its water would involve costly litigation, and its use would deprive an area tributary to Los Angeles of its water supply. As early as 1892, Fred Eaton, long-time City Engineer (and Mayor, 1899–1900), was familiar with the Owens Valley. Some forty creeks, fed by melting snows, carried water down the eastern slopes of the Sierra Nevada where at the crest precipitation ranged from thirty to forty inches a year. What did not percolate through the gravel alluvial fans ended up in the Owens River which emptied into the highly salty Owens Lake. He had also noticed the course of an ancient river bed located in such a position that it would simplify the problems of bringing the water south. Uninterested at first, Mulholland, now in charge of the City Department of Water, traveled northward with Eaton during the dry year of 1904. An inspection of the terrain convinced him that an aqueduct could be built to carry water by gravity flow across the Mojave Desert and through the San Gabriel Mountains into the San Fernando Valley. A delegation of city officials agreed, and the proposal was announced to the citizens by an article in the *Los Angeles Times,* July 29, 1905.

A period of lively and acrimonious debate followed. Opponents charged that the main beneficiaries would be large landowners in the San Fernando Valley, that it would be too expensive, that it was too charged with alkali to be useful, and that water was available from other sources. As electric power could be produced cheaply as the water flowed downhill to Los Angeles, the private power companies were opposed to the whole idea. But most of the newspapers and leading citizens were for the project. They emphasized the benefits of the enterprise to Los Angeles—an ample water supply, abundant electricity, and that the sale of electricity alone would pay the interest on the bonds for the entire project. Together the water and power would make possible an increasingly industrialized city. Proponents also benefited from the fact that the years were dry. In the end, on two separate occasions, the citizens voted for the aqueduct with unprecedented enthusiasm. A bond issue to purchase land and survey the route was passed in September, 1905, by a majority of fourteen to one. After the project had been discussed for two more years, funds to build the aqueduct were approved by voters in June, 1907, by a majority of ten to one. One can only conclude that pluralities of this magnitude favoring bond issues were a tribute to an amazing optimism and vitality of the inhabitants of the small city (of perhaps 200,000 people).

Construction of the aqueduct began in 1908 and five years later, November 5, 1913, the great project was completed. The aqueduct ended in an aerating mountainside cascade, water emerged from a tunnel, and splashed in an open ditch down the ridge of an artificial slope into a reservoir at the northern edge of the San Fernando Valley. On the day the water arrived a civic celebration was held and 40,000 persons are reputed to have witnessed the event. As soon as the reservoir was full, water entered a large main leading to tunnels through the Santa Monica Mountains and a second reservoir in Franklin Canyon. By July, 1914, Los Angeles city mains were filled with Owens Valley water.

The building of the Los Angeles Aqueduct is universally recognized as an outstanding engineering feat. Noteworthy, too, is the fact it was completed on schedule and within the projected cost estimates. Comprising open ditches, many tunnels, steel pipe, and siphons, it stretches two hundred twenty-three miles from the Owens River to the San Fernando Valley. Five hundred miles of roads and trails were built simply to provide access to the route, a cement plant was constructed at Monolith to supply that needed material, two hydroelectric plants and one hundred seventy miles of transmission lines provided power for the construction machinery. The Southern Pacific Railroad extended its line north of Mojave and contracted to do some of the hauling. The vast construction project provided many colorful stories for national magazines, and Los Angeles received additional publicity as a city of opportunity. As recently as 1971 the aqueduct was designated a National Historic Civil Engineering Landmark by the American Society of Civil Engineers. (A later construction, St. Francis Dam, built as a storage reservoir in 1926, was not so distinguished. On March 12, 1928, it collapsed; a wall of water rushed down the Santa Clara River through Piru, Fillmore, and Santa Paula to the sea. The disaster killed more than four hundred persons and destroyed 1,250 homes and 7,900 acres of farmland. Los Angeles paid $15,000,000 in claims. The blame was assumed by the designer of the dam, William Mulholland.)

Owens Valley water gave the city five times the amount of water previously available, and a board of engineers was appointed to suggest a program for the rational use of the surplus. They recommended that first consideration be given to irrigation in the San Fernando Valley. Ground water recharge from agricultural use, they reasoned, would be an estimated twenty-seven and a half percent of deliveries, and would eventually return to the Los Angeles River where this "reclaimed" water could be used a second time. Second priority was assigned to the coastal plain between the Santa Monica Mountains and the Baldwin Hills; third priority, Pasadena, South Pasadena, Alhambra, and some other local communities. The report pointed out that these later districts, however, would not yield any return waters by seepage for use elsewhere in the city of Los Angeles. Further, the engineers recommended: (1) annexation to Los Angeles as a condition for the allocation of surplus water, (2) all districts be required to pay in advance the cost of the main distribution conduits to be constructed by the city, and (3) that they assume their proportionate share of taxation to cover the cost of the aqueduct. Reaction to real estate speculation in the San Fernando Valley caused the report to be ignored for a time. Land in the valley had increased in value tenfold with the hope of water and, as much of the land was held in large parcels, a relatively few people realized large profits.

An alternative plan for using the water was developed. It involved selling the water to the highest bidder, thus presumably assuring its highest economic use and also bringing the city the largest possible financial return. Inherent in the plan, however, was the requirement that no water rights were to be involved, for the water could always be purchased by someone else who would pay a higher price for it. It was soon realized that this procedure had the potential for enormous human and legal problems. So the city officials reluctantly gave their support to the earlier plan worked out by the engineers.

Residents of the San Fernando Valley quickly formed "County Water District No. 3" and approved the issuing of bonds for a distribution system, and, in March 1915, voted to join Los Angeles by a vote of six hundred eighty-one to twenty. On May 4, 1915, the annexation of one hundred seventy square miles of the valley was approved by the voters of Los Angeles, 37,662 for, with 24,982 against. At the same time the annexation of the Palms area (seven square miles) was approved, 38,829 to 20,845. Later annexations of Westgate (forty-nine square miles, from Beverly Hills to Santa Monica) in 1916 and West Coast (twelve square miles around the airport) in 1917 brought much of the westside into the city. A proposal to sell water to the cities of Santa Monica and Sawtelle (then an independent city) was defeated in 1916. Annexation as the price of water became the settled city policy.

The residents of the Owens Valley, meanwhile, were not so delighted by these developments. The valley had been surveyed in a preliminary way by the embryonic Bureau of Reclamation early in the century, and there was a possibility that it would be chosen for one of its first irrigation projects. Instead, representatives of the city of Los Angeles quietly bought up land and water rights, and the Bureau was directed by President Theodore Roosevelt to spend its money elsewhere. The federal government also acceded to the wishes of Los Angeles and strategic public lands were withdrawn from public entry to prevent speculation, and a right of way for the aqueduct through public lands was granted. Owens Valley residents were particularly incensed because no large storage dam was constructed in the valley where enough water could be stored to both irrigate the valley and serve the early needs of Los Angeles. No such dam had been planned, and none was built, since Fred Eaton (formerly both City Engineer and Mayor) owned the site and set his price at one million dollars. Mulholland considered this a rip-off of city taxpayers' money and for many years refused to recommend that the city buy it.

Additional bitterness leading to violence was generated in the 1920s when, during a series of dry years, the city began buying additional land and water rights in the valley. This touched off the "Owens Valley Water War"— the aqueduct was dynamited on numerous occasions and in one instance it was "captured" and for two days the water turned out into the desert. The feeling seemed to be that the city should either buy all of the land in the valley or no more, and in 1925 the city agreed to the purchase demand. As the city gradually acquired the land (today it owns 242,000 acres, about 98.5% of the valley floor) the population declined and the merchants in Independence, Lone Pine, and Bishop demanded reparations for loss of trade. After a long dispute, in 1929, the quarreling parties agreed to a three-man arbitration committee to fix prices on the remaining ranch property. Further, an agreement was reached to purchase the land and improvements of the town properties, which were then leased back to the original owners. During these lengthy negotiations the valley suffered the final blow—the chain of banks serving the area failed because the funds were embezzled by the owners—Mark and Wilfred Watterson, leaders in the valley's fight against Los Angeles. This was long before the days of federal deposit insurance and many residents lost all of their savings.

Much has been written about the Owens Valley controversy, some appears to be objective, much seems to be emotional and biased. Remi A. Nadeau, who has written about the events in great detail and with access to a wide variety of sources, sums up one side, the case against the city:

"It is true that some city officials used questionable political methods to kill federal development in the Owens Valley, gain rights-of-way, and hold water filings; that they failed to build a reservoir at the head of the aqueduct which would have prevented the need of desolating Owens Valley; that for several years they had no settled land-buying policy, causing loss of confidence among valley citizens; that they hurt business in the towns by the purchase of farms but refused to assume responsibility for such losses. Such are the grievances of valley people" (Nadeau, 1974, p. 107).

On the other hand, it is doubtful, in retrospect, if the irrigation project that Owens Valley "lost" could have been justified from a national point of view. The amount of arable land is now known to have been grossly overestimated, and is about 56,000 acres rather than 155,000, as thought in the preliminary survey. In addition, the high altitude makes for a short growing season—alfalfa can be cut only twice, compared to three or four cuttings normal for other California areas. Most fruit trees bear in only one year out of five because of late spring frosts. Finally, the market they were looking to, the miners around Tonapa and Goldfield, soon departed. It is possible that its limited natural resources and isolated location would have brought disappointment to the Owens Valley residents, irrigation or not.

In 1933, W. A. Chalfant concluded in his *Story of Inyo* that the county has "been driven to a status unique in California, that of facing a hopeless future" (Chalfant, 1933, p. 337). It is doubtful if anyone would make that statement today. For today it is recognized that the area contains one of the most "impressive and spectacular landscapes in the United States." Because the valley floor is largely owned by the city of Los Angeles and the mountains by the federal government, much open space remains "where the majesty of the valley and its surrounding mountains can be savored and understood with a minimum of cluttering and interference from human development." Further, it is likely that the income from recrea-tion, estimated at $60 million a year, mainly from vacationers from southern California, is considerably greater than any potential agricultural income. (Still, today, some 15,000 acres of alfalfa are irrigated annually, and cattle are grazed on some ranchland.) Too, the city of Los Angeles pays 50 to 60 percent of the property taxes in the county. Since the period of the "hopeless future," the population of the valley has increased from 6,555 in 1930 to 17,371 in 1980 and some would argue that the greatest present danger to the area is uncontrolled growth on some of the remaining privately-owned parcels. In general terms, the valley retains the natural beauty it possessed when first seen by Joseph Walker in 1834 and has not developed into just another region of plowed fields and row crops, as have most of the interior valleys of California.

The Mono Valley Extension and a Second Barrel for the Aqueduct

Drought conditions in the Sierra Nevada in the 1920s demonstrated that there was insufficient water to fill the aqueduct during a dry cycle. Further exploration revealed that additional water, enough to add twenty-five percent to the total resources of the aqueduct, could be diverted from creeks entering the Mono Basin, located farther north. Bonds to pay for the extension of the aqueduct an additional one hundred five miles (including an eleven mile tunnel through Mono Craters) were approved in 1930. Now the moisture that falls on the eastern slope of Mt. Lyell serves Los Angeles, whereas that which falls on the western side provides water for San Francisco.

Forty years later, in the 1960s, it became increasingly evident that water from the Owens-Mono Valleys, from the standpoint of cost, energy, quality, and reliability, was the city's best source. In years of normal rainfall, more water was available in the valley streams than could be accommodated in the original aqueduct. Consequently, a second "barrel" was completed in June 1970. It has the capacity to increase deliveries from the High Sierra by nearly fifty percent.

Rainfall is not normal every year, however, and sometimes dry years come in cycles. Then water from the open creeks is supplemented by pumping from more than a hundred wells in the Owens Valley—it too has a vast underground aquifer. Pumping occurred in the 1920s, again in the 1930s. In 1977, water was again being pumped, and again there was controversy. This time the question was how much water can be pumped without harming the natural vegetation of the Owens Valley.

Water from the Colorado River and the Creation of the Metropolitan Water District

Rapidly increasing population and the dry years of the 1920s accentuated the need for more water throughout the entire Metropolis. Low runoff from the Sierras reduced the flow of the Los Angeles Aqueduct from four hundred to two hundred sixty-two cubic feet per second. Furthermore, outlying communities that were dependent on local water supplies were experiencing extreme water shortages. Most were dependent on underground sources, and massive overdrafts were common. Water in Pasadena could be pumped from a depth of only one hundred fifty-four feet in 1899, but it was down to two hundred twenty-three feet in 1926 and two hundred forty feet three years later. Santa Monica was getting water from wells with a water table below sea level—the intrusion of sea water forced it to drill new wells inland, beyond its municipal limits. Inglewood, founded at the site of the flowing Centinela Springs, was now pumping water from a depth of one hundred fifty feet. The three hundred fifteen square mile artesian area around Los Angeles over a forty year period had shrunk to almost nothing. The 1930 Census reported only one artesian well in the Los Angeles River Basin, none

in the San Gabriel River Basin, and a total of only twenty-one in all of Orange County. Clearly, it seemed, additional water from outside the region was needed.

Meanwhile, in 1921, a bill had been introduced in Congress which authorized the building of a dam at Boulder Canyon on the Colorado River to prevent a repetition of disastrous flooding of the Imperial Valley. (Some years previously—1905-1906—as the result of an engineering failure the Colorado had emptied its entire flow into the valley for sixteen months, ruining much farmland and creating the Salton Sea.) The dam would also make possible the construction of an "All American" irrigation canal and provide irrigation water for the Imperial Palo Verde, and Coachella Valleys. Mulholland headed an investigative party charged with assessing the feasibility of bringing Colorado River water to the local area. They reported it was a possibility, and in 1924 the City of Los Angeles filed an application with the State Bureau of Water Rights for water: 1,500 cubic feet per second from the Colorado between Parker and Blythe.

Many years of political argument and compromise were to ensue before any action would be taken. First a "Colorado River Compact" was signed by all of the affected states, save Arizona, appropriating the water of the Colorado River among them. Six years later the Boulder Canyon Project was authorized, over the continuing opposition of Arizona, the private utilities of southern California, and the *Los Angeles Times* (whose owner Harry Chandler had large holdings of cotton land in Mexico). It provided for the building of Hoover Dam and a 1,300,000 kwh power plant. The federal government would advance the funds for the dam but only if there were firm contracts to purchase the power so that the construction costs, plus interest, would be paid back within fifty years. Contracts were signed by communities and utilities in southern California but construction did not start until 1931.

Organization was also necessary in the local area. After some hesitation, the state Legislature created a new entity—the Metropolitan Water District. Its purpose was to construct an aqueduct, build the necessary reservoirs, and act as a wholesaler of the water. It was to be financed by property taxes and revenue from the sale of water. The city of Los Angeles transferred its preliminary surveys of aqueduct routes as well as its Colorado water rights to the District. In addition to Los Angeles, original members were Anaheim, Beverly Hills, Burbank, Glendale, Pasadena, San Marino, Santa Ana, and Santa Monica—they were quickly joined by Fullerton, Long Beach, Torrance, and Compton.

The building of Hoover Dam, an immense structure 1,282 feet high, was one of the largest construction projects in the world at that time. Six large companies contracted to do the work, and an entire community, Boulder City, was created to house the 10,000 workers. Water behind the dam would form the largest artificial lake in the world. It was an engineering feat of the 1930s equivalent to the space program of the later decades.

Of more direct concern to the local communities was the building of Parker Dam and the two hundred forty-two mile Colorado Aqueduct. For this, the thirteen cities voted a $220,000,000 bond issue in 1933, which was approved by a majority of five to one. The aqueduct itself was a challenging engineering enterprise; water had to be pumped out of Lake Havasu, and then over or through six mountain ranges with a total rise of 1,600 feet. Although it was about the same length as the Los Angeles Aqueduct it cost nearly ten times as much. Operation was costly also. For here there was no gravity flow, instead water had to be pumped over the intervening mountains. In a recent year this required 1.6 billion kwh of electricity and cost 4.8 million dollars (1979–80).

In 1941, the first water was delivered (to Pasadena), and the major concern of the District in its early years was to sell enough of it to make payments on its bonds. With the population surge following World War II, however, all of the water was soon spoken for as city after city and water district after water district applied for membership. Today the Metropolitan Water District extends beyond the borders of the Metropolis from Oxnard to San Diego and serves one hundred twenty-two cities and large chunks of unincorporated territory. More than half the population of California is served by its water supplies.

Deliveries of Colorado River water to the Metropolis are scheduled to be reduced in the future. In the agreements made among the states in the Colorado River Compact and later interpretations, more water was allocated to the various users than there was actual water in the river. Lengthy court battles were the result, and in 1964 the Supreme Court decided against California's claim and, in effect, gave more water to Arizona. When the Central Arizona Project is completed, perhaps sometime in the 1980s, the Metropolitan Water District's entitlement of 1.2 million acre feet will be cut approximately in half.

The California State Water Project

Water problems of all kinds plagued California in the 1950s. Northern rivers occasionally flooded, with tragic results—in 1955, the Feather River devastated Marysville and Yuba City. In Kern County wells were going dry; the aquifer was being overdrawn at the rate of two hundred sixty billion gallons a year. The Supreme Court's decision reducing by half California's share of Colorado River water was anticipated. Even so, much acrimonious north-south bickering took place before a California Water Plan was approved by the voters in 1960. It includes a large dam on the Feather River at Oroville, the California Aqueduct extending four hundred forty-four miles along the west side of the San Joaquin Valley, and pumps that will lift some of the water almost 2,000 feet to a tunnel through the San Gabriel Mountains to deliver water to the Metropolis and to San Diego. The dam is designed to reduce flooding on the Feather River, provide water-oriented recreation, enhance fisheries and wildlife, control salinity in the Delta, and furnish 4.2 million acre-feet of water for various users. Some will go to cities in the south Bay and Central Coastal areas (ten percent), some to irrigate six hundred square miles in the San Joaquin Valley (forty percent), and some to provide additional water to southern California (fifty percent).

Feather River water is not inexpensive. It is sold to the wholesaling agencies at a price that reflects the cost of delivering it to that point. In a recent year an acre-foot of water cost residents of Yuba City $10.10; Alameda County, $30.98; Kern County, $21.73; and the Metropolitan Water District, $60.43. Furthermore, these are open-ended contracts that will reflect any future increases in transportation costs. The Metropolitan Water District, in addition, will pay about two-thirds of the capital cost of the project. Although the project produces considerable electricity at Oroville, much energy is required to raise the water over the San Gabriels, and the system is a net consumer of power. (Full operation will produce an estimated 5.3 billion kwh and require 13.8 kwh for pumping.)

The Use of Used Water: Water Reclamation for the Metropolis

The urbanization of a formerly irrigated arid land has many bonuses. An acre of homes uses less water than an acre of most crops. Water used for industry is much more productive of jobs than water used for agriculture. Finally, water used in a home, store, or factory ends up in a sewer system, in a captive state, with the possibility for reclamation. Water used for irrigation, or the watering of landscaping, has a less certain fate. Some may evaporate in the irrigation process, some is used by plants and transpired into the atmosphere; in either case, it is used "consumptively" and lost to the system. Whatever fraction of irrigation water seeps into the underground aquifer, however, may be recaptured for reuse at some nearby well. What of that portion of irrigation water applied to lawns and shrubbery that actually falls on sidewalks or streets, and runs down the gutters to storm drain entrances? What evaporates is lost, of course, but the fraction that runs into the storm drains in many areas of the Metropolis finds its way into a settling basin where it seeps to the underground aquifer where it, too, can be recovered at a later date. All of the water from home, store, or factory that enters a sewer ends up at a sewage disposal plant with the potential for reuse. In fact, the main sewer lines that converge on the three large sewage plants in the Metropolis are by far the largest freshwater streams in the region.

The proportions of water in the Metropolis which meet these varying fates is uncertain. Some estimates indicate that up to fifty percent of an urban water supply is used consumptively or incidentally lost; another twenty to thirty percent of the original supply is needed to carry off concentrated wastes and to prevent the concentration of salts in the soil. This would leave only about twenty to thirty percent of the initial supply for possible reclamation. Others feel that a city with an effective sewer system and a low usage for plant growth may have as much as ninety percent of its water available for reuse.

If water is to be reclaimed it is important that the fresh water be of good quality to begin with. A single cycle of water use adds about 300 milligrams of salts per liter (mg/l) of water. The recommended limit for salts in municipal water supplies is 500 mg/l, although some standards find 1,000 mg/l acceptable. Colorado River water has an average salt content of 717 mg/l, and, even if softened, a single use would cause the salt content to approach the accepted limits. Water from the Owens Valley averages 280 mg/l, State Water Project water, 220–325 mg/l, and local water ranges from 300 to 600 mg/l.

If there is to be much enthusiasm for reclaimed water, its cost must be reasonably competitive. Comparative water rates are unusually elusive and constantly changing, usually upward. For example, any water that has to be pumped (essentially all of it except that from the Owens Valley) is subject to increased pumping costs. Power contracts expire for the State Water Project in 1983 and Hoover Dam in 1988. Greatly increased power costs are anticipated. Obviously, the following comparisons should be thought of as only rough generalizations, subject to rapid change. In 1980–81, the Metropolitan Water District was delivering untreated water at the following rates: domestic, $90 an acre-foot (af); agricultural, $51 af; for underground replenishment, $60 af; for treated water (softened, chlorinated, filtered) the price was $25 af more in each category. There is a catch, however: the Metropolitan Water District gets a substantial portion of its revenue from taxes in the area it serves. In 1980–81 for example, its revenues from water sales were about one hundred forty million dollars, and revenue from property taxes, about fifty-five million. Owens Valley water costs considerably less, and no taxes are involved. Locally pumped water may cost even less, perhaps $20 af. A California Department of Water Resources Bulletin in 1975 estimated the total cost of reclaimed water from a new plant, through secondary treatment, would be $65 af, with carbon absorption $111 af, and more, if additional treatment was required. However, some of the plants already in operation report much lower costs, some in the $20–$40 af range, some even less. With all costs, but particularly power costs, due to rise in the future, accurate prediction is difficult. However, if the total cost of Metropolitan

Water District water is computed, it seems evident that reclaimed water, at many installations, will be competitive on a cost basis alone.

There is a final problem. Although a recent survey indicates that more than forty percent of the people in California are willing to drink, cook, and bathe in reclaimed water, it is illegal to do so. State law forbids direct connection of reclaimed water to a domestic water system. So its uses are limited, mainly to irrigation, industrial use, and groundwater replenishment through separate distribution systems. Our cautious approach is explained by the Department of Water Resources. Recent years have seen "the development of a wide range of organic compounds for industrial, agricultural and household uses which find their way into public water supplies. . . . Many of the complex compounds do not break down into simpler forms and persist for a long time. As long-term effects of ingesting even minute amounts of these compounds are unknown, an effort is made to avoid using water containing the compounds. Similar concerns exist regarding viruses which may not be fully eliminated in waste water treatment and reclamation processes." (State of California, 1974, p. 43.)

As might be expected in an arid land, local communities in the Metropolis have been national leaders in water reclamation. The city of Pasadena utilized the effluent from a sewage treatment plant for irrigation as early as 1924. Two years later a treatment plant for the cities of Pomona, Claremont, and La Verne produced reclaimed water that was used for the irrigation of citrus orchards, pasture lands, and the recharge of groundwater basins. Los Angeles, in 1930, built a pilot plant in Griffith Park specifically designed for the reclamation of water rather than the disposal of sewage. It is reported that its operator, Mr. R. F. Goudey, would drink the product of this plant, much to the amazement of visitors. The first plant in California designed to reclaim industrial waste water was put into operation by the

Kaiser Steel Corporation in Fontana in 1942. Some 750,000 gallons of both sanitary and process waste water are reused daily.

Today there are at least fifteen water reclamation plants in the Metropolis. The ten in Los Angeles and Orange Counties in 1981 were producing about 135,200 acre feet a year (afy) of tertiary-treated wastewater. Presently, 53,000 afy is being applied in a number of ways including industrial processes such as paper manufacturing, greenbelt and park irrigation, agricultural irrigation, groundwater recharge, and saltwater intrusion control barriers. The remaining 82,000 afy is being released to the San Gabriel or Los Angeles River channels. This is only a little more than five percent of the total water used in the area, however; some 1,066,000 af of waste water was discharged to the sea. Reclaimed water from sewage, logically, is the property of the sanitation district that is involved, and a more detailed discussion of current water reclamation efforts will be found in the chapter entitled "The Disposal of Urban Waste."

Water Use and Conservation

It is clear that water is a limited resource that will become more valuable in the future and that thoughtful conservation efforts should become widespread. Additional sources available to the Metropolis are few, speculative, and costly. Seawater desalination is unlikely with present technology because of the high cost of power necessary for the operation. Towing an iceberg into Santa Monica Bay is more imaginative than practical. Additional California water, via a flexible plastic underwater aqueduct lying on the continental shelf and carrying water from the mouths of northern rivers seems unduly speculative. Clearly, conservation, which permits a limited supply of water to be spread out among more users, should be an essential feature of water management in the Metropolis.

Conservation is already further advanced in the Metropolis than in many areas. For example, perhaps the single most effective conservation device is the water meter: where meters are installed, there typically results an immediate reduction in water consumption of from forty to fifty percent. The Metropolis, however, is essentially one hundred percent metered, so this tool has already been used. Seemingly obvious waste reducers, meters are required only for large industrial customers in New York City, are unknown in Chicago, and even in the arid West are not used in Sacramento, Fresno, Bakersfield, or in many other cities in the Central Valley.

Water use, on a per person basis (and this is the way it is always measured), varies considerably. If all water delivered by the city of Los Angeles during a year is divided by its population, the consumption works out to 175 gallons per capita per day, a figure that has remained about the same for the last twenty years. However, water use is strongly affected by seasonal and regional temperatures. The San Fernando Valley uses more water (per capita) than the other parts of Los Angeles; in that area consumption is about three hundred percent higher in the summer than in the winter. Other factors also influence water consumption—generally, areas with single-family houses on estate-size lots, with high incomes and many water-using appliances, consume the most water. Thus in Beverly Hills the average is 301 gallons per capita per day (gpcpd); in Claremont, 289 gpcpd; in Glendale, 180 gpcpd; in Long Beach, 172 gpcpd; in Santa Monica, 169 gpcpd; and in Santa Ana, 162 gpcpd. The trend toward a greater proportion of the population living in apartments reduces water use, but the increasing use of waste disposals, automatic dishwashers, and automatic clothes washers are forces in the opposite direction.

Beyond the common per capita consumption figure, how is water actually used in a city? In the city of Los Angeles average water consumption over the last ten years has been distributed as follows: residential, forty-six to forty-nine percent; commercial and apartment, thirty-four to thirty-eight percent; governmental, seven to eight percent; and industrial, about one percent. It is clear that individual families, house and apartment dwellers combined, consume perhaps seventy to seventy-five percent of all water delivered. Individual conservation efforts are important.

Further, individual savings apparently will come mainly through education for it has been found that simply raising water rates does little to affect consumption. Presumably, the low-income families are already using relatively little water, and higher water rates for middle- and high-income groups are still only a minor fraction of their total expenses. Much water in residences is used for landscape irrigation and some have suggested that a shift to native species, which require little water, would be an appropriate conservation response. Some would argue, however, that water for such amenities as lawns, trees, fountains, and parks should be disturbed only with caution. Although a lush tree may, from one point of view, be considered a luxury in an arid land, a well-watered tree can reduce air temperatures on a hot day by as much as five degrees, and a single tree is reported to provide a cooling effect equivalent to five average-sized room air conditioners running twenty hours a day.

6. *Suggested Readings*

Englebert, Ernest A. and Ann Foley Scheuring, eds. *Competition for California Water: Alternative Resolutions.* Berkeley: University of California Press, 1982.
Outgrowth of a conference whose goals were "to identify competing needs and demands for water in California, to seek out realistic water policy options, and to point out areas where cooperation and compromise can help in developing state water policies."

Hoffman, Abraham. *Vision or Villainy: Origins of the Owens Valley-Los Angeles Water Controversy.* College Station, Texas: Texas A & M University Press, 1981.
Written by a professional historian, almost seventy-five years after the event, this volume is a scholarly and balanced account of a much discussed subject.

Kahrl, William L. et al. *The California Water Atlas.* Sacramento: State of California, 1979.
The product of contributions from more than fifty authorities, many revealing maps and written material. Many good photographs.

Nadeau, Remi A. *The Water Seekers.* Santa Barbara: Peregrine Smith, 1974. 2nd edition.
First published in 1950, tells the story of the search for water from both the Owens Valley and the Colorado River.

Outland, Charles F. *Man-Made Disaster, the Story of the St. Francis Dam.* Glendale: Arthur H. Clark, 1977. 2nd edition.
A detailed account of the failure of a reservoir on the Los Angeles water system in 1928, the resulting destruction and investigations.

Smith, Genny Schumacher. *Deepest Valley.* Los Altos, Calif.: William Kaufmann, Inc. 1978.
A guide to the Owens Valley, its roadsides, trails, geology, plants, and wildlife. Includes a section on the water controversy, mainly in the 1970s.

CHAPTER 7

Flood Hazard in a Land of Little Rain

Figure 7.1. Flood waters rushing down an eastern channel of Tujunga Wash endanger the Southern Pacific Railroad bridge and that of Sherman Way. View to the northwest on March 3, 1938. (Photo courtesy Spence Collection / Department of Geography, UCLA.)

"January 17, 1770 . . . we . . . arrived at the (Los Angeles River) and forded it, observing on its sand, rubbish, fallen trees, and pools on either side, for a few days previously there had been a great flood which had caused it to leave its bed. . . ." Juan Crespi (Bolton, 1927, p. 270).

"There are basically two means to prevent flood damage. They are, stay out of the way of floods or keep the flood flows in defined channels. . . ." California Department of Water Resources (1974, Vol. II, p. 23).

"Few localities in the United States have flood problems as difficult of solution as those inherent in the geological, topographical, climatological relations of the terrain in Metropolitan Los Angeles." Samuel B. Morris (1941, p. 86).

A semi-arid landscape and a lack of flowing streams are the dominant impressions of the Los Angeles Metropolis, particularly striking to the migrant from the humid East. Thus conditioned, it is not surprising that local settlers have failed to realize that the urbanization of the area would create one of the most concentrated, difficult, and expensive flood hazards in the United States. The hazard from flash floods results from the record high rainfall intensities, the steep gradients of the streams together with the large population and wealth of improvements which occupy the alluvial fans and flood plains, and occasionally encroach upon the stream channels.

Even experienced dry land explorers have been unable to comprehend the severity and scope of the region's floods. The first exploring party, returning through the area, crossed the Los Angeles River in January, 1770. They observed "fallen trees, rubbish, and pools of water on either side," and commented understandingly, "a few days previously there had been a great flood which had caused it to leave its bed." Yet, when a member of this expedition located a mission a few years later, he chose a site so close to the San Gabriel River that the crops were regularly flooded out and the mission had to be moved to its present location, some six miles back from the stream.

Historic Floods of the Nineteenth Century

Since the Los Angeles Metropolis was first settled, numerous floods have caused increasingly severe damage. Until 1825, the Los Angeles River, then a perennial stream, spread over much of the lowland south of Los Angeles forming lakes, ponds, and marshes, and provided moisture for extensive willow thickets. What water reached the sea ran out through Ballona Creek into Santa Monica Bay. In 1825, during a period of heavy flooding, the course of the river was changed: a new channel was formed near the foot of the hills at Dominguez and the river then emptied into San Pedro Bay. The marshes gradually drained and the groves of trees dried up and died.

The flood of 1861–62 is remembered as one of the great floods of the Los Angeles area. During this flood the entire lowland from Los Angeles to the sea, both to the west and the south, was a great lake. The San Gabriel River also overflowed its banks, creating a new channel west of El Monte and joining the Los Angeles River. Today this channel is called the Rio Hondo. The Santa Ana River was a raging torrent, completely inundating the communities along its banks, destroying orchards, vineyards, and grain fields. Anaheim, four miles from the river, was under four feet of water which spread in an unbroken sheet to Los Coyote Hills, three miles beyond the town. The Arroyo Seco, swollen to a mighty river, brought down from the mountains and canyons great rafts of driftwood which were scattered over the plains below Los Angeles. They furnished fuel for the poor of the city for several years.

The 1880s were wet years, with several seasons, particularly that of 1884, ranking as major flood years. Forty inches of rain fell in downtown Los Angeles, much more in the mountains. All the bridges across the Los Angeles River, save one, were washed out. Many houses were swept away, several people drowned. In the downtown area, the water came up to First and Main, and at Maple and 24th Street the water was four feet deep. Water ran westward down Washington and Jefferson, then southwest into Ballona Creek and into Santa Monica Bay. The area around La Cienega was a great lake, as was the section back of Venice. The San Fernando Valley was flooded from Glendale to Chatsworth, and the Southern Pacific Railroad was washed out in many places.

A four-day storm in February, 1914, brought nineteen inches of rainfall to the San Gabriels, three inches along the coast. In one hour 1.5 inches of rain fell in Los Angeles. The ground was already soaked from previous rains, and water and tons of debris rushed down the steep mountain canyons. The flood discharge of the Los Angeles River equaled the normal flow of the Colorado, and the San Gabriel River was carrying almost as much water. Water swept over the river banks and into the built-up areas, hundreds of people became refugees, rail service was totally disrupted. Long Beach was an island. Four million cubic yards of silt were emptied into the harbor. Damage was estimated at more than ten million dollars. Floodwaters which had run freely over the lightly populated plains were severely damaging populated areas. Within a week, the County Board of Supervisors created a County Board of Engineers on Flood Control. Plans were made for the first time to attack the flood problem.

More than seven square miles of the slopes of the San Gabriels above the La Canada Valley were burned clean in November, 1933. The last three days of the year were rainy, with a veritable deluge occurring in the early morning hours of January 1, 1934. Water, mud, and rocks poured down the canyons. Eyewitnesses insisted the mixture had the consistency of wet concrete with "boulders riding on top of the wave that seemed to leap clear of the water" (Troxell, 1936, p. 23). The mass was a wall twenty feet high when it reached Foothill Boulevard. Boulders weighing several tons were carried more than a mile below the mouths of the canyons. Automobiles were rolled over and over by the rush of the water. Houses were filled with mud one to three feet deep, some were washed from their foundations. It was calculated that in less than twenty minutes, 600,000 cubic yards of debris were deposited on the valley floor, devastating citrus groves, vineyards, towns, and highways. La Crescenta and Montrose were particularly hard hit—more than forty persons died. (Water came down the Arroyo Seco, through

the pedestrian tunnels, and filled the Rose Bowl to the height of the lower box seats. The rain lessened, the flow was diverted, and fire engines were called to help pump out the stadium. The turf, when it appeared, was reported an "emerald green." The game went on as scheduled, although only 35,000 determined fans could force their way through the flooded streets to the stadium. Scalpers took a beating, as tickets went for fifty cents. Columbia upset Stanford 7 to 0.)

Heavy rains from February 27 to March 3, 1938, caused the most severe flood for which records are available. Many stations reported twenty to thirty inches during this five day period, with a peak of thirty-two inches at Kelley's Kamp, in the San Gabriels. It is believed the peak discharges of the major streams exceeded any since those of the floods of 1861–62, the greatest previously known. Water and debris poured out of the steep mountain canyons and inundated almost 300,000 acres of land bordering the Santa Ana, San Gabriel, and Los Angeles Rivers. Areas near the mountains were covered with debris, citrus groves along the lower courses of the streams were inundated, many homes were destroyed. The area around Colton was under water, as were parts of San Bernardino and Riverside. Flood waters spread around the city of Santa Ana. Large tracts of the San Fernando Valley were inundated; much damage was done along the Los Angeles River; bridges, highways, and railroads were severely damaged. Water rose so rapidly that many people in the threatened areas could not be warned; eighty lives were lost, mainly along the Santa Ana and Los Angeles rivers. Damage was estimated at more than seventy-eight million dollars.

But that was a long time ago, surely it can't happen today. No? Then read the following account of a flood of recent vintage (Rantz, 1970, pp. B5–B8).

89

Table 7.1
Summary of Precipitation Data at Selected Stations

Precipitation station		Precipitation, in inches, for dates shown				
Name	Altitude (feet)	Jan. 25	Jan. 25–26	Jan. 18–21	Jan. 23–26	Entire storm Jan. 18–26
Big Bear Dam	6,800	11.05	18.59	13.60	21.82	35.42
San Bernardino................................	1,100	2.53	4.99	3.35	6.08	9.43
Mount Baldy	4,280	11.04	21.42	20.08	27.54	47.62
Glendora West	820	6.00	7.35	8.28	9.22	17.50
Opids Camp	4,250	15.56	21.11	21.01	24.16	45.17
Burbank..	680	4.43	5.98	7.10	7.16	14.26
Topanga	745	9.54	12.18	12.98	14.20	27.18
Matilija Dam	1,050	9.15	14.76	20.84	17.17	38.01

The Flood of 1969

"Southern California, until January 12, 1969, was experiencing an unseasonal winter drought, and the moderate precipitation that occurred on January 13–14 gave little indication that the drought was soon to be broken. The series of storms that was to plague the region did not begin until the evening of January 17. Precipitation was relatively light until January 19 when intensities increased sharply. The center of the east-moving low-pressure area that generated the storms stagnated about 700 miles off the coast on January 21, with the result that a succession of storm waves passed over southern California. Except for a lull on January 22, heavy precipitation occurred during most of the period January 19–26, and this was climaxed by the intense downpour of January 25. During most of the storm period the freezing level was at an altitude of 7,000 feet; precipitation occurred as rain below that altitude and as snow at the higher altitudes. Table 7.1 summarizes precipitation data for selected stations throughout the area. Some of the storm totals exceed the heaviest January precipitation previously recorded at the stations. The wide range of precipitation values in the table reflects the general decrease of precipitation with distance from the storm center and the local increase of precipitation with altitude.

"Heavy rains during the 4-day period January 18–21 brought widespread, but generally minor, damage to southern California. Damage was severe, however, in localized areas. Streams rose but even those that were uncontrolled by reservoirs generally stayed within their banks and flooding was localized. Ten campers, however, lost their lives when trapped by the rising waters of Sespe Creek in Ventura County, and four other drownings were reported elsewhere in the region. Transportation was snarled as floodwaters in Cajon Canyon cut the main east-west lines of the Southern Pacific and Santa Fe Railroads, and more than 100 Los Angeles streets were blocked by felled trees. The greatest monetary damage occurred in the Glendora-Azusa foothill area of the San Gabriel Mountains. A brush fire in August 1968 had burned off erosion-retarding vegetation in the canyon area above the town of Glendora. The 4 days of rain on the bare soil were climaxed by a local precipitation burst of 2 inches in 3 hours, which brought down a torrent of sediment- and debris-laden water. Streets were boulder-strewn and sediment spread over streets and lawns and into homes. In places the streets were covered with sediment to depths of as much as 4 feet. Damage in Glendora was estimated at $2 million.

"It was with a feeling of relief, therefore, that southern Californians viewed the rainless skies of January 22. The relief was short-lived, however. The rains of the preceding 4 days had saturated the ground and had produced a condition favorable for heavy runoff from ensuing rains; the stage was set for the deluge that was to follow. The rains started again on January 23 as the second 4 day phase of the storm arrived. Not only were antecedent conditions favorable for heavy runoff, but the time distribution of precipitation during this phase was conducive to high peak discharges, because the heaviest precipitation came near the end of the storm when streams were already swollen.

"In Los Angeles County, flooding was confined primarily to the headwater tributaries of the principal streams—the San Gabriel and Los Angeles Rivers—and to the smaller canyon streams that are directly tributary to the ocean. The heavy runoff of the San Gabriel and Los Angeles Rivers was stored in flood-control reservoirs and released at rates compatible with the capacity of downstream flood channels. In the mountain and foothill areas, however, the rapidly rising tributaries of those two rivers left their banks and created havoc. Bridges, roads, and streets were washed out and homes were destroyed or damaged; thousands of persons were evacuated. The sediment and debris carried by the streams added to the misery. Debris flows occurred again at Glendora to add to the damage suffered in the earlier phase of the storm. Damage of a similar nature, but not as severe, occurred in Highland Park, Sherman Oaks, Verdugo Hills, Brentwood, Bel-Air, Hollywood Hills, Encino, and Glendale. Landslides, more aptly termed mudslides, also created much damage in those towns and buried seven persons alive in their beds when the slides entered their homes. Topanga Creek, a small stream, directly tributary to the ocean, swelled to the size of a river. Almost 1,000 persons in Topanga Canyon were isolated when homes and roads were destroyed by water and mudslides, and three persons were smothered when mud swept through their home. On the coastal plain, street flooding occurred in many towns such as Manhattan Beach, El Segundo, and Long Beach.

"East of Los Angeles County, in the Santa Ana River basin, major flooding was confined to the upper reaches of the river and its mountain tributaries. The rampaging waters of such creeks as Cucamonga, Deer, Day, and Cajon damaged or destroyed by erosion an aggregate of several hundred miles of improved flood channels. Roads and bridges were washed out, and the main lines of the Southern Pacific and Santa Fe Railroads, which had received emergency repair after being cut during the first phase of the storm, were severely damaged as a result of repeated attack by the waters of Cajon Creek. Nor were homes spared by the deluge; in the town of Cucamonga alone, flooding caused the evacuation of 1,000 persons. Farther downstream, near the junction of the San Bernardino, Riverside, and Orange County lines, the Santa Ana River was effectively controlled by storage in the Prado flood-control basin, and released flows were within the capacity of the river channel downstream through the populous areas of Orange County.

"In general, the flood of January 1969 was comparable to that of March 1938. The 1938 flood had been the most damaging flood of recent times in southern California and its peak discharges are usually used as a standard for comparing flood magnitudes. West of Los Angeles County peak discharges were greater in 1969, and east of Los Angeles County the 1938 peak discharges were greater. In Los Angeles County itself, the relative magnitude of the two floods varied somewhat randomly, but more commonly the greater peak discharges were those that occurred in 1938."

Obviously floods occur in the Los Angeles area with disturbing frequency. On the basis of somewhat scanty historic records it is believed that a "great" flood, approaching the probable maximum, covering the entire flood plain, will occur once in a hundred years; while a large flood, inundating the low-lying valley and coastal plain, may occur six times in a century. Moderate floods may come about once every ten years. These are rough averages; in the past, sizable floods have occurred at intervals of from one to twenty-three years. No one can tell when a flood will come, but it is certain that the future will bring more of them, occasionally of devastating magnitude.

Natural Conditions Make Flooding Inevitable

The unique combination of topography and climate makes floods a natural phenomenon in the Los Angeles Metropolis. Surrounding the area is an arc of high mountains; their crests, where the rivers have their origins, are more than 10,000 feet high and less than sixty miles from the sea. Stream gradients down these mountains are extremely steep, and even the valleys have considerable slope. The Los Angeles River, for example, is only fifty miles long (not counting the mountain tributaries). Yet it has a greater fall flowing from

Canoga Park to San Pedro Bay than does the Mississippi from St. Paul to the Gulf of Mexico (seven hundred ninety-five feet as compared to seven hundred five feet).

Average annual precipitation ranges from about ten inches near the coast to some forty inches in the high mountains. However, in some years almost no rain falls; in others, there are many severe storms. For example, precipitation in the 1975–76 rainfall year was only forty-eight percent of "normal," but in 1977–78 it was two hundred twenty-three percent of "normal." Annual averages are almost meaningless. Further, the region is subject to occasional torrential winter storms, usually violent, erratic, and of short duration. Rainfall at some mountain stations has exceeded an inch in five minutes; a station in Santa Anita Canyon has the record for twenty-four hours of rainfall in the United States, twenty-six inches. Torrential downpours occurring within extended periods of precipitation are responsible for the area's damaging flash floods. In addition, major floods are almost always preceded by earlier storms which have saturated the ground. When a second period of heavy rainfall arrives, no more moisture can be absorbed and massive runoff occurs.

Water rushes down the mountain slopes, through the steep canyons, over the alluvial fans at their mouths, across the washes to the rivers, and out to sea. The descent from mountain to valley takes only a few hours at most, sometimes only a few minutes. As a further complication, the precipitous slopes of the mountains are largely underlain by decomposed igneous rocks, readily erodable material. Thin soils and scanty summer rainfall have produced only a sparse vegetation cover. The velocity of the water enables it to carry with it much silt, sand, and rock from the crumbly slopes, eventually even large boulders weighing several tons. As the rushing, debris-laden water slows and spreads out crossing the alluvial fan, the large boulders and rocks are deposited, perhaps causing the stream to seek a new and easier route over the fan. In the valleys the riverbanks are low and easily breached; during periods of flood streams do not remain within these narrow dry season channels but spread widely over the adjacent landscape. As the velocity of the water is further decreased, the streams deposit their loads of gravels, sand, and silt on orchard, street, or lawn.

Flood Control

Although floods have occurred with distressing regularity in the Los Angeles area, little thought was given to reducing the damage until relatively recently. Actually, the damage in earlier periods was minimal. The Indian simply walked to higher ground, and so did the cattle of the Rancho Era; even the early farmers took their losses as one of the many hazards of a speculative endeavor. Water occasionally reached the main streets of downtown Los Angeles. The flooded merchants dried out their stock, replaced the dissolved adobes of their buildings and began anew. It was not until the flood of 1914 that occupance had reached the stage where it appeared to the citizens that some action was necessary.

Within days county engineers were instructed to draw up plans to reduce damage from future floods. A Los Angeles County Flood Control District was formed. Its boundaries, significantly, were confined to the metropolitan area and its mountain watershed (instead of all of Los Angeles County) apparently to avoid the necessity of a two-thirds majority on any vote authorizing bond indebtedness. Future events confirmed the wisdom of this strategy. For, although the taxes to pay for flood control construction would fall equally on all property in the District, the land in the path of floods would be disproportionately benefited. In addition, the people who lived on high ground had little sympathy for those in the path of floods. In the face of this community controversy, engineer

J. W. Reagan drafted the proposal artfully—all of the projects were lumped together in a $5 million bond issue; any neighborhood that wanted to approve some nearby improvements had to approve those for other parts of the region too. The election was called, on short notice, for February 20, 1917. The bond issue just squeaked by, 34,346 in favor, 34,295 opposed, a majority of only fifty-one votes. This was in sharp contrast to the huge majorities that approved bond issues for bringing water into the area only a few years earlier. Flood control remained a local activity until the passage of several Federal flood control acts, beginning in 1936. Since that time, many of the major flood control structures in the area have been built by the United States Corps of Engineers.

The basic objectives of flood control in the Metropolis are about as follows: slow down runoff in the mountains, reduce erosion and the debris carried by the running water, store some of the excess water temporarily in reservoirs, and then move the rest of the water to sea as expeditiously as possible. All of these activities are designed, first of all, to protect the lives and property of the inhabitants of the area. The Los Angeles County Flood Control District has a second objective: to conserve as much water as possible by allowing it to percolate into the underground reservoirs. Conservation is not a concern of the Corps of Engineers, and, in any event, the conservation concern has had to be subordinated to the more important goal of preserving life and property. It is a big job. One engineer described the task as "well nigh impossible of complete solution on the one hand and a necessity on the other" (Rantz, 1970, p. B4). Exactly what has been accomplished?

Flood control in the mountains is designed both to retard erosion and to reduce and slow down surface runoff. A thick vegetative cover is of major assistance in this program, and regulations that keep the mountains in forest cover are an important beginning. Vegetation is valuable in many ways. It breaks the force of the raindrops, shielding the soil from their direct impact, and thus reduces sheet erosion. Roots bind the soil together and help hold it on the slopes. Litter from the vegetation slows the flow of any running water. Furthermore, the decaying leaves and the fine roots add to the pore space in the soil and increase its capacity to absorb water. Prevention of forest fires is an important flood control measure. Should a fire occur, prompt reseeding to rapidly growing grasses gives some erosion protection while the larger plants are reestablishing themselves. In addition, stream channels in the canyons are stabilized where necessary, and many small "check dams" have been built in the mountain streams to slow down their flow and reduce their load of debris.

Even the heaviest vegetation cover, the spongiest soil, and the most efficient system of check dams cannot contain the intense rainfall of the occasional large winter storm. As an additional control measure, large dams and reservoirs have been constructed, designed to store as much of the flood water as possible. The purpose of these reservoirs is to absorb the flood peaks, retain some of the debris carried by the flood waters, and regulate the release of relatively silt-free waters. Within the Los Angeles County Flood Control District there are twenty large dams, ranging from thirty-three to three hundred sixty-five feet in height. The first, Devils Gate Dam on the Arroyo Seco, was built in 1920; other early structures were Pacoima Dam, Big Tujunga Dam, and San Gabriel Dam. The early dams, it will be noted, were built in mountain canyons. Later dams, Hansen, Sepulveda, Santa Fe, and Whittier Narrows, for example, were built farther downstream on the rivers, and have many square miles of land behind them that might be inundated during a flood. In practice, none of these large downstream structures has ever "spilled"—even in the 1969 flood they were only from fifteen to forty-five percent full.

The steep mountainous slopes and generally loose surface material, as we have noted, are conducive to massive erosion. The huge quantities of silt, sand, rocks, boulders, branches, and even tree trunks which are carried along with the flood water complicate flood control in an expensive way. The debris tends to settle behind the dams, filling them up to the point where they are no longer capable of storing any water. In an attempt to reduce this problem, "debris basins" have been constructed near the mouths of canyons—ninety in Los Angeles alone. Their function is simply to retain the debris, allowing the water to pass downstream. After every flood the debris has to be removed to make room for the load carried by the next flood and this is both a difficult and costly job. The canyons are often steep and narrow, and the problem is to dump the cleaned out debris someplace where it will not simply be washed downstream again during the next flood. For example, in 1969 the District let a contract to remove nine million tons of silt, sand, and tree trunks from debris basins in a narrow canyon. Normally, trucks are used in the operation, but here the contractor used one hundred sixty-four conveyor belt units to transport the material three and a half miles up the winding canyons. Runoff water was to be diverted under the debris, piled in a side canyon, through a pipe five feet in diameter. The job cost the district $5.5 million.

Crossing the lower slopes of the alluvial fans were from five to twenty main channel lines which, on the valley floors, separated into dozens of old flow channels. Once out of the mountain canyon, a "river" had no permanently defined channel in most cases, but storm flood-water followed the lowest gradient down the slope of an alluvial fan. As one storm deposited sediment to fill a channel, the next flood took any lower channel across the fan, debouching onto the lowland at some point near or far from the channel last used. Each river had, therefore, a wide channel zone, given the name "wash" in local parlance. Such "wash" zones on valley floors, in the early twentieth century, were as much as two miles wide. Early main highways crossed these "wash" zones on long bridges. During the summer months, any permanent stream flowed in the narrow lowest channel. The length of these bridges over such tiny summer streams often amazed easterners, who sometimes became frightened at the sight of the whole channel zone under turbulent flood in winter. In the San Fernando Valley, a "wash" channel zone draining Big Tujunga Creek, in 1915, occupied the broad stretch today containing the residential communities of Arleta, Panorama City, and Sepulveda. The Big Tujunga and Hansen dams, plus storm drains emptying into Sepulveda Dam, now control the floods that formerly raged across that lowland sector. In the period after World War II, land developers began laying out housing and business developments on what formerly had been several "wash" flood drainage zones but which, at the time of development, were broad, open zones of empty country. If human beings are going to occupy these flood drainage zones, the stream channels must be stabilized and confined in such a way as to prevent the wide-spreading flood that follows a severe winter storm. Flood control engineers have straightened and lined with concrete some four hundred fifty miles of river channel to facilitate the rapid and safe movement of flood waters over the lowlands. The upper reaches of some alluvial fans, and the lower courses and mouths of some canyons, into which settlement has now penetrated, are more difficult to control, so that such areas still are subject to flood problems.

Water Conservation Versus Flood Control

Given the necessity of providing flood protection to the citizens of the Metropolis, how do you also conserve as much as possible of the winter rainfall? Clearly, the need to replenish the underground water supply of the region is a vital one. The techniques of flood control and water conservation, however, are difficult to reconcile.

Substitution of concrete channels for the natural sand and gravel stream beds, of course, effectively prevents the percolation of water into underground aquifers as it runs down the streams. So, wherever it was considered safe, concrete paving was omitted from the stream bottom. For example, the San Gabriel River has only a sand bottom from its canyon mouth to beyond Whittier Narrows, and the stream bed is occasionally scarified with special ditching plows to pulverize the surface and encourage percolation. In addition, the channel of the Los Angeles River is paved with stones for seven miles (from Riverside Drive through the Glendale Narrows), a condition which permits some water to seep through.

More importantly, as a means of adding additional areas of porous surface for water percolation, a total of 3,126 acres (about five square miles) of spreading grounds have been constructed. Located adjacent to the streams, these consist of some thirty-five gravelly, leveled areas surrounded by low levies where water can be diverted and allowed to sink into the subsurface basins. The largest recharge facility is the Rio Hondo Spreading Grounds of five hundred ninety acres, located, along with the San Gabriel Spreading Grounds (one hundred eighty-one acres), below the Whittier Narrows Dam to spread run-off from the San Gabriel Valley. When in use they look something like rice paddies.

Water from small storms can simply be diverted into the spreading grounds as it flows down the stream channels. However, considerable ingenuity is necessary to conserve water during large storms because of the high peak flow and the large amount of silt in the water. As silt would plug up the settling basins, the water diverted into them is mostly from the rising stage when the water is reasonably clear, and from the receding stage when the debris-laden flow is past and the water becomes clear again. Recently flocculation facilities (which convert silt into large lumps) have been installed in several spreading grounds, allowing conservation of silty water which would have been bypassed earlier.

Normally, the full capacity of the spreading grounds is used during every winter rainfall. In addition, much of the mountain runoff is retained behind dams for post-storm release to the spreading areas. During a year with average rainfall, about 140,000 acre feet of water, with a value of perhaps $7 million is conserved for future use. Since their program began, the Los Angeles County Flood Control District estimates it has saved some four million acre feet in its spreading grounds, and, if channel percolation is included, the figure would rise to seven million acre feet. (An additional three million acre feet of imported and reclaimed water have been conserved through the spreading grounds.)

Anything approaching complete conservation of storm water, however, raises some difficult problems. If it were not for the hazard floods present to life and property, considerably more storm water could be saved. Once flood waters have been impounded behind a dam, the District finds itself in a dilemma. In order to provide maximum protection to the people in the area, the reservoirs should be emptied as rapidly as possible to prepare them for another possible heavy rain. To conserve as much water as possible, however, any one flood volume should not be released any more rapidly than the spreading grounds can absorb it. There is never enough capacity in the spreading grounds to absorb a whole season's flood water, so that in extended wet spells much water is "wasted" by being allowed free passage into the ocean. Adding additional spreading grounds today is at best costly, for the price of land is high everywhere in the Metropolis. Often no suitable land is available. Most of the land is already occupied with humanly-created structures. Further, many areas are underlain with an impervious material such as clay and are, therefore, of no use for settling purposes.

Even so, little of the precipitation which falls on the Metropolis normally is lost to the ocean. In the drainage basin of the San Gabriel River, for example, it is estimated that less than one percent of the water which falls upstream of Whittier Narrows is lost to the sea. In the Los Angeles River area, where geologic conditions are not good for spreading grounds about ten percent of the precipitation ends up in the ocean.

National Flood Insurance Program

In the past decade the National Flood Insurance Program has gradually added an additional element to the flood control effort in the Metropolis. Communities with flood prone areas are virtually mandated to participate in a new flood plain management program. Detailed hydrologic studies have been made to identify areas subject to flooding by the "base flood"—one that may occur once in a hundred years. Communities are required to adopt ordinances aimed at protecting lives and new construction from future flooding. Virtually all new construction is forbidden in designed "floodways," while in the flood plain fringe new dwellings must have their first floor above the water surface of the one-in-a-hundred-year flood. Commercial buildings may be "flood-proofed" or elevated. Once a community has implemented its flood plain management plan, property owners can purchase flood insurance at rates reflecting the structures' risk. The program is "virtually mandated," because if any mortgage money is borrowed from a lending institution insured, regulated, or supervised by the federal government (and that includes almost all financial institutions) flood

insurance is required. Most communities in the Metropolis have either adopted a flood plain management plan, or are in the process of doing so. For most of the Metropolis, however, the program has come too late to be of much help in land planning as the flood-prone lands are already almost completely developed.

7. Suggested Readings

Bigger, Richard. *Flood Control in Metropolitan Los Angeles.* Berkeley: University of California Press, 1959.
A small, scholarly volume that tells the story of the beginnings of flood control in the area and its development over four decades.

California Department of Water Resources. *California Flood Management: An Evaluation of Flood Damage Prevention Program. Bulletin 199.* Sacramento: Department of Water Resources, 1980.
A recent publication that provides a good general review of the flood problem of the state and modern thinking about damage prevention.

Los Angeles County Flood Control District. *Biennial Reports.*
Every other year the District reports on floods, debris removal, water conservation, weather, and other items that are pertinent to the agency's activities. Technical *Hydrologic Reports* are also issued biennially.

Turhollow, Antony F. *A History of the Los Angeles District, U.S. Army Corps of Engineers, 1898–1965.* Los Angeles: U.S. Army Engineer District, 1975.
Although the story of this organization includes harbor improvement and shoreline protection, much of this volume is devoted to the agency's role in flood control.

CHAPTER 8

Disposing of Urban Waste:
Sewage, Garbage, Rubbish

Figure 8.1. Water from the Los Coyotes Water Reclamation Plant in Cerritos is used to irrigate the Iron Wood 9 golf course. (Photo courtesy County Sanitation Districts of Los Angeles County.)

"An underground river rushed into Hyperion. Its purity of 99.7 percent exceeds that of Ivory Soap . . . but two-hundred million gallons are a lot of water, and the three thousandth part of that daily quota represents a formidable quantity of muck. . . . The chemical revolution begins . . . From something hideous and pestilential the sludge is gradually transformed by these most faithful allies (bacteria) into sweetness and light—light in the form of methane, which fuels nine . . . diesel engines, and sweetness in the form of an odorless solid which, when dried, pelleted, and sacked, sells to farmers at ten dollars a ton . . . And meanwhile another torrent, this time about 99.95 percent pure, rushes down through the submarine outfall and mingles . . . with the Pacific. The problem of keeping a great city clean without polluting a river or fouling the beaches, and without robbing the soil of its fertility, has been triumphantly solved." Aldous Huxley (1956, pp. 163–65).

"The six million metric tons of anchovies off southern California produce as much fecal material as ninety million people, that is ten times as much as the population of Los Angeles, and the anchovies, of course, comprise only one of hundreds of species of marine life . . . The sea is starved for the basic plant nutrients, and it is a mystery to me why we should be concerned with their thoughtful introduction into coastal seas in any quantity that man can generate in the foreseeable future." John D. Issacs (Bascom, 1974, pp. 21–24).

From Private to Public Responsibility

In the Los Angeles Metropolis, as in other urban areas, waste disposal began as a personal responsibility. Kitchen scraps were fed to chickens or hogs (yours or your neighbors). Human wastes were received by privies (politely called "outhouses"). Other trash was taken, by good citizens anyway, to the edge of town and dumped into a convenient arroyo. As time passed, however, two factors pressured for change in this tolerant system. One was simply the greatly increasing urban population and the accompanying increase in the volume of waste produced. The second was the gradual realization that diseases were caused by germs, a concept that is surprisingly recent, dating only from the 1880s.

Public waste disposal systems developed in response to the varied nature of urban waste. The extension of piped water to residence and shop and the gradual introduction of the flush toilet produced waste water (or sewage) with disposal requirements peculiar to liquids. The accumulation of kitchen scraps (or garbage) odoriferous and attractive to flies, but nutritious for hogs, was solved by a separate collection for about seventy-five years. Then, with the advent of the in-sink garbage disposer, it too became part of the liquid sewage system. Solid waste: ashes, metal, bottles, cans, and other materials, was a later concern of the municipalities and collection of these non-combustible items gradually became widespread. The disposal of anything that would burn, the combustible part of residential trash, remained a personal responsibility throughout most of the Metropolis until 1957.

The story of the area's waste disposal, therefore, is one of a gradual shift from private to public responsibility. A second theme soon becomes apparent—with increasing knowledge, disposal systems which were considered adequate or even exceptionally fine become condemned as woefully insufficient or even dangerous in a later era. Sanitation standards and practices are in a constant process of evolution.

Today's Sewage Systems

Hidden from view beneath our urban streets are many thousands of miles of sewers, essential elements in the existence of a large concentration of population. Without a quick and efficient means of removing body wastes cities would become deadly and plague-ridden. Sewers and sewage treatment plants are our protection against diseases caused by improper disposition of human waste, such as diarrhea, cholera, typhoid, paratyphoid, and enteritis, among others.

Today the Metropolis is served by three extensive and one small sewer systems terminating in ocean outfalls, some smaller inland systems, together with a number of water and reclamation plants, most of the latter located high on the collection lines. The city of Los Angeles and the communities in the drainage area of the Los Angeles River upstream of that city are served by one massive system with its terminus at a sewage treatment plant at Hyperion (on Santa Monica Bay just south of the Los Angeles International Airport). The San Gabriel River drainage area is generally served by the Sanitation Districts of Los Angeles

County and its even larger Joint Water Pollution Control Plant at Carson. The Orange County Sanitation District serves that political entity and has a set of treatment plants near the mouth of the Santa Ana River. These three systems discharge three hundred forty, three hundred seventy-one, and one hundred thirty million gallons a day of at least partially treated water into the ocean. The Terminal Island Treatment Plant, a much smaller facility, generally serves the communities of San Pedro and Wilmington. More than ninety-nine percent of all wastewater discharged into the Pacific from the Metropolis comes from these four plants.

The Cities Take the Sewage

The primitive attitude toward sanitation in early Los Angeles is revealed by Harris Newmark, who wrote (1970, p. 119) that in the 1860s he connected his bathtub drain to a *zanja* (irrigation ditch) at the back of his lot by means of a wooden pipe. The Bella Union Hotel, too, is reported to have connected its drains with a *zanja* in 1860 and this was the "first sewer in Los Angeles" (Newmark, 1970, p. 265). Early public concern with sanitation generally focused on the location and maintenance of privies. In the same vein, Riverside prohibited the location of cesspools (covered pits for receiving sewage) within the first 1,000 feet of the upper side of canals and four hundred feet on the lower side.

Public sewers began in Los Angeles in 1875, when the population was but 7,000. However, at first an attempt was made to use "*Zanja* Number 9" as the main sewer, but it did not drain properly, and the sewage simply collected in low spots. Even so, in 1874 the Pico House was advertising: "The unpleasant odor of gas has entirely disappeared with the building of the new sewer" (Newmark, 1970, p. 469). A proper sewer for the town was constructed in 1876, and wastes were flushed to the southern part of Los Angeles. The sewer was soon extended to the southern city limits where "the South Side Irrigation Company disposed of the sewage in return for the right to sell the sewer water" (Fogelson, 1967, p. 32). The customers were the Cudahy Ranch and other landowners in the vicinity of Slauson and Central Avenues.

Spurred by the boom in population in the 1880s and the city's desire to retain its reputation as a health resort, Los Angeles ordered Fred Eaton, the City Engineer, to devise a comprehensive sewer plan for the city. Its main features were three interceptor sewers and a ten mile outfall generally following the old course of the Los Angeles River to Santa Monica Bay. Although an advance in sanitation, the outfall was considered by some to be not only overly expensive but also a waste of water. As an alternative, the Pacific Sewerage Company was organized by local entrepreneurs. It offered, for an appropriate bonus, to build a sewer system and accept the city's sewage, expecting to screen out the impurities and sell the water for irrigation. Considerable debate followed. The argument that "sewage should be used and not wasted" had many followers, and the Sewer Commission recommended this solution. However, a Board of Engineers, while admitting that the use of sewage for irrigation would be "theoretically ideal," concluded that for the municipality, "an outfall to the sea, which requires a minimum of care and attention . . . is to be preferred" (Fogelson, 1967, p. 33). Eaton believed that sanitation and irrigation were incompatible, and the City Council, perhaps remembering the problems with a private water company, recommended the outfall solution. The voters were harder to convince and several attempts were necessary before a two-thirds majority would support the needed issue.

The outfall was completed in 1894 and the city's raw sewage now flowed into Santa Monica Bay at Hyperion. A second outfall was completed to the same site in 1908.

Pasadena Uses a Farm

Pasadena, the area's largest suburb, was installing sewers too, but it was thirty-five miles from the sea and an ocean outfall seemed out of the question. The city's solution in 1887 was to purchase three hundred acres of land in Alhambra, four and a half miles from the center of the city. An outfall was built along Garfield Avenue to the property located south of Mission Road and in 1892 operations began on the "sewer farm."

After some experimentation it was determined that English walnuts, pumpkins, corn, barley, and wheat were ideal crops. The sewage was simply used for irrigation as it came from the outfall, although a settling tank was provided to collect any solids. However, it was reported that "usually one can approach the streams and stand upon their very edge without realizing that they are sewage. In the early morning, when night sewage is discharged, the flow is frequently perfectly clear; later in the day it is discolored and has a soapy appearance." All paper was reported dissolved by the long journey, and the settling tank caught nothing but rags. About the only other noticeable solids were "coffee grounds and corks—the former contributed by coffee drinkers, and the latter by other drinkers" (Jones, 1904, pp. 39–47).

The operator of the farm, formerly a "prosperous Iowa farmer," ran the sewage for seven to ten days on one section, then, when the soil was sufficiently dry, it was cultivated, usually by plowing. He was careful not to irrigate after the seeds were put in (for the pumpkins and grain) but the corn was irrigated between the rows. Two crops a year could be grown "because sewage is an excellent fertilizer and soil conditioner." More than one hundred acres were in walnuts, and the farm was so successful—the income was about twice as great as expenses—that an additional one hundred sixty acres were purchased. The land was eventually surrounded by five rows of eucalyptus trees, one hundred feet high. The operator lived in a farmhouse on the land, and "The men at the farm who have worked for years in the sewage irrigated fields are the healthiest mortals imaginable. They never feel an ache or pain. . . ." Yet, nothing "was raised for human food that could in any possible way come in contact with the raw sewage" (Jones, 1904, pp. 39–47).

Pollution in the Bay

Only a few years after the Los Angeles outfall began discharging sewage into Santa Monica Bay the cities along the shore began complaining about polluted beaches. In 1915 the State Board of Health ordered Los Angeles to correct the problem, but all bond issues to improve the facility were defeated. The "West Coast Annexation" in 1917 brought the beach at Hyperion, and the area through which the sewer line was routed, into the city. Now, at least, the disposal system was within the city limits. Complaints continued, and the Board of Health began to take legal action. It was not until 1922, however, seven years after the trouble started, that the voters agreed to spend the required funds. Before the new plant could be completed, however, the Board of Health quarantined the beaches at Venice. In May 1924, the Hyperion facility was completed. It consisted of simple screening devices and a new mile-long concrete submarine outfall. In the meantime, other cities in the Los Angeles River drainage basin were beginning to construct sewers and the obvious engineering solution was simply to connect with the Los Angeles system. Vernon, Culver City, and Glendale started the trend, and they were soon joined by San Fernando, Beverly Hills, Santa Monica, and Burbank. Eventually, all cities and unincorporated territory north and west of Los Angeles sent their sewage into the Los Angeles lines.

Up-Grading in the Interior

As sewage technology progressed, and the hazards of disease spread by untreated sewage were more widely realized, some of the earlier disposal methods were up-graded. Pasadena, for example, joined South Pasadena and Alhambra in 1924, to construct an *activated sludge* treatment plant. In this process, air is pumped into raw sewage, and bacteria and fungi decompose the organic materials. A settling phase permits removal of much of the organic material as sludge—about two percent solid material—which can be dried and used as a soil conditioner "as inoffensive as leaf mold." The clear effluent (treated wastewater) is then chlorinated to kill bacteria. The Pasadena plant produced 3,000 tons of dried sludge per year which found a ready market for use on the nearby orange groves. The effluent was used for irrigation on the city's old sewer farm. Pomona, Claremont, and La-Verne also banded together to build an activated sludge plant in 1927. It was reputedly the first installation designed specifically to produce irrigation water for sale. The operators boasted that the dissolved nutrients in the effluent of one day's production were equal to 8,750 pounds of horse manure to the irrigators buying the water. Orchardists in the vicinity of Walnut built a pipeline five miles long to carry the liquid to their groves. Other cities, Covina for example, also used a sewer farm; still others, such as Arcadia, continued with individual cesspools until the 1940s. In fact, numerous cesspools are still in use. In the early 1970s, for example, only sixty percent of the homes in the upper Santa Ana watershed (north of the Santa Ana Mountains) were connected with sewers, whereas the lower watershed, generally Orange County, was ninety percent sewered.

At Hyperion "Los Angeles Aims at Perfection"

Meanwhile, back at Hyperion, where raw sewage was being pumped in increasing amounts into Santa Monica Bay, all was not well. Because of the population growth of the war years, the plant once again was inadequate for its load of sewage. Raw sewage, discharged only one mile from the beaches, was being washed ashore and gases and odors from cracks in the outfall were fouling the air. Beginning in 1943 the State Board of Health quarantined more than ten miles of beach from Hermosa Beach to Venice. Because of the large number of cities which shared the sewer outfall and lack of agreement over how the costs of a modern sewage treatment plant were to be shared among them, construction was delayed until 1948 and the new plant was not completed until 1951. Writers lauded its design; "Los Angeles Aims at Perfection" was the title of a typical story about the Hyperion plant (Huxley, 1956, p. 163). It was described as the largest and most modern activated sludge plant in the world. The famous author, Aldous Huxley, quoted at the beginning of this chapter, reflected the euphoric feeling. Everyone was certain that sewage pollution in the area was finally a thing of the past.

However, only three years after the new plant was opened it was being used to capacity—any additional sewage could not receive secondary (activated sludge) processing. Too, the market for dried sludge could not absorb the production of this gigantic plant and its salvage became a money-losing operation; the drying of sludge was stopped, and the liquid sludge was discharged into the bay. The plant was upgraded in 1957 when two much longer underwater pipelines were built. One, carrying sludge (but only about one percent solids) was seven miles long, ending at the head of a submarine canyon. The other, used for the effluent, was a conduit twelve feet in diameter and five miles long with diffusers at the end to better mix the effluent with the sea water at a depth of one hundred ninety feet. A gigantic structure, it carries what is sometimes said to be the largest freshwater stream in southern California.

The Hyperion system remains today much as it has just been described. About three million people are served by some 6,500 miles of mainline sewers which focus on the plant where more than three hundred fifty million gallons of wastewater are treated each day. Today only about a third of this volume can be given the full anaerobic treatment so two-thirds is simply screened and pumped out to sea. A small proportion of the clear, chlorinated effluent of the secondary process is used to irrigate the landscaping around the plant. The methane produced in the digesting process is used much as Huxley described twenty years ago: it provides power for most of the treatment operations and the surplus is sold to a city of Los Angeles power plant located next door.

The city of Los Angeles also operates a small sewage treatment plant on Terminal Island serving the communities of Wilmington and San Pedro. It is currently being upgraded to provide secondary treatment to all of its sewage. The effluent is discharged into the outer harbor.

Joint Outfall System

Even larger in size than the system just described, the Sanitation Districts of Los Angeles County operate the Joint Outfall System (JOS) which serves the sewage treatment needs of all or part of seventy-two cities and forty-five unincorporated communities housing about four million people and 8,000 industrial companies. It generally comprises the San Gabriel River drainage basin and includes the coastal plain south of Los Angeles for a total of about six hundred fifteen square miles. A unified network of some 1,000 miles of trunk line sewers collects wastewater; seventy-seven percent is currently handled at a Joint Water Pollution Control Plant at Carson, the rest at five water reclamation plants located higher up on the system.

The Carson plant was built in 1928, with the first outfall constructed in 1937. Today the plant receives some three hundred twenty-five million gallons of wastewater per day for treatment. Only primary treatment is provided with the effluent pumped through two tunnels (one eight feet, the other twelve feet in diameter) six miles to the coast at Whites Point, west of San Pedro. The waste is discharged through two submarine outfalls approximately one and three quarters miles off the Palos Verdes Peninsula, at a depth of two hundred feet. At this location a classical continental shelf does not exist; deep waters are located a short distance off shore amid a complex system of basins and troughs.

In the Joint Water Pollution Control Plant the solid material which settles in the primary clarifiers is anaerobically digested and then dewatered with centrifuges. These dewatered solids are spread to dry in windrows, most of which is sold to a private company and marketed as "Kellogg's Gromulch," a soil conditioner. The rest is hauled away for burial in a sanitary landfill.

The anaerobic digestion, as at Hyperion, produces a reclaimable gas, mainly methane. Some five million cubic feet of this "digester gas" are recovered daily and used both to power the effluent pumps and to heat the boilers. Altogether, reclaimed gas supplies about fifty percent of all electrical power and about eighty percent of the total energy consumption at the plant. Any gas in excess of daily need is sold to a nearby oil refinery.

Orange County Treatment Plants

The Orange County Sanitation District operates two interconnected sewage treatment plants. Treatment Plant No. 1 is located about four miles from the coast (in Fountain Valley) adjacent to the Santa Ana River and has a capacity of about sixty million gallons a day (mgd). Plant No. 2, located about 1,500 feet from the ocean at the mouth of the same river, has a capacity of about one hundred seventy mgd. Most of the sewage is given only primary treatment, chlorinated, and pumped through a new outfall, shared by both plants, which extends five miles into the ocean.

In conjunction with this disposal system, the District has been operating Water Factory 21 since 1975. The plant treats some fifteen million gallons of water a day and produces an extremely high quality water. In addition, about one third of this water receives additional treatment in the "world's largest reverse osmosis" facility to lower its mineral level. The reclaimed water is then injected into the groundwater basin to reduce seawater intrusion.

Upstream Reclamation Plants

The two largest sewage disposal systems, in addition to their ocean outfalls, also have an increasing number of upstream water reclamation plants. A recently completed addition to the Los Angeles system is the Los Angeles-Glendale Water Reclamation Plant with a capacity to reclaim twenty mgd. Located on the main sewer interceptor near the border of the two cities, the plant provides secondary and tertiary treatment (i.e., the effluent is filtered and given a long duration chlorine treatment). Glendale's share of the reclaimed water is used for cooling in their municipal power plant. Los Angeles uses its share to irrigate a portion of Griffith Park, with any surplus discharged into the Los Angeles River for percolation into the underground aquifer. The sludge is simply returned to the sewer line for processing at Hyperion. Burbank also operates a water reclamation plant, reclaiming some seven million gallons of water per day mainly for use as cooling water in their municipal power plant.

A more ambitious undertaking, a water reclamation plant in Sepulveda Basin, is currently under construction. It is designed to perform secondary and tertiary treatment for some forty mgd. The solids removed will be returned to the existing outfall system for treatment at Hyperion. The reclaimed water will be used for irrigating the recreational land in Sepulveda Basin and for groundwater recharge. Construction of the badly needed plant was delayed for a decade by conflicts with the State Resources Agency (which pushed for a smaller plant) and the federal government which held up needed funding until the controversy over ocean dumping of sludge was resolved.

Five water reclamation plants are located upstream on the Joint Outfall System sewer lines. Currently, they provide secondary treatment for about ninety-five mgd, about twenty-seven percent of the total flow of the system. A location relatively high on the system's lines has several advantages. In this position they intercept high quality domestic wastewater which presents few problems for reclamation. (The main sewage plant receives the waste from the heavily industrialized areas.) A further advantage of high elevation is that it permits the treated water to be distributed by gravity flow or low-lift pumping to areas of use.

The oldest of these plants, built in 1962, is in the Whittier Narrows; a more recent addition is located at San Jose Creek some two miles away. The treated water from these plants is used mainly for the replenishment of groundwater basins and what is not used for this purpose goes into the San Gabriel River Flood Control Channel. The waste solids are returned to the sewer for centralized treatment in the main downstream plant. At a third plant in Pomona water is given an additional tertiary treatment, producing water described as "crystal clear." The city of Pomona sells the water for irrigation to California Polytechnic University and the Bonelli Regional Park. Two additional plants, Los Coyotes and Long Beach, discharge their effluents into the San Gabriel River and Los Coyotes Creek.

Controversy Concerning Ocean Disposal

At the present time all of the sewage disposal systems in the Metropolis are in the process of trying to conform to federal and state legislation which will make necessary drastic and expensive changes in their operations. The Federal Water Pollution Control Act and the State Ocean Plan, in practice, require secondary treatment of wastewater destined for ocean discharge and tertiary treatment at all upstream reclamation plants. Perhaps more importantly, they effectively ban the dumping of sewage sludge, no matter how well digested, into the ocean after 1985. The local sanitary districts have massive spending and construction programs underway in an attempt to meet their legal requirements.

However, the need for such drastic changes is questioned by many of the local people involved. As a result, we are treated to an interesting controversy among scientists. For example, the ban on ocean disposal of sludge raises the question of acceptable alternatives, particularly considering that sludge will be produced in vastly increased quantities by the required secondary treatment facilities. (Today, about nine hundred tons a day of sludge are disposed of by the three large agencies; this is expected to increase by almost ninety percent if secondary treatment is provided for all wastewaters.) The wisdom of the legislation itself is questioned by some scientists. They believe it was designed basically to clean up the polluted rivers, lakes and shallow waters of the Atlantic Coast and feel it is not needed in the West where deep, cool water of the Pacific comes close to shore. Secondly, there is concern with the high cost: cost in dollars, cost in energy consumed, and cost in environmental impacts of the additional treatment facilities and the land disposal of sewage sludge.

The controversy can be illustrated by arguments in the *Final Summary, Environmental Impact Statement of the Joint Outfall System Facilities Plan* of July, 1977. Since 1937, the JOS has discharged primary-settled wastewater and a portion of stabilized sludge to the ocean. It is agreed that over the years a portion of the solid particles settled to the bottom of the ocean, resulting in an organically enriched deposit as much as eight inches deep in the immediate vicinity of the diffuser pipe. Industrial metals and pesticide residues in this deposit "have contributed to, or are suspected of contributing to, a number of ocean problems" (U.S. Environmental Protection Agency, 1977, p. 7). The greatest single offender was DDT discharged in large quantities prior to 1969—which entered the sewer system from the nation's largest manufacturer of the chemical. The DDT entered the food chain in the ocean water and endangered the California Brown Pelican. In addition, the discharge of the effluent "is considered by some investigators to have been an important factor in the disappearance, around 1959, of once-extensive kelp beds off the Palos Verdes Peninsula" (U.S. Environmental Protection Agency, 1977, p. 7). Further, Dover sole living near the ocean outfalls are characterized by the prevalence of fin damage. Too, there have been general ecological changes—an increase in the quantity of life around the outfalls, and a decrease in species diversity, for example.

However, the JOS has made important improvements in its operation in recent years. In 1969 the discharge of DDT into the sewers was banned, and "the nesting count of the California Brown Pelicans on Anacapa Island has increased from near zero levels in 1970 to three hundred in 1974." Too, the diversity of organisms near the outfall has improved, although the fin-erosion of the Dover sole remains. Kelp beds have been established and are increasing in size, although the sea urchin, which grazes on them, has to be artificially controlled. Some scientists argue that the "elimination of the sea otter in the last century," together with "intensive fishing of sheeps head and other predator fish, has allowed the grazers of kelp to multiply unrestricted by predators," and hence the disappearance of kelp can be explained, at least in part, in this way (U.S. Environmental Protection Agency, 1977, p. 7).

The U.S. Environmental Protection Agency, however, points out that the JOS in the past has been a contributor to serious problems off the Palos Verdes peninsula of the sort described earlier. The Agency takes the position that, "to protect the marine environment from the adverse long term impacts of known as well as yet unidentified toxicants," secondary treatment is necessary. They also point out that the waste sludges may be converted to usable energy ("a study is underway toward this goal") and used as a soil conditioner. Further, in spite of the high mineral content of the water at the JOS plant, making it uneconomic for reclamation at this time, perhaps conditions will change in the future (U.S. Environmental Protection Agency, 1977, p. 9).

The Los Angeles County Sanitation Districts engineers, however, if it were not for the legal requirements, would consider treatment alternatives which, they argue, would provide "essentially equivalent benefits to the marine environment at substantially lower costs and with less negative impacts on basin air quality and energy requirements." Partial secondary treatment, they argue, would reduce harmful materials "below any known chronic or acute toxicity levels for marine organisms." Such things as DDT can be and have been controlled at their source. Concentrations of toxic material have been reduced already to less than five percent of the pre-1970 levels. "To achieve additional removals by adding full secondary treatment will impact basin air quality by the addition of 100 lb/day of hydrocarbons, 1000 lb/day of nitrogen oxides, and 500 lb/day of carbon monoxide—and increase the use of energy by 360 barrels of oil per day" (U.S. Environmental Protection Agency, 1977, p. 9). Furthermore, much of the nutrient value of the wastewater for increasing productivity of the nearshore marine environment will be lost. (See the Issacs' quotations at the beginning of the chapter.)

Plans for Compliance

The three major waste disposal agencies, after years of engineering studies, have settled on disposal systems that meet the no-ocean-dumping-of-sludge requirement. The city of Los Angeles will enlarge its Hyperion plant and add much new equipment. After anaerobic digestion the sludge will be mechanically dewatered (by centrifuge), further dried by the energy efficient Carver-Greenfield dehydration method, and finally combusted (burned) in a starved-air multiple hearth reactor. The remaining char/ash, seven to ten truckloads a day, will be hauled to a sanitary landfill. At various stages of the operation, gases will be produced that can be burned to produce steam for the generation of electricity, and the entire process is thought to be energy efficient. The burned gases will be passed through an "advanced air cleanup train." "Systems considered to accomplish pollution reduction include bag houses . . . for particulate removal, NO_x reduction using ammonia injection, and SO_x removal by wet chemical scrubbing. . . . Flue gases will be directed to a stack (between fifty to a hundred feet high) for atmospheric dispersion." (LA/OMA Project, 1980, p. VI-80.) Rube Goldberg (famous for his cartoons showing fabulously involved machinery for simple operations) would be pleased. There is a further problem: the Hyperion site is not large enough for all of the equipment that will be needed. It is possible that the plant can be expanded northward onto some of the vacant land west of the Los Angeles International Airport runways. Construction in this area, however, may conflict with the legally established critical habitat of the El Segundo Blue butterfly.

The Los Angeles County Sanitation District has somewhat similar plans for a portion of its sludge. Three "process trains" are proposed. Part of the sludge will be processed and sold as a soil-conditioner as at present. A second portion will be handled in the same complicated way as at Hyperion. Surplus sludge from the two operations will be dried and hauled to a sanitary landfill: the third "process train." The Orange County Sanitation District, apparently because nearby space is available, is able to utilize a land-based non-thermal processing alternative. Anaerobically digested sludge will be dewatered and trucked to Round Canyon, air dried, and then trucked to a nearby landfill.

Garbage—From Hogs to Sewage

Garbage, or food waste, includes scraps from the home kitchen, as well as larger volumes from restaurant operations, markets, or wherever food is handled or processed. Garbage collection began in Los Angeles in 1902. It was disposed of in what was called a garbage "crematory" which was reportedly successful before it burned down. Again, for a brief period, 1915–1921, the city sold its garbage to the Southern Pacific Reduction Company. It processed the garbage in an expensive plant, dehydrating it with naphtha and steam and producing grease (used to manufacture soap) and a residual tankage, which was sold as feed for chickens and hogs or as fertilizer. The company made money during World War I when prices were high, but failed in 1921.

At that point the city went back to a practice it had instituted earlier and sold its garbage as hog feed. By 1928 Los Angeles garbage had made Fontana Farms the largest hog feeding operation in the world. The garbage was loaded on gondola railroad cars and shipped fifty-five miles to the ranch in San

Bernardino County. From five hundred to six hundred tons of garbage was available each day, enough for from 40,000 to 60,000 hogs. When they reached their full weight the hogs were sent to Los Angeles for slaughter and sale as pork. The waste from the hog farms and hog pen cleanings was made into fertilizer and sold to orange growers. Everything seems to have been recycled. (Incidentally, a city ordinance forbade hotels and restaurants from selling garbage to private collectors—presumably the city system could not have functioned without their rich leavings.) Other cities sold their garbage to small hog feeders located around Buena Park, Palmdale, and Saugus.

Fontana Farms went out of business in 1950, and by that time the neighboring counties had ordinances prohibiting the movement of garbage into their jurisdictions. New hog farms were started in the relatively isolated Saugus-Newhall area and half a dozen feeders purchased the garbage from Los Angeles and a number of surrounding cities. Public Health groups were concerned about the possibility of the spread of trichinosis from poorly cooked pork, and, spurred on by an outbreak of a virus disease among the hogs, the feeding of raw garbage was prohibited in 1953. Sterilization by cooking was then necessary. By 1954 the hog feeders were feeding about 1,050 tons of garbage a day. In return, some 1.2 million pounds of meat were marketed in the Los Angeles area annually, some ten percent of its pork consumption.

The hog farms, however, were gradually forced out. Two factors were responsible for their demise. In the first place they are not good neighbors, producing powerful odors, and generating traffic, both of huge trucks and trailers of garbage, and trucks of live hogs. Then, too, with the spread of the household garbage disposers the garbage went down the drain into the sewer system and was no longer available for collection. This shift in disposal methods eliminated the moving of garbage through the streets. On the other hand, it added a large volume of waste to be processed at sewage disposal plants. In addition, of course, it eliminated the possibility of recycling a large volume of organic matter through hogs and back to human food.

The Disposal of Solid Waste

Solid waste—rubbish, refuse, trash—the general non-edible, non-liquid waste of urban civilization has been handled separately down through the centuries. Ancient urbanites disposed of much of their unusable wastes by dumping things into the mud streets, where they sank out of sight, or by piling things into backyard rubble heaps, to the delight of contemporary archaeologists. Early modern disposal methods brought forth the occupational calling of the rag picker, the dump scavenger, and the junk collector. Only in the more recent decades of this century have sophisticated disposal techniques been developed in response to changing cultural concepts. For many years solid waste was considered to be composed of two categories, combustible and non-combustible. What would burn was the responsibility of the individual householder until very recently. However, as early as 1912 the city of Los Angeles began collecting all solid waste that would not incinerate—ashes, bottles, broken crockery, glass, tin cans, stones, concrete, and the like.

The collected urban waste, at first, was simply dumped on city-owned land. In 1924, however, a contract was awarded the Los Angeles Foundry Company (later, the Los Angeles By-Products Company) to receive the waste. At their plant at 25th and Alameda in Vernon the metals and glass were salvaged. The cans were de-tinned, shredded, baled, and shipped to Arizona for use in ore extraction process at copper refineries. By 1930 some 1,000 tons of shredded cans a month were shipped to the mines. At the same period the broken glass was shipped to China for reuse as colored glass; later the flint and amber

"cullet" was remelted in local glass factories. For many years dead animals were collected separately and delivered to the Los Angeles Fertilizer Works. In 1927 "two Ford trucks collected 56,000 dogs, 54,000 cats, and 450 large animals." Non-salvageable rubbish and street sweepings were simply dumped and used as fill for low areas.

When, in an attempt to reduce air pollution, home incineration was forbidden in 1957, the collection of combustible rubbish was provided for residents throughout the region. In Los Angeles two massive incinerators were opened, one on Gaffey Street in the harbor area, another on San Fernando Road at Lacy Street. However, neither could meet the strict air pollution standards and they operated for only a short time. Collection and salvage of metal and glass continued—their value appeared to rise as fast as the cost of labor—and the continuation of the operation seemed assured. By the mid-sixties, however, salvageable material had declined to less than thirty percent of its earlier volume, partly because of the replacement of canned by frozen foods. Similarly, home garbage disposal units were becoming widespread and collecting the scanty garbage for hog feeding became only marginally profitable. It perhaps was not surprising, therefore, that in 1965 the city of Los Angeles began the combined collection of all household refuse and ended its salvage activities. The catalyst was a successful mayoralty campaign in which the major issue seemed to be that "Los Angeles housewives should no longer have to segregate their garbage." Combined collection of all solid waste has become universal throughout the Metropolis.

Solid Waste Management

Solid waste in the Metropolis is produced at the rate of about 6.5 pounds per person per day. Residential waste accounts for 2.51 pounds of this; the rest is commercial and demolition waste. For the Metropolis this

Table 8.1
Contents of Typical Household Refuse

Type	Percent of total
Mixed paper	27.0
Tree trimmings	21.5
Grass and dirt	11.6
Newspaper	10.7
Glass	7.3
Garbage	5.3
Ferrous metals	5.2
Cardboard	3.6
Textiles	2.0
Lumber	1.6
Molded plastic	1.2
Plastic fiber	0.9
Ceramics	0.8
Non-ferrous metals	0.8
Leather and rubber	0.5
	100.0

Source: City of Los Angeles, Board of Public Works, Bureau of Sanitation. *Liquid and Solid Waste Collection, Treatment, Disposal by the City of Los Angeles,* no date.

Table 8.2
Input to Landfills, Los Angeles County

Type of Refuse	Percent of Total
Household refuse	35
Commercial waste paper	11
Small wood and lumber (2 × 4 and smaller)	15
Large wood and lumber (timbers, utility poles, etc)	2
Garden waste and brush	3
Miscellaneous	5
Solid fill	29
	100

Source: City of Los Angeles, Board of Public Works, Bureau of Sanitation. *Liquid, and Solid Waste Collection, Treatment, Disposal by the City of Los Angeles,* no date.

means that some 32,500 tons of waste are produced a day or 11,865,500 tons a year, a prodigious volume to be collected and disposed of. Today, collection is by either private or municipal collectors, and disposal is almost universally by sanitary land fill.

Residential waste accounts for only thirty-eight percent of the total, but it is the stuff which we see collected in the neighborhoods and hauled down the streets and an analysis of its composition might be instructive. A recent survey of residential refuse for the city of Los Angeles reveals the following proportion by weight (Table 8.1).

Paper of all sorts is the largest single component of the refuse, comprising about forty percent of its total weight. Tree trimmings, grass, and dirt add an additional significant volume—about a third of the weight. On the other hand, garbage, which spoils and grows rotten, is a minor, perhaps vanishing, fraction of residential waste. The survey also revealed that residential waste is sensitive to such vari-

ables as the season of the year with more yard waste in the summer which makes that the large volume period. Too, per capita waste quantities tend to increase with economic status of the neighborhood and to decrease as the proportion of apartments increases.

Although we have no data on the composition of the region's commercial and demolition waste, it can be inferred fairly clearly from the input of the landfills in Los Angeles County (Table 8.2).

Aside from household refuse, previously analyzed, the major item, twenty-nine percent of the entire landfill receipts, is "solid fill," apparently mainly demolition waste: old concrete, asphalt, plaster, plaster board, dirt, rocks, and so on. The second major non-residential item is wood and lumber, seventeen percent of the total, if both small boards and large timbers are included. Finally, commercial waste paper forms another eleven percent, a surprisingly large fraction, as many offices run their own salvage operations.

Sanitary Landfills

With the demise of the incinerator, public as well as private, and with open burning banned, the disposal of solid waste in the Metropolis for the last twenty years has been almost universally by sanitary landfill. The method was facilitated by the existence of a large number of man-made pits and mountain canyons and by procedures developed through the years to minimize any adverse environmental impact. Although sanitary landfills are basically a controlled dump and cover procedure, they are a far cry from the traditional city dump. The solid wastes are deposited under close supervision, spread and compacted into thin layers by bulldozers and covered with at least six inches of soil at the end of each day. Any water that seeps through the fill, the "leachate," is caught and diverted to the sewer system so as to prevent possible contamination of the underground aquifer. When completed, a three to four foot layer of dirt is added. The filled pits and canyons, now valuable publicly owned open space, can be converted into parks, golf courses, or, in one instance, a botanic garden.

The sanitary landfill is not without its critics, the most vocal of whom tend to be the homeowners in the vicinity. They object to noise, complain about blowing dust, and fear the invasion of rats and flies. All of these objections, however, can be minimized, if not eliminated, by proper operation of the landfill. Bulldozers can be effectively muffled, water trucks can keep down dust, and "snow fences" can catch any blowing paper. Landscaping and decorative fencing can shield the operations from view. Methane gas produced by the decaying fill, once a problem, is now caught and used for its energy. Landfills, too, have subsidence problems, minimized by their open space status.

There are about thirty sanitary landfills in operation in Los Angeles County today, many quite large, with remaining active "lives" of from five to fifty years. A few, however, have been filled and put to use. The city of Montebello, for example, has a playground on a landfill, and Burbank has added to its level land in Stough Park with filled land. The most unique use of a completed landfill, however, is the South Coast Botanical Gardens in Palos Verdes. Formerly a diatomite mine, it was used as a sanitary landfill between 1957 and 1965 and some 3.5 million tons of trash were deposited in depths ranging from five to one hundred sixty-five feet. Today, eighty-seven acres of this fill have been converted into a botanical garden.

A recent study of the Southern California Association of Governments (SCAG) indicates that disposal by sanitary landfill is likely to be with us for many years. Suitable mountain canyons seem to be available in the region. Best of all, waste disposal costs by sanitary landfill are relatively low although the total involved is $300 million a year, and rising. The major portion of the cost is collection, with costs ranging from $8 to $24 a ton, with the mean around $14. (These collection costs would be relatively constant, regardless of the means of disposal.) The landfill operations themselves are not costly, varying from $0.80 per ton to about $2.00 per ton, with the mean about $1.30. A recent nationwide survey reported that waste disposal costs in Los Angeles were the lowest of any major city, about $15 per ton, compared to those of New York (which was high) of $55 a ton. Any region which can boast that its operations are "least costly in the nation" for any municipal service is not likely to change that service quickly.

Salvage and Reclamation

Salvage and reclamation of reusable materials from the waste stream is socially desirable for many reasons: it is a way to preserve scarce materials, it may reduce total costs (if materials can be sold for more than the cost of salvage), and, if a portion of solid waste material is withdrawn for salvage, the landfills will not be filled quite so quickly. At the present, however, the financial and legal climate does not encourage the salvage of scrap once it has entered the solid waste stream. Most salvage that does occur takes place in industrial and commercial establishments, some of which produce a great deal of salvageable paper or metal. Only an estimated two or three percent of the total paper used by households is salvaged, mainly through paper drives by service organizations. However, the salvage of aluminum beverage containers is increasing rapidly, spurred by a local aluminum manufacturing firm active in recycling.

The Southern California Association of Governments has recently pointed out that if salvage and reuse is to be possible, government at various levels must take positive action. The organization recommends the following: (1) a container tax designed to reduce the volume and overall environmental impact of containers and promote the reuse of these items; (2) a virgin material tax or penalty—the provision of a penalty for the use of over a given percentage of virgin materials; (3) reclaimed material subsidy. A direct subsidy could be provided to those manufacturers employing all or a substantial fraction of reclaimed materials in their product.

8. Suggested Readings

LA/OMA Project. *Draft Facilities Plan/Program. Proposed Sludge Management Program for the Los Angeles/Orange County Metropolitan Area.* Los Angeles: LA/OMA Project, 1980. Not paged consecutively.
This report is a description of proposed land-based sludge disposal methods for the three major wastewater facilities in the two-county area.

Los Angeles, Department of Public Works, Bureau of Engineering. *Wastewater Facilities Plan.* Los Angeles: City of Los Angeles, 1977.

A series of volumes detailing a twenty-five year plan to serve the projected wastewater needs of the city of Los Angeles. Perhaps the *Summary* is all the average reader will need.

Orange and Los Angeles Counties Water Reuse Study. *Facilities Plan.* Volumes I and II. Los Angeles: OLAC Water Reuse Study, 1982.
This "Facilities Plan" is the final report of the OLAC Water Reuse Study—a four year, $4 million effort to determine how best to incorporate water reuse into the total water supply program of Southern California.

Sanitation Districts of Los Angeles County. Solid Waste Management Department. *Puente Hills Landfill. Environmental Impact Report and Appendices.* Whittier: Sanitation Districts of Los Angeles County, 1982.
Although this report focuses on a single site, it is a revealing example of the issues that must be considered whenever the opening or expansion of a landfill is contemplated.

Sanitation Districts of Los Angeles County. *Final Environmental Impact Statement and Environmental Impact Report for the Joint Outfall Facilities Plan.* Volume I, II and Summary. Whittier: Sanitation Districts of Los Angeles County, 1977.
This three volume report reflects the step by step planning, alternative proposals, citizen input, and so on, that went into the redesign of the Districts' sewage disposal system.

CHAPTER 9

Electrical Energy for the Metropolis

Figure 9.1. Castaic Power Plant, a 1,250,000 kw pumped storage peaking facility is located about twenty miles northwest of Los Angeles at the upper end of Castaic Lake. (Photo courtesy Los Angeles Department of Water and Power.)

"Those who enjoy, as a matter of course, an average day of 16 or 18 light or lighted hours, can hardly imagine the boredom and frustration of earlier times when sunset meant the end of general activity. The increase in the hours spent usefully or pleasantly by millions whenever electricity sheds its light is one of the greatest blessings of mankind. If to this are added the endless hours of drudgery which electrically driven labor-saving devices spare housewives, farm families, and other workers, one gains some idea of the scope of this boon which has come to mankind. . . ." Erich W. Zimmermann (1951, p. 596).

111

Metropolitan areas are massive consumers of energy and Los Angeles is no exception. Gasoline is used in automobiles, kerosene in jet airplanes, diesel fuel in trucks, natural gas or fuel oil in the heating of homes, schools, and offices, and for the operation of factories. In addition, natural gas, fuel oil, coal, falling water, and nuclear energy are used to produce electricity. Electricity, in turn, is also widely consumed in urban areas for lighting, air conditioning, powering elevators or escalators, and operating motorized equipment and appliances of all sorts.

Although it accounts for only slightly more than one-fifth of all energy consumed in the Metropolis, electricity is the focus of this chapter, and some of the other energy sources are considered elsewhere. The consumption of electricity is directly related to the operation of the Metropolis, and its cost is a characteristic of the local economy. A portion of the electricity we use is produced within the Metropolis itself and has significant environmental impacts. Finally, when electric shortages are imminent, as they have been in the recent past, they affect this Metropolis in an individual way.

The Two Giant Utilities

Electricity for the Metropolis is supplied almost entirely by two giant power companies, the Southern California Edison Company (SCE) and the Los Angeles Department of Water and Power (DWP). The SCE is the nation's fourth largest power company, and the LADWP is the largest municipal electrical utility in the country. Small municipal companies serving Burbank, Glendale, and Pasadena also have a limited generating capacity, whereas the cities of Anaheim, Azusa, Colton, Riverside, and Vernon distribute power, but purchase it wholesale from SCE.

The city of Los Angeles found itself in the power business almost by coincidence. Water in the Los Angeles Aqueduct drops 2,617 feet on its way to the San Fernando Valley, and several hydroelectric plants were built to furnish low cost power for the aqueduct's construction. (It was reputed to be the first major engineering project in America to be constructed primarily by electric power.) When the aqueduct was completed the power was available for sale to help pay for the project. In 1911 the citizens of the city voted (by a majority of 9 to 1) in favor of public distribution of power, rather than leasing the plants to private companies, and out of this action came the "power" portion of the DWP. By 1939 the city had purchased the electric distribution facilities of three private utilities operating in Los Angeles and was the sole distributor of electricity in the city.

The predecessor companies of the Southern California Edison Company, too, began as producers of hydroelectric power. The first hydroelectric plant in California was built near Etiwanda in 1882. Small dams and generating plants were built along the streams of the San Gabriel Mountains, transmitting electricity to such foothill communities as Riverside, Pomona, San Bernardino, and Redlands in the 1880s. However, the first electricity in Los Angeles was produced by a steam plant and used for street lights on seven tall "masts" in 1882. Power from a generating plant near the mouth of San Gabriel Canyon was delivered to Los Angeles twenty miles away in 1893. Other similar lines were built, and in 1904 they were extended to power sites on the western slopes of the Sierras one hundred thirty miles to the north, including a site on the Kern River. A decade later a hydroelectric plant on the San Joaquin River, still farther north, was put "on line." At first several small companies were involved, but by 1917 most had been consolidated into the Southern California Edison Company. With the availability of aqueduct power in Los Angeles, the SCE soon relinquished power sales in that city and concentrated on the suburban communities and their even larger market.

The area's hydroelectric power was greatly increased after 1936 by the construction of Hoover Dam, whose financing was made possible by contracts committing the utility companies serving the Los Angeles area to take all of the electricity the dam would make possible. The DWP also constructed additional hydro facilities along the Los Angeles Aqueduct, at San Francisquito Canyon, in the San Fernando Valley, and in Franklin Canyon. Similarly, the SCE developed the "Big Creek" tributary of the San Joaquin River in such a way that water passes through five power plants before it is stored in Friant Reservoir for irrigation use. Steam plants, where electricity was generated by steam turbines fueled by oil or gas, were built at an early date, too, but they were considered as an emergency reserve for dry years or for periods of greatly increased demand. As recently as 1940 an amazing ninety-seven percent of the electricity distributed by the DWP was hydroelectricity, and the SCE was also essentially a hydro company, with about seventy percent of its power from this source. For more than fifty years clean and cheap electric energy, produced without smoke or fumes, was a distinctive characteristic of the Los Angeles Metropolis.

Hydroelectricity might be thought of as a form of solar power: it is produced by the gravitational energy of water, energy supplied by the sun, through the precipitation of water on land at some elevation. The power produced by running water is proportional to the rate of discharge of the stream and the height of the fall. California has a variety of suitable power sites, some where small streams occur in the high mountains, some where large streams (such as the Colorado) are found at low elevations. Falling water, historically, was considered to be the ideal power source: the "fuel" is free (although much capital must be invested to utilize it), it is a renewable resource, there are no air pollutants, there is no need for cooling water. Furthermore, it is an extremely efficient one-step conversion of mechanical to electrical energy, with an efficiency of more than ninety percent. It is ideal as an element of a power grid, for the production of hydroelectricity can be started and stopped quickly, as needed. Of course, if a storage dam has to be built on a river, that portion of the river is no longer "wild," although now a "lake" is available for recreation. Too, dams are barriers to migrating fish, and "fish ladders" are only a partial solution to that problem. If the stream is silty, silt will be deposited behind the dam, gradually reducing its utility. The advantages of hydroelectricity are so great, however, that most of the obvious power sites have long since been developed.

Hydroelectricity no longer powers the Los Angeles Metropolis. Today, only about fifteen or twenty percent of the electricity consumed in the area comes from hydro sources and much of that is imported from the Pacific Northwest. All of the old hydro plants remain; in fact, new ones are added occasionally: along the barrel of the second Los Angeles Aqueduct and at Castaic Lake, for example. However, the enormous increase in demand for electricity in the area since 1940 has made other sources essential. The 1950–60 period saw the construction of numerous steam plants, fueled by natural gas or low sulfur oil, and located within the Metropolis. In the 1970s, coal-fired plants, built in conjunction with a consortium of utilities, and located outside the Basin, were added. One company, the SCE, also has one nuclear installation. Table 9.1 lists the major sources of power for the two dominant companies, and the maximum generating capacity of each installation.

The Perishability of Electricity and the Peak Load Problem

A basic characteristic of electricity is that it is extremely perishable—except in very small quantities it cannot be stored economically. It

Table 9.1
Generating Capacity of Metropolitan Utilities
Southern California Edison—Resources

Station	Capacity (megawatts)
Thermal Generation	
Oil and Gas	
Alamitos (Seal Beach)	1,950.0
Redondo	1,602.0
Ormond Beach (Oxnard)	1,500.0
El Segundo	1,020.0
Huntington Beach	870.0
Etiwanda	904.0
Long Beach	686.0
Cool Water (Daggett)	628.0
Mandalay (Oxnard)	430.0
Other (inc. turbine peakers)	845.8
Subtotal	10,435.8
Coal	
Four Corners (48% share)	768.0
Mojave (56% share)	884.8
Subtotal	1,652.8
Nuclear	
San Onofre (80% share)	348.8
Total Thermal Generation	12,437.4
Hydro Generation (36 plants)	877.3
Firm Purchases/Exchanges	1,802.7
Total Generation Capacity Resources	15,117.4

Source: Southern California Edison Company, *1980 Annual Report*, p. 19.

Los Angeles Department of Water and Power—Resources

Station	Capacity (megawatts)
Thermal Generation	
Oil and Gas	
Haynes (Seal Beach)	1,583.0
Scattergood (Playa Del Rey)	642.0
Valley	519.0
Harbor	397.1
Gas turbines	76.0
Subtotal	3,217.0
Coal	
Navajo (21.2% share)	550.0
Mojave (20% share)	316.0
Coronado	210.0
Subtotal	1,076.0
Hydro Generation	
Department of Water and Power	193.0
Hoover Dam	511.0
Pacific Northwest	525.0
Subtotal	1,229.0
Pumped Storage	
Castaic	672.0
Total Resources	6,194.0

Source: City of Los Angeles, Department of Water and Power, System Development Division. *1982-2002 Resource Plan, April, 1982.* p. 10.

must be consumed as it is produced. This quality creates serious problems for a power company. It means that a generation system must have enough capacity to meet the highest demands (peak load) of system customers whenever that demand occurs. Such capacity adds greatly to the cost of the system and, therefore, to the cost of electricity.

The DWP, for example, finds its greatest demands are in the summer months (with August normally the peak month) when much electricity is used for air conditioning. Its lowest demands are in the spring (bottoming in April) when days have begun to lengthen, reducing the need for constant lighting, and while the temperature is still moderate enough to require little refrigeration of the air. Less electricity is used on weekends than on working days. The peak demand on a Sunday in April, for example, may be no more than 2,500 megawatts; a weekday in that same month, 3,200 megawatts; but a weekday in August, 4,000 megawatts. Too, there are great variations in demand during a single day. On June 17, 1981, the daytime temperature reached 104 at the Civic Center and 105 at Burbank Airport. On that day, the peak load was 4,343 megawatts at 3:00 P.M., whereas at 5:00 A.M. on the same day, the load had been only 2,033 megawatts, less than half the demand of the peak period.

How does the DWP, or any electric utility, meet such wide variations in demand for its non-storable product? To a certain extent it can start, stop, and slow down its generators, depending on its particular situation. Hydro plants are particularly good for "peaking" as water can be allowed to accumulate behind the dam during hours of low demand and run through the turbines when electricity

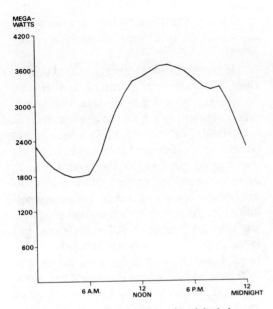

Figure 9.2. Varying demand for electricity in Los Angeles during the course of a hot summer day. Data from Los Angeles Department of Water and Power.

is needed. The DWP has recently completed the Castaic Power Project on the California Aqueduct that may serve as an example. Here California Aqueduct water drops more than 1,000 feet from Pyramid Reservoir through a tunnel thirty feet in diameter. When fully developed, there will be six turbine generators with a total capacity of 1,250,000 kilowatts. Water which would normally flow steadily through the aqueduct is stored in Pyramid Reservoir and then is channeled through the turbine generators during peak demand periods, six to ten hours a day in summer, three to six hours a day in winter. This does not end the story. The six generators are reversible as motors, so that the turbines will work as pumps, and some water can be lifted back to Pyramid Reservoir in off-peak periods, using surplus energy from steam plants, for reuse during hours of greatest demand. By means of this "pumped storage" the usefulness of both the steam and hydro plants is increased.

The linking together of several power companies, so that electricity can be exchanged among them as the need arises, is another solution to the peak demand problem. All of the local companies are linked together; in fact, most of the electrical utilities in the state are tied together. An extension of this idea is the "Pacific Intertie," an eight hundred forty-six mile, direct current line connecting California power companies with Bonneville and other Columbia River hydroelectric power plants. It is reputed to be the "longest distance, highest capacity, direct current transmission line in the world," and makes 1,400,000 kilowatts of electricity available to the DWP and SCE, as well as the municipal utilities of Burbank, Glendale, and Pasadena. It is designed to make use of the seasonal variations in power supply and demand for electricity between the Pacific Northwest and southern California. For example, in summer demand for power is high in the south for air conditioning and irrigation; production is high in the north because of heavy runoff. In winter, demands are lower in the south, but high in the north (for heating and lighting) at a time when its river runoff is reduced. The energy available from the Northwest is currently partly firm peaking capacity and partly temporarily surplus electricity. It can be returned at off-peak periods, or it can be paid for. In recent years, there has been a surplus of energy in the north, so the local utilities have received considerable cheap hydro power the year around. (The drought year of 1977 was an exception.) It is expected, however, that little surplus power will be available from the Northwest after the late 1980s because of increasing requirements of the region.

Thermal Generating Plants—Our Major Power Source

The major source of power for all of the local electrical utilities over the past several decades has been steam-driven generating plants burning oil or natural gas and located within the Metropolis. The capacity and locations of the largest of these plants are included in Table 9.1. In an average year they supply from sixty to sixty-five percent of the total electricity used in the region. Steam generating plants are ideally located near the customers they are designed to serve, and with easy access to the vast amounts of water needed for cooling. Eight of the ten large plants have such a location—within the Metropolis and adjacent to the ocean.

Thermal electric plants require some high-quality water for steam generation, which may require distillation in areas of impure water. Plant operation, however, requires incredible amounts of water for the cooling and condensing of generated steam. The condensing of steam creates a vacuum that produces a pull effect on turbine wheels while the superheated steam is pushing from the opposite direction. Illustration of the amount of cooling water needed is striking. The two pipes bringing in sea water to the DWP Harbor Plant (a smaller facility) have a capacity of six hundred seven cubic feet per second (cfs), which is larger than the four hundred thirty-five cfs capacity of the Los Angeles Aqueduct. The SCE Alamitos plant requires more than two million acre feet of cooling water per year. All water delivered to the Metropolis by the MWD in an average year amounts to less than one million acre feet.

Plants that can use the unlimited supplies of cool ocean water and use it only once are the most efficient. However, concerns about the marine environment (water is returned to the ocean about ten degrees centigrade warmer than when it was removed) and the esthetics of coastal plants have reduced the possibilities of additional construction in these locations. Plants in non-coastal locations, such as the DWP Valley plant, must tap fresh water supplies, and this plant is connected to the city water system by a forty-eight inch pipe. To conserve water it is continuously recirculated by means of eight redwood cooling towers, but

these tall structures with their plumes of rising steam are considered unsightly by many people.

In recent decades natural gas has been the chief fuel of the local thermal plants. It is by far the least polluting of all fuels, and air pollution regulations require its use whenever it is available. In the late 1960s about eighty percent of all fuel burned in the local plants was natural gas. As gas shortages began to occur in the 1970s, however, all the plants had to use more low sulfur fuel oil, increasing pollution. By the late 1970s natural gas produced less than ten percent of SCE's electricity, but in the early 1980s it was producing about one-third. Local thermal plants seem destined to shift back and forth between oil and gas, burning as much gas as is available in any given year.

A new addition to the thermal plant group is a nuclear-fueled plant at San Onofre, in Camp Pendleton, just south of the Metropolis. The plant, in which SCE has an eighty percent interest, is located on the ocean and uses sea water for cooling. However, unlike the other thermal plants, its heat is provided by fission of enriched uranium. Clean and smog free, it might seem to be the ideal method of power production for the region, but it has to contend with the well-publicized questions of safety and spent fuel disposal. Commercial production of power at San Onofre began in January, 1968. Two additional units are under construction and are expected to begin operations in 1982 and 1983, respectively.

Other novel, though minor, sources of power are also being utilized. For many years the excess methane gas produced at the Hyperion sewage treatment plant has been used as a supplemental fuel at the adjacent DWP Scattergood steam plant. This amounts to only about one percent of its requirements. Since 1974 methane from the Sheldon-Arleta Landfill in Sun Valley has been used to power a two hundred kilowatt generator on an experimental basis. Fifteen deep wells were drilled into the landfill, and the methane collected is being burned in the nearby Valley Steam Plant. It is thought that if all landfills in the area were developed (when they are all completely filled) as much as 50,000 kilowatts could be produced from the extracted methane. Another unique source of local power is being developed in the DWP in conjunction with the Great Lakes Carbon Corporation in Wilmington. Here, waste heat (high temperature gas being exhausted into the atmosphere) is salvaged and used to run a steam generator, a process called cogeneration. The plant completed in 1979 has a capacity of 60,000 kilowatts, but the amount of electricity produced depends upon the scale of operations of the carbon plant.

A small but growing proportion of the power for the Metropolis comes from coal-fired steam plants located outside the region. The increasing scarcity of natural gas, a reluctance by the utilities to become dependent on foreign sources of oil, and the difficulty in meeting stringent anti-pollution standards of the Los Angeles Basin are some of the forces behind this trend. Both the DWP and SCE are members of multiple utility consortiums which have built large coal-burning plants relatively near the source of coal. Several installations are based on coal from the Kayenta mine at Black Mesa in Northeastern Arizona on land leased from the Hopi and Navajo Indian tribes. One plant is located at Navajo Station, near Page, Arizona, and a seventy-six mile rail line has been built to carry coal to the power plant. Most of the power produced here is destined for Arizona, but the DWP has a twenty-one percent interest, enabling all users to benefits from the economies of scale. (Water for cooling is drawn from Lake Powell, but it is recycled by means of cooling towers and is not returned to the lake.) The DWP has a twenty percent interest and the SCE a fifty percent interest in a second coal-fired plant called the Mojave Project. This plant, located three miles south of Davis Dam on the Colorado River (at the eastern tip of Nevada) also uses coal from the Kayenta mine. Because the plant is located two hundred seventy-five miles from the mine, however, the coal is transported by pipeline in slurry form—a mixture of half coal and half water. The water is recovered and forms a portion of that needed for cooling purposes; the remainder comes from the Colorado River. As its site is only fifty miles south of Hoover Dam, electricity can be transmitted to the Metropolis via existing transmission lines. In addition, the SCE receives electricity from a coal-fired plant in the Four Corners area, in which it has a forty-eight percent share.

The Expansion of Generating Facilities

One does not have to embrace the growth projections of the power companies, or subscribe to a general growth scenario for the region, to conclude that for the Los Angeles Metropolis additional supplies of electricity are likely to be necessary in the future. It is probable, for example, that the ultimate elimination of smog will require the substitution of electricity for the fuels currently being burned in the Basin, including gasoline in automobiles. Even with the most sophisticated conservation program, this would require large additional amounts of electricity. Expansion poses formidable problems. Earlier expansion plans of the local utilities have come to naught because of environmental concerns: a nuclear plant in the San Joaquin Valley, a coal-fired plant at Kaiparowits, Utah, additional dams and hydro plants on the Colorado River are but a few recent examples. Today, it is against national policy to construct new facilities that burn natural gas or fuel oil. As there are no economically developable coal resources in California, seeking a site for coal-fired plants near the coal source—Utah or Arizona—forces the local utilities into the role of interlopers and despoilers.

In spite of the difficulties, several proposals for expansion are currently under way. The DWP, Utah Power and Light, Anaheim, Riverside, and many small local utilities are involved in the construction of a large 3,000 megawatt coal-fueled steam electric plant near Lynndyle, Utah. Known as the Intermountain Power Project, it will use coal from nearby central Utah mines and get its water from the Sevier River. The DWP will have a thirty-four percent interest in the plant, Anaheim slightly more than ten percent. Commercial operation of the first phase of the plant is scheduled for 1986. In the planning stage is a 1,500 megawatt coal-fueled, steam electric generating station to be located in eastern Nevada near Ely—the DWP has a 39.1 percent interest. Known as the White Pine Project it is tentatively scheduled to begin operation in 1989.

Another expansion strategy is to buy into existing power plants, those already approved and under construction in neighboring states. The DWP, for example, has purchased a thirty percent interest in the coal-fueled Coronado generating station recently completed at St. John's, Arizona. It also has an 11.6 percent interest in the 3,666 megawatt Palo Verde nuclear generating station being built near Phoenix, Arizona. SCE, similarly, has a 15.8 percent interest in the plant, scheduled to begin producing electricity in 1983.

Energy for the Future

Future energy possibilities include the utilization of solar and geothermal sources. The Metropolis has long sunny days, and the use of this abundant solar energy to serve a portion of its needs is inevitable in the near future. The technology for heating water and swimming pools is already with us, and the heating of homes themselves has been successfully demonstrated. Some applications are being made to larger units: apartments, schools, and offices. Only the high cost is holding back extensive application, a situation that may be remedied shortly as mass production of the necessary equipment becomes possible. However, used in this way, solar energy is more likely to displace natural gas than electricity.

Solar photovoltaic cells, which can turn sunlight directly into electricity, are already in existence, but they are expensive and generally considered impractical for extensive use. However, the "world's largest solar photovoltaic electric generating facility" is located on a twenty-acre site near Hesperia, in Apple Valley. It consists of one hundred separate photovoltaic panels mounted on units designed to track the sun, and produces one megawatt of electricity, enough for about four hundred homes. The Atlantic Richfield Company, a major producer of photovoltaic cells, owns the facility, and sells the electricity to SCE.

The sun's energy is also used in a "solar thermal central receiver" power plant recently completed in the desert at Daggett. Dubbed "Solar One," it consists of 1,818 movable "heliostats" (a set of twelve mirrors, twenty-three feet square) designed to track the sun and focus its rays on a giant receiver/boiler atop a three hundred foot high tower. The fluid in the boiler is heated and produces steam which is then used to generate electricity in a turbine system. The heliostats occupy a one-hundred-acre semi-circle surrounding the tower. Both the SCE and DWP are involved in the experimental project, as is the United States Department of Energy. During the daylight hours the facility produces ten megawatts of electricity, enough for about 5,000 homes. A thermal storage system provides for production of electricity at a reduced rate during periods of cloud cover and in the early evening hours. In addition, a private corporation is building a somewhat similar facility on an adjacent site. In it, solar energy will be collected and concentrated by 5,300 parabolic trough collectors, with the heat used to generate steam for an electric turbine. It is designed to produce twelve megawatts of electricity for sale to SCE.

The use of solar energy for heating, cooling, and the production of electricity has a great deal of appeal. It is non-polluting, inexhaustible, and free for the taking. Skeptics, however, insist that even under the ideal conditions of the sunny Southwest, wringing energy from the sun is inefficient with present technology. For example, the energy requirements for the production of silicon photovoltaic cells is high, equal to the electricity they will produce in five years of operation. As their useful life is only ten years, and other energy consuming materials are needed in constructing the facility, their inefficiency is obvious. Similarly, it is calculated that the energy required to produce the materials in a solar thermal electric plant is equivalent to five years production from the plant. The useful life of the plant is unknown; it may be several decades. On the other hand, conventional power plants "pay back" their energy requirements in two or three years and have a useful life of thirty years. One reason for governmental subsidies for solar facilities is to test the accuracy of these figures.

Geothermal energy—energy from the heat of the earth's core or magma—is another possibility for the future. Here the technology is further advanced. Electricity has been produced from geothermal heat at The Geysers in northern California for more than twenty years. DWP and SCE have contributed to the financing of a number of "wildcat" exploratory wells in the Mono Lake region and around Lake Crowley. All were failures. The Imperial Valley, however, appears to be a reliable source of geothermal energy. Even so, there are problems. At The Geysers superheated steam is available. In the Imperial Valley, by contrast, the geothermal resource is hot water, a much less efficient source of energy. The water contains high concentrations of salts which clogs

and corrodes the pipes. There is also the possibility of air pollution from non-condensable gases such as hydrogen sulfide which are present in the thermal fluids. In addition, the problem of disposing of large quantities of mineral waste is formidable. Land subsidence apparently can be avoided by injecting the unwanted waste water into the producing zone of the reservoir. Considerable noise is also characteristic of geothermal operations. Nevertheless, geothermal development is under way. Both the DWP and SCE are involved in a ten megawatt demonstration facility near Brawley already in operation. Several other plants of similar size are under construction near the Salton Sea.

The Metropolis is not noted for high and constant winds; just the opposite is true. However, SCE has several experimental wind turbine generators located in San Gorgonio Pass just west of Palm Springs, one of the windiest spots in the Metropolis. In addition, the company is soliciting proposals from private developers who will install their own generators, and will purchase wind power from any commercial "wind-park" in the SCE service area.

Consumption of Electricity

How is electricity used in the Metropolis? Table 9.2 illustrates the consumption of electricity in the city of Los Angeles, a pattern that is probably about typical for the region as a whole. It is significant that commercial users consume forty-eight percent of all electricity utilized. These users include office buildings, shopping centers, wholesale houses, schools, public buildings, and hospitals. Residential use—single-family homes and apartments—amounts to much less, twenty-seven percent. Most of the remaining power is used by industry, amounting to twenty-three percent. The vast majority of customers, though, are the residential users, each consuming a relatively small amount of electricity as compared to other users. Historically, utilities have

Table 9.2
Los Angeles Department of Water and Power
Retail Electricity Sales, 1981

	No. of Customers	Av. Consumption in K.W.H.	K.W.H. in Billions	Percent
Residential	1,037,735	4,642	4.8	27
Commercial	148,333	57,009	8.5	48
Industrial	22,150	181,193	4.0	23
Street lighting and other	6,195	-----	0.4	2
Total	1,214,413	---	18.7	100

Source: Los Angeles Department of Water and Power, *Annual Report, 1980–81*. p. 27.

Table 9.3
Residential Uses of Electrical Energy in Los Angeles

Use	Percent
Refrigerators and freezers	29.5
Lighting and other appliances	27.7
Air conditioners	13.1
Television	11.6
Resistance heating	5.2
Water heaters	3.3
Pool filter pumps	2.8
Range	2.5
Clothes washers and dryers	2.0
Dishwashers	1.7
Evaporative coolers and heat pumps	0.6
Total	100.0

Source: LADWP, *Consumer Guide to DWP Services*, 1981, p. 20.

charged these small customers higher rates, justifying this procedure on the basis that constructing and maintaining lines, installing and reading meters for these small users is relatively costly compared to serving the relatively few commercial users who, in a sense, buy electricity in bulk lots.

Whereas the commercial users form the major consumers, the collective citizenry commands more than one-fourth of the region's electricity. Table 9.3 illustrates how the average home puts this electricity to use. Note that if the electricity used for refrigerators and freezers and air conditioners is combined, more than forty-two percent of all electricity used in the home is accounted for. In Los Angeles, cooling is the big item. Lighting and small miscellaneous appliances are the next largest users with nearly twenty-eight percent. Television sets consume nearly twelve percent. Water heating and resistance heating (the sort of heaters often found in bathrooms), perhaps not the most efficient way to use electricity, have declined to only about eight percent. Any plans for conservation must take into account these proportionate uses.

The Management and Conservation of Electricity

For the years ahead a program emphasizing the efficient management of electricity use is clearly called for, and conservation should be an important part of the program. The careful use of electricity has not been a major goal of our architects, engineers, and designers until recently. Many improvements can be made, given new priorities. The design of any building, home, office, or whatever, should be such that summer sunlight would never fall on a glass surface—each floor of a multistoried building might have an overhang, for example. Outside windows could be made of thermal panes or solar reflective glass. All homes and buildings should be thoroughly insulated; even the choice of exterior colors is important. Air conditioning thermostats can be set at seventy-five degrees and the system designed in such a way that they use outside air whenever the temperature makes it possible. More efficient lighting systems are available—fluorescent lights use appreciably less energy than incandescent lamps, and, for commercial purposes, sodium vapor lights are even more efficient. For commercial and industrial buildings various peak-load controlling devices that shed less essential loads are considered helpful. For example, a device may automatically shut off the water heater while the elevator is operating, turn off machinery when it is not in use, and so on. These latter devices do not reduce the total demand for energy, but help control the critical peak load problem. Other new additions to local building codes include interlock heating and cooling equipment to prevent simultaneous operation, automatic closing doors leading to all commercial and industrial air conditioned space, and prohibition of new "air curtain door" installations.

Other conservation methods are tied to rate incentives and penalties for the misuse of energy. Energy conservation results when a master meter for an apartment complex is replaced with individual meters. The SCE has submitted a proposal to the California Public Utilities Commission to institute time-of-day pricing for commercial and industrial users; that is, to charge more for electricity during periods of high system use and less for electricity used in non-peak periods. Another proposal is for "rate incentives," where rates rise sharply after some average "base" amount of electricity is used. The increase in efficiency of electrical appliances might be encouraged through publicity or legislation. For example, if all the window air conditioners in Los Angeles were of the most efficient brand, it would save the system some 250,000,000 kwh annually, or enough electricity for 50,000 average residential customers. The prohibition of automatic defrost refrigerators would similarly save enough electricity to serve 20,000 people.

It should be emphasized, however, that many conservation practices are difficult to achieve. Often they require an additional outlay of money; an energy-efficient appliance may cost more than one that wastes energy, for example. Although they may save money in the long run, that inducement may not be enough to encourage the initial expense. Similarly, attempts to lower peak demand through time-of-day pricing have all sorts of practical difficulties. Commercial users, for example, resist the concept by arguing that they need to have their air conditioning going, lights burning, and escalators running when the customers are present—a time that often coincides with peak demand hours. They insist that higher electric costs will simply be shifted along in the form of higher prices. Factories might adjust by shifting more work to the "graveyard shift," but any savings in electricity might be balanced by increased labor costs. However, if a factory can shift energy-consuming operations to off-peak hours, some real economies may be possible.

9. Suggested Readings

The current sources and future plans for electrical energy for the Metropolis can be found in the Annual Reports of the Southern California Edison Company, and the Los Angeles Department of Water and Power. The publications of these utilities are replete with data and describe the events of the past year in some detail.

Useful information applicable to the region can also be found in the various publications of the California Energy Conservation and Development Commission. Two publications, *Energy Challenges and Opportunities for California. Biennial Report,* 1981, and *Electricity for Tomorrow, Final Report,* 1981, are particularly useful. They review the ten year resource plans of each utility and make suggestions as to which plants might be shut down, where expansion might take place, and discuss the role of conservation in energy demand forecasts.

10

The Metropolis before the Gringo

Figure 10.1. San Gabriel Mission, one of the most prosperous in California, is shown here in a lithograph by G. and W. Endicott, circa 1820s. (Photo courtesy California Historical Society/Title Insurance and Trust Co. (L.A.) Collection of Historical Photographs.)

"The earth grew ever to the southward and the people followed," Gabrielino creation legend. Bernice Eastman Johnston (1962, p. 3).

"A short gallop over the hills brought us in sight of the "Pueblo de los Angeles," situated about three leagues from St. Gabriel, and about twenty miles from the bay of St. Pedro. The population of this town is about fifteen hundred. . . . In the vicinity are many vineyards and cornfields, and some fine gardens, crossed by beautiful streams of water. The lands being level and fertile, are capable of great agricultural improvement; and several Americans, taking advantage of the resources of the place, are living here, having storehouses, and are engaged in business." A description of Los Angeles in 1829. Alfred Robinson (1971, p. 25).

Indians Occupy the Land

No one knows for how many centuries human beings have drifted through or occupied the land of the Metropolis; it may be in the order of 10,000 years, perhaps much longer. At the time Europeans arrived it is estimated that from 5,000 to 10,000 Indians were living in the local area. These were comparatively recent arrivals, residents for perhaps 1,000 years and a separate linguistic group. The languages spoken in the San Diego and Ventura areas were completely different. The local tribes were spread from Malibu to Laguna Beach, the northern limit was the San Gabriel and the adjoining mountains and included the offshore islands—a region that generally coincides with our modern Metropolis. They lived in villages, small collections of round, symmetrical huts, "like half an orange," made of tules over a frame of willow branches. The exact number of settlements is unknown, there may have been about forty, clustered along the coast and beside the rivers. Although a definite group they had no name for themselves. As a result, they have been called the *Gabrielino* after their assignment, by the early Spanish missionary fathers, to the Mission San Gabriel, the final event in their tribal life.

The Gabrielino were one of the most advanced tribes south of the Tehachapi. Krober spoke of them as beyond question the "wealthiest and most thoughtful of all of the Shoshoneans of the state" and asserts they "dominated (other tribes) civilizationally whenever contacts occurred. Their influence spread even to alien peoples. They have melted away so completely that we know more of the fine facts of the culture of ruder tribes, but everything points to these very efflorescences having had their origin with the Gabrielino." For example, the religious use of a drug made from the Jimson weed was widespread, but the cult, its mythology, "the ritual actions and songs that constitute its body, were worked out primarily if not wholly by the Gabrielino. . . ." (Krober, 1925, p. 621). It would appear that initiating fads and inventing religions is an old Los Angeles custom.

The Gabrielino were industrious hunters and gatherers and made effective use of the food resources of the southern California landscape. They were not farmers; there seems to have been no need for them to be. In fact, their activities sustained a population density surpassed in only two other places in the United States. There was plenty of food available in the wild landscape, especially acorns in the valleys and shellfish along the shore. A staple was the acorn, of which tons were produced by the local oaks. The nuts could be pounded to a meal in mortars, and the bitter tannin leached from it in leaf-lined baskets set into sand basins. The mush was then boiled and eaten cold. The seeds of many grasses and bushes could be parched in a basket of hot coals. Other vegetable food included the pits of wild plums ground into meal, yucca shoots, cactus fruits gathered with tongs, and even the "honey dew" left by the aphids as a sticky secretion on the plants they fed upon.

Animals, too, contributed to the Indians' nourishment. Bernice Johnston (1962, p. 33) describes the variety in their eating habits. "Every small and large animal that roamed the plains and foothills . . . was hunted or snared to add to the Gabrielino diet. Deadfalls with acorn triggers yielded small game, communal drives sent scores of rabbits into waiting nets, rats' nests were burned and gophers lured from their holes. Hunters went out for deer and antelope, equipped with head and back disguises of the animals' antlers and skins and a knowledge of every mannerism of the quarry to make possible the close approach necessary for a clean arrow shot. The range of fish and bird and insect ran from the stranded whale downward to the yellowjacket larva and the caterpillar, which was served after toasting to a crisp." Shellfish, fish, seals, and sea otter were important items in the diet of the villagers who lived near the sea.

It seems to be agreed that the men wore no clothing, whereas the women had a skin wrapped around the waist. This might be a deer skin in the valleys, the skin of a sea otter near the coast. Both groups were covered at night by rabbit skins, "sewn together in the form of a bedspread." The women wove beautiful baskets and made pots from the steatite, or soapstone, found on Catalina Island. These were superior to pottery utensils. "One could hardly induce food to burn in them, they could be mended with asphalt if broken, or a handle affixed to turn a large fragment into a frying pan" (Johnston, 1962, p. 31). Steatite was also used in making beads, pipes, carvings of fish, seals, whales, and ceremonial bowls. The men near the sea, particularly those in the islands, made sewn plank boats, used for fishing. The wood was split from the trees by whalebone wedges, smoothed on the wet sand of the beach, holes made in the planks with chert drills, laced together by deerskin cords, and caulked with hot bitumen. Although these boats made sea voyages to distant places like Saint Nicholas Island, sixty miles from San Pedro, constant bailing, using large abalone shells, was necessary.

The Gabrielino often worked hard, whenever it was necessary, especially during the season for harvesting acorns or seeds. They never worked longer than they had to, however. They used their leisure playing games, "endless variations of cat's cradle, archery practice, a lively hoop and pole game" (Johnston, 1962, p. 72) and a gambling game involving guessing which hand held the prize. Further, according to Johnston (1962, p. 35), "sun bathing was a recognized and respectable occupation, and basking in warm springs a luxury for which every Indian yearned." The goal of the good life, it would seem, has been a natural occurrence in these lands for thousands of years.

Today these Indians have disappeared, leaving few if any survivors. What then is the significance of their centuries of occupance to the present Metropolis? It was their presence, and their reported docility and friendliness that brought the Spaniards into the area originally. They located the missions—the padres built them where the Indian population was the most dense. They provided the labor at mission and pueblo alike. As McWilliams (1946, p. 23) puts it, "They cleared the ground, planted the first vineyards, constructed the irrigation ditches and canals, and built the Missions." Later they were to provide the labor for the ranchos. Their usefulness was immense and their helpfulness can be inferred from the report that they easily learned to speak Spanish without an accent. They were familiar with the land and showed the explorers the easy routes through the mountains—some of these early trails have become today's highways. A few Indian place names survive in Spanish-American spellings of the original sounds: Topanga, Pacoima, Saticoy, Cucamonga, Azusa, Cahuenga (Place of the mountain), and Malibu (Place where mountains run out to the sea). Further, some would argue, the availability of docile Indian labor made possible a system of agriculture noted for its backwardness and its dependence on cheap labor, a pattern which to some extent still exists. Finally, McWilliams (1946, p. 23), writing in 1946 felt that "the brutal treatment of Indians in southern California in large part explains the persistence of an ugly racial arrogance in the mores of the region of which, alas, more than a vestige remains."

Envoys of Spain Discover and Describe the Los Angeles Coast

The year was 1542. Only fifty years earlier Columbus had sailed across the Atlantic and discovered the New World. Only thirty years had passed since Balboa had first seen the Pacific from a peak in Darien. Cortez had conquered the Aztec capital at Mexico City only twenty years before. Although much of the land mass had been occupied, great stretches of the Pacific side of New Spain were still unknown. Ships were built in the waters of the west coast to aid in its exploration, and Juan Rodríguez Cabrillo was given command of two of the vessels. He was directed to sail northward to look for "Cathay" and to search for the "Strait of Anian," the supposed water route to the Atlantic.

What Cabrillo found was California. A summary of his journal exists and it records the first European impression of the southern California landscape. Cabrillo, it should be noted, was no ordinary sailing captain. He had been with Cortez during the capture of the wondrous Tenochtitlán and was one of the conquerors of Guatemala, El Salvador, and Nicaragua. He had seen much of the New World, was a sophisticated observer, and no longer was easily impressed.

Cabrillo and his two ships left San Diego Bay October 3, 1542 and continued northward along the coast for three days. During this time "they saw many valleys and plains and many smokes and sierras inland" (Wagner, 1941, p. 46). They visited the islands of San Clemente and Santa Catalina, anchoring and going ashore (at Avalon?). Here, "a great number of Indians came out of the bushes and grass, shouting, dancing and making signs to come ashore." They went and "everybody felt very secure." In addition, the Indians launched "a fine canoe containing eight or ten Indians" which came out to the ships (Wagner, 1941, p. 46).

On the 8th of October, "they came to the mainland in a large bay (San Pedro) which they named 'Baia de los Fumos' on account of the many smokes they saw there. . . . The bay . . . is an excellent harbor and the country is good with many valleys, plains, and groves of trees" (Wagner, 1941, p. 47). Again, they encountered friendly Indians in a canoe. The following day they continued up the coast

"anchoring in a large *ensenada,*" presumably Santa Monica Bay. They sailed further along the coast, stopping next at what is thought to have been Point Mugu. Here they "saw on land an Indian town close to the sea with large houses like those of New Spain, and they anchored in front of a large valley on the coast. Here many fine canoes holding twelve or thirteen Indians each came to the ships . . . they named the town 'Pueblo de las Canoas.' The people wear some animal skins, are fishermen, and eat raw fish as well as maguey. The country within is a very beautiful valley, and the Indians explained that inland in that valley there was much maize and food. Beyond this valley some high, very broken sierras were visible" (Wagner, 1941, p. 47). The party landed, took possession and stayed for several days before moving on. The ships continued northward along the coast discovering more "beautiful and well populated valleys" and "good country with fine plains" (Wagner, 1941, p. 48). Cabrillo died on the voyage, but Ferreli, his pilot, reached at least Point Arena before heading back to New Spain.

Vizcaíno Selects the Place Names

Although ships returning from Manila to Acapulco sometimes coasted California, they seldom stopped, and when they did it was not in southern California. The next thorough exploration of our coast was postponed for sixty years (1602–3), when a merchant contractor, Sebastian Vizcaíno, sailed northward, surveying the shore in detail from Acapulco to Oregon. The names he gave to places, often taken from the calendar of saints, have remained on many coastal features.

Vizcaíno and his three ships spent ten days in San Diego Bay (which they named). Reconnoitering the coast, which "was very verdant," they passed an island they named San Clemente and anchored at another island they called Santa Catalina. Indians, "well built and

126

robust" in eight oared, plank canoes ("they go flying") met the expedition. They were invited to come ashore and at a village were given "roasted sardines and small fruit like sweet potatoes." The women are described as being "well featured and well built, of good countenance . . . affable and smiling." Houses were "like cabins . . . they cover these with a mat of rushes very tightly woven. . . ." The people "live by buying, selling and bartering." They were given a grain in "wicker baskets very well made," and noticed water vessels resembling flasks, "ratten inside and thickly varnished outside." A fishing device like a harpoon by which sea otters were taken is also described. They "saw many fires, both on the mainland and on the island" and thought they were "signals for ships to enter." They concluded, "The Indians are affable, friendly, and eager to know what is going on" (Wagner, 1929, pp. 234–239, Bolton, 1930, p. 85).

On November 29, 1602, Vizcaíno entered a bay which he named San Pedro. On December 1st, the ships sailed northward, through a fog, and passed a point they called "Conbersion," but this name did not stick. It is now Point Hueneme. He went on to discover Monterey Bay, which he touted as an excellent harbor, and created an interest in that spot which lasted for two hundred years.

One of the diarists on Vizcaíno's expedition wrote of finding ambergris (a waxy secretion of sperm whales) at San Diego and thought it would be a possible source of wealth along the entire coast. He also felt that because of the golden flowers growing there they would surely find gold nearby. But even without such speculation, an objective reading of the diaries of these two expeditions gives one a positive impression of the coast. It had many fine harbors, verdant valleys which seemed to be producing much food, a rich sea life, and friendly Indians who appeared to have a reasonably high standard of living gained from resources near at hand. The mountains in the background would provide a steady source of water. The many smokes might have been a puzzle—they still are. Were they signal fires, grass fires to aid in hunting, or wildfires in the brush? In a covering letter to the Viceroy, one of Vizcaíno's diarists characterized the contents of his volume as "containing an Account of the Riches, the Temperate Climate, and the Advantages of the Realm of the Californias" (Bolton, 1930, p. 105).

The First Land Party— 1769

Cabrillo and Vizcaíno had described the California coast in optimistic terms, and their accounts were not forgotten, but were incorporated almost verbatim in the most popular navigation guidebooks of the era. Activity in the rest of New Spain occupied the conquerors, however, and more than two centuries passed before a land party was sent into the area. Even then it was forces outside the region—exaggerated reports of Russian (and perhaps English) activity in the north Pacific—that moved the authorities to action, rather than the intrinsic attractions of southern California. The Council of War that convened in May, 1768 ordered an expedition to occupy the port of Monterey and to secure it for the crown through the founding of a presidio and mission.

Don José de Galvéz, the Visitor General of New Spain, sent out the expedition in four parts, two by land and two by sea, to rendezvous in San Diego. They were to explore and settle, if possible, the port of San Diego on the way to Monterey. The ultimate goal was to incorporate the territory into the Spanish domain by making friends with the Indians and founding missions to spread the faith and advance civilization.

The two land parties had a rugged trip pioneering a trail up the Baja peninsula, and the two ships had a disastrous journey, arriving with most of both crews sick or dying. Captain Gaspar de Portolá, as officer in charge of the entire project, determined to press on to Monterey and started out from San Diego July 14, 1769 "with that small company of persons, or rather say skeletons, who had been spared by scurvy, hunger and thirst" (Cleland, 1929, p. 123).

Actually, for an exploring party on the far frontier it seems to have been reasonably large (sixty-seven men) and well supplied. It was also well organized. Riding far ahead was Sergeant José Francisco Ortega, a "great scout," who located Indian trails the group could follow and selected the streams for overnight camps. The order of march of the main party, as reported in Costansó's diary was as follows:

"At the head rode the commander (Portolá) with the officers (Lt. Pedro Fages, Miguel Costansó, color-sergeant of engineers and cosmographer, Father Frey Juan Crespi, chaplain and official diarist, and Father Francisco Gómez), the six men of the Catalan volunteers, and some friendly Indians with spades, pick-axes, crowbars, axes, and other implements used by sappers to cut the brush and to open a passage whenever necessary. Next followed the pack train (of 100 mules) which was separated into four divisions, each one with its muleteers and an adequate number of soldiers of the garrison as an escort. In the rearguard came Captain Fernando de Rivera, with the rest of the soldiers and friendly Indians, convoying the spare horses and mules" (Cleland, 1929, p. 123).

Although they were marching into *terra incognita,* they were not completely ignorant of what lay ahead. They had as a guide book the standard navigators' handbook, *Navegación Especulativo y Práctico,* that summarized all known information of the coast, mainly from the voyages of Cabrillo and Vizcaíno, including descriptions of coastal islands, headlands, and ports, complete with their latitudes. So they hugged the coast on their journey, not only because they were heading for Monterey, but because they could take advantage of the information in their guidebook. For example, Crespi, on a hill near El Toro, wrote of seeing two islands which "must be San Clemente and Santa Catalina"

and then reasons "the bay of San Pedro must be about five leagues distant from our camp" (Bolton, 1927, p. 138). Farther on, Costansó, the other diarist, arriving at the coast on the Oxnard Plain, saw a large town: "We thought that this was the town which the first Spanish navigators, among others Rodríquez Cabrillo, named *Pueblo de Canoas"* (Teggart, p. 17).

Entering the Metropolis

As the party entered the area now part of the Metropolis at about El Toro, they followed the base of the Santa Ana Mountains northward, feeling that there the streams would have more water in them than out on the plain. (Remember, they had spent the preceding months plodding up the dry length of Baja.) They named Santiago Creek, which Crespi described as "an arroyo of running water, although it was evident that it was diminishing because of the drought and little by little the waters were being absorbed by the sand." Coming to the Santa Ana River they found "a bed of running water about ten varas wide (thirty-five or forty feet) and a half a vara deep. It is not at all boxed in by banks. . . . It is evident from the sand on its banks that in the rainy season it must have great floods which would prevent crossing it." Even in July they "crossed the river with much difficulty, on account of the swiftness of the current." And the San Gabriel River was "a good channel of water, which when measured was found to have a volume of three quarters of a square yard . . . in order to cross the arroyo it was necessary to make a bridge of poles, because it was miry" (Bolton, 1927, pp. 140–144).

The land and its vegetation was also of interest. As they arrived south of Santa Ana they "entered a large plain, the end of which we could not see. . . ." The bed of the Santa Ana River "is well grown with sycamores, alders, willows and other trees we have not recognized." In the vicinity "is a great deal of good land which can easily be irrigated." To the northeast, "near the river the mountains have many prickly pears and much sage, but afterwards all the land continues fertile and is well covered with good grass." As the party crossed the Puente Hills looking toward El Monte, Crespi writes, "We then descended to a broad and spacious plain of fine black earth, with much grass, although we found it burned." The San Gabriel River was flowing "among many green marshes, their banks covered with willows and grapes, blackberries and innumerable Castilian rosebushes loaded with roses." The next day they traveled "through brush and low woods, which delayed us a long time, making it necessary to cut the brush down at every step that was taken" (Bolton, 1927, pp. 139–145).

Indians appeared in abundance, reflecting the productivity of the land. In the El Toro area they visited a village where the Indians "have houses made of willows and large baskets of reeds so tightly woven that they hold water." On the right bank of the Santa Ana River was a village of "prosperous Indians." "Fifty-two of them came to camp" asking the explorers to stay and saying that they would provide "food, such as antelope, hares and seeds." They exchanged presents, for beads and a silk handkerchief receiving "two baskets of seeds, already made into pinole, together with a string of beads made of shells such as they wear." At La Brea Canyon north of Fullerton, a "whole village, which numbered more than seventy souls, came to visit us." Along the San Gabriel River the soldiers "brought in an antelope, with which this country abounds . . . I tasted the roasted meat, it was not bad" (Bolton, 1927, pp. 139–146).

While camping on the Santa Ana River Crespi wrote, "I called this place the sweet name of *Jesus de los Temblores,* because we experienced here a horrifying earthquake, which was repeated four times during the day. The first, which was the most violent, happened at one in the afternoon and the last one

about four." Just two days later, "In the afternoon, we felt another earthquake." And the next day, "At half past eight in the morning we felt another earthquake." And the next day, too, August 1st, "At ten in the morning the earth trembled. The shock was repeated with violence at one in the afternoon, and one hour afterwards we experienced another" (Bolton, 1927, pp. 142–146). And the next day they were to feel three more in the afternoon and night. So there seem to have been thirteen earthquakes within the span of a few days. Costansó describes the reaction of a local resident. "One of the natives who, no doubt, held the office of priest among them, was at the time in camp. Bewildered, no less than we, by the event, he began, with horrible cries and great manifestations of terror, to entreat the heavens, turning in all directions, and acting as though he would exorcise the elements" (Teggart, p. 17). Apparently the "priest" had experienced earthquakes before and knew just what to do.

During the next four days the party crossed the Los Angeles lowland and moved into the San Fernando Valley. It seems worthwhile to quote the words of the first European observers verbatim, first from the diary of Juan Crespi, and for the last day from that of Miguel Costansó. Actually, the accounts of these two men are remarkably similar.

The Diaries of Crespi and Costansó

"Wednesday, August 2—We set out from the valley in the morning and followed the same plain in a westerly direction. After traveling about a league and a half through a pass between low hills, we entered a very spacious valley, well grown with cottonwoods and alders, among which ran a beautiful river (Los Angeles River) from the north-northwest, and then, doubling the point of a steep hill, it went on afterwards to the south. Toward the north-northeast there is another river bed which forms a spacious water-course, but we found it dry (Arroyo Seco). This bed unites with that of the river, giving a clear indication of great floods in the rainy season, for we saw that it had many trunks of trees on the banks. We halted not very far from the river, which we named Porciúncula. (Camp probably near North Broadway in Lincoln Heights.) Here we felt three consecutive earthquakes in the afternoon and night. We must have traveled about three leagues today. This plain where the river runs is very extensive. It has good land for planting all kinds of grain and seeds and is the most suitable site of all that we have seen for a mission, for it has all the requisites for a large settlement. As soon as we arrived, about eight heathen from a good village came to visit us; they live in this delightful place among the trees on the river. They presented us with some baskets of pinole made from seeds of sage and other grasses. Their chief brought some strings of beads made of shells, and they threw us three handfuls of them. Some of the old men were smoking pipes well made of baked clay and they puffed at us three mouthfuls of smoke. We gave them a little tobacco and glass beads, and they went away well pleased.

"Thursday, August 3—At half-past six we left the camp and forded the Porciúncula River, which runs down from the valley, flowing through it from the mountains into the plain. After crossing the river we entered a large vineyard of wild grapes and an infinity of rosebushes in full bloom. All the soil is black and loamy, and is capable of producing every kind of grain and fruit which may be planted. We went west, continually, over good land well covered with grass. After traveling about half a league we came to the village of this region, the people of which on seeing us came out into the road. As they drew near us they began to howl like wolves; they greeted us and wished to give us seeds, but as we had nothing at hand in which to carry them we did not accept them. Seeing this, they threw some handfuls of them on the ground and the rest in the air. We traveled over another plain for three hours, during which we must have gone as many leagues. In the same plain we came across a grove of very large alders, high and thick, from which flows a stream of water about a buey in depth. The banks were grassy and covered with fragrant herbs and watercress. The water flowed afterwards in a deep channel towards the southwest. All the land that we saw this morning seemed admirable to us. We pitched camp near the water. (Ballona Creek, west of La Cienega.) This afternoon we felt new earthquakes, the continuation of which astonishes us. We judge

that in the mountains that run to the west in front of us there are some volcanoes, for there are many signs on the road which stretches between the Porciúncula River and the Spring of the Alders, for the explorers saw some large marshes of a certain substance like pitch; they were boiling and bubbling, and the pitch came out mixed with an abundance of water. They noticed that the water runs to one side and the pitch to the other, and that there is such an abundance of it that it would serve to caulk many ships. This place where we stopped is called the Spring of the Alders of San Estevan.

"Friday, August 4—At half-past six in the morning we set out from the camp, following the plain to the northwest. At a quarter of a league we came to a little valley between small hills and continued over plains of level land, very black and with much pasturage. After two hours' travel, during which we must have covered about two leagues, we stopped at the watering place which consists of two little springs that rise at the foot of a higher mesa. (Perhaps where University High School is now located.) From each of the two springs runs a small stream of water which is soon absorbed; they are both full of watercress and innumerable bushes of Castilian roses. We made camp near the springs where we found a good village of very friendly and docile Indians, who, as soon as we arrived, came to visit us bringing their present of baskets of sage and other seeds, small, round nuts with a hard shell, and large and very sweet acorns. They made me a present of some strings of beads of white and red shells which resemble coral, though not very fine; we reciprocated with glass beads. I understood that they were asking us if we were going to stay, and I said "No," that we were going farther on. I called this place San Gregorio, but to the soldiers the spot is known as the Springs of El Berrendo because they caught a deer alive there, it having had a leg broken the preceding afternoon by a shot fired by one of the volunteer soldiers who could not overtake it. The water is in a hollow surrounded by low hills not far from the sea" (Bolton, 1927, pp. 146–150).

"Saturday, August 5—The scouts who had set out to examine the coast and the road along the beach returned shortly afterwards with the news of having reached a high, steep cliff terminating in the sea where the mountains end, absolutely cutting off the passage along the shore. This forced us to seek a way through the mountains, and we found it although it was rough and difficult.

"We then set out from the Ojos del Berrendo in the afternoon, and, directing our course to the northwest towards the point where there appeared to be an opening in the range, we entered the mountains through a canyon formed by steep hills on both sides." (Presumably Sepulveda Pass.) "At the end of the canyon, however, the hills were somewhat more accessible and permitted us to take the slope and, with much labor, to ascend to the summit, whence we discerned a very large and pleasant valley." (San Fernando Valley.) "We descended to it and halted near the watering-place, which consisted of a very large pool." (Near Encino.) "Near this there was a populous Indian village, and the inhabitants were very good-natured and peaceful. They offered us their seeds in trays or baskets of rushes, and came to the camp in such numbers that had they been armed, they might have caused us apprehension, as we counted as many as two hundred and five, including men, women, and children. All of them offered us something to eat, and we, in turn, gave them our glass beads and ribbons. We made three leagues on this day's journey. To the valley we gave the name of Santa Catalina;" (or Valle de los Encinos) "it is about three leagues in width and more than eight in length, and is entirely surrounded by hills" (Teggart, p. 23–25).

The main description of the area ends at about this point. They rested at Encino the next day, received many visitors, some of whom drew a map on the ground showing the shape of the channel islands, and indicating the route of ships they had seen. The following day they marched about three leagues northward across the San Fernando Valley, camping northwest of the future site of Mission San Fernando "in a very green valley grown with large live oaks and alders." The next morning they crossed San Fernando Pass to Newhall, then down along the Santa Clara River to the coast at Ventura. They saw many Indian villages, received many presents of seeds, acorns, nuts, and pine nuts, found many canoes in the water, and August 13 felt two more earthquakes. On the coast they found "a real town," and pitched their camp a short distance away.

After journeying north they discovered San Francisco Bay, but were so unimpressed with Monterey Bay that they almost missed it. The party returned in January, traveling rapidly. This time, on the advice of Indians, they entered the San Fernando Valley through Calabasas Pass, left by Cahuenga Pass and camped above the present Hollywood. From there, "on entering the plain we saw towards the east a chain of mountains covered with snow." As they crossed the Los Angeles River they observed "on its sands rubbish, fallen trees, and pools on either side, for a few days previously there had been a great flood" (Bolton, 1927, pp. 269–271).

And so they returned to San Diego. They had not founded a settlement on Monterey Bay, but they had discovered the more important bay at San Francisco, and they pioneered a trail up the California coast that was to form the broad outline of *El Camino Real*.

There was no more talk of amber and golden flowers indicating gold. Nevertheless the comments of the travelers indicate they felt they had found a promising land. It had streams for irrigation, something generally lacking in Lower California. There were fertile valleys which could be irrigated, grass was abundant in the winter, and the natives were numerous and friendly. True, distances were great, and transportation and travel difficult, but a land route had been placed through Baja and all the way to beyond Monterey. The only disquieting features were the almost continuous earthquakes in the Los Angeles area, but even these had ceased by the time the party returned.

A Chain of Missions Is Created: Including San Gabriel

A mission and presidio were established at San Diego while Portolá was on his journey north, and on a second trip he established a presidio at Monterey June 3, 1770, and founded Mission San Carlos nearby. A new group of Franciscans arrived the next year enabling Mission San Antonio de Padua to be founded one hundred twenty-five miles south of Monterey. Mission San Gabriel was founded September 8, 1771. Although in all twenty-one missions were founded along El Camino Real, in the area of our concern San Buenaventura was not founded until 1782, and San Fernando was a late addition, coming in 1797.

Father Junípero Serra, president of the missions, sent two of the Franciscans, Fathers Somera and Cambón, to San Diego by ship. Here they were joined by their guards and set out for the "River of Earthquakes" to found Mission San Gabriel on the site of Portolá's earlier camp. However, they did not find the location on the Santa Ana suitable and continued on to a spot on the present Rio Hondo (at about the point where that stream is crossed by San Gabriel Boulevard). However, the crops were "drowned out" the first year, and trouble reoccurred in the second year, also.

Father Fermín de Lasuén, a proven administrator, was put in charge to develop the "unusual farming opportunities" that were thought to exist at San Gabriel. Arriving in 1772, he found a group of small structures made of poles and roofed with grass, ten neophyte huts, all enclosed in a stockade. He proposed moving the mission to a more suitable place he seems to have picked out. It was about five miles away, at the site of the present mission. The relocation was accomplished in 1775. A few more years of struggle passed, but nine years later seven hundred thirty-nine neophytes were on the mission rolls, and some 4,000 livestock roamed its extensive ranches. Its growth was steady, and for fifty years it was to be a major center of activity in southern California.

Los Angeles Is Founded as a Pueblo by Governor Felipe de Neve

August 4, 1781, is considered to be the founding date of Los Angeles, but the genesis of the city is much earlier. It was in 1777 that de Neve, the new governor of California, transferred the seat of government to Monterey. On his journey north along Portolá's trail he inspected the three presidios and eight missions along the way. What was missing, he felt, was sufficient food-raising capacity, a lack that could be remedied by adding a few country towns—pueblos—of farmers and stock raisers. His experience in Baja had taught him that prime requisites for agricultural communities were a year around supply of water and arable land that could be irrigated, and he noted several such locations along the trail. He asked that he be sent some farmers and proposed that two pueblos be established, one on the Porciúncula River (Los Angeles) near Mission San Gabriel, and the other on the Guadalupe (San José) near Mission Santa Clara. A few farmers were identified among the soldiers at San Francisco and Monterey, and the pueblo of San José was founded forthwith. Los Angeles would have to wait until some new families arrived from Mexico.

It was not until February, 1780, that Captain Rivera began recruiting an authorized twenty-four married settlers and their families for the Los Angeles settlement. They were to be offered lands in California, ten pesos a month for three years, plus a daily allowance of rations. Complete personal outfits from saddles to shoes would be furnished each settler, as well as his farming needs: two cows, two oxen, two horses, three mares, one mule, two ewes, two goats, and tools, and equipment. Repayment was to come out of future production. Surely this was a generous bounty that might attract an immigrant in even today's affluent society.

Recruiting the first civilian settlers for California proved extremely difficult. Perhaps the standards were too high, "Men of the soil. . . . Healthy, robust and without a known vice or defect. . . ." (DeCrois, 1931, p. 12). More likely the distance was too great, the location too isolated, and the unknowns too significant. In any event, Rivera traveled about five hundred miles over a period of a year among the settlements of Sonora and Sinaloa and was able to recruit only fourteen families before giving up in despair. Even so, two of these deserted before the small group left their rendezvous at Los Alamos. The recruits came from the most poverty-stricken groups in the area, and were all illiterate. Racially, "only two could claim to be Spanish, the rest being Indian, Negro, and mixed blood" (Caughey, 1970, p. 140). After more than six months on the road, and the loss of one settler to smallpox, they set up a temporary camp at San Gabriel July 14, 1781. The group now comprised eleven families, forty-four persons in all.

De Neve had been in residence at San Gabriel since May and apparently had picked out the exact site for the Los Angeles settlement. He also compiled detailed instructions for the laying out of the pueblo.

The town, he directed, should be located so that the boundary would include all the irrigable area, and the weir placed so the water would reach as much land as possible. The plaza and residences were to be placed as close to the river as feasible for the convenience of the settlers and so they could see their fields, but the town must be on ground high enough to be safe from floods. The plaza was to be two hundred feet wide by three hundred feet long, with its corners pointing to the cardinal directions of the compass so that the streets extending from them should not be exposed to the four winds. Around the plaza building lots of twenty by forty varas (fifty-five by one hundred ten feet) should be given out. The adjoining land across from the plaza on the east should be reserved for the church and government buildings. A vacant space, two hundred varas wide, should be left between the town and the planting fields to be given out as the population grew. The planting fields should be two hundred varas long and two hundred varas wide, as this size of tract could be planted with one bushel of corn. Each settler should draw in a lottery one building lot, two adjoining planting fields that were irrigable, and two that were not. All the rest of the land should be held in reserve in the name of the King and should be awarded gratuitously to later settlers. Each settler should have a share in the common water, pasturage, firewood, and lumber.

Settlers were also exempted from tithes or other taxes on their produce for five years. In return they were obliged to complete their homes, cultivate their fields, increase their stock, construct a weir and other public works. They were also obliged to sell their surplus at a fair price to the presidios and to reimburse the royal treasury for their initial assistance. It should be added that the land holdings of the pueblo contained four square leagues (about twenty-eight square miles) and the boundaries of the grant ran a league distant, "North, South, East and West from the center of the church door." This area, incidentally, became the original incorporated city of Los Angeles.

The settlers must have been taken to the site fairly soon after their arrival, the lots surveyed, and the work of clearing the brush begun. The assignment of the building plots and planting fields was then done by lot. On September 4th they left their temporary camp and moved to their new location. By the end of October the *Zanja Madre*, or main water ditch for diverting waters of the river, had been constructed, and the settlers were working on their homes. Corrals for the cattle and horses had been constructed, but the animals had not yet been distributed in order that the settlers would first devote their time and energy to completing the pueblo building. When that was completed they would begin leveling their fields and sowing grain. By November they had constructed their homes "which for the present were built of palisades, roofed with earth."

Five years later Sergeant José Dario Argüello arrived from the presidio at Santa Barbara and, on September 4, 1786, confirmed titles to the house lots, and planting lots, and recorded each settler's brand. None of the heads of families were able to write; all signed by making the sign of the cross.

The Los Angeles River entered the plain a few miles above the townsite, and at that time discharged a clear, steady flow from the saturated gravels underlying the San Fernando Valley. The stream constituted the overflow from a subterranean reservoir so its volume, though not large, was fairly constant as far down as the pueblo and beyond. Occasionally, in the winter, it was swollen by flood waters, becoming a turbulent river, filling its arroyo from bank to bank.

In selecting a site that could be irrigated but would escape winter flooding de Neve chose a terrace about half a mile west of the arroyo's edge and backing up against a range of low hills. A weir of brush and poles was constructed about two miles upstream where the river rounded the steep bluff of the Elysian Park Hills, and from here the water was dispersed into zanjas (ditches) over the surface of the terrace to the pueblo lots and the planting lots farther south. The ground was smooth, but with sufficient slope to insure good drainage.

The main irrigation ditch had to tap the river far enough above the pueblo so that the diverted water could flow by gravity to the terrace which was elevated above the stream level. Thus, the original intake was located north of the present North Broadway bridge. From this point the main ditch ran southward, following the base of a low scarp (Alameda Street?) to a point above the plaza. Here it divided into two major ditches, one of which carried the domestic water supply to the pueblo, the other, the irrigating water to the fields. The route of one of these ditches can still be seen crossing Olvera Street.

Agricultural Village, 1781–1821

The Pueblo of Los Angeles was founded as an agricultural village and for the first forty years of its development that is what it remained. The settlers were all recruited as farmers and were occupied in cultivating their irrigated fields and raising their stock. Their numbers steadily increased and they gradually built permanent homes. Two missions prospered in the hinterland, functioning as competing focal points, and indeed engaging in at least some manufacturing. A few ranchos gradually developed with sizable herds of cattle and horses. Still, in the pueblo itself, there was but a single occupation—agriculture. Here, as in much of the world, the farmers did not live on their land, but in the village—even the first rancho grant contained the clause that the grantee would "sleep at the pueblo" (Caughey, 1970, p. 88), that is, live in town. Theirs was a subsistence economy. There seem to have been no merchants; in fact, Bancroft (1886, II, p. 420) insists of the 1811–1820 period "Retail trade there was none. . . ." There appears to have been no commercial manufacturing although everyone raising grapes presumably made wine and brandy. The only professional was an occasional teacher for the village school.

Agriculture developed nicely. Slowly at first, and beset with discouragements such as "devastations of locusts," the pueblo soon was an agricultural success. As early as 1790 the pueblo "produced . . . more grain than any of the missions, except San Gabriel" (Bancroft, 1886, I, p. 461). Again, problems—in 1805 "all the corn, beans and pease (were) destroyed by the *chapule*" (Bancroft, 1886, II, p. 111). However, in 1810 the pueblo was reported to be producing between 3,000 and 4,000 *fanegas* (about 1.6 bushels) of wheat and corn. By 1817 Solá, the governor, was reporting that the settlers "had excellent lands, supplied much produce to the Presidio (Santa

Barbara) and, in fact, produced all there was a market for" (Bancroft, 1886, II, p. 350). Grapes were also becoming an important crop, and the Solá report for 1818 stated that the pueblo had 53,686 vines. By 1823 it was reported that Los Angeles had 10,623 cattle, 2,851 horses, one hundred eighty-three mules, ninety-six asses, and four hundred sixty-eight sheep. All in all a commendable achievement amply fulfilling the purpose of its founding.

The pueblo grew considerably in size and gradually took on a permanent look. From the eleven families and forty-four persons of the founding group the population had grown to one hundred forty by 1790, and more than doubled (to three hundred fifteen) in the next decade. The 1800–1810 period saw only modest growth, to three hundred sixty-five (including those on ranchos), but perhaps as many as fifty young men had been recruited to join the soldiers at the presidios. Boys could join the army when sixteen years old. Daughters often became wives of soldiers. On retirement, many returned to the pueblo. This cycle repeated itself, often for several generations. By 1820, the pueblo and ranchos held six hundred fifty persons.

This population was housed in a significant accumulation of buildings. One story, adobe structures, unpainted, with dirt floors, and with only hide covers for window and door, they were an ingenious use of local building materials and well-suited to the climate. Visitors invariably noted the roofs: flat, made of poles and reeds, covered with earth and then waterproofed with a layer of tar from the nearby tar pits. A plaza existed, but without public buildings or commercial structures to give it significance. There was no further mention of the town's adobe wall, presumably long since dissolved by the winter rains and not necessary for an inland village located among friendly Indians.

The Embryo Town, 1822–1846

Two unrelated events in 1822 signaled the beginning of the urban phase of pueblo life. One was the completion of a church on a new plaza, which would provide the attractive force necessary to give form and structure to the settlement. The second was the change in allegiance from Spain to Mexico, which removed many economic controls, reduced the competition of the missions, made possible the presence of an increasing number of foreigners, and allowed the development of considerable trade.

The completion of a church and the development of a new plaza were events of prime importance in the urban development of the pueblo. Since its founding the villagers had had to travel the seven miles to San Gabriel for religious services; the priests seldom visited the pueblo, a point of controversy between the two groups. Preliminary efforts to start building a church date from 1811, but nothing much happened until 1818. At that time Governor Solá ordered the site of the proposed church changed from the old plaza to a new one which would be laid out on uncluttered higher ground "near the comisionado's house." The work was done by Indians from the Missions San Gabriel and San Luis Rey. It was near enough to completion to be dedicated in December, 1822.

For the first time the town had a focal point. The new church, imposing for its time and place, facing a pristine plaza, became the center of attraction of the town. Desirable building sites were created surrounding this open place. Beginning with José Antonio Carrillo, citizens with the most influence began to compete for these favored sites. Previously the distribution of houses must have been rather haphazard. Now, gradually, the houses of the "best" people in the town surrounded the plaza. Los Angeles began developing an urban form typical of Mexican cities everywhere.

Urban Economic Developments

On April 11, 1822 the Californians transferred their allegiance from Spain to Mexico. California became a Mexican Province, free from the tight economic structures of Spanish rule. Much smuggling of foreign goods had occurred during the long revolutionary period, and now "to accommodate the citizens of Los Angeles" (Bancroft, 1886, III, p. 25) San Pedro was excepted from regulations restricting the entry of foreign goods. Ships appeared more often, goods for trade generally became available, and some of the ships' personnel occasionally remained as residents of the town. Further, in the 1830s, trading parties from Santa Fe arrived annually, bringing in blankets, American goods, and silver, and leaving with horses and mules and "China silks." The missions were secularized, many more ranchos were created and the population of the hinterland increased; so did the number of people living in the pueblo, increasing from seven hundred seventy in 1830 to 1,110 ten years later, and reaching an estimated 1,250 in 1845.

Considerable trading was done on shipboard directly with the ranchers, but enterprising merchants soon had goods on sale every day in Los Angeles stores—fine cloth, tools, and other manufactured goods were available from all over the world. As a result of these changes some genuine urban features appeared: retail stores were established, specialized craftsmen offered their services, a few professional men appeared, and some manufacturing outside the home began. Symbolically, but only incidentally, the pueblo was officially raised to the status of a *ciudad* in 1835 and at the same time was named the capital of the territory; the actual movement of the government did not occur until 1845.

Perhaps the best source of objective data on the urban development of the pueblo are the *Padróns* (census) of 1836 (Layne, 1936, pp. 81–89) and 1844 (Northrop, 1941, pp. 360–417). The first of these was compiled fourteen years after the urban period began, so it should reflect the changed conditions of the settlement. Fortunately, the *Padrón* of 1836 appears to have been compiled carefully. Summarized in Table 10.1 it reveals the magnitude of the nonagricultural occupations. Seventy-five residents were listed as having urban occupations, one hundred forty-six were in various agricultural pursuits, whereas ninety-nine were classified as servants, vagrants or prostitutes, occupations that were neither clearly urban nor rural. This division assigned the eleven persons listed as property owners and the seventeen ranchers living in the pueblo to the agricultural sector. Even so, the urban occupations now accounted for a third of the urban-rural total, an impressive proportion for a settlement that had been an agricultural village only a few years previously.

Not only was the urban labor force of goodly proportions but the occupations were of the sort that are characteristic of urban settlements everywhere. Sixteen persons were classified as merchants and five more were associated with them as *subordinates*. In addition, six tavern keepers should be added to the group of general retailers. It is possible that some of these establishments were small, but the operations of John Temple and Abel Stearns must have already been of considerable size although previously (1829) Tiburcio Tapia had been reported to be the principal merchant in the town. Some Californians appear to have understood the workings of trade, for five of the merchants, four of the *subordinates,* and five of the tavern keepers were "Californians" (persons born in California or in other parts of the Spanish empire and, therefore, presumably citizens of California).

Artisans and craftsmen offering specialized skills typical of the commercial structure of nineteenth century towns comprised a second large group of townsmen in 1836. One segment produced custom-made clothing, the

Table 10.1
Occupations from *Padròns*

Spanish	English Equivalent	1836	1844
comerciante	merchant	16	15
subordinate	clerk	5	—
tabernero	tavern keeper	6	1
cosinero	casino operator	—	2
zapatero	shoemaker	7	11
sastre	tailor	6	5
sombrerero	hatter	3	3
platero	silversmith	3	2
carpintero	carpenter	7	3
cigarrero	cigar maker	1	2
albañil	mason	1	4
tonelero	cooper	2	1
encalador	lime pit (operator)	1	—
panadero	baker	—	1
médico	doctor	2	1
soldado (militar)	soldier	4	1
escribiente	scribe	1	2
prof. de leng.	prof. of language	1	—
cocinero	cook	5	2
jabonero	soap maker	1	—
bordador	embroiderer	1	—
sacristian	sexton	1	—
empleado	employee	1	—
cajero	cashier	—	1
cirujano	surgeon	—	1
herrero	blacksmith	—	1
proprietario	property owner	11	2
labrador	laborer, farmer	65	170
L.P.	laborer-proprietor	40	59
campista	farm worker ranch hand	—	40
ranchero	rancher	17	16
hortelano	gardener	2	—
arriero	muleteer	1	—
vaquero	cowboy, herdsman	10	—
ninguna	vagrant	68	19
sirviente	servant	18	49
mala vida	prostitute	13	—

Source: Compiled from J. Gregg Layne, "The First Census of
the Los Angeles District," *Historical Society of Southern
California Quarterly*, 18:81–89, and Marie E. Northrop, ed.
"The Los Angeles Padrón of 1844," *Historical Society of
Southern California Quarterly*, 42: 360–417.

only kind available anywhere in the 1830s.
Seven shoemakers, six tailors, and three hatters plied their crafts in the pueblo. To this
group should be added one embroiderer creating ornamentation for the locally produced
garments. In addition, the town boasted three
silversmiths, a craft necessary in the production of jewelry, decorations for saddles and
harnesses, as well as religious and household
items. Seven carpenters were available to
manufacture furniture, carts, or other objects
of wood. One cigar maker was also present.
Two coopers produced the barrels essential in
the aging and storage of wine and brandy. One
man, presumably a tanner, although not identified as such, operated a lime pit. Another
made soap. The services of a mason were
available. These are the kinds of occupations
found in towns the world over.

The local craftsmen were dominated by
Californians two to one. Only in the wood-
working trades did foreigners have majorities:
six of the seven carpenters, both of the coopers. The lime pit operator was an American.
In the other crafts, foreigners were poorly represented: one of the three hatters, one of the
six tailors, and that was it. The seven shoemakers, three silversmiths, the embroiderer,
the *cigarrero*, soap maker, and mason were all
Californians.

The professions and services were not
strongly represented; they never are in small
towns. There were two medical doctors, however, and one "professor of language." In addition, the *ayuntamiento* had a professional
scribe (or clerk) and a sexton cared for the
church. Four soldiers were stationed in the
town. The five cooks seem to have been employed in private homes although where they
worked or if the homes took in boarders is not
clear. Nationalities were mixed in three
groups. The two doctors were Americans,
whereas the language teacher was French.
Three of the cooks were foreigners (English,
American, Canadian); two were not. The sexton, scribe, and soldiers were Californians.

The *Padrón* of 1844 seems to have been less carefully done, and its compiler less perceptive. For example, in his view there were no longer any prostitutes, and the idle vagrants had almost disappeared. If the father was a *labrador* the same term was applied almost indiscriminately to his family members—girls from twelve to fourteen years of age and to boys as young as ten. The listing of occupations, too, seemed less detailed than in 1836, although the urban activities it reflected were substantially the same. The total, however, had now dropped to fifty-nine. This data also appears in Table 10.1.

A few changes may be worthy of note. One of the doctors now listed himself as a surgeon. The number of tavern keepers was reduced sharply, but a new category, *casiono* (dancing hall operator) now appeared. Other newly listed occupations included a baker, a cashier, and a blacksmith. Incidentally, among the rural occupations, no *vaqueros* (cowboys) were listed as living in town, but the term *campista* (skilled agricultural worker or ranch hand) was applied to forty residents.

During the 1830s the city's finances and the activities of the council (*ayuntamiento*) reflected this growing commercial importance. By the middle of the decade the city was receiving much of its revenue from monthly licenses on taverns, clothing stores, billiard parlors, grocery stores, and on the sale of liquor. In addition, a fee was charged for putting the city seal on the measuring *varas* used in clothing stores. In 1835, "owing to scandalous irregularities existing in the stores to the detriment of . . . the consumer who through necessity is compelled to daily provide himself with the necessaries of life," a series of reforms were proposed by the president of the council. "Those selling by weight and measure" were warned to obey the law; "a pound and a quarter shall contain 16 *almudes* or measures of grain and the measuring *vara* shall be 36 inches long." A committee was "to review all stores and taverns every eight days."

On the "second day of January the committee shall seal the weights and measures." Finally, "bread and other edibles sold shall be announced upon a tablet placed upon the door of each store stating the value, quantity and quality of each" (Los Angeles City Archives, n.d., pp. 18–51). These activities no longer reflected the regulations of a subsistence agricultural village. Rather, they were a response to the needs of a commercial town.

Ranchers Graze Their Cattle on the Land

Only three years after the pueblo was founded, several soldiers, looking to their retirement, asked for unoccupied grazing land in the Los Angeles area. Juan José Dominguez received the land from Redondo to Wilmington, Manuel Nito's grant stretched from Long Beach to Whittier, and José María Verdugo was given the Glendale area. At first only informal grazing permits, these magnanimous gifts soon evolved into full-fledged grants. No money changed hands, the land was free, presumably given in recognition of government service. A formal procedure evolved. Applicants had to petition the governor, describe the lands, produce a crude map of it. If the request was approved, he then had to occupy the land, stock it with cattle, build a house, plant some trees, and the land was his. Eventually, the boundaries were "surveyed" by the pueblo's alcalde—the officials rode the boundaries on horseback, indicating the landmarks—"a cactus patch," "a bullock's skull," and so on. Some fifteen other ranchos were granted before 1833. After that date the Mexican governors passed out parcels of land with increasing liberality. These blocks ranged in size from less than one to more than one hundred eighty square miles. Eventually, there were fifty-five of these ranchos in the local area.

The ranchos soon became additional focal points of activity, along with the pueblo and mission. In fact, in the 1830s and 1840s, about half the population of the area was living on

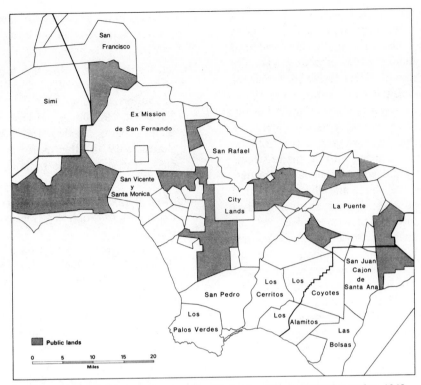

Figure 10.2. Ranchos, city lands and public lands of the Los Angeles region, 1848.

the ranchos, the other half in the pueblo. The location of the rancho headquarters was chosen with care—presumably at spots where there were springs or other sources of year around water. Usually, a rancho supported about twenty or thirty people, but the number varied widely—one rancho housed more than two hundred people, a second more than a hundred, a third was worked by a single couple. In any event, these fifty-five rancho headquarters were centers of economic and social activity. Trails connected them to the pueblo, to other ranchos, and to the landing at Wilmington. They were the places of origin and destination of much of the movement in the region. For decades they were important landmarks and place names on a generally empty landscape. And most ranchos, their titles confirmed (albeit after long delays), were continued intact into the American period.

However, the rancho economy was not to survive for long in the American period; within a couple of decades it gave way before agricultural and town-founding activities. What then remains in today's landscape as a reminder of these old ranchos, so prominent in the area's life of yesteryear? Not as much as one might expect. The rancho headquarters, focal points for half a century of pastoral life, have faded away as activity centers in the urban landscape. In not a single instance did a town spring up around a rancho headquarters—towns were located with their centers elsewhere. The rancho buildings that are still standing—some are fine adobes, today's historic monuments—have to be sought out, and are often found in out-of-the-way places. Their early site advantage—perhaps a flowing spring—was quickly lost with the development of more sophisticated water supply systems.

What has survived prominently into today's landscape, surprisingly, are the rancho boundaries, once so casually surveyed and generally ignored. Miles of county and city boundary lines coincide with the boundaries of earlier ranchos; they were handy, already existing lines, readily available for legislative use. As rights-of-way for roads were dedicated by adjacent property owners, many rancho boundary lines coincide with the major streets of today: Sepulveda, Ramona, Whittier, Washington, Wilshire, and Pico Boulevards are some examples. Further, many of today's streets are interrupted, or are offset, or continue at an angle, as they cross rancho boundaries. Finally, in some instances, the present street pattern within the entire area of an earlier rancho is oriented to conform to the boundaries of the rancho. An example of this is a portion of modern Burbank, formerly Rancho Providencia, as can be observed on any map showing local streets.

10. Suggested Readings

Bowman, Lynn. *Los Angeles: Epic of a City.* Berkeley: Howell-North Books, 1974.
Although a general history of Los Angeles, Bowman's knowledge of Spanish has made the sections on the Spanish-Mexican land grants particularly useful.

Heizer, Robert F. and Alan J. Almquist. *The Other Californians.* Berkeley: University of California Press, 1971.
Subtitled, "Prejudice and Discrimination under Spain, Mexico and the United States to 1920," this useful volume discusses the state of the Indians, Mexican Californians, Chinese and Japanese.

Johnston, Bernice E. *California's Gabrielino Indians.* Los Angeles: Southwest Museum, 1961.
A well written and authoritative study of the local Indians. Includes a map showing the presumed village sites at the time of the Portolá expedition.

Reid, Hugo. *The Indians of Los Angeles County.* Los Angeles: Southwest Museum, 1968.
A reprinting of letters written in 1851 to the *Los Angeles Star.* Reid had twenty years' experience in the area and his wife was a Gabrielino.

CHAPTER **11**   The Americanization of Los
                                  Angeles

Figure 11.1. Pasadena, founded in 1874 as an orange growing colony, had developed a commercial district along Colorado Boulevard by the early 1880s. This view looks west toward Fair Oaks. (Photo courtesy California Historical Society / Title Insurance and Trust Co. (L.A.) Collection of Historical Photographs.)

"The City (of the Angeles) is the product of one era of barbarism, two or three kinds of civilizations and an interregnum. . . . You meet native Californians, wide-hatted Mexicans, now and then a Spaniard of the old blue stock, a sprinkle of Indians and the (Chinaman) in his shirt and cue. . . . You hear somebody swearing Spanish, grumbling German, vociferating in Italian, parleying in French, rattling China and talking English. . . . It is as many tongued as a Mediterranean seaport, and hospitable as a grandee." Benjamin F. Taylor (1878, p. 261).

"The gold rush made northern California a real part of the United States; the boom of the eighties did precisely that for the south. Where once the 'cattle of the plain' had grazed in silence over rich acres, now the American citizen built his trolley lines, founded his banks, and irrigated his orange groves. The boom was the final step in the process of making California truly American." Glenn S. Dumke (1944, p. 276).

Table 11.1
Population Growth in Los Angeles and San Francisco, 1850–1900

Year	Total Population Los Angeles	San Francisco	Rate of Growth Los Angeles	San Francisco
1850	1,694	34,776	---	---
1860	4,385	56,802	159%	63%
1870	5,728	149,473	31%	163%
1880	11,183	233,959	95%	57%
1890	50,395	298,997	351%	28%
1900	102,479	343,782	103%	15%

Source: U.S. Bureau of the Census, *Fifteenth Census of the United States: Volume 1, Population*, Table 11, pp. 18–19.

The first half century of Los Angeles as an American city was to see it evolve from a sleepy Mexican town into a bustling western city. Its development is recorded in its growth of population decade by decade (Table 11.1). Beginning as a small town, it grew rapidly in the prosperous fifties, stagnated in the next decade, spurted in the seventies, and then took off like a rocket in the boom of the eighties. In relative terms, however, the population of Los Angeles was continuously small; San Francisco dominated the urban scene in California. In addition, it should not be forgotten that even San Francisco's population was insignificant compared to that of many an eastern city. By 1890, New York had a population of about 2,500,000 and both Chicago and Philadelphia had over a million inhabitants each.

The Americanization of Los Angeles, 1848–1867

No map of the Pueblo existed, and the Americans hired Lieutenant E. O. C. Ord to make a survey in 1849. He found a rather typical Mexican settlement with a small church facing the plaza, surrounded by several hundred one-story adobe structures that lined the dirt roads, trails really, that led out to the ranchos in the neighboring valleys. It had the appearance of a Mexican desert town, with only two trees showing against the yellow walls of the town buildings: one the famous sycamore that gave Aliso Street its name, the other

a lacy pepper. Yet it had an oasis quality too, with vineyards, orchards, and irrigated fields filling the land between the town and the river. A few of the dwellings near the plaza were more pretentious; three had two stories, five were roofed with tile. These dwellings with the prestigious plaza locations were the homes of the town's prominent families: Del Valle, Lugo, Olvera, Carrillo, Sanchez, Sepúlveda, and Pico. One of these, the house of Francisco Avila, still stands a few yards up Olvera Street, the only remaining adobe residence in downtown Los Angeles.

Using the church door as the center of the city, Ord attempted to make some order out of the chaotic arrangement of buildings (1849). He surveyed Main Street (Calle Principal) south from the river, past the church and the Bella Union Hotel. The adobes on this street from the Plaza to First Street, built originally as houses, now housed a fair number of small businesses. Southwest of the Plaza the alignment of the buildings allowed only a narrow lane connecting with Los Angeles Street. This was the well-known "Negro Alley," notorious for its gambling dens, "houses of ill fame," and frequent killings. Apart from the cluster of buildings in the immediate vicinity of the plaza, the area south of Main Street was in farms. The Zanja Madre (mother ditch) ran along the slope between Los Angeles Street and Alameda Street, with branches running off toward the river forming a veritable network of canals. The land to the north of Main was higher, difficult to irrigate, and vacant. Ord blocked out the portion of this area that was reasonably level into city-sized blocks and lots. A few years later (1852) Henry Hancock made a new survey adding a number of thirty-five acre lots in the outlying parts of the city.

In this motley collection of adobes the census taken in 1850 found 1,694 people: 1,610 whites, seventy Indians, twelve blacks, and two Chinese. The population of the surrounding ranchos was only slightly larger: 1,920 whites, two hundred sixty-four Indians, and one black. Only about three hundred of the town's population were of American ancestry in 1850 and, as was usual in frontier towns, men outnumbered women by three to one. But the fifties were halcyon days in Los Angeles and by the end of the decade of the 1850s, the population had grown to 4,358, an increase of one hundred seventy-two percent.

The growth of the fifties reflected the prosperity of southern California. "Everybody in Los Angeles seemed rich, everybody *was* rich," is the famous phrase of Horace Bell (1881, p. 10) who was on the scene. The wealth came as a by-product of the gold rush. Although the action was four hundred miles to the north, the miners provided the first genuine market for the cattle of the local ranchers. Cattle that formerly were only useful for their parts, hides, horns, and tallow, could now be sold for from fifty to seventy-five dollars each at the diggings. From 1852 to 1856 the purchasing power of the rancheros soared beyond their wildest expectations. Now these retired soldiers and governor's favorites had incomes to match their grandiose land holdings. The bubble was soon to burst, but while it lasted Los Angeles boomed.

The growing town began to improve its connections to the outside world although its relative isolation was by no means over. The stagecoach line of Phineas Banning replaced the traditional oxcarts connecting the town to ships at the San Pedro landing. From there it

was a three-day steamboat ride to San Francisco or a month's journey to New York. In 1857, Wells Fargo established a stage line to San Francisco—again, a three-day ride. The next year the city had its first direct connections with the east when the Butterfield Stage arrived from St. Louis via El Paso. "That was one of the longest stage routes in the world. . . . I rode over it from here to St. Louis on my wedding trip in 1860, a distance of 1900 miles, traveling night and day for eighteen days and twenty hours . . ." wrote H. D. Barrows (1893, p. 55). Wholesalers were using Los Angeles as their headquarters for trade throughout the southwest. A local newspaper estimated that during the first three months of 1859 "there has left this city not less than one hundred and fifty wagons loaded with goods for Utah." (Thompson and West, 1880, p. 95.) Banning, the teamster with government contracts, regularly sent his freight wagons loaded with supplies to the army garrisons at Tejon, Yuma, and Tucson. A telegraph line connected Los Angeles with San Francisco in 1860. In that year the last bullfight was held in Los Angeles; old customs were fading away.

Slowly, American ways began to prevail. The *zanjas,* source of both domestic and irrigation water, carried only a trickle; worse, residents and their livestock bathed in it. The Americans felt this was unsanitary and wasteful and leased distribution rights to private individuals, hoping for improvements. One lessee built a water wheel in 1857, a storage tank in the plaza, and constructed a distribution system of wooden pipes. Under Mexican law, all vacant land within its borders belonged to the Pueblo in common. If a man wanted a building lot he petitioned the Ayuntamiento (Council) for a grant of the land. If he failed to use the lot it was taken from him. In addition, no one had written title to the land; surveys were nonexistent or inexact. After 1860, with surveys complete, land parcels could be bought and sold in the normal American manner. There was great pressure to get the land into private hands and onto the tax rolls; land sales were held regularly. For a few years the thirty-five acre parcels of the Hancock survey were on the market for thirty-five dollars. There were few takers. Other institutions were changing, too. The community was formerly homogeneously Catholic, but in the 1850s regular services were held by Jews, Methodists, Presbyterians, and African Methodists. Both the Hebrew Benevolent Society and the Catholic Sisters of Charity date from the first American decade. Schools had been conducted in the Pueblo in the homes of hired teachers, but the system had been disrupted by the gold rush. The earlier practice was revived until 1855 when a two-story brick schoolhouse was built on the northwest corner of Spring and Second, "rather 'out in the country.' "

Outlying Towns

During the first twenty years of American occupance, urban activity generally was confined to Los Angeles itself. However, four outlying towns were founded which have persisted and become parts of the Metropolis. Each was founded for a special purpose, and none reflected a need for dispersed urban service centers. The earliest, in 1851, was a settlement of squatters, called El Monte after the willow groves in the vicinity. Immigrants, mainly from Texas, settled "at the end of the Santa Fe Trail" where many springs near the San Gabriel River made farming easy. In the same year San Bernardino was founded as the last unit in a chain of Mormon settlements reaching from Salt Lake City to the Pacific, presumably as a gateway for gathering of the saints from Europe. The 100,000-acre Rancho San Bernardino was purchased and a stockade built. The townsite, eight large blocks with lots of one acre, patterned after Salt Lake City, was surveyed the next year. There were some five hundred original settlers, but the group was recalled to Utah in 1858. Some two-thirds of

the original settlers left in response to the recall, and only gradually did other settlers take their places.

Anaheim was founded in 1857 by the Los Angeles Vineyard Society as a grape-growing venture by "50 Germans from San Francisco." George Hansen, a prominent local surveyor, chose the site: the lower end of an alluvial fan just below the point where the river comes out of Santa Ana Canyon. It was easy to irrigate, but also subject to flash floods. Finally, Phineas Banning, who ran a freighting and staging business between the harbor and Los Angeles, built a new landing on inner San Pedro Slough in 1858 and founded the town of Wilmington. It was six miles closer to Los Angeles than San Pedro and was soon built up with Banning's warehouses, wagon manufacturing shops, and corrals. The Civil War assisted its growth considerably, as a depot for the Quartermaster Department was located there, with several thousand soldiers stationed in "Drum Barracks" (named after Adjutant-General Richard C. Drum). Towns were not yet really in demand, and no more were to be founded for ten years.

The Natural Calamities of the Sixties

If the fifties were happy days in Los Angeles, the sixties were remembered as years of natural calamities. The winter of 1861–1862 brought thirty days of continuous rain, widespread flooding, and the crumbling of many of the city's adobe buildings. The Los Angeles River overflowed, and vineyards and orchards were washed away. Merchants in Mellus Row (on the east side of Los Angeles Street between Aliso and First) worked in water up to their waists trying to salvage their goods. In the fall of 1862 an epidemic of smallpox visited the city; by February there were two hundred seventy-six cases in Los Angeles. Newmark pointed out that vaccination was not yet compulsory, and the disease was especially bad among Mexicans and Indians. "For a time fatalities were so frequent and the nature of the contagion so feared that it was difficult to persuade undertakers to bury the dead. . . ." (Newmark, 1926, p. 322).

The next two years were marked by unparalled drought. During the entire winter of 1862–63 no more than four inches of rain fell. In Los Angeles County, seven out of ten cattle in the herds of the ranchers died of starvation. The drought continued through the next year and the plains around Los Angeles in all directions were strewn with carcasses and bleaching bones. The cattle still alive could not be sold as no one could feed them. Abel Stearns, one of the larger ranchers, lost from 40,000 to 50,000 head of cattle. The settlers at Anaheim, although surrounded by a "great fence of willow trees," had to station guards to keep the hungry and thirsty cattle from stampeding their irrigated acres.

The Failure of the *Rancheros*

The drought of the early sixties was the *coup-de-grace* of the ranching economy of southern California. Before the drought the old families still owned essentially all of the land; after it, only a quarter of the parcels worth more than $10,000 were in the hands of the Californians. As Pitt wrote: "A mean and brassy sky thus eventually did in the south of California what lawyers and squatters had accomplished in the north—the forced breakup of baronial holdings, the transfer to new owners, and the rise of a way of life other than ranching" (Pitt, 1971, p. 248). But even before the hot sun scorched the pastures of wild oats, mustard, and filaree, the ranching economy of the southland had grown feeble and frail. The Americans were transforming the Mexican province into an American state and the old Californians and their way of life could not survive for long.

Perhaps basic was the need to adapt to a money economy, a difficult adjustment for a people familiar with bartering hides and tal-low for their necessities. Money was now needed for everything. Property taxes were imposed for the first time. They amounted to about twenty-five cents an acre, rather high in terms of the prices of the times, and, if tens of thousands of acres were involved, the total could be considerable. Money was also needed to pay the Indian laborers who had previously been worked more or less involuntarily. Money was needed to hire lawyers to appear before the Land Commission and present proof of title. Lawyers on the frontier were costly and some of the suits were lengthy. It took eighteen years and seventy-eight lawsuits before the Sepulvedas had a clear title to Rancho de los Palos Verdes.

The old families were a generous group and not familiar with money management, a dangerous combination. As Horace Bell explained: ". . . the Californian was so fullhanded and happy that he gave no heed to the sore foot and the rainy day, and when he needed money it was more convenient to go to the money lender than to deny himself imaginary necessities, and thus he gave the . . . userer . . . an easy seat astride his neck and was never able to shake him off. The California Spaniard was so over-generous that he would thus raise money for his friends in sums great or small. He knew not the value of money or the crushing power of compound interest . . ." (Bell, 1927, p. 476).

An actual case was related by Leonard Pitt in the sad tale of Don Julio Verdugo: "Feeling in a bullish mood in 1861, Don Julio decided to mortgage Rancho San Rafael (today's Glendale and part of Burbank) and use the money for sprucing up his casa, buying provisions and paying taxes. He signed for a $3,445 loan at 3 percent monthly interest, which by 1870 had ballooned into a debt of $58,750 and ended in foreclosure, a sheriff's sale, and ruination. At the public auction Verdugo's lawyers bought the 36,000 acre San

Rafael for themselves . . . Verdugo also had to yield Rancho La Cañada to other gringos . . ." (Pitt, 1971, p. 252).

A further problem was the nature of the Californian's traditional life style which included much entertaining, lavish spending, and a "widespread, deep rooted passion for gambling that led to spectacular wagers and ruinous losses." Fiestas were common, "dancing, singing and eating proceeded all night and well into the following morning." The wedding of Petra Pilar Sepúlveda in 1853 lasted five days and nights, "its lavishness . . . made a deep impression on the gringos" (Pitt, 1971, p. 129). When the rancheros had money they spent it freely on themselves and their friends. The gringos were startled that Don Lugo owned a bridle inlaid with $1,500 worth of silver and put it to everyday use even when he was strapped for money.

More than anything else the Californians loved horse racing. There were constant match races between the leading rancheros—the Yorbas, the Avilas, Sepúlvedas, and Picos. In October, 1852, the populace of the city witnessed the most famous horse race in California's history. The race was between Pío Pico's "Sarco" and José Andres Sepúlveda's "Black Swan." The latter horse had just been imported from Australia and ridden down from San Francisco. The race began "on San Pedro Street near the city limits, and running south a league and a half and return"—a distance of nine miles (Newmark, 1926, p. 160). Californians came from all over the state to witness the event. Betting was heavy, twenty-five thousand dollars, in addition to 1,000 horses, 1,000 cattle, and five hundred sheep were said to have been bet on the race. Sepúlveda's wife gave each of her servants $50 to wager on the race. The two owners rode the horses themselves, and Sepúlveda's "Black Swan" won by seventy-five yards. Pico, we are told, lost $1,600 in cash and three hundred head of cattle.

Los Angeles in 1868

Although much was changed after twenty years of American rule, much remained the same. The population had grown considerably to perhaps 5,000 persons, but the cosmopolitan mixture of a frontier town was still evident. With no rail connections, many immigrants still came by sea—Americans from New England, Texas, and other seaboard states, for example. But there were also numerous Europeans: French, Germans, and Italians, with the French particularly numerous, attracted by their early success as vintners. The French population was important enough, with perhaps six hundred residents, so that beginning in 1859 a French Vice Consul was stationed in the city. But the above groups still formed a minority. More numerous were the native Californians, now becoming landless, but remaining important on the Los Angeles scene. To this group might be added more recent immigrants from Mexico (mainly from the state of Sonora), some of whom had worked earlier in the northern mines. Indians were present, too, living in "a miserable village near the Los Angeles River." They still did much work in town in the vineyards and orchards. We are told that they were paid with *aguardiente* (brandy), got drunk over the weekend, were regularly arrested on Sunday and held until their "employers advanced the fines against next weeks' work." Bell called it a "slave mart . . . only the slave at Los Angeles was sold fifty-two times a year . . . bought up by the vineyard men and others at prices ranging from one to three dollars, one-third of which was to be paid the peon at the end of the week" (Bell, 1927, p. 35).

The urban economy was growing. Wholesaling was becoming important as the town was the entry point for goods to Fort Tejon, the Owens Valley, Salt Lake City and the Mormon settlements, as well as Fort Yuma and much of Arizona territory. Manufacturing, too, contributed to the economy of the growing town. The 1860 and 1870 census show that the vintners dominated the economy. The six wineries in 1860 contributed $132,000 in wages, more than ten times any other activity; by 1870 the number of wineries had increased to forty-three. Carriage and wagon-making was the second most important employer of the period, and the town had several firms manufacturing saddlery and harness, six flour and meal mills, six bakeries, three breweries, two brick kilns, and a furniture factory, a foundry, a tinsmith, an oil refinery, a tannery, and manufacturers of such things as soap and brooms. In 1860 Los Angeles County recorded eight active gold mines with fifty "hands" at work, as gold had been discovered the year previously in San Gabriel and Santa Anita Canyons.

The appearance of the town was changing, but only slowly. The business district was concentrated along Main and Los Angeles Streets, from the Plaza south to Temple, and cross streets, Arcadia, Aliso, and Commercial. (This area is now occupied by a portion of the Civic Center and Santa Ana Freeway, changing the alignment of the cross streets.) At the head of Main on the Plaza, Pío Pico was finishing the finest hotel in southern California, the three-story Pico House (still standing). A handsome brick building, with arcades over the sidewalk, built around a large patio, with flowers, birds, and a fountain, it had eighty rooms, gas lights, and a bathroom on each floor. Other Californians had also invested their ranching profits in business buildings. Particularly imposing was Temple's Court House on Main Street, the Arcadia Block, the "first modern brick business block in town," sporting an iron balcony, constructed on Los Angeles Street by Abel Stearns. Two additional hotels, the Lafayette and the United States were built on Main Street. Beginning in 1867 gas was manufactured from tar, and twenty-five street lamps were a proud feature of the business district. The new brick kilns were kept busy, as we are

told that in a single year, 1859, thirty brick buildings were built. Presumably, most were residences.

A residential district of homes set in gardens, indicating the preference of Americans and Europeans, was growing between First and Fourth. Guinn wrote: "The aristocratic residence streets of the city were San Pedro and the west side of Main. The wealthier residents on Main owned through the block and fronted their stables on Spring." (Guinn, 1893, p. 64.) However, Andrew Boyle had purchased a vineyard along the river together with the bluff above it and on the heights had built a two-story brick home. As a result the old bluff became known as "Boyle Heights." But the dominant buildings in town remained the "broad-brimmed, thick-walled" adobe structures, with flat roofs of asphalt and sand. They lined the streets around the plaza, in "Sonoratown" to the north, and were found on side streets everywhere. In the business district, covered "verandas" jutted out from brick building or adobe alike, so the pedestrian, stumbling along the dirt sidewalks, could avoid the summer sun or winter rain by keeping under these block-long spans of wooden awnings. Looking at the town as a whole, Pitt put it nicely: "Los Angeles was Californian in the center, Mexican toward the east, Yankee in the west, and cosmopolitan everywhere. 'Semi-gringo' Horace Bell dubbed it, a town of mixed essences" (Pitt, 1971, p. 121).

The Sunny Seventies

About 1868 a series of events occurred that forecast prosperous times for Los Angeles in the decade ahead. The ranchos were breaking up, immigrants began to arrive in droves, new markets appeared for agricultural produce and general supplies. All of these events stimulated the urban activities in Los Angeles. The Los Angeles and San Bernardino Land Association, trustee of Don Abel Stearns, the largest of the landowners, subdivided his seven ranches totalling two hundred seventy-seven square miles. They were divided into parcels of from twenty to one hundred sixty acres and put on the market at from $5 to $13 an acre. Maps showing the available property were distributed widely around the United States and in Europe, together with glowing accounts of opportunities in southern California agriculture. Within eighteen months, 20,000 acres had been sold and put under cultivation.

The timing could not have been more propitious. The restless years after the disruptive Civil War were a time of massive westward migration. Some of the migrants came overland, and canvas-topped prairie schooners arrived from the east daily—all the vacant space around the town was taken up by their camps. Others came by rail to San Francisco (the Central Pacific was completed to that city in 1869) and moved southward. On the Pacific Ocean, the little passenger-carrying sidewheeler from San Francisco was always full, and passage had to be booked weeks in advance. Farmers, flooded out of the Central Valley by the deluge of 1868, drifted southward in search of dryer lands. The large number of newcomers provided plenty of buyers for the newly available farmlands.

The favorite crops of the newcomers were barley and corn. They needed little water and yielded income the first year. Barley was sown with the first rains, harvested in the spring. The land was then planted in corn so the farmer could get income from two crops in the first year. Simultaneously, interest in agricultural land was stimulated by the discovery of an artesian well in the Compton neighborhood—water shot two feet in the air, giving promise of irrigation water for lands far from any stream.

Happily, just at the time barley and corn became plentiful in the Los Angeles area a local market developed which was to absorb the entire surplus. Silver and lead had been discovered at Cerro-Gordo in the Inyo Mountains east of the Owens Valley. By the middle of 1868 several wagons arrived in Los Angeles carrying bars of the metals. Although Los Angeles was a long distance from the mines, its port was the cheapest port from which bullion could be sent to market. From 1870 through 1875 the Inyo silver trade dominated the commerce of Los Angeles. The 1,200 mules engaged in its hauling provided a market for all the barley the farmers could grow, and local production of fruit, nuts, potatoes, and corn helped supply the miners. The wholesalers on Los Angeles Street were busy handling the local produce as well as imported whiskey, tools, clothing, and everything else needed to keep a full-fledged mining camp in business. In an average year the freight bill alone was reported to be $470,000, perhaps half of which was spent in Los Angeles. Supplies for the mines were the basis for much of the city's wholesale business, reported to amount to $5,000,000 a year.

The main freight line to Cerro Gordo was operated by Remi Nadeau. Nadeau devised a freighting system which involved a dozen stations set up from thirteen to twenty miles apart, with two wagons each pulled by fourteen mules shuttling between them on a schedule almost equaling that of a stage coach line. By 1873, he was operating eighty teams, each pulling mammoth wagons with massive wheels five feet high and six inches wide. As the wagons came down from the mines they appeared to be empty as the lead and silver bars barely covered the wagon floors. On the northward trip, however, they were piled high with bales of hay, sacks of barley, barrels of whiskey, and other bulky goods, and were in danger of blowing over in strong winds. In that same year Nadeau consolidated his corrals, barns, stables, blacksmith shops, and wagon-repair facilities, so that they occupied almost the entire block bounded by Broadway and Hill between Fourth and Fifth. He also improved the route northward by shifting his teams from the steep Cahuenga Pass to a new road he cut through the brush jungle and impenetrable wilderness of the narrows where the Los Angeles River emerges from the San Fernando Valley, creating what is now San Fernando Road.

The optimism generated by the Cerro Gordo trade was eclipsed in the seventies by the excitement of railroad construction that would break, it was hoped, the area's long handicap of isolation. The Central Pacific had begun its transcontinental runs to San Francisco in May, 1869, but that terminus was four hundred fifty miles of dusty trail or choppy ocean away, and the event meant little to Los Angeles. However, the Southern Pacific was building a rail line down the San Joaquin Valley, destined to be a second transcontinental route to the East, and Los Angeles hoped to be on that route. In 1869, however, the most traveled route out of Los Angeles was to the harbor, and it was proposed to build a railroad to Wilmington, "as the first link with the Southern Pacific." After much debate the city and county authorized a bond issue to finance the line (the vote was seven hundred for and six hundred seventy-two against). "Los Angeles and San Pedro Railway," as it was called, ran down the present day Alameda Street twenty-one miles to the wharves at Wilmington. Beginning in October, 1869, two trains a day traveled the route, the passenger fare was $2.50 for the hour's journey, and the cost of moving freight to and from the port was reduced considerably.

The easiest route east for the Southern Pacific, once it had crossed the Tehachapis, was to head over the level plain of the Mojave directly toward Needles. The battle to convince the Southern Pacific to add fifty miles and much expensive tunneling to its route in order to serve Los Angeles was long and acrimonious. The railroad was extracting treasure and advantage from every town it entered in the San Joaquin Valley; it would be the same for Los Angeles, and then some. To induce the line to build by way of Los Angeles, the city gave the railroad its controlling interest in the Los Angeles and San Pedro Railroad, a subsidy equal to five percent of the assessed valuation of the county (amounting to $600,000) and a sixty acre site for a railroad station and yards. In return, the Southern Pacific agreed to build its route to the east through Los Angeles, and to construct, within fifteen months, twenty-five miles of road north toward San Fernando Mission, the same length of road east toward Arizona, and a third line to Anaheim.

Work began in June, 1873, and the branch lines were completed as scheduled. However, work on the San Fernando tunnel was difficult and hazardous to the point where at times completion was in doubt. A local newspaper headlined it as "The Greatest Project Now Under Construction," and perhaps it was. At times 1,500 men were thrown into the battle, including 1,000 Chinese tunnel diggers. The tunnel was 7,000 feet long (more than a mile and a quarter), the longest tunnel ever built in the West. Finally, the tunnel was complete, and, on September 6, 1876, a golden spike was driven as the last rails were laid in Soledad Canyon. At long last Los Angeles was linked with northern California and the rest of the United States.

While all of this was going on, another railroad venture was under way in the area. John P. Jones, a rich Nevada mining tycoon, founded Santa Monica and built a railroad to Los Angeles. Called the Los Angeles and Independence Railroad it was planned as part of a road through Cajon Pass to Jones's mine at Panamint in the Owens Valley. No rails were laid farther than Los Angeles. In any event, Los Angeles now had two railroads running to the sea, one connecting with San Francisco, another heading east with transcontinental possibilities, and a fifth building south. From a city with no rail lines only seven years previously, Los Angeles had developed into what its boosters saw as the railroad center of the West.

The Cerro Gordo trade and railroad building not only brought money and people into the area but also stimulated urban growth. Many new buildings were built and new businesses established. The retail district expanded, moving from Main Street to First and spreading over to Spring and into the cross streets between the two. In 1875 the highest priced real estate in Los Angeles, however, was on both sides of Main Street between Arcadia and Temple Streets. St. Vibiana's Cathedral had been completed on Main below Second in 1876, adding to the southward movement of activity.

The new two-story brick buildings housed the usual firms of a trading town: there were stores selling dry goods, groceries, clothing, jewelry, drugs, furniture, tobaccos, stationery, and bakery goods, as well as hotels, banks, restaurants, saloons, barber shops, real estate, and insurance offices. There were also livery stables, harness and saddlery shops, gunsmiths, blacksmiths, wagon and buggy shops, and the Wells Fargo Express Office. Two newspaper offices were in the area, the *Star* and the *Express,* both with offices on Spring Street. Some of the stores had names that were to remain for a long time among the city's retailing firms: Desmond's Hat Store, Coulter's Dry Goods, and Germain's, a dealer in garden seeds. In the second floor offices were the doctors, lawyers, architects, and other professional men. Sidewalks were of wood, or packed earth held in place with curbs of boards.

Somewhat outside the main retail district, the New York Brewery was located at Third and Main. Adjacent to it was the "Round House" in the "Garden of Paradise," a cool, tree-shaded bower with a bar under the trees, reminiscent of a European beer garden, and the site of the city's elaborate Fourth of July Celebration, 1876. A second firm, the Philadelphia Brewery, was located on Aliso Street. Los Angeles Street was the location of wholesale grocers, wholesale liquor firms, dealers in hides, and various commission merchants.

Below the "Round House" on Main Street was a high class residential district with the best houses close in and smaller houses built regularly out at least as far as Ninth. Small acreages and suburban homes were occupying the easily irrigable land southward to the city limits and westward south of about Seventh. Horse-drawn street cars were going south as far as Washington and Figueroa and west to Ninth and Alvarado, encouraging the building of houses along their lines. Horse cars also went eastward across the river to East Los Angeles and Boyle Heights. East Los Angeles, laid out in 1873, within a few years was called "the principal suburb." It is described as having "a handsome school" and of the three or four hundred persons who lived there "all, or nearly all, are engaged in business in Los Angeles proper" (Thompson and West, 1880, p. 113). Boyle Heights, in 1880, seems to have been about the same size. (Both were within the corporate limits of Los Angeles.) Prudent Beaudry, a local subdivider, had piped water to the lots he owned on Bunker Hill and houses were being built on that highland also. Several years later (1882), when electric lights were installed to illuminate the town, they were mounted on high towers located within an area bounded by the Plaza, Seventh, Main, and Grand. Presumably this included the most important sections of the built-up town.

With the Easterners' taste for greenery and a more extensive irrigation system, the town was beginning to take on a lush look. "Bordering the sidewalks," wrote Salvator, "are many peppers . . . slender eucalyptus, castor bean plants, and frequently the stately, full weeping-willow. . . ." The same trees were found in the gardens. "Frequently, too, are seen formal plantings of tall cypress, together with almond and orange trees. The Norfolk Island Pine and the rubber tree flourish everywhere. Houses on the street side are usually enclosed with fences. Holloday's Patent Mills (a windmill) often stand near the houses . . ." (Salvator, 1929, pp. 125–126).

Brick and artificial stone were still used for many of the structures of the most wealthy. But now the "unaccustomed fragrance of new lumber" was often in the air, lumber ships were arriving at Banning's docks at Wilmington, and owning a lumber yard was a profitable business. As Adler summed it up, "The vogue for 'Carpenter Gothic,' a plentiful supply of (Douglas fir) and carpenters to assemble these into stylish residences by means of the newly available machine-made nails" (Adler, 1963, p. 15) were on the Los Angeles scene in time to be reflected in the building boom of the 1870s. The adobe hacienda gave way to styles that permitted bay windows, balconies, porches, and high pitched roofs supported by fancy brackets.

"Sonoratown" remained as a sector completely built up with adobes. Horace Bell, a colorful local resident, approved of this traditional architecture. "This writer stands by the adobe house as the coolest house, the warmest house, the cheapest house, and the most earthquake-proof house (?), and the best house for fandangos that ever existed in this old city of yours. Nothing but an adobe house could have stood an old-fashioned fandango . . ." (Bell, 1927, p. 199).

Outlying Towns of the 1870s

An increased agricultural population and activity related to the railroads stimulated urban development in the 1870s. A few developments were simply speculative townsites laid out in anticipation of finding buyers and settlers. Compton, though founded in the closing years of the previous decade, was a classic example. A partnership of several promoters subdivided seven square miles of raw land into twenty and forty acre farms and at its center surveyed a townsite. Santa Ana (1870), Tustin (1869), and Newport were also towns founded in the midst of newly occupied farming land. Other towns grew out of the activities of agricultural colonies: groups of settlers

organized to finance the expensive irrigation works and land development costs needed to start an agricultural enterprise in an arid land. Riverside (1870), Cucamonga (1872), and Pasadena (1874) were classic examples of this type of town.

Railroad building stimulated additional town-founding activity. Charles Maclay bought the northern half of the San Fernando Valley and in 1874 laid out the town of San Fernando on the Southern Pacific's northern line. In less than two weeks, more than $6,000 worth of lots had been auctioned off for about $10 each. The town, at the end of the rail line during the building of the San Fernando tunnel, was also stimulated by the construction of an oil refinery at Pico Canyon. Santa Monica got off to a good start, too, as it was laid out as the ocean terminus of a proposed rail line to Independence. Other "railroad towns" of the seventies were Downey, Norwalk, Garden Grove, and Orange, on the Anaheim branch, and Alhambra and Pomona on the route toward the east.

An Austrian Archduke Describes Los Angeles

Ludwig Louis Salvator, Archduke of Austria, spent the winter of 1876 in Los Angeles and published a book on his observations. *Eine Blum aus den Golden Lande ober Los Angeles*. He was an extensive traveler and a compulsive writer, publishing at least thirty-five books. His work on Los Angeles has been translated by Marguerite Eyer Wilber as *Los Angeles in the Sunny Seventies, A Flower From the Golden Land* (Salvator, 1929, pp. 127–138), and a portion of his description gives us a first hand view of a foreigner:

"Los Angeles is the seat of the county government and now has . . . a population of 16,000. These are about equally divided among Americans, Europeans, and Californians. Americans and Europeans, however, have given the greatest impetus to the present development. The former own the most houses and the land in the city; the latter control the bulk of the commerce. In the latter branch, the Irish and Germans have also been notably successful. The native Californians, on the other hand, have gone in largely for ranching, sheep-herding, and the raising of vineyards and orange trees. Despite the cosmopolitan nature of the inhabitants—on the streets are heard spoken English, French, Spanish, German, and Italian—the community spirit predominates, being strengthened by a mutual interest in the city's advancement.

"Comfortable accommodations for strangers have been amply provided in Los Angeles. There are several hotels which are generally filled to capacity during the winter season by travelers who come out to enjoy the mild climate of Southern California. The best of these is the Pico House, which, like all the four leading hotels, is down Main Street. . . .

"One particular section of Los Angeles is known as Sonora, so-called because most of its inhabitants were originally from Sonora in Old Mexico. This, which is the Californian quarter of Los Angeles, extends north from the Catholic Church on out through the valley. Sonoratown has two tramways. One of these runs down the center of the broadest street toward the Catholic cemetery; the other, after crossing the wide bed of the Los Angeles River via a wooden bridge, runs over into East Los Angeles. From the opposite bank of the river, where castor-beans grow rankly, the view over the Los Angeles Valley with its green alder-bushes is magnificent. Here, high up on the gently rolling ground, are scattered the houses that comprise East Los Angeles. This is a comparatively new part of the city, but it will soon develop into one of its finest sections. . . . In this tract, lots were sold only on condition the purchaser erect a fence and set out a definite number of trees. Eight-inch pipes connect this section of the city with the Los Angeles water system. . . .

"The streets of Los Angeles fairly teem with activity. Because of its mixed population, they are always colorful and interesting. Street-cars cross the principal streets and travel according to the American custom, down to the terminus, returning in the opposite direction. On the streets numerous vehicles and carriages are seen—four-seated carriages with heavy springs, light American vehicles, and frequently small carriages driven by Chinese. In Los Angeles, the Americans usually drive in place of riding horseback. Many riders, however, are in evidence, for the Spaniards, Frenchmen, and Italians prefer riding to driving. Spanish boys are often seen galloping gaily. Young Californians, brown as Arabs, also ride by, sometimes stopping their horses near the fruitstores and then galloping rapidly away, followed by their bulldogs, up the dusty streets.

"A gay crowd of men and animals is constantly coming and going on the streets. Innumerable bronze-colored half-breeds from the Mexican province of Sonora wearing plug hats on their dusky heads, tanned Scotchmen in straw helmets, distinguished Spaniards in riding clothes, and animated, laughing girls in large cotton capes and broad straw hats pass by. Upon passing on down the street strange sights are constantly being encountered: barber shops where customers stretch out nonchalantly; elevated seats where men lean back smoking cigarettes while their shoes are being polished; Chinese laundries bearing strange inscriptions advertising their activities; political notices posted from one end of the street to the other; vendors driving carts and selling fish. The streets are at the peak of their activity in the evenings, especially at the entrance to the opera-house where there is so much pushing and shouting going on that it is difficult to get through. In highly-lighted bars groups of ranchers drink gaily in an effort to forget the trials and tribulations of the past week.

"In summer, the dust is distinctly disagreeable; however, in the morning the streets are frequently watered from sprinkling carts. The dust on the sidewalks is settled by using a hose attached to water connections inside the house. Only two public gardens, in addition to the small city garden . . . exist in this city. One of these, which is at the terminus of the Spring Street car-line, is called Washington Garden (and) . . . contains 35 acres. It has many fruit trees, a large vineyard trained over a wooden trellis, and, in the center, an octagonal-shaped covered platform for music and dancing. There are also several rows of fine orange, fig, and olive trees, as well as pomegranates. In addition to these is a large dance-hall, an airy building decorated with 7 flat arches which has seats on either side. This is used for many kinds of entertainment. Back of this hall is a young orange grove and a small menagerie where a lioness, a bear, a leopard, an eagle, and several monkeys are exhibited. . . . This garden is extremely popular with the public at large and is the principal place of amusement.

"Out beyond in the same general direction (this will soon be connected by tramway) after passing several windmills, a second garden, called the race-track, or Agricultural Park (Exposition Park) is located. This is where the races are held. The park is a mile in circumference and is completely enclosed by a board fence. Within, in a setting of eucalyptus trees, is an inn and bleachers for spectators. . . .

"Behind the City of Los Angeles stretches . . . a row of hills. On these, homes are already beginning to rise. . . . Over on these hills are several cemeteries—those on the farthest hills being Catholic—and the city burial ground where the Jews and Chinese also have their graveyards. . . . From these heights there unfolds below a magnificent panorama of the middle and western sections of Los Angeles, with its stately buildings, luxuriant fruit orchards and, winding off to the right as far as the eye can reach, the Los Angeles River. Far off toward Santa Monica glimpses of the ocean may be had in three directions, over Wilmington, the Pacific Salt Works (at Redondo) and behind Ballona. On clear days the distant island of Catalina may be seen silhouetted against the horizon. . . ."

The Role of the Health Seekers 1870–1900

"From my personal observation I can say that at least an extra ten years' lease on life is gained by a removal to this coast from the Eastern states: not ten years to be added with its extra weight of age and infirmity, but ten years more with additional benefit of feeling ten years younger during the time." Dr. Peter C. Remondino (1892, p. 118).

The Los Angeles Metropolis was to experience innumerable waves of migrants over the years, motivated by the hope of a better life and economic advancement. The force behind the first of these waves was even stronger, however: the search for good health. In the nineteenth century medical opinion prescribed a change of climate for such illnesses as "consumption" (tuberculosis of the lungs),

asthma, and rheumatism. By the 1870s southern California was becoming accessible to the East, and the fact that it had the same kind of climate as the health centers along the French Riviera was gradually becoming well-known. In the 1870s, 1880s, and 1890s, "tens of thousands of invalids, driven by the urge for self-preservation, flocked west and permanently changed the area," as John E. Baur put it in his history of that period, *Health Seekers of Southern California* (Baur, 1959, p. xi). Solid figures are unavailable, but some scholars estimate that at least a quarter of those who arrived in southern California during these three decades were health seekers.

The "climatic-good health" message was spread through numerous books of the era, such as Nordhoff's famous 1872 book *California for Health, Pleasure and Residence*. It was also spread by local propagandists with exaggerated claims. "Invalids come here by the hundreds, and in every case, where they are not past all hope, they speedily find that precious boon which they have sought in vain in every other clime . . ." (Baur, 1959, p. 14). There was also much writing by doctors, such as Dr. Remondino quoted above, and many others. But perhaps the most effective boosters were the migrants who found the health they were seeking and enthusiastically spread the word to others back home.

Whereas many of the seriously sick who came to southern California died here as quickly as they would have back home, many, somehow, did get better. Many of those with lung problems could be helped by rest, sunshine, and pure air. Many, after giving up their hectic lives in the East, lived the simple life in their new home, hiking and hunting in the canyons. Many followed their doctors' advice, ate a wholesome diet, managed daily exercise, and took advantage of the sunshine. If the sufferers recovered, they might send an account to the local newspapers, or more likely to the newspapers back home.

Los Angeles claimed to be the "Capital of the Sanitarium Belt" and its hotels and boarding houses did host many of the health seekers. Those in search of good health, however, had a greater impact on some of the outlying communities. The founders of Pasadena were impressed with its healthful aspects. San Bernardino was reputed to "offer optimum conditions for tuberculars" (Baur, 1959, p. 74). Redlands was "built by the sick" (Baur, 1959, p. 74) and nearby Mentone was named for the famous health resort on the French Riviera. Monrovia was "a gathering place of tuberculars" (Baur, 1959, p. 60) apparently because many doctors who had the disease moved there. It was said of Riverside, "its settlers are principally invalids—sufferers from lung disease" (Baur, 1959, p. 121). Even its most famous resident, Mrs. Tibbets, who introduced the navel orange to the area, was an asthmatic.

No place, however, was more closely identified with the health seekers than Sierra Madre. It all began with Sierra Madre Villa, built as a sanitarium in 1875, consisting of a hotel and cottages, with the main building featuring a two hundred foot long veranda with sliding windows. In 1880 a state committee suggested that Sierra Madre would be the ideal location for a state tuberculosis sanitarium but nothing was built. Health seekers filled up the Villa to overflowing, and the overflow founded the town in 1882. By 1900 it was said that the majority of its 2,000 residents lived there for health reasons.

Other famous sanitariums included the Pottenter Sanitarium in Monrovia, reputed to be the first modern institution in the area. Altadena had a Vina Sanitarium, and toward the end of the period Kellogg's Battle Creek Company purchased an estate near Glendale for a sanitarium. About the same time the great Barlow Sanitarium, located on twenty-five acres adjoining Elysian Park in Chavez Ravine, was incorporated as a non-sectarian organization to care for the county's indigent tuberculars.

As a sidelight to the health boom, springs and spas became popular during this period. Dr. J. E. Fulton, boring an artesian well in 1874, discovered sulfurous waters. He promptly built a two-story hotel and Fulton Wells became famous; however, when the Santa Fe arrived the spa was rechristened Santa Fe Springs. On the other hand, Arrowhead Springs had been used by the Indians, and during the expansive period of the 1880s a resort covering one hundred eighty acres was opened. Other spas some distance from Los Angeles included Temescal Warm Springs, Murrieta Hot Springs, and Carlsbad, whose waters claimed to be almost identical in mineral content to the similarly named European Spa.

The migration of the health seekers petered out as the nineteenth century ended. More was understood about tuberculosis—it was realized that it could be contagious and tuberculars were no longer automatically welcome. More importantly, with new medical discoveries patients were treated in sanatariums near home. But the thirty year migration was important to the Metropolis. Many of the health seekers were middle-aged, brought their families, and were men of wealth and property seeking to prolong their lives in a milder clime. As David Starr Jordan wrote, "It is true that 'one-lunged people' form a considerable part of the population of southern California. It is also true that no part of our union has a more enlightened or more enterprising population and that many of these men and women are now as robust and vigorous as one could desire" (Jordan, 1898, p. 800).

The Boom of the Eighties: A City Platting Craze

The "Boom of the Eighties" was the grandest boom in southern California's flamboyant real estate history. For decades it was referred to as "The Boom," a milestone, with local events identified as occurring before the boom or after it. The Southern Pacific had completed its line eastward in 1881, extending it to New Orleans two years later. But as a monopoly it charged "all the traffic would bear." The boom of the eighties was touched off in March, 1886, by the completion of a second road, the Santa Fe Railroad, into the city. Now two competing lines were open to the east. Fares to Mississippi Valley points immediately dropped from $125 to $95. This was the beginning of a rate war between the two railroads, each railroad undercutting the other's fares, cumulating in a rate (for a day) of one dollar from Kansas City to Los Angeles. More importantly, for more than a year the fare from Missouri River points remained below twenty-five dollars. Freight rates, too, were lowered drastically, profits went up on exported products, and locally the cost of living was reduced. "The result of this," according to Netz, "was to precipitate such a flow of tentative migration, such an avalanche rushing madly to Southern California as I believe has no parallel" (Netz, 1925, p. 56).

People arrived in droves. "In 1887 four trains a day reached Los Angeles from the east, depositing in that year alone some 120,000 tourists, health seekers, farmers, artisans and business men." With the migrants came a hoard of boomers fresh from the land speculations of Kansas and elsewhere, "fellows who left their consciences—that is if they had any to leave—on the other side of the Rockies" (Guinn, 1890, p. 15). Subdivision and town founding began at once.

The railroads were not the only motivating factor in the boom. Profitable agriculture, advertising, and the belief among many that the southern California climate would bring better health were important, also. But the railroads were doubly important. Their promotion and low fares brought in the migrants,

and the location of their lines influenced the alignment and provided the focus of many of the new subdivisions. Guinn, who observed the boom, explained: "Before the close of 1887, between the eastern limits of Los Angeles city and the San Bernardino County line, a distance of thirty-six miles by the Santa Fe road, there were twenty-five cities and towns, an average of one to each mile and a half of road. Paralleling the Santa Fe on the line of the Southern Pacific, eight more towns claimed the attention of lot buyers, with three more thrown in between the roads" (Guinn, 1890, p. 15). These "cities and towns" were ephemeral things. A promoter would buy a parcel of ranch land, stake out streets and mark off lots, perhaps build a flimsy hotel, have ornate maps printed up of the "town," and he was in business.

The years of the boom brought a kind of real estate madness. Dumke described the scene, "Men stood excitedly in line for days at a time in order to get first choice of lots in a new subdivision. Flag-draped trains hauled flatcars jammed with enthusiastic prospects to undeveloped tracts far from centers of settlement. Exuberant auction sales accompanied by brass bands and free lunches helped sell $100,000,000 of southern California real estate during the boom's peak year. . . . More than two thousand real estate agents paced the streets of Los Angeles, seizing the lapels of prospects and filling the balmy air with verbiage . . ." (Dumke, 1944, p. 4).

A typical boom time "town" was Chicago Park, south of Monrovia, in the sands of the bed of the San Gabriel River. Here streets with names like "State" and "Dearborn" were surveyed, and plat map after plat map was filed as lots were sold off by the hundreds. It is said that "posters showing steamers on their way up the rippling waters of the San Gabriel were used to advertise the town" (Dumke, 1944, p. 181). People would buy lots of any kind;

after all, they simply intended to sell them to someone else at a profit, that is, they expected to find a "bigger fool." At one time there were reported to be "2,289 lots and one resident" in Chicago Park. Eventually he left, too. Another boom town was Gladstone, between Glendora and Azusa, advertised as the "Business Center of the Valley," with the main street, "Citrus Avenue," nine miles long. Excursions were run to auctions of the property and at least $100,000 worth of lots were sold. But the partners squabbled over the ownership of the land, and somehow they had managed to locate the tract two miles from a railroad right-of-way. Soon Gladstone vanished from even the local maps of the area (Dumke, 1944, pp. 182–187). Most of the towns platted during the boom had similar fates. "Of more than one hundred towns platted from 1884 to 1888 in Los Angeles County, sixty-two no longer exist except as stunted country corners, farm acreage or suburbs" (Dumke, 1944, p. 175).

A few of the boom towns, however, did not die completely and have remained to the present day. Azusa began as a typical boom town on the Santa Fe line. Although Jonathan S. Slauson owned 4,000 acres of the old Rancho Azusa, much of it good agricultural land, he platted the town "where it was practically all sand, gravel and boulder wash." When somebody asked him why he placed it at that particular spot, he remarked, "If it's not good for a town, it isn't good for anything!" (Nadeau, 1960, p. 79.) The spot did seem to be good for a town, at least in 1887. It was advertised to a point, we are told, "that buyers stood in line all night before the sale opened; the person who held second place in the line supposedly refused an offer of $1,000 to give it up. . . . Lots totaling $280,000 found buyers the first day . . . nearly half the town lots platted were disposed of during the first three days" (Guinn, 1890, p. 15). Guinn asserted: "Not one in a hundred had seen the townsite. Fewer still expected to live there" (Guinn, 1890, p. 16). The promoters estimated their profits at the end of two months as $1,175,000. In celebration, Slauson erected a brick building and a hotel in the town. There were several hundred people living in Azusa in 1890, and, in spite of the fact that "it was an excellent example of a town which had nothing to recommend it save publicity," it continued to grow.

Although much of the boomtime action involved the creation of new towns, land within the city limits of Los Angeles was also subdivided at a record pace. In 1888, for example, there were 1,700 tracts of lots advertised in Los Angeles. One was the famous Wolfskill Orchard tract, originally one hundred twenty acres lying near the river. A strip of land was donated to the Southern Pacific for a station, and the portion lying between Alameda, San Pedro, Third, and Seventh divided into lots and put on the market. The lots were advertised as being covered with orange and walnut trees and even the cheapest lots near the river brought $500. Another tract, this one near the western city limits, comprising the four blocks just beyond the wasteland that was to become Westlake (now MacArthur) Park, was subdivided by a local socialist, H. Gaylord Wilshire. He surveyed a wide road down the center of his tract and gave it his name. It apparently seemed a desirable location, for the first lot at Wilshire and Parkview was reportedly sold to Col. Harrison Grey Otis. It became the site of his townhouse, "The Bivouac;" today, it is the home of the Otis Art Institute of Parsons School of Design.

Effects of the Boom

By the middle of 1888 it was clear that the boom was over; lots that had been eagerly snapped up just a few months previously were unsaleable at any price. Hundreds of thousands of lots went back to their original owners. "The little white stakes that marked the corners of the innumerable lots in the numerous paper cities and towns . . . (were) . . . buried by the plowshare and the sites of the cities themselves forgotten" (Guinn, 1890, p. 13). Hotels, so optimistically built in the boom towns, stood empty, their owners bankrupt. The boomers moved on. The Los Angeles County Assessor counted sixty ghost towns and argued for a twenty-five percent reduction in the county's assessed valuation. It was estimated that "in these 60 towns about 80,000 acres had been platted into 500,000 lots sufficient for 2,000,000 people, but their combined population in July, 1889, was a mere 2,351" (Guinn, 1890, p. 70). Fortunately, however, the collapse of the boom slowed the economy down but did not ruin it. For example, the local banks did not fail and most businesses were able to carry on as before. The greatest loss, of course, was in anticipated profits. "I had half a million dollars wiped out in the crash," one of Van Dyke's citizens observed, "and, what's worse, $500 was in cash." (McWilliams, 1946, p. 123.)

The Los Angeles *Times,* while the boom was in full frenzy, pointed out some of its evil effects. Agriculture, the mainstay of the region, was being neglected as farmers became more interested in real estate promotions than in tending their orchards. It was clear that the boom was based on speculation and was not a legitimate business enterprise. Los Angeles was growing so rapidly that municipal improvements were not keeping pace with the need for them. In Pasadena, "orange groves, once her pride and boast, had been mostly sacrificed on the altar of town lots" (Guinn, 1890, p. 21). Dumke added that the boom gave undue emphasis to town lots rather than to productive agricultural acreage and faults its leaders for doing nothing to encourage the de-

velopment of industry. The census of 1890 found only six hundred fifty persons employed in manufacturing in all of Los Angeles County.

But the boom had some positive effects as well. The population of the established towns increased a great deal. Los Angeles spurted from 11,000 to more than 50,000; Los Angeles County tripled in population, in spite of its loss of the 30,000 persons in Orange County, which split off (another effect of the boom). Pasadena's population increased more than tenfold (391 to 4,882). Perhaps as important as the numerical change was the change in kind. For the first time Americans dominated the scene. The earlier cosmopolitan group was engulfed by migrants from New England and other Eastern and Midwestern states. Los Angeles would never be the same.

Although many boom towns existed only on paper, some boom capital was invested in bonafide improvements. Scores of irrigation districts were organized, ditches were dug and flumes were built to bring water to the new townsites—many remained as viable operating entities. L. M. Holt, of Riverside, pointed to other benefits, "during this wild speculative craze there were established many solid improvements that have since been turned to good use. . . . There is no section where good cement sidewalks in cities and towns begin to compare with those of Southern California . . . where cities and towns have so good a . . . system of domestic water service. . . . There is no section where there are so many rapid transit railroads" (Netz, 1925, p. 68).

The boom left other permanent effects on southern California. Information about the area was carried to all parts of the world. Advertising methods developed by the railroads and the local promoters set the model for years to come. In addition, the area developed the publicity-consciousness which has characterized it since and which has had an important effect on its later growth.

Finally, although most of the boom towns passed out of existence, as we have seen, it is significant that almost forty towns remained as nuclei for modern growth. The list includes many of the cities and neighborhoods now important in the Metropolitan scene: Alhambra, Arcadia, Avalon, Azusa, Belvedere, Buena Park, Burbank, Chino, Claremont, Corona, Covina, Cucamonga, Eagle Rock, Fullerton, Gardena, Glendora, Hawthorne, Hollywood, Inglewood, La Verne, Lynwood, Monrovia, Puente, Redondo Beach, Rialto, Rivera, San Dimas, Sawtelle, Sierra Madre, South Pasadena, Sunland, Tujunga, Verdugo Hills, Vernon, Watts, and Whittier.

Los Angeles at the End of the Century

The years toward the end of the century saw many changes in Los Angeles. The business district continued to move southwestward. In 1882 Remi Nadeau had opened "a grand hotel" at First and Spring, outside the old business district. The "Nadeau" was a four-story building and had an elevator—both firsts for the city. Within the next few years the "Hollenbeck" was built at Second and Spring, the "Angeles" at Fourth and Spring, and the "Winchester" at Fourth and Main. Directly across from it the "Van Nuys" opened in 1897, a hostelry destined to be the city's new social center. The movement of the hotels was similar to that of other retail businesses. In 1890, retail firms were concentrated on Main, Spring, and Commercial, a connecting street; the plaza area had long since been abandoned by progressive merchants, and the buildings above First were becoming old. Guinn insisted that the boom of the eighties created such a demand for offices, accompanied by drastic increases in rents in the area bounded by Temple, Second, Main, and Spring, that this "virtually drove merchants to seek new locations farther south" (Guinn, 1902, p. 280).

Broadway (then Fort) was being built up with business blocks, too. Harris Newmark built a commercial building on his home lot at 95 Fort in 1886, and when the first streets of the city were paved the next year, the chosen ones were Main, Spring, and Broadway. Still, we are told that as late as 1896 locating a department store on fourth and Broadway was "entirely . . . out of the business district" and "too far south for all but the most adventuresome merchants" (Kilner, 1927, p. 87).

Bunker Hill in the 1890s was one of the fashionable neighborhoods, and houses in the New Queen Anne and Eastlake styles were rapidly built on that height. "Houses were decorated by corner towers, spindled verandas, second and third floor balconies, and here and there a prideful bit of stained glass," as Adler put it. She continued, "They had diagonal stripes of siding, whorls of round-ended shingles, parti-colored roofing, and English chimneys. They were painted a 'tasteful' brown or gray" (Adler, 1963, p. 21).

High class residences were moving southeastward and to the suburbs as well. The area around U.S.C. then known as "College Heights" was building up, as was "Pico Heights" west along that street. A sample of addresses listed in the *Los Angeles 1894/95 Blue Book* indicates many of these "fashionable" people lived, in order of decreasing numbers, on Figueroa, West Twenty-Third Street, Grand, Hill, Broadway, West Seventh, West Twenty-Eighth, Main, West Adams, and so on. Harris Newmark was then living on Grand at Eleventh. Some idea of the built up residential portion of the city can be seen from a map of the Los Angeles Railway System in 1898, Figure 11.2. The street car lines reached the city limits in every direction save toward the north, and, in addition, they ran out Pico and Washington to a newly annexed portion of the city.

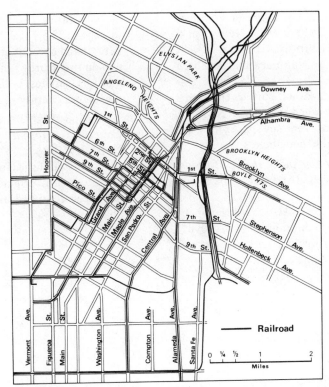

Figure 11.2. The Los Angeles Railway (streetcar) system in 1898. Source: Redrafted from data in *Street Railway Journal.* June, 1898, p. 6.

11. Suggested Readings

Baur, John E. *Health Seekers of Southern California.* San Marino: Huntington Library, 1959.
A detailed account of the "health rush," a migration of large proportions in the 1870–1900 period.

Bell, Horace. *Reminiscences of a Ranger or Early Times in Southern California.* Santa Barbara: W. Hebberd, 1927.
A sprightly, exaggerated, first-hand account of the 1850s in old Los Angeles by a controversial attorney and journalist. First published in 1881.

Clelland, Robert G. *Cattle on a Thousand Hills: Southern California, 1850–1880.* San Marino: Huntington Library, 1941.
The story of the impact of American institutions on the life of the Spanish-Californians, and the conversion of ranchos into farms and towns.

Dumke, Glenn S. *The Boom of the Eighties in Southern California.* San Marino: Huntington Library, 1944.
The classic account of this historic event during which established towns grew rapidly, and raw rangeland was converted into more than a hundred alleged "towns," and thousands of lots sold to eager buyers.

Nadeau, Remi. *City-Makers: The Story of Southern California's First Boom.* Costa Mesa: Trans Anglo Books, 1965.
A readable account of the 1868–1876 period emphasizing trade with Cerro Gordo and the building of the first railroads.

Newmark, Harris. *Sixty Years in Southern California, 1853–1913.* New York: Knickerbocker Press, 1916.
A diary kept by Newmark that has been expanded by Dr. Perry Worden. Although from its form it appears the events were recorded when they occurred, much has been added from newspaper files; extremely valuable nonetheless.

Pitt, Leonard. *The Decline of the Californios.* Berkeley: University of California Press, 1971.
Subtitled, "A Social History of the Spanish Speaking Californians, 1846–1890," it has much revealing material gleaned from the Los Angeles area.

Smith, Sara Bixby. *Adobe Days.* Cedar Rapids, Iowa: The Torch Press, 1925.
A firsthand account of life in Los Angeles and on two nearby ranches, Los Alamitos and Los Cerritos, in the latter part of the nineteenth century.

Thompson and West. *History of Los Angeles County, California.* Berkeley: Howell-North, 1959.
Originally published in 1880, profusely illustrated with "original sketches," it has now been reprinted and is widely available.

12

An Agricultural Base
for the Metropolis

Figure 12.1. Orange groves dominated the landscape for scores of miles along Foothill Boulevard. This view is from Glendora toward Mount Baldy, March 6, 1941. (Photo courtesy Spence Collection/ Department of Geography UCLA.)

"From San Bernardino and Redlands, Riverside, Pomona, Ontario, Santa Anita, San Gabriel, Pasadena, all the way to Los Angeles, is almost a continuous fruit garden, the green areas only emphasized by wastes yet unreclaimed, a land of charming cottages, thriving towns, hospitable to the fruit of every clime; a land of perpetual sun and ever-flowing breeze, looked down on by purple mountain ranges tipped here and there with enduring snow. . . . The development of the country has only begun." Charles Dudley Warner (1890, pp. 820–21).

For more than half a century the area now urbanized as the Los Angeles Metropolis was the scene of a remarkable and unique agricultural development. Although a wide variety of crops were raised, its agricultural achievement was so successful that a single fruit, the orange, became the area's dominant export. Astonishingly, this exotic and almost unknown fruit was quickly promoted into an American breakfast necessity—perhaps the earliest example of the impact of the Los Angeles Metropolis on our national life. It was orange growing, too, that helped create the regional image of exotic lushness—a tropical oasis, a land apart from the rest of the country. The orange was an attraction for the tourist and a stimulus to migration. Further, agriculture in general provided the support for a large network of towns and influenced their character, and agriculture stimulated the manufacture of needed supplies and equipment. Finally, it was agriculture that made the Los Angeles Metropolis one of the state's most important economic areas. It is not surprising that such a long and well developed period of agricultural dominance has left a significant impression on the modern urban landscape, and a noticeable mark on the nature of the present metropolis.

The Los Angeles agricultural achievement did not come easily or quickly. The sight of brown hills and treeless plains convinced the newly arrived Easterner that he had arrived in a barren land. This impression was quickly dispelled, since almost everything would grow if it were given water. It required years of trial and error, however, to discover which crops could be reliably matured and sold profitably in a market two thousand miles away. Experience in farming in the East, or even in the Midwest, proved of limited value in a radically different environment. Little was known about growing conditions in the surprisingly varied southern California environment. As McWilliams (1949, pp. 116–17) has pointed out, there were no soil maps, no climatic maps,

no books on cultural practices, no information on pests or plant diseases, and no reference works on irrigation. Everything had to be discovered experimentally. It is no wonder that more people lost their fortunes than made them in the early days of southern California agriculture.

Institutional and Technological Developments

The transition from a ranching to an agricultural economy was facilitated by a number of institutional and technological developments. For example, in 1872 California repealed the "No Fence Law," resolving the conflict between open-land grazing and fenced field irrigation in favor of the irrigator. No longer did the irrigator have to build costly fences around his field, as at Anaheim where the entire tract was fenced by six foot willow cuttings planted one foot apart. The grazer became responsible for damage caused by his cattle or sheep to irrigated-crop fields. Similarly, the enactment of the Wright Act, in 1887, reversed the doctrine that riparian owners held title to all water in streams bordering their lands. The continuance of water law under the concept of riparian rights would have been fatal for agricultural development in an arid land where water was needed for irrigation away from stream-border lands. There was substituted the legal concept of appropriation under reasonable beneficial use, which separated right to water from right to land, thereby permitting the transportation of water to any point in the hinterland. The new law also provided for the organization and government of irrigation districts in each county. Within three years eleven districts were formed in Los Angeles County, and seven in San Bernardino County.

Other discoveries and new introductions also aided irrigation agriculture. In 1868 the search for water was augmented by the discovery near Compton of the area's first artesian well, a well that flows without pumping by means of hydrostatic pressure. Artesian areas were found in many places in the Los Angeles district, and by 1885 five hundred artesian wells had been drilled in the San Bernardino area alone. Wells that would not flow naturally could always be pumped, and after 1868 the metal bladed windmill became a common feature of the Los Angeles landscape. Increased irrigation brought about improved techniques. Concrete irrigation tile, which drastically reduced loss of water, became common after 1882.

Another vital need, access to the eastern market, was gradually achieved as connecting railroads were completed. The Southern Pacific built an extension to Los Angeles in 1876, but as products had to travel east via San Francisco its value was limited. The Southern Pacific completed its line from Los Angeles to New Orleans in 1883, and four years later the Santa Fe established direct connections between southern California and Chicago. With competing lines, freight rates fell, and for the first time an effective connection with the market was possible.

Earlier Successes: Grapes, Wine and Brandy

Grape cuttings were brought to the San Gabriel Mission by the Franciscans, and by 1830 from 400 to 600 barrels of wine and 200 barrels of brandy were produced annually. Although this bounty was for consumption by residents, grapes and their products became the area's first commercial agricultural success and its first significant export. Grapes did well in the Los Angeles climate, and could be grown without irrigation in the "wetter" (sandy soil) sections. More importantly, grapes could be turned into wine or brandy *(aguardiente)*, the popular drink of the populace. Both products had the advantage of being concentrated items, with good keeping qualities, relatively valuable, easy to store and ship, and

much in demand. Dominating the limited agricultural scene in the 1830s and 1840s, they were increasingly important in the 1850s and 1860s as California's expanding population created a growing market.

Commercial production of grapes in Los Angeles began in 1824 when Joseph Chapman set out 4,000 vines, using cuttings from the mission. He was followed by Jean Louis Vignes, who arrived from the Bordeaux region of France in 1831, purchased 104 acres of land south of Aliso Street east of Alameda, and set out El Aliso Vineyard with imported cuttings. Another major producer was William Wolfskill who planted his vineyard in 1838 and eventually had a cellar with a capacity of 60,000 gallons. In addition to these prominent producers, twenty-four other vineyards of from two to six acres were growing within the Los Angeles city limits as early as 1831. But both in landscape impression and in long term influence Jean Louis Vignes was clearly the leading figure. His El Aliso Vineyard featured a grape arbor, perhaps ten feet in width and fully a quarter of a mile long, extending from his adobe to the river, and the scene of many early Los Angeles celebrations. By 1836 he had a vineyard of 40,000 vines, a good cellar, and many oak barrels—he himself cut the trees and made the casks. He exported wine and brandy to Santa Barbara, Monterey, and San Francisco in 1840, receiving $2.00 a gallon for white wine and twice that for brandy. Before Vignes died in 1862 it is thought that at least thirty wine growers had been lured to California by his letters.

The massive influx of population into northern California during the gold rush created a large new market and stimulated production of grapes and wine. Large scale commercial vineyardists and wine makers included the Sainsevain Brothers of Los Angeles who produced 115,000 gallons in 1858, Matthew Keller, credited with 55,000 gallons in the same year, and Benjamin D. Wilson, whose

Oak Knoll Vineyard in what is now San Marino, produced 20,000 gallons in 1859. The total wine production of the county was estimated to be 500,000 gallons in 1859.

To facilitate trade most of the Los Angeles commercial vintners established depots in San Francisco. The firm of Kohler and Frohling, one of the largest shippers, is reported to have had 100,000 gallons of wine and 20,000 gallons of brandy in storage in 1862. In Los Angeles, the firm rented the entire basement of the City Hall building, as well as the storage vaults at the Wolfskill vineyard to house its products. Its wines were marketed all over the world. Among the principal wines were a "credible" white, a red—"strong and earthy"—Port, Champagne (popularized by the Sainsevain Brothers), Angelica (a sweet wine made by adding brandy to grape juice) and the every popular *aguardiente*.

One result of the wine boom was the organization of the Los Angeles Vineyard Society, a cooperative organization that founded Anaheim in 1858 as a wine producing venture. The members were Germans from San Francisco, and for their colony's name they took the name of the river (Ana) and combined it with the German home, heim. Four hundred thousand vines were planted the first year on twenty acre plots, and by 1872 there were nine hundred acres of bearing vines, and its eight wineries were producing over a million gallons of wine annually. There were occasional problems. *The Los Angeles Star* reported (December 11, 1877) "Internal Revenue Collector Hall swooped down on an illicit distillery at Anaheim one day last week and captured 1,000 gallons of grape brandy spirits."

Commercial viticulture seems to have been in the hands of recent immigrants, or at least men of capital. Although not much land was required for a commercial vineyard, considerable money was needed to prepare the land, to purchase and plant the cuttings, and to finance the cultivation and yearly pruning of the vines the three or four years before they began producing a crop. Further, picking and crushing the grapes, tending the wine making process, testing, storing and bottling the wine, and marketing the product required further financial investment. In 1855 an estimated one million dollars was invested in grape growing and wine making in Los Angeles County. And when in 1855 the Vignes vineyard and winery were sold to two nephews, Jean M. Vignes and Pierre Sainsevain, for $43,000, the transaction was reportedly the highest price paid for any piece of Los Angeles real estate up to that time.

Los Angeles, Anaheim, and Sonoma (in northern California) were the three major grape and wine areas of the decade of the 1860s. In the local area production reached 3,838,000 gallons of wine in 1868, and in 1869 advanced to nearly four million gallons. Even so, Sonoma County passed Los Angeles in 1869, and leadership was to shift to the north in the 1870s when viticulture became a California mania with massive overproduction. The resulting low prices caused many vineyards to be pulled up and planted to other crops. This was stimulated by the invasion of a number of pests and diseases. At Anaheim, a mysterious ailment (now known as Pierce's Disease) killed all the vines in the 1880s. The vineyards were never replanted, the land being used instead for the growing of walnuts and Valencia oranges.

Although an isolated example, the Anaheim transition was symbolic. Grape production never again regained its preeminence in the Los Angeles area. Although a suitable crop, it had a fatal flaw, since grapes could be produced almost everywhere in California, in the small valleys in the north as well as in the relatively cheap land of the vast San Joaquin Valley. More profitable and unique crops were to displace grapes, although not immediately or completely.

Grapes remained a profitable crop on a portion of the area, generally on land not suitable for citrus, mainly in the Etiwanda, Guasti,

Fontana triangle, and for a time on the northern floor of the San Fernando Valley. Today the former area remains as the last refuge of the old industry. Here, on the sandy surface of the Cucamonga alluvial fan, where hot or cold air, in season, blows down from Cajon Pass, are some 15,000 acres still in grapes, down from a post-prohibition high of about 33,000 acres in 1940.

Wheat in the San Fernando Valley

For some forty years wheat was grown on the level floor of the San Fernando Valley in operations on a vast scale. Isaac Lankershim, a wheat grower from northern California, noting the good stands of wild oats growing in the valley, organized the San Fernando Farm Homestead Association and bought half the valley (south of Roscoe Boulevard, exclusive of Rancho Encino), in 1869 for $2.00 an acre. Sheep were raised for a number of years with flocks reaching 40,000 head, but this venture was ended by the drought of 1874–75.

Wheat in the Los Angeles area had been plagued by a fungus called "rust" which was particularly severe in locations exposed to the moist ocean air. But the valley was inland, the air was dryer, and a new rust and drought resistant wheat variety, Odessa, became available. By the fall of 1875 Isaac N. Van Nuys, Lankershim's foreman (and future son-in-law), had 10,000 acres planted to wheat, the season looking promising, and plans were made for marketing their first crop. Shipping rates via the Southern Pacific from San Fernando were high, and the farmers determined to find a cheaper way to get their grain to tidewater. A new port was being constructed in Santa Monica Bay, and Lankershim built the first real wagon road through Sepulveda Canyon (the first road over the mountains west of Cahuenga Pass) making the valley accessible to the Santa Monica area. However, when the

grain was ready for shipment the Southern Pacific lowered its rates and the grain went by rail to San Pedro after all.

Wheat was dry farmed (grown without irrigation) and after the first rain in the fall the land was plowed, harrowed, and seeded, in a single operation. In the spring, if the rains had been bountiful, the crop was ready and by June the harvesters were moving through the fields. At first the machines were pulled by eight to thirty-six horses, but later steam power became popular.

From 1875 to 1915 wheat covered the valley, its level monotony broken only by widely scattered groves of aging eucalyptus and pepper trees marking ranch buildings. Van Nuys, for example, divided his company's operations into seven large ranches, each with a headquarters. One remains, the Workman Ranch buildings preserved as the Shadow Ranch Park, 22633 Van Owen Street, Canoga Park. Two were located at the focal points of modern communities: the Patton Ranch, at the junction of Reseda and Ventura Boulevards (Tarzana) and the West Ranch, at Sherman Way and Reseda Boulevard (Reseda). The Home Ranch was located two miles west of the present center of Van Nuys, and the Kestor Ranch about a mile and a half southwest of that same community. The Old Sheep Ranch, comprising the land between Ventura Boulevard and the Los Angeles River, had its headquarters in the vicinity of the present Bullock's Fashion Square. And the Clyman Ranch was part of the 12,000 acres sold by the Association in 1888 to be laid out as a townsite (first called Toluca, then Lankershim) now North Hollywood.

Although the Lankershim-Van Nuys operation was the valley's largest, other wheat and barley ranches existed. Benjamin and George Porter (the Porter Land and Water Company) farmed much of the valley north of Roscoe Boulevard, eventually selling a portion of their land to H. C. Hubbard and F. W.

Wright (Mission Land and Water Company). Wheat reigned until water was available for irrigation. In 1919 the entire Lankershim-Van Nuys operation was sold and the ranching equipment auctioned off. An era of the valley was at an end.

With water available and a distribution system completed (1915) irrigated agriculture quickly replaced wheat. The large holdings were split up into small farms or home acreages and a variety of crops were introduced. A central belt, generally from Canoga Park to Van Nuys, specialized in sugar beets, lima beans, melons, pears, apricots and other crops. The southeastern section was devoted to peaches, apricots, walnuts, grapes, melons, pumpkins, alfalfa, and some green vegetables. Along the northern rim, east and west of San Fernando, important plantings of oranges and lemons were made, later spreading to the western section of the valley's rim. Below the orange and lemon belt, on lands that suffered from winter frost, was a linear zone that produced lettuce, cabbage, tomatoes, and other vegetables for the urban fresh-produce market. The raising of chickens, for eggs and fryers, was also important in several sections of the valley floor on small farms that also grew a variety of fruit. This varied irrigated agriculture was to dominate the valley until the building boom following World War II.

Agricultural Experiments That Failed

As the New England seafarer sailing unknown seas clawed his way to fortune by his willingness to "try all ports," similarly the Los Angeles agriculturist tilling in an unfamiliar environment hoped for the same success by being willing to try all crops. Such varied crops as cotton, silk worms, coffee, tea, castor beans, opium poppies, and eucalyptus trees were tried. All failed, though most would grow and some enjoyed prosperity for a year or two.

Cotton first appeared in Los Angeles during the Civil War growing on a small plot belonging to William Workman. Matthew Keller tried growing cotton on a six acre irrigated plot lying west of Figueroa, from Ninth to Adams. It reportedly grew luxuriously and produced abundantly, but labor was scarce and markets distant. Around 1870 a Col. J. L. Strong, a cotton planter from Tennessee, leased six hundred acres along the Santa Ana River. He reportedly grew much cotton but made no money. Seemingly, growing cotton with irrigation in the area was a possibility; the rub was picking, ginning (presumably there was no gin) and finding a profitable market for the lint, which grew so luxuriously without irrigation elsewhere.

Silk was another fiber that had a brief popularity with Los Angeles experimenters. The chief promoter was Louis Prevost, trained in the art of sericulture in France. He had produced silk in San Jose in 1860 from silkworm eggs brought from China and mulberry trees grown from seed imported from France, and propagandized silk growing by a series of letters to newspapers. He succeeded in getting the state legislature, in 1864, to pass an act giving a bounty of two hundred fifty dollars for every plantation of 5,000 mulberry trees two years old, and three hundred dollars for every 100,000 merchantable cocoons produced. Some two hundred acres in the Los Angeles area were planted to two million mulberry cuttings. Prevost had a planting of fifty acres on South Main Street, a mulberry tree nursery, and near it a large cocoonery. The California Silk Center Association was formed and in 1869 bought 4,000 acres (now part of Riverside) for the purpose of establishing a colony of silk growers and weavers. Indian women were to be trained to the delicate task of unwinding the cocoons. There was considerable speculation in silkworm eggs, which sold from three to ten dollars per ounce; money was made in the sale of the silkworms and in collecting the state bounty. However, the bounty was re-

166

pealed (1867), Prevost, the only man who knew how to operate the industry died (1869), the price of eggs declined and the producers went bankrupt. The key to silk production was abundant, highly skilled, but cheap labor, a non-existent commodity in a frontier community. Although mulberry trees grow easily in California and elsewhere, the activity was doomed from the beginning.

The eucalyptus tree had been brought from Australia as a shade tree, and attempts were made to grow the tree on a large scale for lumber. A "Forest Grove Association" was formed in 1874 and 100,000 trees were set out on a sixty acre tract of land near Florence (south of Los Angeles). Remi Nadeau had a grove in the same area totalling eighty acres and A. Bullock had forty acres in eucalyptus near the San Gabriel River. In five years the trees grew to a height of thirty to forty feet and were cut for fire wood with the stumps sprouting a second crop. But even the fast growing gum tree could not turn southern California into a lumbering community, since eucalyptus grew with a twisted grain pattern that made poor lumber.

The castor bean was grown for a time for its oil. In 1866 the local crop was reported to be 5,000 bushels and a small castor-oil factory was in operation the next year. The crop increased to 24,000 bushels in 1875, and four years later three hundred fifty acres were said to be in castor beans. However, they were reported to "ruin" the land, and were in fact hard to stop growing, as a volunteer crop grew wild for years along the zanjas. Even today, castor beans are occasionally seen growing as "weeds" in vacant land and along roadsides.

Many other crops were tried in a minor way. Tobacco was grown on a small scale, so were sugar cane, peanuts, and hops. All the grains were tried, and most of the fruit and nut trees. Even such exotic items as opium poppies were given a try at Riverside. These, however, were damaged by Santa Ana winds and did not prove profitable. Most of the or-chard plantings of exotics were pulled out and served only to replenish the woodpiles of the farmer. A truly successful crop for the area seemed unaccountably elusive.

Oranges: Agricultural Dominant, 1890–1940

In 1877 Joseph Wolfskill sent a boxcar of oranges from Los Angeles to St. Louis. It took the car (routed through San Francisco) a month to arrive; Leland Stanford, president of the road, made the arrangements personally and the bill for the freight was five hundred dollars. The fruit was in good condition in spite of the crude packing methods and apparently found a welcome market. Thus began a regional trade that, within a decade, enabled oranges to become the king of the agricultural enterprises of the Los Angeles Metropolis. Within five years five hundred carloads were shipped east annually, and forty years later 50,000 carloads of citrus fruit were marketed yearly in the eastern states. Acreage devoted to citrus rose steadily decade by decade until in 1950 it reached a peak of more than 237,000 acres (more than three hundred seventy square miles) in citrus groves. The industry became highly organized, using advanced advertising techniques, and, producing only a few standardized varieties of oranges and lemons, was able to overcome high costs of production (land, labor, water), the hardship of a long distance to markets, and occasional losses from frost and wind. The Los Angeles Metropolis became the premier orange growing region in the world and the area's orange growers came to epitomize American commercial agriculture. Yet their road to success was difficult and uncertain in the early experimental years.

Early Plantings

The first local orange grove was planted in the irrigated garden of Mission San Gabriel about 1804, and at one time it may have consisted of four hundred trees. Oranges gradually became a common dooryard tree in the

Pueblo, producing fruit for home use. As early as 1834 Louis Vignes began planting a grove on Aliso Street using seedlings from the mission and Manuel Requena also had a grove of commercial size. William Wolfskill set out seedlings in 1841 on the east side of Alameda Street between 4th and 6th, gradually increasing it in size to twenty-eight and then to seventy acres. Also in the early forties, a grove was planted a few miles north of the mission and it eventually became the property of Benjamin Wilson.

Stimulated by the gold rush (which created a lucrative market, as Los Angeles goods could be shipped by water to San Francisco), other plantings were made in the fifties. One orchard was planted across Alameda from Wolfskill's grove, another in San Bernardino, a third near Highland. In 1867 there were 15,000 orange trees in the Los Angeles region. Even so, they could not begin to satisfy the demands of the northern market. Of the 3,250,000 oranges imported by San Francisco in 1866, only 250,000 came from Los Angeles, the rest from Mexico and the islands of the Pacific. However, in the decade of the seventies the development of citrus plantings increased, especially around Riverside, which had 17,000 orange trees, second only to Los Angeles. Pasadena was founded in 1873, and many of its ten to thirty acre lots were planted to oranges. Grapes were still the dominant fruit crop in the area, and the horticulturists were divided as to which was the most profitable.

Developments of the 1870s

The lack of rapid response to the newly available northern market may have been caused by the inherent characteristics of the orange growing operation. The orange grower must have considerable capital, not only for land but for growing costs and living expenses during the five to eight years before a crop is produced. Further, the orange is a native of the humid tropical forest and the trees require large amounts of water and a constantly moist soil, the crop being damaged by only brief intervals of delay in irrigation. Essential is a reliable source of two to three acre feet of water per year (enough to cover an acre of ground two to three feet deep), in addition to at least fifteen inches of natural rainfall.

Early expansion was also hampered by uncertainty over the quality of the bud stock available at nurseries. Many orchardists found that when their trees finally began to bear they matured fruit irregularly, had litle resistance to frost, and the fruit was of such poor quality as to be almost unsaleable. "In 1875 nothing worthy of the name orange could be seen in California. Thick-skinned, sour, pithy and dry, it was an insult to the noblest of fruit . . ." was the comment of one observer (Van Dyke, 1890, p. 31). This problem was resolved almost by chance. A missionary in Bahia, Brazil, had discovered an amazingly fine orange: sweet, flavorful, large, hardy, regular maturing, almost completely seedless, and with a "navel." Some seedlings were sent to the U.S. Commissioner of Agriculture in Washington, and two budded trees were forwarded to Mrs. Luther Tibbets of Riverside, who had asked for help in selecting fruit trees suitable for her new home. Planted in 1873, and first fruited in 1878, this orange, known as the Washington Navel, became the basis for the winter orange industry in California. Somewhat similarly, two nurserymen, A. B. Chapman and George H. Smith, received an unmarked package of orange trees from England in 1876; one of these turned out to be a Valencia, which in California did not ripen until the April-September season. The Valencia became the standard summer orange, going to market when demand was the highest, whereas the Washington Navel was marketed in the December to May period. By the end of the decade, therefore, experiments in the selection of varieties had met with success, and some fine fruiting trees were filling the southern California orchards.

The Location of Citrus Districts

Oranges could be grown in downtown Los Angeles and were successful early in Riverside and Pasadena, but they would not flourish everywhere in the area. Eventually through trial and expensive error the minor variations in relief, climate, water conditions, and soil were discovered that were hospitable to citrus production in contrast to those that were not, and the area's citrus districts were delineated. Most of the districts had sharply defined margins and wide stretches of land between them with no citrus trees. Where oranges would do well they were extensively grown. Several districts had solid plantings of 25,000 acres or more, with scarcely a plot of other crop intermixed.

Generally the citrus plantings in the Metropolis were located on the higher margins of the interior valleys and along the inner margin of the coastal plain. One belt from one to six miles wide stretched irregularly for about eighty miles in front of the San Gabriel and San Bernadino Mountains. Most of it could be seen on a drive along Foothill Boulevard between Pasadena and Redlands. A smaller area was located on the north facing alluvial slopes around Corona, Arlington, and Riverside. A second major district was on the piedmont alluvial plain west of the Santa Ana Mountains in Orange County. At one time, large citrus groves existed along the south side of the Santa Monica Mountains. Hollywood was a lemon producing community, for example, but this district was one of the first to fall to the subdivider.

Climate

Climate is the principal environmental factor restricting commercial citrus growing to a few small portions of the world, and variations in the microclimates of the Los Angeles Metropolis are the prime determinants in the location of the citrus districts described above. Winter frosts, summer heat, and desert winds are all involved. Radiation frosts on calm, clear nights are common in the area in winter. The sloping valley margins tend to have less frost than the valley floors, as the cold heavier air drains off the slopes and accumulates in the valley bottoms. This fact is the prime reason for the location of citrus groves on the higher lands of the basins. To combat these frosts the orchardist scattered heaters throughout the grove, at the rate of about one heater per tree, as only a thin layer of air near the ground was involved. "Smudging" in the early years left a dense cloud of smoke over the orange districts, much to the discomfort of the residents. Later, "wind machines," which stir up the cold ground-hugging air layer, mixing it with warmer air above, served the same purpose. Although an added expense, the orange crop is so valuable that if only one crop is saved from frost, it will frequently pay for all the cost of the operation for several years.

In order to fight freezing temperatures successfully the orchardist must know what temperatures are to be expected each night during the frost season. To provide this vital data, the Weather Bureau developed an efficient system of frost forecasting, with the predicted temperatures announced over the telephone (later the radio) for each citrus district.

High winds, particularly of the Santa Ana variety, can also be destructive to the citrus crop, blowing the fruit from the tree, and drying the leaves. Where winds are a frequent problem, as in the vicinity of Cajon Pass, citrus are not planted. In other areas windbreaks are used, and row after row of tall eucalyptus and dense cypress trees were characteristic features of many citrus districts.

Although the search for suitable varieties of oranges and appropriate locations for citrus groves can be described in a couple of paragraphs, the human effort and monetary loss that resulted from this unavoidable experimentation should not be forgotten. At one time it was said that as many acres of citrus had been pulled out as failures as those acres of trees that had been successful.

Insect and Disease Problems

The fickleness of agriculture was once again revealed to the area's orange growers in 1885. Their expanding groves were suddenly threatened by an insect parasite, the cottony cushion scale. Entering California originally on fruit imported from Australia, the parasite could denude a grove in a single season. Hundreds of acres of trees were destroyed, including the famous Wolfskill grove. In desperation the growers sent an entomologist to Australia, who discovered that in that country the scale was held in check by a natural enemy, the ladybird beetle. Thousands of beetles were sent to Los Angeles and released in the infected groves. So rapidly did they multiply in the presence of an almost unlimited food supply that within a year they had the scale under control. This operation has been called the "most nearly perfect example of biological control of an insect pest that man has thus far been able to bring about" (Batchelor, 1948, p. 604).

The broad belt of mountain and desert that separate Los Angeles from other citrus districts was a big help in preventing the introduction of many pests. So has been the exclusion of fresh citrus from outside the area. Plenty of pests have appeared anyway: black scale, red scale, red spider, aphids, and other insects that suck the juices from the leaves, stems or fruit, or secrete damaging substances. The grower's battle against them has been constant and costly, and spraying and fumigation of citrus trees has become a big business.

Railroads Supply an Economical Link to Market

High quality oranges produced in abundance would have been of little economic value without low cost transportation to a populous market. The northern California market was limited and eventually oversupplied. With the completion of the Southern Pacific line a route to the east, however circuitous, was open. However, as competing railroads began building, rates began to tumble, and shipping volume increased, with the first complete trainload of oranges shipped in 1886.

The railroads quickly established a symbiotic relationship with the orange growers. The roads needed additional freight and joined the growers in publicizing the novel fruit. Early joint efforts included an exhibit at the 1885 New Orleans World Fair, and the next year exhibits were placed in Chicago and Boston, where passers-by could see displays of California oranges. The railroads similarly publicized the region to stimulate passenger traffic, emphasizing the potential of the area for orange production.

Marketing and Advertising

Marketing and advertising of oranges both had their experimental phases. Early marketing was handled by commission houses. However, in years of heavy production the fruit was often handled on consignment and a glutted market resulted in heavy losses for the growers. After repeated crises the growers experimented with various cooperative associations that by 1895 evolved into the Southern California Fruit Growers Exchange. A federation of local exchanges, it was designed to direct marketing, controlling when and where all oranges were shipped. It was immediately successful, and was soon handling the bulk of the area's fruit. An important southern California institution, it exists today as the Sunkist Growers, Inc.

Its advertising campaigns became legendary for their ambition and ingenuity. The goal was no less than to change the breakfast habits of America. One early experiment in advertising by the exchange was begun in 1908 with Iowa as a pilot project and the Union Pacific as a partner. As the crop rolled to market, trains crossing Iowa bore gaudy banners proclaiming the merits of oranges. Orange Week was announced, and city newspapers, country weeklies, and farm journals carried full page displays. Iowans responded by buying fifty percent more oranges than previously and at higher prices.

If advertising was to benefit the local product and not Florida oranges also, a distinctive label was necessary: the brand name "Sunkist" was adopted in 1908. As the technique for printing the trademark on the orange was not yet developed, it appeared on the tissue paper wrapper, and it was hoped that the retailer would display the fruit in its distinctive covering. To encourage this, the Exchange advertised that it would send the housewife gifts of silverware for the return of wrappers—one spoon for twenty-five wrappers. These "orange spoons" designed for eating halved fruit became "hot items" and within a decade the Exchange became the largest silverware buyer in the world. Later, a campaign was launched to convince consumers to squeeze the fruit and drink the juice, as a full glass required several oranges. In 1916 juice ads offered housewives a glass hand juicer for ten cents; eager buyers sent in their dimes.

A Unique Agricultural System

Gradually, a simple system of agriculture expanded into a complex agricultural economy, accompanied by a household domestic consumer system, both focused on the orange. The combined systems were unique in America, remarkable in their commercialization and systematization. Individual holdings were usually small, from five to twenty acres, often places of retirement of businessmen from the eastern states. Essentially all services were contracted through the Exchange so that there was nothing arduous in the undertaking. Commonly the grower had his entire acreage in oranges, with only the space of a city lot reserved for house and garage. Even fences were uncommon as they would take up valuable space. The owner kept the ground cultivated, fertilized, and watered, although these services could be contracted for from the Exchange. The Exchange would pick, store, grade, and market the fruit, and the grower received the average price of the season for his grade of fruit. Often the value of the land was high, as much of it was recognized as having subdivision possibilities, and usually profits were not large. But the life was nice, the location was pleasant, and the prestige was great.

Other Important Agricultural Crops

The orange was king, but there were other lordly crops that made Los Angeles the most important agricultural county in the U.S. from 1919 to 1949. Almost all of the lemons produced in the U.S. came from the area, as did many of the avocados and olives. English Walnuts were so important they became known as California Walnuts, and peaches and apricots were grown in abundance. Alfalfa and sugar beets were important field crops grown with irrigation, wheat and barley where irrigation was not possible. Row crops were numerous, particularly, lima beans, a wide variety of vegetables: cabbage, cauliflower, cucumbers, lettuce, melons, onions, tomatoes, and celery. Flowers were raised commercially in isolated spots. For many years Los Angeles County was the leading dairy county in the country.

These crops were found in recognizable zones, responding to a complicated pattern of microclimates, soil areas, and water conditions. But, generally speaking, alfalfa, grain, sugar beets, and lima beans, the field and annual row crops—crops not injured by frosts— were located on the valley floors. On nearby sloping well-drained land were located the walnuts, peaches, and apricots. Farther up the slopes often in the form of a dark green horseshoe around the rim of the valley was the orange belt. Still higher on the slopes were the lemons and avocados, and on land so high that winters are cold, apples were grown.

The citrus industry increased its acreage annually, reaching its peak in about 1940, when the Metropolis boasted 190,000 acres of oranges and 48,000 acres of lemons. Even in the depression year of 1930 it was estimated that 200,000 persons were supported by the industry, and that it brought $130,000,000 into the area. Groves stood in solid stands, with some districts containing as many as 25,000 acres, scarcely interrupted by any other crop.

However, with the urban explosion since 1945 and the high assessed valuation of land that had subdivision potential, acreage in citrus decreased to about 118,000 acres in 1980, and most of this is in the far reaches of Riverside and Ventura Counties. Some of the growers have moved to the eastern foothills of the San Joaquin Valley, others have succumbed to competition from Florida. Now that the main market is in frozen juice the superior appearance of the California orange is no longer important.

The English or California Walnut

The walnut was second in importance only to the orange in the local orchard scene. Small bearing walnut orchards were reported in Los Angeles in 1854, with some large trees estimated to be more than twenty-five years old. Presumably the seeds for these trees came from the Franciscans. They were reported as "plentiful" in southern California in 1867, and in 1885 were recognized "as staple an article of export as any other well known California product." By 1920, when reliable statistics became available, there were about 75,000 acres of walnuts in the Los Angeles area, second in magnitude to that of the orange. Large, leafy, but deciduous trees, walnut groves had neither the sunny aspect nor the perpetual beauty of an orange grove. They did not become a symbol of luxurious living as did the orange and lacked their exotic mystique.

Walnuts do best on deep, well drained soils. As a deciduous tree, the walnut needs winter chill and can tolerate frost during the dormant season. Extreme heat in summer can damage the nuts. Although they require frequent irrigation in summer, they are injured by a high water table and alkali soils. Walnut districts thus developed on the higher, well drained portions of the interior valley floors in the vicinity of Chino, Pomona, Puente, and West Covina, and also on the coastal plain, from El Monte to Whittier, La Habra and Rivera. Some were grown in the San Fernando Valley, as well as in the more distant Simi Valley, around Moorpark, and on the upper portions of the Oxnard Plain.

The walnut grower's problems were somewhat similar to those of the citrus producer. The trees became full bearing only after twelve or fourteen years, although by then they were very large, so in the early years they were sometimes intercropped, often with lima beans. Imitating the successful orange producers, the California Walnut Growers Association was formed in 1912, evolving into the Diamond Walnut Growers, Inc. Sized, dried, and sacked at local processing plants, walnuts were shipped to the Association's headquarters and shelling plant at 1745 East 7th Street. It was a massive seven story building that could shell more than twenty million pounds of nuts annually.

Although as late as 1936 sixty-five percent of the bearing orchards of the state were in the Metropolis, acreages began to decline after 1940, and today there are less than 4,000 acres in the area, mostly in Ventura County. Not only did subdivisions move rapidly into the walnut areas, but some orchards became decadent, others were of obsolete, low yielding varieties. In 1956 the Association moved its headquarters to Stockton, and another era was at an end.

Other Crops

Other important tree crops, particularly in the first three decades of the twentieth century were peaches and apricots. Deciduous fruits, they could stand winter frost, enjoyed

172

summer heat and were grown in the interior valleys, often below the citrus groves. Peaches were grown in the San Fernando Valley, around Pomona, Alta Loma, Chino, and Mira Loma. Apricots, requiring less water than citrus, were located in such places as the Hemet Valley and the Santa Clara River Valley and adjacent valleys in Ventura County.

Less important in total acreage, but somehow more characteristically Californian, olive production also flourished. San Fernando Mission was famous for its olives and olive oil, but commercial production came relatively late. A large grove of 1,600 acres was planted at Sylmar at the northern corner of the San Fernando Valley in 1894 and at the time was reputed to be the largest olive grove in the world. In 1934, it was still producing a crop of 1,000 tons of olives annually, five percent of the state's production. In that year the owners, the Sylmar Packing Corporation, canned from 25,000 to 50,000 gallons of ripe olives annually and also produced olive oil. There were nearly 6,000 acres in olives in the region in 1920, declining to 3,500 by 1950. The olive tree is long-lived, and tolerates both neglect and poor soil conditions. As olive groves were abandoned, the trees proved popular as decorative planting around homes, and most of the old orchard trees, by the 1970s, had been scattered throughout the Metropolis.

Manufacturing in the Agricultural Age

Manufacturing was relatively undeveloped in the agricultural period. What little there was often involved the processing of agricultural products or producing materials and equipment needed for the agricultural operation. Wineries and distilleries dominated the industrial scene in the early years. In 1860 wineries accounted for nearly half of the capital invested in Los Angeles industry and their payroll of over eighteen thousand dollars was considerably higher than that of any other industry. By 1870 there were forty-three wineries in the county, and they employed four hundred thirty-eight persons, seventy-seven percent of all the manufacturing employment. Flour milling also had some importance early. For example, Lankershim and Van Nuys purchased the old S.P. depot at the southwest corner of Commercial and Alameda Street and established the Los Angeles Milling Company in 1878. These were only minor enterprises in the overall economy—Oscar Winter in appraising "The Rise of Metropolitan Los Angeles 1870–1900" (Winter, 1947, pp. 391–405) says nothing at all about manufacturing.

One reason for this was that processing the now dominant agricultural products was not considered manufacturing. Oranges were simply sorted and packed. Walnuts were dried, sorted, sacked, or shelled. Employment in these operations, though considerable, was not "manufacturing." Only items that were processed by canning contributed to the manufacturing statistics. Multipurpose canneries that could process, by harvesting sequence, apricots, peaches, tomatoes, and pumpkins-squash, and such winter-ripening vegetables as carrots, beets, and pickling cucumbers were of localized importance and were scattered around the agricultural fringes of the metropolis. In 1933, for example, a pack of 60,000 tons of fruit and 20,000 tons of vegetables was reported. Besides Los Angeles, important canning operations were carried on in Van Nuys, San Fernando, Burbank, Ontario, Cucamonga, Colton, Santa Ana, Riverside, Hemet, and Banning. All their supplies, except the wooden boxes, were manufactured locally. One example, the Los Angeles Can Company on San Fernando Road, made cans for fruit, vegetables, and tuna.

Agriculture and Urbanization

The agricultural age created a large number of towns dependent on agriculture. As the region has become urbanized, this system of settlements has become an integral part of the Los Angeles Metropolis. For example, a line of orange belt towns developed on the north slope of the San Gabriel Valley—Pasadena, Arcadia, Sierra Madre, Duarte, Azusa, Glendora, and Covina. To the south and west Pomona, Claremont, Upland, Ontario, Redlands, Riverside, and Corona were also citrus towns, with economies originally independent of Los Angeles.

Each town had a character of its own. A number were founded as colony settlements and often attracted people with the same backgrounds, means and "refinement," with the capital necessary to purchase land and finance irrigation systems. Mutual association was necessary to develop irrigation, and later they were brought together by their common activity—raising the same crop for the same market. Their towns were reported to be clean and conservative, but they were two class towns: the owners and the laborers. Much labor was required for work in the fields and packing houses. McWilliams reported that the work was first done by Chinese laborers, from 1900 to 1910 by Japanese, and then, at the peak of the industry, by Mexicans or Mexican Americans who had always been present in some numbers. These workers were said to be more conscientious, available for lower wages, and more willing to do all kinds of intermittent work than Anglo Americans. A few of the larger growers maintained camps for their workers, but most lived in town, often literally on the other side of the tracks. McWilliams, writing in the 1940s, put it this way: "Throughout the citrus belt, the workers are Spanish-speaking, Catholic, and dark-skinned, the owners are white, Protestant, and English speaking. The owners occupy the heights, the Mexicans the lowlands" (McWilliams, 1946, pp. 218–219).

Remnants of the Agricultural Era in the Modern Landscape

In a Metropolis now highly urbanized, what remains to remind us of these many years of agricultural prominence? It is true that agriculture itself has not entirely vanished. Working orange groves remain, largely in the distant districts around Riverside and Redlands, and lemons are still important in Ventura County. In addition, an occasional "relic" grove remains: as of 1981, a working orange grove could be found within half a mile of the Promenade Shopping Center in Woodland Hills, occupying a hillside north of Oxnard Street. Beyond that, some urban oriented aspects of agriculture flourish, many "dry lot" dairies are located around Chino, and nursery stock is grown widely in the area. Similarly, growing of cut flowers has become an even more important activity.

As we have seen, the communities that grew up in the agricultural era are with us still, with changed functions. Some names reflect an earlier day: Orange Grove Avenue, the traditional "Millionaires Row" of Pasadena, and Orangethorpe in Anaheim. Then there are the cities of Orange and Walnut, Orange County and Walnut Valley, and many institutions, Olive View Sanitarium, for example. Further, numerous orange trees remain, struggling to survive where subdivision lawns have replaced the open cultivation of their early years. Similarly, larger walnut trees are occasionally visible in their formal rows, now only showing above the rooftops. Lines of pepper trees, cypress or pine border an occasional city street, remains of the windbreaks of an earlier era. Finally, the fully mature olive trees that landscapers have moved into decorative locations, often spent their earlier years as part of a commercial grove.

12. Suggested Readings

Ewing, Paul. *The Agricultural Situation in the San Fernando Valley*. Washington: U.S. Department of Agriculture, 1939.
One of the rare descriptions of the local agriculture during the period when the San Fernando Valley was considered to be the garden of Los Angeles.

Nadeau, Remi. "Wheat Ruled the Valley," *Westways,* 55 (April, 1963) 18–21.
An account of wheat growing in the San Fernando Valley, 1869–1910.

Patterson, Tom. *A Colony for California.* Riverside: Press-Enterprise, 1971.
A detailed history of Riverside, one of the most significant of the region's agricultural communities, noted particularly for its leadership in orange production.

Teague, Charles C. *Fifty Years a Rancher.* Los Angeles: Ward Richie, 1944.
A personal account of the expanding knowledge of a migrant who became importantly involved in the development of both the citrus and walnut industries in southern California.

Zierer, Clifford M. "The Citrus Fruit Industry of the Los Angeles Basin," *Economic Geography,* 10 (1934) 53–73.
The classic analysis of the citrus industry by a geographer who came to UCLA in 1925, early enough to get a firsthand view of this world-famous agricultural district.

CHAPTER 13

Twentieth Century Growth of the Metropolis

Figure 13.1. Building activities in the early 1950s created "instant cities" on formerly agricultural land. Shown here is Lakewood rising out of the bean fields, February 17, 1953. The view is to the northwest. (Photo courtesy Spence Collection/Department of Geography, UCLA.)

"To a northern European entering Pasadena . . . or parts of Los Angeles in winter is like entering a vast conservancy, whose domed roof is the cloudless blue and in which a sumptuous array of floral splendour is on view." Arthur T. Johnson (1913, p. 26).

"Actually Los Angeles has not grown, it has been conjured into existence . . ." Carey McWilliams (1946, p. 134).

Tourism: Pasadena the Prototype

Tourism had its roots in the developments of the 1880s and increased considerably in the early part of the twentieth century. Stimulated by scores of books on the area, railroad and Chamber of Commerce advertising, as well as by the nation's increasing wealth, tourism became an important business. This was the era of railroad travel, tourists came by Pullman car, and winter was the tourist season. The typical tourists were wealthy Easterners free to flee the rigors of the grim Northern winter.

The Eastern visitors expected comfortable accommodations and a number of tourist hotels were soon built in many of the most attractive spots in southern California. (Early examples, outside of the Metropolis, were the Arlington in Santa Barbara and the Coronado in San Diego.) No city was to have a hotel development rivaling that of Pasadena. The first and most famous of the Pasadena Hotels was the Raymond, owned by the Boston travel agency, Raymond and Whitcomb, and built on the city's southern border in 1886. Located on "Raymond Hill" it had twenty-five acres of gardens and could be seen for miles. With more than two hundred suites and over forty "water closets" it was said to be the largest and most luxurious hotel in the West. A recently completed rail line, part of the Santa Fe system, stopped just outside; the trip from New England's snow to the Pasadena sun became fashionable—35,000 tourists were entertained in its first six months of operation. Another large hotel, Hotel Green, was located in downtown Pasadena. Constructed by a patent medicine millionaire, G. G. Green, in 1890, it eventually covered two city blocks and also included landscaped gardens (now Central Park). It too had its private railroad terminal across the street. Other Pasadena hotels, though not so famous, also had their advocates: the La Pintoresca north of town, the Maryland (1903), the Vista del Arroyo (1905), and the Huntington (1914).

Although the tourist hotels often had elaborate grounds and a program of activities to occupy their guests, Pasadena soon developed additional attractions exploiting the nature of the region itself. The nearby San Gabriels had offered hiking and hunting for years before a toll road was graded to the summit of Mount Wilson in 1891. The region's most famous tourist attraction featured a cable railway up the mountains, constructed by Thaddeus S. C. Lowe, balloonist, inventor, and promoter. Beginning at Lake Avenue and Woodbury road, the line ran to the bottom of Rubio Canyon, which was developed with the Rubio Hotel, a pavilion and trails among lakes and waterfalls lit with 2,000 Japanese lanterns. Here one transferred to the cable line which climbed 2,682 feet to the top of Echo Mountain, the site of many paths, walkways, and the three story Chalet Hotel (later called the Alpine Inn). The line eventually was extended another three and a half miles, "curving in and out among pungent pines, and skirting deep canyons" (Taylor, 1928, p. 61), to Crystal Springs (and another hotel) on a peak that became Mount Lowe. On the inaugural trip, July 5, 1893, the first car was reserved for the Pasadena City Band. We are told that as the car moved silently upward, powered by noiseless electric power, it soon disappeared into a cloud bank while the band played "Nearer my God to Thee" (Seims, 1976, p. 54). The entire hotel complex with its unique trip "from the oranges to the snow" became an obligatory event for tourists and was popular with the local residents as well. In 1928 a visitor described the scene from Mount Lowe. "If the day is clear you can see beyond the shores of the Pacific to Catalina Island. Doll houses are there below you, with the orchards like checkerboards, and wheat fields dotted with microscopic haystacks. Comes evening with the sparkle of newborn lights, like the stars in inverted heavens, and behind you bulk the dark, friendly mountains" (Taylor, 1928, pp. 61–62). The line remained in operation for more than forty years.

A second magnet for Pasadena tourists was the Busch Gardens. They were created in 1903 as a part of a luxurious winter establishment Adolphus Busch created on the grounds of his home on Orange Grove Avenue. He landscaped seventy-five acres from Orange Grove to the stream in the Arroyo Seco, and, on the lower thirty acres, adjacent to the water course, the Gardens were developed. They consisted of both formal gardens and natural woodland. The former were landscaped with a wide variety of exotic plants and shrubs, tropical trees stocked with rare birds, pools, lawns, and miles of trails. One observer wrote, "Particularly unique are the groups of gnomes and fairies scattered in shady nooks, tableauing the more familiar fairy tales. One unforgettable group is gathered convivially about a microscopic table, set with bottles which bear the unmistakable label of Anheuser Busch" (Taylor, 1928, p. 82). Later the Gardens were to be the locale of many movies including the Errol Flynn "Robin Hood," before they were finally subdivided in the 1940s.

Busch was just one of the numerous wealthy families that came to Pasadena to spend the winter, liked it, and finally established permanent homes. A favorite location for their mansions was South Orange Grove Avenue, which both overlooked Arroyo Seco and had a fine view of the San Gabriels. So many built there that it became known as "Millionaires' Row." Busch himself bought the Thaddeus Lowe house, an enormous three story structure containing some 24,000 square feet of space and said to have been the largest residence in California. Other wealthy Easterners followed: William Wrigley, Hulett Merritt, Charles Gamble, Thomas Warner, and thirty or forty more. For many years Pasadena was reputed to be the richest city per capita in America. As recently as 1939 a study rated it first among American cities in "general goodness of life."

Although Pasadena was the main goal of the early tourists the entire region was attractive to winter visitors. There were a myriad of sights to be seen and many places to visit. Most of these were located at places reached by the Pacific Electric Interurban lines, and the PE advertised tours with suggested stops along the way. One could take the "Balloon Route Excursion," for example, and see the lushly landscaped Soldier's Home at Sawtelle, visit the beach at Santa Monica, ride the gondolas at Venice, and visit the Carnation Gardens, and gather moonstones at Redondo Beach. One could attend the Chautauqua at Long Beach, and cross the channel to Catalina and ride the glass-bottomed boats, see the flying fish, and observe the "underwater gardens." One could visit Cawston's Ostrich Farm in South Pasadena, take an ostrich-cart ride, and feed the birds oranges. To the east were the San Gabriel Mission, Lucky Baldwin's Santa Anita Ranch, and the Mission Inn in Riverside. McWilliams insisted that from 1900 to 1920 Los Angeles itself was essentially a tourist town. "With its peep-shows, shooting galleries, curio shops, health lectures, and all-night movies, Main Street became a honky-tonk alley that never closed. During the winter months, Los Angeles was, in fact, a great circus without a tent." (McWilliams, 1946, p. 133.)

The All Year Club and the New Tourists

Tourism, as we have seen, became a big business for the Metropolis. There were some problems, however, in the earlier period. Owners of apartment houses, for example, complained that whereas their units were filled in winter they were empty in summer. In response, the "All Year Club of Southern California" was founded in 1921, and began an advertising campaign. Aimed particularly at the neighboring inland states, one of its slogans was: "Sleep under a blanket every night

Table 13.1
Population Growth of the Metropolis 1900–1980
(In Thousands)

Year	City of Los Angeles		Los Angeles County		Outlying Counties		Total Metropolis	
	Number	Rate	Number	Rate	Number	Rate	Number	Rate
1900	102		170		67		237	
1910	319	211%	504	193%	120	79%	624	163%
1920	577	81	936	86	181	51	1,117	79
1930	1,238	115	2,208	136	333	84	2,541	127
1940	1,497	21	2,785	26	393	18	3,179	25
1950	1,970	32	4,152	49	665	69	4,817	52
1960	2,479	26	6,038	45	1,501	126	7,539	56
1970	2,816	14	7,032	16	2,627	75	9,659	28
1980	2,967	5	7,476	6	3,588	37	11,064	15

Source: U.S. Bureau of the Census, *Volume 1. Population.* Various years.

all summer in Southern California." The ploy seemed to work and by 1924 the Club claimed that the number of summer tourists equalled winter visitors. The proportion who have come in the summer has been increasing ever since. By the 1940s about twice as many tourists were thought to come in the summer, although those in winter stayed longer and spent more.

Actually, even without the blandishments of the All Year Club, technological developments were changing American travel habits. Transcontinental highways with all-weather surfaces were being built, automobiles were now reliable and cheap enough for almost every family. Americans took to the highways and it is said that in 1923 and 1924 a one-way stream of automobiles could be seen moving westward. The spread of paid vacation time in many industries increased the possibilities for movement. Summer tourists were not of the wealthy class of the earlier visitors, so that it was the vast middle class that was arriving to see southern California.

The Metropolis continues as a tourist attraction to the present day. The Southern California Visitors Council estimated that in 1950 over 2.5 million tourists visited the area. By 1980 more than thirteen million tourists arrived, mainly in the summer, spending an estimated eight billion dollars in the region.

Oil: Source of Energy and New Wealth

One of the most exciting events of this period was the discovery that the Metropolis was underlain with some of the nation's most productive oil deposits. A miner from Colorado, Edward L. Doheny, after investigating various tar deposits in 1892, took a partner and dug a well by hand at the corner of Glendale Boulevard and Second Street. They struck oil and the city's first oil boom began. The Los Angeles City Field, bounded by Figueroa, First, Union, and Temple, became a forest of derricks, and by 1895 its production dwarfed that of all other California fields. By 1900 the field had been expanded to include a strip two blocks wide running from Elysian Park to the intersection of Vermont Avenue and Wilshire Boulevard. About 1,150 wells were in operation and production exceeded 1.3 million barrels annually. Oil was discovered near the Rancho La Brea Tar Pits in 1902, and the Salt Lake Field, bounded by Wilshire, Beverly, La Brea, and Fairfax, soon became the region's largest producer. Later, 1908, the Beverly Hills Field was brought into production. Demand was not great at first as petroleum was mainly refined into kerosene to be used for lighting purposes. Too, the quality of the oil was not high. With the dramatic increase in supply, prices fell rapidly. For the first time the area had a local source of fuel and energy. Soon both the Santa Fe and Southern Pacific converted their locomotives from coal to oil, and some oil was used for paving. Massive demand from factories, power plants, and above all, automobiles, was still in the future.

The years 1920–1924 saw sensational oil developments in the Los Angeles region. Seven major fields were discovered during this period; three were huge pools of petroleum: Huntington Beach (1920), Santa Fe Springs on the Alphonso Bell ranch (1921), and Signal Hill (1921). These fields were so productive (totaling 650,000 barrels a *day* in 1923) that they completely swamped existing storage capacity and upset the national price structure. Other local fields were discovered later, but only one was of "world class." The Wilmington field (1932) has produced a total of more than 1.6 billion barrels, reached its peak only in 1970, and its 2,300 wells still give it the lead over all other California fields in annual production. (It is also the scene of the world's largest water injection project, and the only field in California being administered under the Subsidence Abatement Act.) Fortunately, by the time these gigantic fields were discovered, petroleum could be marketed in the East via the newly opened Panama Canal, and automobiles were creating an increasing demand for gasoline.

Petroleum meant more to the Metropolis than just a local source of energy, although that was important enough. In the 1920s, it constituted a large part of the area's non-agricultural exports, bringing in income to purchase goods not produced locally. The developing oil fields provided employment for a large number of persons. It brought to the landowners, mostly residents of the area, much wealth. It has been the basis for an important refining industry since that time. Closely related to the industry is the manufacture of oil well tools and equipment, a branch of manufacturing in which the Los Angeles area ranks second in the nation. Petroleum has created a landscape, or "oilscape," of tank farms, refineries, smokestacks, as well as "grasshopper" pumps that mark the site of some wells, all within the Metropolis. Petroleum still brings in wealth in the 1980s. Today's drilling rigs or pumps are at work near the business district, on the Beverly Hills High School grounds, along Pico Boulevard, on the grounds of the Veterans Administration, as well as on artificial islands in Long Beach Harbor, where the structures are camouflaged as skyscrapers, complete with nighttime lighting.

The Movies and the Creation of Hollywood

Motion pictures, a development as unexpected as the discovery of oil, were to help transform the area in the twentieth century. The invention of the motion picture camera made possible, for the first time, the concentration of the entertainment industry in one place. That place was to be Los Angeles and it was an industry appropriate beyond the area's wildest dreams. It fit the area precisely. Motion pictures required no raw materials, and the finished products were so light they could be shipped from anywhere—the isolation of Los Angeles didn't matter. The industry produced no smoke or fumes, but had an enormous payroll. The movies were monopolistic and the industry was not affected by the business cycle. As McWilliams said, it was "made to fit the economic requirements and physical limitations of the region like a glove" (McWilliams, 1946, p. 339).

"One-reelers" were being produced as early as 1903 around New York, but the film was "slow" and needed bright sunshine. Too, wet and cold weather interfered with outdoor production. As early as 1907 William Selig of Chicago leased the roof of a building in downtown Los Angeles to shoot scenes for "The Count of Monte Cristo." In 1913 Cecil B. DeMille rented a barn at Vine and Selma Streets for his partners Jesse Lasky and Sam Goldwyn to use as a studio. The next year D. W. Griffith was shooting "Birth of a Nation" in the Hollywood Hills, and by about 1920 all the major movie producers had moved to southern California. Kenneth Macgowan (1956, p. 274) explained some of the factors involved:

"Movie makers found in Los Angeles another attraction almost as powerful as the California sunshine. This was the city's proximity to a great many different kinds of landscapes that could not be enjoyed in the East. From San Diego to San Francisco and eastward to Arizona there was almost every variety of mountain, valley, lake, seacoast, island, desert, countryside and plain that a story might call for. Much of the seacoast was barren of habitations. Where there were houses, the type of local architecture provided Mediterranean atmosphere. 'Westerns,' which began to be popular even before the days of the first feature films, could be shot in Griffith Park or San Fernando Valley. The silent film delighted in real exteriors, and the studios built up elaborate photographic card catalogues of 'locations' throughout the Southwest."

The first studios were built in the Edendale section and the Silver Lake district just to the west, within an easy street car ride from downtown Los Angeles. However, the little community of Hollywood, a mixture of citrus groves, wooden bungalows, and open fields soon became the favorite location and early clusters of studios appeared on Sunset Boulevard and on Melrose Avenue. As the industry grew and prospered so did the community, land values rose, and as early as 1915 studios were being built in other locations. Soon they were widely scattered—MGM in Culver City (1915), Universal in Universal City (1915), Warner Brothers in Burbank (1928), Republic in Studio City, Disney in Burbank, and Fox in Westwood (1928). In spite of the early dispersal of the studios, however, "Hollywood" continued to be used by writers to refer to the movie production community regardless of geographical location.

Movies quickly became big business. As early as 1922 more than 12,000 people were continuously employed in the industry and perhaps 150,000 extras were on call. Some fifty-two studios were in operation, wages totaled $30 million and an additional $20 million was spent in the area on equipment and operations. Four years later employment reached 35,000 and payrolls were more than $1.24 million weekly. With the success of sound in Al Jolson's film, "The Jazz Singer," in 1927, an additional group of technicians were added to the payrolls, and soundproof stages of steel and concrete replaced open-air sets. The advent of color after 1932 added still another group of specialists. Too, in an era when "spectaculars" were in vogue, thousands of employees were engaged in building sets, developing "props," designing and producing costumes, and so on. Clearly the industry was characterized by labor intensiveness, a great asset to a growing community. All through the 1930s and into the 1940s, the industry boomed, with perhaps seven hundred pictures started each year. As recently as 1945 over four billion tickets of admission were sold in the United States alone, and, in this country, about eighty-five percent of all expenditures for spectator amusements were spent on the movies.

Movies no longer dominate the American amusement scene and the industry itself has changed greatly. Many films made by American producers are shot abroad—centers such as London, Rome, Paris, and Madrid rival Hollywood. Many foreign countries provide subsidies for locally produced films. Taxation and employment problems in the Metropolis have been discouraging to local film making. As costs have gone up, the demand for feature films has been declining. The production of films and shows for television has taken up some of the slack and a number of the old movie studios have been taken over by the television producers.

There is some evidence that the worst is over, however; Los Angeles has passed an ordinance to facilitate filming in the city. The state is revising its tax laws. The number of feature films produced is on the rise. The independent production companies, now in fashion, are not tied to any studio and are free to film anywhere in the world, wherever they can make the best deal.

Hollywood still has some assets for film making. It is the location of a large supply of professional and technical talent and all sorts of supporting facilities. Film labs, costume-outfitting, sound production facilities, electronic lighting equipment, scenery and "prop" construction, and various other types of equipment and supplies are readily available. Supply and repair facilities are close at hand in emergency situations. It is a reassuring place to work and the combination of supporting elements reduces the financial risks.

Radio and Television

The motion picture industry contributed more to the region than just jobs and income, although these were important enough. It promoted the region's image of glamour and make-believe in every city and hamlet in America and in much of the world—a circumstance discussed elsewhere. In addition, the presence of motion pictures in the area was a magnet that was to attract other activities. The first such, and most obvious example, was radio broadcasting.

Radio was another industry new in the twentieth century, dating only from 1920. Gradually networks of stations were formed, and the first coast to coast broadcast originated in Los Angeles when, on January 1, 1927, NBC broadcast the Rose Bowl game to the nation. The early west coast headquarters of the networks was San Francisco. However, with the development of sound in the movies, the broadcasters quickly realized that they could attach themselves to the Hollywood glamour by utilizing motion picture talent. More and more broadcasts began to originate in Hollywood. In 1938, CBS dedicated its west coast headquarters at "Columbia Square" on Sunset Boulevard. In the same year, NBC finished its "Radio City" not far away, and the network that became ABC had a studio on Vine Street. As the industry grew the city gained new significance as a producer of radio shows, and Los Angeles and New York rapidly became the two national centers of radio program origination. In addition, national and regional advertising agencies opened new offices or expanded old ones to service shows produced in the area.

Later, with the development of television in the 1940s, the networks shifted to producing television shows, and Los Angeles again was to be a major center of activity. The foundation of the industry, as with radio, was the vast reservoir of talent in the region, as well as the numerous production facilities and skilled technicians that could be drawn from both the motion picture and radio fields.

Aircraft-Aerospace

A third industry, previously unknown and beyond the range of any forecast, also brought world leadership to Los Angeles in the twentieth century: the aircraft-aerospace industry. In the early days of the airplane these frail craft required almost perfect weather to be flown safely. The dependably clear skies, light winds, and mild winters of the Metropolis fulfilled these needs. The region's assets for all-year flying were on exhibit in January, 1910, when it was the host of the nation's first air meet, a ten-day affair at Dominguez Field. The early aviators were also the manufacturers, and Glenn Martin had already built his first airplane in an abandoned Santa Ana church, earning part of his needed capital by stunt flying for the movies. Moving to Inglewood in 1915, he was soon producing ten planes a month. An employee, Donald Douglas, secured a contract to build planes for the Navy, and began production in an old movie studio in Santa Monica in 1916. At about the same time, two brothers were building planes in a garage on the beach at Santa Barbara, later moving to the area, first to Hollywood and then to Burbank. They founded Lockheed Aircraft Corporation. By 1928 the area was second only to New York in the manufacture of airplanes. North American Aviation moved from Baltimore to Los Angeles in 1934, giving as their reasons the fine climate, the many parts plants, a trained labor supply and low building costs. Northrup Aircraft was founded in Hawthorne in 1939. As World War II was beginning in Europe, the area had moved into undisputed first place in aircraft assembly. (Historically, engines and propellers were made by separate firms and brought to the site of the airframe for final assembly.)

The aircraft industry expanded phenomenally during World War II. Large amounts of capital were invested, new plants were constructed and old factories were expanded. Thousands of laborers, skilled and unskilled, poured into the Metropolis from every state in the union but many were from the Midwest and South. For the first time the industry became a volume manufacturer. Although the industry declined briefly after the war, since 1950 it has evolved into a business giant known as the aerospace industry, growing to peaks unknown even during its wartime expansion.

Soon after World War II, the industry added electronics to its capabilities but after 1958 the emphasis on the "space race" revolutionized the old aircraft firms and new organizations entered the picture. The complexity of missile and space projects necessitated an increased emphasis on research and a change in the nature of the work force. The industry was now reputed to have assembled the greatest concentration of mathematicians, scientists, engineers, and skilled technicians in the United States.

The scientific shift of the industry utilized both old traditions and new arrivals. A large pool of scientific talent oriented to aviation had been developing over many years. Professor Theodore von Karman at the California Institute of Technology had been involved in all scientific aspects of aviation, rocketry, and space exploration for several decades, and an aeronautical laboratory had existed on that campus since 1928. This was the predecessor to the World War II Jet Propulsion Laboratory and its commercial spin-off, the Aerojet-General Corporation. Two former students of von Karman, Simon Ramo and Dean Wooldridge returned to the area during the war, working for Hughes Aircraft on various electronics projects. In the post-war period they organized their own firm, Thompson-Ramo-Wooldridge, or TRW, together with its scientific offspring, Aerospace Corporation. Somewhat similarly, a scientific "brain trust" organized by the Air Force at Douglas Aircraft during the war evolved into the independent and non-profit research organizations, Rand and SDC.

For almost three decades after World War II the aerospace industry—the aircraft-missile-electronics complex—functioned as the foundation of the region's economy. At its peak in 1967 it furnished employment for about a half million persons, nearly forty-three percent of the total manufacturing employment. Since that time the industry has declined in importance, and in 1979, a fairly typical year, the employment in the industry was 325,000 out of a total manufacturing employment of slightly more than one million.

Growth Thresholds and Branch Plants

Over the years local manufacturing endeavors faced two serious handicaps. One was the small size of the local market. The other was vast empty spaces between Los Angeles and the densely populated eastern part of the country which made it uneconomic to market locally produced goods in the distant East. However, as population grew in the twentieth century so did the potential of the local market. Now these long distances proved to be a benefit rather than a handicap. Gradually, for first one industry and then another, critical market thresholds were reached. It then became more profitable to build a branch plant in the Los Angeles area rather than to ship goods to this market from the distant eastern manufacturing belt. Gradually, and then with accelerating speed, literally hundreds of branch plants of eastern firms were established in the Metropolis.

Automobiles and Rubber

An early and prominent example of the proliferation of branch plants was in automobile assembly. The first to come was Ford, a pioneering advocate of decentralization. Engines, body panels, frames and other major components were shipped from the East, with final assembly taking place near the market. Henry Ford opened his first assembly plant in Los Angeles in 1917, moving to a tide-water location in Long Beach in 1927 and, after that site was affected by subsidence, to Pico-Rivera. Willis-Overland, an important early manufacturer, began assembling automobiles in the Maywood vicinity in 1927, and Chrysler Corporation located on a nearby site in 1932. Studebaker established its first branch plant anywhere in Vernon in 1936, and in that same year Buick-Oldsmobile-Pontiac came to South Gate. So it went: by 1950 all the major manufacturers were assembling automobiles in the area (including Kaiser-Frazer in Long Beach, Nash in El Segundo and Chevrolet in Van Nuys) and the Metropolis was second only to Detroit in volume of production. Developments in the industry since that time have resulted in the demise of many of the earlier companies, and the consolidation of production in fewer plants.

The multiplication of automobile assembly plants in the Los Angeles area created a considerable demand for parts and accessories. The most important of the automobile suppliers that located factories in the area were the producers of tires, perhaps because they had a large secondary market in the region as well. The Goodyear Tire and Rubber Company opened a branch plant in Los Angeles in 1920. Other firms followed: Firestone and Goodrich, both in 1927, and the United States Rubber Company in 1930. These were the "big four" of the business, and again by 1950 the area was second in the nation (after Akron, Ohio) in tire manufacturing. The Metropolis had some additional advantages in the production of tires. The natural rubber used in this period came from Southeast Asia and could be imported economically through Port Los Angeles; similarly, the cotton for the cord was grown in the nearby Imperial Valley.

Iron and Steel

Iron and steel production in the Los Angeles area is also market-oriented. The oil discoveries of the twenties stimulated the construction of four small steel mills, based almost wholly on reprocessing local scrap. However, the first integrated steel mill on the West Coast was the Kaiser Steel Corporation's Fontana Plant. It also may be considered to be market-oriented. Built to supply a local wartime market in the West Coast shipbuilding industry (financed by a federal loan) and under governmental direction to locate at least sixty miles inland, it at first prospered and expanded. Although it is near the market, its raw material, with the exception of scrap, comes from considerable distances. The iron ore is mined at Eagle Mountain, near Desert Center in Riverside County, one hundred sixty-four miles from the plant by rail. When mined, the ore runs about fifty percent iron and is beneficiated to from fifty-six to fifty-eight percent iron before it is shipped. Coal is imported from company-owned mines near Sunnyside, Utah (eight hundred miles distant) and from Raton, New Mexico. Limestone comes from Cushenbury, in the Lucerne Valley, seventy-five miles away. Scrap, however, is available in the Los Angeles area, the largest and cheapest source in the West. Large quantities of scrap find use in the open hearth furnaces. Water, although used very efficiently, is pumped from company wells, and is neither overly cheap nor abundant. After postwar expansion this integrated works consisted of three hundred fifteen coke ovens, four blast furnaces, nine open hearths, plus three oxygen furnaces, for a total capacity of about three million ingot tons annually, the largest production west of the Mississippi. Nearly half of its production—plate, strip, pipe, structural shapes, and tin plate—is marketed in the Metropolis, another quarter finds its way to the San Francisco Bay region. With cost escalations in recent years, and steel from abroad making inroads on the West Coast market, the Kaiser Steel Corporation's operations are suffering the same problems as other American steel companies, and the future for the plant is uncertain.

Developments after World War II

Market thresholds for many industries seem to have been reached with the massive influx of population following World War II. For example, in the seven year period 1950–57 manufacturing employment more than dou-

bled, increasing more than twice as rapidly as the expanding population. By 1960 the proportion of the labor force in manufacturing was almost exactly the same as that for the average large American metropolitan area. The Metropolis appears to have reached manufacturing maturity.

An additional important component of local manufacturing followed logically from the large population increase. These were the industries producing the supplies, fixtures, equipment, and other components necessary to build up the expanding "urban plant." This involved houses, schools, offices, ships, factories, utilities, streets, freeways, and so on. Beginning early, and growing larger with every boom, these manufacturers expanded rapidly after World War II. Soon the Metropolis became first in the nation in the production of such things as home heaters, water heaters, kitchen ranges, plumbing equipment, cabinets and doors, and was high in plaster products, household furniture, and so on. In a real way, growth itself has stimulated additional growth.

Population Growth and Real Estate Booms

Continued expansion of agriculture, the unexpected oil discoveries, the growth to world importance of the movies and the aircraft-aerospace industries, and the continued American desire for the good life, at one time or another stimulated real estate expansions reminiscent of the legendary "Boom of the Eighties." Speculation in urban land seems to be endemic in southern California. With the rapid growth of population, of course, there was a steady legitimate need for new building lots, although the supply put on the market by the hopeful speculators always far exceeded the demand.

The early part of the century was marked by a small boom in real estate. Ocean sites became popular. Hermosa Beach was opened in 1902, Naples in 1905, and speculation in Re-

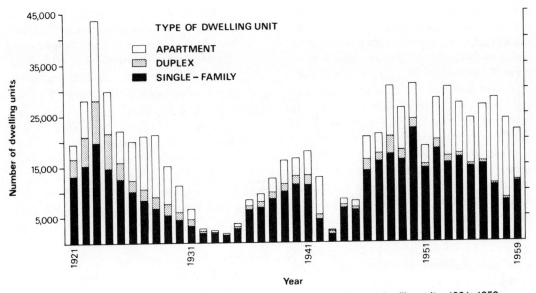

Figure 13.2. New residential construction in Los Angeles, by number of dwelling units, 1921–1959. Source: Redrafted from: City of Los Angeles, City Planning Commission, *Accomplishments*, 1959. p. 6.

dondo Beach lots (founded in 1887) was rife in 1906. However, the most spectacular subdivision was the work of Abbot Kinney, who bought a one hundred sixty acre tract of sand and marsh, and proposed to build an American Venice (1905), with canals, gondolas (manned by Venetian gondoliers), homes, and an amusement pier. He actually accomplished his dream and Venice remained a popular seaside resort until petroleum was discovered in the area in 1929. Other successful subdivisions were Hollywood and Beverly Hills. Hollywood was subdivided in 1903, the Hollywood Hotel was built on the corner of Hollywood Boulevard and Highland Avenue, streets and sidewalks put in, and trees planted along the walks. Beverly Hills was laid out in 1907, although nothing much happened until 1912 when the Beverly Hills Hotel was built in the middle of a bean field.

Later, with the hope of Owens Valley water, subdividing activity shifted to the San Fernando Valley. Zelzah, now Northridge, was the first community, surveyed in 1910 at a site

on the Southern Pacific's Coast Line. The next year the Los Angeles Suburban Homes Company, which had purchased much of the Lankershim-Van Nuys holdings, subdivided the towns of Van Nuys, Lankershim (North Hollywood), Marion (Reseda), and the appropriately named Owensmouth (Canoga Park).

Boom of the Twenties

In 1920 the city of Los Angeles had a population of 575,000. It is estimated that in the next five years the population doubled—the city was clearly the fastest growing in the nation. Stimulated by the burgeoning motion picture industry, major petroleum discoveries, and the new ease of travel, the population explosion touched off the region's last genuine real estate boom, the "Boom of the Twenties." The peak year of the boom came in 1923 when 11,608 acres were subdivided and 1,057 tracts were put on the market in the city of Los Angeles alone. The same year saw the "construction of three hundred mercantile buildings, four hundred industrial buildings, and 25,000 single and double dwellings." It is said that 43,000 real estate agents roamed the streets. The Janss Investment Company was offering lots in Westwood for $950 and up. Will Rogers at that time was writing a syndicated column with a Beverly Hills dateline. In discussing the boom in 1923 he wrote, "Lots are sold so quickly and often here that they are put through escrow made out to the twelfth owner. They couldn't possibly make a separate deed for each purchaser; besides he wouldn't have time to read it in the ten minutes he owned the lot."

Many of the boom towns failed. For example, Victor Girard, who had developed the West Adams district, purchased 2,886 acres around the junction of Ventura Boulevard and Topanga Canyon in 1923. Under the title of the Boulevard Land Company he laid out 9,826 lots, planted thousands of trees and named the place Girard. His real estate office, a spectacular mosque-like structure, stretched for two blocks along the south side of Ventura Boulevard. It was simply a false front, his subdivision was wildly premature, and even his name was ephemeral—the community is now known as Woodland Hills, and it grew only after World War II.

The boom collapsed in 1925, with a wave of bankruptcies, foreclosures, empty buildings, and subdivisions abandoned to the farmers.

13. Suggested Readings

Clark, David L. *Los Angeles, a City Apart.* Woodland Hills: Windsor Publications, 1981.
Perhaps the best of the lavishly illustrated histories appearing in the Los Angeles Bicentennial year. Covers many of the same topics considered in this chapter.

Fogelson, Robert M. *The Fragmented Metropolis, Los Angeles, 1850–1930.* Cambridge, Mass: Harvard University Press, 1967.
Originally a dissertation in history at Harvard, this book is particularly valuable for its discussion of such things as the development of industry, the spread of the city over the landscape, and the beginning of city and regional planning.

Gebhard, David and Harriette Von Breton. *L.A. in the Thirties, 1931–1941.* Santa Barbara: Peregrine Smith, 1975.
Emphasis on architecture, many pictures. Produced for an exhibit at the Art Galleries, UCSB.

Lavender, David. *Los Angeles Two Hundred.* Tulsa, Okla.: Continental Heritage Press, 1980.
Another fine bicentennial history, beautifully illustrated with historic and modern photographs.

Rintoul, William. *Spudding In: Recollections of Pioneer Days in the California Oil Fields.* San Francisco: California Historical Society, 1976.
Although state-wide in scope, contains considerable material on early Los Angeles oil men and oil fields.

Seims, Charles. *Mount Lowe: The Railway in the Clouds.* San Marino: Golden West Books, 1976.
A large, lavishly illustrated account of the area's famous tourist attraction from its inception to the removal of the last rails.

Torrence, Bruce. *Hollywood, the First 100 Years.* Hollywood: Hollywood Chamber of Commerce, 1979.
Don't be put off by the publisher, Torrance knows his stuff and has produced a valuable book. More than 300 fine photographs.

Weaver, John D. *Los Angeles: The Enormous Village, 1781–1981.* Santa Barbara: Capra Press, 1980.
Traces the development of the city of Los Angeles in a popularly written, anecdotal, humorous fashion.

CHAPTER 14

Downtown Los Angeles: Is
There a There There?

Figure 14.1. Some of the world's tallest buildings have been added to the Los Angeles Central
Business District. (Photo courtesy Greater Los Angeles Visitors and Convention Bureau.)

"Take one survey of downtown Los Angeles and it is evident that there is available anything
that money can buy. Los Angeles is the shopping center for all of the smaller outlying districts,
for people living within a hundred mile radius of the city come here to buy. Merchants must cater
to every conceivable taste, and perhaps that is one reason for the development of the superior
department stores. There is no city in the West which can compare with Los Angeles in the quantity or quality of these stores. They are palatial, modern to the last appointment, showing styles
which are not only up to the minute but a second or two ahead. For the shopping sex they are

among the show places of Los Angeles . . . the larger stores are clustered around Broadway and Seventh, whose intersection marks the new center of town. West Seventh is rapidly becoming the Fifth Avenue of the Pacific Coast." Katharine Ames Taylor (1928, pp. 44–48).

"For casual visitors and Angelenos alike, downtown is the center for daytime civic and commercial business. The streets are crowded and active by day, less so at night . . . some of the tallest buildings in the world are in this area." Richard Saul Wurman (1981, p. 12, 21).

Los Angeles Develops a Typical Downtown

The Los Angeles Central Business District has passed through three distinct phases in the twentieth century. The first thirty years of the century saw its rapid development into a busy and vigorous district. Next came a thirty year period of decentralization, although what had been built earlier downtown remained operational, with a minimum of growth or change. However, during the last twenty years, not only has the downtown been the scene of significant growth and revitalization, but there has also been an almost revolutionary shift of the specialized districts within it. Perhaps the one consistent characteristic has been a general migration of the retail district to the south and west. We will first examine the central business district of Los Angeles in the sixty year long "classic period," next discuss the decentralization of some of the downtown firms and, finally, analyze the new central business district of the 1980s.

In the early years everything in Los Angeles was clustered around the Plaza: the church, retail stores, wholesale houses, residences of prominent people, and whatever else there was. As the little city grew and business houses vied with each other for an accessible location, specialized districts began to develop, and residences were gradually forced toward the margins. Businesses generally migrated south and west, on Main, Spring, and eventually Broadway. In the early twentieth century Broadway quickly became the location of the majority of retailers and theaters,

and soon some of the more adventurous were moving out on Seventh as well. At the same time, Spring Street was developing into a specialized financial-office district. North of First, the Los Angeles City Hall and County buildings formed the nucleus of a Civic Center. The Los Angeles Public Library was built on Fifth between Grand and Hope (on the site of an earlier Normal School, the parent of UCLA). Bookstores and clubs clustered along the streets to the south of it. Bunker Hill (north of Fifth, west of Hill) was a topographic barrier whose slopes were not easily climbed by pedestrians. It long remained as a relic residential island, while business activities migrated around it, keeping to the level land. Wholesalers moved into the old buildings vacated by retailers near the Plaza and on Los Angeles Street, and the beginnings of an apparel industry appeared in the lofts of South Los Angeles and adjacent streets.

Mass transit both stimulated and responded to these central business district developments. The Los Angeles Railway, the local streetcar line, had its major arteries on Spring, Broadway, and Seventh; The Pacific Electric, the interurban to the suburbs, disgorged passengers at the Pacific Electric Building at Sixth and Main or in the Subway Terminal Building at 415 South Hill, with most of the lines from the west reaching it on Hill Street itself. By 1924, a traffic survey found that 1,200,000 persons entered the downtown daily, an amazing situation for the population of the city of Los Angeles at that time was only about 750,000 people. These downtown visitors were producing traffic jams with black automobiles vying for space with the yellow streetcars and the red interurbans. This vast influx of people crowded the sidewalks and surged into the stores and theaters, producing a bustling, vibrant American downtown. No wonder it was, by the 1920s, the most concentrated and valuable area in southern California.

The Los Angeles Downtown in its Classic Period

Broadway and later Seventh Street were transformed in the twentieth century into the most exciting portion of the Los Angeles downtown. The pioneer department store to locate on Broadway moved to the west side of that street below Fourth in 1896, and fittingly took "Broadway" as its name. The next year, The City of Paris, the largest department store in town, left Main Street and moved to Broadway between Third and Fourth (now the site of the Grand Central Market). Hamburger's People's Store (later, The May Company) abandoned its upper Spring Street site in 1906 for a large new building quite far down Broadway—at Eighth. Bullock's opened as a new store at Seventh and Broadway in 1907. Thus, before 1910 the department stores which were to anchor the retail district on Broadway for more than fifty years were all in place. Between these stores swarmed the complementary retail establishments catering to the same customers. There were variety stores—F. W. Woolworth, J. J. Newberry, S. H. Kress, W. T. Grant—plus innumerable apparel shops, dress shops, shoe stores, millinery (hat) shops, tailor shops, men's clothing stores, jewelry stores, drug stores, cigar stores, and candy shops. Interspersed among these retail outlets were many theaters—legitimate, vaudeville, and movie. Broadway was without question the most glamorous street in all of Los Angeles. It was the pedestrian's delight for on this busy, lively street were located the most elaborate window displays, the fanciest facades, the most ornate marquees, the brightest of lights. It was swarming with crowds of shoppers and theater-goers both day and night.

A few of the more adventurous retailers began moving to locations on Seventh Street—perhaps to be adjacent to the street car lines that were bringing in customers from the rapidly growing west side. Robinson's was the first, moving from First and Broadway—too far north—to Seventh and Grand in 1914. Coulters, one of the oldest and largest retailers in the city, moved from an obsolete location at Spring and Temple to Seventh and Olive in 1917. Later, during the euphoria of the Boom of the Twenties, Barker Brothers, located the farthest out, at Seventh and Flower (1928). Soon Seventh, too, became a lively, exciting, busy retail street.

The saga of Arthur Letts, the founder of the Broadway Department store illustrates nicely both the migration of the retail district and the activity on Broadway during its classic period. Letts arrived in Los Angeles in 1896 and took over the stock of a store at 146 North Spring Street, a location that was beginning to suffer because of the migration of businesses southward. He found a vacant store to rent at Fourth and Broadway which at that time "seemed out in the country." However, his store was successful from the start and Letts was able to expand almost annually, into space next door, into the upper floors and then into adjoining buildings. It was the custom of downtown department stores to have a special showing of new fashions each spring and fall. At the Broadway's showing in the spring of 1903 more than 30,000 people visited the store in one evening, a tribute to the vitality of the downtown of a city with a total population of about 130,000. Letts continued to prosper, and in June, 1915 a new, large, and luxurious store was opened on the same site, nine stories high with fourteen acres of floor space, served by fourteen passenger elevators—60,000 persons visited the store on its opening day. This glamorous new store featured, in addition to its many departments, a spacious cafe that opened onto an Italian Garden, a men's grill, an auditorium, a nursery, a hospital, writing rooms, and "a 'silence room,' where women under stress of weariness or nerve strain could retire for complete rest in absolute silence" (Kilner, 1927, p. 154). Letts also took over an uncompleted department store building at Seventh and Broadway in 1907 and, to avoid confusion named it after its first manager, John Bullock. In 1919, Letts leased the opposite corner to Loew's Theaters; at the time it was thought to be the most valuable corner in California. (The same year he bought the 3296 acre Rancho San José de Buenos Ayres—it extended from Pico to Sunset, from the Los Angeles Country Club to the Veterans Administration Home. It was said he was the only man in southern California who could come up with the asking price: two million dollars in cash.)

Department stores and other retail shops drew large crowds to Broadway and it was only natural that it soon became the entertainment street—the "Great White Way" of the growing city. Vaudeville houses were the first arrivals. In 1910 Alexander Pantages built a theater in the style of an English music hall at 534 South Broadway and named it after himself. (It is now the Arcade Theater.) The Orpheum, the largest of the vaudeville circuit companies, opened a theater by that name at 630 South Broadway in the same year; it remains as the Palace. A decade later another of the nationwide companies dedicated a grand house at Seventh and Broadway—Loew's State Theater. As an introduction of more modern things to come, a "nickelodeon," a silent movie house with a five cent admission, was opened a few doors from the Pantages in 1917, called Clunes Broadway Theater, now the Cameo. It was with the flowering of the movies that the era of ornate and luxurious theaters reached their peak; they were truly "motion picture palaces."

Sid Grauman opened one of the first of these palaces anywhere, on Broadway at Third, calling it flamboyantly, The Million Dollar Theater. It opened in 1918, could seat 2,000 persons, and had a "lush Churrigueresque exterior . . . complemented by an equally sumptuous baroque interior . . ." (Gebhard and Winter, 1977, p. 215). Other theaters quickly sprang up on Broadway—the State, the Globe, and the United Artists, for example. Some deserve special mention. The Tower, opened in 1927, was built in the Spanish Style and was the first theater in the city specifically designed for sound. Its premier film, as one would suspect, was the first of the sound movies, Al Jolson's "Jazz Singer." The most opulent picture palace ever constructed on Broadway, appropriately called the Los Angeles Theater, was still to come. Opened in 1931 at 615 South Broadway, it featured a restaurant, a ballroom, a "sound proof" crying room for mothers with noisy children, an oval lounge with a series of mirrors reflecting the picture for those waiting to be seated, and a fabulous ladies' room with individual rooms instead of stalls, each decorated in a different marble. The last of the downtown theaters to open was the Roxie at 518 South Broadway, in 1932. An era was over, but for a generation and more Broadway was the region's "Great White Way," lit at night to almost daylight brightness by the signs advertising its exciting shows. (A few theaters chose locations on adjacent streets—a second Pantages on Seventh at Hill, 1929, and farther south on Hill, The Mayan, 1927, and the Belasco, 1920.)

Beginning about 1910, the city's financial institutions, previously scattered north of First on Main, Spring, and Broadway, started to migrate to Spring Street. Soon Spring, from about Third to Eighth, was the location of many banks, title and trust companies, stock brokers, savings and loan concerns, and other financial institutions. The street was to be lined by a double row of solid-looking buildings thirteen stories high—bringing them to the maximum height of one hundred fifty feet then allowed by law. These were not just ordinary banks, or purely local savings and loan companies. They were large concerns, the state or regional headquarters of these growing financial institutions. One of the important institutions on the street was the Los Angeles Stock Exchange. The cornerstone for a new building for the Exchange at 615 South Spring, in a masterpiece of bad timing, was dedicated with a large and festive civic celebration in late October, 1929—the next week the stock market crashed. Actually, not every building on Spring housed a financial institution. The Alexandria Hotel, opened in 1906 as "the first completely fire-proof building in Los Angeles," was a prominent local landmark. It boasted five hundred rooms, a two hundred car basement garage, and an interior palm court with a stained glass ceiling. For years the Alexandria was the premier hotel in the city and it quickly became its social and banquet center, and the meeting place of the newly acceptable motion picture producers. However, Spring Street was to remain the "Wall Street of the Metropolis" for half a century. As recently as 1959 the United California Bank constructed its headquarters building at Spring and Sixth. This was a last, dying gasp, for change was already in the air.

Decentralization of Downtown Functions

In 1930 three-fourths of all of the commercial and professional activity in Los Angeles was carried on downtown. Change was to take place quickly. With the rapid spread of ownership of increasingly reliable automobiles, businesses were soon freed from dependence on mass transit to bring their customers to them. The motion picture exhibitors were the first to sense that patrons could be lured to outlying areas. Hollywood Boulevard became a theater district in the 1920s, the location of "four of the most beautiful theaters

in the country" (Torrence, 1979, p. 127). Grauman's Egyptian was opened in 1922, "named the year the discovery of King Tutankhamen's tomb created an instant society of Egyptologists," Warner Brothers Theater in 1926, Grauman's Chinese in 1927, and the most fabulous of all, the Hollywood Pantages. It is said that when it opened in 1929, "it was the largest (2,812 seats), most original, and certainly the most ornate" in the region (Torrence, 1979, p. 128). Theaters, of course, were opening in other parts of the city too; the Fox Wilshire, for example, dates from 1919, and the area's first drive-in theater was opened at Pico and Westwood in 1934.

Other downtown businesses began moving toward their customers. The area's most notable example of decentralization came from the decision of Bullock's, for decades located at the very apex of the traditional downtown, to build a new store two and a half miles to the west, in the heart of a wealthy residential neighborhood. The new store was to be located at 3050 Wilshire Boulevard and was to signal an upgrading of merchandise; it was given a new name—Bullock's Wilshire. This handsome store incorporated several firsts: it had a dual "frontage," with the traditional display windows facing Wilshire, but also with an elaborate facade and the "real" entrance facing the parking lot behind the store. The customer drove his auto into the rear *porte-cochere* where a valet parked the car; on departing, packages were delivered to the rear entrance by conveyor belt—the ultimate in automobile shopping. It opened September 26, 1929, and was visited by 300,000 persons on opening day. Other downtown department stores followed the trend: Desmond's, a clothier, to 5519 Wilshire in the same year. The Broadway opened a branch on Hollywood Boulevard in 1931, and in Pasadena in 1940. Sears, new to retailing, built its first Los Angeles store, including three levels of parking, on Pico and Western, in 1938. The May Company joined the trend with a new store on Wilshire at Fairfax in 1940—the architecture featured a gold tower, a "real '30s perfume bottle," at the corner. By 1941, all the major department stores except Robinson's had suburban branches, and several stores, Desmond's and I. Magnin, had abandoned the downtown altogether. Sales of the downtown department stores, which had accounted for seventy-five percent of the county's retail sales in 1919, and for fifty-four percent of them as late as 1939, fell to twenty-five percent in 1956.

Hotels also were locating outside the downtown. The Beverly Hills Hotel opened in the middle of a bean field in 1912—but it was easily accessible by car from Hollywood. Other hotels were soon built on the west side. The largest and most famous was the Ambassador, completed on Wilshire in 1921, with its Coconut Grove nightclub, and featuring a swimming pool with white sand beaches.

The New Downtown

The "old" or classic downtown, the central business district described previously, remained generally static for many decades. Commercial growth took place elsewhere. Suddenly, major events of the 1950s and 1960s sparked a revitalization of the entire downtown and were responsible for a series of shifts so pronounced that they are easily visible to the most casual observer. Five forces can be identified as contributing to these revolutionary changes:

1. The population of the metropolis more than tripled in the thirty years after 1940, so that the downtown had an enormous new population to serve.
2. A network of freeways was built focusing on the downtown core, making it more accessible to more people than ever before.
3. The location of the freeways in relation to the downtown was completely different from that of the public transit lines, creating pressures for new alignments within the core area.
4. The removal of the one hundred fifty foot height limit on buildings made possible the introduction of the modern skyscraper into the downtown core area.
5. The enactment of federal legislation permitting the creation of redevelopment districts facilitated changes in several sections of the downtown.

The most striking change in the downtown is the appearance of a skyscraper skyline. Today, a score of office towers ranging up to sixty-two stories tall mark the location of a new financial-office district and reflect the increased business activity of the area. For years, only the Los Angeles City Hall was permitted to penetrate the one hundred fifty foot height limitation, about the height of a thirteen story building. By the 1950s, modern engineering practices made the "skyscraper," common in cities the world over, appropriate for even earthquake-prone Los Angeles. Furthermore, the land adjacent to the new Harbor Freeway, previously poorly served by the major mass transportation lines, became newly accessible and thus a prime downtown location. At about the same time, Bunker Hill was cleared and regraded and became available for redevelopment.

The Union Bank was the first to respond to these forces, opening the Union Bank Plaza in 1968, featuring a forty-two story building on Figueroa between Fourth and Fifth, immediately adjacent to the freeway. In the same year the Crocker Bank completed a building of similar height at Sixth and Grand. Next, in 1972, appeared two black twin towers, fifty-two stories high, the Atlantic Richfield Plaza

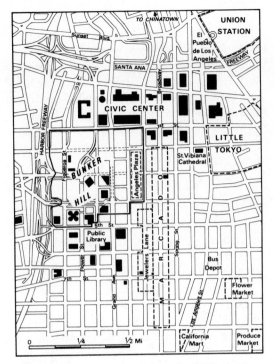

Figure 14.2. The Los Angeles Central Business District.

(one of the towers housed the Bank of America). Covering the entire block between Figueroa and Flower and Fifth and Sixth, The Plaza included a large, two-level, underground shopping mall. The next year the sixty-two story First Interstate Bank building was completed at Hope and Wilshire, and in 1974 the Security Pacific Plaza opened a fifty-five story tower at Flower and Third. Other buildings ranging from seventeen to thirty-two stories were going up at the same time. As this is written in 1981, additional financial towers are under construction in the same neighborhood: Crocker Center and the Wells Fargo Bank building. Some scoffed at these new developments. A banker is quoted as saying, "It was a matter of vanity, a contest to produce the biggest phallic symbol" (Forbes, 1973, p. 67). This new construction has had far-reaching effects. It has meant that the financial district,

formerly on Spring Street, in effect has leap-frogged the old retail district along Broadway, and a new financial-office district has been created between the Harbor Freeway and Grand, from Third to about Sixth Street. More than a simple shift is involved; the new developments represent a massive increase in office space. Perhaps surprisingly, even this increase in space has not been enough to satisfy the demand. One office planning firm in 1978 was advising its clients to avoid Los Angeles as rents for space were higher than for similar space in either Chicago or New York. As a result, prices of land in the area are reported to have increased as much as fifteen times in the last decade, and purchasers from around the world bid on any buildings which are put up for sale. Even the site of the earthquake-damaged St. Paul's Cathedral at Figueroa and Sixth has been sold recently for office development.

The change in the downtown retail district has been nearly as drastic. It has bifurcated, or divided itself into two quite different parts. Broadway, almost as busy as in its golden era, is now a grand *Mercado,* the major shopping street of the local Hispanic population. The buildings that once housed the merchandise for the suburban Anglo housewife now are occupied by firms that carry goods designed to appeal to the Mexican-American shopper, and their aisles are as crowded as ever. The motion picture palaces now run Spanish language films and retain much of their old-time gaudiness. Latin music is heard from the record stores. And in characteristic Latin fashion, activity on the street picks up on Saturdays and Sundays, when even the parking lots become bazaars full of vocal vendors and eager shoppers.

Seventh Street, on the other hand, has remained a traditional downtown retail street, the shopping street convenient to the nearby office workers and to an occasional suburban housewife. Its retail function was strengthened and the western movement along it accentuated by the opening of the Broadway Plaza on Seventh, between Hope and Flower, in 1973. A truly remarkable event, the development was said to be the largest department store to be built in any central city for forty years. It houses not only the "flagship" department store in the Broadway-Hale chain but also the attached "Galleria," a multi-level shopping mall, lit by a spectacular skylight. The block-long megastructure includes a six-story parking garage above the store, a Hyatt Regency Hotel with a revolving restaurant on top, and a thirty-two story office building. Today's trends seem destined to continue: Bullock's, a fixture at Broadway and Seventh for nearly three-quarters of a century, has announced plans to move six blocks westward to a new super-block office complex, on Seventh between Figueroa and the freeway (immediately south of the Los Angeles Hilton).

Large new hotels, too, have been built in recent years, mainly in the new financial-district on the west side. For many decades the Biltmore, has been unrivaled as the "grand dame" of Los Angeles deluxe hotels since it opened in 1923. Located on Olive opposite Pershing Square, it featured a spectacular Renaissance lobby, with an ornate cathedral-like vaulted ceiling. Its position has been used by some as forecasting the western movement of the downtown hotels. However, a clear indication of this movement awaited the opening of the Los Angeles Hilton, on Wilshire adjacent to the Harbor Freeway, in the 1950s. For a time this hotel, which turns inward to a subtropical garden, was the largest of the downtown hotels. It is now eclipsed by the most spectacular of the downtown hotels, John Portman's Bonaventure, a "twenty-first century" building, with five cylindrical bronze glass towers rising in the block bounded by Flower and Figueroa, Fifth and Sixth. The guests leave its gigantic atrium lobby, with its

one-acre lake, hanging gardens, and trees, via glass-covered outdoor elevators, like tiny space craft, for a view of the city on the way to their rooms. The central thirty-five story tower is topped by a revolving bar. An additional luxury hotel, the Plaza Forte, is under construction adjacent to the freeway, diagonally across Figueroa from the Bonaventure. As part of this hotel cluster, the Hyatt-Regency, previously mentioned, should be included.

Hill Street as Jewelers' Lane

Within the last decade a new specialized retail district has sprung to life in the Los Angeles downtown, Hill Street, from Seventh to above Fifth, has become a "Jewelry Lane." By 1980, it was reported that an unbelievable six hundred retail jewelers were operating in a relatively few specialized buildings along or adjacent to that street. For decades wholesale jewelers had existed in the buildings in that general area, and about a dozen years ago an entire structure at 607 South Hill was converted into a building catering exclusively to the needs of jewelry manufacturing and wholesaling. However, beginning in 1976 when the plaza level and basement of that building were divided into retail booths, retailers have proliferated up and down the street. Now there are hundreds of retail jewelers in the converted buildings on Hill between Sixth and Seventh, with names like Los Angeles Jewelry Center, Jewelry Design Center, The New York Jewelers Exchange, Theater Jewelry Center, Western Jewelry Mart, and the Milano Jewelry Plaza. Other buildings are planned on spaces formerly used for parking lots. In addition, the entire block along Hill facing Pershing Square (between Fifth and Sixth) is to be developed into the Jewelry Mart, a twenty-story twin tower structure, planned with retail booths on its first floor—space for wholesalers and manufacturers above. Comparative shopping is the name of the game in the jewelry business, and this district is one of the best examples to be found anywhere. Its appearance at this time is reportedly linked to the rapid influx of jewelers to Los Angeles, owing to unsettled conditions in much of the world, resulting in the migration of jewelers from Lebanon, Iran, Egypt, Israel, and the Far East.

The Los Angeles Civic Center

On the north edge of the downtown, extending in a mile long band between First Street to the Santa Ana-Hollywood Freeway, is the large and thriving Civic Center. Expanding from a small nucleus around the Los Angeles City Hall, it now consists of some eighteen governmental and public buildings. Anchored on one end by the Department of Water and Power Headquarters, and the Music Center, it continues with a rather stark row of city and county buildings facing a grassy mall (with parking beneath) and cumulating in Parker Center, the police headquarters, at the other end. It is the work place of about 25,000 persons and the destination of some 35,000 others on an average day, a busy vital portion of the new downtown.

Several features are worthy of special note. On the north end, next to the DWP Headquarters, lies the Music Center, a three building focus of many of the region's cultural events, the magnet of large evening crowds. The major structure, the Dorothy Chandler Pavilion, is the home of the Los Angeles Philharmonic, but also the scene of everything from Cinco de Mayo celebrations to swearing-in ceremonies for new citizens. Included also are the Ahmanson Theater and the Mark Taper Forum, with its own Center Theater Group. At the other end of the Civic Center is the Los Angeles Mall, featuring underground parking, shopping areas, and a park with the Triforium, a structure designed to produce music coordinated with the flashing lights of 1,494 glass prisms. The whole complex is a bit isolated from the "real" downtown. Although an attempt had been made to tie the group of buildings together, the fact that it is bisected by some half dozen north-south streets has made much unification difficult.

Little Tokyo

Little Tokyo, for more than half a century a center for Japanese residents, merchants, and cultural activities, is an additional downtown district with its own distinctive activity and life. It began in the older buildings on the edge of downtown early in the century, survived the deportation of the 1942–45 period, and is now a flourishing area, generally concentrated along First and Second Streets between Los Angeles Street and Alameda. The "Little Tokyo Redevelopment Project" has been underway since the 1960s, and today numerous new buildings rise above the older structures. Scores of restaurants, markets selling produce and fish, retail stores of all kinds, gift shops, and a variety of professional offices line the busy streets. Almost all of the shops are owned by Japanese. Today, not only the Japanese population but other local visitors and out-of-town tourists are present in large numbers. Even so, the streets seem to be maintaining both their ethnic quality and local character.

Most impressive of the new structures is the twenty-one story New Otani Hotel which opened in 1977 overlooking Los Angeles Street. Complete with restaurants and shopping arcade, it features both American and Japanese style rooms and a dramatic roof garden with carp ponds, water falls, and stone lanterns. Another new complex includes the Sumitomo Bank Building (location of the Japanese consulate) with a basement restaurant that is famed for "the longest sushi bar outside Japan." Prominent also is the Japanese Village Plaza, which meanders between First and Second Street and is lined with many small shops characteristic of a Japanese village. It is a handsome development, with blue tile roofs, red glazed tile walkways, and a theme fire tower on First. Another new structure, Little Tokyo Towers (on Third between Central and San Pedro), is an apartment house for Japanese senior citizens. Almost hidden down a narrow entrance driveway on First is the Koyasan Buddhist Temple, one of three Buddhist temples in Little Tokyo.

Bunker Hill Redevelopment

The elevated area known as Bunker Hill has been an urban redevelopment project since 1959. The hill is a one hundred thirty-six acre area generally bounded by the Harbor Freeway and Hill Street, and extending south from the Civic Center to Fourth or Fifth Streets. During the 1880s it was built up with Victorian houses and an occasional wooden hotel. By the 1950s these had become increasingly dilapidated, however, and most had been turned into apartments or rooming houses. It was an oasis of residence near downtown, and Angels Flight made climbing the slope unnecessary for its residents. The Redevelopment Agency cleared away the houses and regraded the hill to a level just above the tunnels that carried the street traffic under the hill. Few builders were interested in the newly cleared

sites at first and rebuilding has been slow. Today, the south half is the site of some of the major office buildings and hotels mentioned previously, and near the Civic Center rises the Bunker Hill Towers, consisting of three highrise structures. Almost all of the parcels on Bunker Hill have now been sold, a senior citizens' complex on Hill Street is nearing completion, and Angels Flight, long in storage, may fulfill earlier promises, and run once more.

14. Suggested Readings

Literature specifically on the Los Angeles downtown is essentially non-existent. Some of the general works listed after Chapter One have useful sections: *LA/Access* provides a guide to many of the buildings and sub-regions, and *Above Los Angeles* has a number of fine air views of the downtown. Ironically, there are a number of nostalgic reminiscences featuring pictures of the Bunker Hill of an earlier day, a part of the downtown that is no longer there. Among the best of these are William Pugsley, *Bunker Hill, Last of the Lofty Mansions*. Corona Del Mar, Calif.: Trans-Anglo Books, 1977, and Arnold Hylen, *Bunker Hill: A Los Angeles Landmark*. Los Angeles: Dawson's Book Shop, 1976.

CHAPTER **15**

Metropolitan Jobs and Districts: Manufacturing and Wholesaling

Figure 15.1. A DC-10, the "Super 80," one of a new generation of efficient and quiet airliners, on the final assembly line at the McDonnell Douglas Long Beach factory. (Photo courtesy McDonnell Douglas Corporation.)

"It (Los Angeles) is a city of hedonists, their faces to the sun; it is also a city of millions of workers, whose energy is as unmistakable and as unremitting as the night-and-day hum of cars on the freeways . . ." Brendon Gill (1980, p. 119).

"Expertise is the stock in trade of this metropolis, and behind the flash and the braggadocio, solid skills and scholarship prosper. There are craftsmen everywhere in L. A. . . . For somewhere near the heart of the L. A. ethos there lies, unexpectedly, a layer of solid, old-fashioned, plain hard work. This is a city of hard workers." Jan Morris (1980, pp. 87–88).

Table 15.1
Estimated Number of Wage and Salary Workers in Non-Agricultural Establishments, by Industry, 1980

Industry	Number	Percent
Manufacturing	1,213,000	24.5
Services	1,105,600	22.3
Retail Trade	811,600	16.4
Government	714,100	14.4
Wholesale trade	327,500	6.6
Finance, insurance and real estate	312,000	6.3
Transportation and public utilities	253,100	5.1
Construction	198,400	4.0
Mining	19,500	0.4
	4,954,800	100.0

Source: State of California, Economic Development Department, Division of Employment and Research. *California Employment and Payrolls.* Table C.8.

Employment in the Metropolis

The importance of each major category of employment in the Metropolis is revealed by the data in Table 15.1.

These figures, of course, change somewhat from year to year, the proportions less than the raw numbers. Manufacturing is clearly the most important employer in the region furnishing about one quarter of all the jobs. The service sector has been expanding in the last few decades and is now in second place with more than a fifth of total employment. Retail trade is third, with government a close fourth. However, if retail and wholesale trade are combined, trade becomes almost as important as manufacturing in the region. Much less important is the triple category of finance, insurance, and real estate; the transportation-public utility category; and contract construction. Mining, which includes oil field workers, is insignificant in terms of total regional employment.

Job Locations

The locations of the area's nearly five million jobs are widespread throughout the Metropolis. Retail stores are found in every part of the region at sites near their customers. Jobs in services, too, are generally located where the

people live who have need of their ministrations. Government service activities are also widespread, although there is a major concentration of governmental workers in the Los Angeles Civic Center. Construction workers, uniquely, seldom assemble in the same location for long; the housing tract, apartment complex, or office building are soon completed and the workers move on to a new project elsewhere. Generally considered, manufacturing and wholesaling jobs exist throughout the Metropolis also. These two activities, however, occasionally have specialized locational requirements. Several types of wholesaling, for example, are characterized by a close cluster of firms, often in or near downtown Los Angeles. Some manufacturing firms, as well, find particular sites within the Metropolis advantageous locations for their plants. This chapter, therefore, will concentrate on manufacturing and wholesaling, emphasizing not only their importance but also their characteristic locations within the Metropolis.

Manufacturing Districts

The location of the work places of the region's 1,213,400 persons employed in manufacturing can be roughly inferred from Figure 15.2 showing the distribution of industrial land

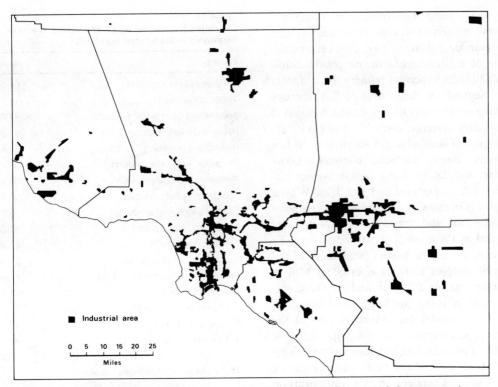

Figure 15.2. Major industrial areas in the Los Angeles Metropolis. Source: U.S. Department of Commerce, National Oceanic and Atmospheric Administration. *A Study of Earthquake Losses in the Los Angeles, California Area.* 1973. p. 295.

in the Metropolis. As compared to other metropolitan areas, less industrial land is found in the central part of Los Angeles and more is located in the margins and in the suburbs. There are several reasons for this. Producing motion pictures takes much space and filmmakers found the room they needed on the city's outskirts. Petroleum refineries generally favored harbor locations—some twenty miles from downtown Los Angeles. Aircraft assembly must take place adjacent to an airport large enough to handle the company's product—and these were all located far from the city center. Importantly, too, manufacturing came relatively late in the development of the Metropolis and close-in land was already occupied. Finally, in the last few decades of rapid expansion, manufacturers have favored efficient, one-story plants, with large parking lots, often

elaborately landscaped—all of which require the sort of space that is available only near the edges of the Metropolis.

It is difficult to explain in detail the distribution of industrial areas in the Metropolis (as shown in Figure 15.2) but a number of generalizations are possible. Industry at first found the flat land between downtown Los Angeles and the river attractive—it was well served with railroads. This district was extended across the river and several miles southward in the 1920s by favorable zoning and low tax rates in the city of Vernon, and in more recent years eastward into Pico Rivera and the City of Commerce. When Los Angeles developed a harbor twenty miles from its center after 1900, the harbor itself as well as the extensive lowland behind it attracted space-consuming industries, particularly petroleum refineries. Nearby Torrance, founded as a planned industrial city, also became the home of many manufacturing plants. Standard Oil built its second refinery in California at El Segundo on Santa Monica Bay, thereby starting another city destined to be dominated by industry. Aircraft assembly brought industrial uses to land adjacent to airports in Los Angeles, Santa Monica, Burbank, Hawthorne, and, lately, Long Beach. Newer airports such as Ontario and the John Wayne Airport (Orange County) are also surrounded by industrial land, a rational use for districts plagued by the noise of airport operations. To the east, the entire district from south of the Ontario Airport to the Kaiser Steel Mill in Fontana, mainly stony ground on the Cucamonga alluvial fan, has been zoned for industry. Too, considerable industrial land in the Metropolis appears as sinuous strips along the region's railroads, and, to a lesser extent, along some freeways. Many early manufacturing plants were dependent on rail transportation and sought locations with rail connections. Today, this is much less true, but the railside land remains industrially zoned. Planners, in the years of expansion after World War II, rezoned much agricultural land for industry in the San Fernando Valley and Orange County. Although some of this land was adjacent to rail lines, the electronics plants and other light industries that have been attracted to these sites are little concerned with shipment by rail.

Manufacturing Activity in the Metropolis

Manufacturing activities are commonly classified by both state and federal agencies into categories as illustrated by Table 15.2. However, to understand Metropolitan manufacturing it is useful to divide these activities into quite different groups. A metropolitan area may process local raw materials for a larger market. For example, it may freeze orange juice, can fish, or refine petroleum and

Table 15.2
Estimated Number of Wage and Salary Workers Employed in Manufacturing–1980

Industry	Number
Food and kindred products	66,200
Textile mill products	13,300
Apparel and other textile products	84,700
Paper and allied products	22,300
Printing and publishing	69,800
Chemicals and allied products	41,400
Petroleum and coal products	13,300
Rubber and plastic products	50,700
Leather and leather products	9,200
Lumber and wood products	17,200
Furniture and fixtures	47,900
Stone, clay and glass products	31,800
Primary metal industries	41,600
Fabricated metal products	102,200
Machinery (except electrical)	132,600
Electric and electronic equipment	193,800
Transportation equipment	195,500
Instruments and related products	52,400
Miscellaneous manufacturing industries	27,500
	1,213,400

Source: State of California, Economic Development Department, Division of Employment and Research. *California Employment and Payrolls.* Table C.8.

sell the products outside of the area. Conversely, a region may import raw materials and process them for use of local consumers—either people or factories. Furniture making and aluminum casting are examples of this kind of manufacturing. Finally, a metropolis may import raw materials, perform the manufacturing process, and market the finished product outside the region—nationally or even internationally. Some consider this the highest and most sophisticated type of manufacturing. "Sophisticated" industries in the Metropolis include aerospace (and all of its components—electronics, computers, etc.), apparel, motion pictures, and others. In real life, of course, these categories are not clear cut. The petroleum refineries, for example, today use both imported and local crude and sell their products both within and outside the region. Furthermore, locally produced movies are shown in the Metropolis as well as worldwide, apparel made in the Metropolis is also sold here, and so on. Even so, the industries of the first and third categories are classified as "basic industries"—they bring money into the region from the outside. Los Angeles, as someone put it, cannot exist by washing each other's cars or taking in each other's mortgages; it must earn money from without the region. Aerospace, apparel, and motion pictures are obvious major "money earners."

Aerospace: The Leader by Far

The aerospace industry in all of its ramifications is clearly the region's most important activity. Aerospace provides employment for about 325,000 persons, one out of every four of the region's manufacturing workers. Further, among these employees are tens of thousands of engineers, a group that commands high salaries. In addition, many skilled workers—electronics technicians, computer specialists, master mechanics, and hosts of others—form a labor force with above average salaries. Clearly, the financial impact of the aerospace payroll is even greater than the number of its employees might indicate. Finally, aerospace has given the region its industrial fame and even today it is likely that no other urban complex in the world has a comparable assemblage of aerospace firms to match those of the Los Angeles Metropolis.

We have previously discussed the historic, climate-related beginnings of the aircraft industry in the Metropolis, its explosive growth during World War II, and its continued importance in the "cold war" years. However, advances in technology during the past three decades have changed the industry drastically. As recently as 1950 it was a fairly simple industry based on the assembly of engines and propellers, produced elsewhere, into the aircraft structures constructed by the local aircraft concerns. Since then the jet engine has made possible much larger aircraft, and the development of avionics, guided missiles, rockets, spacecraft, and satellites have complicated the picture enormously.

The development of the jet engine caused the first major change in aircraft manufacture. This engine is an extremely powerful device. It can propel a huge, heavy aircraft at high speeds, or smaller aircraft at supersonic speeds. When commercial airlines switched to jet-powered fleets in the 1960s, following the lead of military aviation, the "tin bending" days of aircraft assembly became obsolete. Aluminum sheets and bars were now much heavier and had to be laboriously shaped by milling machines—sculpted really—before they were assembled. If supersonic speeds were involved, even stronger, heat-resistance components were required. Some critical parts were formed of a stainless steel "honeycomb-sandwich," other parts were made from titanium, or molded of an epoxy-graphite material to secure the required lightness and strength. All of these advances required manufacturing procedures that were precise, difficult, almost handicraft operations, and, needless to say, costly.

During the same period the aircraft industry was moving rather naturally into the production of unmanned missiles, rockets, and reentry vehicles. It was a logical transition since the guidance systems were similar, and the engineering problems and manufacturing operations had much in common. This new branch of the industry began slowly after World War II, but accelerated quickly after the Russians launched their "Sputnik" in 1957. As the "space age" began, the aircraft companies received contracts for the launching rockets and space vehicles that were needed to put a man in orbit and on the moon. The National Aeronautics and Space Administration (NASA) was created in 1959 to accomplish

Table 15.3
The Aerospace Complex

SIC	Industry	Employees
372	Aircraft and parts	100,000
366	Communications equipment............	60,000
376	Guided missiles, space vehicles......	60,000
367	Electronic components and accessories...................................	50,000
357	Office and computing machines	25,000
382	Measuring and controlling devices ..	20,000
365	Radio and tv receiving equipment ...	10,000
		325,000

Source: U.S. Department of Commerce, *County Business Patterns, California, 1979.* Table 2. Data modified to conform to boundaries of the Metropolis.

this task. Shortly thereafter the term "Aerospace" became the generally accepted name for the entire aircraft and space complex.

A quantum leap in the amount and sophistication of available electronic equipment produced a third revolution. Early World War II bombers had several thousand electronic components, the later B-17 (Flying Fortress) had 28,000, and the B-58 (1957) had some 95,000 electronic elements. With the development of the guided missile and satellites their use was further multiplied. Electronic parts amounted to twenty percent of the cost of an airplane but were at least fifty percent the cost of a missile. Aerospace firms, like it or not, were involved with electronics. Electronic expertise was needed to integrate the airframe and electronic subsystems, if nothing else. Some aircraft firms, in addition, spun off their own divisions to develop and manufacture the needed electronic subsystems. At the same time, companies specializing in the production of electronic equipment grew, and many developed divisions specializing in "avionics," as electronics for aircraft use came to be known.

The numerous elements of the present day aerospace complex, as defined by the Research Department of the Security Pacific Bank, as well as employment in 1979, are summarized in Table 15.3.

Aircraft Manufacturing—The Traditional Companies

Of the early aircraft manufacturers, five remain among the region's leading employers, although most now are divided into several divisions. Employment in 1980 was about as follows: Hughes Aircraft, 52,000; Rockwell International (originally North American Aircraft), 28,000; Lockheed California, 28,000; McDonnell Douglas, 26,000; and Northrop, 15,000. These five are still assembling aircraft in the Metropolis—the activity that brought the region its early manufacturing fame. McDonnell Douglas (former Douglas Aircraft) has moved from Santa Monica to more spacious Long Beach Airport. Here it produces large numbers of several commercial passenger planes, the DC-9, and the larger DC-10, as well as a military/tanker adaptation. The "Super 80," a "stretched out" version of the popular DC-9 designed to meet the 1985 federal noise standards, is also going into production. Lockheed is in business in its traditional Burbank location (Burbank Airport) assembling several types of manned military aircraft. One, the P-3 Orion, is "the Navy's primary long-range anti-submarine patrol plane" used by several foreign air forces also. The TR-1, a tactical reconnaissance aircraft, derivative of the famous U-2, is assembled at the company's "off-limits" development location—the "Skunk Works." Lockheed's newest commercial aircraft, the L-1011 "TriStar," however, is too large to be flown comfortably from Burbank, and is assembled at Palmdale. Northrup Corporation, adjacent to the Hawthorne Airport, currently is turning out manned military planes, including the F-5G, advertised as "the most widely deployed supersonic fighter built in the U.S." Hughes Aircraft is beginning an order for five hundred thirty-six "Advanced Attack Helicopters" for antitank applications, at its plant in Culver City, with final assembly at the Los Angeles Airport. North American produces military aircraft at its plant on the south side of the same airport.

These are not simple, small-scale operations. Constructing an aircraft is something like putting together an extremely complicated, compact building that will fly. Though an assembly operation, it is totally different from the automobile industry where a finished car may come off the line every sixty seconds. Northrop, for example, completes five military planes a month. Douglas produces a DC-9 every 4 1/2 working days, a DC-10 every six days. Still, total numbers are impressive. By 1980 Douglas had delivered about 1,000 DC-9s, half to domestic buyers, half to foreign airlines, and more than three hundred DC-10s.

Subassemblies: Division of Labor

Now come the complications, first subassemblies. Northrop's Hawthorne plant makes the "center and aft fuselages, the two tails and everything inside" for the Douglas F/8–18 Hornet fighter. Currently two "shipsets" a month are being produced. Eventually 1,366 of these planes will be constructed for the U.S., and one hundred thirty-seven for Canada. For another manned fighter, the F/A-18L, the two companies will switch roles, with Northrop the prime contractor and Douglas making some subassemblies. For a number of years Northrop has also been turning out the fuselage for Boeing's 747 wide-bodied transports at a rate of seven a month, shipping them to Seattle for final assembly (about five hundred delivered so far). The fuselages for the Douglas commercial passenger planes are assembled in San Diego (by Convair) and then shipped to Long Beach by barge. This division of labor is a common practice, so, in addition to the final assembly of aircraft, local plants are normally manufacturing portions of aircraft with the final assembly to be done by others, within or without the Metropolis. In addition, Lockheed Aircraft Service Co. has an "aircraft maintenance and modification" facility at the Ontario International Airport. They will rebuild—modify—any aircraft to suit the current owner's needs. A number of other firms do similar work.

Subassemblies, complex or simple, are also produced by scores of local companies that do not assemble aircraft themselves. This is not surprising as the Metropolis has been the scene of aircraft assembly for fifty years. For example: Menasco, Inc. (Burbank) specializes in landing gears; Weber Aircraft (Burbank) in aircraft interiors; Bendix (Van Nuys) in hydraulic equipment; Nordskog Industries (Van Nuys) in aircraft galleys; Rohr (Riverside) in engine pods; Lear Siegler (Santa Monica) in aircraft automatic flight control and stabilization systems; Transport Dynamics (Santa Ana) in heat, refrigeration and ventilating systems; Tridair Industries (Torrance) in specialty fasteners for aircraft— "captive fasteners, self-locking studs, self-threading bolts, latches and alignment pins," by the hundreds of thousands. And so it goes. Firms are not restricted to the local market. The Garret Corp. (9851 Sepulveda), for example, builds jet engines for corporate and commuter aircraft. It also manufactures "most of the environmental control systems, actuation and auxiliary power units for the Boeing 727, 737, and 747," and it is the "largest producer of automatic turbochargers in the world," turning out more than 800,000 in 1980.

New Divisions, New Locations and a Myriad of Products

Most of the aerospace firms we have discussed so far have been old line firms associated with the traditional aircraft industry, but with the coming of missiles, rocket engines, satellites, space capsules, and the like, old companies have "spun off" new divisions, often at new locations. North American's rocket group became Rocketdyne, with its plant at Canoga Park, handy to its engine test site in the Santa Susana Mountains. It has become the world's leading producer of liquid rocket engines and is currently producing the engines for the "Space Shuttle" as well as the 4th stage engine for the new MX missile. Another division of the same company (Rockwell International) is producing the "Space Shuttle Orbiter" in Downey, for final assembly in Palmdale. McDonnell Douglas Astronautics Company (Huntington Beach) is producing "spacecraft, launch vehicles, and ground support equipment." At El Segundo the same company produces satellites, both communications and meteorological, for private companies and various governments. General Dynamics makes "shoulder launched infrared and surface to air guided missiles" at its Pomona plant. TRW makes telecommunications satellites in Redondo Beach. Many other similar plants are located all around the region.

Missile and satellite production is also an assembly process, bringing together much sophisticated electronic equipment, much of it supplied by still another group of subcontractors in the region. Some are familiar names, some are not. Litton Industries makes internal navigation systems, gyroscopes, and accelerometers in Woodland Hills. Aerojet ElectroSystems (Azusa) constructs "advanced electro-optical, electro-acoustical and microwave sensor systems, and real-time data systems;" Whittaker's Tasker Systems produces antenna tracking devices, tactical radar jammers, and radar simulators in Chatsworth. Of course, these subassembly manufacturers do not make all of the components that go into them but purchase from an additional layer of firms the needed printed circuits, displays, umbilicals, capacitors, relays, solenoids, oscillators, microcomputers, photodetectors, electrical optical cameras, and so on and on. These items, too, often consist of assembled components, many of which are purchased from yet another layer of suppliers.

Most of the elements and components used in avionics have nonaerospace uses, and over the years the firms that make them also have turned to the civilian market. For example,

firms making communications equipment for aircraft, Hughes International and Litton's Data Systems, supply land-based non-military systems as well. Computers are used extensively in missiles and satellites but also have burgeoning use in all industry and business. Similarly, electronic components, microprocessor chips, semiconductor memories, and so on are in demand by companies manufacturing commercial and household equipment as well as by aerospace firms. Engineers skilled in avionics can shift easily to many branches of electronics. The presence of these enormous resources in the Metropolis—firms, components, engineers, skilled labor—has facilitated the growth of a whole series of high technology industries.

Finally, the changing requirements of the armed forces have created yet another layer of companies, many located in the Metropolis. Military contracts often call for the "research, development, test and evaluation" of a weapons system. Old line aircraft manufacturers may pool their efforts in the development and production of the required plane or missile. However, as research and development have become more important, special companies or divisions may specialize in this aspect of the contract, TRW's Defense and Space Systems Group and the Aerospace Corporation, for example. In addition, another series of firms concentrate on the supervision of weapons contracts and the evaluation of the product after it is manufactured—Hughes International is one of these.

The years ahead should see continued growth of the Metropolitan aerospace industry. The commercial airliners now being manufactured offer considerably greater fuel efficiency than their predecessors. Too, their engines are much quieter and produce much less air pollution—features needed to meet strict governmental regulations that will go into effect in 1985. Similarly, expenditures for military aircraft, missiles, and military and civilian satellites seem likely to increase, both in the U.S. and abroad. Then, too, the high technology firms related to the aerospace activity appear to be expanding. All of this should translate into growing employment in this already dominant manufacturing category.

Sportswear Capital of the World

For several decades the Los Angeles Metropolis has been second only to the New York City region in apparel manufacturing. However, it has become a much more respectable second since 1970, experiencing increasing sales and employment, while New York City has been declining slightly. Beginning in a small way in the 1920s and 1930s, the industry capitalized on the glamour of California and Hollywood. Company names are suggestive: "Hollywood Blouse, Inc.," "Holly-Mode of California," "California Sophisticates," or, alternatively, "Campus Casuals of California." The California label today is reputed to indicate "an imaginative use of color and pattern as well as style and originality." Los Angeles apparel manufacturers, reflecting the relaxed lifestyle of the region, claim to have introduced pants for women, pedal pushers, culottes, and the bikini. Even today local manufacturers assert, "New York doesn't think much about pants (for women) . . . they have allowed us to capture a total marketplace." As the rest of the nation "becomes more leisure minded and drifts toward the Sunbelt" the products of the Los Angeles apparel industry are increasingly in demand.

Today about 85,000 persons work in all branches of the garment industry. It is thus second in employment only to the aerospace complex. Currently, the local garment industry is broadly diversified, with some activity in all apparel categories—men's clothing, undergarments, and even standard items. However, swimsuits, women's dresses, pants, sportswear, and sportshirts for men, the branches of the industry with the longest history, still command the largest share of the national market. The success of the Los Angeles apparel industry, however, owes to more than the style of clothing. Wage rates are low here and only a few of the workers are unionized. Too, getting started in Los Angeles is easier than in New York. Rents are lower and the California Mart gives new lines instant visibility. In addition, bank lending is reportedly much more liberal; for example, Manufacturers Bank reportedly makes forty percent of its commercial loans to clothing companies.

The "apparel industry" includes many individuals and firms performing a wide variety of operations. The production of a dress, for example, may proceed something like this. The manufacturer begins by selecting a design— an original sketch may be made or a copy purchased. The garment is first sewn up in muslin, fitted on a manikin, and analyzed for costs and profits. If approved, materials will be selected and samples sewn up and shown at the California Mart; hopefully, orders will accumulate from retailers and production can begin. The muslin original is taken apart and the pattern maker makes paper patterns of the parts, cutting them in as many different sizes as the dress is going to be made up. Now bolts of cloth are unrolled, the material inspected and folded in perhaps one hundred layers on the cutting table, making a stack many inches high. The paper patterns are then fitted on top as closely together as possible to avoid waste, lines marked with chalk on the material, and the cutter with his electrical cutting tool (like a saber saw) cuts the many layers of material with one pass. The pieces of the dress are now sorted, numbered and bundled, and are ready for sewing. The manufacturer with an "inside shop" does his own sewing; if he lacks sewing capability, this operation must be contracted out. Operators stitch the pieces together with high speed machines into dresses. If the material requires it, the garment may be sent to a presser; if hand work is necessary, it will be done by a finisher. Finally, the dress ends up in the shipping room where it will be packed and the orders shipped to the retailer.

In real life, things are often not quite so simple and smooth. Textiles come from mills in the East; fabrics and patterns have to be chosen and ordered many months in advance. Because of the necessary lead time, a manufacturer may begin producing the dresses before he has his orders in hand. Retail buyers usually buy slowly and in small quantities at first to see which garments sell the quickest, then reorder only the most popular lines. The manufacturer must be able to fill these reorders rapidly (they can always be cancelled) and it is in these reorders where the most profit lies. It is a great temptation, and sometimes necessary, to have the garments made up in advance. Then, if fashion is fickle and reorders do not come, the possibility of getting caught with thousands of unsold garments "on the rack" is great. The garment manufacturer needs not only talent but also luck to survive, and the turnover is high. Almost one out of five go out of business each year.

Because of the vagaries of fashion and the premium on speed and flexibility, the apparel business is typified by small operations and much subcontracting. A manufacturer swamped with orders for a "hot item" not only runs his own operation at top speed but will contract out much of the work—cutting, sewing, pressing. In recent years there has been an increasing tendency toward larger, professionally managed firms. There is a trend toward advertised brands, and only large companies can afford the necessary advertising. Too, department stores like to deal with firms that can fill large orders. However, for high-style items the large firm takes high risks. "Big companies can't turn on a dime the way a small company can," one manufacturer points out, "with the largest firms there is so much involved that they can't take a chance on a new item doing well because before they turn around they have 100,000 of them, and they are hanging on the rack" (Business Week, 1978, p. 187).

The dress designer may have a glamorous job, but most work in the garment industry is hard, monotonous, and poorly paid. Wages comprise a large proportion of the costs of a garment, and wage rates are traditionally low. Work tends to be seasonal and the manufacturers desire a reservoir of labor with the requisite skill to draw on when they step up their production. It is an industry that historically has employed the most recent immigrants, as language skills are not a barrier to work. In Los Angeles, many workers are Mexican-Americans, Mexican nationals, blacks, and Orientals; most are women and, on the average, older than the average worker. Much work is piecework, and wages in 1978 averaged $3.88 an hour, reportedly thirty-one cents above the national industry average, but lower than for manufacturing workers in general.

The Garment District

Los Angeles Street has long been considered the "Seventh Avenue" of the Los Angeles garment district. The district has only vague boundaries, but extends from about 4th to Adams, and from Hill to Alameda Streets. Within this sprawling district of mostly rather low and old buildings are an estimated seventy-five percent of the apparel manufacturers of the region and a much higher proportion of the firms that are associated with them. Here is the de facto headquarters of the Los Angeles apparel industry, the gigantic California Mart. Here are the suppliers of sewing machines, cloth cutters, cloth spreaders (folders), cutting tables, and so on and on. Here are the mechanics who know how to repair these machines. The representatives of several hundreds of textile mills have offices in the area—dozens in one building, the California Textile Mart (819 Santee). Here, too, are the purveyors of thread, fasteners, snaps, and hangers. The button and buttonhole makers are here as well as other specialized subcontractors—"Expert cutting, marking, grading—pickup and delivery." And, importantly, in this district are the banks that are familiar with the financing needs of the apparel manufacturer. Some banks specialize in factoring—the factor buys accounts receivable so that the manufacturer gets his money as soon as he ships his goods, rather than waiting for the retailer to pay. For many garment manufacturers a location in the garment district offers numerous advantages. Everything he needs or is likely to want on short notice is near at hand. Then, too, the laborers he will need to recruit are familiar with its location and are accustomed to riding the RTD buses that serve the district. All of these things together are called "external economies"—economies outside of an individual firm.

Many of the region's largest apparel firms, however, are not located in the garment district. It is crowded, the buildings are old, and crime is a problem in some sections. Too, the industry has been expanding for a decade, and space within the area is getting expensive and hard to find. Cole of California (five hundred employees) makes swimsuits and sportswear in a plant in Vernon, and the Encino Shirt Company (six hundred) manufactures sportshirts in Chatsworth. Catalina, Inc. (2,000) makes swimwear and sportswear in plants in Commerce, Fullerton, and Montebello, while Mode O'Day (five hundred) produces sportswear in Burbank and San Bernardino, as well as within the district—1368 E. 15th Street. These are all large firms and many have moved to new, modern, air-conditioned plants—facilities impossible to find in the garment district. Many small firms also spurn external economies to locate near a source of labor. Scores of sewing contractors, for example, operate in Chinatown and in numerous Latino communities. Conversely, not all firms have moved out of the central area, and the district itself has been expanding. One of the largest employers, Tobias Katzin Co. (1,400), makes men's and boys' slacks at 1300 Santee Street, and Alex Colman (four hundred fifty) produces dresses and sportswear at 2100 South Figueroa, on the eastern and southern margins of the garment district, respectively. These large firms do not really need the garment district's external economies. They are large enough to employ their own repairmen, and they do not often find it necessary to run across the street for a dozen zippers.

Hollywood: Are You Still with Us?

The community of Hollywood is second only to Disneyland as the region's most popular tourist attraction. The sidewalk along Hollywood Boulevard is embedded with gold-colored stars honoring motion picture greats. Grauman's (now Mann's) Chinese Theater is a mecca for visitors today as in years gone by. The Hollywood sign on the background hills has been lovingly restored. What of the motion picture industry itself, the activity that made Hollywood its world-wide symbol?

All of the nation's major studios' production facilities and three-fourths of its production employment are located in the Metropolis. There are seven major production companies and, in addition, in 1980, seven independent producers: the latter may be established concerns or they may be formed to make a single film. The three networks also produce film in the Metropolis, as do numerous other companies producing television programs, commercials, and films for educational and industrial use. Total employment in all phases of the industry—production, distribution, and exhibition—in 1980 was about 65,000.

Of the producers, Universal is the giant with about 7,000 employees; the others, Paramount, Walt Disney Productions, Twentieth Century Fox, Metro-Goldwyn-Mayer (MGM), and Warner Brothers, employ from one to two thousand, and Columbia, about two hundred fifty. In addition, many associated firms, vital to film production, are located in the area. For example: Warner Brothers Studios (a separate firm) provides crew and studio space; William Morris and International Creative Management are theatrical agencies that represent actors, writers, and directors; Panavision makes and rents movie cameras and lenses; Petite Caterers supplies food to film locations; Western Costume furnishes theatrical costumes; and Cary Limousine Service provides transportation to actors and executives alike. In addition, if the shooting takes place within the Metropolis, the economy is stimulated further—many extras are hired; lodging may be needed; food, gasoline, and building materials are consumed.

Although the industry worries about increasing costs, the future appears bullish. Annual movie attendance has been increasing since its low point in 1973, the industry is resistant to economic contractions, and, in spite of rapidly increasing ticket prices, movie-going is still a relatively inexpensive form of entertainment. Fewer but more profitable films are being released. Selling a film's rights to television and film distribution companies can bring in substantial revenues. The growth of pay-TV, video cassettes, and videodiscs should further increase the demand for Hollywood products. Finally, the industry seems firmly entrenched in its original homeland, and the external economies of producing films in the Metropolis are still significant.

Local Raw Materials Processed for Export

The Los Angeles Metropolis has become essentially an urbanized region and no longer produces much in the way of raw materials in the traditional sense. Some agricultural land is still tucked away among the subdivisions, and a few citrus groves remain. Tuna and albacore are yet landed at San Pedro, albeit in smaller quantities than before. Local oil fields include the state's most productive—Wilmington and numerous others, although today imports exceed regional production and exports are relatively small.

Processing Agricultural Products

Packing fresh oranges in crates in the traditional way was never considered "manufacturing." However, making wine or preserves, canning fruit, and even freezing orange juice earns a "manufacturing" classification, and a small segment of this industry remains in the Metropolis. Today, the largest food processor in the region is Kern Foods, Inc. (1,200 employees), located in the City of Industry. It is a relatively unspecialized operation, producing a wide variety of items: preserves, jellies, fruit nectar, frozen strawberries, tomato juice, catsup, and other items. Sunkist growers have a Lemon Products Division (five hundred fifty) in Corona, producing lemon juice products, lemon oil, pectin, dried lemon pulp, and pharmaceuticals. Treesweet Products (four hundred) cans and concentrates citrus juice in Santa Ana, while Vita-Pakt (two hundred ten) in Covina and the Paramount Citrus Association (two hundred fifty) in San Fernando do similar kinds of things. One winery in the area, the Brookside Vineyard Co. in Guasti, employs a respectable number, some three hundred; the other local wineries are much smaller with payrolls ranging from eight to seventy.

Tuna Canning for Humans and Pets

Los Angeles became the nation's leading fishing port in the 1920s as tuna and albacore gained popularity with the nation's consumers. Within the last decade about a dozen canneries were operating on Terminal Island. Today, however, only two firms remain: Star Kist Foods (2,000), specializing in canning tuna and pet food, and Pan Pacific Fisheries (2,000), which adds mackerel, fish meal, and oil to its product line.

Petroleum Refining: Much Space, Massive Equipment, Few Workers

Petroleum refineries are highly visible industrial operations. Their jumble of towers, pipes, and tanks produce one of today's weirdest-looking industrial landscapes. Furthermore, seldom is a human being to be seen—these acres of industrial "spaghetti" seem almost to operate by themselves. This impression is fairly accurate. The twenty-one refineries in the Metropolis in 1980, operating twenty-four hours a day, employed only about 7,000 persons. As these refineries have a capacity of 1,373,000 barrels of crude a day, this must represent the greatest output per man of any of the region's industrial operations. To take one example: only 1,600 workers are needed to operate the region's largest refinery, the Chevron plant in El Segundo, with a capacity of 405,000 barrels per day—thirty percent of the total. In spite of the maze of equipment, the refining process is basically simple and the workers mainly watch dials and turn valves. Heat is applied in a distillation process; all but the heaviest crudes flash into vapor which rises in a "fractionating tower" and condenses on trays according to the temperature at which portions of the vapor become liquid—gasoline, jet fuel, diesel, lubricating oil, and so on. Asphalt remains as a residue.

Petroleum refining began in Los Angeles to process the crude produced by its "world class" petroleum discoveries of the 1920s. Most of the gasoline, kerosene, and other products were exported, and harbor locations were favored. Today, although the Los Angeles region produces twenty-five percent of California's oil and the Wilmington field is the state's second largest producer, local demand for petroleum products greatly exceeds the local supply, and the region's refineries process much imported crude. Thus, refineries that started out refining local crude mainly for distant markets, now find themselves processing mainly imported crude mostly for the local market.

Fortunately, sites near the harbor remain advantageous. Much petroleum comes in by tanker and some of the refined products are sent out by ship also, although most are dis-tributed by pipeline. Shell, Texaco, and Union have refineries in Wilmington, ARCO is in Carson, and Mobile is in Torrance—all are near the Twin Ports. Chevron, located in El Segundo, has no harbor, but uses underwater pipelines extending about a mile to large steel mooring buoys in Santa Monica Bay for its tanker connections. The exception to this locational pattern is Gulf which operates a refinery on the old Santa Fe Springs oil field, more than ten miles by pipeline from the harbor. Together the local refineries have about eight percent of the nation's refining capacity. This is enough for the region's needs and produces a surplus for sale to other parts of California as well as to Arizona and Nevada.

Manufacturing for the Metropolitan Market

Some types of industries find a location near the market advantageous. With a population of more than 10.5 million, the Los Angeles Metropolis provides an attractive location for thousands of these firms. A sample of market oriented industries includes bakeries, both large and small, soft drink bottlers, breweries, and meat packers, as well as the producers of tin cans, glass and plastic bottles, paperboard boxes, and the container industry in general. Newspaper publishers and commercial printers also find a location near their customers essential. Furniture, too, for home and office, can advantageously be manufactured near its market. Finally, there are a number of industries, currently declining in the United States, in which factories may have been built with wider distribution in mind that now can compete best near the location of their plants—iron and steel is a Metropolitan example.

Bakeries: Local and Metropolitan

If manufacturing employment were mapped, small clusters of industrial workers would appear in almost every residential neighborhood. These would be employees of the local bakeries. Neighborhood bakeries produce custom orders of specially decorated cakes for birthdays, weddings, and other celebrations as well as a daily baking of breads, rolls, cakes, and cookies. Often they have their national specialties—French, Italian, Mexican, Danish—or other types of baked goods, or they may emphasize particular items—croissants, carrot cakes, bagels, cheesecake, or whatever. However they may differ, their goal is the same—to deliver their rapidly perishable products to their customers within hours after they are produced. A neighborhood location is vital.

Today, much bread, rolls, cake, cookies, and other standard bakery items are found on the shelves of every supermarket in the region. The rise of mass merchandising, improved preservation, and delivery by truck have been accompanied by the development of the giant bakery; for these factories the entire Metropolis is the market. The region's largest individual bakery is Van De Kamp's Dutch Bakery (1,400 employees) located on Fletcher Drive just off the Golden State Freeway. Continental Baking Co. (1,700) has two plants in the area, one baking bread and buns, another specializing in cake and sweet goods. Oroweat Foods (two plants, nine hundred employees), Barbara Ann-Langendorf Bakeries (four hundred), and a Safeway Stores-Bread Plant (three hundred) are the region's other large concerns.

(Another perishable food item, soft candy, also benefits from a market location. Within the Metropolis, Sees Candy Shops is dominant, with 2,000 employees at its plant at 3423 S. La Cienega. Significantly, the company has a branch plant in the San Francisco area.)

The Beverage Industry: It's the Water?

A classic example of a local industry, where a cheap, ubiquitous, bulky material—water—is the chief ingredient, is the beverage industry in all of its subdivisions. The bottling of soft drinks is one of the most widespread of American industries. Historically, every respectable city had its own brewery and, in spite of enormous consolidation in the industry, a metropolitan location is still a major asset. Finally, locally-produced or purified water is occasionally bottled for retail sale.

In brewing, barley is combined in a chemical process with small quantities of malt, corn, rice, sugar, and hops, and large amounts of water to produce beer. Beer itself is mostly water and is a bulky product, relatively inexpensive but with relatively high distribution costs, whether packaged in bottles, cans, or barrels. In recent years, four breweries have been operating in the Metropolis: Anheuser-Busch (eight hundred) and the Joseph Schlitz Brewing Co. (six hundred), both in Van Nuys, Miller Brewing Company in Azusa, and Pabst (two hundred fifty) at 1920 N. Main Street, a long-time location of a local brewery. Currently, Anheuser-Busch is expanding its Van Nuys plant with the goal of doubling its capacity. Los Angeles city water is used by the three breweries within the city; local supplies are also tapped at Azusa. A common characteristic of all four sites is a rail siding, needed not only for receiving barley and other ingredients, but also for the distribution of beer.

Of equal importance in terms of employment is the bottling of soft drinks. This is a simple process: syrup, often patented and imported from some national manufacturing center, is combined with local water, carbonated, and then canned or bottled. Clearly, a location near the market is advantageous. There are also important economies of scale and most plants produce a multitude of products. Pepsicola Bottling Company of Los Angeles (eight hundred employees) has plants in Torrance, Baldwin Park, and Buena Park. Coca-Cola has its architecturally classic plant on Central Avenue (it is designed to look like an ocean liner) as well as a branch at Downey. In addition to Coke, it bottles Tab, Fresca, Bubble-Up, Canada Dry, and Arrowhead Bottled Water. Arrowhead, actually a division of Coca-Cola, has eight plants scattered around the region bottling water. The effect of economies of scale is illustrated by the Dr. Pepper plant (five hundred) in Gardena, which also produces Squirt, Vernon's Ginger Ale, Orange Crush, Dad's Root Beer, and Nestea.

Meat Packing—Mainly in Vernon

Although the Union Stock Yards that operated in Vernon from 1922 to 1963 have been closed for nearly two decades, considerable meat is still packed in the old neighborhood. Only one packer still butchers hogs—the Clougherty Packing Co., the largest employer with 1,100 workers, which sells under the trademark, "Farmer John." The other packers, about forty-five firms, process beef, purchasing the animals from feedlots mainly in the Imperial and San Joaquin Valleys, and selling the meat to the local supermarkets or, if butchered under rabbinical supervision, selling it at kosher butcher shops. Some firms still import the animals live, others process the animals near the feedlots, and then age the meat in their local refrigeration plants. Another group of firms, such as Oscar Mayer (eight hundred employees), specialize in processing meat into sausage, salami, and a wide variety of prepared meats.

One of the unique features of the meat packing industry is its concentration. About thirty of the forty-five plants are in Vernon, most along a short stretch of Vernon Avenue or nearby side streets. This concentration makes it easy for buyers to "shop the market," but it also reflects long standing zoning patterns on streets adjacent to the former Stock Yards. Closely associated industries also cluster in Vernon; Kal Kan Foods producing dog and cat foods, nine rendering works (processors of fat, tallow, bones), and a number of dealers in hides; several, including the Vernon Leather Company, operate tanneries. Other users of by-products are nearby: The Pacific Soap Company, Los Angeles By-Products Co., Swift Adhesives, and the Academy Candle Company, as well as a firm that advertises, "Meathandlers, Ltd.—Commercial Loading and Unloading of Trucks."

Cans, Bottles, Boxes: By the Billion

To package the soft drinks, beer, orange juice, catsup, fish, pet food, lubricating oil, paint, and everything liquid, perishable or small that is manufactured in the Metropolis, billions—literally—of cans, bottles, bags, and boxes are needed. Then, too, these containers and most everything else produced in the Metropolis are packed in paperboard boxes for shipment. Containers are a lot bulkier than the sheet steel, aluminum, glass, plastic, or paperboard that comprise the raw materials. Manufacturing near the place of use is clearly indicated.

The container industry is well developed in the Metropolis, with all of the major companies represented. Often these firms produce a wide variety of containers. The American Can Company has five plants in the area, including a metal can plant in the harbor district adjacent to the tuna canneries, plastic container plants in Glendale and Alta Loma, and a Dixie products plant in Anaheim. Continental Can has four plants in the area making steel and aluminum cans, one plastic container plant, another making corrugated boxes. National Can has four plants; Reynolds Metals, one (a large plant with seven hundred employees) in Torrance. General Can has three plants, and the Container Corporation of America has five, producing mostly corrugated and solid fiber shipping containers.

Manufacturing glass containers is a specialized branch of the industry with a separate series of companies. In this industry, basic raw materials are used; sand is mixed with lime, soda ash, and "cullet" (broken glass being recycled) and heated in large furnaces to a temperature of over 2,500 degrees F. It now has a molasses-like consistency and can be blown into the desired container shape by automatic machines. Plants tend to be large; each company has only one in the region. Of the eight plants, four employ more than five hundred persons: Kerr Glass in Santa Ana, Owens-Illinois in Vernon, Thatcher Glass in Saugus, and Ball Glass in El Monte. Typically, these plants produce bottles for beer and other beverages, all sorts of bottles and jars for foods and pharmaceuticals, and occasionally glass containers for home canning.

Printing and Publishing

Printing and publishing is an important activity with about 70,000 employees in the Metropolis. Characteristically, the branches of the industry that are well-developed are those that benefit from a location within the region that they serve. Newspapers traditionally are tied to their local markets; they feature local news, get their revenues from local advertisers, and, if the papers are to be delivered quickly, subscribers cannot live too far from the printing plant. Similarly, much commercial printing is done on a tight time schedule; telephone directories, advertising brochures, company reports, lawyers' briefs, concert programs, and so on are seldom prepared much in advance—the printer ideally should be just around the corner from the customer. In addition, the customer normally needs to be consulted time and again during the production process—layouts must be approved, type selected, proofs corrected, and the like—so a nearby location is essential.

In the Metropolis the major employer in both newspaper publishing and commercial printing is The Times Mirror Company. "The Los Angeles Times" has its headquarters adjacent to the Los Angeles Civic Center, at "Times Mirror Square," and employs some 6,000 persons. The newspaper circulates over a million copies daily and Sunday, blanketing not only the Metropolis but also all of southern California, and asserts that it is "without question the world's most financially successful newspaper." Satellite printing operations have been built in Orange County; others are planned. Other local newspapers are also important employers: the "Long Beach Independent Press-Telegram" (nine hundred), "Los Angeles Herald Examiner" (eight hundred), "Daily News" in Van Nuys (seven hundred), the "Daily Breeze" in Torrance (six hundred), and so on, with an additional fifteen newspaper publishers employing more than one hundred persons. Magazine and journal publishing is relatively poorly developed in the area. However, Volt Technical Corporation in El Segundo produces a variety of technical publications and has 2,000 employees. Too, perhaps appropriately, the Peterson Publishing Company (seven hundred), publisher of "Motor Trend," is located in the Metropolis on Sunset Boulevard.

Commercial printing is also well developed in the Metropolis, with both letter press and lithographic divisions represented. Again, the Times Mirror Press, 1115 S. Boyle Avenue (adjacent to the Santa Monica-Santa Ana Freeway interchange) is the largest, but with eight hundred employees is not so dominant. More than a thousand firms are represented; about thirty have more than one hundred employees, most have fewer than ten. Specialties include banknotes, business forms, letterheads, business cards, telephone directories, and record jackets.

Furniture for Home and Office

Furniture is still produced in many of its traditional centers—Grand Rapids, Michigan, High Point and Thomasville, North Carolina, for example. It is, however, a bulky product, more expensive to ship than the wood, steel, or fabric from which it is made. It is not surprising, therefore, that the large and growing Metropolis has attracted an important furniture industry that employs about 47,000 persons. Plants are generally small; of the 1,000 plants producing household furniture, for example, only nine have more than five hundred employees, most have less than fifty.

214

All branches of the industry are represented, producing everything from wooden kitchen cabinets, dining and bedroom furniture, and upholstered furniture to metal household fixtures. The largest concern, Brown Jordon Co. with headquarters in El Monte, employs about 1,000 persons in three local fabricating plants and specializes in "aluminum and rattan patio, poolside and living room, dining room, bedroom and terrace furniture." (Reversing the usual procedure, it has branch plants in Arkansas, Florida, and Virginia and advertises nationally.)

Other segments of the industry produce everything from office furniture to mattresses and springs. Most of the manufacturers in these categories, as in the household furniture group, seem to be local concerns. However, occasionally a branch plant of a national firm appears. Steelcase, Inc., for example, the largest manufacturer of office furniture in the nation, headquartered in Grand Rapids, has a factory in Tustin with eight hundred employees producing steel desks, filing cabinets, and office chairs.

Iron and Steel, Aluminum,
and the New Realities

The manufacture of iron and steel, once considered vital to an area's industrial importance, had a spurt in the Metropolis during World War II, but today seems vulnerable to competition from imports from Japan. The Kaiser Steel Corporation (discussed in detail on page 185) still employs about 6,000 persons in its integrated plant in Fontana, but appears to be in financial trouble. Other steel mills, operating by melting down local scrap or imported pig iron, are also feeling the competition. United States Steel, for example, operated a plant in Torrance from 1916 to 1979, when the facility was dismantled and the land put up for sale.

Bethlehem Steel, on the other hand, with local roots going back to the late 1890s, currently produces 600,000 tons of steel annually and employs 1,800 persons in its Vernon plant. Steel scrap, plus some pig iron and limestone, is melted in three electric furnaces to produce steel. Finishing mills then roll the steel into structural sections, bars, and rods. These items can be used directly or they may serve as raw materials for further processing by local firms. Rods, for example, are used directly in vast numbers as reinforcement in concrete construction, but they can also be manufactured into all kinds of bolts and nuts. In addition, wire mills draw rods into various types of wire to be used for fencing, stucco netting, upholstery springs, staples, tie wire, and other items. Bars are shaped into oil field tools, springs, blades, and so on. Several smaller steel mills operate in similar fashion in the Metropolis.

However, most of the several score local companies that list themselves as "steel mills" do not produce steel. Some are fabricators. For example, Bethlehem has a second plant, this one in Torrance, that fabricates steel into structural shapes to be used in the construction of bridges and buildings. Most, however, are simply "mill warehouses," not manufacturers at all. Typical is Latrobe Steel in the City of Commerce. Although it employs 1,800 persons, it does little fabricating locally, but concentrates on selling specialty steel to the region's tool and die shops, forge shops, the aerospace industry, and so on.

There are two aluminum plants in the Metropolis, the Aluminum Company of America (1,600) in Vernon and Martin Marietta Aluminum (1,300) in Torrance. Their function is to melt aluminum scrap purchased locally together with imported ingots and to form it into aluminum castings, bars, rods, etc. These can then be rolled into shapes needed by local consumers, mainly the aerospace industry.

Wholesaling: Occasional Concentration

Wholesale trade, "the sale of goods in large quantities, as for resale by a retailer," is well developed in the Metropolis. About a quarter of a million persons are employed in wholesaling, putting the region third in the U.S. in wholesale employment, behind only the two large distribution centers of New York and Chicago. Traditionally, the wholesaler assembled large quantities of each item in a central warehouse and then shipped out smaller batches to retailers. Today this function is sometimes assumed by "a manufacturer's representative" who may display samples and have the order shipped directly from the company warehouse to the retailer's store. Both methods of selling will be considered wholesaling here.

Wholesaling developed early in Los Angeles. Local firms were supplying army posts in Yuma and the Mormon settlements in Utah in the 1850s and 1860s, and in the 1870s the main economic activity in the city was supplying the needs of the miners at Cerro Gordo. As rail lines were built into the city the wholesalers located their warehouses near the freight stations and express offices—particularly in the area between Los Angeles and Alameda Streets. Recently, with the rise of truck transportation, freeways, and a new understanding of the efficiencies of one-story buildings, many wholesalers have built their warehouses in outlying locations. In 1980, for example, Certified Grocers opened a new single story dry-grocery warehouse the size of thirteen football fields in the City of Commerce. Located near the junction of the Santa Ana and Long Beach freeways, it is completely automated, and eighty-one trucks and eleven railroad cars can be handled simultaneously.

However, the needs of all wholesalers are not alike. In spite of the attractiveness of roomy, suburban sites, a number of wholesalers remain clustered, often in or near the traditional downtown location. Some have packed themselves tightly into a single building, or a few adjacent buildings. The wholesalers of flowers, produce, apparel, jewelry, home furnishings, furs, and textiles, among others, are located in close clusters. Why?

What do these wholesalers have in common? First, all deal in non-standardized items, items difficult to describe precisely, where appearance, freshness, quality, or style are of overriding importance. These characteristics encourage the purchaser to "come to market," and a compact location, convenient for these professional buyers, is needed. Wholesalers not located in a handy cluster are not likely to be much visited. In addition, in the flower and produce markets, the price depends on supply and demand and, as the produce is perishable and cannot be kept for long, the price is likely to vary from hour to hour. To efficiently "clear the market" it is important for all sellers and buyers to come together, hence the close clustering.

On the other hand, if the wholesaler handles standardized items, groceries for example, the buyer places his orders by phone, or mail, or computer. He knows what the boxes and cans he sells look like, the prices remain stable for weeks and months, and he has no need to go to market. Wholesale grocers are located in widespread locations around the Metropolis at sites convenient to rail sidings and freeway entrances. Hardware and drug wholesalers handle standardized items, too, receive their orders as described above, and are located broadly around the area. Nevertheless, there is some advantage for one hardware wholesaler to be near another one. These dealers carry an enormous variety of items, 100,000 different things by one estimate, and to complete a retailer's order they may have to go to their competitor for a few missing items. However, in analyzing the Metropolis, we are particularly interested in activities that form specialized districts, and so will discuss a few of the wholesalers that cluster.

The Produce Market—Consolidation
and Modernization

Early every weekday morning, between 2:00 and 3:00 A.M., the trucks arrive with their loads of freshly harvested tomatoes, celery, carrots, potatoes, oranges, apples, or most any fruit or vegetable. As they are rapidly unloaded, "swampers" wheel the carts to their designated stalls, and the vendors inspect the day's stock to be ready for the haggling that soon will begin and continue on until about noon. Another day's cycle at the Los Angeles Produce Market has begun.

In the nineteenth century, growers used to haul their produce to the Plaza where their wagons could be easily visited by the grocers, restaurant chefs, and other buyers. By 1901, their rigs were so numerous they were declared a public nuisance and they were forced to move. Today, the produce market is found in two semi-adjacent downtown locations. One, the Seventh Street or Terminal Market, occupies twelve acres owned by the Southern Pacific, bounded by Alameda, Seventh, Central, and Eighth Streets. Several decades ago, because of overcrowding, a second market was established on a site bounded by Ninth, San Pedro, Eleventh, and San Julian—the "Ninth Street Market." As the two markets are half a mile apart this makes for inconvenience and inefficiency.

The Los Angeles produce market, measured in terms of carloads of goods handled, is second in size only to New York, and serves an area extending to San Luis Obispo, Fresno, Las Vegas, Phoenix, to the Mexican border and beyond. The large size of the market is surprising because many of the supermarket chains buy their produce "in the field" directly from producers, bypassing the market entirely. In fact, only about twenty-five to thirty percent of the fresh produce consumed in the Metropolis comes through these market stalls. But this is twenty-five percent of an enormous volume, and the market grosses about $300 million annually.

The produce market is composed of a conglomeration of small market companies, located side by side, often specializing in one or several products, whatever it is they know best. The market, an auction really, is extremely

sensitive to supply and demand—produce does not remain fresh for long, and the urge to "clear the market" each day is strong. Whatever is left late in the selling day is apt to be offered at sharply reduced prices and often purchased by peddlers who can dispose of the produce quickly from trucks in their habitual neighborhood locations. As quality as well as price varies from day to day, from hour to hour, and from vendor to vendor, the need to visit the market is apparent. It is an industry based on personal contacts and trust, and produce companies seem to remain in the same families for generations. The wholesaler spends much time building up contacts with the growers on one hand and with buyers on the other. Most buyers are seeking produce for small stores, large restaurants, institutions that serve meals, and small supermarket chains. Some may be agents for large, more distant customers, and even the buyers for the large chains come by to check the price and quality of produce available to their competitors. Actually, anyone can purchase produce here, provided he can use a large quantity, a crate or more.

A visitor to the produce markets will notice obvious problems: many of the streets are too narrow to accommodate the large produce trucks, the space for unloading, storage, and selling is cramped and obsolete (with no room for fork lifts, for example), often dating literally from the "horse and buggy days." Produce markets in other cities have often been moved to a suburban location when new quarters were needed, and for several decades the possible consolidation and future location of the market has stirred much controversy. Those who want to move allege the area is crime-ridden, among other things; arguments for staying include the fact that the produce trucks operate mainly at night and do not add to freeway rush hour traffic. In any event, in mid-1980, Mayor Bradley announced the receipt of a federal grant to aid in modernizing the area and in building a new combined market on a much expanded site—twenty-two acres of warehouse and open air space—at the location of the present Terminal Market. The action was described as "the first in the nation for the retention and expansion of a central city market." The city of Los Angeles will thus retain some 5,000 jobs, and it is thought another 1,000 jobs will be created in the expanded market. When completed, the new market will be owned by the city, managed by a non-profit corporation, with space subleased to the vendors.

The produce market has a special demand for goods and services, and a number of ancillary industries, firms, and activities have been attracted to its environs. Its many trucks are serviced by several major truck terminals, one using the space under the raised Santa Monica Freeway—between Figueroa and Santa Fe. Several service stations designed especially to service trucks are located on Alameda Street. Sambo's Restaurant on Olympic and Alameda is used by truckers and vendors as a spot to recruit free-lance labor, as are also the corners of Alameda and 7th, and along Olympic and San Julian or Towne. Packaging concerns abound: Con Paper at 6th and Central, the Golden State Box Company, 810 S. Kohler, and Custom Container Corp., 1919 E. 7th Place, for example. In some European cities the early morning operations and the colorful displays of fruit and vegetables, have given the markets exotic reputations. Both the now-abandoned Covent Garden in London and Les Halles in Paris, for example, attracted many early morning vistors, locals and tourists alike. There is some thought that the new L.A. Market may, too. In the meantime, knowing visitors breakfast with the locals at Vickman's (1228 E. 8th), open from 3:00 A.M. to 3:00 P.M.

Flowers: By the Thousands of Dozens

Vendors in the Los Angeles Floral Market, located in the two blocks bounded by Seventh, Eighth, Maple, and San Julian, spend the early morning hours busily arranging their products for sale. The nine rather drab, barnlike sheds, and the lines of nondescript vans parked on Wall Street (which bisects the area) give little hint of the colorful sight to be found within the buildings. Inside, hanging in bunches from overhead wires and piled high on tables, are not dozens, but thousands of dozens of every flower grown by southern California's prolific nurserymen. These two blocks are the location of the largest cut-flower wholesale market in the nation, with gross sales of about $40 million dollars annually. Buyers begin arriving about midnight and the selling is at its peak between 5:00 and 7:00 A.M.; prices are not fixed; all transactions are by haggling. Flowers begin to show their age quickly, prices change just as rapidly, and, as the market is mainly a Monday, Wednesday, Friday affair, an effort is made to "clear the market" each selling day. As purchases are made the blooms are trundled out to the vans of the local florists or "route men" for delivery within the Metropolis or to the airport for long-distance shipment.

The Los Angeles Floral Market is operated by the Southern California Flower Growers Association and has been located at this Wall Street site since 1923. About ninety firms participate in the wholesaling activities and perhaps eighty percent of them also manage growing operations (in contrast to their counterparts in the Produce Market). Sales are only to members or affiliates of the Southern California Floral Association (about 1,000 persons)—sales to others would require collection of sales tax. Hybrid tea roses are the volume leader, followed by carnations, pompom chrysanthemums, gladioli, and standard chrysanthemums. Potted plants account for perhaps ten percent of the market's sales. About seventy-five percent of the flowers go to retailers in the Metropolis; perhaps half of the rest are shipped out of state and the rest go to other retailers in California or to street peddlers.

The floral market is not without its problems. Fewer retailers are personally visiting the market, trusting to standing orders or the telephone. Thus, the wholesalers complain, impulse sales are lost and the number of buyers bidding for the flowers is reduced. However, in spite of some movement of large growers to peripheral locations and increased direct shipping to Eastern buyers, the volume of the market has doubled in a recent fifteen-year period. Too, the facilities have grown inadequate and obsolete, with poor security, inefficient loading arrangements and insufficient refrigeration and assembly space. One study suggested the market should move to a suburban location in Orange County. However, at the present time (1980) a new two-story building, with rooftop parking, is under construction. When completed it will occupy the entire block between Maple and Wall and will double the amount of available selling space. Thus, the improvement of the floral market on its traditional site has begun, and retaining it and its 2,000 jobs in the central city seems assured.

"Cal Mart" and 40,000 Fashion Buyers

Traditionally, buyers from department stores and apparel stores haunted Los Angeles Street and its environs shopping for clothing in the latest style and fabric. This was the "Garment District" and apparel manufacturers were located in the area partially for the convenience of these buyers. However, with the building of the California Mart, buying convenience has been carried to its logical conclusion—now it can be done within a single building. The symbiotic relationship between the local apparel industry and the California Mart may partially explain the rapid growth of the industry in the Metropolis at a time when it has been losing ground in other parts of the country.

Constructed in stages from 1964 to 1979, the California Mart consists of four interconnected fourteen-story towers and covers an entire block between 9th and Olympic, Main and Los Angeles Streets. Within what is the downtown's largest building are more than three million square feet of display and exhibit space, divided into showrooms and offices for some 2,000 tenants. These tenants are not only the local garment manufacturers—apparel firms from all over the country use the facilities to display their latest fashions. Different floors are devoted to specialized displays: dresses, sportswear, jeans, swimwear, lingerie, men's wear, boys' wear, girls' wear, infants' wear, coats, accessories, textiles, couture, and so on. From 30,000 to 40,000 buyers appear for the showing of spring fashions in October and again for the fall styles in April. However, the Mart is open every week, and special shows such as "Western Children's Bandwagon," "Shoe Market Days," and "Holiday Accessory Market," occur regularly. It is reported that more than two billion dollars worth of merchandise is sold through the Mart annually, about fifteen percent of the nation's apparel business.

The California Mart is a privately-owned enterprise, the brainchild of Harvey and Barney Morse, geared to the needs of apparel manufacturers and retail store buyers. Included in the building, in addition to the exhibit rooms, are a "Market Mezzanine" with seventy-five individually furnished showrooms for trade shows, a 600-seat "Fashion Theater" used for style shows and banquets, and an "Exhibit Center" with room for three hundred display booths. Some 7,000 persons work in the building and to serve them are nine restaurants, three in-house caterers, three banks and many other service firms. Included also are firms that serve the specialized needs of tenants and buyers, an interior designer for the fashion trade, and a firm offering new-store-opening service, for example. The Mart is reported to be "the largest merchandise center of its kind in the world," and the prototype of others in Chicago, Atlanta, and Dallas.

(A few blocks away is located an unassociated, yet related, institution, "The Fashion Institute of Design and Merchandising." This is a two-year college with 2,000 students, and offers AA degrees in "Merchandising, fashion design and interior design." The location was chosen, its brochure reports, to be close "to the corporate offices of the major retail stores and the center of apparel manufacture that focuses on the California Mart." Many of its students work in the showrooms, others attend classrooms the college maintains in the Mart, and advanced seminars are taught by Cal Mart lessees in their showrooms. Many graduates, we are told, find full-time jobs in the area.)

Hill Street—The Wholesale Jewelry Center of the West

Hill Street, from 7th to 4th, well-known today as a retail "Jewelers Lane," is also the location of a large and rapidly expanding wholesale jewelry industry. For many years, four buildings, two on Hill, and two around the corner on 5th, housed the vast majority of the region's wholesale jewelers. Recently, four more buildings on Hill Street and several others on nearby streets, were converted for use by this specialized activity. The Pantages Theater at 7th and Hill is now the Theater Jewelry Center; other conversions include the Los Angeles Jewelry Center, the Western Federal Building, and the Jewelry Design Center. Today (1980), a block long building with twin twenty-story towers is rising on Hill Street fronting Pershing Square—the International Jewelry Center. Still another building, the Western Jewelry Tower, a twenty-five-story structure, is going up at 625–27 S. Hill. The site (a parking lot) was reportedly purchased in 1979 for $214 per square foot, thought to be the highest price ever paid for downtown land.

Clearly, the wholesale jewelry industry represents a vigorous and growing element in the Los Angeles Central Business District.

Today it is estimated that there are more than a thousand wholesale, importing, and manufacturing firms located in this small area. Many are recent arrivals from such troubled areas as Beirut, Iran, and Thailand. Optimists believe the Hill Street District will eventually rival New York as the nation's largest jewelry center.

Wholesale jewelers deal in non-standardized, small, and valuable items as well as diamonds and other precious gemstones. Pieces are often custom-made, so considerable manufacturing is associated with wholesaling, and many stonecutters, diamond setters, polishers, and engravers work in the district. As one jeweler puts it, "People in this business are so interdependent. One person may design a piece, then send it to someone for casting, someone else to set the diamonds, another person may be the polisher." (Simross, 1979, Part IV, p. 1.) Buyers come to the wholesale market to personally examine the varied offerings and to compare prices. Clustering is therefore the order of the day—not only for the buyers' convenience, but because being near other jewelers means your offerings will be seen by many buyers. In addition, insurance rates are a significant factor in the cost of doing business, and these rates are considerably less in buildings with specialized security systems—which all of these buildings have. Finally, it is not an accident that the district has developed within easy walking distance of the downtown hotels.

Home Furnishings: Los Angeles Mart, the "Blue Whale" and Environs

Buyers of home furnishings at wholesale come from two groups—professional buyers for retail stores or interior decorators, who buy for individual customers. Both types of buyers go to "the market"—to compare style, quality, and price. But there is a major difference between the two types that affects the location of those who cater to them. The home furnishing (and giftwear) buyer will typically make several buying trips a year and may come to Los Angeles from almost anywhere in the Southwest. The interior decorator, on the other hand, is usually a local professional and will have dozens of clients during the year, necessitating numerous trips to the wholesaler. On many occasions he will want to take his customers along on the viewing expedition. Furthermore, the interior decorators (architects, specifiers, or whatever) are likely to maintain offices near their customers—the well-to-do segment of the Metropolitan population.

The Los Angeles Mart has been constructed to efficiently serve the retail store home furnishing buyer. It is a large, twelve-story building, centrally located in the Metropolis and reasonably near the downtown hotels, on Broadway at Washington. More than a thousand wholesalers exhibit their wares in its showrooms—furniture of all styles, floor coverings, fabrics, lamps, draperies, accessories, china, as well as a large variety of giftwear. Although open all year around, it has its seasonal "Market Days" for buyers of home furnishings, and others for giftwear buyers.

The Los Angeles Mart is open to interior decorators but their major activity is elsewhere. The vast majority of the wholesalers used by decorators are located in an area just east of Beverly Hills. They may be in individual shops on Robertson, Melrose, and Melrose Place, and on nearby streets, or clustered together in the massive Pacific Design Center at Melrose and San Vicente. The offices of many of the region's interior decorators themselves are in the area, and it is near the homes of many of their wealthy clients. Many of the wholesale showrooms are in small buildings within walking distance of each other; others are in the relatively new Pacific Design Center, known as the Blue Whale because of its size and its distinctive blue glass exterior.

15. Suggested Readings

Cunningham, William G. *The Aircraft Industry, A Study in Industrial Location*. Los Angeles: Morrison, 1951.
Although the book is thirty years old and surveys the aircraft industry on a nationwide basis, there is much material on the Los Angeles area in it that is still useful.

Rand, Christopher. *Los Angeles, the Ultimate City*. New York: Oxford, 1967.
Originally a series of articles in the New Yorker, this volume is particularly good in its description of the developing aerospace industry.

Security Pacific National Bank. Research Department. *Monthly Summary of Business Conditions, Southern California*.
Each issue of this publication includes a detailed discussion of some economic topic or an analysis of one of the sub-regions in southern California. Free. To get on mailing list write Research Department, Security Pacific National Bank, Box 2097, Terminal Annex, Los Angeles, CA 90051. The bank also publishes occasional items on various aspects of the local economy, for example, *Southern California: Economic Issues of the Eighties*.

CHAPTER 16

The Twin Ports: The Human Answer to a Niggardly Nature

Figure 16.1. An eight mile breakwater creates a harbor for the Ports of Los Angeles and Long Beach. View is from February 3, 1967. (Photo courtesy Spence Collection/Department of Geography, UCLA.)

"Why, where are all the ships?" inquired the Senator from Maine. "As near as I can make out, you propose to ask the government to create a harbor for you almost out of whole cloth. The Lord has not given you much to start with; that is for certain. It will cost four or five millions to build, you say; well, is your whole country worth that much? . . . Well, it seems you have made a great mistake in the location of your city. If you Los Angeles people want a harbor, why not move the city down to San Diego? There is a good harbor there." Senator William P. Frye of Maine, of the Committee on Commerce as he stood on the barren San Pedro headlands after the thirty mile ride from Los Angeles in October, 1889. (Quiett, 1934, p. 288.)

"It was in this spirit of brash self-confidence that Los Angeles undertook the construction of . . . the deep-water harbor at San Pedro. The . . . undertaking . . . required a bold imagination and hard-headed foresight, for it involved the conversion of a region nature had designed for mud flats and sand dunes into one of the greatest man-made harbors of the world." Robert Glass Cleland (1947, p. 111).

Today the ports of Los Angeles and Long Beach form one of the great harbor complexes of the nation. Although divided by a municipal boundary and with quite different histories, they form a single geographic and economic terminal and when taken together are often called the Twin Ports. For many years they have served more ships and handled more tons of cargo than any other west coast port, and, even in this modern era of massive petroleum imports, few locations in the United States report greater tonnages. There was no natural harbor here, however, and considerable controversy developed as to whether San Pedro Bay or Santa Monica Bay was better suited to the building of an artificial landing. As an added handicap Los Angeles itself did not border the sea, it was an inland city twenty miles from deep water.

Even though the coast lacked a harbor, from the beginning of settlement supplies could be brought in easier by ship than overland. Gradually, too, a few products of the region were available for export and some trade developed. From the earliest days ships anchored in San Pedro Bay where the Palos Verdes Hills offered some protection from the west. Ships arriving legally came only from Mexico, but in 1805 the *Lila Bird,* out of Boston, exchanged cloth, sugar, and manufactured goods for badly needed provisions. More ships were to arrive via the Cape Horn route and from Mexico, and the San Pedro anchorage was on the line of this north-south movement of goods. Deep water did not come close to shore, and even the small vessels of the pre-American period had to anchor out in the bay and transfer their cargos to even smaller boats before they could be landed on the beach.

"We All Agreed It Was the Worst Place We Had Seen Yet"

Richard Henry Dana (1911, pp. 115–120), quoted above, was involved in bringing cargo ashore at San Pedro in 1825. He wrote with feeling about the primitive conditions of the landing in his best selling book, *Two Years Before the Mast.*

". . . doubling a high sandy point (Point Fermin) we let go our anchor at a distance of three or three and a half miles from shore . . . we thought we might as well have stayed at Santa Barbara and sent our boat down for the hides . . . there was no sign of a town, not even a house to be seen. What brought us into such a place, we could not conceive. No sooner had we come to anchor, than the slip-rope, and other preparations for southeasters, were got ready; and there was reason enough for it, for we lay exposed to every wind that could blow, except the northerly winds, and they came over a flat country with a rake of more than a league of water. As soon as everything was snug, the boat was lowered, and we pulled ashore. . . . As we drew in, we found the tide low, and the rocks and stones, covered with kelp and seaweed, lying bare for the distance of nearly an eighth of a mile. . . .

"Having made arrangements for a horse to take the agent to the Pueblo the next day, we picked our way again over the green, slippery rocks, and pulled toward the brig, which was so far off that we could hardly see her in the increasing darkness. . . . We all agreed that it was the worst place we had seen yet, especially for getting off hides, and our lying off at so great a distance looked as though it was bad for southeasters.

". . . in a few days . . . we loaded our long-boat with goods of all kinds, light and heavy, and pulled ashore. After landing and rolling them over the stones on the beach, we stopped, waiting for the carts to come down the hill and take them; but the captain . . . ordered us to carry them all up to the top. . . . The hill was low, but steep, and the earth, being clayey and wet with the recent rains, was but bad holding ground for our feet. The heavy barrels and casks we rolled up with some difficulty, getting behind and putting our shoulders to them; now and then our feet, slipping, added to the danger of the casks rolling back upon us. But the greatest trouble was with the large casks of sugar. These we had to place upon oars, and lifting them up, rest the oars upon our shoulders, and creep slowly up the hill with the gait of a funeral procession.

"Now, the hides were to be got down, and for this purpose we brought the boat round to a place where the hill was steeper, and threw them off, letting them slide over the slope. Many of them lodged, and we had to let ourselves down and set them a-going again, and in this way became covered with dust, and our clothes torn. After we had the hides all down, we were obliged to take them on our heads, and walk over the stones, and through the water, to the boat. The water and the stones together would wear out a pair of shoes a day, and as shoes were very scarce and very dear, we were compelled to go barefooted. At night we went on board, having had the hardest and most disagreeable day's work that we had yet experienced. For several days we were employed in this manner. . . . "

Although more than fifty years separated Dana's traumatic experience at the San Pedro landing and Senator Frye's caustic comments quoted at the beginning of the chapter, the condition of the harbor had changed only marginally. The account that follows is an attempt to describe the painstaking process through which a modern port has been developed for the Metropolis, to understand the nature of its operation, and to assess its present day significance.

Americans Arrive and Improve the Landing

Phineas Banning, one of several teamsters operating wagon and stage lines from San Pedro to Los Angeles, significantly modified the landing procedure in 1857. Between the mouth of the Los Angeles River and San Pedro

waves and currents had formed a low, east-west strip of sand dunes known as Rattlesnake Island. Behind it was a large expanse of mud flats and shallow water, San Pedro Slough, connected to the Bay by narrow, shallow channels. Banning purchased land at the head of the main channel, built a dock and founded the town of Wilmington. After a bit of dredging, lighters could bring cargo through the winding channel to the dock at Wilmington which was four or five miles closer to Los Angeles than the San Pedro landing. The Federal Government gave the new settlement status by building a supply depot (Drum Barracks) there during the Civil War. The supremacy of the Wilmington landing was assured in 1869 when a railroad was built from the location to Los Angeles, twenty-one miles away.

The Wilmington landing (part of the Los Angeles inner harbor today) had one serious flaw. Although the channel was six to ten feet deep at high tide, a sand bar at the entrance was only eighteen inches below the surface when the tide was out. Because of this, ocean-going vessels still had to anchor out in San Pedro Bay and the cargo had to be transferred to small boats to be landed, an expensive and time consuming process. Congress was petitioned for aid. The Army Engineers built an ingenious jetty connecting Rattlesnake Island with Deadman's Island, a rocky outcrop near San Pedro. The tide rushing through the newly narrowed channel scoured out the offending sand bar. Traffic through the port increased considerably. However, the Southern Pacific took control of the original rail line in 1872 and the rates for shipping goods to Los Angeles were raised steadily. In 1881 the road extended its line across Wilmington Lagoon to the old San Pedro landing, giving it a complete monopoly on the shipment of freight from the port.

The presence of several new railroads in the Los Angeles area, however, and the increasing dominance of San Francisco as the major market and supply center on the Pacific

Coast made possible unexpected competition for the traditional landing. Santa Monica Bay was just as close to Los Angeles as San Pedro Bay and considerably nearer to San Francisco, a condition recognized by several promoters. First to act was John P. Jones, the "Nevada mining Midas," and U.S. Senator from that state. He built a pier in 1875 at Santa Monica Bay, a rail line into Los Angeles, and at the foot of the pier, with R. S. Baker, platted the town of Santa Monica and auctioned off lots. Landing at the Santa Monica wharf shortened the journey from San Francisco by several hours and Jones' landing intercepted considerable trade which would have gone to Wilmington. The Southern Pacific monopoly was broken, and freight rates from Wilmington to Los Angeles were cut in half. This was not to last, however, for Jones soon found himself in financial difficulties. Within two years (1877) the Southern Pacific purchased the Santa Monica railroad and shut down the pier. Freight rates from Wilmington to Los Angeles were quickly raised to record heights.

In a similar move, the Santa Fe Railroad built a line to "Port Ballona" (located where Marina del Rey was to be built later) but failed in an effort to make a channel in the slough. Instead, a rail line was extended to Redondo in 1889 where a pier already existed and where a deep submarine canyon enabled ocean vessels to tie up at a short wharf and unload directly into railroad cars. By 1892, Redondo was handling sixty percent of the ocean trade of Los Angeles excluding coal and lumber, which, in any event, were mostly destined for use by the Southern Pacific itself.

Finally, in 1891, an eastern group representing the Union Pacific Railroad, in an action of long-range significance, bought a portion of Rattlesnake Island. Next, the Union Pacific's "Terminal Railroad Company" built a line from Los Angeles, through Long Beach across the mouth of the Los Angeles River and along the island to its westward end, in an at-tempt to get a share of the lucrative traffic. As the company hoped to make the location the terminus of a transcontinental railroad, Rattlesnake Island was renamed "Terminal Island."

Huntington Builds Port Los Angeles

The Southern Pacific, under the new leadership of Collis P. Huntington, tired of competition from Redondo (and perhaps anticipating the loss of its monopoly on San Pedro Bay), made its move in 1890. Huntington secured a three-fourths interest in the Jones' holdings in Santa Monica in 1890 and purchased all of the beach between the Palisades and the ocean as far north as Temescal Canyon, as well as a two hundred fifty acre site on the bluffs (1891). Next, he built a railroad from his Los Angeles connection, through a tunnel under Ocean Avenue and along the shore to a point north of Santa Monica Canyon. Finally, at that point he constructed the "Long Wharf" extending nearly a mile out into Santa Monica Bay, reputed to be the largest and longest wharf in the world. It was indeed a massive affair, ending in a vast platform one hundred thirty feet wide on which were constructed waiting rooms, dining rooms, several large coal bunkers, storage sheds, and so on. Audaciously named "Port Los Angeles," the wharf was open for business in 1893. It was a success from the start. Some three hundred vessels arrived the first year, the Pacific Coast Steamship line moved its terminus from San Pedro to Port Los Angeles and other shipping lines left Redondo for the new facility. At Santa Monica the Southern Pacific clearly had a monopoly, since by purchasing the strip of beach Huntington had made it impossible for any other rail line to come down to the harbor, and the mountains made it unfeasible for anyone to build a landing farther up the coast in the direction of San Francisco.

Although the Metropolis now had multiple landings it still did not have a decent harbor. Merchants and shippers in Los Angeles, hoping to share the Oriental trade, had been petitioning Congress for years to provide a deep water harbor for the city and had endorsed a proposal of the Army Engineers to construct an artificial harbor protected by a breakwater across San Pedro Bay. Huntington, too, would need a breakwater to upgrade the open roadstead at Port Los Angeles. Redondo, also, was hoping for federal improvements. Unable to resolve conflicting claims, Congress commissioned a special Board of Engineers to determine the best location near Los Angeles for a deep water harbor. The Board concluded that whereas either San Pedro or Santa Monica were possible choices, San Pedro was the preferred location. Its position was superior, its capacity was greater, its inner harbor was improved, and the breakwater here would be cheaper. Huntington intervened to block the proposed Congressional appropriation for a San Pedro breakwater.

The Free Harbor Contest

The blocking action of the Southern Pacific touched off a ten-year battle known to local historians as the "Free Harbor Contest." The name came from the conviction of Los Angeles shippers that the Southern Pacific effectively controlled the waterfront at Santa Monica and would have a lasting monopoly if that location became the area's harbor. On the other hand, at San Pedro two railroads were already in place, offering the possibility of competition. On one side of the struggle was the Southern Pacific, the *Santa Monica Outlook,* and the landowners on the west side. On the other, the Los Angeles Chamber of Commerce, the *Los Angeles Times,* and landowners on the south side. Over the years additional assessments were ordered; all of the reports favored the San Pedro site, although people like Senator Frye, quoted at the beginning of the chapter, remained unconvinced. Port Los Angeles was a single pier jutting out into open Santa Monica Bay; behind it lay a sea cliff almost two hundred feet high. It was clearly an unsuitable place to develop a major port. San Pedro, by contrast, had a number of advantages for the creation of an artificial port. It was protected from the west winds by the Palos Verdes Hills. More importantly, however, inland was San Pedro Slough, a vast area of tidal flats, ideal for dredging out the miles of channels and basins necessary for the construction of a port.

After years of national controversy, during which the monopolistic power of the Southern Pacific and Huntington became important issues, money was finally authorized in 1899 for the construction of a breakwater at San Pedro. In retrospect, one would have to agree that the choice was a wise one, of long term advantage to all sections of the urban area. The warehouses, tank farms, refineries, and factories, generally associated with a large port, were well suited to the flat, flood-endangered land behind Wilmington. Residential development, on the other hand, is clearly a wiser use of the more elevated land of Santa Monica, Brentwood, and the Pacific Palisades. Huntington's own holdings, a tract of land directly behind the Long Wharf and intended for industrial development, remained vacant as the "Huntington Estate" until 1926. At that time it was purchased by the Pacific Palisades Association, given the name "Huntington Palisades," and subdivided into large residential lots.

The construction of the San Pedro breakwater was regarded as an engineering feat of world renown. The first barge load of granite from a quarry on Catalina was dumped in 1899, and its first phase was complete in 1910. One writer (Kenkul, 1965, p. 28) described it this way, "If the water were drained away from it, a wall more than two miles long, nearly 200 feet thick at the base and fifteen to twenty feet

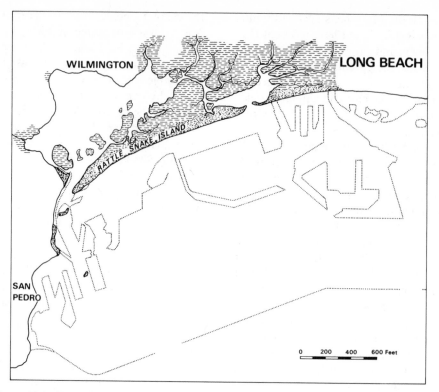

WILMINGTON

LONG BEACH

RATTLE SNAKE ISLAND

SAN PEDRO

0   200   400   600 Feet

Figure 16.2. The west San Pedro Bay shoreline of 1872 and modern developments. Source: From *Port of Long Beach General Plan. 1973.*

thick at the top, as high as a four story building, would be exposed." With its completion the western end of San Pedro Bay was transformed from an open roadstead into a safe harbor, able to furnish protection to the largest ocean vessels.

Through the years the original two-mile long arc has been extended so that it is now eight miles in length and extends, with two gaps left for entrances, almost across the entire bay. In addition to building the breakwater, a great deal of dredging has taken place. The outer harbor has been deepened, and the inner harbor has been deepened repeatedly, widened, and provided with several turning basins. The material dredged up has been used to enlarge Terminal Island to more than three times its original size, providing needed space for port activities. As the island was widened

by the addition of fill, however, summer homes of prominent Los Angeles residents, once located on a popular beach, found themselves more than a mile from the waterfront and their properties useless for the original purposes.

The Development of the Harbor: Port of Los Angeles

Los Angeles, it is said laughingly but truthfully, had a Harbor Commission (1907) before it had a harbor. There is an explanation for this. The breakwater construction and dredging activity were within the city limits of San Pedro and Wilmington, two small incorporated towns with extremely limited financial resources. To construct a major seaport would require the building of docks, warehouses, transit sheds, railroad tracks, roads, cranes, and other expensive installations. The situation was critical for, during the long harbor fight, the facilities of the port had deteriorated and trade had languished.

It soon became clear that if the Metropolis was to reap the benefits of a modern port, the city of Los Angeles would have to pay for its development. Los Angeles had the wealth and the desire—indicated by its creation of the Harbor Commission. But the city was inland; to develop the port it would have to go to the ocean and unite with San Pedro and Wilmington, a legally unprecedented task. As cities must consist of contiguous (touching) territory, Los Angeles, as the first step, proposed to annex a "shoestring strip." This was a band of agricultural land about sixteen miles long and half a mile wide, extending south from Los Angeles to the border of Wilmington which, in turn, was contiguous with San Pedro. The vote in this strip for annexation was close—two hundred eight yes, two hundred two no. The next step was more difficult: state law did not provide for the consolidation of two cities already incorporated, so that a new law had to be passed. Eventually the legal barriers were cleared away and consolidation elections were held in 1910. There was less opposition than had been expected. In San Pedro the vote was one hundred seven yes, sixty-one no, and in Wilmington, seven hundred twenty-six yes and two hundred seventy-seven no. The Los Angeles voters were enthusiastic; 13,737 voted yes and only two hundred twenty-one no. (While this was going on Long Beach annexed about half of Terminal Island.)

Why would cities vote to give up their independence and consolidate with a much larger unit, even though this might be to the region's advantage? Only because they had been promised major improvements. If consolidation carried, Los Angeles agreed to do some things the smaller cities wanted very badly. Los Angeles would spend $10,000,000 on harbor improvements. The city would build a truck highway from the city to the waterfront. The road, the present Alameda Street, was originally called "Harbor Truck Boulevard." Too, the cities were to be terminals for rate-making purposes. Finally, Los Angeles would provide the same level of services as to police, fire protection, parks, libraries, and so on, for the new areas as existed in other parts of the city.

The construction of a first class, municipally-owned, regional harbor was to be delayed until one additional problem was resolved. The newly consolidated city owned only about one hundred acres of waterfront, whereas the Southern Pacific held title to a thousand acres of tidelands. Fortuitously, however, the railroad's title was found to be invalid, and in May, 1911, the California Legislature granted the tidelands to the city of Los Angeles. Four years after its formation, the Los Angeles Harbor Commission finally had a genuine harbor to administer.

When the Panama Canal was opened in August, 1914, the harbor was ready for the expected boom in trade. The initial dredging of the inner harbor was about finished; numerous piers, docks, wharves, and warehouses were in place; much of the tidelands had been reclaimed; and a turning basin had been completed. World War I, unfortunately, had just begun and much of the world's shipping was diverted to that cause. Even so, the long struggle for an improved harbor seemed to be paying off. Mulholland reported that the opening of the Canal resulted in the immediate reduction in the cost of iron water pipe by $2.00 a ton. Tonnage handled in the harbor increased from 1.1 million tons in 1907 to 2.4 million tons in 1917.

The 1920s were booming years at the harbor. More than 7,000 ships arrived each year. One can hardly imagine what the region would have done without the improved port. Even so, the region was nearly awash with oil, the product of numerous bonanza petroleum strikes. Production totaled one-fifth of that of the entire world during the decade. There were no pipelines leading out of California and all of the oil had to be shipped through the port. As a result, petroleum essentially monopolized the export capacity of the port, accounting for more than ninety-five percent of the outbound tonnage. At first the exports were of crude oil, but ten large refineries were quickly constructed in the harbor area and by 1925 ninety percent of the exports were gasoline, kerosene, and lubricating oil. Most of the petroleum products were shipped by tanker, but kerosene was also packed in millions of five gallon cans for shipment as fuel for the lamps of China. It was this enormous volume of petroleum, 27.2 million tons in 1923, that enabled the new Los Angeles port to surge ahead of all others on the Pacific Coast in that year, a position only recently challenged by the even newer Port of Long Beach.

As the oil tankers steamed out of the harbor they met lumber ships coming in, for lumber dominated the import scene in almost the same way as petroleum did the exports. The building boom of the Twenties was in full swing, a new house was being built every five and a half minutes in Los Angeles, and more were under construction in the suburbs. The lumber for this unprecedented construction activity came from the Pacific Northwest and was shipped almost entirely by sea. Lumber companies fought with the oil men for space on the docks.

Observers in the Twenties continued to stress the importance of the Panama Canal to the local area. The canal, it was pointed out, brought Los Angeles 7,700 miles and twenty-one sailing days closer to the eastern seaboard. Too, the region seemed to be taking advantage of the new facility. In 1925, no less than seventy percent of all shipping passing through the Panama Canal originated at or was destined for Los Angeles. Further, local spokesmen proclaimed that the harbor and canal were great boons to Los Angeles manufacturers, putting Los Angeles, in terms of shipping costs, as close to the New York City market as Buffalo.

Few Los Angeles manufacturers, it may be presumed, were actively competing in the New York market in this period. The harbor itself was an attractive location for manufacturing plants—not only refineries sought waterfront locations. As early as 1923 there were four shipbuilding yards in the harbor, employing some 20,000 persons. Fishing was booming, too, and soon a dozen large canneries were built to handle the catch. As early as 1925, more tuna were packed in the Los Angeles harbor than in any other place in the world. By 1929, Los Angeles had displaced Boston as the nation's most productive fishing port. Other manufacturing concerns building facilities in the harbor area in the decade included Pacific Borax Company, Procter and Gamble, and the Los Angeles Soap Company (a copra oil and meal plant).

The Development of the Port of Long Beach

Today the Port of Long Beach handles as much or more traffic as the Port of Los Angeles. Its history, in comparison, is much compressed, with the building of the port occurring almost entirely after the 1920s. As recently as 1965, although billing itself as "the largest dry cargo port on the west coast," Long Beach handled only half the total tonnage of its elder twin. Its development since World War II has been phenomenal and, as a result, the port is one of the newest and most modern in the nation.

Long Beach, founded as a real estate promotion in 1882, was only a small town at the turn of the century. At one time its ambitions to be a port involved consolidation with Wilmington and San Pedro. A private company, beginning in 1906, attempted to develop a harbor among eight hundred acres of lagoon and tidal marsh lands around the east end of Terminal Island, and dredged a channel through Cerritos Slough. The Los Angeles

River emptied into the bay at about this location, however, and the thousands of cubic yards of silt and debris carried down in one year of flooding could fill channels dredged out over many years. As a result, the company, on the verge of bankruptcy, relinquished its holdings to Long Beach and, in 1910, the city annexed a portion of Terminal Island. The city issued bonds to raise the funds needed to complete the dredging, and by 1911 a municipally owned pier and cargo shed had been completed. Silting was a continuing problem, however, and for many years the Port of Long Beach was a small, one berth, lumber terminal.

The reopening of the Panama Canal after World War I stimulated trade and Long Beach issued more bonds to further deepen the channel and to reclaim more land. The most important event of the decade, however, was the permanent solution to the silting problem. In 1923, the Los Angeles County Flood Control District, through a system of dikes and levees, channelized the mouth of the Los Angeles River and diverted its flow eastward away from the harbor. With that, dredging became worthwhile and the Cerritos Channel was deepened, opening the harbor to deep draft vessels. Trade increased considerably. In addition, the extension of the San Pedro breakwater eastward in 1928 created a quiet-water ship anchorage. This made possible the development of the Long Beach outer harbor. In the same year the city opened a "Navy Landing," encouraging naval vessels to anchor in the outer harbor, an event that marked the beginning of a close association between the Navy and the Port of Long Beach.

The decade of the 1930s was also one of events significant to Long Beach Harbor. Pier A, which also functioned as a breakwater for the inner harbor, was constructed. "Pierpoint Landing," a commercial development on its seaward tip, became the most popular sports fishing terminal of the region. Several oil companies, a gypsum company, and the Ford Motor Company built facilities in the harbor. But perhaps the most momentous event for the port's future was the discovery of oil in the harbor area in March, 1938. Within a decade the Long Beach Harbor Commission became the fourth largest producer of oil in California. Oil revenues were devoted to harbor improvements and, finally, Long Beach had financial resources equal to those of its larger neighbor. For thirty years money pouring in from oil royalties was used to develop an enormous expanse of modern piers, wharves, and storage sheds.

The years of World War II were years of extreme activity in the Twin Ports; however, the lasting effects of the period were important to Long Beach. A U.S. naval station and shipyard were under construction as the war began and were finished toward its close. Included are a mole-type breakwater forming a "middle harbor" and three major drydocks for the repair and remodeling of large naval vessels. For the years of the 1950s the shipyard was far and away Long Beach's largest industrial employer, with some 7,000 workers. For many years, too, it functioned as a naval base, the headquarters of the U.S. Fifth Fleet.

The Twin Ports Today

The prime function of a port is to expedite the transfer of cargo from ship to trucks or trains, or vice versa, speedily, cheaply, and safely. Most of the 9.2 square miles of land area of the port is used for this specialized activity. Certain manufacturing activities, as we have seen, find a port location advantageous, and a considerable area is used for their facilities. The easy access to quiet water makes the harbor attractive for small boat marinas. Finally, the bustle of port activities and the glamour of ships sailing to distant ports attracts tourists and visitors in general. To serve them, a fraction of the port space has been developed as shopping centers with nautical themes, restaurants, and the berthing of the "Queen Mary."

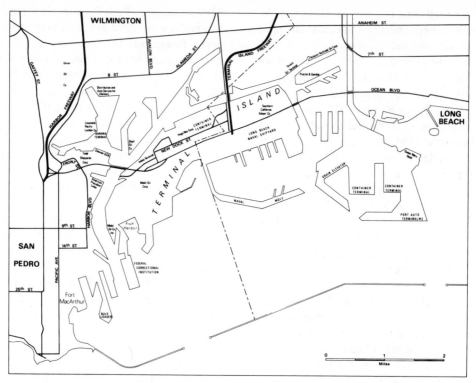

Figure 16.3. The Twin Ports: Los Angeles and Long Beach.

The Harbor of Commerce

The twin ports have an advantageous location and configuration for commerce. San Pedro is close to the great circle route from Panama to the Orient and thus is a convenient and economical place for vessels to stop for fuel and cargo. Further, the ports lie two hundred miles farther east than any other major Pacific Coast port, making them an economical place to land cargo destined for interior U.S. points. Once ships leave the open ocean, all berths in Long Beach are within one to three miles of the sea, and those in Los Angeles are all within 4.5 miles. Main channels are thirty-five feet deep in Los Angeles and a spacious sixty feet in Long Beach; the latter depth can serve all of the world's ships except the very largest of the supertankers.

The Twin Ports are equipped to transfer almost any imaginable cargo. They have specialized docks, spacious transit sheds, and ample loading space for trucks and trains. A wide variety of handling equipment is also available, and many of the one hundred ninety-three docks are especially equipped to cope with specific kinds of cargo: petroleum, vegetable oil, molasses, grain, ore, automobiles, or bananas, for example. Other berths are equipped with cranes and slings to deal with mixed loads of general cargo. Recently gigantic cranes of the sort designed to move containers have been installed in some areas. Passengers, of course, have their specialized terminals. Each of these docks has its specific handling equipment: pumps, vacuum hoses, endless belts, gangplanks, cranes of all sorts with attachments of magnets, slings, hooks, and so on. Specialized storage facilities are also available: tanks, silos, refrigerated transit sheds, ordinary transit sheds, or the acres of surfaced space necessary to receive containers, automobiles, or on which to store the pyramidal piles of white salt, yellow sulfur, black coal, red iron ore, or whatever. Because of the ports' modern facilities, turnaround time is short, averaging about 2.5 days for conventional cargo ships, twenty-four hours for container ships, and 1.8 days for bulk carriers.

Ports are continually revamping their facilities to accommodate the changing requirements of transcontinental shippers. The most recent development in ocean trade is the container concept for shipping general cargo. Items to be shipped are loaded into a standardized container at the manufacturer's door, transported by truck or train to the port, loaded on the vessel, shipped to the port of destination, and then sent by rail or highway to the customer. All the while the product is sealed in a tamperproof, weatherproof aluminum box or "container," designed for economical, speedy handling. Docks to handle containers, however, need gigantic cranes which can lift the twenty or forty foot long rectangular boxes, as well as space to store thousands of them while the transfer is made. The Port of Long Beach, for example, has one container dock with storage space for 5,000 or 6,000 containers within reach of the unloading crane (which cost $2.12 million).

As automobiles have become a major import of the Twin Ports, specialized unloading docks have been built for the major companies. Toyota, for example, has leased thirty-five acres in the Port of Long Beach, which not only provides space for unloading the autos, but also has room for offices, warehousing, dewaxing, repairing, and accessory installation. There are 28,000 square feet under roof and storage space for 6,000 automobiles. Adjacent to it, "Port Auto Terminal No. 2," operated by the Pasha Group, is even larger with space for 21,250 automobiles.

Many other kinds of cargo require special facilities. Many docks are equipped with the gigantic hoses, pumps, and pipelines to storage tank-farms that are necessary to handle petroleum for the ten refineries importing crude oil through the port. Others have many of the same facilities but specialize in other liquids: molasses, tallow, or coconut oil. Some dry cargo also needs unloading machines designed for its peculiarities. Bananas, for example, require electrified unloading machines—canvas slings on an endless belt—as well as their own warehouses divided into cold storage and ripening rooms. Other docks are used primarily for single products: cotton, lumber and plywood, newsprint, or scrap metal.

There are still a good many docks which are used for general and miscellaneous cargo. Here the stevedore continues to operate his traditional crane, handling goods in barrels, bales, boxes, sacks, or cans. They are lifted out of the ship's holds in rope slings, and rattled away on small carts for storage in the transit sheds.

In addition, two sections of the Port of Los Angeles are used by commercial fishermen. One, "Fisherman's Dock" in the San Pedro section, is run by the fishermen's cooperative, and distributes fish locally. The other, "Fish Harbor," on Terminal Island, is used by the tuna fleet and serves the adjacent fish canning plants.

Several passenger terminals also serve the port. Ocean-going passenger liners and cruise ships use the "Matson" or the "American President Lines Terminals" in Wilmington and San Pedro, respectively, the only docks specifically designed to accommodate passenger ships. In fiscal 1975–76 some four hundred fifty passenger ships arrived in the harbor, about 70,000 persons arrived and 61,000 sailed. Usually almost an additional half million passengers sail from the harbor to Catalina each year, and for decades the "Catalina

Terminal" in San Pedro was a busy place, particularly in summer. Since 1975, however, "The Big White Steamer" U.S.S. Catalina has been inoperative; smaller boats make the trip, from both San Pedro and Long Beach.

There are four major civilian shipyards in the harbor, of which only one, the Todd Shipyard Company, covering some ninety acres in San Pedro, is actively engaged in the building of ocean-going vessels and naval ships. In recent years, for example, they have constructed cargo passenger liners, tankers, and destroyer escorts in their two five hundred twenty-four foot building ways. The three other yards, Bethlehem Steel and the Harbor Boat Building Company on Terminal Island, and the California Shipbuilding and Drydock Company in Long Beach, do an extensive business in repair and remodeling. A fifth facility, the Long Beach Naval Shipyard, is devoted to the logistic support of surface ships of the U.S. Navy and is normally busy in the alteration and repair of anti-submarine and anti-air warfare surface ships of the fleet. It has three graving (repair) and three floating drydocks at its disposal. In addition to the shipyards, the port also has a full complement of machine and ship repair companies which work on ships at the customers' piers, some specializing in propeller service, others in tank cleaning, and so on. Other areas of the piers, docks, and wharves are used for mooring, marine service and repair, conversions and shipbreaking (scrapping). Numerous ship chandlers (dealers in ships' equipment), bunkering companies, towage and salvage concerns, barge operators, and pilot services are also available. Several piers are used for water taxi service and as public landings.

Three categories of manufacturing traditionally are attracted to harbor locations: those which use raw materials from the sea, those whose raw materials arrive by sea (or whose finished product is to be exported), and those whose product is used on the sea itself. Shipbuilders are the most obvious examples of the latter category, and four examples were listed in the preceding paragraph. During World War II Howard Hughes built a gigantic wooden flying boat, affectionately called the "Spruce Goose," in the harbor area. The plane is currently being prepared for exhibit near the anchorage of the "Queen Mary." Products of the sea are processed in several fish canneries on Terminal Island (Star-Kist Foods, Inc.; Van Camp Sea Foods Co.; and Pan Pacific Fisheries, for example). These factories attract other satellite activities, and facilities of the Continental Can Company and the Pan-Can Company are located nearby. In years past a kelp drying plant has also functioned in the harbor. For many years Procter and Gamble have processed imported copra into vegetable oil for soap, shortening, and cooking oil, and the Kaiser Cement and Gypsum Company has manufactured imported gypsum into wallboard. Too, for many years the Sun Lumber Company has operated a lumber mill in the area. Reversing the procedure, the West Coast's largest scrap exporter, Hugo Neu-Proler Company, operates an automobile crusher and shredder and processes more than 350,000 automobiles into scrap during an average year.

Finally, the port area is attractive for certain kinds of recreational activities. To serve the small boat enthusiast, each of the Twin Ports has devoted extensive areas to small boat marinas. In a recent year, for example, there were 3,115 privately-owned boats moored in the Port of Los Angeles, and Long Beach provided moorings for 1,000 more. The Port of Long Beach has the "Queen Mary" on display, and a hotel and restaurant complex has been built nearby. In addition, a park has been provided where "people can come to fish, picnic, and watch the ships and sail boats." Sports fishing landings are also available at the "Queen's Wharf." On the Los Angeles side, "Ports of Call"—"Whaler's Wharf"—"Norm's Landing," a complex of shops and restaurants attract an estimated three to four

Table 16.1
Leading Commodities Handled by the Twin Ports

Inbound		Outbound	
Commodity	000 tons	Commodity	000 tons
Crude Petroleum	26,625	Petroleum products	6,485
Petroleum products	6,421	Petroleum coke	3,227
Iron and steel, shapes, etc.	2,024	Grain (mainly corn)	2,091
Building cement	1,001	Iron and steel scrap	937
Lumber and plywood	901	Basic chemicals, etc.	854
Motor vehicles and parts	725	Crude petroleum	829
Iron ore and concentrates	669	Raw cotton	680
Limestone	553	Non-metalic minerals	638
Fresh fruits and nuts	524	Waste paper and scrap	561
Electrical machinery	484	Fresh fruits and nuts	410
Paper and paperboard	418	Prepared animal feeds	341
Fabricated metal products	404	Plastic materials	242
Machinery, except electrical	315	Phosphatic chem. fertilizers	228
Rubber and plastic products	194	Meat, fresh, frozen	145
Salt	150	Tallow	110
Apparel	132	Machinery, except electrical	105
Alcoholic beverages	110	Nonferrous metal scrap	105

Source: Department of Army, Corps of Engineers. *Waterborne Commerce of the United States, 1979*, Part 4, pp. 4–7.

million visitors per year. Moored near the same location are a fleet of fast, modern sportsfishing boats, harbor cruise vessels, entertainment showboats, and the floating ship restaurant, "Princess Louise." Cabrillo Beach, where the breakwater touches the shore, features Cabrillo Museum, displaying ship models and items of marine biology—it had 350,000 visitors in 1973. In addition, plans are under way to turn the old "Municipal Ferry Building" in San Pedro into a Maritime Museum.

Commerce through the Twin Ports

The major commodities that move through the Twin Ports normally rank about as they appear in Table 16.1. As individual items are commonly measured by weight (tons), heavy items have a prominent place in the rankings—as they do in a visual image of port traffic. Petroleum dominates both the inbound and outbound traffic of the Twin Ports as it

has for fifty years. Today it accounts for an amazing two-thirds of the total inbound tonnage and petroleum products (including petroleum coke) comprise more than half the outbound shipments. It should be pointed out, however, that whereas most of the crude petroleum comes from foreign ports, much of the refined product, fuel oil mainly, enters the coastwide trade.

Other "weighty" items rank high. Steel mill products: bars, plates, pipe, and tube, in demand by local manufacturers and builders, lead the "also rans" on the import list. Lumber nowadays arrives in Los Angeles mostly by truck or train, but enough still follows its traditional route down the coast to give it fifth ranking. Other "heavyweights" include cement, iron ore, limestone and paper. Bananas are an important "fresh fruit," as they can be unloaded only where specialized equipment is available and are distributed from the Twin Ports throughout the Southwest.

235

Table 16.2
Ten Leading Trading Partners in Total Trade
Southern California Customs Districts 1980

Exports		Imports	
Country	Value in Millions	Country	Value in Millions
Japan	$3,800	Japan	$8,200
Mexico	1,500	Indonesia	2,000
United Kingdom	1,200	Taiwan	1,900
South Korea	1,100	South Korea	1,050
Taiwan	900	West Germany	1,000
West Germany	800	Mexico	850
Hong Kong	600	Hong Kong	850
Singapore	500	United Kingdom	700
Malaysia	400	Malaysia	600
Indonesia	200	Singapore	400

Note: This table includes the San Diego Customs District whose trade is mainly with Mexico.
Source: Compiled from, Security Pacific Bank. *Summary of Business Conditions/Southern California.* April 30, 1981.

Measurement by tonnage clearly understates the importance of some of the imports of the Twin Ports. Motor vehicles (automobiles, small trucks, and motorcycles) for example, are the most valuable category of imports although they rank only sixth by tonnage. Ranking second in value is electrical machinery, a category that includes television sets, stereo equipment, radios, and a wide variety of electronic components. Petroleum ranks only third in value, only slightly ahead of machinery and mechanical equipment.

Outbound ships, once the petroleum products have been accounted for, carry a wide variety of items, with agricultural products and raw materials dominant. Grain, mainly corn, leads the list, with cotton from the San Joaquin and Imperial Valleys also of major importance. The tonnage of citrus fruits is also significant. Iron and steel scrap, a natural product of one of the largest concentrations of automobiles in the world, ranks high, as does waste paper, another product of millions of consumers.

If exports were ranked by value, such categories as machinery, both electrical and nonelectrical, would rank right after petroleum products. (Airplanes, an important export of the Los Angeles Customs District, do not show up on port statistics as they are simply flown to their destination.) Other high ranking exports in terms of value include clothing and accessories and iron and steel.

Trading Partners

The Los Angeles Metropolis has for decades had the ambition to serve as the nation's window to the Orient and, although that day may not yet have come, about two-thirds of the value of the trade through the Twin Ports normally is with the Asian region. Japan for many years has been the region's dominant trading partner, and four countries—Japan, Taiwan, Indonesia, and South Korea accounted for about half the trade passing through the Twin Ports in 1980. Note that Table 16.2 is concerned with value of trade, not tonnage, and that it includes data from all of the Southern California Customs Districts. Most of Mexico's trade comes through San Diego and can be discounted here. Trade through the airport includes aircraft sold to foreign customers and is a complicating factor.

The nature of trade with the countries of Asia varies considerably. Imports from Japan include automobiles, motorcyles, television sets, electronic equipment of all kinds, and textiles. Exports are mainly food, raw materials, and machinery, but also include aircraft, not involved in port traffic. The Twin Ports receive textiles, electrical machinery, footwear, and sporting goods from Taiwan, exports to it include cotton and chemicals. Korea sends clothing, textiles and cement, and a wide variety of small manufactures (cameras, etc.) and receives machinery and cotton, among other items.

Newly important among countries from which imports arrive are the oil producers. In fact, Indonesia, which produces a low-sulfur petroleum much desired in this smog-plagued region, ranks second, just behind Japan.

The United Kingdom and West Germany dominate the European trade. Imports from the United Kingdom are mainly Scotch whiskey, gin, and automobiles; exports to that country include such things as computers and computer equipment. Automobiles dominate the imports from Germany; shipments consist mainly of technologically sophisticated capital goods, and agricultural products.

Significance of the Twin Ports

The advocates of an improved harbor for Los Angeles in the last century argued that only through the existence of a modern port could the city become the premier metropolis on the west coast. That was an oversimplification, and it is difficult to document the effect the port actually has had on the subsequent growth and prosperity of the Metropolis. That it had an effect is unquestioned. For example, the early refineries and other manufacturers which located in the port were important centers of employment. Too, many service personnel who passed through the Twin Ports during World War II were attracted to the region and vowed to make it their home in later years—some did. But to try to quantify the importance of these effects is impossible.

It is easier to assess the importance of the port to the modern Metropolis. For the purchaser of imported items such as an automobile, the price in the immediate vicinity of the port is less than farther inland, since expensive land transportation charges are not added to the bill. Similarly, local manufacturers can reach coastal and overseas markets economically. But beyond these simple effects, what is the overall impact of the port on the local economy?

A local research concern, Williams-Kuebelbeck and Associates, Inc., was engaged by the managers of the Twin Ports to study this very problem in 1976. Using a series of questionnaires, multipliers, and so on, their goal was to "prepare a current assessment of the economic impacts generated (in the Metropolis) by the flow of waterborne commerce through the two ports" (Williams-Kuebelbeck, 1976, p. 1). They concluded that waterborne commerce-related firms generated 121,476 jobs, and that an additional 97,251 jobs were provided by industries that received income from the first group for a total employment impact of 218,727 jobs. Further, they concluded that the maritime commerce of the ports, both directly and indirectly, generated $2.5 billion in payrolls, $9.8 billion in gross business revenue, and $3.9 billion in local business purchases in the Metropolis. Put in a different perspective, these figures comprise 5.3 percent of the total employment in the area and 7.6 percent of the total wages and salaries. In addition, local, state, and federal governments derived $260.3 million in direct tax revenue from industries related to waterborne commerce (Williams-Kuebelbeck, 1976, pp. 8–9).

Administration of the Twin Ports: Rivalry and Duplication

The Port of Los Angeles is administered by a five member Board of Harbor Commissioners, appointed by the Mayor, subject to the approval of the City Council. Similarly, the Port of Long Beach is administered by a five member Board of Harbor Commissioners, appointed by the City Manager, with the approval of the City Council. In each instance the Board directs the Harbor Department Staff and is responsible for the operation, development, and planning of the harbor. So we have two sets of Harbor Commissioners and two Harbor Departments, each managing, in a sense, one half of the port.

The divided authority obviously makes for much duplication but perhaps also stimulates efficient operation. The duplication is easy to identify; we have already noted the two Boards, two Departments, and two staffs. Further, to a certain extent expensive facilities are duplicated, too; if one port installs a new improved bulk loader, the other, to remain competitive, feels it must install one, too, a situation that may lead to unnecessary and costly expansion. On the other hand, the ports, in competition for the same shipping, each try to provide speedier, more efficient, and more economical service than the other. If a shipper is unhappy with his treatment in the Port of Los Angeles he can move his operations to the Port of Long Beach. There may be some merit in the current arrangement.

For many years agencies interested in economy and efficiency have advocated consolidation of the ports. Decades ago, when a portion of the breakwater was to be funded, the federal government agreed to make the appropriation only if the two ports were to consolidate. They did not, but the breakwater was built anyway. As recently as 1974 a report to the Los Angeles City Council recommended "discussing with the appropriate officials of the City of Long Beach the operation of the two ports . . . as a single entity under one board representing both cities" (Ruhlow, 1974, p. 3). Nothing has ever happened. Although the ports do cooperate on matters that concern them both and a permanent liaison committee exists, it seems doubtful that the present arrangement will be changed soon. Civic pride is strong and the force of inertia is great.

16. Suggested Readings

Board of Harbor Commissioners, Long Beach, Los Angeles. *Annual Report.*
> Both of these agencies issue *Annual Reports* that summarize the activities and developments of each port, as well as numerous other brochures designed to inform both the shipper and the general public about their facilities.

Kenkuk, John H. "Development of the Port of Los Angeles," *Journal of Transportation History.* 7 (1965) 24–36.
> This is a detailed account of the development of the Los Angeles portion of the Twin Ports to 1965.

Lewis, Leland and Peter Ebeling. *Sea Guide, Southern California.* Newport Beach: SEA Publications, 1973. 3rd ed.
> Although written for the sailor, and including landings from Santa Barbara to Ensenada, this book has good maps and some material on the Twin Ports.

Marquez, Ernest. *Port Los Angeles, A Phenomenon of the Railroad Era.* San Marino: Golden West Books, 1975.
> A lavishly illustrated account of the development of a landing in Santa Monica Bay, this book includes a section on historic San Pedro as well.

17   **Metropolitan People and Neighborhood Complexity**

Figure 17.1. Neighborhoods of similar houses were the product of each building "boom." On April 25, 1924, development had reached out West Third to Rossmore. (Photo courtesy Spence Collection/Department of Geography, UCLA.)

"The world's image of Los Angeles . . . is of an endless plain endlessly gridded with endless streets, peppered endlessly with ticky-tacky houses clustered in indistinguishable neighborhoods, slashed across by endless freeways . . . and so on . . . endlessly." Reyner Banham (1971, p. 161).

"Blacks from the South, Latinos from Ecuador, Chinese from Hong Kong—they are coming to Los Angeles in waves, bringing new cultural richness, ethnic pride and civic complexity.

"To a city accused of aimless sprawl ethnics are bringing neighborhoods—indeed cohesive communities. Infinite variety. Irony." Richard E. Meyer (1980, p. 1).

" 'Los Angeles,' said Dr. Franklin Murphy, one of the sovereign wise men of that city, 'used to be a dull gray city of transplanted Midwesterners. Now it's an Oriental carpet of colored stripes.' " Theodore H. White (1982, p. 350).

A Multitude of People

The Los Angeles Metropolis, as the decade of the 1980s begins, is called home by about 11,500,000 people. In America it is thus second in size only to greater New York, with its population of about 17,000,000, and comfortably ahead of the eight-county Chicago region with its estimated 7,000,000 inhabitants. Furthermore, the Los Angeles Metropolis is almost unique in that it is still growing— albeit not as spectacularly as in previous decades. From 1953 to 1963, the population shot upward by about 300,000 persons per year. Then a period of declining growth set in, reaching a minimum of some 30,000 persons in 1972. Beginning the next year the growth rate increased, however, and now the Metropolis has about 170,000 more people annually, a figure that represents twice the national rate. This persistent growth sets the Metropolis apart from most of the other large urban areas in the United States. The New York region lost population, perhaps half a million, during the past decade, and the Chicago area is just about holding its own.

Furthermore, much of the recent growth of the Metropolis has been through immigration, producing a cosmopolitan mix of nationalities and ethnic groups. Today there are about 3,500,000 Latinos in the area, mainly of Mexican heritage, but including many from other Latin countries, of which perhaps 1,000,000 are "immigrants not on the citizenship track." Asians: Japanese, Chinese, Koreans, Filipinos, Vietnamese, Thais, Indonesians number almost 500,000. There are perhaps 100,000 Armenians in the Metropolis, 100,000 Israeli, 50,000 British subjects, 50,000 Norwegians, and so on and on. In addition, there are about 1,150,000 blacks in the area, a number that has changed only a little in the past decade. It is also estimated that about 50,000 American Indians live in the Metropolis. No wonder Jan Morris (1980, pp. 91–95) recently exclaimed " . . . Los Angeles is a haven, to whose doors people have come from all over the world. It is a fraternity of refugees." Actually, not all of these "refugees" are recent arrivals, far from it; many members of the groups mentioned above have been residents of the Metropolis for generations and are in a real way part of the "native" population. Further, one should not lose sight of the fact that about half the population of Los Angeles County and about sixty percent of the people in the entire region are Anglos, and generally the only thing they or their forebears were fleeing was some cold place "back East."

Additional cosmopolitan variety of the Los Angeles population is reflected in its wonderfully complex mix of religions. The long time reputation as a Protestant stronghold was never completely justified, for the city has a long history of "sprouting cults, sects and rites like vivid fungi," to further quote Jan Morris (1980, p. 93).

The "mainline" religions are well represented also. There are more than 2,000,000 Roman Catholics in the area, and about 1,500,000 people are affiliated with some Protestant church. These are divided into perhaps 250,000 Baptists, 225,000 Lutherans, 210,000 Methodists, 200,000 Latter Day Saints (Mormons), 170,000 Presbyterians, 110,000 Episcopalians, and 70,000 Seventh Day Adventists. Another 270,000 or so belong to scores of smaller, lesser-known Protestant denominations. Even the major churches are not united, of course; there are numerous Baptist Conventions, Lutheran Synods, Methodist Conferences, and so on. Many other persons are members of Orthodox churches of various national backgrounds. Jewish temples and synagogues have a membership of about 125,000 (out of an estimated Jewish population of 550,000). There are a large number of Buddhists of various traditions. There are numerous Scientologists, Spiritualists, Swedenborgians, Theosophists, members of the Vedanta Society and Self-Realization Fellowships. It is enough to cause one local resident to exclaim, "New psychiatric movements come and go here like wildfire . . . there are probably more religions in Los Angeles now than there have ever been (in any one urban area) in the whole history of mankind."

Comparisons of ethnic and religious groups in the Metropolis with those elsewhere cry out for the superlative. The Mexican-American population is the largest concentration of Mexicans aside from Mexico City, the Japanese-American population is the largest on the continent, and no other urban area outside Korea has so many Koreans. There are more American Indians in the Metropolis than in any other urban area, and so on. Similarly, in the United States only New York and Chicago have more Catholics, the Jewish population is the third in the world behind New York and Tel Aviv, and there are more Mormons in the Metropolis than in Salt Lake City. It would seem that the image of the area as a home of Protestant Midwesterners is mistaken, at least today.

A provincial image would have been erroneous a century ago as well, for then Los Angeles was almost as cosmopolitan as it is today. Ludwig Salvator, the Archduke of Austria, in his 1878 volume, *Eine Blume aus dem Goldenen Lande oder Los Angeles* (A flower from the golden land of Los Angeles), reported that the residents of the county were about equally divided among Americans, Europeans, and Californians (Mexicans), and "on the streets are heard spoken English, French, Spanish, German, and Italian." As McWilliams (1946, p. 142) pointed out, "Long before Iowans invaded Southern California . . . Polish intellectuals, British remittance men, Chinese immigrants, Basque sheepherders, French and German peasants, and German-Jewish merchants and financiers were on the scene."

The Metropolis did miss the effect of the inpouring of the vast throngs of European immigrants that engulfed the cities of the East and Midwest at the turn of the century. As a consequence, Los Angeles did not experience the era of the large ethnic enclave so typical of many other American cities. There were no "Little Italys," "Deutschlands," or "Swedetowns," here. Too, although many cities came to be dominated by immigrant European Catholics, Los Angeles was, as reputed, filling up mainly with Protestant migrants from the states "back East." The earlier open and polyglot atmosphere was replaced by a narrow, provincial aura. "Puritanism is the inflexible doctrine in Los Angeles . . . Los Angeles is overrun with militant moralists, connoisseurs of sin, experts in biological purity," (Wright, 1934, pp. 90–92) lamented a writer in 1913.

The situation is now turned upside down. Today the population of many of the older Eastern urban areas has stabilized, and the ethnic enclaves of yesterday have all but disappeared. Since the immigration laws were revised in 1965 the proportion of entrants from Asia and Latin America has increased dramatically. Others have arrived as refugees from war, disorder, or economic privation. Perhaps not surprisingly, Los Angeles is the goal of many of these "new immigrants." The Los Angeles International airport and San Ysidro are today's Hoboken or Ellis Island. Los Angeles as well as New York is the nation's melting pot. Furthermore, the ethnic neighborhood is reappearing. The second or third generation Chinese, Mexican-Americans, and Japanese are witnessing the renewal and expansion of their older centers by new immigrants. The traditional Chinatown and Little Tokyo are not only expanding (albeit in different ways) but are also cloning new neighborhoods in the suburbs. The East Los Angeles barrio is bursting outward in all directions; well-established suburban barrios are also growing and new ones are developing. In addition, a Koreatown and Little Armenia have appeared, and significant clusters of Filipinos, Thais, and Indonesians can be observed. Again, as in long ago, a gaggle of languages are heard on the streets of Los Angeles, people from many lands are appearing in increasing numbers in its work places as well as its public places: school, sidewalk, park, museum, or beach.

Indistinguishable Neighborhoods of Ticky-Tacky Houses?

What is characteristic about the Los Angeles neighborhoods, of course, is their infinite and obvious variety—although the world's view may be otherwise. There are neighborhoods that date from many eras: a few were built in the late nineteenth century, more extensive blocks of houses date from the early 1900s, others were created during the boom of the twenties, and most numerous of all are the neighborhoods that were constructed during the years of massive growth following World War II. There are neighborhoods of Victorian houses, California Bungalows, Spanish Stuccos, California Ranch houses, and newer Townhouse condominiums. There are apartment neighborhoods, block after block of two or three story structures, plus an occasional node of "highrises." There are opulent neighborhoods, rich neighborhoods, middle class neighborhoods, and neighborhoods that are poor or very poor. There are neighborhoods of mostly old people, there are neighborhoods that have more than their share of children. In addition, there are Latino barrios, black neighborhoods, Japanese, Chinese, or Korean neighborhoods, Jewish neighborhoods, Armenian neighborhoods, Anglo neighborhoods, mixed neighborhoods, on and on, the variety seems endless. One wonders how this diversity can be indistinguishable to anyone.

One of the most obvious characteristics of a neighborhood, even to a casual observer, are its houses, particularly if many of the houses are of a similar style. Admittedly, the Los Angeles Metropolis is famous for the eclectic style of an occasional house. It is true, too, that every architectural tradition known to man seems to be represented. There are New England saltboxes, French mansards, Swiss chalets, and English thatched roof cottages. In addition, architects of world renown, Irving Gill, Richard Neutra, Frank Lloyd Wright, R. M. Schindler, and many others worked in the area, and the houses they designed are identified in guidebooks and much visited.

All of these houses, in a broad sense, are unique. What is characteristic, and thus important, is that from time to time an occasional style of house "caught on," became almost a craze. These houses would then be duplicated, with slight variations, by the tens of thousands, often filling entire neighborhoods. Generally not designed by architects, the dwellings were constructed by carpenters from mass-produced blueprints or from memory, with modification to fit the lot, the taste of the owner, or the whim of the builder. These were not the homes of the rich, usually, but of the masses. In due time, after a number of years the "fad" would pass, and another favorite style of domestic architecture would take its place. Many of these houses remain today, and, as different styles had a dateable period of popularity, they provide an accurate key to the years during which a neighborhood was built.

The Spanish-Mexican adobe was the first house type to characterize the region, but the population was very small, and that was a long time ago. Only a few relic adobes remain, often much modified, sometimes isolated and difficult to find. Americans brought with them a preference for a framed, wooden house, copying styles popular "back East," including a fair number of Queen Anne/Eastlake (Victorian) structures. At first, when labor was cheap, these were typically three stories high, with steep-pitched roofs, fanciful gables, dormer windows, some rounded corners, spacious porches, and trimmed with docked shingles, fancy scroll work, and spindly pillars—gingerbread. Later, as costs went up, more two-story houses were built and the exterior noticeably simplified. Victorians were built during the waning years of the nineteenth century and a few remain near downtown Los Angeles; others sit in isolated splendor in some of the older suburbs. Occasionally some have been lovingly restored, as along Carol Avenue in Angeleno Heights.

From about 1908 to 1923 the most common house built in the Metropolis was the "delectable" California Bungalow, a type introduced to the nation from this state. Most were one story, with horizontal wood siding, low-pitched roof, wide eaves decorated with simple two-by-four-inch brackets, and front porches, with a lower gable roof, supported by tapering cubical columns. They were airy houses with many windows, and the living room was heated by a fireplace, often with an outside chimney. Two-story modifications also became common. Tens of thousands of these homes were built, many with individual variations, and many neighborhoods are still dominated by them. They remain on the westside in a broad band from Hollywood running southward to USC, for example, and exist in large sections of Glendale, Pasadena, and all of the other suburbs that were built up during the period of their popularity.

Beginning about 1923, in the midst of the building boom of the twenties, a new house type appeared and became immediately popular. It was a Spanish stucco and tile house (Mission Revival) whose trademark was a stucco exterior, and the decorative use of red roofing and floor tile. Arches, round-topped windows, and a small patio were common. Located in neighborhoods built up in about the 1923–33 period, they form still another ring on the Los Angeles westside and characterize extensive neighborhoods in many suburban communities.

Home building stagnated during the depression of the 1930s and the war years that followed. The post-war period, from 1947 on into the 1970s, was a period of massive construction. The "tract system" was perfected

and what we might generalize as the California Ranch House became the characteristic house type. It was a one-story, low and sprawling structure, built on a cement slab, with a low-pitched roof covered with asphalt shingles and an elongated front porch supported by simple posts. The exterior might be combinations of stucco and wood, often with corner windows with a horizontal dimension. The California Ranch House varied from the plain and simple version to more elaborate houses with shake shingles and decorated with bracketing, pigeon lofts, or most anything. Over the years the ranch house has been modified with an infinite variety of exteriors into what one is tempted to label simply Contemporary American.

House styles that are going to become popular are not always easy to spot immediately. However, what seems likely to become the dominant style of domestic architecture during the eighties is the Townhouse. Usually of two stories, rather narrow for its height, with garage underneath, it is built in rows and clusters, with condominium ownership. Normally the exterior is stucco and often the roof is of tile, but the type is still in the evolutionary stage.

Although famous for its preference for the single family house, the Metropolis has always had its apartment neighborhoods and today in some areas almost all of the new construction is multiple family dwellings—apartments or condominiums. Early apartments were often square box-like affairs of wood or brick. But along with the California Bungalow came the "Bungalow Court," a multiple family development consisting of a cluster of bungalows facing a central sidewalk. The same form was later built in the Spanish Stucco style, also. But along with the stucco house came the ubiquitous stucco apartment, evolving into a "garden type" with much space given over to flowers, lawns, and trees. These developments are space-consuming, seldom over three stories tall, often hollow in the center to accommodate pool, sauna, and patio, and occasionally form clusters that include tennis courts. The multiple dwelling has dominated new construction in the 1960s and 1970s in the city of Los Angeles, and in the older suburbs and in many areas they have replaced earlier neighborhoods of California Bungalows or Spanish Stuccos.

Another obvious distinction among Metropolitan neighborhoods is their wealth, or lack of it. This quality is most easily measured by home values, a characteristic that usually reflects the fortunes of their residents as well. There are opulent neighborhoods in the Metropolis; other sections are obviously poverty-stricken; most of the neighborhoods rank some place in between.

Perhaps the most spectacular sector of opulence in all of America is the string of communities built on or near the south slopes of the Santa Monica Mountains: Beverly Hills, Holmby Hills, Westwood, Bel Air, Brentwood, Pacific Palisades, and Malibu. Sunset Boulevard is its *Champs Elysees,* and the Mercedes, Ferraris, and Rolls-Royces that follow its winding track between lushly wooded estates turn southward to the homes of the rich or swing into the canyons to the north—the lair of the super rich. Here only the tops of the mansions are visible above the high walls and banks of vegetation which guard the "concentrated privacy" that characterizes the neighborhoods of the very wealthy. Residence in these secluded neighborhoods is the goal of many of the wealthy families from the troubled areas of the world—a safe haven in the sun—and the ambition of fortunate Americans as well. One realtor serving the area explains that whereas in the past most of their clients were "affiliated with films—actors, directors, screenwriters—or with other areas of the entertainment industry. . . . Today 70 percent of the buyers are non-Californians and foreigners. . . . There's one section of Beverly Hills—Trousdale Estates—that's now more than half foreign-owned." Buying into

the area is an expensive undertaking. A writer accompanying a realtor in Beverly Hills remembers her ticking off the home values as they drove by, "One point four, two point five, one point eight five," she casually murmured, listing recent selling prices in millions (Reeves, 1979, p. 75). These are for just ordinary homes; Pickfair, described as "The Buckingham Palace of the West," was purchased recently by Laker owner Jerry Buss for $5.4 million, and the late Conrad Hilton mansion, on eight acres overlooking the Bel Air Country Club, is listed as $16.5 million. In Westwood, a condominium development on Wilshire Boulevard is offering its units at prices ranging from $1.5 to $11 million. Other areas of opulence are found on the Palos Verdes Peninsula, in the older, aristocratic city of San Marino, and at Newport Beach (reputed to have the largest Rolls-Royce agency outside England).

At the other end of the scale, neighborhoods of "cheap" houses are not lacking in the Metropolis, just as they are not lacking in any other large urban entity. They are generally in the older sections of the region, within the original city limits of Los Angeles, southward, generally between Vermont and Alameda to Compton, in East Los Angeles, and in the older parts of suburban areas. Often the occupants are members of minority groups. However, even the poorest neighborhoods do not have the appearance of the slums that are found in Eastern cities. There are almost no tenements, no districts of multistory "rabbit warrens." Two-thirds of the houses in even the meanest areas are single-family dwellings (occasionally run-down, rented shacks), and even the public housing projects consist of one or two-story stucco buildings.

Residential values somewhere in the middle range are characteristic of the majority of neighborhoods. These are located, generally, over much of the floors of the San Fernando and San Gabriel Valleys, and the flatter portions of Orange County. These areas, by and large, were the scene of most of the post-World War II construction, locations of extensive tract development and the ubiquitous California Ranch House.

Segregation by age and "geriatric ghettos" are not new. In the Metropolis pockets of the aged have existed in the downtown area, around the Veterans Hospital in Sawtelle, in the Venice of an earlier day, in Long Beach, and in a few other areas. These have been the elderly poor, by and large. Today, in an era of urban insecurity and an increasing number of elderly people, this segregating tendency has been commercialized and extended to the middle class and the affluent. The "retirement village" has been invented. In our area these developments are represented by Rossmore Leisure World and, on the margins, Laguna Hills, Sun City, and Leisure Village. In addition, the proportion of the population over sixty-five is also high in a number of older, established neighborhoods. The elderly reside in a broad band from the Los Feliz district and downtown Los Angeles westward to Beverly Hills, and in Santa Monica, Long Beach, Glendale, Pasadena, Alhambra, and other suburbs with retirement homes and many apartments. Conversely, districts with a low average age are also present. These districts include South-Central Los Angeles, East Los Angeles, much of the San Fernando Valley, and many sections of Orange County.

Many Peoples: Many Neighborhoods

The people themselves often contribute a great deal to neighborhood variety. In a Metropolis still dominated by Anglos this neighborhood uniqueness is most striking when minority groups are involved, particularly those groups with a distinctive urban tradition. Latinos have a well-established and distinctive pattern of urban living and a vibrant street life. Asians, too—Chinese, Japanese, Koreans, and others—produce distinctive urban forms with specialized services and shops that create recognizable districts. Neighborhoods produced by blacks, on the other hand, are almost indistinguishable from Anglo neighborhoods of similar economic status—presumably because of a common centuries-long American heritage. *Jewish Los Angeles* asserts that, "Jews naturally like to cluster in neighborhoods" (Reisner, 1976, p. 7). Although this characteristic may have some validity in today's Los Angeles, except for a few blocks along Fairfax Avenue, Jewish neighborhoods are indistinguishable from those of gentiles.

The Return of the Mexican

The Los Angeles Metropolis was part of Mexico for its first seventy years of European settlement, and the Spanish names on the land, streets, and cities give the region a Latin flavor. The original Mexican residents remained an important part of the region's society and economy for several decades of American rule—longer here than elsewhere in California. Their numbers were relatively small, however, and they were rapidly submerged by the tide of Anglos that arrived during the boom of the 1880s and later decades. A few Mexicans, however, began to arrive in the area early in the twentieth century, and unrest in Mexico in the 1910–1920 period strengthened the flow. Others were recruited into the area as laborers on the railroads, as migratory agricultural laborers, or as workers in the expanding citrus industry. The 90,000 persons "born in Mexico or with parents born in Mexico" in 1920 had tripled to 275,000 ten years later. As Cary McWilliams (1946, p. 69) recognized, "Even as sentimental Americans were performing funeral rites for the departed Mexican, the tide of Spanish influence began to sweep up the coast."

In recent decades, however, the Latino population has reached a different order of magnitude. The 1970 census reported 1,700,000 persons of "Spanish heritage" in the

245

Metropolis, a figure widely believed to be an inaccurate undercount. Today, if undocumented workers are included, the estimates are about twice the 1970 numbers, perhaps 3,500,000. Not all of the recent Latino population increase owes to immigration. Data for a seven year period, 1970–77, indicates a natural Latino increase of 305,000 in Los Angeles County alone, seventy percent of the population increase in the county. (Anglos accounted for two percent of the increase in the same period.) In 1850, Los Angeles was described as the largest Mexican town in the United States. Clearly it is again today.

Population groups are not only difficult to count, but the individuals that comprise them are not always agreed on what they should be called. Older Mexican-Americans usually do not call themselves Chicanos. It is thought that about eighty-five percent of the Spanish-surnamed (a census term) population are of Mexican heritage, so sometimes that label is used in an all-inclusive way. On the other hand, a portion of the group is from other Latin American countries, or Cuba; hence, the increasing popularity of more general words such as Latino or Hispanic. We will use all of these terms interchangeably.

Latinos represent both the oldest and newest groups in Los Angeles, a situation made for irony. In the decades prior to World War II, migrant farm workers would converge on Los Angeles each winter. The local newspapers would regularly proclaim the event a "Mexican problem" and deplore the relief and hospital load created by this annual influx. Mexican-Americans long were barred from municipal pools, and as late as 1943 the area was the scene of a "zoot suit" race riot, directed especially toward Latino boys who wore this distinctive style of clothing. But during this same period the area was discovering and romanticizing its Spanish heritage. Starting with Helen Hunt Jackson's *Ramona* (written in 1885), a myth was created glorifying an imaginary life of the "mission days" (an activity

which, incidentally, resurrected their crumbling remains). By 1900 this movement was well under way, symbolized in that year by the construction of a hotel in Riverside that became famous as the "Mission Inn." Its style of architecture was copied widely by builders throughout southern California. Furthermore, numerous cities sponsored annual fiesta days, often including a colorful pageant called "the ride of the *Rancheros Visitadores.*" This is seen today in a different form in the bands of riders with embroidered suits and tasseled sombreros, seated on silver-encrusted saddles, who embellish the Tournament of Roses Parade in Pasadena each New Year's Day.

Today's pattern of the distribution of the Spanish surname population also has its anomalies. Early studies show that Mexican-Americans (along with Asians) were even more severely segregated than blacks. Now the situation is much more complex. Latinos live in widespread fashion throughout the Metropolis and are present in significant numbers in every neighborhood, even every census tract. This can be explained in part by the fact that many Latinos have lived in the Metropolis for many generations and many have been completely assimilated. Furthermore, many recently arrived Latinos work as live-in domestics in Anglo households. But, perhaps more importantly, the urbanization of the Metropolis has engulfed scores of previously outlying Mexican settlements of agricultural laborers, brickyard or railroad workers that were widely scattered in an earlier period. As a result, a recent survey revealed that fully one-third of the Latino population lived in census tracts where the population was fifteen percent or less Latino, another third in tracts that were forty-five percent or less Spanish-surname. Only ten percent lived in tracts that were more than seventy-five percent Hispanic. However, distinct barrios do exist, and it is thought that they house a larger proportion of the Latino population today than they did previously.

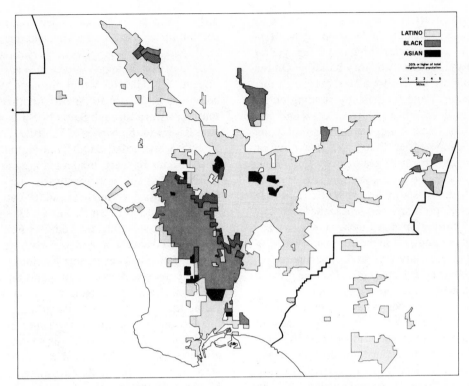

Figure 17.2. Neighborhoods with thirty percent or more Latinos, blacks or Asians. Drafted from 1980 census data.

"East Los Angeles" is the common name given to the region's major barrio. It dates from about 1910 when the inhabitants of the adobes of old Sonoratown east of the Plaza (close to the railroad employment centers) spread across the river into Lincoln Heights. It expanded in the 1930s, gradually replacing a Jewish neighborhood in Boyle Heights and City Terrace, and finally moved into the unincorporated county territory of East Los Angeles itself. This group of communities has now coalesced into the nation's largest barrio, about fifteen square miles in area. It is the cultural center of the Latino population, the home of its mural artists, and one of several entry points for undocumented persons. Here Latinos comprise more than ninety percent of the population.

Much of the social life of the barrio takes place on the street, reflecting the Latin lifestyle and love of urban living. Brooklyn Ave-nue is the main street of Boyle Heights barrio and its intersection with Soto Street is its hub. Here residents of all ages wait for buses, do a little *chalandro* (boy or girl watching), and wander off, as down a village street, to visit the restaurants, *panaderias* (pastry shops), *discotecas,* or to haggle with the proprietors of the clothing stores, shoe shops, *farmacias,* or food markets that line Brooklyn Avenue. Signs in second-story windows announce the presence of various services—doctors, dentists, immigration counseling, and the *Oficina del Concejal* (City Councilman). Credit is often available in the shops and defaults are few. Spanish is the language of the street and window signs, although most residents are bilingual. Fanciful murals decorate an occasional windowless wall.

First Street is a less developed commercial artery, although the location of the *Mercado del Los Angeles*. This is a large, yellow stucco and red tile, two-story building. On the first floor are various food markets (and a tortilla factory) and the balcony running on all four sides is mainly occupied by cafes and *tavernas*. Mariachi groups stroll and play on weekends. Whittier Boulevard is the major commercial thoroughfare of East Los Angeles, particularly in the section between the Long Beach Freeway and Atlantic. It is also the barrio's cruising street where the local "low riders" parade up and down, slowly, on appointed evenings, if the *police* permit. Evening dances at Kennedy Hall and rock concerts at East Los Angeles Community College provide some neighborhood unity. As Mario Casteneda (1975, n. p.) points out, however, that although to an outsider the barrio may seem to be a single neighborhood populated by Latinos, it is, in reality, divided into distinct "turfs" often characterized by *varrio* activities (gang action), with the geographical limits of each turf indicated by *placa* writing.

Secondary barrios in the Metropolis are numerous and widespread, usually an expansion of an earlier "Mextown" that was often located literally across the tracks from the Anglo neighborhoods. The San Fernando barrio, for example, began as a cluster of workers near the citrus and olive packing plants of that town. Additional clusters were at Pacoima, Van Nuys, and Canoga Park. Cities in the citrus districts—Azusa, Pomona, Riverside, Santa Ana, and Norwalk, to name a few—had similar settlements. Other barrios had different origins: a colony of brickyard workers in Montebello (separated from the rest of the world by a high wall), employees of the Pacific Electric in Santa Monica, and other clusters of laborers in San Pedro, Wilmington, and La Puente. Often these *vecindades* had local names reflecting their location: *La Raya* (the frog—on marshy land), Dogtown (near an animal shelter), and so on. These older settlements have generally expanded, and today communities where Latinos are dominant extend from East Los Angeles in every direction. A band of Hispanic population runs eastward into the San Gabriel Valley through Montebello and El Monte to Azusa. Another goes south-eastward through Santa Fe Springs and Pico Rivera to the fringes of Whittier. A third extends westward through Huntington Park to the Santa Barbara Boulevard area around USC, and again, northwestward along San Fernando Road through Glendale and Burbank to the city of San Fernando. One could drive in a big swinging arc from San Fernando to Azusa, a distance of perhaps forty miles, and almost literally never leave a barrio.

The massive Mexican immigration of the last decade and the expanding barrio is providing the Metropolis with its closest approximation of the European newcomer and the ethnic enclave of the turn of the century eastern city. But it is a different era, a different place, and, perhaps, a different immigrant. The Mexican newcomer often has arrived after a rather inexpensive land journey, meaning to return to his homeland when he has earned a "stake" or if he is dissatisfied. He is coming to a place with a landscape similar to his homeland and to a land once part of his background. He is not always a legal immigrant, and, even if he is, he is sometimes slow in becoming naturalized or is simply disinterested in the process. He is in no hurry to give up the Spanish language or to abandon his cultural values. For these reasons, and perhaps because of a lack of acceptance by the dominant Anglo society, he has proven difficult to "melt" into the American "melting pot," and, after all, has arrived at a time when the value of blending does not have universal acceptance.

The Mexican-American in the past was described as being almost invisible, part of a dual lifestyle, lost in an unseeing city. It is true that as the largest minority for many decades, Mexicans have not influenced Los Angeles the same way the Irish affected Boston, or the

Italians, San Francisco, or the Jews, New York. Yet today, in an Anglo Metropolis, the Latino is ubiquitous and omnipresent. Hispanics care for the children, clean the house, bus the dishes, mow the lawn, fix the car, sew the clothes in the garment factories, and furnish the labor for many assembly lines and construction projects. On weekends Latinos are prominent in the amusement centers, parks, museums, galleries, and beaches. Furthermore, their cultural artifacts are all about. Mexican restaurants are widespread. Mexican food is present in every supermarket, and tacos, burritos, and enchiladas are standard items in every school cafeteria, factory vending machine, or institutional food stand. Twist the dial of a radio or television set and Spanish voices are heard on many stations. Dodger games have been broadcast in Spanish for more than twenty years. R. T. D. buses invite the rider with "Bienvenidos." Scores of theaters show Mexican films in many neighborhoods. The Spanish language daily newspaper, *La Opinion,* circulates widely. Spanish is taught increasingly as a second language in local schools. And Broadway, the main retail-theater street of the downtown's glory years, has become a grand *Mercado,* its "Million Dollar Theater" a Los Angeles icon throughout Mexico.

Blacks Discover the Metropolis

In comparison with many American urban areas, the black population of the Metropolis is both relatively recent in origin and of modest proportions. Even so, the black community has long had its well-known places—Central Avenue and the Hotel Somerville were nationally famous in the 1920s. Internationally recognized also is the Watts neighborhood that blazed into prominence as a black ghetto in the violent year of 1965. Some of its citizens, the late Ralph Bunche and Tom Bradley, for example, are also known around the world.

Although blacks were important in the tiny group that originally settled Los Angeles, there were only a dozen in a city of 1,600 persons in 1850. The modern black community had its beginnings in the booming period of the 1880s when blacks increased from one hundred two to 1,285, to comprise 2.5 percent of the population. Significantly, this proportion changed only slightly during the next half century. The fact that the 2,841 blacks in Los Angeles in 1900 made it the largest black settlement on the Pacific Coast is an indication of the small attraction the region had for blacks in the early years.

Black neighborhoods in Los Angeles became widely dispersed in the decades after the turn of the century, housing a population that reached 7,500 in the rapidly growing city of 1910. One black neighborhood developed on the southeastern edge of the business district (along Weller Street between First and Second), and others formed in several directions from downtown: along Temple Avenue (near an abandoned oil field) to the north, along Jefferson Boulevard on the west (between Normandie and Western), and, in a farflung outlier to the south, the Furlong Tract, or "Mudtown" (between 51st and 55th, and Alameda and Central). Perhaps this generally widespread pattern of residences was the result of the small population of the city, its rapid expansion, and the limited amount of old housing located in any one area. These same factors, however, did not prevent a much higher degree of segregation among the few Japanese and Chinese (and the more numerous Mexican-Americans) in the city.

By 1920, although the proportion of blacks to whites was no larger than it had been forty years previously, most blacks were living in a segregated area. It then stretched about thirty blocks down Central Avenue from the original downtown settlement. The city of Watts at this time was a new small rural outlier, and was annexed by Los Angeles in 1926. This marked change in residential pattern was created by the increased use of deed restrictions and other forms of white resistance. The district iself in this decade was still quite mixed in its population, however, with many whites interspersed among the blacks. Central Avenue with its churches and businesses became one of the most notable black streets in the country. By 1925 the main black community had reached Slauson Avenue, which was to remain an impenetrable barrier until World War II. For fifteen years this area of black residences was surrounded by established white areas closed to black occupancy by restrictive covenants, although the black population had expanded to about 65,000 by 1940. Efforts to establish black residences in some of the beach cities were also effectively blocked.

The booming growth of the Metropolis during World War II and its aftermath also saw the beginning of a change in black-white ratios of fifty years' duration. In Los Angeles County the white population increased by forty-one percent in the decade of the 1940s, the black population increased by one hundred twelve percent, and blacks accounted for 5.5 percent of the total by 1950. Similarly, in the decades of the 1950s and 1960s, the proportion of blacks increased somewhat—to 7.6 percent in 1960, and to 10.8 percent in 1970. The decade of the seventies, however, saw only a slight change, to an estimated 11.4 percent, indicating some black out-migration from the county, as higher than average birth rates continued. The percentage of black population in the Metropolis is only about half of the proportion in other large metropolitan areas such as Chicago, Detroit, New York, and Philadelphia. Similarly, Los Angeles, the central city, has a population that is only about 18 percent black, far lower than most cities of its size class. (It should be noted, however, that Los Angeles has a much larger area than most cities.)

Spatially, the World War II period saw the breaching of the Slauson Avenue barrier, although the density of the black population remained vastly higher north of that street than south of it. It also witnessed a large increase of black population in the Watts area. A Jefferson Avenue outlier also expanded, and some significant black population also appeared in the suburbs, particularly in an area of older black settlement in western Pasadena/Altadena.

By 1960, the three largest black neighborhoods had coalesced: Central Avenue/Furlong Tract, Watts, and West Jefferson. Two decades later, the district stands as a massive segregated area, stretching from downtown Los Angeles southward more than a dozen miles and reaching from three to seven miles westward. Alameda Street, with its railroad tracks (and generally unfriendly white suburbs beyond), has been a stable eastern boundary through the years. As Ronald Lockmann (1982) puts it, "There is soul food and soul music on one side and country music and rednecks on the other." Expansion, therefore, has been southward and westward. Much of the area is within the city of Los Angeles or unincorporated county territory (Willowbrook and Florence, for example), but at the southern limit the city of Compton is about eighty percent black (and in this city blacks live east of Alameda). On the west the black district has expanded into Inglewood. To the northeast it is "merging with and possibly transforming" an area predominantly Jewish in population. The Pasadena/Altadena neighborhood (beginning with a settlement of domestics and gardeners handy to that wealthy community in the 1880s) has also grown. Today, perhaps twenty percent of Pasadena's population is black, as is perhaps a third of Altadena's. Other outlying centers are located in Pacoima, in portions of Long Beach, Monrovia, and Santa Ana. At present, the main black neighborhood, sometimes collectively referred to as South Central Los Angeles, is generally stable. However, Latinos are moving south and west from the downtown vicinity into the Santa Barbara area around USC, and Koreatown is also pushing south. Further expansion, if any, seems possible mainly to the west and south.

As is to be expected in an area of nearly forty square miles, much variety is present in the main black district of South Central Los Angeles. The Harbor Freeway bisects the area and, generally speaking, the older and poorer areas are to the east, particularly the original Furlong Tract and the Watts neighborhood. West of the freeway much of the area is distinctly middle class and, on its northwestern edge, the Baldwin Hills neighborhood includes many fine homes, often with swimming pools. Yet the standards of living and economic opportunities are still limited. According to the Community Analysis Bureau, in 1977 the median income for black families was $8,430, for Latino families $8,969, and for Anglo families $17,834. As in other metropolitan areas, whites are significantly better off than blacks, and in the Los Angeles case the Latino population has a position similar to blacks.

Some decades ago, when the black community was much smaller, a single street could be identified as its focus. In the 1920s Central Avenue was its "Main Street," famous around the country. Activity was concentrated at 12th and Central, but its most enduring landmark was at 4233 S. Central, the Somerville Hotel. Opened in 1928, it began its career by hosting the national convention of the National Association for the Advancement of Colored People. For years it was "the hotel for black Los Angeles," both as a transitory home for celebrities (who were excluded from other hotels) and as a night club. In its early days, such distinguished entertainers as Louis Armstrong, Ella Fitzgerald, Lena Horne, and Duke Ellington performed in its club. Today, known as the Dunbar Hotel, it is an Historic Monument, and is being developed as a "Museum in Black."

Now the region is much larger, encompassing many neighborhoods, with few strong focal points. Too, street life here is not as important as in the Latino barrio, for example. Major north-south arteries such as Central, Broadway, Figueroa, and Vermont carry bus routes going downtown, and where they are crossed by major east-west streets—Manchester, Florence, 103rd, Compton, and so on—small commercial nodes have developed. One major shopping district is also in the area—Crenshaw Shopping Center at Crenshaw and Santa Barbara. Blacks, of course, have been a part of American society for centuries, and shopping streets here have little to distinguish them from others of similar economic status elsewhere. Minor items, newspapers such as the *Los Angeles Sentinel* or the magazine *Ebony,* might characterize the district, as well as some of the advertised market specials, but that is about all. The area has its share of large established churches, but it also has a considerable number of small store-front religious establishments that perhaps appeal to the newer migrants from small towns who might feel lost in the large congregations of the main-line churches.

Asians: A Few Oldtimers, Many Newcomers

Asians in the Los Angeles Metropolis include some of the oldest minority groups and some of the groups that have increased the most rapidly since 1965. Chinese go back to the nineteenth century, although then their numbers were small and almost entirely male. Early in the twentieth century the Japanese became the region's largest Oriental group and, at the moment, they still are. In the last several decades, however, Chinese, Koreans, Filipinos, Thais, Indonesians, and others have been far and away the most numerous newcomers from Asia. For more than half a century, it was mainly the Japanese who gave the Metropolis what Oriental flavor it possessed.

Japanese: Out of the Fields and into the Offices

Japanese migrants to America for many decades have shown a remarkable preference for the Los Angeles area, and from 1910 to the present the Metropolis has had the largest Japanese population of any urban area on the American mainland. There were only about 1,000 Japanese in the area as the century began, but ten years later the figure had zoomed up to 8,500, more than doubled to 20,000 by 1920, and rose again to 35,000 in 1930. Early arrivals were laborers, farmers, and fishermen with settlements downtown, in rural areas, and at the harbor. Many Japanese laborers were brought down from San Francisco to work on the strike-bound Pacific Electric in 1903, and others followed after the earthquake there three years later.

Agriculture was to be the foundation of much early Japanese enterprise and prosperity. Citrus groves and sugar beet fields furnished many early jobs. More appealing, however, was an intensive type of agriculture in which small plots of land and much labor could produce crops of high value. As early as 1910 Japanese growers had a "virtual monopoly" in berry production, and by 1912 eighty-five percent of the vegetables consumed in the area were produced by Japanese. Others began growing flowers and still others started nurseries. By 1915 nearly half of the nurseries in the metropolis were Japanese. All of these agricultural activities could be successfully pursued on small parcels of leased land; sometimes close-in plots held by whites for future subdivision, sometimes parcels set among oil refineries and under power lines, sometimes larger acreages. Many Japanese farmers eventually operated farms in the Gardena Valley, on the slopes of the Palos Verdes Peninsula, and on the flat land in an arc around it. Agricultural knowledge could also be utilized in contract gardening. In 1915 some three hundred gardeners in Los Angeles were Japanese; by 1935, there were 2,500.

Japanese growers and truck crops soon made the logical move into marketing, both wholesale and retail. First selling flowers from baskets door-to-door, the growers soon established retail florist shops, and by the 1930s about one hundred Japanese-owned florist shops were reported. In 1914 Japanese growers organized the Southern California Floral Market, first with fifty members, soon with twice that many and a wholesale sales building on Wall Street. Similarly, truck farmers began by selling produce from stands, along rural roads, and in the city. Again, in the 1930s, there were reported to be about 1,000 Japanese-operated fruit and vegetable stands in the area, about seventy-five percent of such stands. Finally, in a report from about the same date, we are told that "distribution of the bulk of vegetable products raised by the Japanese farmers of the Southland is being handled largely by the Japanese produce merchants in the two gigantic wholesale terminals in Los Angeles. . . . "

A small Japanese fishing village grew up in Santa Monica Canyon, and a much larger one, eventually to have more than 2,000 residents, was located on Terminal Island, directly across the channel from San Pedro. Commercial fishing for albacore, bonita, and mackerel was originated by several Japanese fishermen off Whites Point about 1900; thirty years later about two-thirds of the catch, processed by two American and one Japanese canning firms, was caught by Japanese fishermen. Despite growing competition from Italians and Slavs, Japanese fishermen were able to remain dominant for another decade, owing to their head start and their ability to bargain as a group with the canneries. The settlement, located immediately north of the canneries on Fish Harbor, had a thriving commercial district on Tuna Street and was reported to be "one of the most interesting ethnic settlements in southern California" (McWilliams, 1946, p. 322). It remained until

1942, when it was removed by the Navy because of its nearness to its base, well before the general evacuation conducted by the army. It was not reestablished after the war.

The center of Japanese life in the early period focused on "Little Tokyo." This was a typical ethno-centered community where immigrants who could not speak English could use their native tongue and where many of the special goods and services needed by the newcomers could be obtained. Little Tokyo began developing as early as 1905 in a low rent area of mixed uses, abutting Chinatown and a black district, along East First and San Pedro Streets. Gradually the area became a cluster of Japanese-owned restaurants, boarding houses, and labor contractors, bamboo shops, art and curio stores, billiard parlors, grocery stores, and so on. Many resident Japanese lived in the boarding houses, small hotels, and in rooms above the retail stores. From the very first, Little Tokyo served both a Japanese and a non-Japanese population; its restaurants, for example, were patronized heavily by workers of all types from the nearby industrial neighborhoods.

The occupations of many Japanese made surburban residence convenient, however. For example, nurserymen and contract gardeners clustered in Hollywood and Sawtelle. Many Japanese farmers were located in the Gardena Valley, and several other places. Too, although the "Issei," first-generation immigrants, born in Japan, depended on the centrally-located Little Tokyo, the "Nisei," American-born, second-generation Japanese, had little reason to regularly patronize the central ethnic district. Midori Nishi (1964, p. 25) has pointed out that by 1940 at least six outlying Japanese communities, each with its commercial center, language school, and church and temple, could be recognized. They were Boyle Heights, Westside, Olympic Boulevard area, Hollywood-Virgil, West Los Angeles, and Harbor. After Pearl Harbor, 34,141 Japanese, citizens and aliens alike, were forcibly resettled in camps away from the coast. After the war most returned, however, even though they were not compensated for their huge financial losses.

Today, there are perhaps 140,000 persons of Japanese descent in the Los Angeles area. Little Tokyo still exists, much modernized through redevelopment and the infusion of capital from Japan. It now includes The New Otani Hotel, several high-rise office structures, the Japanese Village Plaza and several other shopping malls, and numerous restaurants and retail stores lining First and Second Streets. Also in the area is a six-story Japanese-American Cultural and Community Center, the twenty-two story "Little Tokyo Towers" for retired residents, and numerous churches and temples. Almost no residential space, however, is available around Little Tokyo today. The Japanese population, in general, is widespread throughout the Metropolis, although some suburban clusters can be identified. The traditional Westside-Olympic Boulevard neighborhood now has a shopping center: Crenshaw Square. The considerable Japanese population in Gardena has developed two Japanese owned and oriented centers: the Town and Country shopping center and the nearby newer and larger Pacific Square Mall (near Western and Redondo Beach Boulevard). The latter center includes not only Japanese banks, restaurants, and a market, but also the Pacific Square Inn, a hotel that caters to Japanese businessmen from the mainland. In the surrounding several square miles the population ranges from fifty to sixty percent Japanese and, in addition, the area houses some Chinese and Koreans. Sawtelle retains some of its Japanese population, anchored by the location of the West Los Angeles Buddhist Church and the West Los Angeles Community Church.

One writer has asserted that the Japanese in Los Angeles make up a "miniature New York Jewish community" (Rand, 1967,

p. 120). Cultural values emphasizing hard work and achievement have been coupled with the effective use of the public school system, including higher education opportunities in law, finance, and medicine. The Japanese nursery and gardener still exist but are no longer typical, although the Japanese style of garden with its clean simple style and serene feeling has had a marked influence on landscaping throughout the area.

Chinese: Early Laborers and Recent Arrivals

One of the founders of Los Angeles is reported to have been Chinese, and a Joseph Newmark employed a Chinese domestic as early as 1854. However, it was only after Central Pacific laborers drifted into the city that Los Angeles became the home of a significant number of Chinese. Most of the laborers that built the San Fernando Tunnel in 1867 were Chinese; the city reported about 1,000 Chinese residents in 1880, increasing to 4,000 after the boom years of that decade. These "sojourners" began as cooks and houseboys in town and on ranches, and also found a niche as vegetable farmers. They soon branched out into vegetable peddling, and in Los Angeles in 1880 fifty of the sixty vegetable sellers were reported to be Chinese. Ten years later they were growing as well as distributing "nearly all" of the vegetables in the Metropolis. They established "wash houses" early, and during the early tourist period Chinese were "practically the only servants employed" in the hotels. In the 1890s they provided the "know-how" and the labor for a new celery industry in the marshlands of Orange County. They also worked in the citrus groves in such communities as San Gabriel, Riverside, and Redlands.

The labor of the Chinese was not appreciated. In 1871, nineteen Chinese were killed in a shootout in the Los Angeles Chinatown in what McWilliams (1946, p. 91) described as "one of the worst race riots in Los Angeles history." The Orange County celery workers had to be protected by stationing armed guards at the corners of the fields. In 1893, the National Guard was summoned to Redlands to protect the Chinese citrus workers. Armed protection could not be provided forever and, by 1900, virtually all Chinese had been driven from the groves and from many other activities as well. In many lines of work they were to be replaced by Japanese and Mexicans, although never completely.

While all of this activity was occurring in the rural areas, Chinese in Los Angeles clustered for safety and companionship into a "Chinatown." The "crumbling adobe warrens" of "Nigger Alley" south of the plaza were gradually occupied by the hand laundries, restaurants, grocery stores, curio shops, and "joss houses" of the urban Chinese. The population was all male, mainly "sojourners," and Chinatown developed the usual vices of a transitory, masculine population. The Dakin Atlas of 1888, for example, labels some of the buildings with "gambling" and "opium joint." As the Chinese population grew, Chinatown expanded outward, especially into a dilapidated neighborhood toward the east. Too, after 1900, Chinese were also living around the City Market (at 9th and San Pedro) where Chinese produce wholesalers had a forty percent interest, and along San Pedro as far as Adams. Others were living in their grocery stores, often located in minority areas. The early decades of the century saw a gradual normalization of sex ratios and the transformation of Chinatown from a dependence on gambling, prostitution, and opium, to legitimate tourism, featuring restaurants, gift shops, and so on. When Union Station was built in the 1930s, much of the old Chinatown was destroyed. Some shops and residences remained north of Olvera Street, and this section was developed as "China City." However, in 1938 a large new "Chinatown" was built with Chinese capital, further north on Broadway. It was designed as a tourist attraction from the first, with Chinese architecture, interior courtyards, and "a grand archway from the stage set of the popular Pearl Buck movie, 'The Good Earth.' "

There were only a few Chinese in Los Angeles during this period, 2,500 in 1920 and 2,750 in 1940, but with World War II they were to witness unexpected change. With the United States and China now allies, many things happened. Immigration laws were relaxed slightly; the Chinese Exclusion Act of 1882 was repealed, as were the alien land laws. In addition, things Chinese, for the first time, were seen in a favorable light. Restaurants, which had already modified Chinese dishes and invented others to suit American tastes, now prospered. Gift shops and import-export businesses thrived. Too, a second generation of American-born Chinese, for the first time, outnumbered the "sojourners." As Wong (1979, p. 48) remarks, "In one generation, the old stereotype of unassimilability was replaced by a new stereotype of super assimilability." During the post-war years the Chinese population increased enormously, to about 20,000 in 1960. But in that year only about 1,000 were living in Chinatown; most Chinese were moving out to the suburbs and there was a feeling that Chinatown itself might not survive.

With the passage of the Immigration Act of 1965, however, the Los Angeles Chinese community was to experience revolutionary changes. The Chinese population doubled in a decade to 40,000 in 1970, and it is thought to have exploded to about 100,000 by 1980. Chinatown is no longer merely a tourist attraction; it is now the center of a bonafide Chinese community. The retail district extends a third of a mile on Broadway between Sunset and Bernard, with additional development on Hill. Banks, offices, and community centers have been added, as well as a new commercial complex, "Chunsan Plaza." The latter, as well as much else that is new, has been financed by Hong Kong businessmen.

Scores of apparel factories are tucked into the lofts, basements, and spare rooms of the area. The Chinese residences (perhaps housing 20,000 persons) encompass a triangular area, generally bounded by Alameda, Sunset, and the Pasadena Freeway, but Chinese also are moving into the area south of Dodger Stadium. Fifteen years ago about eighty percent of Chinatown's trade depended on tourists; today from eighty to ninety percent of the people one sees on the streets are Chinese. In recent decades, the Los Angeles Chinatown has served as a point of entry for new immigrants from Taiwan and Hong Kong, and these newcomers have the usual problems with language and general cultural shock.

Increasing population pressure and soaring land values have resulted in considerable movement outward from Chinatown. Today, about eighty percent of the local Chinese live in other neighborhoods. Chinese are moving into the southern fringes of downtown, to the Silverlake-east Wilshire area, and to the more distant Alhambra. It is Monterey Park, however, that has become the nation's most important suburban Chinatown. Already the home of some Latinos and Japanese, Chinese began moving into Monterey Park about twenty years ago. It is only a short distance away from Chinatown via the San Bernardino Freeway, and a large number of houses built since World War II are available. First favored by local Chinese entrepreneurs and professionals, they have recently been joined by well-to-do Chinese immigrants from Hong Kong and Taiwan, in whose papers it is advertised as the "Chinese Beverly Hills." Chinese capital is also revitalizing Garvey Boulevard, with four Chinese-backed shopping centers, three Chinese banks, and many restaurants. A hotel and office building is being planned. The estimated Chinese population of Monterey Park is about 15,000 out of about 52,000.

Koreans: The Most Recent Asians

Koreans have increased proportionately more in the last decade than any other national group. From a modest 1970 figure of less than 10,000, the Korean population has burgeoned to an estimated 100,000 or more today. A study two decades ago found that Los Angeles had the largest concentration of Koreans outside Korea, but the writer was discussing only about 2,000 persons. Clustering in those days was not pronounced, although a small Korean community was identified "between Vermont and Western, Adams and Slauson," a neighborhood already occupied by a few Japanese and Chinese. However, the area's most famous Korean, Dr. Sammy Lee, who gained national fame by winning the Olympic gold medal for high platform diving in 1948 and 1952, practiced medicine and ran a diving school in Santa Ana.

Immigration of Koreans into the United States in the late 1970s reached about 30,000 a year; most, reportedly, came to Los Angeles. The attraction was "other Koreans who can speak Korean, markets where they can buy Korean food," among other things. As a result, a distinct Koreatown has developed, a bit north of the earlier node. It extends from about Washington north to Wilshire and from Hoover to Crenshaw, and has an area of about five square miles. Olympic Boulevard is Koreatown's main street, *Han'gul* (Korean alphabet) signs indicating grocery stores, restaurants, barbershops, hardware stores, wig shops, travel agents, import-export firms, and gas stations occur frequently along a three-mile stretch of the street. On a few blocks, *Han'gul* signs grace every single establishment, and many stores have been built or modified in the Korean style of architecture. Most stores serve both ethnic and neighborhood needs, but they do not seem particularly oriented toward tourists—although some restaurants may be the exception.

Western Avenue is the principal north-south artery of Koreatown. In this section the Wilshire barrier has been overcome. In fact, the neighborhood seems to be growing northward along Western toward Beverly and beyond. The important Korean Community Center, focus of local power and influence, is located at 918 South Western, and the Korean Television Productions, the Korean language station, Channel 22, is headquartered at 5225 Wilshire. Christian churches were influential in unifying the early Korean community, and scores are located in Koreatown today as well as numerous Buddhist temples. A number of Korean language newspapers such as *The Joong-ang Daily News* and *The Dong-A Ilbo* circulate widely. Not all Koreans live in this district, of course. Many are found in outlying communities such as Monterey Park and Garden Grove as well as in other neighborhoods in Los Angeles—around Alvarado and Wilshire and near the Crenshaw Shopping Center, for example.

Armenians: Half Old-Timers, Half Newcomers

It is estimated that more than 100,000 Armenians live in the Metropolis. Perhaps half of these are established residents who have been in the area for many years. The other half are recent arrivals, immigrants of the past decade, generally from either Soviet Armenia or war-torn Lebanon. Taken together, the local Armenian community is thought to be the largest and fastest growing in the nation. As is the case with many immigrant groups, Armenians in Los Angeles run restaurants and a variety of small businesses. Often these are family operations, owned by an established Armenian and providing jobs for many relatives. The *Los Angeles Times* recently catalogued some further economic contributions of this community. "Many Armenians in Los Angeles are professionals. . . . The downtown Jewelry Mart is dominated by Armenians. And, in line with another ancient heritage, many Armenians still sell rugs (Carpeteria, one of the largest rug outlets in the nation, is Armenian owned) . . . the American Armenian National College is located in La Verne." (Stumbo, 1980, pp. 1–3). The Agajanian family has been important in the waste disposal business for many years, especially around Montebello where many Armenians live.

Immigrants tend to settle first in Hollywood, and a typical low-income, overcrowded ethnic enclave has developed, locally known as "Little Armenia." Little Armenia is located generally between Hollywood and Santa Monica Boulevards and extends from the Hollywood Freeway to Vermont. In this area of less than a square mile of run-down bungalows and aging, low rent apartment houses are thought to live as many as 30,000 Armenians, clustered into clannish subcultures based on the nation, and sometimes even the village, of origin. The main street of Little Armenia is Santa Monica Boulevard, with a half dozen grocery stores, cafes, other ethnic shops, and cultural organizations. Occasionally a painting or poster of Mt. Ararat is seen, a nationalist symbol. For many, Little Armenia is simply a port of entry. When they have learned English and found a job, they will move to other locations in the Metropolis, to other Armenian neighborhoods in Glendale or Pasadena, for example, or simply melt into non-Armenian society.

Diaspora in the Sun

Los Angeles today has considerable Diaspora status as the home of nearly one out of ten American Jews. The Jewish Federation Council estimates that there are about 500,000 Jews in Los Angeles County, with perhaps another 50,000 in the outlying areas of the Metropolis, mostly in Orange County. Although this represents only a tiny fraction of the total population (a little more than five percent, less than half that of New York), the Jewish population has been influential in the motion picture industry; the apparel industry is largely a Jewish business, and Jewish businessmen are important in the consumer goods, wholesale trade, and building industries, as well as in the professions. Much of the Jewish influx occurred in the fifty year period 1920–1970 and has added a traditionally urbanizing force to the area's population.

A Jewish element was important in the early days of Los Angeles, with Horace Bell (1927, p. 10) reporting that in the early 1850s "most of the merchants were Jews." But total numbers were few, an estimated 2,500 in 1900 and a modest 20,000 twenty years later. The boom of the twenties brought many Jews to Los Angeles, and the troubled years in Europe between the wars accelerated an exodus from that area. One estimate had the Jewish population tripling to 70,000 in 1930 and doubling again to about 150,000 in 1940. The influx continued during and after World War II and by 1950 the estimated Jewish population was about 330,000, continuing at an unabated rate until 1967 or so, and then leveling off at the present 550,000.

At first Jews lived downtown, as did everyone else, but by 1910 Temple Street was reportedly the "Jewish Main Street." As one writer puts it, "Jewish community institutions like Kaspare Cohn Hospital, the offices of Jewish Federation Charities, Mendelsohn Settlement House, and the Olive Street Schul dotted the Temple Street and Bunker Hill neighborhoods" (Reisner, 1976, p. 7). Old-timers were already moving out toward Western and into Hollywood. However, the number of people involved during this period was not large.

During the twenties and thirties the newcomers were mainly from Russia, Poland, and Germany. These immigrants settled mainly east of downtown, across the railroad tracks and the Los Angeles River, in Boyle Heights and adjacent areas. Here, along Brooklyn and

Wabash Avenues, and the nearby City Terrace District, a bona fide Jewish neighborhood developed. Yiddish was the language of the streets; kosher butchers, grocers, delicatessens, and bakeries shared space with institutions like the Hebrew Sheltering Home, the Breed Street Schul, and the Menora Center. Saturdays and holidays were marked by closed businesses and a festive appearance throughout the neighborhood.

Other, acculturated Jews were already moving into Westside neighborhoods. The oil wells of Gilmore's Rancho La Brea were almost exhausted and the land was being built up with homes, duplexes, and small two-story apartment buildings. Jews from older neighborhoods moved in, some of the Boyle Heights residents did also, and still others from the East and Midwest found this community conveniently located. The prices were reasonable and the Pacific Electric provided easy access to work locations such as the Westside motion picture industry and the garment industry downtown. By 1945 there were "more than a dozen synagogues, several religious schools, a community recreation center, ritual bath houses, numerous social . . . clubs, and many stores, clustered along Fairfax Avenue and Beverly Boulevard, which catered to traditional East European tastes and culture" (Reisner, 1976, p. 10). Fairfax had become what it still is, "the symbolic Jewish neighborhood of Los Angeles."

Today, the neighborhoods with the highest concentrations of "Jewish households," the term used by the Jewish Federation Council, remain on the Westside and in the San Fernando Valley. An area extending from Hollywood to Wilshire, and from Beverly Hills to Cheviot Hills, perhaps five square miles in all, has an estimated Jewish population of from thirty to sixty-eight percent. Within this area the heaviest concentrations are in Beverlywood, Beverly-Fairfax, West Hollywood, and Beverly Hills. Migration farther west has also occurred, particularly to such high class neighborhoods as Westwood, Brentwood, and Pacific Palisades. The San Fernando Valley, since the 1950s, has become a major center of Jewish population. Today, more than 200,000 Jews live in the Valley, mainly in the communities of Sherman Oaks, Encino, Van Nuys, Tarzana, and North Hollywood.

17. Suggested Readings

Bond, J. Max. *The Negro in Los Angeles*. San Francisco: R. and E. Research Associates, 1972.

Bond's doctoral dissertation, written in 1936, was the first effort to tell the story of the developing black area. A more recent study of the same topic can be found in Laurence B. De Graaf, "The City of Black Angels: Emergence of the Los Angeles Ghetto, 1890–1930." *Pacific Historical Review*, 39 (1970) 323–352.

Fellows, Donald Keith. *A Mosaic of America's Ethnic Minorities*. New York: Wiley, 1972.

This wide-ranging volume includes considerable material on Los Angeles, particularly on the Japanese community in Sawtelle.

Griswald del Castillo, Richard. *The Los Angeles Barrio, 1850–1890*. Berkeley: University of California Press, 1979.

This is an excellent study of the origin and development of Los Angeles' largest barrio. Unfortunately it ends before most of the growth occurred.

Reisner, Neil, ed. *Jewish Los Angeles—A Guide*. Los Angeles: Jewish Federation Council, 1976.

Although written for a larger purpose this paperback includes a short history as well as some information on changing locations of Jewish neighborhoods.

Rubin, Barbara. "A Chronology of Architecture in Los Angeles," *Annals of the Association of American Geographers.* 67 (1977) 521–537.

The neglected story of the changing styles of the ordinary house in Los Angeles is the subject of this pioneering article.

Vorspan, Max and Lloyd P. Gartner. *History of the Jews of Los Angeles.* San Marino: Huntington Library, 1970.

This well-known book is historically organized but contains considerable geographic material.

Weber, Msgr. Francis J. ed. *The Religious Heritage of Southern California.* Los Angeles: Interreligious Council of Southern California, 1976.

Essays on half a dozen of the major religious groups of the region are included in this volume. The emphasis is on their beginnings and early development.

Winter, Robert. *The California Bungalow.* Los Angeles: Hennessy & Ingalls, Inc, 1980.

Fine pictures and authoritative text characterize this small book. The author is a professor of the History of Ideas at Occidental and "lives in a bungalow."

CHAPTER 18

Transit in the Metropolis: Horsecars, Cablecars, Streetcars

Figure 18.1. Spring Street was crowded with streetcars in 1905, horse drawn vehicles added to the congestion as did bicycles and an early automobile. View looks north from Third. (Photo courtesy California Historical Society / Title Insurance and Trust Co. (L.A.) Collection of Historical Photographs.)

"The system of electric 'trolly cars' . . . the lines of which radiate like the strands of a spider's web from the heart of the city to the sea on one side and to the summit of Mount Lowe on the other, is, in its scope, management and comfort the best I have ever seen in any land." Arthur T. Johnson (1913, p. 22).

"Railroad men, a canny lot, began as early as 1910 to view the automobile with considerable suspicion. Not knowing just what to make of it, they decided to mark time and see what the potential competitor would do. They are still marking time, and as a result there has been no appreciable improvement or expansion in the rail transportation system in the Los Angeles area since that date." E. E. East (1941, p. 93).

"It seems a transcendent irony . . . that Los Angeles has . . . become notorious for having one of the least adequate public transportation systems of any great city. In other days, it almost invariably showed up in the very forefront, embracing the most improved means for facilitating the movement of people." Robert C. Post (1967, p. 301).

Today the Los Angeles Metropolis is almost unique among cities in the industrialized world in its reliance on the automobile for transportation. Almost every other large city—New York, London, Mexico City, Tokyo, San Francisco—and scores of others depend heavily on electrically powered, grade-separated, mass transit vehicles. Los Angeles uses the gasoline-burning, individually operating automobile. Even today, when Washington, D.C., and Atlanta are building rapid transit systems and Baltimore and Pittsburgh are actively planning them, Los Angeles is unable to initiate anything of the sort. Even federal transportation officials have done little to encourage Los Angeles to build this mode of transport. Why is Los Angeles so different?

Strangely, in view of today's situation, in earlier years Los Angeles went through the same transit stages as every other city, and there was nothing different about it at all. In many ways it was a leader in mass transit innovation. It was willing to adopt new modes of urban transit when its population was much smaller than most cities.

In this section we will briefly consider the changing methods of urban transportation in America—the omnibus, horse car, cable car, electric streetcar and interurban. The bulk of the chapter, however, will discuss the evolution of these modes of transportation in Los Angeles and their effect on the shaping of the modern city.

American Urban Transit History

The colonial city was small, crowded, compact, and everyone walked to work. Only the rich could afford the luxury of a horse and buggy. If transport was essential, one hired a hack. The first change came with the introduction of the horse-drawn omnibus in Boston in 1826. At first simply an urban version of the stage coach, it evolved into a much lighter vehicle carrying about twelve passengers. It quickly became popular, and the next twenty-five years might be thought of as the age of the omnibus. By 1850 more than five hundred of the vehicles were going up and down the streets of New York. The steam locomotive, which made possible an enormous advance in travel between cities, was little used on city streets, as it was smoky, noisy, and frightened the horses.

The second major advance in urban transit came in 1832 when Abraham Brower put an omnibus on iron rails running down Fourth Avenue in New York City. Popularly called the "horsecar" this remarkable development did not diffuse around the urban scene until the 1850s when suddenly scores of cities were provided with them. As their iron wheels moved smoothly over the iron rails instead of jouncing among the cobbles, the horsecar provided a smooth, quiet, accident-free ride. Furthermore, they carried from two to four times the number of passengers as the omnibus and moved at greater speed. Their greater efficiency made possible lower fares, and an era of mass transit began. Although they seem primitive today, horsecar lines were the first form of transit that affected the general citizen. In 1840, in Boston, some one million passengers were carried on the city's omnibus lines, but in 1860 more than 13.5 million passengers rode the new horsecar lines. Population moved out of the congested cities along these street railway routes, and the outlying land owners, often in league with the transit promoters, began mass subdivisions.

The horse-drawn streetcar, however efficient on generally level terrain, did not work well in hilly country. (A car that chased a horse down a hill usually caught it.) In San Francisco, which had hills, Andrew S. Hallidie, a manufacturer of wire rope, designed a "cable car" in 1873 and installed it on Clay Street. Using steam power from a central plant, the cables, sometimes several miles long, were pulled continuously in a slot under the street and the cars could attach themselves to the cable by means of a "grip." Although enormously expensive to install, the cable system was characterized by speed, safety, cleanliness, and operating economy. Cable cars spread quickly to some forty American cities, particularly in the 1880s, and, as with horsecars, property values along the cable routes soared.

At the very time American cities were installing cables an invention that would revolutionize mass transit was being perfected. A streetcar propelled by electricity first ran on the streets of Montgomery, Alabama, in 1886, and an improved version operated in Richmond, Virginia, in 1888. Within four years some two hundred electric systems were being built in American cities or were on order. It was easy and inexpensive to electrify an old horsecar or cable line—wires could simply be strung overhead, above the existing rails. Electrics were fast, reliable, and thrived on the five cent fare. Many more people could afford to ride; urban population moved rapidly to the city's outskirts; and the street railway companies were often as active in the real estate business as they were in transit operations. For about fifty years the electric streetcar, more than anything else, gave shape and form to American cities. Urban sprawl was well underway and the subdivider, lot salesman, and builder became important elements in the suburbanization process.

As traffic increased and the city center became congested, thought was given to separating the transit lines (as well as the railroad lines) from the regular surface street traffic. For example, tracks were elevated in Chicago in 1892 and in Boston in 1894. Too, Boston built a mile of trackage in a subway in 1897, greatly reducing congestion in its business district. New York started its extensive subway system, that was to total one hundred miles, in 1904; Philadelphia began its subways in 1910.

It was inevitable that someone would electrify rail lines between cities and the interurban railroad became a popular form of transport, particularly in the 1900–20 period. Nearly 6,000 miles of track had been built by 1904 and within a few years that would double. With its track often laid on a private right of way or by the side of a highway, the interurban equipment was larger, heavier, and faster than the streetcar. But as Hilton put it, "Few industries have arisen so rapidly or declined so quickly, and no industry of its size has had a worse financial record" (Hilton and Due, 1964, p. 3). Interurban lines reached their peak in the 1920s but ten years later they were rapidly being abandoned, an early victim of the automobile.

Transit Comes to Los Angeles

On September 22, 1873, Charles Dupuy carried his first Los Angeles passenger on the "Pioneer Omnibus Street Line." The horse drawn "buses" ran on Main Street from the Plaza to Washington Avenue, the location of Washington Gardens, a popular beer garden and dance pavilion. The vehicles ran on a half hour schedule, and tickets could be purchased twelve for a dollar. During "Fair Week" in November the line was continued on to Agricultural Park (now Exposition Park). Apparently successful, Dupuy's original stock of two buses was soon augmented by a third.

The next year the first street railway was built in the city when Robert M. Widney organized the Spring and Sixth Street Horse Railroad Company. Iron tracks were laid down from the Plaza in a zigzag route to Sixth and Figueroa. The route ran by Widney's house and we are told he owned property near the end of the line (Post, 1967, p. 11). Operations began July 1, 1874; the car made a round trip every half hour, and the fare was ten cents for a single ride although five tokens could be purchased for twenty-five cents. The horse-drawn streetcar proved as popular in Los Angeles as elsewhere, and lines were soon built in various directions. The Spring and Sixth extended its line up to the new Southern Pacific Depot site in 1876, where it met a line that crossed the river and followed North Broadway to Lincoln Park Avenue. The latter was built by Dr. John Griffin who was subdividing his extensive holdings in East Los Angeles. Another line displaced Dupuy's Omnibus, running down Main and out Jefferson and Figueroa to Agricultural Park. In 1877 the Aliso Avenue Street Railway was built across the river to Boyle Heights, greatly stimulating real estate sales in that subdivision. It began to make a profit, it is asserted, only when it was extended to the nearby Evergreen Cemetery. The City Railroad of Los Angeles built to Washington and Figueroa and eventually to Ninth and Alvarado. Well within the first decade of street railways in Los Angeles their lines were radiating in four directions from the Plaza. The streets that were served by the horsecars were precisely those that were being built up rapidly. The commercial focus of the town was moving steadily southwestward along the horsecar lines, and the neighborhoods served by them, particularly those beyond Washington and Figueroa, were experiencing remarkable growth. By the end of the next decade, horsecar lines were also appearing in the suburbs; Pasadena, Santa Monica, Pomona, Ontario, and Riverside, for example, often associated with real estate developments.

A Railroad Scheme for the Hills

It was during the real estate "Boom of the Eighties" that the next transportation advance, the cable car, made its first appearance in Los Angeles. Bunker Hill had effectively blocked residential expansion to the northwest, but with Hallidie's cable device, the grade over the hill was no longer a problem. First in operation, October 1885, was the Second Street Cable Railroad that ran a mile and a half to Crown Hill at Second and Belmont. Seemingly well located, it had a thriving business center at one end, including the new City Hall and the Hollenbeck Hotel at Second and Spring, and the Los Angeles Investment Company had 1,400 lots for sale at the other end of the line. All the lots were sold within a year and it was reported that real estate values increased by half a million dollars along Second. Service was good—the cars ran sixteen hours a day with twelve minute headways. Patronage of the line was increased by the Cahuenga Valley Railroad, a short steam line that connected the Crown Hill Terminal with Colgrove (within the borders of present-day Hollywood). However, five years later the Second Street Cable Railroad was to succumb to hard times, competition, and winter storms that regularly filled the cable track with mud from the unpaved streets.

The competition was the Temple Street Railway Company which paralleled the earlier line only several blocks away. It, too, was designed to sell property along the line. Beginning operation on a small scale in 1886, two years later the cable reached three miles to Dayton Heights at Hoover Street (then the city limits). Profitable in itself, it was carrying a million and a half riders by 1890.

The most extensive cable system was the property of the Los Angeles Cable Railway. Constructed in the late 1880s, by the end of the decade it formed a giant X through the city. One cable ran from Westlake (now MacArthur) Park, under Seventh Street, up

Broadway and out First to Evergreen Cemetery in Boyle Heights. Another cable began at Jefferson, ran under Grand and up North Broadway to Gates in East Los Angeles. There were twenty and a half miles of cable in all; and the cars crossed the Southern Pacific tracks on the Cape Horn Viaduct, twenty feet high and fifteen hundred feet long, and reportedly was the first elevated cable road in the nation. It was a first-class operation, cars ran eight miles an hour, from 5:30 A.M. to midnight; headways were only two and a half to five minutes and the fare was five cents.

Electric Streetcars for Los Angeles

Meanwhile, electricity was being used to power streetcars experimentally and a local promoter, F. T. Howland (who had brought electric lights to Los Angeles in 1882), quickly introduced the new invention to the city. Howland owned two hundred eighty acres of land on Pico at Vermont, just west of the city limits, which he artfully named "The Electric Railway Homestead Association." Then, on January 4, 1887, he opened an electrified streetcar which not only went westward on Pico to his tract, but also down Maple to the Santa Monica Railroad tracks at 32nd Street. The land promotion was a success, apparently, for 1,210 lots were sold at his first auction, shortly after the line opened. His plans for the electric street railroad were premature, however; the equipment was primitive, and the line went bankrupt and shut down in October 1888. The residents of Howland's tract had to walk a short distance to catch the West Ninth Street horsecars.

Even so, by 1890 Los Angeles had shown remarkable progress in public transit for so small a city. Although with a population of less than 50,000, Los Angeles was among the very first to adopt both the cable car and the electric streetcar. In fact, it did so at a time when both Boston (448,000) and Philadelphia (1,047,000) still depended on horsecars. Further, the lines served most of the city reasonably well. They ran to virtually every populated neighborhood, to each of the major parks, to all of the depots, and to all of the principal cemeteries. In Los Angeles travel by mass transit to the places people wanted to go was possible remarkably early, especially considering the small size of the urban population.

More was to come. Improvements were made rapidly in the electric streetcar, and the electrification of the Los Angeles lines began in earnest in the next decade. Prime movers were Moses Sherman (remembered today in Sherman Oaks and Sherman Way) and his brother-in-law Eli P. Clark. The two began buying up existing lines in 1890, beginning with Howland's defunct Pico Street property. At about the same time they built a new line to the Crown Hill neighborhood. The route ran mainly over West First to Alvarado and then south to Westlake Park. (It was asserted that more people assembled in Westlake Park via the electric line on July 4, 1891 than had ever been together in any one place in Los Angeles' history.)

Before the year was out, Sherman and Clark had electrified five of the Los Angeles streetcar lines. Old lines were extended as electrics, new lines were built, and much of the cable system was taken over in 1893. By then their company, the Los Angeles Railway, was operating thirty-eight miles of electric tracks on seven routes, twenty miles of cable and nine miles of horsecar lines. The company was reorganized in 1895, freeing capital, and the next year saw the electrification of the rest of its lines. Los Angeles Traction, however, a small rival company, operated a cable railroad until 1902.

The years around the turn of the century saw the extension of electrified streetcar lines in all directions. In 1898 when the "Los Angeles Railroad" was purchased by Henry Huntington and Isaias W. Hellman, there were one hundred three streetcars running on seventy-two miles of track. The lines extended outward from downtown Los Angeles to Eagle Rock, East Los Angeles, Boyle Heights, Vernon, Inglewood, and Pico Heights. When Huntington took sole control after 1911, the company had expanded to five hundred twenty-five cars operating over one hundred seventy-two miles of double track on twenty-seven different routes. The yellow cars of the Los Angeles Railroad served the built-up area of the city as well as any similar sized company in the nation. It seemed destined for continued success and indeed was to remain profitable for many years.

Angels Flight

As a footnote to the Los Angeles streetcar scene it should be noted that at about the time the last street cable car was being electrified, a new "inclined cable railway" was opened. This was the legendary "Angels Flight" billed as the shortest paying railroad in the world. It was built in 1901, was three hundred fifty feet long, and rose one hundred feet up Bunker Hill from the southwest corner of Third and Hill. Designed with three rails and an automatic turnout system, the riders reported a little extra thrill when the cars suddenly dodged aside just as they seemed about to collide midway in their course. It was so well counterbalanced that the two cars, the Olivet and Sinai, could be moved by a ten horsepower motor. Each car held ten people, standing was not allowed, and the tickets were five cents each, three rides for ten cents, ten rides for twenty-five cents, and one hundred rides for one dollar. (Both the tourist and the resident were satisfied.) The cars made a trip every minute. At the top, where the ticket taker was located, was "Angels Rest," a small structure surrounded by a flower garden from which the city could be viewed. For an additional five cents one could climb an iron tower "Angels View" and perhaps see Catalina on a clear day.

(A similar, but little-known line, ran from Broadway to Court Street and was called "Court Flight." It burned in 1944.) Angels Flight was taken down in 1969, as Bunker Hill was regraded. Currently in storage, it reportedly will be installed again someday when the development of the hill is complete.

Interurban Travel and the Pacific Electric

Although it was the yellow streetcars of the Los Angeles Railroad that carried the most passengers, it was the "Big Red Cars" of the Pacific Electric interurban that stirred the imagination of the populace and has had continuing nostalgic remembrance. Beginning in 1895 the interurban lines were to radiate in every direction from downtown Los Angeles, and for some decades they provided the region with a fast, clean, and modern transportation system. Commuters took them to work, housewives could run into the city from Long Beach or Pasadena for shopping, on weekends they could be used to go to the beaches or mountains, and tourists found them indispensable for sightseeing all around Southern California. At their peak their tracks stretched for more than five hundred miles throughout the region and they carried nearly a million passengers a day. Although they looked like massive, overgrown streetcars, they were operated like single car passenger trains: you could buy tickets and check baggage, for example. Based on a standard gauge, the system, like an ordinary railroad, also had freight operations.

Sherman and Clark (who had earlier built streetcar lines) built the area's first interurban in 1895, up the Arroyo Seco from Los Angeles to Pasadena. Pasadena was the largest of the suburban cities with more than 5,000 people, had prospered considerably during the "Boom of the Eighties," and was only ten miles away. Traffic was so heavy the line was double-tracked within a year.

The line was called the Pasadena and Pacific, and in order to lend veracity to their company's name they hoped to lay tracks to Santa Monica. As an inducement to that end two large property owners in the Santa Monica area, Jones and Baker, in lieu of cash, gave the interurban line two hundred twenty-five acres of land. The company, needing cash for the construction, sold the tract to subdividers, and it was promptly platted as Sawtelle. Generally following the route of the present-day Santa Monica Boulevard, the line carried its first passengers in the spring of 1896. Santa Monica property values soared and the population tripled within a decade (but this was also the time of the Port Los Angeles development).

Just after the turn of the century, Henry Huntington, already involved with the Los Angeles streetcars, became interested in interurbans. His involvement was to spark a decade and more of rapid transit extension of interurban lines throughout the region. Huntington's first line was completed to Long Beach July 4, 1902. It was built on a private, eighty-foot right-of-way, much of it donated by property owners who expected the value of their adjoining land to appreciate. They were not disappointed. The line was an immediate success, and more than one hundred trolleys a day ran up and down the high-speed line, one every fifteen minutes. Long Beach, a town of only 2,000 people, was to grow to nearly 18,000 in ten years, a rate of growth higher than any other city in the country.

The next few years, particularly the 1903–1907 period, saw the building of lines to many old settlements as well as to new interurban-inspired real estate developments. In many instances Huntington would purchase large tracts of likely looking land and then have his engineers survey a route for an interurban into the area. Lines were completed to Alhambra, Monrovia, and Whittier in 1903, to Glendale, San Pedro, and Huntington Beach in 1904. At the latter community Huntington had purchased an existing townsite and changed its name. His lines reached Santa Ana in 1905, Sierra Madre in 1906, and Glendora and Covina in 1907.

Meanwhile, the Sherman and Clark forces, now operating as the Los Angeles Pacific Railway, were not entirely inactive. They built a second interurban line to the ocean, terminating at Abbot Kinney's Venice of America, an amusement-cultural development, complete with canals and gondolas. Known as the Venice Short Line (running generally out the present Venice Boulevard) it became the most popular route from Los Angeles to the beaches. It was soon to be continued down the beach to Redondo.

Huntington countered by extending his Long Beach line to Naples in 1905, a subdivision in the form of an oval island with internal canals, complete with arched bridges, located in Alamitos Bay. In addition, he purchased the Redondo Land Company which controlled ninety percent of the land at Redondo Beach and also the Redondo Railway Company. He quickly electrified the line, and, during a few weeks in July 1905, was able to sell off three million dollars worth of lots in the beach community. It was thought that this one brief spurt of sales enabled him to recoup his entire investment in the community.

Huntington's interurban building and land subdivision philosophy was well expressed in this 1904 quotation. "It would never do for an electric line to wait until the demand for it came. It must anticipate the growth of communities and be there when the home builder arrives—or they are very likely not to arrive at all, but to go to some other section already provided with arteries of traffic" (Clark, 1981, p. 77). The Huntington Land and Improvement Company was reputed to be the largest land owner in the Los Angeles area, and when the "home builder arrived" Huntington (or occasionally others, Sherman, perhaps) would be there, ready to sell him a lot or two.

Figure 18.2. The Los Angeles Railway (streetcar), Pacific Electric (interurban), and steam railroad lines in the region in 1925. Source: Kelker, De Leuw and Co. *Comprehensive Rapid Transit Plan for the City and County of Los Angeles.* 1925.

Reorganization and Growth

The early years of the century were not only a period of building but also one of consolidation and reorganization of the local transport companies. When the main thrust of this activity ended in 1911, considerable change had occurred. The street railways were consolidated into one company, the Los Angeles Railway, and its sole owner was the interurban king and premier subdivider, Henry Huntington. Further, Huntington's interurban lines, as well as those of Sherman and Clark, were consolidated into the Pacific Electric, and its new owner was the Southern Pacific Railroad. The consolidations were helpful for the efficient operation of the lines as unified systems, but the long-term effect of the change of ownership is harder to access. It is alleged, for example, that the Southern Pa-

cific was never terribly interested in running a passenger line, but was more concerned with the lucrative freight side of the business.

The Pacific Electric, however, seemed to continue its expansionist policies as of old; in the next fifteen years the length of the lines was nearly doubled. For example, the San Gabriel Valley line was extended to Claremont, Upland, and eventually San Bernardino, in 1914. As part of the promotion of the partnership that subdivided the southern San Fernando Valley (south of Roscoe Boulevard), the "Los Angeles Suburban Homes" Syndicate paid a "substantial sum" to have the Pacific Electric extend a line into the valley. Through Cahuenga Pass, it reached Lankershim (North Hollywood) and Van Nuys in 1911. Westward from Van Nuys Boulevard, along Sherman Way, the main street through the subdivision, a line was extended to Owensmouth (Canoga Park) during the next year. In 1913 a line was extended along Van Nuys Boulevard to San Fernando. These interurban lines must have contributed to the spurt in valley land values almost as much as Owens Valley water, for now parcels could be sold as town lots instead of agricultural land.

In the 1920s, when the Pacific Electric system was at its zenith, it operated eight hundred passenger cars and had some 6,000 scheduled runs. In 1924, its best year, it carried nearly 110,000,000 passengers. More than a thousand trains a day left the Pacific Electric Building at Sixth and Main or the Subway Terminal on Hill north of Fifth. These two stations were focal points of a network of lines that ran out from the city in many directions. One set of lines ran westward to Santa Monica, and the other ran southward to Long Beach and San Pedro. A major artery branched off at Watts, running to the Orange County cities as far as Santa Ana and Orange; another served the beach cities, including Newport Beach and Balboa. Eastward, the San Gabriel Valley was well served, with one line curving down to Yorba Linda, another ending in Glendora, and the main line running all the way to San Bernardino, with branches to Riverside and Corona. North of Los Angeles the lines served Glendale and Burbank, and an additional line ran over Cahuenga Pass with branches to Canoga Park and San Fernando. You could ride the Big Red Cars from Lake Arrowhead to the Pacific, and from Canoga Park to Redlands. From downtown Los Angeles you could reach Pasadena or Glendale in forty-five minutes, Long Beach in fifty minutes, and Santa Monica in an hour.

The Decline and Disappearance of Electric Transit

The consolidation of the Los Angeles transit enterprise into two systems in 1911 created companies that seemed destined for success. Management was competent and operated without the problem of local governmental scandals that were common elsewhere. More importantly, the transit lines served the area where the people were; in fact, the direction of growth had been guided by their presence. The Los Angeles Railway had a five cent fare, the Pacific Electric also maintained competitive rates. Generally, the service was reasonably swift and reliable. Only one future problem was identified early. The *Examiner* was already complaining in 1911: "It (took) more time to get from the station at Sixth and Main to Aliso Street . . . than to run the balance of the trip to Pasadena" (Fogelson, 1967, p. 164). Yet, in less than fifteen years both transit systems would show symptoms of illness, so serious that without drastic changes the disease might be fatal. What happened? Perhaps the best account of the changing circumstances of the lines can be gleaned from three governmental reports from the years 1914, 1919, and 1925.

A study of the transit systems by the local Board of Public Utilities in 1914 was full of optimism. The Board expected the earnings of the companies to "increase at a remarkable rate" as the population increased in the area they served. The Board, however, made two assumptions: that costs would remain constant in the future (as they had in the past), and that the companies would continue to monopolize the area's urban transit (for only the affluent could afford automobiles). Both assumptions were quickly invalidated, the first by America's entry into World War I and the second by the invention of the jitney.

"Auto Snipers and Trolley Cars" was the way *Sunset* magazine put it. (Sunset, 1915, p. 47.) They were reporting on a new form of transit that appeared on the streets of Los Angeles July 1, 1914—the Peoples Five-Cent Auto Car Service, quickly nicknamed the "jitney." Running down the major streets, these privately-operated automobiles picked up passengers for a five-cent fare. It was every man for himself, cars cutting in to the curb to "snipe" passengers ahead of the trolleys and then driving pell-mell down the street. Anyone with an automobile ("hundreds of owners of cheap cars") could earn a little extra money—as much as ten dollars a day for a full-time operator. Operating on no schedule and on only the most travelled routes, free of taxes and any kind of regulation, they were universally opposed by the streetcar companies. By the end of the year it was reported that there were over seven hundred jitneys in service in Los Angeles, and the "craze" quickly spread to other cities in the nation. In 1915 alone, patronage dropped by 17.7 million on the Los Angeles Railway and by 8.6 million on the Pacific Electric, a decline attributed to the spread of the jitney. Eventually, the jitneys were regulated as public utilities, required to carry insurance and to conform to a number of standards. The rules made their operation unprofitable and they vanished from the streets in 1917. By then, much needed revenue had been forever lost to the transit lines.

Our second clue to the changing status of the local transit lines, this time right after World War I (1919), appears in a report of the California Railroad Commission in response to a request for rate increases (Fogelson, 1967, pp. 168–69). As the Southern Pacific was already subsidizing the money-losing Pacific Electric, they were granted a fare increase. The Los Angeles Railway, however, was not. The recommendation, instead, was to reduce expenditures by rerouting lines and introducing cars operated by one man. The first suggestion was taken, but the city of Los Angeles refused to permit one-man cars, citing the line's poor safety record. Other recommendations, too, were beyond the authority of the Railway to implement. For example, the Commission recommended that the cities remove the streetcar company's obligation to pave the streets adjacent to their tracks. Paving was not only expensive, but in effect it required the streetcar lines to provide surfaces that benefited only their competitors—auto-

mobiles and trucks. However, cities were not eager to assume this new expense and no action was taken.

A final recommendation was that outlying communities prohibit motorbus competition with the Pacific Electric. Bus lines started about 1914 and drained away much needed revenue from the rail lines. The Commission felt that the buses had the capacity to disrupt without being able to supplant the rail lines (Fogelson, 1967, pp. 169–70). There was still no conception, by either the rail lines or public agencies, of the menace of the automobile to rail transit. The majority opinion in 1919 was still that automobile congestion in the center of the city was reaching a saturation point and that the delays and discomfort of driving would soon force the drivers back to the streetcars and trolleys.

The early twenties were years of explosive growth for the Metropolis, and the fortunes of both lines seemed a bit brighter. Their ridership did not increase as fast as the registration of automobiles, however, and many of the patrons found the rail service infrequent, inefficient, and slow; and the lines were still not profitable. So a third full-scale study was ordered. The California Railroad Commission released its report in 1925 (Fogelson, 1967, p. 172). It repeated most of its earlier recommendations and, in a clear indication that the lines were in serious trouble, suggested what had earlier been unthinkable: that the lines combine under municipal ownership. Combining the two lines would make for more efficient operation and eliminate duplicating lines. Public ownership would have many advantages. It would eliminate the state's five and a half percent gross revenue tax as well as the city's paving requirement. In addition, the city's credit would make possible the retirement of the line's high interest bonds and the issuance of bonds at much lower rates. All in all the potential savings would be enormous. And why not? The city already had municipally owned power, municipal water, and a municipal harbor. Further, city-owned transit was already operating in both New York and San Francisco. The idea was generally accepted, and the local civic and political leaders drew up a contract in 1925; negotiations began, but it was never signed. One unexpected problem arose: Huntington died, and his executors were not interested. Many students of the local transit scene believe that with the failure of municipalization in the 1920s, the Metropolis lost its best chance for a successful rapid transit system.

Plans for Traffic and Transit of the 1920s

The early 1920s were halcyon days for Los Angeles; oil wells and the motion picture industry helped fuel the greatest real estate boom ever seen in the area. Optimism was everywhere. Predictions that Los Angeles would become a great metropolis were coming true, population growth for the future seemed assured. With growth problems of transit and traffic multiplied, plans for their future development seemed essential. At the urging of a citizens committee in 1923, two outside firms were engaged. One was to produce a plan for streets and automobile traffic; another, the firm of Kelker, De Leuw and Company, was charged with providing a "Comprehensive Rapid Transit Plan for the Metropolis." The document would also satisfy a provision of the new Los Angeles City Charter, adopted in 1924, which called for the city to formulate a "comprehensive elevated railway and subway plan" (Los Angeles, City of, 1929).

The Kelker, De Leuw report (1925), released in 1925, recommended a coordinated system of rapid transit lines, with lines extending outward from Los Angeles, running in subways or on elevated tracks near the center and at-grade in sparsely populated areas. Street railways and bus lines were to act as feeders to the rapid transit portion of the system. The portions of the lines running at-grade could be gradually improved as elevated lines as the area grew. The financing was to be by general obligation bonds issued by the city at large, but with the car riders and the owners of the property benefited, also assessed their share.

The transit plan, as might be expected, was supported by the downtown business community and by individuals who were appalled by the congestion of the streets and who were convinced that easy connections with the downtown were important for the health of the entire region. It was opposed by the outlying merchants and by those who felt that Los Angeles did not have to develop as had other cities in the East. The Los Angeles City Club, a municipal reform group, was a spokesman for this latter idea. It deplored increasing concentration in American cities and the ever higher buildings this generated. In addition, they argued that rapid transit would never be self-supporting, and was, in fact, a traditional solution unnecessary in an age of "cheap power, the universal use of the telephone, and the automobile. . . ." Instead, it opted for improvements in automobile movement through rerouting of streetcars and interurban and suggested "a serious study of the bus as a public transportation unit." Further, it "defended the outside business center idea as against the downtown theory" (Dykstra, 1926, p. 397). The public seemed to agree with this analysis, and the Kelker, De Leuw plan was put aside. (The street traffic plan will be discussed in the next chapter.)

In an unrelated but ironically-timed move, the two local rival systems organized the Los Angeles Motor Coach Company in 1925. Through it they established bus lines to serve new areas and to provide feeder service to the rail lines. Buses appealed to the companies for they were inexpensive to establish—requiring no separate right-of-way as they simply used the city streets. The Pacific Electric also formed a second bus line, the Metropolitan Coach Company.

In hindsight, the demise of the rail systems could have been forecast from about that date. For example, the Los Angeles Railway had made no attempt to serve the newer sections of the city annexed in the great period of city growth, 1913–1925. It did not serve Hollywood, the San Fernando Valley, or the western part of the city. Furthermore, much of the equipment until the mid-twenties was primitive, with wooden seats and half the car open to the California weather. Fully seventy percent of their equipment was pronounced obsolete in 1932. The Great Depression of the 1930s applied the *coup-de-grace* to the transit systems in many cities, Los Angeles included. Patronage and revenue tumbled; costs generally remained fixed. The company began abandoning unprofitable lines, reducing the frequency of runs, and raising fares. These moves usually resulted in additional loss of riders, making necessary an additional round of fare increases, service reductions, and so on. World War II delayed the final demise a few years, but, with the end of the wartime boom, the Los Angeles Railway Company collapsed. On January 10, 1945, Huntington's estate sold it to the Los Angeles Transit Lines, whose parent company, National City Lines, was owned by General Motors, Standard Oil of California, Firestone Tire and Rubber Company, among others.

The company had been buying streetcar lines around the country and converting them to bus systems. However, in Los Angeles, their first move was to order forty new streetcars and, in general, to improve the line. True, many lines were soon converted to diesel buses. On two routes electric buses with rubber tires, sometimes called "curbliners" replaced streetcars. These vehicles, which received their power from two overhead lines, ran on rubber tires and could be steered like a bus—they could pick up passengers at the curb instead of out in the middle of the street, maneuver

like a bus around slower traffic, and yet had the quick acceleration, quietness, and lack of fumes of electric motors. (Incidentally, what is supposed to be the "First Trackless Trolley in America" ran up Laurel Canyon from Sunset Boulevard to "Bungalowtown," a real estate development in the hills, beginning in 1910 and running for some months.)

With the patient in its terminal illness, everyone agreed on municipal ownership, and the streetcar and buslines were purchased by the Los Angeles Transit Authority in 1958. Within two years, the streetcar service was reduced to the lines served by modern cars, and the trend toward diesel buses accelerated. There were five streetcar lines still operating at a profit in 1963 when they were abandoned in favor of two hundred new buses. The last streetcar ran in Los Angeles on March 31, 1963. It was called the "Crying Trolley," as painted tears were pictured streaming from painted eyes on the car's front. An era of almost ninety years was over.

The Pacific Electric was following a parallel downhill course. Its lines in operation in 1925 were essentially the same as in 1915, although there had been massive population increases throughout the region. Furthermore, they were using the same equipment as a decade earlier, and their service had deteriorated—it was no longer very rapid transit, particularly as the trains neared downtown. One grade separation had been accomplished—a one-mile tunnel from the Subway Terminal Building on Hill Street to Glendale Avenue. It was opened in 1925, shortening trips to the north and west by fifteen minutes. It also removed seven hundred seventy-eight cars each day from Hill Street and three hundred one from Sixth. But efforts to elevate the main lines to the south and east failed; there were objections in some quarters, and in any event the Pacific Electric had no money to finance them.

World War II doubled the number of riders on the Pacific Electric, bringing a ray of hope. However, the bulky cars found street traffic increasingly intolerable. When the Hollywood Freeway was in the design stage, the Pacific Electric, in a final effort to modernize, sought state and city funds in July 1947, to help finance construction of a Red Car right-of-way in its center. The officials pointed out that two lines of tracks could handle more passengers than the eight lanes of freeway. But the addition would cost twenty million dollars; no money was available under the current laws, and the median lines were eliminated from the final plans.

Beginning in 1950, in the face of massive deficits, rail service was abandoned on one line after another. Key portions of the Pasadena line were condemned for construction of the San Bernardino Freeway. In 1953 the Pacific Electric sold its passenger operations to the Metropolitan Coach Line. However, a few rail sections were still operated to Bellflower, Long Beach, and San Pedro as well as the lines through the subway to Glendale and Hollywood. In 1958 the Metropolitan Transit Authority (already operating the local buses) purchased the Metropolitan Coach Lines. Rail service was abandoned rapidly with the last of the Big Red Cars running to Long Beach April 8, 1961. It was the last operating line west of Chicago, and interurbans are now gone with the other wonders of yesterday. *Sic transit gloria.*

18. Suggested Readings

Crump, Spencer. *Ride the Big Red Cars: How Trolleys Helped Build Southern California.* Los Angeles: Crest Publications, 1962.
This large-sized book presents a detailed and affectionate account of the interurban lines of the region and is illustrated with many maps and photographs.

Hilton, George W. and John F. Due. *The Electric Interurbans in America.* Stanford: Stanford University Press, 1960.
This volume is the standard history of the rise and decline of the interurban railroads and in it the Pacific Electric can be seen in its national perspective.

Myers, William and Ira L. Swett. *Trolleys to the Surf: the Story of the Los Angeles Pacific Railway.* Glendale: Interurbans Publications, 1976.
From 1896 to 1911 the Los Angeles Pacific served the area between downtown Los Angeles and Santa Monica Bay, and the history of this line also tells much about the development of that region.

CHAPTER **19**

Los Angeles Takes to the Automobile and Bets on the Freeway

Figure 19.1. Freeways wove their way through the Metropolis in the 1950s. This view, July 9, 1958, shows the San Diego Freeway completed to just north of Sunset Boulevard. (Photo courtesy Spence Collection/Department of Geography, UCLA.)

"A population can be spread out without rapid transit or street car facilities. The private automobile and the bus have turned the trick. . . . The development of the motor truck and the availability of electric power for manufacturing will continue to decentralize the industrial district. There can be developed in the Los Angeles area a great city popoulation which . . . lives near its work, has its individual lawns and gardens, finds its market and commercialized recreational facilities right around the corner and which, because of these things, can develop a neighborhood with all that it means.

"Under such conditions city life will not only be tolerable but delightful—indefinitely more desirable and wholesome than the sort induced and superinduced by the artificially stimulated population center which constantly must reach higher and higher into the air for light, air and a chance to see the sun." Clarence A. Dykstra (1926, p. 398).

"She drove the San Diego to the Harbor, the Harbor up to the Hollywood, and the Hollywood to the Golden State, the Santa Monica, the Santa Ana, the Pasadena, the Ventura. She drove it as a riverman runs a river, every day more attuned to its currents, its deceptions. . . . Again and

275

again she returned to an intricate stretch just south of the interchange where successful passage from the Hollywood onto the Harbor required a diagonal move across four lanes of traffic. On the afternoon she finally did it without once braking or once losing the beat on the radio she was exhilarated, and that night slept dreamlessly." Joan Didion (1970, p. 13–14).

We have seen how the Los Angeles Metropolis evolved in the normal American way through the building of an extensive streetcar and interurban network. But the area did not take the logical next step toward elevated trains or underground subways. Instead, it left the mainstream of American urban development and clutched the newly invented automobile to its breast with unusual passion. Automobiles became numerous in the region at a time when they were rare and impractical novelties elsewhere. Apparently originally purchased more for a weekend trip to Idyllwild or Redlands than for the drive to work on Broadway or Hollywood Boulevard, they soon began to have commuting utility as well.

Los Angeles, it is important to note, grew to metropolitan size only after the age of the automobile had arrived. So Los Angeles had a choice not available to older cities. One school of thought, as expressed by Clarence Dykstra in the paragraph quoted earlier, felt that a better city, dispersed and airy, could be built now that this new form of transportation was available. However, there was probably little in the way of deliberate "choosing" of the automobile over mass rapid transit. Funds were readily available through gasoline taxes and registration fees for public roads; the privately owned transit facilities had neither the money nor credit to carry out plans for modernization. So "motorways" were designed and built and the streetcar and interurban lines declined and eventually were abandoned.

The Early Automobile Finds a Congenial Home in Los Angeles

Automobiles appeared in the area in the 1890s as curiosities for the wealthy and toys of the mechanically inclined. By 1900 there were enough drivers in the region to organize the Automobile Club of Southern California, and ten years later it had attracted 2,500 members. Agitation by bicyclists, particularly, had resulted in the improvement of many of the area's roads at the turn of the century and by 1919 the *Los Angeles Evening Express* could write, "It is getting to the point where you have to hunt a good while to find a dirt road of any length anywhere in Los Angeles." (Brilliant, 1964, p. 230.) Responding to this, the first mobile Angelenos seem to have thought of their automobiles as a means to explore southern California rather than as a commuting vehicle. Congress thought so too, officially classifying the auto as a "pleasure vehicle" in 1918. The Auto Club published its first tour book the next year, an impressive volume of three hundred eighty-eight pages, covering most of the roads in the state. By 1920 the Club had increased its membership more than tenfold to 30,320.

Both the climate and the housing pattern made southern California the natural home of the early automobile. These primitive vehicles were fragile things, essentially inoperable in cold and snowy weather. Early cars were hard to start in the cold, and, open to the weather, they were miserable to ride in on days of low temperature. Even as closed cars became common, heaters were rare or ineffective. Too, roads in much of the country were impassable for anything more demanding than a horse and buggy (or sleigh) during the snow season. In the East the cars were put in storage ("up on blocks" as the saying went) for the winter. This was not necessary in Los Angeles and local observers explained the popularity of the autos in this way: "There is no day in the year when it is impossible or even uncomfortable to ride in an open car. The widely scattered population and the almost universal housing in detached single family dwellings situated on lots large enough to admit housing automobiles encourages their use."

Automobile historians consider the year 1919 to be the turning point in the development of the automobile. Earlier models were the products of an experimental era; autos built in later years had real utility. By 1920 they were reliable and useful; for example, the electric starter replaced the hand crank and buttoned on "side curtains" were superseded by glass windows. In 1919 ninety percent of the automobiles on the road were open touring cars or roadsters, whereas ten years later ninety percent were closed sedans or coupes.

Even during this transitional phase the automobile was purchased in inordinate numbers by southern Californians. Automobile registration in Los Angeles County increased from 110,000 in 1918 to 430,000 in 1923, an amazing increase of four hundred percent in only five years. It is universally asserted that by this time Los Angeles County had the highest ratio of automobile ownership in the world: one automobile for each 2.9 persons. Everyone in the county could go automobile riding at once and, with just a little crowding, could sit in the front seat!

Motor Cars Are Essential

By 1920 the automobile was making a major impact on Los Angeles and during the year both government and private industry reacted to the new challenge. In April, at the urging of the streetcar company whose cars were being delayed in traffic, the City Council banned daytime parking on many downtown streets. On Saturday, April 10, 1,000 tickets for illegal parking were issued, business suffered, and the law was repealed. The *Los Angeles Times* (April 25, 1920) began the story of the event with the headline "Motor Cars are Essential. Two Weeks of No Parking Proves

That Business Can't Do Without Them." This headline was taken by many to be a public recognition of the arrival of the automobile age in southern California. In a more successful effort to regulate downtown traffic, in October, the city installed traffic signals at major intersections along Broadway. As the lights changed a bell rang and little red and green arms moved up and down. The *Times* described them as behaving "like a cross between a railroad semaphore and an alarm clock." As the year ended, the "World's Largest Garage" was to open at Grand and Fifth, a reinforced concrete structure with nine floors, designed to provide off-street parking for more than 1,000 cars. There were unsolved traffic problems, of course. In 1920 there were one hundred seventy-two fatal accidents on the city streets and an additional 5,027 persons were injured. Clearly the problems created by the automobile cried out for solution.

Recommendations were on the way shortly. A citizens' "Los Angeles Traffic Commission" was organized in 1922. It not only tried to cope with daily problems, it also hired three city planners, Harland Bartholomew, Frederick Law Olmstead, and Charles H. Cheney, to draft a major street plan for the city. Incidentally, the Commission also recommended that the city employ a second group of experts to study transit problems. The Kelker, De Leuw report discussed in the previous chapter was the result.

Major Traffic Streets and the Boulevard Stop

The Olmstead-Bartholomew-Cheney report (1924): "A Major Traffic Street Plan for Los Angeles" was presented to the citizens in May, 1924. It noted the rapid rise of automobile ownership in the city and documented their extensive use. Traffic counts revealed that in November, 1923, about 650,000 persons entered the business district every day by automobile as compared to about 750,000 by street railway. This is an amazing statistic considering the newness of automobile transportation. The recommendations were in two parts. One focused on the automobile, the other on the streetcar. Automobiles could move more freely, the report argued, if the streets were widened and opened in accordance with a plan, and if left turns and street parking in congested areas were eliminated. The major recommendation, however, was that streets be classified into "major traffic streets" and minor streets, with "major traffic streets" for through travel, on which a higher speed can be maintained with safety because no one is allowed to turn in from a side street without first coming to a dead stop. This is called the "boulevard stop plan." How revolutionary an idea it must have been. Today it is hard to imagine a city with traffic coming into all intersections with only general "rules of the road" to guide it. The report also suggested that minor streets—those that serve residences—should be "narrower and indirect." Also recommended were a number of parkways, including an Arroyo Seco Parkway ("parkways should be made exceptionally beautiful as a route of pleasure travel") and a new "River Truck Speedway," partially in the bed of the Los Angeles River.

The second part of the plan concerned the streetcar and it too involved a classification of streets: in the downtown area some were to be reserved for streetcars, some for autos. "But the streetcar, owing to its economy of space and low cost of operation per passenger, must take precedence over other forms of vehicles in the congested area, prior to the reduction in surface street use by the still more intensive mass transportation offered by subways or elevated lines." Thus, in 1924, a report on streets gave first priority to the streetcar, and seemed to foresee the development of mass rapid transit, along with growth, in the city's future.

The residents of Los Angeles "accepted" the street plan by voting a $5 million bond issue to finance street improvements in November, 1924. Again, in 1927, they authorized a special property tax to finance street improvements. The need was obvious: in the decade of the 1920s Los Angeles County gained 1,272,037 people and 644,418 automobiles. Additional laws were passed in 1925. Now pedestrians as well as autos were required to obey traffic signals, jaywalking was prohibited in the business districts as were horse-drawn vehicles during rush hours, and illegally parked vehicles could be impounded. By the end of the decade "492 intersections were controlled by semaphore stop signals releasing scores of officers for more important duty." "For the first time in history," as Brilliant (1964, p. 144) put it, "human beings were by common consent obeying the quasi-arbitrary commands of a man-made mechanism." In addition, hundreds of boulevard stop signs were installed.

Miles of new city streets were opened and many existing streets were paved. Usually the move to pave the streets was begun by the property owners, the work done by the city, and the costs charged to the property owners along the streets. By June, 1921, the city of Los Angeles had almost five hundred fifty miles of paved streets within its borders. Two years later an additional one hundred thirty miles of paving was under way. Occasionally, major paved streets were featured in the subdivisions of wealthy developers: Gillis put through San Vicente Boulevard in West Los Angeles and Huntington built Huntington Drive in San Marino. Investors in the Hollywood Hills formed an Improvement District and in 1923 voted bonds in excess of $1 million to build a twenty-one mile roadway they named Mulholland Drive. Its official opening in 1925 was celebrated, according to Brilliant (1964, p. 208) by "an aerial display, a rodeo starring Tom Mix, a costume carnival and street dance on Vine Street . . . a celebration in Hollywood Bowl with a galaxy of movie stars showered with roses from a fleet of airplanes, and the most brilliant street lighting and searchlight display ever seen in southern California."

The automobile was also spawning auxiliary industries. In 1926, for example, the *Times* reported, "the wrecking of automobiles and the salvaging of parts has become an established industry in Los Angeles. . . . There are 66 automobile wreckers in the city and 32 of them are on South Main Street." A major event of 1928 was the opening on Spring Street of a thirteen story Hills Brothers' "Skyscraper Garage," in which 1,000 cars could be stored after being raised and lowered by means of "fast elevators." Its opening was reported to have "materially reduced the critical traffic situation in that section of Los Angeles" (Brilliant, 1964, p. 191).

New Studies Propose the "Motorway"

Automobiles in the area continued to increase, with 960,416 registered in Los Angeles in 1936. Soon there would be a million cars on the streets, and two more transportation studies were commissioned. One was by the Auto Club of Southern California (1937), and the other by the City of Los Angeles Engineering Transportation Board (1939). Although their reports, issued in 1937 and 1939, respectively, came to opposing conclusions about the role of rail transit, both now recognized the primacy of the motor car and suggested engineering devices to cope with their increasing numbers.

Not surprisingly, the importance of the automobile in moving people was emphasized in the Auto Club report. The Los Angeles Railway, it calculated, carried 242 million passengers an average of five miles each in 1936 for a total of 1.2 billion passenger miles. The Pacific Electric carried 64.7 million passengers an estimated average distance of ten miles, totaling 647 million passenger miles. However, automobiles in Los Angeles County (based on estimates projected from gasoline sales), traveled six million miles and, carrying an estimated average of 1.448 (!) persons per auto, accounted for 10.8 billion passenger miles. Even if we discount the accuracy of their

estimates, it is clear the automobile was by then the dominant transport medium in the area.

The survey also asserted that in the past dozen years the pattern of automobile traffic had changed significantly. Previously, some ninety-seven percent of the automobiles surveyed had the downtown as their destination; in 1937 the pattern revealed a good deal of crisscrossing with multiple destinations. Further, the report found that most of the traffic delays were caused by "interference" at intersections. In a change from earlier thinking, the report asserted that the solution to the local traffic problem will "not be found through providing more streets and highways as they simply add to the number of intersections." In addition, "as through streets are opened up, they simply attract land uses that result in increasing traffic conflicts."

What then was the 1937 solution to moving automobile traffic if simply adding more streets and highways would not do the job? "It is recommended that a network of motorways be constructed to serve the entire metropolitan area. They should be on right-of-ways 360 feet wide in residential areas and 100 feet wide through established business districts. They should have 4 to 6 lanes with a physical barrier extending the full length of the motorway dividing opposing lanes of traffic. The remaining land on each side should be planted to trees and shrubs. There should be no crossing at grade at any point. Secondary streets should cross underneath or above; at intersections a structure generally referred to as a cloverleaf should be installed" (Automobile Club, pp. 31–32). There we have the earliest description in any of the local transportation proposals of what we now recognize as a freeway.

Further, the report had some recommendations concerning location suggesting that in business districts the motorways cut through the center of the blocks. It continues, "On this land the so-called motorway building should be constructed. In general, the first and second floors of this building should be devoted to retail business, and the third floor to the motorway proper, and the fourth and fifth floor, and as many additional floors that may be needed to parking, and the remaining floors to office space. Access to surface streets would be provided at convenient intervals." (Automobile Club, p. 32.) Finally, the cost of motorway buildings should be self-liquidating. Any visual image of today's freeway network makes it obvious that this idea was never implemented. Instead, freeways have generally avoided business centers, perhaps much to our future sorrow, for the utility of freeway rights-of-ways for any kind of a rapid transit network is now greatly reduced.

Other sections of the Auto Club plan were more traditional, arguing again for the classification of surface streets, the prohibition of parking on commercial streets, as well as a novel idea: the synchronization of traffic signals. For rapid transit it has short shrift; it recommended the removal of all street railways from the streets and the establishment of an adequate metropolitan motor bus transportation system.

Automobiles, Buses, and Streetcars, Too

The City of Los Angeles Transportation Engineering Board, after a year and a half of study, issued its report in 1939. The report recognized the predominance of the automobile as a means of transit, but it also emphasized the desirability of encouraging greater use of mass transit facilities. Specifically, it recommended the construction of a system of motorways, or freeways, to facilitate rapid movement for *both* the private automobile and mass transit. The intention to encourage mass transit was clear: the system should be designed to permit the operation of express buses on freeways to provide an attractive rapid mass transit service at minimum cost to the public.

"If only 5 out of every 100 vehicles on an express highway are buses, the effect of their greater capacity . . . is to more than double the passenger carrying service performed by the highway. . . ." (Los Angeles, Transportation Engineering Board, 1939, p. 7).

Finally, the Board felt that continued growth would eventually make necessary the construction of a rail rapid transit system to serve the densely settled portions of the city. Subways in the downtown area and rail lines along the median strips of freeways were recommended. A "route to the west . . . along Wilshire Boulevard" was one of the suggested locations. In an opinion at odds with that of the Auto Club "it does not think it appropriate to utilize small capacity vehicles, such as buses, on heavy lines where streetcars clearly could furnish the best service at lowest cost." Interestingly, it suggested that the Hollywood Freeway be built and financed with tolls if necessary as a sample of what freeways would be like, for "the vast program (of freeway construction) may appropriately follow local acceptance . . . through the public use of the facilities proposed!" (Los Angeles, Transportation Engineering Board, 1939, p. 15.) The feeling seems to have been, "If they try it, they will like it."

The Area's First Freeway: "Most Extraordinary"

Even as these two reports were being written, work was underway on what, almost by coincidence, was to become the area's first freeway. A "parkway" from Los Angeles through the parks in the Arroyo Seco to Pasadena had been on the drawing boards at least since 1920. Some work had actually begun in the early 1930s. Los Angeles County eventually applied for federal funds to complete the work and by 1938 construction had started again. In the meantime, because of the many delays, local engineers had had time to study modern highways in the east (Connecticut's

Merritt Parkway and the Pennsylvania Turnpike) and the *autobahn* in Germany. As a result, they revised their design of the parkway to eliminate all intersections and to make it a limited access road. On December 30, 1940 (in time for Pasadena's New Year festivities) a major six mile segment was complete, and Governor Olson dedicated what was called the "West's first freeway." "It takes courage," he said, "to do a thing for the first time." And then, after more reflection, "All this is, to say the least, most extraordinary." (Bozzani, 1941, p. 3.) Little did he realize that within a few decades the type of roadway he was dedicating would be considered not only ordinary but also essential for urban movement. Actually, the Pasadena Freeway, as it is known today, was soon revealed to have been inadequately designed, with lanes too narrow, curves too sharp, shoulders almost nonexistent and merging space at on-ramps completely lacking.

On the next day, with somewhat less fanfare, Gene Autrey, the Honorary Mayor of North Hollywood, cut the ribbon of a short, one mile segment where four lanes of roadway had been built on each side of the Pacific Electric tracks through Cahuenga Pass. By 1942 it was to stretch another two miles, and a segment of the Hollywood Freeway was in place.

Although a Master Plan of Highways, about the same as that proposed by the Transportation Engineering Board, was adopted by the County Regional Planning Commission in 1941, and reconciled with neighboring counties in 1946 and 1947, little building had taken place during World War II (1942–45). With the end of the war, the time was ripe for accelerating freeway construction. New residents by the hundreds of thousands had flocked to the area during the war and in the immediate post-war years, making the need for improved transportation even more critical. Housing for this new horde was going up rapidly wherever land was available, generally on formerly agricultural tracts in the suburbs.

Equally important, large sums of money for highway construction were now available, first from the Federal Government, and after 1947 from an increased state gasoline tax. The need was there, the plan was ready; financing was available. No demonstration project financed by tolls was needed. Everyone seemed to agree that freeways should be built as rapidly as possible. Argument was mainly over who should get their freeways first.

Work on the "stack," the four-level interchange which was to be the focus of the freeways near the Civic Center, was soon begun (completed 1948), and construction of the freeways that were to radiate out from that junction got quickly under way. By 1953 the Hollywood Freeway was completed through Cahuenga Pass and a connection made (at Avenue 22) with the older Arroyo Seco Parkway, now renamed the Pasadena Freeway. Two years later much of the Santa Ana and the San Bernardino Freeways were completed to those cities, although each had small unfinished gaps. When 1960 arrived the Ventura Freeway had been extended westward across the San Fernando Valley (from the Hollywood Freeway), the Long Beach Freeway was complete, and the Harbor had crept southward to Alondra. Many of the remaining freeways were built in the early 1960s: the Santa Monica (surprisingly late), the Harbor finally reached San Pedro, most of the San Diego and the Golden State were complete. Generally, the early freeways, like the Pacific Electric before them, focused on the downtown. Later, circumferential freeways were built: San Diego, San Gabriel River, Foothill. By the mid-1960s, the region had a reasonably complete freeway system permitting circulation throughout the area in many directions without the need of passing through the original downtown interchange.

Throughout the decade of the 1950s particularly, but into the 1960s too, the general concept of freeway building seemed popular with citizen and press alike. Freeways seemed

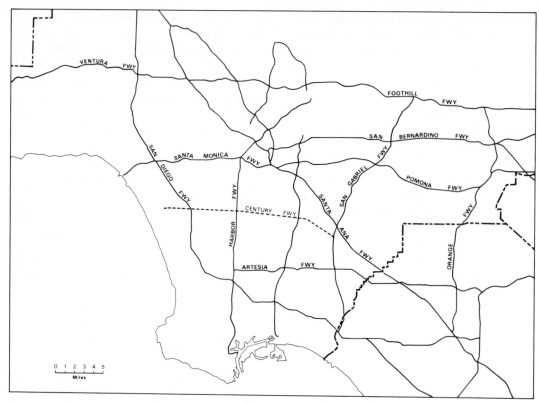

Figure 19.2. The freeway system of the Metropolis.

to increase mobility dramatically in the areas that they served. Opposition, such as it was, came mainly from the homeowners and businessmen whose property was condemned for the freeway rights-of-way. The highway engineers argued that they were doing the best they could, that they tried to disrupt as few homes as possible, and pointed out that they were able to locate the Hollywood Freeway in such a way that forty percent of the land it used had been vacant. This reasoning did not appease the owners of the other sixty percent. Even though they were paid market value for their property, plus relocation expense, the disruption of living patterns was real and sometimes painful. Stories appeared in national magazines about families being uprooted by freeway construction from three successive homes. Some felt that the owners

whose houses were taken were lucky, and that the unlucky ones were those who now found themselves living along the fringe of those eight whizzing lanes of freeway traffic with the accompanying noise and fumes. Unhappy, too, were the people who have lived along quiet residential streets that suddenly were graced with off or on ramps for a new freeway and the thunder of new surface street traffic.

Although the general routes of freeways were laid out in the 1947 Master Plan, specific locations were the responsibility of the engineers of the State Division of Highways and the local planning agencies. The cost of acquiring land for rights-of-way, the engineers insisted, played an important part in the selection of the exact route of a freeway. Thus freeways were often routed across blighted areas rather than through areas with high property values. Concern for costs also, on occasion, resulted in the use of public land for freeway rights-of-way, land such as parks, reservoir margins, or other open land. For cost reasons, too, freeways tended to run through single family residential neighborhoods and to avoid apartment sections and business districts.

Direct public input on freeway routing problems was minimal in the early years, and after *pro forma* public hearings the routes were regularly approved as proposed, one section at a time, by the appropriate City Council. Each decision affected only a relatively small proportion of the citizens of a large city like Los Angeles, for example. Only rarely, as in small El Monte, where most of the city's populace objected to a freeway on a twenty foot high embankment cutting through the town, was construction held up until compromises were made. Again, freeway construction through South Pasadena (another small city where most of the citizens were affected) was stalled for more than a decade owing to a dispute in routing. These were the rare exceptions.

Eventually, the Highway Engineers, stung by public criticism, attempted to make procedures more understandable and open. Hearings began to be held in the communities affected, alternate routes were proposed, the cost and affect on the community of each route was assessed, the material was placed on public display in libraries and public input requested. Perhaps, in the end, the desired route was chosen anyway, but at least the appearance of public participation was maintained.

Have the Freeways Fulfilled Their Promise?

An objective appraisal of the freeway system is difficult. They were built during an era of rapid population growth and an almost explosive proliferation in both numbers and use of the automobile. For example, in 1950 there were an estimated 54.2 million miles of daily travel in the Metropolis (using 3,180,000 gallons of gasoline). By 1970 this had increased to 145 million vehicle miles (using 13,180,000 gallons of gasoline) each day. There is no question that personal mobility, for better or worse, has been expanded greatly by the freeways. One wonders what the region would have been like without them, but that is idle speculation.

One interesting attempt to evaluate the performance of freeways is the M.A. Thesis of Wayne A. McDaniel, "Re-evaluating Freeway Performance in Los Angeles" (1971), written for the UCLA School of Architecture and Urban Planning in 1971. Its goal was to use quantitative data to determine how close our freeways came to fullfilling the stated objectives of their early advocates. These objectives were mainly threefold: to provide sufficient capacity to handle future traffic needs and to remove excess traffic from the surface streets, to eliminate delays to reduce journey times between parts of the city, and to reduce the street accident and fatality rate. Significantly, a study by a traffic engineer in 1960 concluded from the data available at the time that freeways had accomplished all three of these objectives (McElhiney, 1960).

McDaniel, using more recent data, however, came to a completely different conclusion. The first objective, to provide sufficient capacity to handle traffic needs and to remove excess traffic from surface streets, has not been met, he argued. It was agreed that freeways handle traffic well during non-peak hours, but today about twenty-five percent of the local system is subject to bumper to bumper congestion during peak hour use. Surface streets paralleling newly built freeways did at first show dramatic reductions in traffic, but within a few years traffic counts showed increases on the paralleling streets higher than they had been before the freeway was built. Intersecting streets from which on- or offramps were built showed massive traffic increases with the opening of a freeway, that in many instances created new congestion. Finally, McDaniel (1971, pp. 20–21) asserted, the installation of on-ramp meter signals were intended to divert to surface streets those who would not wait at the on-ramp, thus diverting back onto surface streets some volume of traffic. These were the very streets whose lightening of traffic had been the objective for the freeway in the first place. This, McDaniel asserted, was an admission of failure of the freeway system (McDaniel, 1971, pp. 11–12).

An unexpected effect of opening a freeway, according to McDaniel was to induce new traffic. Induced traffic, he said (1971, pp. 21–22), has two sources: trips that previously were made by other modes, such as a bus, and trips that had not been made at all. He quotes a Los Angeles City traffic study that estimated that twenty-nine percent of the traffic on the Santa Monica Freeway immediately after its opening was induced traffic. In the long run newly created traffic will increase still more because of trips originating from new land developments encouraged by the freeway. This created demand is one factor in the seeming inability of a freeway system ever to provide sufficient capacity.

Studies in 1960 had concluded that the freeways had been successful in reducing driving time, the second objective of the freeway advocates. However, later works include statistics which reflect the result of rising traffic demand and the associated congestion. McDaniel (1971, p. 23) concluded, "They indicate that in less than a decade peak hour driving time on five freeways has increased by two or three times." One might add that in some instances freeway driving times have been reduced to surface street times. McDaniel also remarked (1971, pp. 23–25) that the point-to-point times of the data are really concerned with speed, and evidence from other sources indicates that the length of time Angelenos are spending in their cars is actually going up.

The extent to which the third objective, increased safety, has been reached is in dispute. If fatalities are expressed in terms of vehicle miles driven, a favorite statistic of the traffic engineers, then the freeway age has brought significant improvement. For example, in 1939 the Los Angeles rate was 9.5 fatalities per 100,000,000 vehicle miles, in 1957 it was down to 3.4. Too, driving on freeways produced fewer fatalities, by this measure, than driving on surface streets. In 1957 the rate was 3.4 on surface streets and 2.4 on the freeways, and the injury rate was two hundred six on the streets and ninety-eight on the freeways. Comparable data is not available for recent years, only raw figures. In Los Angeles County, for example, in 1976 there were nine hundred twenty-seven fatalities in motor vehicle accidents; one hundred fifteen were on freeways, eight hundred twelve on surface streets. With an estimated thirty-five percent of vehicle miles driven on freeways, their relative safety, by this measure, remains clear.

McDaniel, however, was not impressed with this data (1971, pp. 27–30). He insisted that a motorist is not as concerned with the degree of risk for each mile as he is with total risk in all his travels. The most accurate indicator of total personal risk a Los Angeles resident endures is reflected in "annual fatalities per 100,000 persons." Table 19.1 compares this fatality rate in four large cities over a series of years. This table, McDaniel asserted, indicates a nationwide decline in fatalities for the 1940s and 1950s that is correctly identified by highway engineers as the result of the widespread creation of safety programs. From the 1950s, when Los Angeles freeway construction began in earnest, to the early 1970s, local per capita rates consistently have been fifty to one hundred percent higher than rates of comparably sized cities. This disparity can be explained by a greater reliance on the automobile in Los Angeles. The creation of a freeway system did not succeed in reducing this disparity as the per mile safety advantages of

Table 19.1
Motor Vehicle Fatality Rate (Including Vehicle Related Pedestrian Fatalities)

Year	New York	Philadelphia	Chicago	Los Angeles
		Fatalities per 100,000 persons		
1942	10.8	12.7	13.7	21.3
1945	9.6	9.1	13.9	27.9
1947	9.6	10.2	15.0	21.8
1948	7.5	7.3	12.8	15.5
1951	7.0	8.0	11.5	13.6
1954	7.5	8.9	10.9	14.8
1957	8.1	8.2	8.5	17.8
1960	7.6	8.5	7.6	15.7
1963	8.5	8.7	8.2	13.6
1966	7.4	9.3	9.0	16.2
1969	10.7	10.0	9.4	17.2
1972	11.2	10.7	8.4	15.4
1974	9.0	9.3	8.9	11.3
1975	---	8.9	9.7	9.7
1976	---	---	10.1	11.4
1977	8.6	6.5	9.2	12.2
1978	8.4	6.5	9.1	14.5
1980	9.0	7.5	10.0	15.7

Source: National Safety Council, *Accident Facts*. Published annually.

freeways have been entirely negated because Angelenos have deemed it desirable or necessary to drive many more miles than their counterparts in other cities.

Table 19.1 has been updated, for this chapter, using what data is available from incomplete reports. With the imposition of the national fifty-five mile per hour speed limit in 1974 the fatality rate dropped dramatically for the nation as a whole. In Los Angeles, too, the years from 1974 and on mark a significant change in this measure. For the first time the fatality rate in this city, in 1974, began to approach that of other large centers not so dependent on the automobile. (Their rates, interestingly, show little change.) Perhaps this is due to the reduced rates of speed on the freeways; perhaps other unidentified factors are involved. Although we can be thankful for the reduction in fatality rate, it can hardly be attributed to the presence of freeways, for they were all here in abundance during the period of high fatality rates, of the previous decade.

The foregoing evaluations, said McDaniel, were characterized by a single theme. Freeways have succeeded in producing large increases in corridor capacity, but the three direct benefit objectives of their planners have not been met because of constantly increasing demand. Only the quantity, not the quality of services provided, has been improved.

Why has this been so? The traditional explanation is that an automobile is "an economically superior good." As family income increases the number of automobiles increases, and their use rises. Further, the automobile as a status symbol seems to be a widely accepted concept.

However, McDaniel (1971, pp. 31–35) argued that the two most important factors preventing freeway supply from ever catching up with freeway demand are inherent in the system itself. The first factor pertains to financing in which user charges (an eleven cent a gallon gas tax) have not been effective in restricting freeway usage to socially acceptable levels. The tax, of course, is not selective and is collected from all Californians who buy gasoline, regardless of when or where an automobile is used. This policy has generated significant subsidies to peak hour users, as it assumes the social cost associated with a motorist does not vary with the time or location of the trip. A motorist who uses the Santa Monica Freeway, for example, during peak hours imposes a significant social cost by further congesting traffic flows for all other users, whereas this is not true of a motorist who uses the Freeway at 3:00 A.M. or who uses some other little-used highway. Secondly, the costs associated with serving peak hour users are higher than for non-peak users, since highway planners attempt to design the facilities to accommodate flows at peak hours, adding extra lanes, ramps, and so on, necessary only a few hours a day. By constructing these facilities with funds collected from motorists at large, the financial system embodies a strong off-peak-user to peak-user subsidy. A solution through variable user charges is fraught with many problems.

A second factor, inherent in the system itself, leading to an under-supply of freeway services, is the marked propensity of freeways to create their own demand (McDaniel, 1971, pp. 35–36), not only short run demand, as has been discussed earlier, but also in the long run. This comes through their impact on land development, a process which in turn, creates an increasing need for freeway space.

McDaniel concluded (1971, pp. 39–40) that Los Angeles freeways have not provided sufficient capacity, and knowledgeable observers now agree that they never will; that Los Angeles drivers spend as much time, if not more, in automobiles now as they did twenty years ago; rush hour velocities in many freeway corridors have exhibited a substantial decrease in recent decades; and on a per capita basis, no fewer Angelenos are killed in auto accidents than twenty years ago. He was not arguing that freeways have not contributed toward these objectives, because then one would have to indicate what the situation would be with no freeways at all—an exercise in unfounded speculation. What can be asserted, McDaniel said, is that the system has not performed as was promised in the 1950s and there is no reason to believe that it ever will.

Los Angeles as the Epitome of the Automobile and the Freeway

In the decades of the 1950s and 1960s Los Angeles gained a national reputation as a region where cars and freeways dominated the lives of the residents. Articles in national magazines would assert, even in the 1970s, "Angeleno life is unthinkable without the automobile. People meet friends at the Thriftimart parking lot, they grab a bite at Bob's Big Boy drive-in, they cruise down Sunset Boulevard looking for action, they drive 20 miles for dinner or a movie. It's impossible, they say, to cash a check, buy a quart of milk, get to work or school or play without jumping into a four-wheeled steed. . . ." (Barnes, 1973, p. 13). Local newspaper articles poked gentle fun at the phenomena; in "How I Made a New Friend on the Freeway," the commuter-author relates to the occupant of a green pickup truck whose driving patterns were identical to hers and then fantasizes that her experience may not be so unusual. "Perhaps any given freeway, at any given moment, is fairly teeming with Datsuns relating to Oldsmobiles, Mustangs getting it on with Volvos, Mercedes-Benzes cozying up to Chrysler Imperials" (Lapides, 1974, pt. II, p. 7). And Joan Didion, quoted earlier, has her heroine receive psychological comfort through spending her waking hours constantly driving the freeways. Even the entry for Los Angeles in the newly revised *Encyclopaedia Britannica* insists, "Its hallmark is a network of freeways that provide moving parking places for the county's

Table 19.2
Ratio of Autos Owned to Households for Selected SMSAS

SMSA	1960	1970
Boston	0.91	1.07
New York	0.64	0.75
Philadelphia	0.91	1.13
Pittsburgh	0.93	1.11
Chicago	0.89	1.06
Detroit	1.11	1.32
Cleveland	1.05	1.26
Denver	1.23	1.46
St. Louis	0.94	1.21
Minneapolis-St. Paul	1.10	1.31
Dallas	1.19	1.44
Los Angeles-Long Beach	1.21	1.33
San Francisco-Oakland	1.05	1.22
Seattle	1.12	1.36

Sources: U. S. Bureau of the Census, U. S. Census of Housing 1970, *Detailed Housing Characteristics—U. S. Summary*, HC(1)B1, Table 40; and U. S. Census of Housing 1960, *States and Small Areas—U. S. Summary*, HC(1) no. 1, Table 19.

4,000,000 cars and trucks. Angelenos commute, shop, bank, and breed by automobile. . . ." (Weaver, 1974, p. 107).

It is true that in the 1920s the automobile uniquely dominated the Los Angeles scene, and since then the increase in the number of automobiles has been phenomenal. It is true, too, as will be discussed in the next chapter, that Los Angeles is almost uniquely alone of cities of its size to be without a mass rapid transit system. In the middle 1970s, how unique is the Los Angeles affection for the automobile? If automobile ownership is taken as a criteria, it is not very unique, as Table 19.2 demonstrates. Both Seattle and Denver have more automobiles per household than Los Angeles, and Detroit, Cleveland, and San Francisco-Oakland all have ratios which are not especially different. The old, very large centers, New York, Boston, and Philadelphia, are still relatively low in automobile ownership. Beyond these, the variation in automobile ownership between metropolitan areas is no longer great. Too, most cities today have extensive freeway systems. In addition, the mode

of commuting travel now is dominated by the automobile in most large cities. "The proportion of work trips by automobile ranges between 75 percent in the central city and 86 percent in the suburbs in Los Angeles. In Detroit the percentages are 68 and 86 and in Chicago the range is from 63 to 76. Public transport accounted for an average of only 25 percent of the work trips of the 30 largest SMSAS. . . ." (Nelson, 1976, p. 56). Clearly, automobiles are now common and much used in all large American cities.

19. Suggested Readings

Brilliant, Ashleigh E. "Some Aspects of Mass Motorization in Southern-California, 1919–1929." *Southern California Quarterly,* 47 (1965) 191–208.
The impact of the automobile on the lives of everyone in the Metropolis was analyzed by Ashleigh Brilliant in a Ph.D. dissertation in history at the University of California, Berkeley, in 1964. This article presents a summary of his findings.

Brodsly, David. *L. A. Freeway. An Appreciative Essay.* Berkeley: University of California Press, 1981.
This volume might be described as an attempt to interpret the meaning of the freeway system by a person who grew up with it. In addition, there is much in it about Los Angeles in general and its various forms of transportation over the years.

Foster, Mark. "The Model-T, the Hard Sell, and Los Angeles' Urban Growth: Decentralization of Los Angeles During the 1920s." *Pacific Historical Review.* 44 (1976) 459–484.
This article recounts the story of the growing public preference for the automobile and the development of subdivisions far from public transportation lines at the time of a major real estate boom.

CHAPTER 20

Rapid Transit and the Metropolitan Future

Figure 20.1. Rapid transit in the future may include buses on the freeways. Shown here is the San Diego-Santa Monica interchange, November 23, 1964. (Photo courtesy Spence Collection / Department of Geography, UCLA.)

"However misguided the Bay Area Rapid Transit may prove, one may say with considerable certainty that a similar system for Los Angeles could not possibly be equally successful." George W. Hilton (1967, p. 389).

"But in the long run, say in 50 years when the bonds will have been retired, when everyone will regard BART as just another built-in feature of the region, rather like Golden Gate Park, perhaps no one will question whether BART should have been either built or abandoned. It will then be regarded as a handy thing to have, a valuable facilitator of trips that would not otherwise be made by the elderly and the young, a blessing that enriches the quality of Bay Area life. And who will gainsay then the wisdom of having built a white elephant today?" Melvin M. Webber (1976, p. 39).

The Los Angeles Metropolis, as we have seen, did not adopt the rapid transit recommendations of the 1920s. Instead it drifted off into a sixty year love affair with the automobile and the freeway. But the lure of rapid transit did not die, it was simply dormant awaiting a more receptive era. In the meantime, the Metropolis has seen the opening of rapid transit lines in most of the world's great cities, including recent construction of systems in Toronto, Washington, D.C., and, particularly in that rival to the north, San Francisco. Actually, within the past ten years proposals to construct a rail rapid transit system have been on the ballot in Los Angeles County three times. None have been successful. However, the specter of a national energy crisis, the certainty of drastically higher gasoline prices, and the feeling that a more compact city would be ecologically appropriate have kept the issue alive.

In order to discuss rapid transit we must have clearly in mind what is meant by the term. Emphatically, it is not what is presently furnished by the Southern California Rapid Transit District (RTD) which operates a fleet of buses on the streets and freeways. Rapid transit is defined as "a passenger transportation system using elevated or underground trains or a combination of both." The vehicles must move on a separate right-of-way, uninterrupted by cross streets or other traffic. Rapid transit vehicles are normally powered by electricity and run on a fixed guideway. The guideways are usually steel rails (for steel wheels) but some systems use rubber tires running in a concrete groove. Separate rights-of-way and fixed guideways allow rapid transit vehicles to carry large numbers of passengers at high speeds on reliable schedules.

Rapid Transit Versus the Automobile and the Freeway

The automobile and the freeway as a means of movement in a city have certain inherent advantages, unattainable by any kind of rapid transit system. The automobile is absolutely flexible as to its origin and destination: it can leave from your front door and go directly to any point in the Metropolis (provided you can find a place to park). It is absolutely flexible as to schedule: you can leave when you want and return when you are ready (assuming you are not in a car pool). You have absolute privacy—all alone in a steel cocoon. You travel in comfort—you always have a seat, and normally can regulate the radio and often the temperature to suit your taste. If you have packages to carry, an automobile makes the task an easy one. Normally, too, a journey by car is faster than a trip by rapid transit, although certain rush hour and rainy day situations could be exceptions. Other advantages may not be universally felt. For some, driving is a relaxing-recreational experience. Others feel that a car is a status symbol, although for others a bicycle or riding BART is more fashionable.

On the other hand, rapid transit has some intrinsic advantages of its own as a metropolitan transportation system. It is a more efficient user of space, able to move 30,000 seated passengers an hour per single line of track compared to 6,000 by a four-lane freeway. If underground, it consumes space only at station entrances and hence can go right into the most heavily congested business centers, delivering passengers close to office buildings or department stores. Transit vehicles, unlike cars, do not have to be stored at the passenger's destination; hence, there are no parking problems and parking lots or structures do not dilute the business areas. Rapid transit is one of the safest forms of transportation, the private automobile one of the most dangerous. Rapid transit is useable by almost everyone: those who do not have access to a car, those too young to drive, those too old to drive well, or those who are physically unable or simply disinclined to drive. It may make unnecessary the considerable expense of owning a car. It is efficient in moving people in all kinds of weather and is less of a polluter. The strain of driving is absent. There is more social contact.

The Los Angeles Metropolitan Transit Authority

Convinced by some of the preceding arguments, proponents of rapid transit have never been convinced that freeways were the ultimate solution to the Metropolitan transportation problem. A group of civic leaders, sponsored by the Los Angeles Chamber of Commerce, joined together in 1948 and proposed a Rapid Transit Action Program to the state legislature. The lawmakers were urged to form an agency that would plan rapid transit lines within the framework of the freeway system, existing interurban lines and rights-of-way. However, nothing happened until 1951 when the legislature created the Los Angeles Metropolitan Transit Authority (MTA). It was authorized only to construct and operate an overhead monorail line between the San Fernando Valley, downtown Los Angeles, and Long Beach. No funds were appropriated, the line was to be financed by unsecured bonds repaid out of operating revenues and, incredibly, although a public agency, it was to be regulated and pay taxes as if it were privately owned. (Incidentally, the Bay Area Rapid Transit District (BART), created at the same time, was treated quite differently. The latter was given power to develop a plan for the entire area, and appropriations were authorized to match local funds.) The Los Angeles County Board of Supervisors eventually funded MTA which hired a consulting firm to study the corridor and propose a route. The consultants thought that a monorail from Van Nuys to Compton would be financially feasible if assurances could be obtained "on the matter of damages for occupancy of streets, exemption from tax assessments and exemption from Public Utility regulations" (Coverdale and Colpitts, 1955, p. 70). No legislative action was ever taken to fulfill these needed "assurances" and interest in the monorail concept waned. Additional MTA studies in subsequent years explored the possibilities of buses on freeways, subways in the downtown area for the use of buses and express buses on elevated roadways.

In 1957 the state legislature again moved into the transit arena. BART had completed its area-wide planning mission and the legislature created the San Francisco Bay Area Rapid Transit District, with taxing powers, to finance engineering and development studies. At the same time, the legislature transformed MTA into a countywide public transit authority, but without taxing power. However, MTA was now granted exemption from taxes on its property, it was given power to operate existing transit facilities, and to plan, finance, and develop needed improvements. The next year MTA purchased most of the bus lines in the area, financing the acquisition with a $40,000,000 revenue bond issue.

The MTA also began a series of studies on the feasibility of mass rapid transit for the area, the location of the most appropriate routes, projected revenue, financing possibilities, and so on.

No local financing was available and no federal money was forthcoming. The legislature was repeatedly petitioned to make some kind of tax resources available to the district but with no success. None the less, planning began for a rail rapid transit system. None of the proposals were attractive to private interests. MTA watched in frustration the successful 1962 BART referendum. That agency had what MTA did not have: authorization from the legislature to issue bonds payable from direct assessments of property taxes.

Southern California Rapid Transit District Plan of 1968

Agitation for equity continued and in 1964 the legislature created the Southern California Rapid Transit District (SCRTD or, more

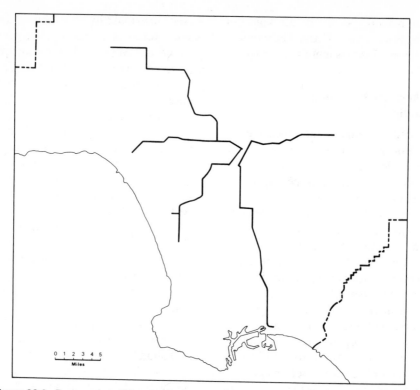

Figure 20.2. Recommended Five-Corridor system. Source: Redrafted from: Southern California Rapid Transit District, *Final Report, May 1968.* p. 10.

commonly, RTD). Its charge was similar to that of the MTA: to operate the bus lines and to plan for and construct a rapid transit system. But there were some important differences. The RTD had the power of eminent domain, and, after a successful referendum, the right to tax and to issue general obligation bonds. Too, the directors were no longer appointed by the governor but were to represent the local governments. There was more to come; in 1966, the legislature actually appropriated funds for engineering and planning studies.

RTD, with considerable fanfare, eventually unveiled its proposal. For the first time, in November, 1968, the region would get a chance to vote for or against rapid transit—and the taxes to pay for it. The proposed system consisted of an eighty-nine mile "dual rail system" of which about twenty miles were subway or tunnel, serving sixty-six stations. The system focused on downtown Los Angeles and had five corridors: Wilshire to Barrington, San Fernando Valley (through Hollywood, Cahuenga Pass, out Sherman Way to Tampa Avenue), San Gabriel Valley (San Bernardino Freeway median to El Monte), Long Beach, and finally to the Los Angeles Airport (extending to Rosecrans Avenue). The proposed line ran in a subway in areas of high property values: downtown Los Angeles, the Wilshire corridor, Hollywood, and through the Santa Monica Mountains. In other areas, it was to be located in a depressed open cut or on elevated "skyways." The trains could reach speeds of seventy-five miles an hour: however, when stations stops were included they would average forty miles an hour. In addition, a network of one hundred fifteen new bus lines consisting of three hundred miles of routes were to feed passengers to the transit stations. The estimated cost of the system was $2.5 billion to be financed by a one-half cent increase in the sales tax.

Citizen interest in the proposal was high and favorable arguments were numerous. Although many freeways had been built, congestion during the rush hour was common. The transit plan was supposed to divert "about 20 percent of the medium and long haul rush hour traffic along the five corridors" (Southern California Rapid Transit District, 1968, pp. cc-3) and thus furnish significant traffic relief. Too, "every trip made by Rapid Transit instead of by auto will make a contribution to the reduction of smog. . . ." Safety would be enhanced: The New York Transit Authority had not had a single fatality in thirty-nine years whereas the Los Angeles County freeways were averaging one hundred sixty-three fatalities every year. The transit system would improve the mobility of the seventeen percent of the households which had no car and the one-third of the county's women of driving age who did not have a drivers' license. The traveler would save time and reduce auto operating and parking costs. And finally, "more than two-thirds of the entire population of Los Angeles County live within ten minutes travel time of the recommended routes" and "42 percent of the estimated 1980 total employment in Los Angeles County will be employed within one mile of the Rapid Transit System" (Southern California Rapid Transit District, 1968, p. RTD-11). Support came from the downtown business community and from others who felt that a city should not be wholly dependent on the automobile. Nearly one-half million dollars was spent to "sell" the rapid transit proposition. The *Los Angeles Times,* however, opposed the proposal.

Opposition arguments, predictably, focused mainly on two issues. The cost of the project and the method of financing were ob-vious targets. The $2.5 billion price tag was said to be the largest ever submitted to a group of voters anywhere. The RTD had originally discussed financing the lines by an increase in property taxes, but switched to what was felt to be a more politically feasible sales tax. However, many argued that as land values around transit stations would soar in value, some means should be devised to tap this new wealth to help finance the line. Others felt the cost was simply too great for the county taxpayers to bear. The second argument was that whereas all the people would pay for the line, the transit system would actually benefit very few people. This would be true not only because many parts of the county were a long way from the lines, but also because the population was too dispersed to be served by any transit system. Anyway, southern California was automobile country and its residents would never leave their cars for rapid transit.

Other complaints were directed to the specifics of the plan. The economics of extending the line beyond Compton to Long Beach were questioned. It was alleged that the extension was political—an attempt to pick up votes from the harbor city. Criticism was directed to the omission of a line along the corridor of the Santa Ana Freeway—apparently a line was not included there because it would primarily benefit the residents of Orange County who would pay no taxes toward the cost of building the line. Residents of the San Fernando Valley were not happy because the line in their area was to be a "skyway," but they were told that to put it underground would be too expensive, particularly considering the pattern of flood control channels and sewer lines which would have to be rerouted. The line to the airport, it was charged, would run through an area of thin patronage, and was put in primarily to serve the airport. If this was so, opponents argued, why should not the airport itself pay some, maybe half, of its cost. Finally, the single focus on downtown Los Angeles was an additional objection.

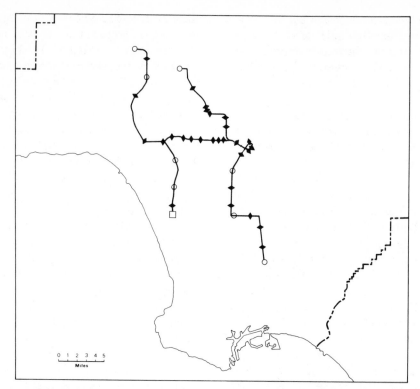

Figure 20.3. The H Plan proposed by Abraham Falick. Source: Based on Abraham J. Falick, *Transport Planning in Los Angeles: A Geo-Economic Analysis.* Ph.D. Dissertation in Geography, UCLA. 1970. p. 270.

All of the years of planning and preparation were for naught. On election day only 44.73 percent of the voters voted yes while a sixty percent majority was necessary for a bond issue to carry. Supporters took some consolation in the fact that over a million persons voted yes. RTD felt the defeat was caused by "a negative reaction to bonding and taxes as such, without regard to the purpose." However, independent analysis of the voting pattern dismissed this reaction as too simplistic. These detailed studies found, for example, that generally voters living within two miles of a station favored the measure by a slight majority, and that "the effect in outlying areas of voters' realizations that they would not be served by the system diminished the total vote by about five percent." In addition, "both low and high-income levels resulted in a more favorable vote than middle-income levels." The poor presumably supported the measure because they thought they might use the line; the rich because they thought it was a good idea and the cost was not a deterrent to them. Blacks were highly supportive, Mexican-Americans less so, and Orientals only slightly more favorable than whites. "When all this is said, the task remains to devise a system that all groups, particularly the numerous middle class, will find appealing." (Stipak, 1972.)

The "H" Plan of A. J. Falick

As an alternative, Dr. Abraham J. Falick, then a Planning Economist with the Los Angeles City Planning Commission, proposed a smaller scale rapid transit system with a quite different alignment. Although never officially adopted by any public agency, Falick's plan (Falick, 1970, pp. 260–302), illustrated by Figure 20.3, brings out some significant rapid transit issues. The H system would extend from California State University, Los Angeles, through the downtown and out Wilshire Boulevard to Westwood. A northeast leg would go up Vermont Avenue, through Hollywood and Cahuenga Pass to a terminal in North Hollywood. A third line would begin downtown, proceed to Exposition Park, down Avalon Boulevard to Watts. The northwest line would extend from Westwood/UCLA through Sepulveda Pass to a terminal west of Van Nuys. Access to the airport would be by a line running south from Century City. An expanded bus feeder line would be an integral part of the system. The line itself would run in a subway under Wilshire and downtown; much of the rest of the line would be a "skyway." Like the RTD plan, the H plan was designed to supplement rather than replace the automobile.

A close examination of the H plan routing reveals that the entire system would be located within the boundaries of Los Angeles and Beverly Hills. This shorter line not only would reduce the cost considerably, but, more importantly, voter approval would be needed only from the voters in these two cities. The large majorities rolled up by the negative voters in the suburban areas could be avoided completely.

The alignment of the H Plan has additional advantages. Instead of a single focus on downtown Los Angeles, this plan has a second point of convergence in the Westwood, Century City, Beverly Hills area. Thus, not only is congestion in the central core reduced, but the Wilshire Boulevard Corridor is given additional stimulus. Secondly, the routes reach into the most densely populated east and southeast parts of the city, tapping the low income Chicano and black residential areas. Further, the plan provides two corridors from the San Fernando Valley to the core areas, not only by way of Cahuenga Pass, but also via the

Sepulveda route. (One reservation must be made here. Ordinary rail transit vehicles cannot surmount the grades in Sepulveda Pass, and Falick proposed using tracked air cushion vehicles instead. If this technology were not available, then expensive tunneling would be necessary.) The Sepulveda route gives the San Fernando Valley residents access to the western core area without going downtown first. Furthermore, the airport line can now serve the entire Wilshire Corridor, the downtown and the west San Fernando Valley.

The treatment of the stations and terminals as active components of the system is another major difference between Falick's H Plan and the RTD proposals. Not only should they be designed to facilitate "across the platform transition" with bus feeder lines, but they should be considered as economic activity points and, as such, generators of considerable revenue. Station or terminal buildings should attract such functions as "a supermarket, medical/dental/legal/ real estate offices, savings and loan and bank offices, and even a child care center or elementary school (for convenience of working mothers)" (Falick, 1970, p. 280). If located with care, it might be possible to lease the air rights above the stations for the construction of office buildings. Leasing of station space and air rights above the stations to businessmen might make individual stations self-supporting. Not only that, the city might create an agency to develop real estate in station areas at a profit and thus reduce the total cost of the transit system.

Although originally planned as a Los Angeles-Beverly Hills system, the H Plan lines are located in such a way that cities outside the system could easily link up with them if and when they wished. Compton, whose voters have always supported rapid transit, might want to build a short connection to Watts. Santa Monica, also favorably disposed to transit, would be able to join via Westwood. Pasadena could link up with the system at the CSULA terminal, and the cities in the San

Gabriel Valley might want to extend that line, conceivably as far as Pomona. The South Bay cities could build north to the Airport. Inglewood might want to construct a line to the Forum-Hollywood Park area, and so on. Extensions could also be considered within Los Angeles, connecting the two Valley terminals, or, if traffic warrants, building westward into the valley. Once a start is made, a system could be put together as conditions and sentiment dictate. Actually, the next transit proposal was not to be restricted to a city or two; rather, it was a large scale system, the product of transportation planners of several counties.

Southern California Rapid Transit District Proposal of 1974

"Public transportation gets another chance at the polls" was the way the newspapers greeted a new RTD proposal of 1974. A product of many years of planning and coordination with neighboring counties, its purpose was "to improve public transportation through the development of a modern rapid transit system and expanded local transportation network" (Herbert, 1974, p. 1). Basically, the ballot measure was a "financial tool" to generate money to enlarge and upgrade the existing bus fleet and to "provide local money to start building a high-speed transit network." The money, $4.7 billion, would come from a one-cent increase in the sales tax. The plans were to buy 1,000 new buses and to begin construction of a one hundred forty-five mile, high speed, fixed-guideway transit network. Orange County had a similar proposal with the same increase in sales tax and its proposed fifty-five mile transit network tied in with the Los Angeles County system. Clearly this was both a better prepared effort and a more ambitious proposal than the 1968 affair. Mayor Bradley, one of its strongest backers, proclaimed, "it is now or never. Either we do it November 5th or we will never see a rapid transit system built in our lifetime." (Herbert, 1974, Oct. 27, p. 5.)

The public attitude was thought to be more favorable toward rapid transit in 1974 than in 1968. There was growing disenchantment with freeways. Concern over the effect of the automobile on the environment was high. The energy crisis had now arrived; memories of gasoline shortages during the Arab oil boycott were fresh in the voters' minds. Gasoline prices had doubled. New air pollution laws required major modifications in gasoline engines, making the automobile less satisfactory to drive. What would the new transit system do about all this? "It reduces our reliance on the automobile; it can turn back the tide of congestion, diminish unnecessary fuel consumption and alleviate air pollution." In addition, matching funds were thought to be available from the federal government provided there were local transit funds to match.

The advocates of the transit measure were well organized and comprised most of the community leaders, including many who in the past had been in the opposite camp. The president of a major oil company was the chairman of a Citizens' Committee organizing the campaign for the proposition. The Automobile Club of Southern California was now supporting rapid transit. The *Los Angeles Times*, in a shift from its previous position, urged a yes vote. The Sierra Club supported it. Tom Bradley had just been elected mayor of Los Angeles as a strong advocate of transit. Several fringe taxpayers groups were opposed. Some planners argued against the measure, feeling Los Angeles was too diffuse and too little focused on downtown for rapid transit to be successful. They also argued that in other cities where transit systems were built most of the riders had been diverted from buses, not automobiles. Some of the routes were criticized. In the San Fernando Valley, the "route is over marginal land such as flood control channels and freight railroad tracks rather than following the strong urban spine of Ventura Boulevard, two miles to the south." Suburban leaders were opposed. The mayors and

Chambers of Commerce of eighteen suburban communities took out a full-page advertisement in the *Los Angeles Times* the day before the election urging a no vote. They insisted that the poor would pay the tax for a system "for the benefit of major corporations along Wilshire Boulevard and downtown Los Angeles who will profit most by so-called rapid transit." (Los Angeles Mayors Committee, 1974, p. 27.)

In the summer of 1974 the national mood was turning pessimistic. Stories about a recession, even a possible depression, were daily newspaper features. Inflation was increasing month by month. Then, in a masterpiece of bad timing, just three months before the election, contract talks between RTD and their employees broke down. All of its bus drivers, mechanics, and maintenance personnel went on strike. Not a bus moved for sixty-eight days, dramatically illustrating the vulnerability of public transit to work stoppages. When the voters went to the polls in November, they turned down the sales tax increase which would have permitted the start of rapid transit by a vote of 43.3 percent for, 56.7 percent against. This was a slightly worse defeat than in 1968. Not all jurisdictions were opposed. The measure carried the city of Los Angeles with a fifty-four percent majority, Beverly Hills had a sixty-one percent yes vote, and Compton was the most supportive with seventy-one percent voting yes. Orange County, on the other hand, voted against the proposal by a wide margin, only 37.6 percent were in favor. The *Los Angeles Times* laid the defeat to the unwillingness of the voter to add to his tax burden in a time of inflation. The paper deplored the result, feeling it was a serious setback to transit plans for the area and making it much more difficult to obtain federal funding for a transit network.

Baxter Ward's Sunset Coast Line

With the defeat of the long-planned and widely supported RTD 1974 proposal most people felt the chance for voter approval of any rapid transit system was remote. Supervisor Baxter Ward, a member of the RTD Board of Directors and a railroad enthusiast, was not discouraged. His staff put together a proposal for a two hundred thirty-two mile rail transit system, the most extensive yet, located along freeways, flood control channels, and railroad rights-of-way. He labeled it the "Sunset Coast Line" and sold it as a modern version of "Big Red Cars." The cost of construction was estimated at $5.8 billion; again financing was to be by a one-cent increase in the sales tax. Unveiled early in 1976, community hearings and the usual planning tools were sidestepped, and the issue put on the primary election ballot of June 8, 1976.

Arguments pro and con were brought to a climax late in May by a series of lengthy articles in the *Los Angeles Times*. Although presenting both sides of the issue and including a piece by Baxter Ward himself, the general tenor of the articles was strongly negative. "Rapid Transit—No Guaranteed Gasoline Savings," "Transit Plan Offers Little Improvement for L.A. Air," "Transit Projects Plagued by Cost Overruns," and "Rail Rapid Transit: the Doubts Persist," were some of the headlines of the articles. In the end, in a switch from its position two years earlier, the *Times* advised a no vote on the transit proposal. "Wrong Way Transit" they called it, objecting mainly to the sole utilization of rails, with the tax money committed entirely to the operation of rail cars and with no provision at all for funding bus operation. Although Mayor Bradley and the Long Beach City Council supported it, the Los Angeles City Council did not. Some planners felt it did not fit into the city's master plan. The Mayor of Pomona, once again, led the suburbs in opposition.

With local leadership once more divided, it was perhaps not surprising that the voters gave the Baxter Ward proposal the soundest defeat yet. Only 665,368 persons voted for it, a mere 40.6 percent of the votes cast. This contrasts with more than a million yes votes in

1968. Of the incorporated cities, only Compton supported the proposal, with a yes vote of fifty-eight percent.

Caltrans, Disciplined Freeways and Diamond Lanes

As recently as July, 1978, the Los Angeles County Transportation Commission, a new agency, surveyed public opinion on the possibility of raising sales taxes to pay for "a rapid transit system and improvements in bus transportation." Fifty-eight percent of those surveyed said they would support a tax increase. Effort during the next few years was concentrated on a "starter" rapid transit line. Beginning at Union Station, it would run as a subway under Wilshire Boulevard as far as Fairfax Avenue, turn north to serve Hollywood, then continue on the surface and on elevated tracks through Cahuenga Pass to a terminal in North Hollywood. This fifteen mile transit line would run through the most densely populated sector of Los Angeles where densities are as great as in cities where rapid transit lines have been successful in the past. While some money was available locally and at the state level, the bulk of the several billion dollars needed to construct the line would have to come from Washington, and prospects of that happening soon seem dubious.

The difficulty of financing rapid transit has shifted the emphasis back to the automobile, the bus, and the freeway. The California Department of Transportation (Caltrans) moved to a policy of building no new freeways, though the closure of a few gaps in the system continued. Caltrans began putting an emphasis upon more efficient operation of the existing freeway system, under the concept of "disciplined freeways." A major feature in this program was the installation of "metered timing" at on-ramps, aimed at controlling the rate of freeway entry in such a way as to maintain a free-flowing traffic pattern. Another goal of metering the on-ramps was the diversion of short distance users off the freeways unto surface streets. In reality, of course, it was the drivers that the planners hoped to discipline.

Cars on the Los Angeles freeways during the rush hours have an occupancy rate of only 1.2 persons. This is a fascinating figure to planners: if it could be increased only slightly, even to 1.4, the freeways could move appreciably more people. How can this be done? As one incentive to car pool, some metered on-ramps have been designed with preferential lanes for car pools and buses, enabling them to drive onto the freeway without waiting. As a further step to induce car pooling and bus riding, in the spring of 1976 Caltrans opened what was to be a one-year experimental project on the Santa Monica Freeway. The fast lanes of the freeway (one in each direction) were marked with diamonds (the federal symbol for exclusive-use high-occupancy roadways) and reserved for the use of buses and cars with three or more occupants during the commuting hours. At the same time, the ramp meters were set to severely restrict the inflow of vehicles with one or two passengers. The purpose, it was announced, was to "conserve energy and reduce air pollution."

All hell broke loose. The Santa Monica Freeway serves a vocal and influential segment of the population, including, apparently, a number of reporters and editors of the *Los Angeles Times*. Ray Herbert, the paper's Urban Affairs Editor, covered the event in depth, reporting the negative reaction of most of the motorists. Editorial followed editorial. "Dishonesty with Diamonds" questioned Caltrans optimistic data, and by June the conclusion was "A Total Flop." The Diamond Lane experiment apparently did shorten the commuting time for bus riders and those in three-member car pools, but these were relatively few—the exact figures were in dispute. However, it had predictable side effects. Motorists were irate at the long delays at the on-ramps—five, ten, fifteen minutes or more. Paralleling streets were jammed. There were appreciably more accidents on the freeway and on paralleling streets. The Highway Patrol was kept busy ticketing numerous Diamond Lane violators. After five months, the experiment came to a sudden end. A judge ruled that it had been put in operation without the filing of a needed environmental impact statement. He ordered all traces of the Diamond Lane removed.

It hardly seems possible that the Diamond Lane experiment could have achieved its goals of reduced air pollution and energy conservation. Although some new car pooling occurred, twice a day tens of thousands of cars were standing with engines idling, waiting to get on the freeway. Furthermore, the design of the experiment seemed fatally flawed. Assuming a downtown Los Angeles work destination, persons who had chosen a residence location that was relatively close in (anywhere east of the San Diego Freeway) and were driving alone were now penalized by long waits at ramp meters. Others, who lived farther out— Santa Monica, the Palisades, Malibu, or Marina del Rey—had no such waits. They could simply enter at the unmetered beginnings of the freeway or via the San Diego interchange. If the Santa Monica Freeway Diamond Lanes would have been made permanent, it would seem that people might be encouraged to live farther from their work rather than closer. Then, too, there was a feeling that the decisions about freeway operation were being made four hundred miles away in Sacramento by persons afflicted with the northern California hostility toward Los Angeles. For example, the *Los Angeles Times* (June 24, 1976) felt that one motive behind the Diamond Lanes was a state and federal governmental notion that Los Angeles' dependence on the automobile is not only excessive but "indeed rather sinful. They would teach us a lesson, these latter-day Prohibitionists: we shall be weaned of our dependency, and a little force will probably do us good."

Americans do not like to be "disciplined." In a survey of some seven hundred persons using the Santa Monica Freeway taken just after the experiment was ended, over eighty-four percent of those interviewed said that if it had been put to a vote they would have voted against the Diamond Lanes. Plans for similar experiments on other freeways apparently have been put aside. A new median strip was constructed on the northbound San Diego Freeway and prepared as a Diamond Lane. The RTD found that its new buses slowed down to twenty-five miles an hour going over Sepulveda Pass (the old buses slowed to twenty). It was obvious they could not maintain speeds needed for the fast lane and, therefore, these proposed Diamond Lanes would be of no use to them. Again, the concept seemed poorly thought out and the whole idea was abandoned.

A Bus Rapid Transit System?

Some transportation planners feel that for regions like the Los Angeles Metropolis, with an extensive freeway system already built, buses could be used as "rapid transit" vehicles. Doing so, they say, would avoid the extremely high capital costs of a rail transit system. (It is claimed, for example, that the actual cost of a ride on BART is $4.00 with fares bringing in an average of only $1.00.) Further, they argue, if buses are comfortable, air-conditioned, with a high probability of seat availability, running on a reliable schedule, and with frequent service and reasonable travel times, they can attract just as many riders as a mass rapid transit system with similar characteristics. They do not believe the notion that commuters are attracted to rail rapid transit because they perceive it as more modern and "urbane" than buses. A reasonable travel time, they continue, could be provided by using bus priority lanes on surface streets, preferred access at freeway entrances, reserved freeway lanes, or even by simply flowing with the traffic on "disciplined" freeways. Buses have an additional advantage—at the end of their run they can circulate on residential streets, offering something not far from door-to-door service. This feature, and the fact that no transfer is necessary (from bus to rail vehicles), eliminates a time-consuming mode change and adds to their travel time advantage.

The bus as a freeway "rapid transit" vehicle immediately faces two major problems—freeway location and the "nonrecurrent event." Freeways were built through sparsely populated areas where land acquisition costs were low. For the same reason, their routes avoid business districts and other employment centers. Rapid transit lines, by contrast, are most effective running through dense population and business concentrations such as the Wilshire corridor and downtown Los Angeles. So the original decision not to run the freeways through business centers via "motorway buildings" has now come back to haunt the transportation planner. For now, to reach the desired destinations, the commuter bus has to leave the freeway and traverse the often congested city streets. For example, to reach Century City from the San Diego Freeway a bus must use crowded Santa Monica Boulevard. And, of course, no freeway serves the Wilshire corridor, an area of high population density and many work destinations. Furthermore, to the extent that buses are forced to mix with the regular traffic on surface streets or freeways, they are subject to delays owing to the "nonrecurrent event." By this delightful term, the planners mean anything from an overturned truck to a stranded blonde, either of which bring traffic to a slow crawl for miles in each direction. As reliability of schedule is one of the most important factors in the decision to shift from automobile to transit, these unpredictable delays could be fatal to bus patronage.

Reasonable travel times and a reliable schedule would be more likely if the bus were given an exclusive right-of-way over as much of its route as possible. One could imagine exclusive bus lanes on surface streets, busways built above or beside freeways, and even subways for buses under the Los Angeles downtown. This would increase the cost of the system considerably and perhaps, if all the suggestions were implemented, it would approach that of a conventional rapid transit system. In a sense Los Angeles already has a sample of the bus as a "rapid transit" vehicle in the eleven-mile El Monte Busway—two separate lanes along the San Bernardino Freeway. Unfortunately, as it nears the downtown, the special lanes end and the buses are forced to join the regular traffic at Mission Road. Even so, bus riders save several minutes of commuting time and considerable money, and within a year after its opening, some 7,750 commuters were using it daily.

20. Suggested Readings

Southern California Association of Governments. *Regional Transportation Plan.* Los Angeles: Southern California Association of Governments, 1979.
This legally required document covers every aspect of regional transportation from bikeways to airports. It is revised periodically.

Southern California Rapid Transit District. *Final Report. May, 1968.* Los Angeles: Southern California Rapid Transit District, 1968.
This report includes a brief history of rapid transit proposals in Los Angeles as well as a detailed discussion of the five-corridor system that was recommended in 1968.

CHAPTER 21

Political Boundaries Divide the Metropolis

Figure 21.1. At least five incorporated cities and several areas of unincorporated county territory are included in this view which looks westward toward Santa Monica Bay, January 19, 1968. (Photo courtesy Spence Collection / Department of Geography, UCLA.)

"Do you remember grandma's crazy quilt? Multicolored splotches of zany shapes on a large square bedcover. Call the whole bedcover Los Angeles County, the zany shapes the outlines of its 78 scattered cities and intervening spaces, areas not included in any city, unincorporated territory." Preston Hotchkiss (1973, p. B–2).

"Digging still deeper into the question of why the metropolitan area is fragmented into competing governmental units, one must ask who gains and who loses from such organization." Risa Palm (1981, p. 73).

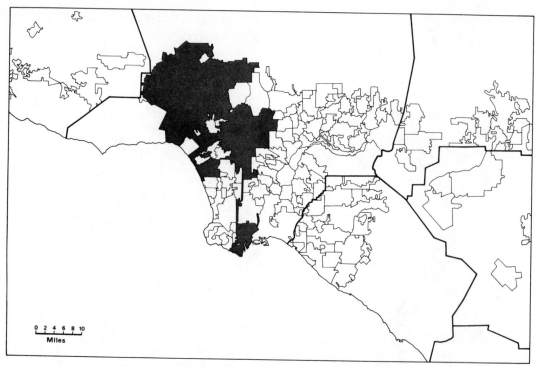

Figure 21.2. The political pattern of the Los Angeles Metropolis.

The Los Angeles Metropolis is considered as a single unit in this book and whenever possible data has been adjusted to fit the whole region. Although the Metropolis as we have defined it has no independent legal existence, considering it as a unit generally makes sense. Similar urban forms—houses, apartments, factories, office buildings, shopping centers—are widespread over its valleys and plains. Its residents treat it as a single "city" for living in their work and play patterns. Automobiles and trucks move at will along its freeways and surface streets from one end of the region to another. The region functions in many ways as a single economic entity. Yet the Los Angeles Metropolis is overlain with a complex web of boundary lines dividing it into a "crazy quilt" of political units of all kinds. It contains parts of five different counties and one hundred eighteen individual incorporated cities. These cities vary in size from slightly more than one to about four hundred sixty-five square miles

and have populations ranging from less than one hundred to almost three million. Even so, scores of communities remain unincorporated. In addition, the region is divided into nearly one hundred school districts, perhaps fifty water districts, and hundreds of other districts providing health services, parks, cemeteries and so on. Each unit provides services, each collects taxes, each has a greater or lesser impact on the life of the people in the region. In terms of political administration the region is hopelessly fragmented.

Yet even the most important of these political lines—county boundaries and city limits—are seldom noticed by the average resident. One moves from Santa Monica to Los Angeles to Culver City and Inglewood, for example, without being aware of passing through these jurisdictions at all. One travels unknowingly from Los Angeles County to Orange County and from Riverside to San Bernardino County. Occasionally, however, a change in the landscape is so sudden and startling that it is noticed by everyone—although the fact that a political boundary is responsible for the shift may not be recognized. Driving eastward on Sunset Boulevard in Beverly Hills a motorist travels through a neighborhood of large, high class residences, surrounded by expansive yards. Suddenly, at Phyllis Street, the scene abruptly changes—now towering multistory apartments, office buildings and commercial buildings crowd the avenue. What has happened? A political boundary has been crossed: the line between the City of Beverly Hills and the unincorporated portion of Los Angeles County known as the "Sunset Strip." Zoning regulations, tax rates, business codes, developmental history have all changed. Numerous examples of this phenomena can be located. For example, the boundary between the cities of Vernon and Maywood (which runs down a narrow alley) separates a wholly residential section from solid blocks of factories and warehouses. Too, a striking exception to freedom of movement and unnoticed boundaries is to be found in the City of Rolling Hills. A white rail fence eight miles long broken only by four guarded gates leading to its private roads marks the boundary of this "horsy" city. But these examples, generally, are exceptions. More often, for even the most sophisticated observer, all that can be noticed in crossing a political line are minor things: street numbers may change suddenly, the street name may change, street signs may be of a different color, fire hydrants may be of a new style, or the pavement may show signs of being of varying ages where the political units meet.

In most cases, however, although there may be little change in the visible landscape, political boundaries have a significant effect on the people involved nonetheless. The *Los Angeles Times* tells the story of a family that moved from a Westlake Village apartment to a Westlake Village condominium four blocks away. "They now live in a city, in a different county represented by different politicians and

serviced by different sheriffs and fire departments and different utility companies charging different rates. If they had children they would have been transferred to different schools" (Willman, 1972, p. 1). "Westlake Village" appears to the observer to be a unified community. Actually, the western section is part of the incorporated city of Thousand Oaks (and in Ventura County); the eastern part, incorporated as Westlake Village, is in Los Angeles County. Unification in the future seems virtually impossible as state law prohibits annexing territory across county boundaries.

Large Units Are Soon Divided and Fragmented

When California was organized as American territory the region's existing political units were simply continued. The original Los Angeles County was of enormous size including all of the Metropolis except the Ventura County portion and extended eastward to the Colorado River. The original American city of Los Angeles had the same area as the old pueblo: four square leagues or about twenty-eight square miles. The seat of government for both county and city was in downtown Los Angeles. Division of the area began with the formation of San Bernardino County in 1853. Thirty-six years later, as agricultural settlement increased, farmers to the south felt that Los Angeles was far away and unresponsive to their needs. Orange County was formed with its seat in Santa Ana in 1889. Still, the counties were large and had the potential for governmental administration on a metropolitan scale. This arrangement was not to last for long.

Small agricultural centers were springing up in outlying areas, many grew rapidly during the boom of the 1880s, and the desire for local government increased. If a resident needed the "law," a sheriff's deputy had to come out from Los Angeles. Any request for road improvement, fire protection, or anything else had to be taken to a distant county seat, a considerable journey in those horse and buggy days.

The state legislature responded to the general desire for "home rule" by passing laws providing for the incorporation and organization of local governments in 1883. Any settlement with a population of five hundred or more was permitted to incorporate. The procedure was simple. A petition signed by one hundred qualified electors was presented to the county supervisors; they could delete but not add territory. An election was scheduled, a majority of the residents voting decided the issue. Soon the number of signatures required was reduced to fifty and the incorporation law remained essentially unchanged for half a century. Annexation, joining territory to an existing city, was also easy, permitted to any contiguous territory whenever the residents or landowners were willing.

The rush to incorporate began. From 1883 until 1930 fifty-five new cities were incorporated in Los Angeles County and another twelve in Orange County. In addition, the city of Los Angeles annexed territory so as to increase its size to some four hundred sixty-five square miles. Less than seventy-five percent of the population lived in incorporated cities at the turn of the century, by 1930 cities contained eighty-five percent of the people. Political fragmentation had begun.

In 1933 the law was changed to make incorporation more difficult. The petition was required to have signatures of residents who represented twenty-five percent of the value of the property in the proposed city. The results were as expected—over a twenty year period only one city was incorporated. Then in 1954 conditions changed again, as will be explained, and in the next twenty years forty-seven new incorporations were formed in these two counties.

Why the rush to incorporate around the turn of the century? Why did it become popular again recently? The desire for local control is an obvious motive through the years although the use to which it would be put varied enormously. Local control would assure local officials who would respond to local desires. Thus they could be counted on to close down saloons, permit racetracks, keep out sewer farms, preserve large estates, permit oil wells, discourage industry or encourage it, as the local folk desired. Fear was often the activating force, fear of losing control through annexation to a larger community, fear of swarms of new residents that might upset traditional patterns, fear of any change that might raise taxes. Occasionally, and with increasing frequency, it became obvious to some that local control, properly managed, could raise property values enormously and generate a great deal of tax revenue which would not have to be shared with the general metropolis. For these later cities it was not so much fear as avarice that provided the incorporation motive.

The Early Wave of Incorporations — 1883–1930

Pasadena, often the leader, was the first settlement in Los Angeles County to take advantage of the new incorporation laws, becoming a city in June, 1886. Although many arguments emphasized the desire for better services, the emotional issue was the need for local control to deal with a saloon on Colorado Street. Once incorporated the temperance-minded citizens promptly closed the offending business. It simply moved to Pasadena's south side, a district that had refused to be included within the new city. At this location the tavern received its license from the Board of Supervisors and "kept open on Sundays and did a thriving business" (Carew, 1930, p. 349). This was too much for the local residents and South Pasadena was incorporated in 1888. Meanwhile, Santa Monica had voted for incorporation in the waning days of 1886, mainly "to check the lawlessness of the Los Angeles hoodlums, both male and female, who report thither by the hundred every Sunday" (Bigger and Kitchen, 1952, p. 82). Pomona, too, was having difficulties, "a man gets just a little too much to carry home conveniently and lies in the gutter, where no one touches him, our constabulary having no power to act," (Bigger and Kitchen, 1952, p. 83) and voted to incorporate in 1888. With similar motives Monrovia incorporated in 1887 and Compton in 1888. Other incorporations of that period, Redondo Beach, Whittier, Azusa, Long Beach, Covina and Alhambra, seemed to be motivated by the desire for better roads and other local services. Significantly, these early cities were separated from each other geographically (even South Pasadena had a hill between it and Pasadena) and usually were surrounded by sparsely populated agricultural land.

Fear of absorption by larger neighbors, the "Big City Bogey," has been the motivating force behind innumerable incorporations, increasing in importance as the possibilities multiplied. The city of Los Angeles, however, began expanding early, and many of the surrounding communities incorporated to maintain their independence. Los Angeles was continuously moving westward and the community of Beverly Hills and its five hundred fifty residents feared absorption by the larger city. Their fears seem well-founded—Owens Valley water was being stored in a reservoir in Franklin Canyon north of the community, pipes from it were being laid under the area's streets. The residents voted sixty-six to thirteen to incorporate in 1914 and have retained their independence although they have been completely surrounded by Los Angeles. The same westward movement motivated the Standard Oil Company to promote the incorporation of land around its refinery as El Segundo in 1917 to keep it from "falling to Los

Angeles." Almost every city that the boundary of Los Angeles now touches incorporated with similar motives. Surprisingly, the one area that appears to have been in the greatest "danger" through the years, "East Los Angeles," adjacent to the original pueblo has not been annexed and remains unincorporated: half a dozen incorporation attempts have failed.

It was not just Los Angeles that could generate fear. Frightened by talk of "Greater Alhambra" the old settlements of San Gabriel and San Marino, wishing to preserve their identity, went the incorporation route in 1913. Similarly, Signal Hill, fearing annexation by ambitious Long Beach, incorporated in 1924. Scene of a "world class" petroleum discovery three years earlier, at the time it became a city it contained perhaps 1,200 oil derricks, one hundred thirty oil companies and 1,800 people. Incorporation, it was argued, would enable it to continue its oil production without the restrictions and ordinances of the average metropolitan city. Long Beach, disgruntled, shut off the water it had been furnishing the area.

Fear, not of annexation, but that a neighbor might use the community as the location of a "sewer farm" spurred several incorporations. The "Tri-Cities" (Pasadena, Alhambra, South Pasadena) planned a joint operation featuring a large sewer farm located between the settlements of Monterey Park and Montebello. To prevent this the entire area was incorporated in 1916. Then, the battle won, Montebello separated from the larger unit, forming a separate city in 1920. Similarly, the city of Covina built a sewer farm in the midst of an agricultural district outside of its borders. Although the area was entirely rural, with no business center, the residents incorporated as West Covina in 1923 and shut down the sewer farm.

Fear of "Southern California's foes of sin, led by the Anti-Saloon League" in neighboring communities reportedly weighed heavily on the mind of E. J. (Lucky) Baldwin in 1903. Baldwin was world renowned as a notorious roué and libertine and owner of Rancho Santa Anita, the location of "stables worthy of the aristocrats of the turf he was breeding" (Glasscock, 1933, p. 236). Nearby was his subdivision of Arcadia and the fashionable Oakwood Hotel. A racetrack, he thought, would fit in nicely, but what would the neighbors think? So Baldwin incorporated the entire area as Arcadia, managing the affair, we are told, by temporarily settling "Huntington's illiterate peon gang" on the site to meet the population requirements. After a feast of watermelon, the story continues, they voted thirty-five to none for incorporation and elected a city council composed of Baldwin and his employees (Bigger and Kitchen, 1952, p. 89). Although he was seventy-five at the time, he is said to have celebrated the victory relaxing "on his cool, vine-clad porch, surrounded by three charming brunettes," discussing with reporters the possibility of Arcadia becoming the Monte Carlo of the West.

Less glamorous but equally significant was the incorporation of Vernon in 1905. Here, just south of Los Angeles, farm owners organized by John Leonis and the Furlong brothers led the fight against annexation to the larger city and instead promoted incorporation. Their goal was to increase the value of their farmland by selling it as sites for industry. However, there was little interest in establishing manufacturing in the area at the time. While waiting, the incorporators conceived the notion of producing revenue for the city and themselves by turning Vernon into a "Sporting Town." Prize fighting was illegal in most places, but world championships were settled in Vernon. Soon an 11,000 seat indoor arena was built. Sunday baseball was "blue lawed" out of respectable communities, but the Vernon Tigers played their home games on Sunday morning. Saloons were unwelcome in many places; in Vernon the "Longest Bar in the World" never closed. Eventually, as the Metropolitan mar-

ket expanded after World War I, industry was attracted to Vernon as its founders had hoped: by 1925 three hundred plants employed 15,000 workers. The attraction was low cost operation and for many decades property taxes were the lowest of any community in California. Services that were needed by industry were well developed, amenities for residents were omitted. There were few residents. Vernon's population has fallen from a high of 1,269 in 1930 to today's eighty-nine, as no residential building permits have been issued for many years. In 1979 property in Vernon was assessed at more than one billion dollars (over $4,000,000 for each resident) and sales tax rebates amounted to almost $50,000 per capita. Perhaps 65,000 persons work within the city limits. Many in the Metropolis learned much from Vernon, and its lessons were to be applied later in the century.

A number of other cities, mainly agricultural centers, also incorporated in this period; La Verne, Sierra Madre, Claremont, Glendora, and El Monte are typical examples. However, during the depression years of the 1930s regulations were changed to make incorporation more difficult. Signatures of residents who represented twenty-five percent of the value of the property of the proposed city were now required. The results were as hoped—over a 20 year period only one city, Palos Verdes Estates, 1939, was incorporated in Los Angeles County. Before we pick up the story of more recent years, the annexation activities of the large cities, particularly Los Angeles, deserve our attention.

City of Los Angeles—Regional Unification by Annexation

While much of the Metropolitan landscape was being split up into small units, the activities of the city of Los Angeles demonstrated an opposing trend. For about seventy-five years the city was busily annexing neighboring territory and consolidating many scattered communities into one massive unit. Los Angeles has grown from its original four square leagues (about twenty-eight square miles) to today's four hundred sixty-five square miles through annexation and consolidation. Annexation means the joining of territory outside a city with the municipality by mutual consent. (If the area to be annexed is inhabited, the action must be approved by popular referendum in both the area to be annexed and the receiving city.) If the area to be joined is already incorporated the technical term is consolidation. In the city of Los Angeles this process began slowly at first, then, from 1906 to 1927, the city virtually exploded over the landscape. But that was its final fling. Since 1927, with the exception of the consolidation with Tujunga in 1932, growth has essentially stopped. Activity in the last forty-five years has mainly involved annexing small parcels of land and detaching others in an attempt to straighten out the city's 315 mile long boundary.

Annexations in the early years were designed mainly to provide irrigation water and other services to adjacent areas where population had spread beyond the city's boundaries. The city's first annexation, in 1859, simply extended its border four hundred yards to the south "to bring valuable farming land within the city's irrigation system." After a court decision forbidding Los Angeles from selling water beyond its boundaries, land previously served quickly annexed. First came the residential neighborhoods now east of the city, Highland Park and Garvanza, including Sycamore Grove in the Arroyo Seco, which also, we are told, needed policing. A much larger area lying south and southwest of the city (south of Slauson, west of Arlington), was also annexed in the 1896–1899 period. Though small in comparison with what was to follow, these parcels increased the city's area by more than fifteen square miles or about fifty-three percent.

Early in the twentieth century came the annexation of the famous "shoe-string" strip during the city's push to the sea to bring within its jurisdiction Wilmington, San Pedro and the new harbor as discussed on page 222. It consisted of a wide section next to the city's southern boundary, then continued as a strip a half mile wide and sixteen miles long to the harbor. A jog was necessary to avoid the village of Gardena. When Wilmington and San Pedro were consolidated as well, an additional thirty-three square miles were added to the city's area.

Funds for the aqueduct had scarcely been approved before annexation to Los Angeles became the goal of many outlying communities wanting an assured water supply. The Los Angeles voters, however, were becoming choosy. Eleven communities voted in favor of annexation in 1907 including Gardena, Eagle Rock and Cahuenga. However, the Los Angeles voters turned them down believing the tax base of these communities would not support the services they would require. Instead, the city accepted Colgrove which lay between the northeast corner of the city and Hollywood. Hollywood, which had incorporated earlier, now needed water, petitioned to join Los Angeles and was accepted. At the same time (1910) the adjoining districts of Los Feliz-Griffith Park were also annexed, as were Bairdstown and Arroyo Seco. These additions increased the city's area by twenty-four square miles bringing the total to just over 100 square miles.

The next massive annexations came after the great debate over the disposition of Owens Valley water discussed previously. Its resolution was that the "price" of water should be annexation. On May 22, 1915, two areas of agricultural land, the San Fernando Valley (including the north slope of the Santa Monica Mountains), about one hundred seventy square miles, and Palms (roughly the area between Crenshaw and Overland), 7.3 square miles, was voted in. In one day Los Angeles almost tripled its size. Annexations of additional large areas quickly followed. Westgate, from Beverly Hills to the ocean (today's Westwood, Brentwood and Pacific Palisades) and including the Santa Monica Mountains west of Stone Canyon, about forty-nine square miles, was accepted in 1916. The West Coast Addition—the present Westchester, Los Angeles Airport and Hyperion—was annexed in 1917. Hansen Heights (the Hansen Dam area) in the San Fernando Valley was added in 1918. Los Angeles had now become the nation's largest city with 365 square miles of territory, a position it was to hold for more than four decades.

In the next six years (1922–28) thirty-four unincorporated areas and five cities joined Los Angeles—most were small parcels, many of less than a square mile. Occasionally their names suggested their locations: La Brea, Ambassador, Sawtelle, Hyde Park, Eagle Rock, Fairfax, Venice, Green Meadows, Watts, Sunland, Tuna Canyon, Mar Vista, and Barns City. Three annexations were of considerable size: Lankershim, now North Hollywood (7.4 square miles), joined the city in 1923; the Laurel Canyon Addition, the south slopes of the Santa Monica Mountains from Cahuenga Pass west to Stone Canyon (13.6 square miles), was annexed in 1923; the next year the land east of Cahuenga Pass extending to Griffith Park, known as Providencia (4.8 square miles), was added. Little further happened until the Tujunga consolidation of 1932 (8.7 square miles), the last major addition to Los Angeles.

By 1928 the expansive period, begun with so much optimism in 1913, came to a virtual halt, never to be renewed. Now the Water Board was warning city officials that the city's water supply could not be stretched much farther. In addition, extending service to newly annexed areas was proving to be enormously expensive. Too, by the late twenties incorporations in the suburbs had formed a ring around the city providing an effective barrier

to much further expansion. Finally, with the promise of Colorado River water, an event largely instigated and financed by Los Angeles, any community could be assured of abundant water by joining the Metropolitan Water District. By this action Los Angeles was instrumental in creating the conditions that made annexation to it unnecessary. For seventy-five years the city had been a powerful force for unification although its growth was halted before the suggested Los Angeles City-County consolidation was achieved. Without its expansionist policy it is clear that the Metropolis would have several score more "fragments" than it has today.

The areal growth of Los Angeles, obviously, was not the product of a well developed plan—the city simply responded to the forces of the moment. As a result the city does not have a rational, compact shape. Just the opposite is true. "The city is grotesquely shaped, like a charred scrap of paper," is the way John D. Weaver describes it (Weaver, 1980, p. 107). Its shape reminds Rodney Steiner of "a one-legged, east facing turkey with feathers ruffled" (Steiner, 1981, p. 5). Not only does Los Angeles sprawl irregularly across the landscape, political islands and enclaves break up its continuity. It has voids within it like holes in Swiss cheese. Enclosed within it are three cities, San Fernando, Beverly Hills and Culver City, as well as several important unincorporated communities—West Hollywood, Baldwin Hills and much of Marina del Rey. It surrounds Santa Monica on its landward sides. All of this disconnection and diffusion makes for inefficiencies and added expense in providing such services as police and fire protection, water, sewer service and everything else.

The expansion of Los Angeles, at first glance, was not much different from what was happening in many other American cities. New York, Philadelphia and Chicago, for example, all grew enormously in area. Philadelphia increased from 2.2 square miles to one hundred thirty in one year, 1854. New York expanded from 38.85 square miles to three hundred sixteen by a single legislative act in 1898. On the other hand, a few cities grew little. Boston was only 43.2 square miles in size when it reached a ring of suburbs uninterested in annexation. San Francisco consolidated its city and county governments in 1856 with an area of 46.4 square miles of land (and 82.6 square miles of water). In California cities cannot cross county lines and San Francisco has the same area today—more than a hundred years later. What set Los Angeles apart from other cities was that it had a relatively small population during its expansion period and the land it acquired was sparsely populated. Therefore, almost alone among large cities in America, Los Angeles had room within its corporate boundaries to accommodate many additional persons, including many of those who flocked to the Metropolis after World War II. Consequently, its population (and tax base) has been increasing in recent decades while in most other metropolitan areas growth has been confined to the suburbs while the central city experienced a declining population.

Another subtle difference from most cities is the official recognition of traditional community names within the city of Los Angeles. As large cities annexed smaller communities the community names persisted to a greater or lesser degree and many are used to identify the areas today. Yet, with the exception of New York's five boroughs, it appears that these community names persist more strongly in Los Angeles than anywhere else. A resident of Los Angeles is likely to say that he is from some community: Pacific Palisades, Hollywood, Van Nuys, Chatsworth, Granada Hills or Canoga Park, for example. Furthermore, this community identity is strong enough so that it has been officially recognized by the U.S. Post Office. Woodland Hills is an official place as far as the post office is concerned, as are many other communities. The official zip code directory lists Woodland Hills as if it were a separate city while in Chicago the community of Hyde Park is listed as Hyde Park Station, Chicago, as is Chestnut Hill Branch, Boston, and so on.

Empires in the Suburbs

Expansion was not confined to Los Angeles, suburban cities had the annexation bug, too. For example, Long Beach has grown from 3.1 to 46.3 miles, Glendale from 2.3 to 29.2 and Pasadena from 5.1 to 22.6. Many other cities have annexed enough territory to more than double their original area. Bigger and Kitchen, two UCLA political scientists, called the phenomena "Empires in the Suburbs" (Bigger and Kitchen, 1952, p. 195).

Pasadena, a city since 1886 and the most populous suburb for many decades, began its expansion in 1904. First, to the west, it annexed the Arroyo Seco, going far up into the San Gabriels as a means of protecting its water supply, and also Annendale, San Rafael Heights and Linda Vista on the far side of the Arroyo to prevent them from falling to Los Angeles. Eastward it annexed Eaton Canyon for its water wells, and took in all territory to the Sierra Madre line. Annexations to the north proceeded smoothly until blocked by the community of Altadena. Although seemingly wedged between Pasadena and the high mountains, Altadena has preferred to remain unincorporated.

Glendale was not incorporated until 1906 and started from a tiny base of only 1.5 square miles but soon dreamed of "Greater Glendale." Its first annexation to the west and south gave it access to the Southern Pacific Railroad and absorbed the community of Tropico (where it blocked the expansion of Los Angeles). It spread northward, too, into Verdugo Canyon, location of much of its water, and gradually expanded until it touched Burbank on the west and Pasadena on the east. In the 1950s Glendale boldly moved across the Verdugo Mountains, absorbed the community of

Verdugo, and then, with a strip a mile wide, spanned the densely settled La Crescenta Valley, thus imposing a barrier between the city of Los Angeles and the unincorporated communities of La Crescenta, Montrose and La Canada.

Of all the suburbs, Long Beach has been by far the most aggressive and audacious in its annexation attempts. As a result it is now the second city in the Metropolis in both area and population. Incorporated in 1887, within a decade it had annexed "Brighton Beach" and a portion of Terminal Island to the west. Although only about a square mile in area, these annexations not only have proved to be underlain with oil but also have become the basis for the city's fine harbor. Next, the city moved northward, first annexing Belmont Heights and adjacent territory plus a second large tract of land. Then the city tried an audacious ploy—it added a strip only a hundred feet wide, running northward for a mile and then extending seven miles eastward to the Orange County line. As all annexations must be of contiguous territory (that is, they must be physically touching) and cannot cross county boundaries, this narrow ribbon served to prevent any neighbor to the north from moving to the sea and preserved the intervening area for future annexation to Long Beach. The seaside communities of Belmont Shore, Alimitos Bay and Naples were indeed added to Long Beach in 1923. When annexed territory reached Signal Hill's boundaries, however, that oil-rich community quickly incorporated. Undaunted, Long Beach continued annexing territory northward to Compton and again sent out narrow strips many miles long both to the east, encircling the "Montana Ranch," and to the west. Again the ambitious city met with failure. The westward encircling ribbon was ordered disincorporated in 1926, and much of the area encircled to the east avoided the Long Beach grasp by incorporating as Lakewood in 1954.

Counties Supply Urban Services

Although the rash of incorporation and the expansion of Los Angeles and other cities absorbed many of the populated portions of Los Angeles County, numerous settled communities remained unaffected. They were able to continue without incorporating because the county began supplying them with urban quality services early and improved these services steadily. County libraries were established in 1913. The County fire department, which began as a service to forest and mountain land, soon evolved the capacity to protect structures in settled areas. Street lights and sanitary sewers were gradually provided to residents of unincorporated communities. The County Sheriff's Department added personnel and modified procedures until it resembled a city police department. Soon the level of services in unincorporated areas became as high as in many cities.

In addition, beginning in 1908, Los Angeles County began providing services to some of the incorporated cities. Cities began "contracting" (paying) the county for such things as the assessment of property, handling elections, ambulance and health services, enforcement of building regulations, street sweeping, engineering surveys, animal care and many other things. As early as 1954 the county had four hundred agreements with the cities within its borders to provide various types of services.

Generally these services were financed by county-wide property taxes, special district taxes or billed directly. However, the precise allocation of the total county costs between the unincorporated areas and the cities created unresolved controversy. At one point the League of California Cities issued a report that estimated eighty-five percent of the cost of city-like services provided to the unincorporated areas by the county were in fact paid for by the residents of the cities. Action by the legislature to remedy this situation failed. The controversy was unresolved in 1954 when to everyone's surprise a second wave of incorporation began.

The "Lakewood Plan" — Home Rule with Economy

The period 1930–1954 had been a dormant one on the local incorporation scene. However, after World War II new residents poured into the Metropolis and farmland was converted to housing tracts almost overnight. By 1954 the population of unincorporated areas of Los Angeles County was estimated at 1,135,000. The scene was set for momentous events. They were triggered by two incidents, neither of which was designed to stimulate incorporation.

In the early 1950s building activities of the Lakewood Park Corporation created an "instant city"—the community of Lakewood with 77,000 residents and a large shopping center—on what had been bean fields. Located just north of Long Beach and almost completely surrounded by a one hundred yard wide shoestring of that city, it was thought annexation was inevitable. Several parcels, in fact, did vote to join Long Beach. However, most of the new residents were satisfied with the services the County of Los Angeles was providing; many feared loss of community identity. Allies were found in the Lakewood Water and Power Company and the Southern California Gas Company which would lose their franchises with annexation. After considerable discussion, Los Angeles County expressed a willingness, for the first time, to supply under contract *all* services an incorporated city would need, including police and fire protection. The community, with this novel alternative, turned down supplications from Long Beach and incorporated as Lakewood. It was said a city could now incorporate without hiring a single employee. This was not quite true, but the large startup costs that normally generated large municipal indebtedness were eliminated.

The citizens of Lakewood were pleased with their arrangement and publicized it widely. The county was happy too, for now department heads and employee organizations had little fear that their operations would be reduced by the multiplication of new communities. Los Angeles County even set up an office to give technical assistance to community groups wanting to incorporate. The incorporation movement was further stimulated by a 1958 state law that allowed a one cent increment in the sales tax to be returned to the city of collection. Taxes collected in unincorporated areas went into the county's general fund, however, residents in these areas had no assurance that locally collected money would be used to benefit their communities. Incorporations boomed; in one four year period twenty-five additional cities were organized in Los Angeles County, more cities than had been created in any previous *decade*. No one at any governmental level had anticipated this new fragmentation.

Not only was there a rush to incorporate, but all except three of the new cities adopted the Lakewood Plan. These "contract cities" as they were called, negotiated with the county for a package of services. The package typically included law enforcement, fire protection, street maintenance and other services with large capital requirements. Rarely were such neighborhood activities as parks or recreational supervision included. Each service was priced—it was said that new cities shopped for services as if in a supermarket. One patrol car on a twenty-four hour basis cost one sum, street cleaning once a week came at so much a curb-mile, and so on. From time to time cities reviewed their contracts, perhaps switching to other suppliers, perhaps setting up their own departments.

Table 21.1
Selected Characteristics of "Normal" and Specialized Cities

City	Population	Area Sq. Mi.	Density Sq. Mi.	Per Capita Assessed Value	Per Capita Sales Tax
Los Angeles	2,950,010	464.88	6,357	$23,748	$62.59
Long Beach	356,906	49.56	7,189	26,642	52.74
Beverly Hills	32,281	5.70	5,667	98,448	219.26
San Marino	13,298	3.75	3,546	43,540	22.21
Bradbury	840	1.99	421	47,619	2.60
Hidden Hills	1,769	1.38	1,285	59,355	2.80
Rolling Hills	2,039	2.98	683	86,316	3.34
Rolling Hills Estates	8,230	3.33	2,469	55,771	0.00
Vernon	89	4.98	18	13,584,269	53,560.56
Industry	806	10.79	75	1,497,518	9,776.30
Irwindale	1,038	9.49	109	380,539	1,337.34
Commerce	10,507	6.56	1,602	120,110	1,046.71
Santa Fe Springs	14,556	8.68	1,677	89,997	529.09

Source: California Controller, *Annual Report of Financial Transactions Concerning Cities of California, 1980-1981.* Sacramento: State Controller, 1981.

Single-Purpose Cities

Of the thirty-four cities created in Los Angeles and Orange Counties during this rush to incorporate, twenty-three appear to be logical organizations of residential communities and formed reasonably "normal" cities. Motives were the traditional mixture: desire for home rule and control of land use, fear of annexation or disenchantment with county services. Eleven cities, nearly a third, however, were specialized, "unnatural," single-purpose cities. They incorporated to preserve "estate type" communities, to gain a tax advantage for industrial property owners, or to promote land appreciation. These cities followed the lead of San Marino and Vernon. Although totally different kinds of cities, they are generally characterized by a small population, low population density, high per-capita assessed property valuations and sales tax rebates. See Table 21.1. These are distinctive patches in the Metropolitan fabric, their characteristics now reinforced by political independence. They fall into three types. The "San Marino" type characterized by semi-rural estates—Rolling Hills, Bradbury, Rolling Hills Estates, and Hidden Hills. The "Vernon-Signal Hill" type where industrial land rules supreme—Industry, Irwindale, Santa Fe Springs and Commerce. A third type is exemplified by "Dairyland-La Palma," where dairy farms were first preserved in a specialized city, then, at a later date, reorganized into a more or less "normal" community. For this last group it is their historical development rather than present situation that sets them apart.

Preservation and Insulation—At a Cost

San Marino incorporated early, 1913, to avoid annexation and to preserve its estate type properties. It zoned out most industry and even today ". . . does not let people suffer prolonged sickness or die in its environs . . . its zoning laws prohibit mortuaries and hospitals" (Gordon, 1965, p. 361). Four new cities had somewhat similar situations and ambitions. Rolling Hills is composed entirely of from one to five acre estates, has no public streets, and allows access only through three guarded gates. Rolling Hills Estates, a middle income community, began its corporate life by rezoning all formerly zoned commercial land for agricultural use. Hidden Hills, scarcely more than a square mile in size, also has private streets, and a guarded gate. Bradbury is another area of expensive pastoral properties and private streets, restricted to its residents.

The "estate cities" retain their characteristics at a considerable cost. Only with private streets can entry be restricted, but state gasoline tax rebates to cities are based on miles of public streets; cities with private streets receive none. Similarly, cities with little or no commercial land generate little or no sales taxes and their rebates in that category are relatively small.

The Dairy Farmers' Two-Step

Dairy farmers in the Artesia area used incorporation as a device to facilitate their two-stage objective: first, to allow them to maintain their dairies free from interference, and, later, to enable them to sell out to subdividers at the highest possible profit. Subdivisions were approaching the area in the 1950s. Lakewood was being built on adjacent farmland, land values were soaring as were property taxes when the assessor recognized the subdivision potential of the land. Furthermore, if subdivision took place gradually, urban dwellers adjacent to dairies were likely to file nuisance complaints against the odors and flies that are a part of the dairy business. To prevent these unwanted events, the dairy farmers incorporated as Dairyland, Dairy Valley and Cypress in 1955–56. At the time the three cities contained about 75,000 cows and 5,000 people. One, Dairy Valley, carved out a U shaped municipality, taking in all of the land zoned for dairies that surrounded the residential and business sections of Artesia on three sides. However, these were holding operations. Within a decade, when the demand for residential land had pushed prices still higher, the farmer-councilmen rezoned their dairies for residential use, sold out to the developers and moved their herds further out. As part of the development stage new city names were cre-

ated, Dairyland became La Palma, Dairy Valley was renamed Cerritos. The success of this approach can be seen in their subsequent growth. Cerritos, for example, had 3,500 residents in 1960, 15,858 in 1970, and 52,592 in 1980. It is far and away the fastest growing city in Los Angeles County, increasing by 233 percent in the last decade.

Industry Yes, People No—Vernon Revisited

The advantages of Vernon with its concentration of industry and wholesaling and absence of people was not lost on Metropolitan landowners. During the incorporation rush in the late 1950s two cities managed close imitations; two others, though dominated by industry, included a considerable population. Industry and Irwindale now occupy most of the land zoned earlier by the Regional Planning Commission for the industrial growth of the East San Gabriel Valley. Industry has been called a "tax shelter for factories and warehouses," and its shape described as "a sausage filled with toothpicks" (Marx, 1962, p. 39). It runs as an irregular ribbon for some fourteen miles along the tracks of two railways and the Pomona Freeway as they follow the San Jose Creek through the Puente Valley. The city limits carefully enclose land zoned for industry along the tracks, wiggle in narrow shoestrings through unwanted residential neighborhoods, and widen out occasionally to take in shopping malls, thereby collecting sales taxes. The old landowners who incorporated the city, desiring to retain political control, so carefully excluded residential neighborhoods that "173 patients in the El Encanto Mental Hospital had to be counted to meet incorporation requirements" (Marx, 1962, p. 39). Within five years after incorporation Industry was the location of one hundred twenty-seven industrial plants that employed 10,000 people. In 1980 it had a population of eight hundred six, and its eleven square miles of industrially zoned sites contained so much vacant land that it seemed likely to soon replace Vernon as the most highly concentrated industrial center in the West. Irwindale, it is alleged, was incorporated by sixteen rock and gravel companies afraid of being "zoned into silence and cleanliness" working the gravel of the arroyos of the San Gabriel River (Gordon, 1965, p. 360). Although containing much land that cannot be developed, including the large Santa Fe Flood Control Basin, a few industrial plants have been built among the gravel pits and the homes of its population of 1,038—mainly Latinos.

The cities of Commerce and Santa Fe Springs have both similarities and differences. Both encompass extensive areas of established manufacturing plants and warehouses, both are surrounded by cities that were anxious to annex portions of this valuable land, both, though clearly not seeking a large population, did not exclude contiguous residential land. Both, therefore, find themselves with considerable population, about 10,000 and 15,000 respectively. Commerce, although including many older industrial plants as well as newer developments, generates large tax revenues, and is reputed to receive the fourth largest state sales tax refund on a per capita basis, and the assessed value of its real property also is high. These revenues allow it not only to pamper industry but also its residents—bus service is free, the city's "Camp Commerce" in the mountains is available for its youngsters, as are two enclosed swimming pools, four parks, four libraries and many other people-oriented amenities. Santa Fe Springs, located on a major oil field of an earlier day, is still the site of a major refinery and considerable heavy industry. The "Santa Fe Springs Industrial League," an association of one hundred seventy industrial firms, sparked the incorporation. It is alleged that the councilmanic districts were drawn so that nearly all of the people were in three of the five, thus giving representation to the "legitimate interests of industry."

Reason Reaffirmed—Local Agency Formation Commissions

Appalled by the "unwise and often detrimental annexations and incorporations serving special interests," the State Legislature established a Local Agency Formation Commission in each county. The objective was to stop the runaway growth of local governments and instead to encourage their orderly formation. Each Commission was to examine all proposals for incorporation in terms of demonstrated need for municipal services, to determine if incorporation would satisfy this need, to satisfy itself that the area had "social and economic homogeneity and cohesiveness," and that the incorporation would not be "a threat to, or be in conflict with, the normal and logical expansion of adjacent municipalities." The Commission had the power to prevent incorporation of "exclusively revenue-producing properties" or any attempt "to preempt a tax base to prevent an adjacent municipality from annexing it," and would reject a proposal to create a territorial sanctuary for ". . . a special interest group seeking to perpetuate its objectives." (Local Agency Formation Commission, 1973, pp. 69–71.) Obviously many of the incorporations of the past would be disallowed today. Since the Commission assumed jurisdiction in 1963 only four cities in Los Angeles County, Carson (1968), Rancho Palos Verdes (1973), Westlake Village (1981), and Agoura Hills (1982), have incorporated.

An Unincorporated Mosaic Remains

In spite of more than one hundred incorporations, the spread of the city of Los Angeles over four hundred sixty-five square miles, and despite the advantages of incorporation that are perceived by many, much territory in the Metropolis remains unincorporated. Furthermore, the remaining unincorporated areas are not just the sparsely settled hillsides or forested mountains. In Los Angeles County about one million people out of a population of nearly 7.5 million still reside in unincorporated areas, in Orange County perhaps 200,000 out of two million. A few of these people, it is true, live in small blocks of residential land unclaimed during neighboring incorporations. However, most live in large, long-settled, familiar communities. East Los Angeles has more than 100,000 residents. Other communities of considerable size, Altadena, West Hollywood, Willowbrook, Malibu, Marina del Rey and Diamond Bar, for example, remain unincorporated. All of these add additional complexity to an already fragmented political pattern.

Incorporation elections have been held in many of these communities over periods spanning many decades—but the "no" votes have always won. Altadena, for example, is a long-settled community of some 42,000 persons with a clear identity—it has a weekly newspaper, "The Altadenan," and many civic organizations. In spite of five incorporation elections from 1905 through 1964, it remains unincorporated. Apparently the voters felt that incorporation (or annexation to Pasadena) would mean higher taxes. East Los Angeles has attempted to incorporate eight times, first in 1925, the most recent in 1974; all failed. In the 1974 election proponents argued that incorporation would give the Latino residents needed identity and prevent the breakup of the community through piecemeal annexation by neighboring cities. Critics doubted that the city could generate enough money to support itself, felt any attempts to increase revenue would have to come from urban renewal projects adding industry at the expense of homes, and that the Anglo and Asian minority did not want to become part of a Latino city.

Too Many Governments?

"Too many governments" has been the cry of a generation of students of the Metropolis. Excessive fragmentation is deplored because it is wasteful, inefficient, unfair and irrational.

These observers wonder, for example, how many police departments, each with their own hierarchy of chiefs, headquarters buildings, purchasing agents, and so on, a region needs. Do not scores of police departments, each patrolling its own limited, often oddly shaped jurisdiction make for inefficiencies? Aren't we missing some economies of administration and scale? Again, how many different fire departments are really needed? Wouldn't fewer be better? What happens when a fire company answers an alarm and the fire turns out to be on the other side of a political line, out of their territory? Do they let it burn? How much does it cost a building contractor to be informed about the differing building codes of scores of different cities? Finally, how can a regional plan be effective when scores of cities have their own plans? How can area-wide problems such as transit be solved when jurisdiction is so divided? The lack of efficiency and wastefulness of fragmentation is apparent to many.

In addition, a cogent argument can be made that the existing fragmentation of the Metropolis is unfair to many residents. State laws relating to local property taxes and the return of a portion of sales taxes to cities are based on the traditional notion that a family lived, worked, shopped and sent its children to school within the boundaries of one unit of local government. This is rarely the case in the Metropolis and is completely unrealistic in many of the specialized cities. Gross inequities result. Vernon, for example, has an assessed value of property subject to the local tax rate of $13,584,269 *per person* and receives a sales tax rebate from the state of $53,561 for *each inhabitant*. Industry has a per capita property value of $1,497,518 and a sales tax rebate of $9,776. The figures for Los Angeles, a more traditional city, are $23,748 and $62.59 respectively. The specialized industrial cities are clearly "shortchanging" the rest of the Metropolis, siphoning off taxes that were conceived as revenue for police and fire protection, libraries, parks and other needs of the general urban population. Somewhat similarly, the wealthy island of Beverly Hills also receives a disproportionate share of metropolitan revenue—its sales tax rebate, for example, is more than three times and its property tax base is more than four times that of Los Angeles on a per capita basis.

On rare occasions action has been taken to reduce these inequities: some services have been put on a countywide basis to distribute their costs over the entire population. Public assistance welfare service, for example, is a function of county government. This makes it impossible for high income cities with few welfare recipients to escape taxation to finance welfare payments. Conversely, the burden does not fall disproportionately on cities with a large number of persons receiving welfare. However, this is the exception not the rule, most citizen-services are the responsibility of individual cities.

Continuing Fragmentation Efforts

Fragmentation may be deplored but forces for breaking away remain strong. For example, in the last decade there have been numerous proposals for splitting up Los Angeles County, several reaching the ballot. First to be proposed was San Gabriel Valley County, then, on two occasions, Canyon County (the Santa Clarita Valley). Finally, in June, 1978, the voters were asked to approve Peninsula County (Palos Verdes Peninsula) and South Bay County. In addition, for many years a group called CIVICC (Committee Investigating Valley Independent City/County) has been active in the San Fernando Valley. The arguments were the traditional ones, alleging officials in Los Angeles were distant and inaccessible, stressing the virtues of home rule, insisting that the areas were paying more taxes than were being returned to them.

The County Review Commission, as required by law, analyzed the proposals. Comments on Peninsula County were typical. "The proposed county is largely made up of affluent, well-educated, white families, wth an extremely low incidence of poverty . . . the residents of the remaining portion of Los Angeles County, on average, will be less affluent, less well-educated and will have a higher percentage of senior citizens, unemployed and minorities" (Keppel, 1978, pt. II, p. 8). Simply put, Los Angeles County would keep most of the high-service population which account for county expenditures, but lose part of its revenue producing base.

To the argument that the residents of these areas were paying more taxes than they were getting back in services, the *Los Angeles Times* (1978, pt. III, p. 4) replied, "That is a price, and indeed a fair one, that all suburbs pay for the economic sustenance they get from the urban core, where the jobs and the commerce and the industry originate to keep outlying areas alive."

To successfully break away from a county (or a city) a majority of voters must approve in both the area that desires to leave and also in the remainder of the county. In recent examples that reached the ballot the voters in the "break away" portions voted favorably, those in the rest of the county did not and the status-quo was preserved. To reduce the number of similar proposals in the future, state law has been changed for areas with small populations (less than 350,000 in Los Angeles County). Now proponents must obtain not only the signatures of twenty-five percent of the registered voters within the proposed county (as at present) but also those of ten percent of the voters in the existing county.

The Los Angeles Metropolis— Not the Most Perfect Union

Over the years some of the evils of metropolitan fragmentation have been reduced by single-purpose agencies formed on a county or even a regional basis. Flood control, a regional problem, has been handled on an area-wide scale since the formation of the Los Angeles County Flood Control District in 1915—other counties followed in the 1950s. The first Regional Planning Commission was established in Los Angeles County in 1922. The Los Angeles Sanitation District was formed in 1923 enabling cities to work together to form a metropolitan waste disposal system. Although the Metropolitan Water District formed in 1928 made continuing fragmentation possible it also developed into a regional agency concerned with a regional problem. Smog, first fought city by city, was significantly reduced only after the Los Angeles County Air Pollution Control District was formed in 1948. These were single-feature districts, federations of local governments in some instances, designed to address larger problems while keeping local independence.

Aside from the pioneering Metropolitan Water District, regional problem solving over larger units than the county have been rare until recently. Often their formation has had its impetus in requirements of the state or federal government. The Southern California Association of Governments, SCAG, was formed in 1965 to meet a federal requirement. Today it comprises six counties and almost all of the cities within them. It is described as "a council of governments" to deal with areawide concerns while maintaining the integrity of local governments. It reviews grant applications to the federal government by its member units. In addition, since its inception it has been responsible for preparing a master plan of the area, plans for transportation, airports, parks and recreation, as well as studies of land use, population, housing, employment and economic trends. The South Coast Air Quality Management District, another regional agency, was formed by the state and shares some of its duties with SCAG.

Not everyone agrees that a fragmented metropolis is undesirable. Some argue that competition among various cities in a metropolitan region is beneficial. It makes possible "a quasi-market choice for local residents in permitting them to select the particular community . . . that most closely approximates the public service levels they desire" in relation to taxes charged. Further, under the Lakewood Plan, with each city functioning as a buyer of services and with an increasing number of vendors of these services, competition may increase efficiency of the production of these services, and the responsiveness of those providing them. Too, many conflicts of regional importance can be negotiated in a variety of ways or sharply defined and resolved by the judicial system. Local issues can best be resolved locally, their doubters would argue, and the economies of scale are always open to question.

Yet innovative ideas to promote regional efficiency and rational local control are not wanting. More than a decade ago, Professor Donald Hagman of the UCLA School of Law, proposed a constitutional amendment with these interesting provisions: the counties of Los Angeles and Orange, and all cities, school districts and special districts within them would be abolished; the area would be reincorporated as the City and County of Los Orange Angeles, with all the powers that the abolished governments were permitted; further, any geographical area within it, under criteria the new unit may establish, could be formed into a sub-unit to be called a borough; the borough would be responsible for local government and education, the City/County as the fund raiser, transferring funds by block grants to the boroughs so that services measured by performance would be substantially equal in all areas (Hagman, 1970, pp. 26–29). Needless to say, this proposal has yet to appear on a Metropolitan ballot.

21. Suggested Readings

Bigger, Richard and James D. Kitchen. *How the Cities Grew*. Los Angeles: Bureau of Governmental Research, UCLA, 1952. This is a classic, full of interesting detail about the incorporation of cities in Los Angeles County and the expansion of the city of Los Angeles.

Crouch, Winston W. and Beatrice Dinerman. *Southern California Metropolis: A Study in Development of Government for a Metropolitan Area*. Berkeley: University of California Press, 1964.
The standard work on the topic, this book is limited to a discussion of Los Angeles County.

Gordon, Michell. *Sick Cities: Psychology and Pathology of American Urban Life*. Baltimore: Penguin Books, 1965.
The author was living in Los Angeles at the time he wrote the book and includes many local examples. Chapters on "Too Many Governments" and "City Limits" are appropriate here.

CHAPTER 22

Los Angeles Faces the Future

Figure 22.1. The Los Angeles Central Business District lies at the focus of the Metropolitan freeway system. (Photo courtesy Greater Los Angeles Visitors and Convention Bureau.)

"(Los Angeles) will represent forever, I think, the apogee of urban, mechanical, scientific man, rational man perhaps, before the gods returned. For it is past its prime already. It has lost the exuberant certainty that made it seem . . . unarguably the City of the Future. The City That Knew How. None of us Know now." Jan Morris (1980, p. 100).

"Two hundred and one years after the Pueblo . . . was founded, Los Angeles has come of age . . . the city stands self-confident and secure. Prosperity is in the air. A cultural dawn is breaking. At 201, Los Angeles has, it seems, at last become a place to take seriously. . . ." John Grimond (1982, p. 3).

No seer, regardless of talent, writing about Los Angeles in an earlier age, could possibly have forecast the nature of today's Metropolis. Who could have predicted that the motion picture camera would be developed or that the industry it created would be centered in Los Angeles? Who could have known that underlying the Metropolis was a vast reservoir of petroleum or that the automobile would come along and provide a market for all the gasoline that could be produced? Who could have guessed that the airplane would be invented or that Los Angeles would become world renowned for its manufacture? The list could be expanded through electronics, satellites, space vehicles, and into "think tanks." The future, in the past, was unforeseen and unforeseeable. There is little reason to believe that times have changed. The future of the Los Angeles Metropolis depends on too many variables, too many possibilities, too many unknown future events on the local, national, and international scenes. The most that can usefully be done is to assess the resources, natural and human, with which the Metropolis enters an uncertain future.

The People

The Metropolis now has more than eleven million people (and is still growing), who not only come from a wide variety of ethnic and national origins, but also include many "new immigrants." Both of these qualities—sheer size and ethnic variety-newness—are viewed with worried alarm by some, but with complacent equanimity by others.

Among the concerned is Theodore H. White, who reports on the population changes revealed by the 1980 census. "Los Angeles had, in effect, ceased to be a community of European culture, although no one could guess what would emerge from a city that now clustered Hindus and blacks, Koreans and Japanese, Mexicans and Filipinos, Vietnamese and Israelis. The city was held together by the old

culture expressed in its two dominant newspapers . . . the laws of the United States, and the roads of American engineering. A new Athens might emerge—or a new Calcutta." (White, 1982, p. 364.)

Troubling others is the difficulty of educating children who, in one high school, are reported to speak thirty-nine different native languages. The millions of Spanish-speaking residents are thought to present a particularly serious problem by those who fear that English no longer will be the unifying force in Los Angeles that it has been in America in the past. A related concern is that there are whole sectors of the economy in which Spanish is spoken, a language that most blacks do not know, and that this will be yet another barrier to black progress.

Anyone with a familiarity with American history cannot help but regard these worries with a sense of *deja vu*. Immigrants, particularly those from "new" regions, have been an old concern in the United States. These worries reached an earlier peak in the 1880–1920 period when the source of immigration shifted from the British Isles, Germany, and Scandinavia to the countries of southern and eastern Europe. Alarms were raised that these "new immigrants" were different in language, culture, religion, and even "race," and that assimilation would be difficult if not impossible. Others argued that the frontier was closed, the nation was "full," and that no additional people could be absorbed.

A contrary school of thought emphasized the contributions of earlier immigrants, their building of the canals and the railroads, their work in the mines, the factories, and on the farms. Furthermore, "The fortunate, deeply rooted and lazy remained at home," one writer insisted, "The American is accordingly . . . the most adventurous of Europeans . . . his enthusiasm for the future is profound." (Santayana, 1921, p. 169.) Not surprisingly, some take the same positive veiw of today's immigrants, "That such migrants, extensively selected by themselves for their initiative and by disaster for their strength, resource and ability to survive, should make a powerful contribution to economic development is hardly surprising." (Galbraith, 1981, p. 280.)

Recent visitors to the Metropolis have seen in the local immigrant groups exactly the same qualities that Santayana and Galbraith would expect. "The Asians are particularly energetic. The Vietnamese are already rising swiftly in the professions. The Koreans have a remarkable business bent . . . Latinos take great pride in personal advancement. . . . Most (migrants) in Los Angeles are also religious . . . and inheritors of a tradition that upholds family values. They are also Capitalists. In short they are model American citizens." (Grimond, 1982, p. 11.) Other observers have pointed out that there is good evidence to indicate that English is indeed the language of the vast majority of second generation Latino families, as has long been true of immigrant groups in the past. Finally, recent immigrants to the Metropolis come from cultures where urban life is understood and highly valued. These newcomers are not encumbered with the ambivalence many older Americans feel toward cities. Residents with an affection for city life and a tradition for using the opportunities cities provide are likely to make wiser decisions concerning future urban developments than those whose ideal is a rural or small town environment.

A second group of critics is appalled by the sheer size of the Metropolitan population. Some of these are "old timers" who long for the earlier days of clear skies, uncrowded streets, and an orange grove in the next block. They are joined by lovers of nature and others who see further population growth as an unmitigated disaster. ". . . Nobody sensibly suggests that Los Angeles will be improved by further population growth. . . . Further growth, even with the best of planning, can only come at the expense of those outdoor amenities which have attracted visitors to Los Angeles." (Dasmann, 1968, p. 211.) Many share the sentiments of that legendary cotter, who daily prayed: "We thank Thee Lord, that by Thy grace/ Thou hast led us to this lovely place/And now dear Lord, we humbly pray/ Thou wilst all others keep away."

Growth, properly planned, would not alarm everyone, however, including Allan Temko, architectural critic for the San Francisco Chronical. "There is room in the (Los Angeles Metropolis) for not 20 but 30 or 40 millions of people if only we have the wisdom to conserve the resources which remain unspoiled and to renew resources which have been wantonly damaged. We must decide where we should build, and where the wisest course would be to leave the land undeveloped." (Temko, 1977, p. 10.) Others argue that some dense clusters of population within the present low density residential landscape might actually increase the quality of life by making rapid transit feasible.

The Land

A few years ago, Richard Reeves, a reporter then new in town, was visiting several local writers in the Hollywood Hills. Sitting on the deck of a house, looking out over the Metropolis, one of these authors exclaimed, "There would be very few people in Los Angeles if they had to live with the energy, the wood, and the water that are naturally here. . . . The city is a triumph of American genius and greed. What we're looking at was once a grassy plain. There were deer and antelope out there. . . ." A second guest continued, in a similar vein, ". . . Los Angeles is not at peace with nature. . . . It's a man-made city. . . . There were people who could make money by putting a city here—the last place there should have been one." (Reeves, 1981, p. 6, 9.) These observations, although tossed off casually in a gathering of friends, are not untypical comments about the Los Angeles landscape.

The significance of these statements, however, is chiefly that they were made about Los Angeles rather than some other large city. Their contribution to the understanding of urban location is minimal. A little reflection leads to the realization that there would be very few people in any city if its residents were forced to live on the natural resources found on its site. The site of every city was once a pristine landscape, populated with the appropriate wildlife. Every city on earth is manmade. Whether more money has been made by the conversion of land to urban uses in Los Angeles than in, say, New York or London, would be hard to demonstrate. A lively argument could be staged, however, over where the "last place" (or the "first place") to build a city might be. (One is reminded of the adage, familiar to Californians, which asserts that if America had been settled from west to east, New England would still be occupied solely by Indians.) Much of what is written about the "triumph of American genius and greed," applies to the American city building process in general. On American city sites everywhere, vegetation was cleared, hills were leveled, swamps and bays were filled in, streams were covered or rerouted, and the land was prepared for sale as urban lots—hopefully at a large profit. Finally, one can only speculate on why it is that otherwise astute people manage to say such inane things about Los Angeles. Other cities do not seem to affect their critics in this way.

Perhaps no city (or town, or farm) is completely "at peace with nature," nor can it be. That state of grace was endangered when early humans learned the use of fire and was likely lost forever when hunting and gathering gave way to agriculture. About all we can do now is to work out an uneasy truce and avoid foolhardy provocations. Building a house within the chaparral, on a steep hillside, or at the bottom of a mountain canyon is a thoughtless challenge to natural forces, and such dares often end disastrously. One of the unique features of the Los Angeles Metropolis must be that many of those who choose to live on the most risky sites are often people who can afford to live anywhere. The rich, in most American cities, do not normally make such decisions. Usually the locations best left in their natural state, such as river flood plains, are occupied by the poor, who can afford no better. Perhaps the prevalence of these "inverted locations" is one of the reasons why Los Angeles is perceived to be built on a more hazardous site than most other cities.

In Los Angeles the most visible and persistent symbol of the lack of harmony between nature and the occupants of the Metropolis is smog. It is also the most famous. When a prized asset such as the Metropolitan climate becomes a stubborn problem, the world takes note. To point out that for some individual pollutants other cities have worse records is not comforting: their air was not earlier so highly valued. The truisms that on some days there is no smog, and that in some locations smog is rare are but small solace. Clearly the Los Angeles atmosphere is a delicate and precious amenity that must be returned to its former glory. The details of the region's atmospheric conditions have been discussed elsewhere. Obviously burning anything in the Metropolis endangers nature's truce; so does the evaporation of any unnatural hydrocarbons. Ways must be found to avoid both. Any slight progress in this direction is to be cheered. Major advances are needed and will come, although the ultimate solution is yet unknown. Possibilities include solar heating, electric energy for transport and factory, with the power generated outside the region. Other and better solutions may arise out of continuing research— let us hope that, here, necessity *can* be the mother of invention.

When the ground trembles the entire population of the Metropolis can sense the fragility of its arrangement with the earth. Everyone is affected: locations astride a fault are obviously the most hazardous, and sites on saturated alluvium can be dangerous, but no place is free of the tremors, they cannot be avoided. On the issue of earthquakes those who view with alarm can be understood: presumably the ideal city location would be in a region unaffected by this hazard. That requirement would exclude much of the earth, unfortunately, including the entire Pacific Rim, a region that has been attractive to city dwellers in many lands. It in unlikely that the residents of San Diego, Santa Barbara, San Francisco, Portland, Seattle, or Los Angeles, for example, are going to abandon their quake-prone locations. Yet, earthquakes almost inevitably will affect these metropolitan areas sooner or later.

The pertinent question seems to be: how can we build cities on earthquake-prone sites so as to minimize the inevitable damage and danger? How can we organize so that relief will be prompt and efficient on that inevitable day? Fortunately, single family houses and small apartments can be constructed so as to be essentially earthquake safe—and have been in the Metropolis since 1933. Little extra cost is involved. Hopefully, the lessons of previous earthquakes around the Pacific Rim have been applied to all of the large, modern structures built in the Metropolis. The vulnerability of many of the region's pre–1933 structures, as well as the area's lifelines, have been discussed elsewhere. We must insist that governmental agencies at all levels be prepared to respond to any seismic event that may come, and we must be willing to pay for the cost of effective preparation.

Although all cities have to import everything to survive, the fact that Los Angeles has to import much of its water is often singled out for worried discussion. By contrast, cities that have to import all of their fuel to enable their residents to live through cold winters are seldom treated with similar concern. Obviously, urban living everywhere depends on successful interaction with regions outside the city, both near and far. A secondary theme concerns the way water is used in the Metropolis. It is suggested, for example, that the traditional Eastern house, located in the middle of a grassy, tree-shaded yard, is inappropriate here. More in tune with the environment would be a residence in the Mexican tradition, with the house built around the edges of a small lot, and an open patio, with perhaps only a tree or two, in the center. There is a certain logic in this notion, and some movement toward this style can be seen. Many small apartment complexes, for example, are designed with their units surrounding an open patio. The patio is likely to contain a pool as well as a tree, however. Many of the newer townhouse styles now being built by the thousands, feature private patios, a central communal area, usually paved and with a pool, and a minimum of landscaping. Traditionally-styled houses are being built on smaller and smaller lots. In general, though, the lush tropical introduced vegetation of the Metropolis is likely to be considered by many to be a precious amenity, worthy of preservation, even at considerable cost. In 1982, for example, the Tree People, an environmental group, and the *Los Angeles Times,* launched a community-wide effort to plant one million new trees in dooryard and parkway, in honor of the 1984 Olympics. This "Urban Forest," it was proclaimed, was not only a way to beautify the city but, when grown large, the trees would aid in filtering smog from the air (Smaus, 1982, pp. 12–13).

"Bring Me Men to Match My Mountains"

The above motto, inscribed on the facade of the California State Capital more than a hundred years ago, remains for all to see. The epigram not only pays tribute to the region's spectacular natural environment but, more importantly, it recognizes the value of humankind. These dual assets are as important to the Los Angeles Metropolis as to the state as a whole. The natural features of the Metropolis—landforms, climate, beaches, and adjacent ocean—the wonders of an earlier age are yet with us. What is spoiled, given time, can be largely reclaimed, what is not, can be wisely cared for. The population is large, hardworking, and mainly self-selected. It includes "the greatest concentration of Nobel prizewinners, scientists, engineers and skilled technicians in the country" (Grimond, 1982, p. 23). Today's inhabitants, perhaps more than in the past, appreciate the opportunities available for them in the Metropolis that has been built in southern California.

It may be, as Jan Morris insisted several years ago, that Los Angeles has lost its "exuberant certainty" and that "None of us Know now." It is hard to believe, however, that this pessimism will be a permanent attitude, willingly accepted by the citizens of the Metropolis. Failure to come to terms with nature, or with each other, does not have to be an ongoing condition. The usefulness of scientific, rational thought may again be recognized, if it has ever been completely ignored. Alternative possibilities seem unattractive and unlikely to be widely popular for long. If, once again, we gradually begin to believe that we Know How, the record of the past would seem to indicate that these solutions would as likely be worked out in the Los Angeles Metropolis as in any other.

22. Suggested Readings

Grimond, John. "Los Angeles Comes of Age," *The Economist,* 283/7231 (April 3, 1982) 3–26. Reprinted in *Los Angeles,* 27/5 (May, 1982) 179–210.

A rather comprehensive and sympathetic analysis of modern Los Angeles, written by an Englishman for an English magazine.

Hirsch, Werner Z. ed. *Los Angeles: Viability and Prospects for Metropolitan Leadership.* New York: Prager, 1971.

An outgrowth of a conference, this volume comprises a series of essays on the topic, "Is Los Angeles the Metropolis of the Future?"

References

Adler, Patricia. 1963. *The Bunker Hill Story*. Glendale: La Siesta Press.

Ainsworth, Ed. 1947. " 'Times' *Expert* Offers Smog Plan," *Los Angeles Times,* January 19, 1947. pp. 1, 8.

Automobile Club of Southern California. 1937. *Traffic Survey Los Angeles Metropolitan Area Nineteen Hundred Thirty-Seven*. Los Angeles: Autosocal Printing.

Bancroft, Hubert H. 1886. *History of California*. Vols. II, III. San Francisco: The History Company.

Banham, Reyner. 1971. *Los Angeles: The Architecture of Four Ecologies*. New York: Harper and Row.

Barnes, Peter. 1973. "Kicking the Auto Habit," *The New Republic*. 169 (24):13–15.

Barrows, Henry D. 1893. "Reminiscences of Los Angeles," *Historical Society of Southern California. Annual*. 3 (1):55–62.

Bascom, Willard. 1974. "The Disposal of Waste in the Ocean," *Scientific American*. 23 (2):16–25.

Batchelor, Leon D. and Herbert J. Webber, eds. 1948. *The Citrus Industry*. Vol. II. Berkeley: University of California Press.

Baur, John E. 1959. *Health Seekers of Southern California, 1870–1900*. San Marino: Huntington Library.

Behar, Joseph V. 1970. "Simulation Model of Air Pollution Photo Chemistry," *Project Clean Air*. University of California Research Report. 4 (Project 4014):17–29.

Bell, Horace. 1927. *Reminiscences of a Ranger*. Santa Barbara: Hebberd.

Bigger, Richard and James D. Kitchen. 1952. *How the Cities Grew*. Los Angeles: Bureau of Governmental Research, UCLA.

Bolton, Herbert E. 1927. *Fray Juan Crespi, Missionary Explorer*. Berkeley: University of California Press.

———. 1930. *Spanish Exploration in the Southwest, 1542–1706*. New York: Scribner's Sons.

Bozzani, Amerigo. 1941. "Governor Olson Dedicates and Opens Arroyo Seco Freeway," *California Highways and Public Works*. 19: 3–20.

Brilliant, Ashleigh E. 1964. *Social Effects of the Automobile in Southern California During the Nineteen-Twenties*. Ph.D. Dissertation in History, University of California, Berkeley.

Business Week. 1978. "Fashion's New Regional Look," 2559; 187–188.

California Department of Water Resources. 1964. *Investigation of Failure of the Baldwin Hills Reservoir*. Sacramento: The Department.

———. 1974. *The California Water Plan, Outlook in 1974*. Bulletin No. 160–74, Volume 2, Summary Report. Sacramento: The Department.

———. 1980. *Ground Water Basins in California*. Bulletin 118–80. Sacramento: The Department.

Carew, Harold D. 1930. *History of Pasadena and the San Gabriel Valley*. I., Chicago: S. J. Clarke.

Castenada, Mario. 1975. *The Barrio Hierarchy of the Los Angeles Area*. Reproduced by the author.

Caughey, John W. 1970. *California: A Remarkable State's Life History*. Englewood Cliffs: Prentice-Hall, 3rd edition.

Chalfant, Willie A. 1933. *The Story of Inyo*. Bishop, Calif: published by the author.

Chandler, Raymond. 1971. "The Red Wind," reprinted in *The Midnight Raymond Chandler*. Boston: Houghton Mifflin.

Clark, David L. 1981. *Los Angeles, A City Apart*. Woodland Hills: Windsor Publications.

Clark, William B. and Carl Hague, eds. 1973. *When . . . The Earth Quakes . . . You Can Reduce the Danger*. Sacramento: California Division of Mines and Geology. Special Publication 39.

Cleland, Robert G. 1929. *Pathfinders*. San Francisco: Powell Publishing Company.

———. 1947. *California in Our Time*. New York: Knoff.

Coverdale and Colpitts. 1955. *Report to the Los Angeles Metropolitan Transit Authority on a Monorail Transit Plan for Los Angeles*. New York: Coverdale and Colpitts.

Crowell, John C. ed. 1975. *San Andreas Fault in Southern California.* Sacramento: California Department of Mines and Geology. Special Report, 118.

Dana, Richard Henry. 1911. *Two Years Before the Mast.* Boston: Houghton Mifflin Company.

Dasmann, Raymond F. 1965. *The Destruction of California.* New York: Macmillan.

———. 1968. *A Different Kind of Country.* New York: Macmillan.

De Crois, Teodoro. 1781. "To Captain Fernando de Rivera y Moncada. Instructions for the Recruitment of Soldiers and Settlers for California Expedition." Marion Parks, translator. *Publications of Historical Society of Southern California.* 15:192.

Didion, Joan. 1971. *Play it as it Lays.* New York: Bantam.

Dumke, Glenn. 1944. *The Boom of the Eighties in Southern California.* San Marino: Huntington Library.

Dykstra, Clarence A. 1926. "Congestion De Luxe— Do We Want it?" *National Municipal Review.* 15:394–398.

East, E. E. 1941. "Streets: The Circulatory System," in George W. Robbins and L. Deming Tildon, eds. *Los Angeles: Preface to a Master Plan.* Los Angeles: Pacific Southwest Academy.

Edinger, James G. 1967. *Watching the Wind.* New York: Anchor.

Falick, Abraham J. 1970. *Transport Planning in Los Angeles: A Geo-Economic Analysis.* Ph.D. Dissertation in Geography, UCLA.

Fogelson, Robert M. 1967. *The Fragmented Metropolis: Los Angeles, 1850–1930.* Cambridge: Harvard University Press.

Forbes. 1973. "Los Angeles: City With an Artificial Heart," 112 (7):67–76.

Ford, John Anson. 1961. *Thirty Explosive Years in Los Angeles County.* San Marino: Huntington Library.

Galbraith, John Kenneth. 1981. *A Life in Our Times.* New York: Ballantine.

Garst, Jonathan. 1931. *A Geographical Study of the Los Angeles Region.* Ph.D. Dissertation in Geography. Edinburgh.

Gebhard, David and Robert Winter. 1977. *A Guide to Architecture in Los Angeles and Southern California.* Santa Barbara: Peregrine Smith.

Gill, Brendon. 1980. "Reflections: The Horizontal City," *The New Yorker.* 56 (30): 109–146.

Glasscock, Carl B. 1933. *Lucky Baldwin.* New York: A. L. Burt.

Gordon, Mitchell. 1965. *Sick Cities.* Baltimore: Penguin.

Grimond, John. 1982. "Los Angeles Comes of Age," *The Economist.* 283 (7231): 3–26.

Guinn, James M. 1890. "The Great Real Estate Boom of 1887," *Historical Society of Southern California. Annual.* 1: 13–21.

———. 1893. "Los Angeles in the Later Sixties and Early Seventies." *Historical Society of Southern California. Annual.* 3 (1):66–68.

———. 1902. *Historical and Biographical Record of Southern California.* Chicago: Chapman Publishing Co.

Hagman, Donald G. 1970. "The Unconstitutionality of Incorporation and Boundary Change Laws as an Impetus for Needed Reform," in *Institute of Government and Public Affairs, UCLA. Mimeographed Report Series.* No. 146.

Herbert, Ray. 1974. "Public Transportation Gets Another Chance at the Polls," *Los Angeles Times.* Oct. 27, Part IX, p. 5.

Hilton, George W. and John F. Due. 1964. *The Electric Interurban Railways in America.* Palo Alto: Stanford.

———. 1967. "Mass Transit and the Pattern of Modern Cities: The California Case," *Traffic Quarterly.* 21:379–393.

Hotchkiss, Preston. 1973. *Herald Examiner,* October 13, 1973. p. A18. reprinted in Local Agency Formation Commission. *County of Los Angeles, Ten Year Report, 1963–1973.* p. 27.

Huxley, Aldos. 1956. *Tomorrow and Tomorrow and Tomorrow.* New York: Harper and Bros.

Jackson, Helen Hunt. 1883. "Outdoor Industries in Southern California," *Century Magazine,* October, 1883. quoted in W. W. Robinson, *What They Say About the Angels.* Pasadena: Val Trefz Press. 1942.

Johnson, Arthur T. 1913. *California: An Englishman's Impression of the Golden State.* New York: Duffield and Company.

Johnston, Bernice Eastman. 1961. *California's Gabrielino Indians.* Los Angeles: Southwest Museum.

Jones, Helen L. 1904. "Description of Pasadena's Sewer Farm," *Pacific Municipalities.* 10: 39–47.

Jordan, David Starr. 1898. "California and the Californians," *The Atlantic Monthly.* 82: 793–801.

Keith, Ralph W. 1980. *A Climatological Air Quality Profile California South Coast Air Basin.* El Monte: South Coast Air Quality Management District.

Kelker, De Leuw and Company. 1925. *Comprehensive Rapid Transit Plan for the City and County of Los Angeles*. Chicago: Kelker, De Leuw and Company.

Kenkul, John H. 1965. "Development of the Port of Los Angeles," *Journal of Transport History*. 3: 24–36.

Keppel, Bruce. 1978. "Proposals for Two New Counties on June 6 Ballot," *Los Angeles Times*. March 29, Pt. 2, p. 8.

Kilner, William H. B. 1927. *Arthur Letts, A Biography*. Los Angeles: Privately Printed.

Kroeber, Alfred L. 1925. *Handbook of the Indians of California*. Washington: Smithsonian Institution, Bureau of American Ethnology. Bulletin 78.

Lane, J. Gregg. 1936. "The First Census of the Los Angeles District," *Historical Society of Southern California Quarterly*. 18: 81–89.

LA/OMA Project. 1980. *Draft Facilities Plan/Program. Proposed Sludge Management Program for the Los Angeles/Orange County Metropolitan Area*. Los Angeles: LA/OMA Project.

Lapides, Ann. 1974. "How I Made a New Friend on the Freeway," *Los Angeles Times*. September, 16, Pt. II, p. 7.

Lelong, Eugene Y. 1974. *Air Pollution Control in California*. Ph.D. Dissertation in Environmental Science and Engineering, UCLA.

Lillard, Richard G. 1966. *Eden in Jeopardy. Man's Prodigal Meddling With His Environment: The Southern California Experience*. New York: Knoff.

Local Agency Formation Commission. 1973. *County of Los Angeles, Ten Year Report, 1963–1973*. Los Angeles: Los Angeles County.

Lockmann, Ronald F. Personal communication. May 1, 1982.

Los Angeles Board of Public Service Commissioners. 1916. *Complete Report on Construction of the Los Angeles Aquaduct*. Los Angeles: Department of Public Service.

Los Angeles City Archives. n.d. *Translations From the Spanish*. Vol. III, 18–51. Available in the vault of the Los Angeles City Clerk, Room 395, Los Angeles City Hall.

Los Angeles, City of. 1929. *Charter of the City of Los Angeles, Adopted 1925*. Los Angeles: City of Los Angeles.

Los Angeles County Mayors Committee. 1974. "Vote No on Proposition A Nov. 5th," *Los Angeles Times*. November 4, Pt. 1, p. 27.

Los Angeles Star. 1877. September 11, p. 1.

Los Angeles Times. 1886. August 13, p. 4.
———. 1888. June 15, p. 1.
———. 1976. "Sin and the Diamond Lanes," June 24, Pt. II, p. 6.
———. 1978. "New Counties: No on C and D," May 30, Pt. III, p. 4.

Los Angeles Transportation Engineering Board. 1939. *A Transit Program for the Los Angeles Metropolitan Area*. Los Angeles: City of Los Angeles.

Macgowan, Kenneth. 1956. "Motion Picture Industry," Chapter 26 in Clifford M. Zierer, ed. *California and the Southwest*. New York: Wiley.

Marx, Wesley. 1962. "As If Los Angeles Didn't Have Enough Trouble," *The Reporter*. 27: 38–39.

McDaniel, Wayne A. 1971. *Re-evaluating Freeway Performance in Los Angeles*. M.A. Thesis, School of Architecture and Urban Planning. UCLA.

McElhiney, Paul T. 1960. "Evaluating Freeway Performance in Los Angeles," *Traffic Quarterly*. 14: 296–312.

McWilliams, Cary. 1946. *Southern California Country: An Island on the Land*. New York: Duell, Sloan and Pearce.
———. 1949. *California: The Great Exception*. New York: A. A. Wyn.

Meyer, Larry L. ed. "Los Angeles, 1781–1981." Bicentennial issue of *California History*. 60: 79.

Meyer, Richard E. 1980. "Exploding Ethnic Populations Changing Face of L.A." *Los Angeles Times*, Pt. II, p. 1.

Morris, Jan. 1980. "Los Angeles, The Know-How City," Chapter IV, in *Destinations*. New York: Oxford University Press.

Morris, Samuel B. 1941. "Water Problems of the Metropolitan Area." in George W. Robbins and L. Deming Tilton, *Los Angeles: Preface to a Master Plan*. Los Angeles: Pacific Southwest Academy. 77–89.

Nadeau, Remi. 1960. *Los Angeles From Mission to Modern City*. New York: Longmans, Green and Company.
———. 1974. *The Water Seekers*. Santa Barbara: Peregrine Smith. Revised edition.

National Research Council, Panel on the Public Policy Implications of Earthquake Prediction. 1975. *Earthquake Prediction and Public Policy*. Washington: National Academy of Science.

Nelson, Howard J. and William A. V. Clark, 1976. *Los Angeles: The Metropolitan Experience.* Cambridge: Ballinger.

Netz, Joseph. 1925. "The Great Los Angeles Real Estate Boom of 1887," *Historical Society of Southern California Annual Publications.* 10: 54–68.

Newmark, Maurice H. and Marco R. Newmark, eds. 1926. *Sixty Years in Southern California, 1853–1913.* New York: The Knickerbocker Press. 2nd ed.

Nishi, Midori and Young Il Kim. 1964. "Recent Japanese Settlement Changes in the Los Angeles Area," *Yearbook of the Association of Pacific Coast Geographers.* 26: 23–36.

Nordhoff, Charles. 1872. *California: For Health, Pleasure and Residence.* New York: Harper and Brothers.

Northrop, Marie E. ed. 1960. "The Los Angeles Padron of 1844," *Historical Society of Southern California Quarterly.* 42: 360–417.

Oakeshott, Gordon B. 1973. "40 Years Ago . . . The Long Beach Earthquake of March 10, 1933," *California Geology.* 26: 55–59.

Olmstead, Frederic Law, Harland Bartholomew and Charles H. Cheney. 1924. *A Major Traffic Street Plan for Los Angeles.* Los Angeles: Los Angeles City and County Traffic Commission.

Palm, Risa. 1981. *The Geography of American Cities.* New York: Oxford.

Parks, Geoffrey A. 1951. "Los Angeles Aims at Perfection: New Hyperion Activated-Sludge Plant," *American City.* 6: 79–81.

Pirsig, Robert M. 1974. *Zen and the Art of Motorcycle Maintenance.* New York: Morrow.

Pipkin, Bernard K. and Michael Plossel. 1973. *Coastal Landslides in California.* Los Angeles: University of Southern California, Department of Geological Sciences.

Pitt, Leonard. 1968. *The Decline of the Californios.* Berkeley: University of California Press.

Place, John L. 1970. *Man's Role in Geomorphic Change on the Shoreline of Los Angeles County.* Ph.D. Dissertation in Geography, UCLA.

Post, Robert Charles. 1967. *Street Railways in Los Angeles: Robert Widney to Henry Huntington.* M.A. Thesis in History, UCLA.

Quiett, Glenn Chesney. 1934. *They Built the West.* New York: D. Appleton-Century Company.

Rand, Christopher. 1967. *Los Angeles: The Ultimate City.* New York: Oxford.

Rantz, S. E. 1970. *Urban Sprawl and Flooding in Southern California.* United States Geological Survey Circular 601–B. Washington: United States Geological Survey.

Reeves, Richard. 1981. *Jet Lag: The Running Commentary of a Bicoastal Reporter.* Kansas City: Andrews and McMeel, Inc.

Reisner, Neil. ed. 1976. *Jewish Los Angeles—A Guide.* Los Angeles: The Jewish Federation Council of Greater Los Angeles.

Remondino, Peter C. 1892. *The Mediterranean Shores of America: Southern California, Its Climate, Physical, and Meteorological Conditions.* Philadelphia: The F. A. Davis Co.

Robinson, Alfred. 1971. *Life in California.* Santa Barbara: Peregrine Press. Reprint of 1846 edition.

Robinson, W. W. 1968. *Los Angeles, A Profile.* Norman, Okla.: University of Oklahoma Press.
———. 1942. *What They Say About the Angels.* Pasadena: Val Trefz Press.

Ruhlow, Jerry. 1974. "Merger of L.A. and Long Beach Harbors Urged in Audit Study," *Los Angeles Times.* February 1, Pt. I, p. 3.

Salvator, Ludwig Louis. 1929. *Los Angeles in the Sunny Seventies, A Flower From the Golden Land.* Translated by Marguerite Eyer Wilbur. Los Angeles: McCallister-Zetlin.

Sanitation Districts of Los Angeles County. 1977. *Final Summary. EIS/EIR Joint Facilities Plan.* Los Angeles: Sanitation Districts of Los Angeles County.

Santayana, George. 1920. *Character and Opinion in the United States.* New York: Charles Scribner's Sons.

Saunders, Charles F. 1913. *Under the Sky in California.* New York: McBride and Co.

Seims, Charles. 1976. *Mount Lowe: The Railway in the Clouds.* San Marino: Golden West Books.

Simross, Lynn. 1979. "Jewelry Lane: A Street Paved With Gold," *Los Angeles Times.* December 27, Pt. IV, pp. 1, 8.

Slosson, James E. 1975. "Effects of the Earthquake on Residential Areas," in Gordon B. Oakeshott. ed. *San Fernando, California, Earthquake of 9 February 1971.* Sacramento: California Division of Mines and Geology. Bulletin 196. pp. 235–256.

Smaus, Robert. 1982. "An Urban Forest by 1984," *Los Angeles Times. Home.* July 25. pp. 12–13, 18, 24.

Southern California Association of Governments. 1978. *Areawide Waste Treatment Management Plan, 1978.* Los Angeles: SCAG.

Southern California Rapid Transit District. 1968. *Final Report, May 1968.* Los Angeles: Southern California Rapid Transit District.

Steiner, Rodney. 1981. *Los Angeles, The Centrifugal City.* Dubuque, Iowa: Kendall/Hunt Publishing Company.

Stipak, Brian I. 1972. *Explaining the 1968 Transit Vote in Los Angeles.* Los Angeles: University of California.

Stumbo, Bella. 1980. "L. A. Armenians: the Trauma of Finding a Self-Image," *Los Angeles Times.* June 8, Pt. II, p. 1.

Sunset. 1915. "Auto Snipers and Trolly Cars," 34:47.

Taylor, Benjamin F. 1878. *Between the Gates.* Chicago: S. C. Griggs and Co.

Taylor, Katherine Ames. 1928. *The Los Angeles Trip Book.* New York: Putnam's Sons.

Teggart, Frederick J. ed. 1911. "The Portolá Expedition of 1769–1770, Diary of Miguel Costansó." *Publications of the Academy of Pacific Coast History.* Vol 2. No. 4.

Temko, Allan. 1966. "Reshaping Super-City: The Problem of Los Angeles." *Cry California.* 1 (2):4–10.

Thompson and West. 1880. *History of Los Angeles County.* Oakland: Thompson and West.

Torrence, Bruce. 1979. *Hollywood: The First 100 Years.* Hollywood: Hollywood Chamber of Commerce.

Troxell, Harold C. and John Q. Peterson. 1937. "Flood in La Canada Valley, California, Jan. 1, 1934," *Water Supply Papers.* No. 796C. Washington: United States Geological Survey.

United States Environmental Protection Agency. 1977. *Final Summary. Environmental Impact Statement of the Joint Outfall System Facilities Plan.* San Francisco: United States Environmental Protection Agency, Region IX.

Van Dyke, Theodore S. 1890. *Millionaires of a Day.* New York: Fords, Howard and Hulbert.

Wagner, Henry R. 1929. *Spanish Voyages to the Northwest Coast of America in the Sixteenth Century.* San Francisco: California Historical Society.

———. 1941. *Juan Rodriguez Cabrillo Discoverer of the Coast of California.* San Francisco: California Historical Society.

Warner, Charles Dudley. 1890. "Our Italy," *Harpers New Monthly Magazine.* 81:820–824.

Weaver, John D. 1980. "Los Angeles," *Encyclopedia Briticannica Macropedia.* 2: 107–113.

Webber, Melvin M. 1976. *The Bart Experience—What Have We Learned?* Berkeley: Institute of Urban and Regional Studies and Institute of Transportation Studies. Monograph 26.

Williams-Kuebelbeck and Associates, Inc. 1976. *Economic Impact of Waterborne Commerce Through the Ports of Los Angeles and Long Beach.* Marina del Rey: Williams-Kuebelbeck and Associates, Inc.

Willman, Martha. 1972. "City in Two Counties Brings Confusion to Some Residents," *Los Angeles Times.* June 18, Pt. M. p. 1.

Wilson, Rexford. 1962. "The Los Angeles Conflagration of 1961. The Devil Wind and Wood Shingles," *National Fire Protection Association Quarterly.* 55: 241–288.

Winter, Oscar O. 1947. "The Rise of Metropolitan Los Angeles, 1870–1900," *Huntington Library Quarterly.* 10: 391–405.

Wong, Charles Choy. 1979. *Ethnicity, Work and Community.* Ph. D. Dissertation in Sociology, UCLA.

Wright, Willard Huntington. 1934. "Los Angeles—The Chemically Pure," (March, 1913) reprinted in Burton Rascoe and Troff Conklin, *The Smart Set Anthology.* New York: Reynal and Hitchcock.

Wurman, Richard Saul. 1981. *LA/Access.* Los Angeles: Access Press.

Zeck, Gerald. 1972. *Images of American Cities: A Cognative Approach to the Study of Environmental Perception.* Ph. D. Dissertation in Geography, UCLA.

Zimmerman, Erich. 1951. *World Resources and Industries.* New York: Harper.

Index

Diamond Growers, Inc., 172
Diamond Lanes, 70, 298–299
Didion, Joan, 276, 282
Discovery, 125–127
Disney, Walt, Productions, 7, 209
Disneyland, 7, 12, 207
Dodgers, 13
Doheny, Edward L., 180
Dominguez, Juan José, 138
Dominguez Field, 184
Dominguez Hills, 18
Dong-A Ilbo, 256
Donley, Michael W., 13
Douglas, Donald, 184
Douglas Aircraft, 184, 205. *See also* Mc Donnel Douglas.
Dover Sole, 104
Downey, 151, 206
Downtown Los Angeles:
  in 1850, 142–143
  in 1876, 151–152
  early twentieth century, 189–193
  "new," 194–197
Dr. Pepper Bottling Company, 213
Drought, 76, 145
Drum Barracks, 144, 225
Duarte, 174
Dumke, Glenn, 141, 155, 157, 159
Dunbar Hotel, 251
Dupuy, Charles, 263
Dykstra, Clarence, 271, 275–276

Eagle Rock, 158, 307–308
Eagle Mountain, 186
Earthquake, 10, 322–323
  faults, 27
  hazards, 28–30
  historic, 23–24, 129, 131
  Long Beach, 24–26
  management, 30
  prediction, 30
  San Fernando, 26–27
East, E. E., 261
East Los Angeles, 150, 152, 241, 244, 247–248, 264–265, 305, 315
Eaton, Fred, 77, 79, 99
Eaton Canyon, 309
Echo Mountain, 19, 178
Edendale, 182
Edinger, James G., 52, 55, 62
El Aliso Vineyard, 163
El Camino Real, 131–132
Electric Railway Homestead Association, 265
Electrical energy, 111–121
  conservation, 120–121
  geothermal generation of, 119
  hydroelectricity, 78, 112–115
  peak load problem, 114–115

solar generation of, 118–119
thermal generation, 115–118
use of, 119–120
El Monte, 144, 214–215, 248, 283, 306
El Monte Busway, 300
El Segundo, 33, 91, 185, 202, 206, 211, 214, 305
El Segundo Blue Butterfly, 106
El Toro, 128–129
Ely, Nevada, 118
Elysian Park Hills, 134
Employment, 11–12, 199–221
Encino, 91, 131, 258
Encino Shirt Company, 209
Encyclopedia Britannica, 286
Engineering Geologist Qualifications Board, 31
Englebert, Ernest, 86
Etiwanda, 74, 164
Eucalyptus, 100, 167
Evergreen Cemetery, 264–265
Ewing, Paul, 175
Exploration, 126–131
Exports, 229–237

Fages, Lt. Pedro, 128
Fairfax Avenue, 245, 258
Falick, Abraham J., 294–296
Falick's "H" Plan, 294–295
"Farmer John," 213
Fashion Institute of Design and Manufacturing, 220
Faults. *See* Earthquake faults.
Feather River, 82
Fellows, Donald K., 258
Field Act, 26
Fifth Street, 190
Figueroa Street, 194, 196, 209, 251
Filipinos, 10, 240–241, 251, 320
Filmore, 78
Financial district, 192–195
Fire. *See* Wildfire.
Firestone Rubber Company, 185
First Interstate Bank, 195
First Street, 88, 150, 197, 248, 253
Fish Harbor, 233, 253
Fisherman's Dock, 233
Fishing, 252
Floods, 11
  control of, 92–94
  historic, 88, 128–130, 144
  insurance against, 96
  natural conditions and, 91–92
  of 1914, 88–89
  of 1934, 48
  of 1938, 89
  of 1969, 90–91
  and water conservation, 94–96

Florence, 167, 250
Florence Avenue, 251
Florida, 171
Flour milling, 173
Flower Market, 218–219
Flower Street, 195
Flynn, Errol, 179
Fog, 36, 39–40, 62
Fogelson, Robert M., 99, 188, 269
Fontana, 66, 68, 85, 165, 185, 215
Fontana Farms, 106
Foothill Boulevard, 13, 89, 169
Foothill Freeway, 281
Ford II, Henry, 59
Ford, John Anson, 59
Ford Motor Company, 185, 231
Forest Grove Association, 167
Forest Lawn Memorial Park, 7
Fort Tejon, 24, 146
Fort Yuma, 146
Foster, Mark, 287
Fountain Valley, 102
Four Corners area, 117
Fox Studios, 182
Fox Wilshire Theater, 193
Franciscans, 163
Franklin Canyon, 78, 113
Franklin Canyon Reservoir, 305
"Free Harbor Contest," 227
Freeth, George, 20
Freeway system, 9–10, 70, 279–287, 298–299. *See also* individual freeways.
Freight rates, 163, 165
French, 146, 166
Fresno, 85
Friant Reservoir, 113
Frost, 34, 37, 40
Frye, Senator William P., 223
Fullerton, 82, 158
Fulton, Dr. J. E., 154
Fulton Wells, 154
Furlong Brothers, 306
Furlong Tract, 249
Furniture:
  manufacturing, 214–215
  wholesaling, 220–221
Future, 319–324

Gabrielino, 123–125
Gaffey Street, 107
Galbraith, John Kenneth, 321
Gálvez, José de, 127
Gamble, Charles, 179
Gamble House, 6
Garbage disposal. *See* Waste disposal.
Garden Grove, 24, 151, 256
"Garden of Paradise," 150
Gardena, 158, 213, 253, 307
Gardena Valley, 252–253